Nuclear Ambush

The Test-Ban Trap

Nuclear Ambush

The Test-Ban Trap

---

by

Earl H. Voss

Introduction by
Dr. Willard F. Libby

HENRY REGNERY COMPANY
Chicago 1963

Foreword

Since 1958, I have been interested in American disarmament policy, but I did not have any idea of writing a book. My interest was that of a practicing newspaperman.

Dr. Stefan Possony, then a Georgetown professor and now Director of the International Political Studies Program, the Hoover Institution, Stanford University, suggested that I write this book as my duty to my country, to the free world and to myself. He also guided me through the problems of academic presentation. Relm Foundation responded to my application for assistance with a research fellowship for an objective study of nuclear testing. Henry Regnery eventually decided to publish it.

Many others have given me their help or support, among them Dr. Harold Brown, John T. Conway, William Gehron, Betty Goetz, Philippe G. Jacques, Dr. Gerald W. Johnson, Albert L. Latter, Richard Latter, Isaac Don Levine, John F. Loosbrock, John A. McCone, Benjamin M. McKelway, John H. Morse, Jr., James T. Ramey, Ronald Spiers, Major General Alfred D. Starbird, Lewis L. Strauss, and Dr. James G. Terrill, Jr.

My wife, Marie, probably spent more hours working on the manuscript than I. It would never have been completed without her faithful help. When the final draft was typed and numbered, the book became a family project in which my father and my children, Steve, Pip and Martha, joined. My chief regret is that neither my mother nor Marie's lived to see the final product.

Another regret, in advance, is for the errors which I must reluctantly assume have crept in. The blame for these is mine, of course. I do not wish to imply, either, that any of the persons named above, in or out of the family, shares any of my views.

EARL H. VOSS

Springfield, Virginia.
December 5, 1962.

Contents

Introduction

The span of events presented by Mr. Voss encompasses the gripping drama of the world struggle for nuclear weapons supremacy in its most bitter and determinative early stages. From the time of United States monopoly to the present, seeming equality, it was the rate of gain of the Soviet Union on our early lead which was the paramount issue. We now know that the Soviets followed a determined policy of both pirating our information and protecting and augmenting their own by whatever means possible—the clandestine work of Fuchs, Burgess, Maclean and many others—and the clever exploitation of a fundamental weakness of a democracy: its inability to assess a technical matter and act upon it in rapid fashion. The Soviets have no difficulty, apparently, in calling their scientists into line whenever it is necessary to present a united front, while the West must endure often embarrassing debate among various factions. Thus were the Soviets able to make fools of us for three years, to culminate this game of words with the largest nuclear test series in history—including the firing of the largest bomb ever exploded—to leave us unprepared for test resumption, and finally to add the insult of insisting that should we reciprocate with our own series of tests, they would begin another group. This direct confrontation finally awakened us.

But three precious years of the race for nuclear supremacy were lost to us while the Soviet weapons laboratories were functioning at full speed, working in the sure knowledge that when preliminary preparations were complete, the actual explosions *would* be detonated.

This book deserves careful reading, not so much by the technical expert (who is probably well informed with respect to the issue, regardless of his own policy preferences) as by the responsible citizen, who by this time must be completely confused after hearing the same scientific experts alter their *technical* testimony from one extreme to another in a span of several months. (This sort of reversal rarely comes as a surprise to a scientist, who is accustomed to subjecting his conclusions to constant revision in the light of new experimental data.) It is to the author's credit that he has made such behavior understandable.

ix

In the most careful and thorough manner, with real objectivity, Mr. Voss tells the story of the Soviet arrestation of our nuclear arms development program for three whole years—and of our consequent gift of an opportunity to catch up, which they have accepted.

The nuclear test ban is a good example of Soviet tactical operations and NUCLEAR AMBUSH is a very good description—objective and revealingly detailed—of how they have succeeded in this activity.

It should be clear, however, that the test ban is just one facet of an overall Soviet strategy pattern which is giving our defense fits. The latest tack of this strategy seems to focus on our Civil Defense Program, which seems certain to die because of a lack of funds or public support. This program appears to be hamstrung by a cleverly improvised play on natural American lassitude, resulting from the same forces which mobilized the "machine" which sent us to Geneva in 1958. We must keep in mind that a "Pearl Harbor" in these next decades will offer no opportunity for counterattack. The Civil Defense issue is one of survival or destruction.

Dr. Willard F. Libby

University of California
December 15, 1962

Nuclear Test-Ban Chronology

1945

July 26	First atomic explosion, Alamagordo, New Mexico
August 6	Hiroshima atom bombed.
August 9	Nagasaki atom bombed.
August 14	Japan surrenders.
October	Eastman Kodak film mysteriously fogged; radio-activity in packing boxes eventually discovered to be the cause.
November 15	President Truman, Prime Minister Attlee, and Premier Mackenzie King decide atomic bomb secrets will not be shared until United Nations adopts control plan.
December 26	Moscow conference attended by Secretary of State Byrnes, Foreign Minister Molotov and Foreign Secretary Bevin, discusses atomic energy control.

1946

February 28	Purple Heart Military Order demands nuclear test ban after President Truman's announcement of intention to test atomic bombs at Bikini.
June 30	United States tests atomic bomb in air drop at Bikini.
July	Demonstrators protest against nuclear tests in Times Square, New York City.
July 24	United States tests atomic weapon under water at Bikini.
December 31	United Nations Commission of 11 nations recommends the "Baruch Plan" sponsored by the United States for international control and inspection of atomic energy. Russia dissents.

1947

June	Soviet Union submits its own version of control plan for ending atomic bomb development; limits international inspection so severely that secret A-bomb production could not be discovered.

1948

April 14	United States tests 36.5 kiloton nuclear weapon at Eniwetok.
April 30	United States explodes 48.7 kiloton weapon at Eniwetok.
May 14	United States conducts 18.2 kiloton explosion at Eniwetok.

May 17   United Nations Commission votes 9 to 2 to suspend work on international atomic control, blaming the Soviet Union.

June 22   Soviet veto prevents Security Council from approving atomic energy control plan backed by a majority.

November 4   General Assembly adopts, 40 to 6, United States-sponsored plan for international atomic control; Soviet opposition makes General Assembly resolution a dead letter.

1949

April 4   NATO treaty signed by 12 nations.

August 29   Soviet Union tests nuclear weapon.

September 24   President Truman discloses Soviet Union has set off nuclear explosion.

1950

January 31   President Truman orders development of hydrogen bomb.

March 19   International Communist movement launches world-wide peace offensive to "ban the bomb."

June 25   Communist North Koreans invade South Korea across the 38th parallel.

1951

January 27– February 6   United States tests five nuclear weapons, air bursts, for tactical information, in Operation Ranger in Nevada.

April–May   Operation Greenhouse, at Eniwetok, tests four weapons in "experiments contributing to thermonuclear research." One of the tests had an explosive power of 46.7 kilotons.

July 10   Truce talks begin in Korea.

September 8   Japanese peace treaty signed in San Francisco by 49 nations.

October 3   Soviet Union sets off second known explosion, reported first by the United States, later confirmed by the Soviet Union.

October 22   President Truman announces the third nuclear explosion by the Soviet Union.

November 7   Great Britain, France and the United States submit "Tripartite Proposals" providing for regulation, limitation and balanced reduction of all armed forces and armaments including atomic weapons.

November 16   Soviet Ambassador Vyshinsky tells the world he "laughed all night" about the Tripartite Proposals. He called for (a) a convention prohibiting atomic weapons, (b) then the five powers, Britain, France, the Soviet Union, the United States and Canada, would reduce armaments and armed forces by one third, (c) then all states would submit information on all their armaments and armed forces, (d) finally an international control organ would be set up.

October 22– November 29   Operation Buster Jangle in Nevada Flats, with seven air, tower and surface or underground bursts of low yield, reportedly tactical weapons. Explosions ranged from 0.1 kiloton to 31.4 kilotons.

1952

April 1–June 5   Operation Tumbler Snapper, in Nevada, tests air and tower bursts with troops participating in some tests.

October 13   Great Britain explodes first nuclear weapon, probably of Hiroshima type, in Montebello Islands.

October 31   Mike shot of Operation Ivy, the first test of a hydrogen device, exploded from a tower 20 feet above the earth with yield of 14 megatons. United States enters themonuclear age.

November 15   King shot of Operation Ivy, air drop from 1480 feet.

November   Asian Conference on World Federation appeals to three nuclear powers to ban their nuclear weapons and to the United States to renounce the H-bomb.

1953

January 20   President Eisenhower, in his first inaugural address, says the United States stands ready to make drastic reductions in armaments by methods providing participating nations with assurances of good faith on all sides.

March 5   Stalin dies.

March 17–
June 4   Operation Upshot Knothole in the Nevada Proving Grounds; 11 tests, air, tower, and one from a 280-millimeter gun. The largest explosions were those on April 18, code-named Simon, 42.7 kilotons, and the Climax explosion of June 4, 60.8 kilotons.

April 16   President Eisenhower outlines basic American policy on disarmament and calls on the Soviet Union to join with free nations in "devoting a substantial percentage of savings achieved by disarmament to a fund for world aid and reconstruction."

May   Representative Stringfellow of Utah urges Atomic Energy Commission to end Nevada tests because residents in the area are alarmed about fallout.

Summer   Civil Defense Administration and Armed Services deny that the record number of tornadoes are caused by nuclear tests.

August 8   Soviet Premier Georgi Malenkov announces United States no longer has a monopoly on the manufacture of a hydrogen bomb.

August 12   Secretary of State Dulles says United States has not yet detected any Soviet hydrogen-bomb test.

August 12   Soviet Union explodes its first (non-deliverable) hydrogen bomb.

August 21   Radio Moscow announces explosion of first hydrogen device.

August 31   Soviet Union conducts fission explosion of the same power as American tests in Nevada.

Fall   India and Australia advocate total ban on nuclear weapons in major speeches at the United Nations.

December 8   President Eisenhower presents to the United Nations General Assembly his "Atoms for Peace" plan, calling for an international atomic energy agency to receive contributions of nuclear materials for peaceful international projects.

1954

January 21	First atomic-powered submarine, the Nautilus, is launched at Groton, Connecticut.
February 18	The United States, United Kingdom, France and the Soviet Union agree at Berlin Foreign Ministers Meeting to exchange views on disarmament and reduction of armaments, as recommended by the United Nations General Assembly.
March 1	The United States explodes second hydrogen device in Bikini Atolls with the power of 15 megatons, the largest explosion until 1961. Marshall Islanders sprinkled with fallout.
March 2–5	Marshallese natives and American servicemen on islands in the test area are evacuated to Kwajalein.
March 1– May 13	Operation Castle, of which the 15-megaton "Bravo" shot was a part, with a total of six tests, four of them on barges and two from the earth's surface.
March 15	Japanese fishing boat, the Fortunate Dragon, docks in Yaizu Harbor with 23 sick fishermen radiated from fallout of the Bravo H-bomb test.
March	104 British Labor MPs sign a motion asking the United Nations to proclaim a ban on H-bomb experiments.
March	President Eisenhower orders release to the general public of color movies of the 1952 "Mike" thermo-nuclear shot.
April	Soviet Deputy Premier Mikoyan reports the Soviet Union has put the hydrogen bomb into the hands of its troops.
	Japanese government turns aside suggestions in Diet that the United States be asked to give up tests—unless the Soviet Union does the same.
	Japanese Socialist Party proposes a complete ban on use of nuclear weapons.
	Dr. Albert Schweitzer writes to the British public from Africa to advocate an H-bomb test ban.
	Pope backs test ban if it can be effectively inspected.
Spring	Japanese find strontium 90 in radioactive fallout.
April	Indian Prime Minister Nehru addresses a personal plea to the United States to end hydrogen-bomb tests; he proposes a "standstill agreement" on tests of nuclear weapons.
	The United States curbs distribution of color films of the Mike shot.
April 19	United Nations Disarmament Subcommittee established with five members, the United States, the United Kingdom, France, Canada and the Soviet Union.
April	Indonesian Premier Sastroamidjojo supports Prime Minister Nehru's call for an end to nuclear tests.
	British House of Commons calls on Prime Minister Churchill, President Eisenhower and Soviet Premier Malenkov to hold talks on control of nuclear weapons.
	Colombo powers in Asia urge suspension of H-bomb tests pending negotiations of a nuclear weapons ban by the United Nations.
May 7	Dienbienphu falls to Communist Viet Minh rebels.
May 25	United States presents detailed program for disarmament in-

cluding provisions for careful inspection. For the first time in United Nations disarmament negotiations the United States does not insist on removal of the veto power in applying sanctions to disarmament violators.

May	Secretary of State Dulles promises to seek "properly safeguarded" agreement.
May 28	Communist World Peace Council launches new campaign to stop nuclear tests.
June	President decides United States should not agree to nuclear-test moratorium but disarmament-policy review should continue.
	British Prime Minister Churchill visits President Eisenhower, discusses implications of H-bomb for world strategy.
June 1–11	Soviet Union repeats old disarmament proposals for elimination of all atomic, hydrogen and other weapons of mass destruction together with "simultaneous" establishment of strict international control.
June 11	United Kingdom and France, with "general support" of the United States and Canada, propose that all states agree to prohibit atomic and hydrogen weapons *except in defense against aggression*. Total elimination of atomic and hydrogen weapons should come *after* major reductions in conventional armaments and armed forces.
September 6	United States launches world atomic pool without the Soviet Union.
September 8	Eight-nation Southeast Asia Defense treaty signed at Manila.
September 23	Aikichi Kuboyama, one of the 23 Japanese crewmen on the Fortunate Dragon which was sprayed by radio-activity from the Bravo test, dies. Japan goes into national mourning.
September 30	Soviet Union accepts in principle the Anglo-French memorandum of June 11.
September–October	Soviet series of nuclear tests, announced by the Atomic Energy Commission on October 26.
October 10	Public funeral for Kuboyama touches off wave of anti-Americanism.
November	Bulletin of the Atomic Scientists publishes plan for nuclear test ban.
Fall	Dr. Ralph Lapp announces his deductions that the Bravo shot was a fission-fusion-fission device releasing alarming amounts of radioactivity.

1955	
January 17	Submarine Nautilus, first atomic-powered undersea vessel, goes to sea.
January 21	Communists launch Vienna Appeal through their World Peace Council emphasizing disarmament themes, including "destruction of atomic stocks," a theme which had been de-emphasized since 1947.
February 8	Marshal Bulganin replaces Georgi Malenkov as Premier of the Soviet Union, Nikita Khrushchev takes over as First Secretary of the Communist Party.

February 14   Khrushchev says "we are willing to accept certain partial steps —for example, to discontinue the thermonuclear weapons tests . . ." in a speech before the 20th Communist Party Congress of the Soviet Union in Moscow.

February 23   President says the United States sees nothing to be gained by a separate ban on thermonuclear tests outside a general disarmament program.

March 19   President appoints Harold E. Stassen as Special Assistant to the President for Disarmament.

February 18–   Operation Teapot in the Nevada Testing Grounds, including
May 15   14 air, tower and underground tests. One of the shots was an atomic trigger for detonating H-bombs. Another was a civil defense test. Another was an "air-killer" test. Shots ranged from 1.1 to 28.5 kilotons.

April 5   Churchill resigns: Eden succeeds him.

April   National Academy of Sciences establishes panel to study fallout and other radiation effects.

Easter   Pope Pius warns of the genetic effects of radiation from nuclear weapons.

April   AEC Chairman Lewis E. Strauss discounts fears of genetic damage from nuclear test fallout.

Bandung Conference endorses nuclear test ban.

May 10   Soviet Union proposes ending nuclear tests when elimination of nuclear weapons begins under a general disarmament program.

Soviet Union acknowledges that detecting hidden nuclear weapons stockpiles is impossible.

May 14   Operation Wigwam, a single American test, 2000 feet under water, of a 30-kiloton weapon.

May 26   Harold Stassen, Special Assistant to the President for Disarmament, presents his first comprehensive report to Mr. Eisenhower. It stresses extreme importance of providing against surprise attack, necessity for effective inspection in any agreement. Elimination of nuclear weapons would be impossible, the Stassen group concluded, because stockpiles could easily be hidden. Test ban ignored.

June 22   United States proposes a world pool of knowledge on the effects of atomic radiation on health.

June   President considers and approves conclusions by his interagency group that "a moratorium on H-bomb testing would not be in the interests of the United States and should not be agreed to except as a part of a comprehensive, safeguarded disarmament agreement."

July 18–25   President Eisenhower and the heads of government from Britain, France and the Soviet Union meet at a Geneva summit conference. The Eisenhower "open skies" proposal is unveiled. "Spirit of Geneva" is born.

July 25   Senate establishes subcommittee of the Foreign Relations Committee to study proposals for disarmament and the control of weapons of mass destruction.

August 4	AEC announces Soviet Union has resumed testing of nuclear weapons.
August 12	Soviet Union announces a reduction in its Armed Forces by 640,000 men.
September 6	United States announces it is placing a reservation on all its positions on disarmament because accumulation of nuclear stockpiles presents special problems in disarmament inspection and control.
September 24	AEC reports another Soviet nuclear test explosion.
September 24	President Eisenhower suffers heart attack.
October–November	Foreign Ministers of Britain, France, the Soviet Union and the United States fail to reach agreement on pursuing the objectives outlined at the Geneva Summit Conference.
October 15	Britain conducts two tests at its Woomera Rocket Range in Australia, the first of them equivalent to 20 kilotons.
November 10	AEC announces a further test of a nuclear weapon by the Soviet Union.
November 11	Secretary of State Dulles states at the Geneva Foreign Ministers Conference that "if agreement can be reached to eliminate or limit nuclear weapons under proper safeguards, the United States would be prepared to agree to corresponding restrictions on the testing of such weapons."
November 23	Megaton-range hydrogen bomb exploded by the Soviet Union. Khrushchev announces it on November 27, stating it was a bomb dropped from a great height from an airplane.
December 3	United Nations General Assembly unanimously approves a resolution creating a scientific committee to study the effects of atomic radiation.

1956

February 22	United States releases 40,000 kilograms of uranium 235 for peaceful uses at home and abroad.
March 21	Soviet Union conducts another nuclear explosion, probably in central Asia, AEC announces.
April 3	Stassen proposes detailed plan for first phase of a comprehensive disarmament program, including limitation, not end, of nuclear weapons tests in the 19th step.
April 12	Atomic Energy Commissioner Thomas Murray proposes "tests of multimegaton thermonuclear weapons should be stopped."
April 21	Adlai Stevenson proposes ending H-bomb tests.
May 4–July 21	Operation Redwing tests at Eniwetok including 13 explosions, one of them in the megaton range.
May 21	First H-bomb dropped by the United States Air Force exploded with a yield reportedly "at least 15 megatons."
June	National Academy of Sciences panel reports genetic and somatic effects of fallout radiation would be slight compared with natural background.
July 13	United States Ambassador James J. Wadsworth tells disarmament commission that "in the absence of agreement to

	eliminate or limit nuclear weapons under proper safeguards, continuation of testing is essential for our national defense and the security of the free world."
August 24, August 30, September 2	Soviet Union sets off series of small explosions in Southwestern Siberia.
September 5	Adlai Stevenson begins his second campaign for the Presidency with a strong plea for halting further testing of "large nuclear devices, conditioned upon adherence by the other powers to a similar policy."
September 11	Premier Bulganin proposes in a letter to President Eisenhower a nuclear test ban without international inspection.
September 27	Britain conducts four tests, tower and air, of new and cheaper kinds of A-bombs at Maralinga Proving Ground, South Australia.
October 6	President Eisenhower defends his nuclear weapons testing policy in public statement.
October 17	Premier Bulganin of Soviet Union, in a letter to President Eisenhower, associates himself with "the opinion recently expressed by certain prominent public figures in the United States" on the prohibition of nuclear tests.
October 21	President Eisenhower protests Premier Bulganin's "interference in our internal affairs, of a kind which, if indulged in by an ambassador, would lead to his being declared persona non grata."
October 23	President Eisenhower issues another public statement defending his nuclear test ban policy.
November 17	Soviet Union sets off small explosion in Southwest Siberia.

1957
January 12	United States memorandum sets forth basic disarmament policy, saying that when future nuclear weapons production is effectively controlled, it will be possible to limit and eventually eliminate nuclear tests.
January 14	Henry Cabot Lodge, United States Ambassador at the United Nations, presents a plan for nuclear disarmament, linking a test ban with a cut-off of production of nuclear weapons materials.
January 19– April 16	Soviet Union conducts seven tests in southwestern Siberia, reportedly to perfect atomic warheads for tactical purposes.
March	President Eisenhower and Prime Minister Macmillan take note of the clamor for stopping tests in a Bermuda meeting but they declare that "continued nuclear testing is required, certainly for the present."
March 15	Japanese Diet unanimously passes resolution "regretting" British plans for H-bomb test at Christmas Island. The same resolution calls for "total prohibition of production, use and testing of atom and hydrogen bombs."
March 18	London Disarmament Subcommittee talks open.
April 30	Soviet Union calls for a break in the "link" between nuclear test ban and production cut-off.

May 17	Britain drops one-megaton H-bomb from Vickers Valiant jet bomber in Christmas Island area.
May 25	President Eisenhower decides to loosen the link between nuclear tests and a cut-off of weapons material production. The United States could accept a temporary suspension of nuclear tests for 10 or 12 months, it was decided, but the inspection systems should be established by that time if the suspension were to be prolonged.
May–June	Joint Congressional Atomic Energy Committee studies fallout hazards.
May	Prime Minister Nehru urges a ban on nuclear experiments to prevent human "extinction."
May 22	Indian Parliament passes a resolution urging a test ban.
May 27	Disarmament negotiator Stassen tells Subcommittee in London the United States is prepared "to move half way" to reach agreement on a first-phase disarmament plan.
May 28	Operation Plumbbob begins in Nevada. Mostly tests in small ranges, perhaps to perfect warheads for rockets.
May 31	Britain explodes second hydrogen bomb in Christmas Island area.
June 14	Soviet Union accepts in principle Western demands for inspection of a nuclear weapons test ban, proposing a two-to-three-year moratorium under the supervision of an international commission, with control posts in the territories of the United States, the United Kingdom, and the Soviet Union, and in the Pacific.
June 24	President Eisenhower told by top American scientists the United States can produce nuclear weapons 95 per cent free of radioactivity; cleaner weapons would be possible with more testing.
July	Soviet scientists attending the first Pugwash Conference in Nova Scotia, sponsored by Cleveland industrialist Cyrus Eaton, press for a test ban.
July 8	Soviet Union rejects new Western proposal for loosening the link between cut-off and test ban.
July 15	Communist Party Boss Khrushchev comments that London disarmament talks are going "badly" and blames West.
August 21	Secretary of State Dulles instructs Mr. Stassen to extend the proposed period of test suspension from ten months up to two years, given certain safeguards.
August 29	Britain, France, the United States and Canada present NATO-approved proposal for partial disarmament, including the stopping of nuclear bomb testing in a broader set of arms limitations measures.
September 6	Disarmament Subcommittee holds its last meeting; the Soviet representative is unwilling to agree on the time or possibility of reconvening.
September 19	United States explodes 1.7-kiloton Rainier test 790 feet underground at Nevada Proving Grounds.
October 4	Soviet Union launches first earth satellite, Sputnik I.
October 7	Operation Plumbbob ends after 26 tests.

November 3   Russians launch earth satellite with dog aboard.
November 4   Senator Humphrey of Minnesota, Chairman of the Senate
              Foreign Relations Committee's Subcommittee on Disarma-
              ment, writes President Eisenhower to urge a separation of the
              test ban from the rest of the first-step disarmament package.

1958
January   Dr. Linus Pauling files with the United Nations a petition
              signed by 11,000 scientists from 49 countries urging "an inter-
              national agreement to stop further testing of nuclear bombs."
January 31   First United States earth satellite, Explorer I, fired into orbit.
February 28   Governor Stassen, having completed his tour as Presidential
              Assistant on Disarmament, advocates lifting the nuclear test
              ban out of the first-step disarmament package in testimony
              before the Senate Disarmament Subcommittee.
February–   Senate Disarmament Subcommittee holds extensive hearings
   June   on nuclear test-ban problems.
March 27   Khrushchev becomes Premier of the Soviet Union with Bul-
              ganin's resignation.
March 31   Supreme Soviet approves a decree abolishing further Soviet
              nuclear testing, providing other countries follow suit.
April 4   Khrushchev writes to President Eisenhower proposing the
              United States and United Kingdom unilaterally "adopt a de-
              cision to renounce further tests," as the Soviet Union had
              done.
April 8   President Eisenhower suggests in a letter to Premier Khru-
              shchev that the Soviet Union join the United States in an
              examination of the technical requirements for inspection of a
              nuclear test ban.
May 9   Premier Khrushchev accepts President Eisenhower's proposal
              for technical talks in a letter to the White House.
July 1   Experts from the United States, the Soviet Union, the United
              Kingdom, France, Canada, Poland, Czechoslovakia and Ru-
              mania begin their "Conference of Experts" on inspection
              requirements for a nuclear test ban.
July 31   United States explodes nuclear weapon, code-named Teak, at
              altitude above 200,000 feet in vicinity of Johnston Island in
              the Pacific. This is a megaton shot.
August 8   United States nuclear submarine Nautilus sails submerged
              from the Pacific to the Atlantic under the North Pole.
August 11   Orange test exploded at 100,000 feet over the Pacific near
              Johnston Island.
August 21   East-West scientists agree inspection of a nuclear test ban is
              feasible within certain limits, recommend 180-station control
              system effective down to five kilotons with an optional and
              partial effectiveness down to one kiloton.
August 22   President Eisenhower announces willingness to withhold nu-
              clear tests unilaterally for one year while negotiations on the
              test ban treaty are conducted, providing Soviet Union does
              not resume testing. He leaves open the chance for extending
              the one-year moratorium, which he says can begin October 31.

September 12   United States begins intensive test series, code-named Hardtack II.

September 30   Two nuclear explosions occur in the Soviet Union, breaking Khrushchev's unilateral moratorium. United States announces that "unless the Soviet Union holds further tests after negotiations have begun, the United States remains prepared to withhold further testing of atomic and hydrogen weapons for a period of one year from beginning of the negotiations on October 31."

October 5   Soviet draft resolution in the United Nations General Assembly calls for permanent end of nuclear tests.

October 30   United States completes 37-test Hardtack II series, 19 of them safety experiments, 17 full-scale weapons shots. Eleven of the 37 shots set off underground, ranging from 1.5 tons to 19.2 kilotons.

October 31   Nuclear test ban treaty negotiations between the United States, Great Britain and the Soviet Union begin in Geneva.

November 1–3   Soviet Union explodes two more nuclear weapons, but United States continues negotiation, withholds further tests of its own.

November 7   Atomic Energy Commission announces nuclear explosions in the Soviet Union on November 1 and 3. President Eisenhower declares the United States is relieved of any obligation to suspend tests but that it will continue suspension for the time being; the United States will reconsider its position unless the Soviet Union renounces testing.

November   Data from Hardtack II test series indicate Conference of Experts had greatly overestimated both the ability to detect nuclear weapons tests and the ability to distinguish them from earthquakes.

1959
January   Dr. Albert L. Latter discovers big-hole decoupling theory by which underground nuclear shots could be muffled to appear one-three hundredth their actual size.

January 16   Department of Defense releases details of the findings of the Hardtack II series. Conclusions of the Conference of Experts found to be 33 per cent incorrect on detection and 66 per cent wrong on identification.

January 19   United States and United Kingdom tell the Soviet Union they will no longer insist that any discontinuance of nuclear weapons tests must depend on progress in other major disarmament.

January 22   Dr. Latter presents his decoupling theory to President's Science Advisory Panel at Lawrence Radiation Laboratory, Livermore, California. Dr. Hans Bethe and Dr. Edward Teller accept its validity.

Late January   Atomic Energy Commission Chairman John McCone proposes to Secretary of State Dulles a new plan for a "phased" agreement on nuclear tests, starting with a ban on detectable atmospheric tests, permitting tests underground and beyond the atmosphere while a more effective detection system is developed.

February 21   Prime Minister Macmillan flies to Moscow for personal talks with Soviet Premier Khrushchev, during which the British leader suggests the United States and Britain might accept a ceiling on the annual number of on-site inspections in return for Soviet abandonment of the veto in the Geneva test-ban negotiations.

March 16   Panel on Seismic Improvement presents its report, outlining methods for increasing the effectiveness of seismic detection of underground nuclear shots, also mentioning vaguely the Latter decoupling theory. Degradation of the 180-station control network after the Hardtack II series is confirmed.

March 19–24   British Prime Minister Macmillan flies to Washington to report to President Eisenhower on his Moscow talks. President is cool to annual quota for on-site inspections suggested by Mr. Macmillan.

April 13   President Eisenhower, in a letter to Premier Khrushchev, offers alternative approach to a nuclear test ban. A nuclear test ban should be put into effect in phases, the President says, starting with prohibition of nuclear weapons tests in the atmosphere up to 50 kilometers. Meanwhile negotiations could continue to seek methods of extending an effective ban underground and in outer space.

April 23   Premier Khrushchev proposes in letters to President Eisenhower and Prime Minister Macmillan setting an annual limit on the number of on-site inspections in any comprehensive test-ban agreement, rejects the Eisenhower "phased treaty" plan. Premier Khrushchev suggests the number of on-site inspections per year should not be "numerous."

May 5   President Eisenhower agrees to "explore" the quota idea for on-site inspections.

May 5   President Eisenhower urges Premier Khrushchev to agree to technical discussions on banning nuclear tests to greater heights than proposed on April 13. The United States is ready, the President writes, to explore at Geneva Premier Khrushchev's proposal for a quota of on-site inspections but insists the number should be related to scientific facts and detection capabilities.

June 12   Findings of the Panel on Seismic Improvement admitted to Geneva conference on nuclear test ban. Findings indicate improved equipment and techniques make it possible to identify a large percentage of seismic events above 10 kilotons equivalent, i.e., with the same degree of accuracy that Geneva report of August 21, 1958 had estimated for seismic events above five kilotons equivalent.

June 22–
July 10   East-West experts study high-altitude detection problem, produce agreed report on requirements for inspection system. The Soviet Union accepts 10 of 11 methods of detecting high-altitude and space explosions proposed by the United

States, six of them to be carried in satellite systems, four to be based on the ground.

August 26 State Department announces that under a Presidental directive the unilateral suspension of nuclear weapons testing by the United States, which began on October 31, 1958 and was to continue for one year, will be extended to December 31, 1959.

August 27 British Government announces it will not resume nuclear tests as long as useful discussions are under way at the three-power Geneva conference on a nuclear test ban.

September 14 Soviet rocket shot to the moon in 35-hour trip.

September 18 Soviet Premier Khrushchev asks general and complete disarmament of all nations in four years in speech at United Nations.

October 25 Governor Nelson Rockefeller of New York suggests the United States should resume nuclear tests.

November 2 Senator John F. Kennedy registers "my own emphatic disagreement" with Governor Rockefeller's suggestions that nuclear tests should be resumed.

November 3 Soviet Union proposes formation of three-power technical working group to draft "objective criteria" for the dispatch of on-site inspection teams to unidentified underground events.

November 22 AEC Chairman McCone says the United States should be ready to extend its 14-month ban on nuclear testing only on a week-to-week basis. "I think it would be impossible," Chairman McCone said, "to detect underground Soviet nuclear tests if they had been held."

November 25– Technical Working Group II seeks to find East-West agree-
December 18 ment on capabilities of the inspection control system for nuclear test ban, ends in wide disagreement after 21 meetings. Soviet Union does agree to all American proposals for improving the system.

Mid-December Operation Cowboy, a program of 17 high-explosive shots in salt cavities near Winnfield, Louisiana, start. They prove the Latter decoupling or "big hole" theory. Tests continue until mid-March 1960.

December 29 President Eisenhower says United States considers itself free to resume nuclear testing after the expiration of its voluntary moratorium on December 31, but that it will not do so without giving advance notice.

December 30 Soviet Premier Khrushchev says in a newspaper interview that the Soviet Union will not resume nuclear testing unless the Western powers do so first. He repeats the Soviet Union is ready to conclude an agreement on the final cessation of nuclear tests at once.

1960
February 11 United States presents "threshold" plan for banning all tests except those in far space and those underground which pro-

duce seismic signals below 4.75 on the universal magnitude scale.

February 13   France explodes its first nuclear device in the Sahara Desert.

March 16   Atomic Energy Commission announces preparations for underground nuclear tests for peaceful purposes in New Mexico in 1961.

March 19   Soviet Union calls special Saturday session of the Geneva negotiations to present counter-proposals to American February 11 position. The Kremlin suggests a treaty banning all tests in the atmosphere, in the oceans, in cosmic space and underground above seismic magnitude 4.75. The Soviet Union also accepts the idea of a research program to improve inspection. The treaty should also be accompanied by a simultaneous obligation not to test below the seismic threshold of 4.75 magnitude. The moratorium should run four to five years.

March 29   British Prime Minister Macmillan and President Eisenhower issue communique after day and a half of conversations at Camp David, responding favorably to the Soviet counter-proposal. The threshold treaty should be signed first, they say, then each of them would be ready to institute a voluntary moratorium "of agreed duration" below the threshold, "to be accomplished by unilateral declaration of each of the three powers." Joint research should start as soon as possible.

April 4   Secretary of State Herter says United States-British joint response to Soviet counter-proposal "brought within reach" an agreement which "could well be an historic turning point in the quest for the agreed arms control measures which would lead to a far greater degree of international peace and security."

April 19–23   Joint Congressional Committee on Atomic Energy hears testimony casting doubt on the effectiveness of inspection and control system projected for the nuclear test-ban treaty.

May 1   American U-2 spy plane downed in Soviet Union.

May 11   Soviet, American and British experts open two-week meeting to plan joint research program to lower threshold for detection of underground nuclear tests. Americans announce plans for both nuclear and nonnuclear explosions, Soviet experts ready to carry out large chemical explosions only.

May 16   Khrushchev torpedoes Paris summit conference because of U-2 incident, withdraws his invitation to President Eisenhower to visit the Soviet Union.

May 27   Ambassador Tsarapkin repudiates Soviet experts and denies Soviet Union plans any underground tests for research purposes.

1961
March 21   Geneva test-ban talks resumed in Geneva with the Kennedy Administration's team in charge of the American delegation. Ambassador Arthur Dean presents the Soviet Union with a list of seven concessions designed to reach quick agreement

with the Soviet Union on a treaty. Soviet Union responds by demanding substitution for the single administration of the control organization of a tripartite board representing the Soviet Union, the Western allies and the neutrals. The board or "troika" should act only in unanimity.

April 18 United States and Britain table complete draft treaty banning tests down to 4.75 threshold. They say they are ready to sign immediately.

May 29 United States and United Kingdom offer "sliding scale" formula for setting the annual ceiling on on-site inspections, instead of the flat quota of 20. Quota of inspections would increase from a base of 12, only if there were more unidentified events than 60. Inspection would increase, one for each five events, up to a ceiling of 20 annual on-site inspections.

June 3–4 President Kennedy spends "a very somber two days" in conversations with Premier Khrushchev in Vienna. Deadlock on nuclear test ban persists.

July 15 United States and Britain take test-ban problem to the United Nations by asking that the 16th General Assembly debate an agenda item entitled "The Urgent Need for a Treaty to Ban Nuclear Weapons Tests under Effective International Control."

Late July Joint Congressional Atomic Energy Committee hears progress report on methods of detecting and identifying underground and high-altitude nuclear explosions. One scientist's conclusion: "The control system currently being negotiated at the Geneva Test Ban Conference has a very limited capability to monitor nuclear weapons tests."

July 27 Soviet Premier Khrushchev tells John J. McCloy, President Kennedy's adviser on disarmament and nuclear tests, that his scientists and military leaders are urging the testing of a 100-megaton bomb that could be carried in a rocket.

August 29 Ambassador Dean returns to Geneva Conference to plead with the Soviet Union to reconsider the test-ban idea.

August 30 United States and United Kingdom offer two amendments to their draft treaty of April 18, 1961. One amendment provides that the administrator could be recalled by a vote of seven out of 11 of the control commission. This would have given the dissenting vote to the three non-associated states which the United States and the U.K. proposed should be on the control commission. The second amendment provides that a certain number of nationals of non-associated states should be sent on inspection teams to investigate unidentified events.

August 30 Soviet Union announces its intention to resume nuclear tests.

September 1 Soviet Union resumes nuclear tests in atmosphere.

September 1–3 Belgrade Conference of uncommitted powers avoids harsh criticism of Soviet Union's resumption of testing.

September 3 President Kennedy and Prime Minister Macmillan appeal to Premier Khrushchev to agree immediately "not to conduct nuclear tests which take place in the atmosphere and produce radioactive fallout." What would be in effect an atmospheric test ban could be instituted without any inspection. The Soviet Union rejected the offer out of hand. The deadline for accepting the offer was September 9.

September 5 President Kennedy announces the United States will resume tests—underground.

September 15 First United States test since 1958 conducted underground at Nevada.

November 2 President Kennedy orders preparations for resumption of atmospheric tests.

November 28 Soviet Union turns its back completely on provisional agreements negotiated since 1958, rejects any idea of international control, proposes test ban with no international vertification of any kind.

1962
March 2 President Kennedy announces decision to resume nuclear testing in the atmosphere in the latter part of April unless Soviet Union signs nuclear test-ban treaty with effective inspection by then.

March 14 United States and Britain resubmit their draft treaty at the 17-nation Geneva Conference on General Disarmament. The United States offers to discuss other concessions, including removal of the 4.75 magnitude threshold. Soviet Union rejects the Anglo-American offer.

April 16 Eight new members of the Disarmament Conference offer joint memorandum to the three nuclear powers suggesting a compromise for reaching a nuclear test-ban treaty agreement. Two of its features were: to use national systems plus international stations and to allow on-site inspections only by invitation of the suspected violator.

April 19 Soviet Union accepts 8-nation joint memorandum as the basis for future negotiations on a test-ban treaty. The U.S. and the U.K. accept the joint memorandum as one of the possible bases for reaching agreement on a test ban.

April 25 United States resumes atmospheric testing at Christmas Island in the Pacific.

July 6 United States fires high-altitude shot from missile launched at Johnston Island, the Pacific.

July 22 *Tass* announces resumption of Soviet nuclear tests.

August 27 United States and Britain offer new draft treaty for a comprehensive ban on all tests, another alternative treaty banning tests only under water, in the atmosphere, and in space. Soviet Union immediately rejects the offers.

Fall Ambassador Arthur Dean reduces requirements for on-site inspections to 8–10 per year.

November 4 President Kennedy announces end of American nuclear test series in Nevada.

December 19 Premier Khrushchev once again offers two to three on-site inspections per year on Soviet territory. He also offers to accept three unmanned seismic stations on Soviet territory.

December 29   President Kennedy sends cordial reply to Premier Khrushchev, suggesting negotiations.

1963
January 7   Premier Khrushchev agrees to immediate negotiations.
January 26   President Kennedy announces suspension of United States underground tests in Nevada.
January 26   Republicans plan campaign to oppose Kennedy Administration's proposal for a nuclear test ban.
January–
  February   Secret negotiations by United States and Soviet Union in New York and Washington. United States asks seven unmanned seismic stations inside the Soviet Union.
February 1   Soviet Union breaks off secret test-ban talks in New York.
  William C. Foster, Director of Arms Control and Disarmament Agency, defends new, long-range detection system for test ban in paper submitted to Republican Conference's Committee on Testing.
February 1   Dr. Edward Teller claims proposed ban would be "virtually unpoliced" and "would endanger our security and help the Soviet Union in its plan to conquer the world."
February 2   President Kennedy announces intention to resume tests underground at Nevada after Soviet Union breaks off secret talks.
  Soviet Union explodes underground nuclear tests at Semipalatinsk.
February 19   United States offers to accept seven on-site inspections per year in the Soviet Union, provided United States and United Kingdom can pick events to be inspected.
February 21   Senator Dodd, Democrat of Connecticut, says he would vote against Kennedy Administration's test-ban proposals if a treaty were submitted for Senate ratification.
March 5–12   Joint Atomic Energy Committee hears testimony of Defense Department and State Department experts on capabilities and deficiencies of the United States-United Kingdom long-range detection and identification system for a test ban.
March 6   President Kennedy pledges the United States will not accept a test ban "which did not give us every assurance that we could detect a series of tests underground."

Part I

FALLOUT—FACTS AND MYTHS

In the heyday of American horror movies, Boris Karloff used to propel hearts to throats when he turned from his steaming test tubes and switched off the light. Only the skeletons of his hands glowed in the darkness. They were luminous from tedious experiments with radium and other sinister radioactive substances out of which he conjured supernatural monsters.

Hollywood's script writers evidently had been stimulated by reports, shortly after World War I, of the lethal effect on watch- and clock-makers of many years exposure to the luminescent, radioactive materials with which they painted the faces and hands of their timepieces.

Horror movies may have been part of the preconditioning for the great waves of fear that drenched the world when radiation effects of atomic bombs first became known. Natural radiation or X rays, administered by doctors, dentists, and shoe clerks, had been much more dangerous for 99 per cent of the world's peoples. But they evoked no such mass misgivings.

A few types of radiation and radioactivity nevertheless were already established as fearsome phenomena when the first atomic bombs were dropped on Hiroshima and Nagasaki in August, 1945. Japanese doctors who survived the blasts told of a hideous radiation sickness that frequently caused piteous, lingering illness, then death.

That was in 1945. Fears of radiation persisted. Civil-defense advocates kept them alive. Obviously, nuclear wars would unleash deadly blankets of radiation. But there was no serious thought given to halting nuclear-weapons development because of the radiation released in tests. No thought, that is, until March, 1954, when the United States tested a 15-megaton hydrogen bomb at Bikini.

An unexpectedly heavy blanket of radioactive fallout from the blast covered 7,000 square miles of the Pacific, including some inhabited islands. Natives on the Marshall Islands and Americans at a weather station in the area were exposed to severe radiation doses. Although their rescue and treatment were not handled in the most expeditious manner, none of them, luckily, was exposed to a lethal dose.

Their misfortune might not have created much of a stir, either, had it not been for the unexpected appearance in Japan, two weeks after the H-bomb explosion, of a boatload of fishermen who had accidentally been dusted with the radioactive fallout.

Fish in the hold of their tuna trawler were found to be contaminated. Other catches brought to Japanese markets reportedly were also radioactive. The price of fish, one of Japan's most important sources of protein, dropped drastically.

A near-panic spread all over the Far East and, eventually, throughout the world. Nuclear-*test* effects were suddenly equated with nuclear-*war* effects. Communist radios and publications screamed warnings for months, casting the United States in the role of careless villain.

The cry was also taken up by respected world leaders like India's Prime Minister Nehru. His complaint, in essence, was that the two nuclear powers, the United States and the Soviet Union, had no right to contaminate the rest of the world even if the contamination were light. It was a telling argument.

As the protests gained in volume, the dangers from testing were progressively exaggerated. The Soviet Union began to sense that the Bikini accident had handed her a powerful new weapon. What the Kremlin's aim was still is not definitely known. Perhaps it was only to sow confusion; perhaps to persuade the West to join in outlawing the use of nuclear weapons in warfare. From this side of the Iron Curtain it appeared that the Soviet Union would gain if nuclear war were outlawed.

If Washington could be persuaded, for moral, humanitarian, and health reasons, to abandon or reduce its reliance on nuclear weapons as the foundation of its military establishment, the Western world would have to depend on non-nuclear forces. Under the iron discipline of their dictatorship, the Communists kept a significantly superior conventional force under arms. The Reds would have a military edge.

Whatever the Soviet motives, the Bikini accident dislodged the first stone in an avalanche of fear that was eventually to smother America's nuclear-weapons development for more than three years—without any assurance (except Nikita Khrushchev's dubious word) that the Soviet Union was similarly hobbled.

When the Soviet Union suddenly jumped back into the atmospheric-testing business in September 1961, thirty-four months after it ostensibly had quit, the United States needed another seven months before it could get back to atmospheric testing.

During the United States' thirty-four months of total abstention there was no way to know if the Soviet Union was or was not testing secretly underground. Results of the impressive Soviet series in September and October 1961 showed progress that could well have been made possible by undetected underground shots.

But even after that open-air series the United States hesitated. The cloud of fear for the health hazards of fallout still lingered over the scene. Policymakers shrank from criticism of the weaker peoples of the world if the United States were to resume. President Kennedy stayed his decision to resume atmospheric testing until March 2, 1962, when he announced his plan to order resumption unless the Soviet Union signed an effectively-inspected treaty by late April.

The first atmospheric shot since October 30, 1958, was fired over Christmas Island on April 25, 1962. Part of the delay in American resumption was privately attributed to lack of preparations before September 1961, when the Soviet Union suddenly began testing again.

Obviously the post-1958 maneuvering hurt the United States and permitted the Soviet Union to gain in the nuclear arms race.

How was the United States sucked in? It is the purpose of this book to take a long hard look at how it happened. Much of the United States' eyes-wide-open movement into the nuclear ambush makes incredible reading.

But before digging into that story, the point should be made more convincingly that radioactive fallout from nuclear weapons tests generated fears that were wholly unfounded.

Chapter 1

Biological Effects of Radiation

Whatever the extent of our ignorance of the biological effects of radiation, we do know that these effects are not unexperienced by the human species, even from the genetic point of view, since it is clear now that persons living at high altitudes on granite rocks always have received extra radiation many times greater than is contained in radioactive fallout from the testing of nuclear weapons, and that even those living on certain sedimentary rocks at sea level always have received ten to twenty times the present fallout dose.[1]

There is no complete understanding of how radiation breaks down human tissue. The suspicion, however, is that radiation disintegrates the cells themselves and the liquid in which they are bathed. If living tissues are exposed to enough radiation, all of them will die. But various organisms of the human body have varying resistive powers to radiation.

One thousand roentgens of X rays or gamma rays spread over the entire body will cause death within a few hours. One of the fearsome things about radiation is that even a dose of this enormous size is not apparent to the victim. Radiation does not hurt when it is absorbed. The senses cannot detect it.

According to past experiences with acute, whole-body doses of radiation,[2] 600 roentgens or more are likely to produce eventual death in all the people exposed. With doses of 300 to 600 roentgens, half the people will die, others will be severely ill, lose their hair, and suffer other long-term effects.

Persons exposed to 200 or 300 roentgens may suffer illness for a period of three months. Those getting 100 to 200 roentgens in an acute dose recover, but they suffer nausea and fatigue and their life span may be shortened as much as 1 per cent.

Sixty-four people accidentally sprinkled with local fallout from a 1954 American H-bomb were exposed to a dose of 175 roentgens and recovered completely; there were no deaths.

If the doses are received over a period of years, somewhat larger radiation exposure can be tolerated.

6

While a dose of 100 roentgens does not directly cause sickness or death, it may still have harmful biological consequences. Susceptibility to bone cancer or leukemia may be increased. Leukemia is a disease in which the white blood cells multiply too rapidly. It is fatal.

A man exposed to 100 roentgens is by no means certain to contract leukemia or bone cancer. He merely *may* contract it more easily during the course of his life. His chances are a matter that health statisticians will now be establishing as they keep close watch over test cases for the rest of this century. So far, information is too scanty to permit categorical statements.

Experiments with generations of mice indicate that tumors and leukemia occur more often among animals exposed to relatively large doses of radiation. But the life span of some mice so exposed was increased about 10 per cent.

Doses of 25 to 100 roentgens produce slight transient effects; they seldom produce disabling sickness. It is possible that there are other undefined and practically unidentifiable delayed effects in the 25–100 roentgen-dose range.

Acute dosages up to 25 roentgens produce no detectable clinical effect. There may be delayed effects, but these are not now known. The threshold for noticeable effects from radiation is generally considered to be 25 roentgens.

Fallout from all bomb tests to 1961 will deliver an average lifetime dose to man only 1/100th to 1/60th this threshold amount.

Man's natural environment gives him a seventy-year dose of radiation seventeen to thirty-five times greater than he will receive from fallout from all tests by all countries of the world up to 1961. During man's reproductive period, the average fallout radiation dose to the gonads from all tests so far will be only 1/60th the dose he receives from his natural environment.

Radiation damage depends upon the power of the dose and the length of time the human body is exposed. It is like sunburn. Strong sun can be tolerated on the skin for a short period of time, but over a longer period it can be extremely damaging. Weaker sunrays can be tolerated on the skin for a longer period.

Radiation from gamma rays, X rays, or beta particles depends on the same two factors, the intensity of the dose and the length of exposure.

Living tissue, however, is not always permanently damaged by radiation. Some tissue has the power of repairing itself, at least partially. It is for this reason that the rate at which the radiation dose is received is important in judging the extent of permanent biological damage.

Some living tissue may lack the power of recovery. Damage to genes, for instance, may be irreparable. The genes control the reproductive processes in man. Ionizing radiation applied to the genes, therefore, could be 100 per cent cumulative in its effect.

Radiation doses are classified as acute or chronic. Acute exposure usually means exposure to one severe dose or a series of doses in a short period of time. Continuous or small doses over a long period of time are referred to as chronic exposure.

Acute exposure results in both immediate and delayed biological effects. Chronic exposure is usually considered to produce only delayed effects.

World-wide fallout causes extremely low potency, chronic exposure with delayed effects. Local fallout, however, in the area close to the detonation of a nuclear weapon, can produce acute exposure with immediate effects.

Local Fallout

Acute exposure and heavy dosages of radiation from bombs are unlikely, except in a nuclear war or in the area close to a nuclear test.

Most of what we know about the reactions of the human body to a single heavy dose of weapon radiation comes from the bomb victims in Hiroshima and Nagasaki. There have also been a few high-roentgen accidents to radiologists in atomic-energy plants.

We also have one case of accidental acute exposure of a group of Marshall Islands natives to heavy local fallout from the American hydrogen bomb in March, 1954. Biological effects from these events were immediate.

Because local fallout is "fresh," it still contains many kinds of radioactivities not found in fallout that has aged. There is a tenfold decrease in activity for each sevenfold increase in time, applying to both beta and gamma activities. Thus the hazard disappears relatively rapidly. Its early intensity can cause serious injury, however, if human beings are caught up in it.

These injuries can range from death-dealing gamma doses at or near ground zero to small doses, producing no visible symptoms, at the edge of the local fallout area.

Mild cases of beta damage resemble sunburn, but heavier cases can result in surface hemorrhages and blisters some weeks after absorption. Beta burns are painful and heal slowly; but the patient does not become ill, unless large areas of the body are exposed to beta radiation.

With advance warning, beta burns can be avoided by wearing clothing that covers all of the skin—for example, coveralls and light gloves and boots, taped over at the ankles and wrists. Fallout that gets on the skin should be washed off to avoid cumulative effects.

Gamma radiation in the local zone is a greater hazard than are beta particles. High doses can cause radiation sickness and death. Small gamma doses do not result in radiation sickness, but they may cause the blood to change, lead to a shortening of the life, or cause genetic damage.

Large gamma-ray concentrations can penetrate 3 or 4 feet of well-packed earth or 2 feet of concrete.

Local fallout doses range downward from thousands of roentgens to a few hundred—compared with an average dose of only a few thousandths of a roentgen from world-wide fallout. Beyond the immediate area of a nuclear explosion, rainstorms may produce "hot spots" where the level rises briefly to 30 or 40 roentgens. But this dies out after a few days. Most of the world gets only 50 or less *milliroentgens* per year.

World-wide Fallout

We have only inferential knowledge of most delayed effects from light radiation doses produced by world-wide fallout, as differentiated from early or immediate effects of heavier radiation in man. Inferences have been drawn from experiments with animals, from statistics, and from a limited number of medical and industrial observations; but the doses always have been 10 to 999 times larger than those attributable to world-wide fallout.

Delayed effects are of two main types, genetic and somatic. Future generations could be damaged by the *genetic* effects. *Somatic* effects, which apply to persons living now, may include leukemia, skin changes, precancerous lesions, abnormal growths like tumors, cataracts, changes in the life span and effects on growth and development.

But these effects are also produced by causes other than ionizing radiation. For the most part, it is impossible to say whether radiation or other causes produced them.

Past experience has shown certain organs of the body to be more sensitive to radiation than others. This experience has come from comparing effects of X rays in humans and animals, from radioisotope experiments in animals, and from observation of the effects of radium and other radioisotopes in man.

The so-called "critical organs" of the human body, with the suspected kinds of delayed effects produced by radiation, are: (1) gonads—genetic mutations that could be damaging to future generations; (2) bone marrow and other blood-forming organs—the leukemias, aplastic anemia; (3) whole body—shortening of the life span; (4) single organs (bone, skin, thyroid, and so forth)—abnormal growths or tumors (neoplasma) and other pathological effects; (5) the lens of the eye—cataracts.

These are the delayed effects that the Federal Radiation Council, appointed in 1960 by President Eisenhower, has considered in assigning guides for external and internal exposure.[3]

The doses man receives from radioactive fallout are far too small for their effects to be noticed. At the peak of exposure in May 1959, people in Illinois are estimated to have been absorbing a dose rate of eight-millionths of a roentgen per hour or one-fifteenth roentgen per year, had the peak dose persisted. The average annual dose from natural background radiation in the United States is one-tenth roentgen. But the Federal Radiation Council has found that "in an individual adult it is difficult or in some cases impossible to detect effects from a single external exposure of less than 25 to 50 r, and from continuing exposure to levels even about two orders of magnitude greater than natural background." [4]

Put another way: Fallout radioactivity would have to deliver doses hundreds of times greater than the present dose to produce detectable effects.

Over his lifetime, man's sensitivity to radiation varies. Doses to the gonads are significant only during man's reproductive period. His overall health can be affected by radiation throughout his whole lifetime, an average of approximately seventy years.

An embryo in a mother's womb may suffer effects to its organ system from acute exposures of 2 to 10 roentgens, or to its skeleton from 24 roentgens.

The thyroid of a youngster is more sensitive than is that of an adult. Cancer of the thyroid has followed acute external exposure of approximately 150 roentgens in children, although similar cancers have not developed in adults until exposures of several hundred roentgens.

Children also have been found to be three or four times as sensitive to X rays on the skin, which studies show produce skin tumors.

A lingering medical mystery, of special significance to fallout study, is the effect of small radiation dosages on humans. Scientists simply have not been able to accumulate any evidence that small radiation doses, below about 25 roentgens, are harmful.

Experiments with animals, using total *acute* doses ranging from 25 to 1,000 roentgens, have shown that, insofar as genetic effects are concerned, damage is directly proportional to dose. Chronic exposures, that is the same doses given in small increments, are only about one-fourth as effective in inducing genetic mutations as is acute exposure.

It is noteworthy, of course, that these experiments have been conducted on such comparatively tiny animals as fruit flies and mice, and that they have been exposed to dosages 100 to 3,000 times higher than humans receive from radioactive fallout.

Despite the imprecision of the experiments, however, most geneticists are agreed that any radiation, no matter how small, has some damaging effect on future generations if it reaches the genes. But proof of their theories has yet to be obtained.

There is less agreement among qualified scientists about the effects of low-level radiation on persons now living, as differentiated from effects on future generations. It has been suggested by some that there is a "threshold" dose, below which there is no damaging effect from radiation. But this is a matter of some dispute, where opposing sides base their views less on fact than instinct.

Those who try to prove that radiation below a certain roentgen value is harmless have only experiments with animals, at high-dose ranges above 100 roentgens, to support them. Extrapolating their results to man at low doses cannot produce reliable estimates.

Those who claim there is an effect from any dose, however small, attempt extrapolations at least as remote. Their data are mainly based on adult leukemia cases that developed after acute exposure above 50 roentgens—500 times the annual fallout dose. From the statistics on these leukemia cases, some have attempted to predict the incidence of leukemia in the general population per roentgen of exposure. But there is no way of knowing from past sketchy statistics whether susceptibility to leukemia varies with age or with the part of the body irradiated, or whether the exposure has been acute or chronic.

Faced with these uncertainties, the Federal Radiation Council has concluded that "the evidence is insufficient to prove either the hypothesis of a damage threshold or the hypothesis of no threshold in man at low dosages." [5]

It is instructive for making a judgment of the fallout hazard to study in more detail, however, how meager the evidence is on biological effects of radiation. These effects are usually divided into two categories, genetic and somatic.

GENETIC EFFECTS

There is no direct evidence from studies of human beings to show that low doses of radiation either do or do not cause damage to future generations.

There is evidence of a proportional cause-and-effect relationship between dose and genetic damage in fruit flies down to exposures of 25 roentgens and in mice down to 37 roentgens. This is a big dose on a small body of an animal with a much shorter life span than man.

The newborn child inherits twenty-four chromosomes from his mother and twenty-four matching chromosomes from his father. Each chromosome is a tiny strand along which the genes, carriers of heredity, are strung like beads. The child receives one gene from each parent for each characteristic of his make-up: the color of his hair, the color of his eyes, etc.

The gene from the father usually differs from that of the mother. When the twenty-four sets of chromosomes with their genes from each parent are fused, compromises are made where genes differ. Sometimes the compromise is "down the middle," other times it favors the characteristic of the father or the mother.

Either parent's gene may be "dominant," or it may be weaker than the other parent's, "recessive"; or a compromise may be struck.

For example, the child of a blue-eyed father and a brown-eyed mother with a recessive blue trait may have either blue eyes, brown eyes, or some other color depending on whether or not the father's gene combines with the mother's dominant (brown) or recessive (blue) gene.

If the genes transferred from the sex glands of either parent in the reproduction process are damaged, offspring can be weakened, malformed, killed, or stillborn.

On rare occasions genes change, either spontaneously or under influences not yet understood. Scientists call this "mutation." These mutant genes form new chemicals or new substances carrying new codes that result in new properties for the child in whom the genes reside.

Science does not yet know many causes of mutation, but radiation is suspected to be one of them. Presumably, beta and gamma radiations have this power.

If the injured gene is recessive or given to compromise, the consequences of human absorption of radiation among individuals capable of reproduction may not appear for several generations.

Ionizing radiation can have three effects on future generations if it occurs in germ cells: The cells could be killed, the chromosomes could be broken, the genes could be changed or mutated.

Destruction of the germ cell, of course, ends the reproduction process and would have no effect on future generations. When chromosomes are broken but do not lead to the death of the cell, the pieces of the chromosomes may reunite in unnatural ways or they may not join at all; in both cases the cell usually dies. If the reuniting of the chromosome pieces is not radical enough to cause cell death, the changed chromosomes, probably with modified genes along their lengths, may be passed on to future generations. The "grafted" chromosomes could then lead to many kinds of occurrences, from miscarriages to grotesque malformations, or to minor malformations in descendants.

It appears likely that large radiation doses will produce either radical changes in the chromosomes or kill the germ cells outright.

Low-level radiations continued over long periods also have some effect, but there is a dispute as to how important they are in causing mutations. Because human germ cells may be capable of repair, some believe that light doses of radiation will have no permanent effect. They say there is some "threshold," below which radiation has no effect on human reproduction. Most geneticists, however, believe there is no "threshold," and that any amount of radiation is harmful. Their explanation of why natural background radiation has not caused a mounting incidence of malformation over past generations is unclear.

Several unknowns add to the difficulty in judging the effects of low radiation doses on future generations: What is the rate of spontaneous gene mutation? What is the over-all rate of all induced mutation rates, from all causes? How do improved health-protection practices affect the accumulation of genetic mutations? Can healthy genes help in repairing sick genes?

International and national groups setting radiation-protection guides have wrestled valiantly with the problem of the genetic effects of radiation at low dose rates. However, their standards have been based chiefly on intuition and experience with acute, rather than chronic, radiation, and on experiments with mice, rather than men.

Recent experiments with mice have shown that the genetic effects of low chronic doses of radiation may actually be less severe than past estimates based on mutation rates in mice after acute radiation.

At a so-called "low-dose rate" of 90 roentgens per *week* from chronic gamma radiation, mice showed fewer gene mutations than at a high-dose rate of acute radiation of 90 roentgens per *minute*. In both cases the total accumulated doses were identical. Experiments with fruit flies also produced fewer mutations at the so-called low-dose rate.

Only one-fourth as many mutations occurred under the chronic low-dose-rate radiation. These "low-dose rates" were still enormous in comparison with fallout doses. The effects of lower doses would not be detectable unless billions of mice were studied and unless hundreds of laboratory technicians were thrown into the project.

According to Dr. W. L. Russell, an Oak Ridge scientist whose experiments disclosed the importance of dose rates, giving doses below 90 roentgens is impractical because results cannot be observed. There was this exchange in the 1959 Joint Atomic Energy Committee Hearings:

> REPRESENTATIVE HOLIFIELD. Let me ask you this question: If you exposed parent mice to 10 roentgens, would you be able to detect somatic effects in their offspring?
>
> DR. RUSSELL. I think this would be extremely difficult at the present time with any kind of practical experiment that we can envision. Our lowest dose in the chronic radiation experiment [given over many days or weeks] was 86 roentgens, and at this point, even with over 50,000 offspring, we are not able to tell for sure that the mutation frequency is higher than the control frequency or even that it is lower than in the acute [one-shot] radiation experiment. We arrived at the difference between chronic and acute at higher dose levels. I think it would be very difficult and would require a tremendous experiment to determine the effect of 10 roentgens.

Another recent experiment has shown that it takes radiation doses of 25 roentgens—250 times the annual fallout rate—to produce fractures in chromosomes of human cells grown in tissue culture. This may lead to the conclusion there is a threshold dose below which no damage is done by radiation.

To summarize findings on the effects of radioactive fallout on future generations: There is no evidence that radiation of this extremely low level produces any genetic damage. The only practical experiments, those on tiny animals like fruit flies and mice whose reproductive periods are much shorter than man's, have been conducted with comparatively enormous doses, from 25 roentgens up to 100 roentgens and beyond—hundreds of times greater than the dose dropped on man's much larger body by radioactive fallout.

Dr. Herman J. Muller, Professor of Zoology at the University of Indiana, and one of the world's leading geneticists, characterized the genetic danger of fallout from H-bomb tests as "relatively minor," in 1957 testimony before the Joint Committee of the Congress on Atomic Energy.[6]

Somatic Effects

Leukemia is a disease in which an abnormal number of white blood cells are produced. Deaths from leukemia have been increasing in recent years, and science has found no dependable cure for it. Part of the rise may be more apparent than real—attributable to improved diagnosis and better statistics. The changing pattern of everyday life may also play a significant part.

Leukemia can be induced in animals by exposing them to radiation, and there is a stronger statistical link between leukemia and irradiation than there is between other supposed somatic effects and radiation.

Most studies of leukemia statistics show that the incidence of the disease on persons exposed to radiation increases with the exposure dose. Above about 50 roentgens of whole-body acute radiation exposure, there is a proportional, or linear, correlation between dosage and leukemia incidence. Thus, the higher the dose the greater the chance of leukemia.

Reports that two to 10 roentgens administered to unborn babies in their mothers' wombs can double the incidence of leukemia have not been supported by subsequent studies.

The rising leukemia rate in the general population is due mainly to the increase of cases of chronic lymphatic leukemia. But there is no satisfactory evidence that radiation produces this type of leukemia.[7]

The nation's highest authority on radiation, the Federal Radiation Council, takes a skeptical view of studies that have found striking correlations between leukemia and radiation exposures. The Council lists these limitations and difficulties in past studies of leukemia-radiation correlations:

a. Dipping into old statistics presents difficulties in accurately determining the radiation dose received.

b. Radiation-recording methods have not been uniform in the past.

c. Statistics on disease and on death rates are difficult to correlate because of varying interview techniques.

d. Selection of cases for study may be overweighted with diseases related to leukemia.

e. The number of persons in the population samples have usually been small.

Leukemia is a rare disease with an incidence of only 5 per 100,000 persons in the general population, and its many varying types make it difficult to compare the various statistics. Effects on the blood such as are seen in leukemia can be attributed to causes other than radiation, and there is no known way to distinguish a radiation-leukemia from others. Some types appear to vary with age, a cause that could easily be confused with radiation.

A clear correlation between leukemia and prior radiation has been demonstrated only where the exposures have been high, such as several thousand roentgens of prolonged intermittent exposure; or 500 roentgens to the bone marrow of adult males for diseases previously contracted; or 50 to 100 roentgens for acute whole-body radiation to the general population of all ages, as in Hiroshima and Nagasaki; or acute doses of 2 to 10 roentgens to the fetus.[8]

The Federal Radiation Council concluded that long follow-up periods are required to judge leukemia experience after low-level irradiation.[9]

> It is unlikely that retrospective studies will definitely solve the question of the shape of the dose-responsive curve at low levels of exposure or the existence of a threshold. . . . The risk of any one individual developing leukemia is small even with relatively large doses. However, when large populations are exposed, the absolute number of people affected may be considerable.

R. H. Mole of the Medical Research Council in Great Britain's Atomic Energy Research Establishment at Harwell, has reported experiments that indicate low-dose rates do not produce leukemia in mice.

At Argonne National Laboratory, strontium-90 was injected into mice. It was found, however, that this internally-deposited strontium-90 is "relatively ineffective" in inducing leukemia in the limited experimentation conducted.[10]

Leukemia experts also have found that varying doses had varying effects, depending on the type of leukemia produced. Thresholds, if they appeared, occurred at different points.

"Present data, though inadequate, are consistent with the concept that there exists a threshold dose below which leukemia will not result from radiation," according to Dr. Lloyd W. Law, Head of the Leukemia Study Section, National Cancer Institute, U.S. Public Health Service. "This threshold dose may be quite different for the different morphologic forms of leukemia." Dr. Law found that chronic radiation, of which global fallout is an example, is "appreciably less effective" than acute radiation in inducing leukemias.

Because of the widespread fears that strontium-90 from fallout would produce leukemia when ingested, the Federal Radiation Council paid

special attention to internal emitters in its study of the leukemia-radiation correlation. Its findings:

> We have no documented evidence that bone depositions of strontium in
> humans have produced leukemia. Statements that radio strontium is leuke-
> mogenic [produces leukemia] are based solely upon studies in mice. Since
> leukemia is a common disease spontaneously occurring in certain strains of
> mice, one cannot accept this observation as necessarily applicable to man.

The FRC also studied effects of internally deposited isotopes of thorium, radium, and iodine. Only a few cases of leukemia have been reported in medical literature following thorium injections, the FRC
found, and dose calculations were complicated by the presence of other
radioactivity. The leukemia cases reported occurred after latent periods
of up to twenty years.

Persons with radium deposits in their bones developed bone cancers,
but no cases of leukemia have been reported. Said the FRC, "This is not
unexpected in view of the fact that radium deposited in bones results
in a relatively small dose to the bone marrow."

So few cases of leukemia were reported in patients treated with iodine-
131 for hyperthyroidism or cancer of the thyroid that the FRC appealed
for "planned large-population studies" on such people.[11]

To summarize, leukemia is one of the most likely effects of low-dose
radiation—if there are any effects—but statistics are so fragile that nothing definite is known. Experiments with animals have had the usual
shortcomings of large doses on small experimental animals.

After large doses, of course, the evidence that radiation causes leukemia
is more convincing. Japanese exposed to the *local* fallout of atomic
bombs in Hiroshima and Nagasaki in 1945 are now more leukemia-prone
than other individuals in Japan. Incidence of leukemia has more than
tripled among the Japanese in these two cities. It took about six years
for the appearance of the leukemia symptoms. The Japanese exposure,
however, was on the order of 50 to 100 roentgens for the whole body,
absorbed in a few days. This is 100 to 250 times the estimated cumulative
seventy-year dose from all global fallout to date.

The United Nations Scientific Committee on Radiation Effects, after
reviewing all available data world-wide in 1958, could not make one
categorical statement about the effects of fallout on leukemia. There are
scientific data available to allow the conclusion, however, that there is a
threshold for leukemia induction.[12]

Other Cancers and Abnormal Growths

There is clinical evidence that radiation can cause cancers of the skin,
thyroid, bone, and lung. But the doses are again two and three orders of

magnitude, hundreds and thousands of times larger, than those given off by radioactive fallout.

Take the widely-known case of the miners in Schneeberg and Joachim-sthal, Czechoslovakia, where an ore containing radioactive pitchblende was extracted. These miners were discovered late in the 1800's to be dying in midlife from a respiratory illness called "mountain sickness." The mountain sickness turned out to be cancer of the lung. Half the miners who died in those Czech cities up to 1939 died of lung cancer. They had been breathing radon, a gas that is the first decay-product of radium, in concentrations thirty times the amount recommended by the International Commission on Radiological Protection. Radon, when inhaled, gives birth to other radioactive "daughter products." The daughter products also can be inhaled directly, attached to dust particles in the atmosphere. If they become lodged in the chest they can irradiate lung tissue for long periods of time.

Radiologists calculated that the miners at Schneeberg and Joachim-sthal absorbed about 1,000 roentgens over a period of seventeen years, the length of time before the lung cancers appeared. This dosage probably was not spread evenly over the surface of the lungs, so some parts may have received up to 10,000 roentgens and more during a miner's working life.

Great Britain's Medical Research Council investigated the hazard that radioactive fallout, on its way down from the stratosphere and tropo-sphere, would be inhaled into the lungs and produce lung cancer. It was found that "not more than one or two particles of the more highly active substances are breathed by any person in the course of a year." This amount is unlikely to "constitute a problem in ordinary civilian life," the British report of 1956 concluded.

In contrast to the lung-cancer hazard from internal emitters, external radiation of X and gamma rays is not considered a source of lung cancer.

Bone Tumors

Several radioactive substances are "bone seeking." Radium and a daughter product of thorium, like strontium-90, tend to lodge in the bone when they are ingested. There they can cause local destruction of tissue.

Cancers of the bones and joints developed among watch- and clock-dial painters in the period from 1916 to 1924. Their habit was to "tip" their brushes with their mouths. They thus swallowed radioactive atoms in radium. Some of the atoms became lodged in their bones. When large amounts were swallowed, death was known to occur in about three years. The victims also suffered severe anemia, hemorrhages, and infections, particularly in their jawbones. Others, who took smaller quantities of paint into their systems, also developed bone diseases that caused "rheumatic" pains or sometimes fractures. In some cases, cancer of the bone followed.

These early doses to the clock-painters, however, were again two or three orders of magnitude greater than might be expected to lodge in the bones of man as a result of test fallout.

The Federal Radiation Council attempted to assemble as much experience as possible on changes in human bone due to radiation. It gathered studies of the radium-dial painters; patients treated medically with radium waters; and persons drinking water with a relatively high radium content. Their information permitted evaluation of thirty-five year exposures from radioactive materials in the bone, an unusually broad set of statistics in this field.

Body burdens in living persons were calculated by analyzing the breath, by measuring the whole-body gamma-ray counts, by analyzing excreta, and by assaying teeth and bone.

So far, the FRC reported in May, 1960, "there is no evidence to establish definitely the presence or absence of a threshold for the effects of radium deposition in the bone." In other words, it is not known if low doses are compensated for by the repair processes of the body.

Using radiographic equipment to detect bone changes in adults exposed to radium, it was concluded that "minimal" changes in the bones occur when the residual body burden of radioactivity, measured several decades after exposure, reaches about 0.2 microgram. Because there was no group of "normal" persons with which to compare these adults exposed to radium, there was considerable doubt as to whether the effect observed was attributable to radium or to other unknown causes.

"There seems to be no doubt that, at 0.5 microgram burden," the FRC reported, however, "changes in adult bones, shown by radiographs, are manifest in some individuals." Where the concentration is as high as 0.8 microgram, the FRC found consistent changes in the bones. Among scientists working on the project, the FRC reported, "there is agreement that bone tumors begin to occur at about a burden of 0.8 to 1.0 microgram." Teeth changes, in the same study, showed up in one young person whose body burden was 0.15 microgram.

Prediction is "hazardous" on the effects of body burdens below 0.1 microgram on changes in bones, the FRC reported.

There is real doubt, it was said, whether the diagnostic methods now being used on humans can show any "damage" below 0.1 microgram. One difficulty is that the latent period for the development of "clinically significant" effects increases as the body burden decreases. The latent period in experimental animals may be so long that the animal will die before any effects are detected.

Information on the effects of other radioactive substances lodged in the bone is scanty. Experiments with mice have shown, however, that radium is ten times as potent as radiostrontium in producing tumors. Man also may get rid of radium more rapidly than mice, so no ratio can be applied as between radium and strontium effects in humans.

"Although bone tumors have been produced by radiostrontium in animals, it should be noted that no cases of bone tumors have been demonstrated in man as due to strontium-90," the FRC observed.

If there is no threshold dose below which bone tumors do not occur, experimental evidence still shows that very few bone tumors will result from low body burdens of strontium-90.[13]

A suggested maximum level for strontium-90 in the bones, for the general population, has been set by the International Commission on Radiological Protection at 66 strontium units. The dose from all artificial radiation sources to the bone, in Western and Eastern civilizations, will vary from 8 to 15 per cent of the suggested maximum.

In 1920, twenty-five years after the discovery of the X ray, radiologists and technicians who had been administering X rays in hospitals and doctors' offices, began to develop cancer of the skin, usually in their hands, forearms, or faces. These were the areas that had been exposed to the biggest X-ray doses from the "slop over" of the diagnostic and therapeutic doses administered to patients.

The latent period for cancer of the skin has been found to be as long as twenty-five years. The average is ten to fifteen years. When doses are accumulated slowly, however, as in occupational exposure, the latent period is greater.

Except in the immediate area of detonation, nuclear weapons fallout will not produce skin cancer or other illnesses of the skin, such as erythema and dermatitis. Early cases of skin cancer were allowed to develop mainly through ignorance of the danger. With modern practices, it is unlikely that anyone will expose his skin to such levels of radiation except in case of nuclear war or a nuclear accident.

The Federal Radiation Council, in its canvass of all available evidence, concluded that relatively high external-exposure levels are necessary to produce cancerous effects in tissues of man. Doses to the skin ranging from 500 to 2,500 roentgens have produced observable cancers in some persons, but these are quantities 1,000 to 25,000 times the lifetime fallout dose.

Life-span Shortening

One of the most difficult tasks for students of radiation effects is to establish a definite cause-effect relationship between radiation and shortening of life. Humans are not subject to the kind of rigid controls that are necessary for rigorous statistical analysis.

The Atomic Energy Commission is spending about $7.5 million annually on studies of the effect of small-dose radiation on the life span.

Besides studies in man, there are also studies in animals: mice, rats, guinea pigs, dogs, burros, chickens, swine, sheep, and monkeys. Several important projects were undertaken with dogs and burros, but the most extensive experimentation has been with mice and rats.

Studies in man involve mainly the effects of the 50 roentgens or more exposure to persons in Hiroshima and Nagasaki from the atomic bombs. Marshall Islanders exposed to 175 roentgens down to 14 roentgens are also being closely watched.[14]

Life-span shortening has been demonstrated in animals, when all other conditions have been maintained identical except exposure to radiation, and when chronic high doses of radiation were administered.

Surprisingly, it was found that very low dose rates might actually lengthen the life span of some animals. The mean life span of mice was found to be lengthened when they were exposed to very low dose rates whose total was about 100 roentgens. The evidence, however, was not conclusive.

At dosages of 100 to 300 roentgens and above, whole-body exposure, the life span of mice was shortened 1 to 1.5 per cent of the total life span per 100-roentgens total dose.

In experiments with dogs, it was found that low-dose rates have less effect than a single acute dose.

Doses ranging from 200 to 1,000 roentgens shortened the lives of animals exposed, but chronic radiation was found to be four to five times less effective per roentgen than a single acute dose.

The sketchy evidence accumulated so far indicates that there is partial recovery from acute radiation injury, but not all of the damage can be repaired, no matter how long the recovery period.

After exposure to radiation, experimental animals died of the same causes they had died of before, but earlier than normally.

As in other effects, there was no evidence to support assumptions that a chronic daily dose of 1 roentgen, or a similar small exposure, would produce any life shortening. The ability of the experimental animals to repair part of the radiation damage interfered with analysis.

The FRC found that preirradiation doses of at least 40 to 50 roentgens were necessary before definitive data could be obtained on the median lethal dose of radiation for animals.

Evidence that the *human* life span is shortened by radiation is even more limited. Mortality rates among American physicians and radiologists exposed to radiation have been compared with the general male population, but no definitive answers have been found.

The best information on the effects for the general population still comes from experiments on animals exposed to large doses of whole-body radiation.

"There are as yet no data in man to answer the questions of quantitative estimates of life shortening effect per rad [roentgen] of whole-body exposure," the FRC found.

Separating from all the physical defects in adults and growing-children those defects due to radiation is a feat science has not yet accomplished. Those of man's congenital defects that are caused by changes in the genes must first be identified. In this smaller group, then, one must find which defects are due to radiation. Among these there *may* be a still smaller group caused by fallout.

Rough guesses by some geneticists indicate that perhaps 0.7 per cent of all congenital defects are due to changes caused by some phenomenon in the environment. Radiation may be one of the factors.

Radiation doses from 25 roentgens up to several hundred or more have shown clear effects on animal-embryo development. Human pre-natal effects from this relatively high amount of radiation, compared with that attributable to fallout, include menstrual irregularities, mis-carriages, and stillbirths; a high postnatal death rate and abnormalities at birth; and late-stage difficulties, "such as subtle changes in physio-logical states."[15]

Experiments with pregnant mice at dosages above 25 roentgens showed that the embryo's brain and eyes are probably susceptible to injury until the last months of pregnancy. The same doses can also produce notice-able skeletal defects.

Studies of human stillbirths have shown that radiostrontium can pass through the placental barrier from the mother and become fixed in the skeleton or other organs of the stillborn child. Presumably, if radioactive materials penetrate the embryo, they would act as "whole-body expo-sure" in such small bodies.

The comparatively enormous dose of 24 roentgens per week of whole-body radiation can decrease the normal growth in body weight of rats. Radiation concentrated in certain parts of the bones at high enough doses will cause shortening of those bones in both humans and animals. Children exposed to the atomic bombs in Hiroshima and Nagasaki, where the doses were of the order of 50 to 100 roentgens, did not grow as fast as average Japanese children.

In all these studies of growth and development, however, there is little to show harmful effects from the tiny-dose rates produced by nuclear-weapons-test fallout. This, then, is another problem that requires per-haps a half century of statistical analysis—or a breakthrough in basic biology—before a solution can be expected.

A study by Dr. Alice Stewart of Oxford University, examining three million childhood cancer and leukemia records in England and Wales, has shown that X rays about doubled the chances of these children for developing cancer or leukemia. But the chances had been rather small to begin with. Most of the children had been exposed to a diagnostic dose of 2 to 4 roentgens whole-body radiation before birth.

Natural background gives the average individual a 7-roentgen radia-tion dose stretched over a period of seventy years. Fallout gives him 0.2 to 0.4 roentgen over the same seventy-year period.

Eye Effects

At least 200 roentgens of acute exposure to X or gamma rays is necessary to produce single-dose opacities or cataracts in the human eye. Again the dosage is several orders of magnitude higher than that produced in fallout, except in the area close to a nuclear-weapon detonation.

An Evaluation

This excursion into the basic science of radiation has shown that the hazard of nuclear test fallout is trifling—3–5 per cent—compared to background radiation hazards the world accepts without question. How distorted the thinking has become can be made clear by comparing fallout with other hazards, using some popular statistical techniques.

Over the past twenty years, in the United States, there have been six fatal accidents and a small number of injuries to atomic energy workers from ionizing radiation. For most of these twenty years automobile accidents have been causing more than 30,000 deaths per year. But each of the four radiation accidents that caused the six deaths among atomic energy workers has received world-wide publicity; the fact that over 100 nuclear-energy workers have been killed in automobile accidents alone during the same period has gone unnoticed.

Smokestacks belch millions of tons of acid, silicone, beryllium, lead, and arsenic—all widely suspected to be cancer agents—while scientists are sifting the air for faint traces of radioactive fallout.

Living in a brick house gives a person twenty times the radiation dose one gets from fallout. But world attention has been concentrated on limiting the strontium-90, not on finding a substitute for bricks. There is no known case of moving from a brick house to a frame house to avoid radioactivity.

Luminous-dial wrist watches give off as much as ten times the radiation dose that fallout produces.

Science suspects automobile exhausts, as it suspects fallout, of producing cancer. But no one has suggested declaring a moratorium on automobile transportation, or even making a multi-million-dollar investigation of auto exhausts.

Principally because of the fallout problem, science has been stimulated to learn much more about radiation as a cause of cancer and other health problems than it knows about almost any other occupational or environmental hazard. Benzpyrene, for instance, was discovered in the early 1930s to be a powerful cancer-producing agent in mice. Combustion of petroleum by autos yields more than enough benzpyrene to produce a cancer hazard. In large American cities, there is so much benzpyrene in the air that it settles on windowsills in measurable quantities. But there has been no scientific investigation of the hazard of benzpyrene at low doses.[16]

"I presume that we want to save thousands of lives in this country every year and we could just abolish the manufacture of automobiles and go back to riding horses," Senator Bourke Hickenlooper of Iowa suggested facetiously in one committee hearing on fallout. "It seems to have struck a balance in the minds of people that transportation is important and we keep making automobiles, people keep getting killed by the thousands on the highway every year. We are all sad about that."

On the East Coast, the annual radiation from natural sources is about 0.1 roentgen per year, while Denver and other large Coloradan cities get about twice that amount from natural background sources. Denver is expanding despite this "health hazard." And New York reports a higher rate of leukemia than Colorado, presumably from causes other than radiation.

In southern Illinois, where the drinking water contains unusual amounts of radium, persons store about ten times as much radium in their bones as those living in Chicago. But there is no significant difference in the bone-cancer rates so far detected.

People living in Albuquerque, N.M., annually absorb much more radiation in their mile-high homes than do people in Washington, D.C. The excess is greater than that received by Washington residents from all bomb-test fallout to date. Yet most of the citizens of Albuquerque continue to reside there.

If the incidence of lung cancer from cigarettes is assumed to be linear, that is, depending on the size of dose, as leukemia is assumed to be linearly proportional to fallout, one scientist has calculated that two cigarettes *per year* can produce as much lung cancer as fallout can produce leukemia.[17]

Using the same statistical technique, pollution of the city air can be regarded as a comparable hazard. A few hours spent in the city by country folks would produce lung cancer to the same extent as fallout produces leukemia.

It would be rash to claim that small radiation doses have no effect on humans in increasing bone cancer and leukemia. But it would seem reasonable to conclude that if there is any increase in the incidence of these diseases because of fallout, it is so slight as to be unnoticeable when compared with other suspected causes of bone cancer and leukemia.[18]

The directly proportional or "linear" theory can be applied to other harmful phenomena in modern society.

One's life expectancy can be reduced about nine years by smoking a pack of cigarettes a day, according to one statistical calculation based on the linear theory.[19] This is equivalent to shortening one's life by one hour for each cigarette smoked.

A sedentary job instead of one involving exercise reduces life expect-

ancy by five years, compared to the one to two days life-shortening due
to world-wide fallout. Being 10 per-cent overweight costs one a year and
a half. Living in the city instead of in the country reduces life expectancy
by five years; so does remaining unmarried.[20]

The point here is that it can be misleading in the extreme to assume
that one suddenly-discovered factor, like fallout, is the sole cause for
some change picked at random from a whole spectrum of causes and
changes.

Nor can it be considered completely valid to contend that all mutations are bad. Students of evolution say that it was genetic mutation—
thousands of years ago, when the natural background level of radiation
presumably was much higher than it is today—which produced man in
his present form. It can only be said that mutations are neither all significant nor all bad.

As more is learned about cancer, doubts are increasing that low
doses of radiation produce noticeable or significant effects. Both cancer
and leukemia are sometimes produced by indirect methods not involving
a "direct hit" by a radioactive particle or ray on a human cell. Many
have assumed that radioactivity makes a direct hit on a single cell and
starts a chain reaction of cancerous cells. If two mutations instead of one
were found to be required to produce cancer, however, then instead of
100,000 cases of leukemia produced over the centuries by fallout, there
might be as few as 100 cases, over millennia.[21]

The theory that cancer is caused by a single mutation that gives rise
to a growing colony of cancer cells was in vogue some years ago but is
passing out of fashion. Scientists advancing the proportional theory in
relation to fallout have been "almost exclusively . . . quite unfamiliar"
with recent advances in cancer knowledge.[22]

Add to these difficulties the imprecise measurements of the fallout
hazard that are possible with present techniques, and there develops a
wide range of uncertainty, mainly on the side of doubt as to whether
there is any health hazard in test fallout at all. Fallout doses are so low
that they cannot be used on mice. As has been noted earlier, millions or
billions of mice would have to be bred in laboratories before any genetic
effects would be noticeable from even such relatively high doses of radiation as ten roentgens.

"Hot spots," or clusters of radioactivity from tests could develop in
populated areas, but in experience since 1945, there is no recorded case of
harm to human or animal life.

Most scientists feel that while past testing has not presented a health
hazard, big megaton explosions of the order of magnitude exploded by
the Soviet Union in 1961 and 1962 could eventually accumulate fallout
hazards of serious proportions. Heavy testing in the atmosphere is
not a realistic prospect, even after the Soviet series of 1961 and
1962, however. The United States has signified its intention of confining

the great proportion, if not all, of its future tests[23] underground, where there will be no radioactive fallout hazard.

The greatest hazard might come from newly emerging nuclear powers if they developed "dirty" weapons. Regulation of their *atmospheric* testing could become an issue in the next decades.

How did the unrealistic fear of fallout get such a grip on the world? A rather detailed study of the test-ban's history shows there were many forces at work, some informed and some uninformed.

Part II

TEST-BAN MOVEMENTS AND
NEGOTIATIONS

Chapter 2

The Background

The notion of the nuclear test ban was raised first unofficially shortly after the first atomic bombs over Hiroshima and Nagasaki ended World War II. Tall tales about the fallout effects of these first two bombs had spread around the world by the time the United States got ready for its first series of postwar tests at Bikini in 1946.

Rumors swept Japan in August, 1945, for instance, that "radioactive poison gas" had been released by the nuclear explosions over Hiroshima. Three days after the first A-bomb over Japan was detonated, Dr. J. Robert Oppenheimer, the leader of the scientists' team that built the bomb, issued a public denial of another American scientist's claim that the explosion had blanketed the city with radioactivity that would be lethal for seventy years.

The phrase "radioactive poison gas" apparently first came into usage in the War Department itself, where there had been a fear at one time, before Germany surrendered, that Hitler might get the A-bomb first.

There was little confidence, even among Americans, that all the possibilities for radioactive contamination had been thoroughly explored by the United States before it had released the bomb. There was a minor flurry at the end of October, 1945, when the President of Eastman Kodak Company, T. J. Hargrave, reported a mysterious fogging of photographic film. Scientists jumped to the conclusion that radioactive clouds from the explosions in Japan had moved over the United States, that fallout had dropped on New York state.

Later it was found, however, that the boxes in which the film had been packed were made of materials that had been affected by local fallout after the first United States test at Alamagordo, New Mexico.

Professor Harold Urey, a Nobel prize winner and leading physicist in the United States, charged before a Senate committee that the manufacture and storing of atomic bombs was poisoning the atmosphere of the entire world.

Plans for new atomic tests at Bikini Atoll in the summer of 1946 brought the first agitation for a nuclear test ban. It came from the Military Order of the Purple Heart on February 28, 1946. The World War II veterans wired President Truman demanding that the proposed Bikini tests be stopped. They suggested that a complete moratorium on testing be proclaimed.

Something of a small bandwagon movement to stop the Bikini test series developed among private organizations. Church groups, internationalist organizations, women's groups, Quakers, Senators, veterans organizations, and Communist fronts set up a cry to put off the Bikini tests scheduled for June and July.

When the agitation reached the Senate level and a committee there investigated informally, President Truman sent a letter to the "Hill" insisting the tests must go on. That didn't exactly end the discussion, but Washington felt no further inhibitions about continuing with the test program.

The Soviet Union, still comparatively unsophisticated in the art of plausible opposition to United States nuclear development, merely attacked the explosions as an exhibition of "militarism" and "lack of ethics." The Soviet army's newspaper called it a "belligerent maneuver." Radio Moscow anticipated an armaments race.

Two months later, a Soviet scientist said the Soviet Union was planning its own nuclear-weapons tests and would invite the United Nations to observe them. Times Square, New York City, was the scene, in mid-July, of a demonstration against nuclear tests. But nuclear testing alone, as differentiated from the broad development of nuclear weapons, was a comparatively minor concern of the world in the early postwar period.

Soviet policy called for a complete ban on all uses of the atomic weapon, both before and after Soviet scientists developed their own atom bomb in 1949.

The next wave of interest in stopping nuclear tests developed in the period during which the United States was preparing to make the new "superbomb," the hydrogen bomb.

Before technology made this quantum jump in the destructiveness of warfare, many thinking men throughout the United States advocated making a new approach to the Soviet Union, to see if the arms race could be stopped.

David E. Lilienthal of the Atomic Energy Commission, for instance, was reported to have urged President Truman to seek talks with the Soviet Union before going ahead. Henry Wallace, Senator Flanders, and Cornell's Dr. Hans Bethe all urged that the hydrogen bomb be used only in retaliation.

The French Communist Party, Frank Lloyd Wright, Prime Minister Nehru of India, the American Women for Peace, the United Lutheran Church of America, Soviet Foreign Minister Vishinsky, all these advocated a complete ban on the use of H-bombs. There was, as yet, little agitation to take the smaller first step of outlawing tests.

When the Communists launched their world-wide peace offensive on March 19, 1950, it was to "ban the bomb," not ban the tests.

However, the argument that raged inside the Truman Administration in the early 1950's on the wisdom of going ahead with H-bomb development stimulated the first tentative examination of the possibility that H-bomb development could be controlled by controlling tests.

Policy-planners in the State Department called together a panel of distinguished scientists to study the possibilities of slowing down or halting the arms race in preparation for the 1951 disarmament negotiations with the Soviet Union. The investigation centered on inspection methods, in the hope that some scheme might be devised to overcome Soviet objections to the espionage potential of disarmament control.

Among the advisers appointed by Paul Nitze, the Chairman of the State Department's Policy Planning Staff, was Dr. Vannevar Bush, chief scientific adviser to President Truman in the weapons field. Others on the panel were Dr. J. Robert Oppenheimer; John Dickey of Dartmouth College; and Allen Dulles, then Deputy Director of the Central Intelligence Agency and a longtime expert in nuclear-intelligence affairs.

In those preparatory meetings, Dr. Bush began forming ideas about an H-bomb test-ban, bringing the problem to the official level for the first time.

He went privately to Secretary of State Dean Acheson in 1952, with the suggestion that the United States should seek an agreement with the Soviet Union to prohibit all tests of hydrogen bombs before any were exploded. So far as is known, he was the first to advance formally the idea of an H-bomb test-ban.

After the first H-bomb was tested, the world would be over some kind of watershed, Dr. Bush argued, past the point of no return in developing the vastly destructive H-bombs, whose power was already known to be at least a thousand times that of the conventional atomic or fission-type bombs.

H-bomb test-control did not present the problem that inspection of the smaller A-bombs presented, Dr. Bush reasoned. Their big bang could always be detected, wherever they might be exploded. He hoped that a halt in the arms race at that juncture would not leave the United States in a strategically disadvantageous position.

At that time, the American nuclear laboratories were pointing eagerly for their first test of the hydrogen weapon, set for October or November, 1952, at the peak of the Presidential election contest between General Eisenhower and Governor Stevenson. The impact of the hydrogen-bomb age would fall not on the decision-maker, President Truman, but on the new President, either Mr. Stevenson or General Eisenhower.

Dr. Bush later mentioned "two primary reasons" for his advocacy of the H-bomb test-ban in the early summer of 1952.

> I felt that it was utterly improper—and I still think so—for that test to be put off just before election, to confront an incoming President with an accomplished test for which he would carry the full responsibility thereafter. For that test marked our entry into a very disagreeable type of world.[1]

In the spring of 1954, Dr. Bush told the Oppenheimer security panel that he

> felt strongly that the test ended the possibility of the only type of agreement that I thought was possible with Russia at that time, namely, an agreement to make no more tests. For that kind of an agreement would have been self-policing in the sense that if it was violated, the violation would be immediately known. I still think that we made a grave error in conducting that test at that time, and not attempting to make that type of simple agreement with Russia. I think history will show that was a turning point, when we entered into the grim world that we're entering right now, that those who pushed that thing through to a conclusion without making that attempt have a great deal to answer for.
> That is what moved me, sir, I was very much moved at the time.

Dr. Bush also had serious questions at that time about the United States need for bombs a thousand times as powerful as the A-bomb.

"To us, with 500-kiloton fission bombs, we have very little need for a 10-megaton hydrogen bomb," he told the board reviewing the Oppenheimer security case. "The Russians, on the other hand, have the great targets of New York and Chicago, and what have you. It is of enormous advantage to them." [2]

Dr. Isadore Rabi and Dr. Enrico Fermi were two other pioneers in the United States atomic-bomb development who wanted to approach the Russians on an H-bomb test-ban. In the same Oppenheimer hearings, Dr. Rabi told the panel he and Dr. Fermi thought the H-bomb development

> raised an opportunity for the President of the United States to make some political gesture which would be such that it would strengthen our moral position, should we decide to go ahead with it. That our position should be such that depending on the reaction, we would go ahead or not, whatever going ahead were to mean.[3]

The State Department was reluctant, however, to take up Dr. Bush's suggestion for embarking on new negotiations with the Soviet Union in 1952. The Korean War was still grinding on.

The Russians knew as well as anyone else that the Truman-Acheson administration would have no power to bind the next administration on H-bomb policy. Moscow seemed in no mood for agreement on anything.

An alternative possibility was to postpone the test of the hydrogen weapon until after the election. Then an urgent conference could be held between President Truman and the President-elect. The thought was that the decision then could be made whether to go forward with the hydrogen-weapons development, seek a test-ban, or proceed in some other direction.

These possible alternatives were discussed by Secretary Acheson and his policy planning chief, Mr. Nitze, with President Truman in the late summer of 1952. The President decided to withhold any go-ahead on testing thermonuclear weapons until the last minute. He would not make up his mind until the full circumstances could be known.

The Democratic Presidential Candidate, Adlai Stevenson, indicated some awareness of the problem. In a September, 1952, campaign speech he urged that the United States push ahead with its weapons development, including the H-bomb program, until the Soviet Union accepted effective control. This was in marked contrast to his 1956 campaign attitude.

In October, 1952, Great Britain joined the nuclear club by exploding her first atomic bomb in a test at Montebello Island, off Australia. Scientists were briefly startled by a report that hailstones, falling some 1,750 miles away, were discovered to contain twice their normal amount of radioactivity.

Fallout was also a concern of the AEC as preparations for the huge thermonuclear "Mike" shot continued. Dr. John Bugher of the AEC Biology and Medicine Division, and Merrill Eisenbud, of the Health and Safety Operations office, believed fallout might be one of the most significant aspects of the thermonuclear test.

In August, they flew to Hawaii with AEC Commissioner Gordon Dean to set up a fallout-monitoring network of broader scope than the modest sticky-paper project that had been maintained previously at Eniwetok.

They arranged for special Air Force flights up and down the Pacific, right after the Mike shot, to try to find the fallout and measure its intensity at various distances from the explosion.

Meanwhile, an unexpected problem emerged for the test. The weather in the Pacific Proving Grounds area grew increasingly uncertain. The most favorable weather was predicted to last only until November 1, three days before the election.[4] After that the winds would make it unsafe to test until spring of 1953. Meteorologists said they could not be sure the weather would hold until after the election.

President Truman, as he relates in his memoirs, finally decided to go ahead on his own with the development of the H-bomb rather than risk what amounted to a six-month delay. He could not know definitely how the Soviet Union was coming along with its own H-bomb development. He was chary of risking a slowdown on U.S. weapons development in the deadly arms race.

The first hydrogen "device" was exploded November 1, only a few days before the election, but public announcement of the experiment was withheld.

It was a "dramatic success," President Truman recalls.

So powerful was the explosion that an entire island was blown away and a huge crater left in the coral. It was an awesome demonstration of a new power, and I felt that it was important that the newly-elected President should be informed about it. And on the day after the election I requested the Atomic Energy Commission to arrange to brief President-elect Eisenhower on the results of the tests as well as on our entire nuclear program.

To the surprise of Secretary Acheson and President Truman, however, the President-elect showed little interest in the implications of the event.

There were other tests at the Pacific Proving Grounds in the fall of 1952, possibly including an airdrop and possibly another H-bomb device, but no details have ever been made public.

A few hours after the November 1 blast, Merrill Eisenbud of the AEC began a fallout-monitoring flight from the South Pacific to Japan. Scintillation detectors aboard the low-flying plane were to signal detectable radioactivity. The signals were recorded on tape while Mr. Eisenbud, on another taped circuit, simultaneously recorded the circumstances, location, levels of radiation, and other information. Flying night and day, Mr. Eisenbud completed the trip within three days.

The mission was largely unsuccessful. Only very low levels of radioactivity—in the range of 10 milliroentgens—were recorded. As Mr. Eisenbud later said, "We never did find the main body of fallout." Whether it all shot into the stratosphere or not is one of the mysteries of the nuclear age.

The failure to locate radioactive debris may have helped lull the high policy-making levels of the AEC and the Administration into a false sense of security, insofar as the fallout problem was concerned. The generally-accepted analysis made by officers on the spot was that the debris had fallen out close by and had been swallowed by the ocean. Mr. Eisenbud himself tended toward this theory.

Although the United States did not officially report the November 1, 1952, thermonuclear test until April 7, 1954, word quickly spread.

Sailors of Joint Task Force 132 witnessed the explosion from about 30 miles away and wrote home about it. Heat from the blast reached them at that distance, they said. The fireball, some 4 miles across, rose 25 miles. The shock wave produced minor damage on an island 20 miles to the southeast. Somehow the Task Force commanders had overlooked censoring the mail.

Before the end of November, Asians were sounding the alarm. An Asian Conference on World Federation issued a public plea that the three nuclear powers ban nuclear weapons and that the United States renounce the H-bomb.

Stalin's death in March, 1953, and the resultant struggle for power in the Kremlin, briefly raised hopes in the West that the Soviet Union would be willing to turn away from the arms race to concentrate on its domestic problems. In an April speech before American editors in Washington, President Eisenhower sought to encourage such a course by offering to join the Soviet Union in applying disarmament savings to a fund for "world aid and reconstruction." He also accepted the Truman Administration's policy of seeking international control of atomic energy and "prohibition of atomic weapons" under adequate safeguards, "including a practical system of inspection under the United Nations."

The new Soviet regime was unresponsive, however, and another series of tests was conducted by the United States that spring in Nevada. Army and Marine troops maneuvered in the area of the bomb blast, approaching as close as 5,000 yards to ground zero.

There were protests from uranium prospectors in New Mexico, claiming that radiation from the Nevada tests hampered their work. Fallout on the St. George area of southwest Utah in late May, 1953, caused Representative Stringfellow of Utah to urge the Atomic Energy Commission to end the tests because the residents in the area had been alarmed.

Rumors about the tests' effect on the weather drew a denial from the Weather Bureau that nuclear blasts were affecting the climate on the East Coast of the United States. The AEC, in turn, published a report saying there was no hazardous radiation in any part of the United States from past tests. It was disclosed that 453 claims for damages had been filed after the first twenty Nevada blasts. But no claim exceeded $1,000, and only a handful were paid.

In June, North Dakota's Republican Senator Langer introduced a joint resolution asking prohibition of nuclear testing in the United States.[5]

A record number of tornadoes in the summer of 1953 prompted one congressman to inquire if they were linked with nuclear tests. Both the armed services and the Civil Defense Administration denied it.

Reasons for Soviet disinterest in disarmament measures became clearer in August. The new Premier of the Soviet Union, Georgi Malenkov, electrified the world on August 8 with an announcement that the United States no longer had a monopoly on the manufacture of a hydrogen bomb.

Official Washington was skeptical. President Eisenhower had no comment. Secretary of State Dulles even announced on August 12 that the United States had not yet detected any burst in the Soviet Union. That was the very day, as it was later learned, that the Soviet Union did test a thermonuclear weapon.[6] Premier Malenkov apparently was so confident of success he could make his announcement in advance of the test.

Pravda announced a successful test of one of "a variety" of H-bombs on August 19. The next day, AEC Chairman Strauss confirmed that the United States had picked up evidence of one test. It was not clear from American evidence whether a weapon had been exploded or merely a device.

"The Soviet Union conducted an atomic test on the morning of August 12," the AEC announced. "Certain information to this effect came into our hands that night. Subsequent information on the subject indicates that this test involved both fission and thermonuclear reactions." First information could have been provided by seismic and acoustic detection methods; confirmation probably came from the radioactive cloud.

There was concern in official Washington that the Soviet Union might have assumed the lead in the H-bomb race. Representative Sterling Cole, then an influential member of the Joint Atomic Energy Committee, went so far as to describe the American situation as "desperate" in a television interview. He declined to say whether the Soviet Union had found a cheap or easy way to make the H-bomb, which the United States did not have, as had previously been speculated, but his pessimism tended to confirm this fear.

Secretary of Defense Charles E. Wilson sought to calm the apprehensions. He claimed that the United States was at least three years ahead of the Soviet Union in A- and H-bomb development. He repeated an earlier claim that the Soviet Union probably did not have a droppable bomb.

Appalled by the sudden pyramiding of nuclear power in the hands of the Soviet Union and the United States, the nuclear have-not nations quickly carried their worries to the United Nations. India and Australia advocated a total ban on nuclear weapons in major speeches during the opening days of the General Assembly.

The Soviet Union blandly repeated its old proposal for an unconditional prohibition of atomic and hydrogen bombs, without any specific controls. Although the issue of inspection still obviously barred agreement, the General Assembly voted on November 28, by a vote of fifty-four to zero, with the Soviet bloc abstaining, to form a subcommittee of the Disarmament Commission to try to find a solution in private.

This set the stage for President Eisenhower's personal appearance before the U.N. on December 8, with his novel, "backdoor" approach to disarmament, the "Atoms for Peace" speech which proposed establishment of an international atomic-energy pool, under United Nations auspices. The plan envisioned a mutual reduction of fissionable-material stockpiles by transferring it to a sort of international "bank," which would loan the material to nuclear have-not nations for peaceful uses. Four days later the Soviet Union agreed to discuss the idea if the West would agree to discuss an unconditional ban on the use of nuclear weapons.

Scientists in the Soviet Union, meanwhile, were claiming they had developed several types of atomic and hydrogen bombs. East German officials said the Soviet Union had jumped into the lead over the United States in nuclear-weapons development.

President Eisenhower, obviously intending to counteract some of the Soviet claims, had disclosed in his U.N. speech that the United States had several H-bombs in its arsenal in ranges of millions of tons of TNT-equivalent.

Seeds of doubt had been planted, however, as to the extent of the United States lead over the Soviet Union in the nuclear field. The United States had exploded only eight nuclear bombs, counting the first test at Alamagordo and the two over Japan, before the Soviet Union broke the American A-bomb monopoly on August 29, 1949. The first five of those represented little if any advance in design. The fourth and fifth shots, at Bikini, were primarily intended to show A-bomb effects on ships, and reportedly were of the same vintage as the Hiroshima and Nagasaki weapons. Nor is there any evidence of a spectacular rise in the American stockpile until the early 1950's. Separation of weapons-grade nuclear material was still a tedious process. Speedier separation techniques were not invented until computers became available to the designers.

BRAVO

Sentiment for a nuclear test-ban became a world-wide force for the first time in 1954. In the past, no clear line had been drawn in public understanding between proposals to prohibit completely the use of nuclear weapons and the relatively infrequent suggestions that only tests of nuclear weapons be prohibited. Confusion of the two was to continue, but the tests became the center of attention after a spectacular Pacific Ocean series of thermonuclear explosions by the United States in March and April, 1954.

The first of these shots, a 15-megaton surface explosion code-named "Bravo," galvanized all of Asia and much of the world into action to prevent further experimentation with the huge bombs.

Warnings that the future of all mankind was threatened by the development of the H-bomb had made a deep impression on peoples of all nations. There was widespread discussion of methods to prevent a world catastrophe which, many feared, would cause the end of the world or at least wipe out the human race.

The United States Bravo shot, on March 1, turned out to be twice as powerful as originally expected. An unforeseen wind shift caused fallout from the explosion to drift over inhabited islands in the Marshall chain, instead of dropping harmlessly into the ocean as planned.

Rongelap Atoll, about 100 miles east of Bikini, was inhabited by 64 Marshallese, living in palm-leaf houses on the southern edge of the atoll.

Slightly to the southwest was Ailinginae Atoll, where 18 Marshallese were camping out during a fishing expedition. On Rongerik, there were 28 American servicemen, living in quonset huts, collecting weather data. Another 200 miles about due east from Rongerik lay Utirik, where another 157 Marshallese were living.

As it happened, all of these atolls lay along the unexpected path of the local-fallout radioactive cloud, which extended about 220 statute miles downwind in widths varying up to 40 miles.[7] About 7,000 square miles of territory downwind, most of it ocean, was seriously contaminated.

A little before noon on March 1, 1954, American servicemen on Rongerik, 300 miles to the east, noticed a misty fallout of powerful radioactive dust. The same kind of mist had been falling since midmorning over Ailinginae and Rongelap, but the natives paid little attention.

The American servicemen suspected what was happening. They stayed inside as much as possible, venturing out only in extreme necessity, and wore protective clothing that covered most of their skin.

The Marshall Islanders, unfortunately, did not recognize it as fallout. They had no geiger counters. Moving freely about in the radioactive mist, they wore no special clothing, so the dust settled on their bare torsoes and in their hair. They walked along the beaches where the fallout was collecting. The radioactive coral dust accumulated between their toes.

Many of the children waded in the ocean as usual, and thereby reduced the amount of radioactive dust that clung to their feet and legs. Some went bathing and unwittingly washed away large quantities of the dangerous dust.

The Americans, on the other hand, took showers as soon as they knew they had been exposed, disposed of the clothing they had worn in the mist, and kept under cover of their aluminum huts.

All the exposed persons, the 64 on Rongelap, the 18 on Ailinginae, the 28 Americans on Rongerik, the 157 Marshallese on Utirik, were eventually evacuated to Kwajalein Naval Station. Why it took so long to remove the people from the islands is one of the untold stories of the historic March 1, 1954, Bravo shot.

Automatic monitors spotted around the islands had shown within a few hours after the Bravo shot that Rongerik and Rongelap had both received heavy doses of radioactive fallout. It wasn't long before the indicator needles swung completely off scale.

At this point things seemed to go wrong aboard the "Estes." The news was quickly cabled to New York, where Mr. Eisenbud was following developments. Next morning, he checked with Washington to learn what emergency measures were being taken. The Chief of the Medicine and Biology Department of the AEC had not been informed of the dangerous fallout situation.

In the forward areas, also, there had been some reluctance to accept the instrument readings. It sounded too fantastic. In the Pacific, after all, it was common for electronic gear to "go crazy" or break down completely. For whatever reason, the recorded intensity of fallout was not confirmed for thirty-six hours.

Dr. Bugher, the Medicine and Biology Department chief, and Mr. Eisenbud had obtained previous approval for evacuation of exposed persons, if necessary. All persons on "hot" islands were to be moved out. But the task force provided no immediate evacuation facilities.

The Americans on Rongerik were picked up in two groups: the first eight men, twenty-eight and one-half hours after the explosion; the other group of twenty men, thirty hours after the explosion.

The Marshallese on Rongelap were not evacuated until fifty-one hours after the shot, those on Ailinginae until fifty-eight hours after. On Utirik the process started fifty-five hours after and was completed seventy-eight hours after the explosion—more than three days later.

The 64 natives on Rongelap are estimated to have absorbed an average dose of 175 roentgens, not a lethal dose but a severe one. The 18 Marshallese on Ailinginae received an average of 69 roentgens, the Americans on Rongerik 78 roentgens and the 157 Marshall Islanders on Utirik 14 roentgens.

Men with radiation-measuring instruments did not go to the exposed islands until a week or so after the explosion. Consequently, exact measurements of the radiation doses could not be obtained.

The exposure of the 28 Americans on Rongerik and the 157 Marshallese on Utirik was minimal, however, so the servicemen were returned to duty and the Utirik inhabitants were sent back to their homes. The 82 Marshallese who had been on Rongelap and Ailinginae had absorbed significant radiation doses, however, and remained under continuous observation for three months. They were checked twice yearly thereafter. Because their home islands retained too much radioactivity, they were moved to Majuro Atoll, where they lived for three years.

The fallout pattern was not uniform, of course. There were "hot spots" on Rongerik Atoll where the radiation dose could have been much higher. If the American weather station had been on the northern side of the atoll, it was later calculated, persons there would have absorbed a 200-roentgen dose.

It was also lucky that the Rongelap natives had been living on the southern edge of their atoll. Toward the northern side, the Bravo cloud had dropped much heavier concentrations of radiation. Only ten or fifteen miles from the Rongelap natives' palm huts the fallout had been so heavy that doses of 400 roentgens would have been absorbed by people staying there. They would have had only a fifty-fifty chance to survive.

On the extreme northern tip of the Rongelap atoll, it was found, the dose would have been over 1,000 roentgens, enough to cause certain death within a month.

According to some reports, evacuation teams of the Joint Task Force 7 were not aware of the extent of injury that had been done by the radioactive fallout. When some of the Marshallese got sick, their vomiting reportedly was mistaken for seasickness.

The Task Force obviously had not been prepared for the quantities of fallout that dropped on inhabited islands after the Bravo shot. The types of monitoring instruments placed on Rongerik were calibrated only up to 100 milliroentgens per hour.[8] Their needles went off scale a half-hour after fallout began settling on the ground, but some technicians on the scene reportedly mistook these alarming indications for equipment failure.

After the natives and the Americans reached Kwajalein, however, the story was different. Qualified medical personnel there recognized the symptoms. Those exposed were washed. The Marshallese's hair had to be rinsed again and again, because coconut oil the natives used made their hair difficult to decontaminate. In many cases heads had to be shaved. Contaminated clothes were taken away.

AEC Chairman Strauss, who came to the Pacific for the second thermonuclear shot in the Ivy series, spent most of his time assuring himself that the Marshall Island natives were getting the best of care. He was alert to the trouble that would lie ahead if any of them were to become seriously ill or die. Knowing that the Marshallese frequently died of white man's diseases, the medical team isolated the natives from all Americans who had even the mildest diseases. Americans with head colds, for instance, were barred from the compound where the Marshallese were being treated.

None of them died or was even seriously ill. Pregnant women had apparently normal babies. One of the babies was born while Admiral Strauss was on Kwajalein. The chief of the Marshallese tribe named the baby after Chairman Strauss' wife. As an expression of his delight, the AEC Chairman presented the newborn with ten pigs, making her the "plutocrat of the islands."

Mr. Strauss returned from the Pacific on March 29 and reported to President Eisenhower. He told the President of the astonishing power of the Bravo shot, which had been almost double the scientists' expectations. Mr. Eisenhower suggested that the Admiral come with him "across the street" [9] the next day to speak with newsmen at a previously-scheduled press conference. Mr. Strauss had special charts prepared, then discussed fallout patterns and other effects of H-bombs with newsmen for about an hour.

To the astonishment of both Admiral Strauss and the President, the newsmen and the general public reacted adversely. The AEC Chairman gave all the answers he knew, promised to provide answers to other questions as soon as the data were available. But he was suspected of holding back on the grim horrors of the H-bomb. The attempt to be candid aborted; it merely confirmed suspicions of many that the Administration was withholding the full story.

While the Marshallese were being evacuated, another silent drama was unfolding to the north. A Japanese fishing boat, the "Fortunate Dragon," had somehow slipped inside—or up to the edge of—the charted danger area without being seen by patrol craft dispatched from Joint Task Force 7 before the shot was fired.

The same "white snow" of radioactive fallout settled on the tuna trawler. The Japanese fishermen had noticed the "bang" of the H-bomb explosion, the premature dawn, and roughly noted its time. But they did not recognize the radioactive fallout as a danger. When it began falling about three hours later, it was allowed to lie on the deck and irradiate its occupants. The strange dust irritated their eyes, lips, and nasal passages. Faced with this sudden discomfort and poor fishing as well, the skipper started for home.

Two weeks after the explosion, the little Japanese boat turned up in Yaizu harbor, in Japan, with twenty-three sick fishermen aboard.

What dose they received is unknown. American scientists were not immediately allowed to enter the area where the ship docked. The best estimate is that the men received about 200 roentgens. One of the fishermen, Aikichi Kuboyama, eventually died—whether from complications following the radiation exposure or from natural causes probably never will be known. The other twenty-two fishermen recovered and returned to steady work.

Word spread quickly around the world that the Japanese fishermen had been "dusted" with radioactive fallout. In Japan itself, the reaction was electric. The only country that had suffered the horrors of atomic war could hardly be expected to react with great tolerance. Hiroshima's horrors came alive all over again.

Soon Tokyo University scientists discovered that fish from the hold of the *Fukuryu Maru No. 5*, the "Lucky Dragon," were radioactive. Geiger counters chattered at all Tokyo fish markets. The Japanese people stopped buying fish. Prices dropped sharply.

In Japan, where fish is eaten morning, noon, and night, this was the kind of accident to motivate a whole nation. Geiger counters tested other catches coming into Japanese ports. These too were reported to have been contaminated with radioactivity.

Japanese police went into the market places of Tokyo and other Japanese cities to find the "Lucky Dragon's" 12,000 pounds of radiation-showered fish. Parliament opened debate on the problem.

The exact position of the Japanese ship at the time of the H-bomb blast became a point at issue. Was it inside the "off-limits" zone set up by the AEC? The Japanese Foreign Ministry released a statement saying the ship was 90 miles from ground zero. The fishermen estimated it at about 70 miles. The United States concluded the ship had been inside

the restricted zone; AEC Chairman Strauss was reported to have suspected the fishermen of spying.

As radioactive fish were discovered, Japanese authorities ordered that
they be buried deep in the ground. Japanese doctors ordered the "Lucky
Dragon" fishermen to return to hospitals, where they had been examined
but released, and thorough radiation tests were made on the "Lucky
Dragon" itself.

United States Ambassador John Allison offered medical and scientific
aid for the injured fishermen. Doctors from the Atomic Bomb Casualty
Commission in Hiroshima offered their services.

Scientists in Japan analyzed new fallout reaching the islands and found
something unknown to the layman: strontium-90. The AEC confirmed
that strontium-90 could cause bone damage, but avoided indicating it was
a new by-product of the tests.

Socialists and other opposition parties in Japan were outspoken in their
criticism of the United States for involving Japan in dangerous "war
preparations." Despite the sharp attacks by the Japanese press and political opposition to the Conservative government, however, the Japanese
Foreign Office deferred issuing a protest.

The Marshall Islanders cooperated fully—and quietly—with the American medical authorities. Those exposed to the heavier radioactivity doses
suffered from nausea, fever, and stomach-ache during the first two days
after the "snow" began to fall. A few vomited and had diarrhea. These
discomforts went away, however, without treatment. Some complained
of itchy skin and a burning sensation on the skin and in the eyes for a
couple of days; these symptoms, too, disappeared. For the next two
weeks there were no apparent effects. Later, however, blisters broke out
on their skin, and hair began to fall out in some cases.[10] But all recovered
swiftly.

Scientists estimated that between 50 and 80 per cent of the beta radiation had an average energy of about 0.3 million electron volts. The outer
layer of dead skin, one two-thousandth of an inch thick, was sufficient to
stop much of this energy. The remaining 20 to 50 per cent of the beta
radiation had a higher energy—0.6 million electron volts—and these rays
penetrated into the deeper layer of live skin.

Any type of clothing, however, was sufficient to stop the beta rays.
Lesions, or blisters, appeared only on those parts of the natives' bodies
that were directly exposed to the fallout. Some also accumulated radioactive particles under their arms, in the creases of their necks, and between their toes; painful sores developed in some cases. A few Marshallese walked on their heels while sores between their toes healed.

Six months after their exposure, however, most of the natives had
regained their hair, and the skin lesions had healed.

Four women on Rongelap were pregnant at the time of the fallout.
Three had normal babies, the other a stillborn child. But the incidence

of stillbirths in Rongelap is normally high; a one in four ratio was not unusual. There was no evidence that the stillbirth had been caused by Bravo fallout.

If the wind had shifted just a little bit farther to the south, all the people on Rongelap, Rongirik, and Ailinginae could have been killed. It was also calculated that 30 miles downwind from the huge 15-megaton explosion persons could have stood in the open, unprotected from the heat and blast effects of the weapon. But they would have absorbed a killing dose of radiation within a few minutes after the fallout started.

Apprehension swept the scientific community in the United States. Had the "militarists" been careless? Did they know what they were doing? What about the fallout carried world-wide? Couldn't the cumulative doses of several shots like Bravo blight all peoples for generations? Fears spread throughout the world. The Bravo shot had repercussions for years to come. It was one of the main stimuli for Adlai Stevenson's proposal in the 1956 Presidential campaign that tests of large hydrogen bombs be discontinued unilaterally. Distinction between the local fallout of Bravo and the greatly diluted world-wide fallout was seldom made.

In Nevada and its neighboring states, there was apprehension about test series at Yucca Flats. By carefully gauging the weather, serious fallout accidents had been avoided in the western United States, despite the scores of tests conducted there. But the excellent safety record made by the test managers was little known. The Bravo accident is the one nuclear test of more than 300 that is remembered, perhaps better outside the United States than inside.

It was probably more luck than careful planning that kept the Bravo fallout accident from turning into a disaster. Monitoring was inadequate. Joint Task Force 7 was not psychologically prepared if, indeed, properly briefed. If the wind's azimuth had been a few points more off the prediction of weathermen, this inadequate preparation could have been more tragic than it was.

The initial secrecy with which the AEC approached it all, justified or not, confirmed the world's suspicion that something frightening was being withheld from view. Imaginations frequently ran wild. What was essentially a true appraisal of the accident by AEC became the target of jeering disbelief.

From data on the Marshallese exposed to fallout [the AEC reported], it is seen that the degree of internal hazard in the exposed persons was small. This is encouraging, since these people lived in a relatively primitive state where maximum probability of contamination of food and water supplies existed. If the hazard was minimum under these conditions, it should be even less under conditions of modern American living. With all the testing of nuclear devices in Nevada and elsewhere, the level of strontium, the most important fission product as far as internal hazard is concerned, is still only about one one-thousandth of the permissible body burden as recommended by the National Committee on Radiation Protection in National Bureau of Standards Handbook 52, for industrial workers.[11]

This type of statement from the AEC, however, was greeted mostly with suspicion, partly because secrecy could have been used to hide the full story, partly because motives of AEC, as the manufacturer of weapons, would logically be to promote more tests, not inhibit them.

Confidence in the AEC suffered another setback when Dr. Ralph Lapp, a nuclear physicist not connected with the government, pieced together evidence indicating the March 1, 1954, shot had produced an unusual amount and a different kind of fallout when compared with earlier nuclear explosions. He deduced the bomb had been a fission-fusion-fission device, triggered by a conventional atomic bomb.

He published some of his findings in the fall of 1954.[12] Disquiet spread as the AEC, for military-security reasons, neither denied nor confirmed the Lapp report.

In the midst of the hubbub at the end of March 1954, President Eisenhower ordered that color movies of the 1952 thermonuclear test be released to the general public. His aim, it was said, was to warn the public of the awesomeness of the H-bomb. While this served a larger purpose of reinforcing the American deterrent, there was at the same time a "backlash" which was immediately to be felt in the Bravo accident case. Fears in Asia were confirmed and the clamor for an end to tests rose.

Beside the Bravo test there were other experiments in the series which have not been fully reported to this day. One, code-named "Yankee," was exploded on May 4, 1954, from a barge and, according to official records, produced a seismic signal of the same size as the Bravo shot. No estimated megatonage has been reported.

Admiral Strauss had publicly announced another thermonuclear shot on March 26, also a barge shot, but no estimate of its yield has been released.

The Bravo accident and subsequent thermonuclear shots prompted India's Prime Minister Nehru to address a personal plea to the United States to end its hydrogen tests. After waiting three days Mr. Nehru proposed in a speech before his parliament that the three nuclear powers accept a "standstill agreement" on tests of nuclear weapons. The first appearance of radioactive rain in India reinforced the feelings of alarm on the subcontinent.

The United States decided to curb its distribution of color films of the Mike blast, for fear that it would increase apprehensions abroad about H-bomb tests continuing in the Pacific.

The British Labour Party suddenly rose in angry opposition to further testing. In the late spring, Prime Minister Churchill made repeated appearances before the House of Commons to reject suggestions that the British ask the United States to end its nuclear-weapons tests. He was urged not only by British Laborites but also by the nation's press to seek a meeting with President Eisenhower and Soviet Premier Malenkov to study a ban on the use of nuclear weapons.

AEC Chairman Strauss, trying to make the distinction between tests and war use of nuclear weapons, acknowledged that an atomic war would make the world a "radioactive cinder." Test-ban advocates seized on such points to press their cause. A Churchill statement that "an undue number" of bomb bursts might seriously contaminate the atmosphere for 5,000 years provided foes of nuclear testing more ammunition. That he was referring to nuclear war, not tests, was obscured. And even with respect to nuclear war his prediction was dubious.

At the end of March, 104 British Labour MP's signed a motion asking the United Nations to proclaim a ban on H-bomb experiments.

Prime Minister Churchill held staunchly to the line that control of H-bomb experiments would be impractical. He pointed to the failures of past negotiations with the Soviet Union to achieve effective inspection and control. In April, the House of Commons held a full-scale debate on H-bomb control. The British Peace Committee, the Science for Peace Committee, and other organizations clamored for an end to tests. Canadian Foreign Secretary Lester Pearson urged a renewal of the United Nations efforts to get control of nuclear tests, but rejected Canadian suggestions that the United States be asked to halt them unilaterally.

The Japanese Lower House followed the British lead early in April. The Diet heard members urge the Japanese Cabinet to seek a regulation of nuclear-weapons tests. But the Government announced that Japan would not ask the United States to give up tests unless the Soviet Union did so too. Foreign Minister Okazaki did say he expected the United States to pay compensation for losses of the "Lucky Dragon" fishermen.

Indonesian Premier Sastroamidjojo backed Prime Minister Nehru's proposal for a halt to nuclear tests pending a U.N. Disarmament Committee study of possibilities of negotiating a test-ban. So did the Soviet Union, whose world-peace resolution was being promoted by Moscow radio and newspapers.

Britain, France, and the United States requested an early U.N. Disarmament Commission meeting to create a subcommittee to study the control problem.

The British House of Commons finally went along with a Labor motion urging British Prime Minister Churchill, President Eisenhower, and Soviet Premier Malenkov to hold talks on control of nuclear weapons. The South African Government quickly joined in.

Apprehensions about radioactivity were kept alive, too, when the Japanese announced they were sending a special survey ship to the southwest Pacific to investigate radioactivity of the ocean. An American observer was invited to make the trip.

The Japanese Socialist Party proposed a complete ban on use of nuclear weapons. Dr. Albert Schweitzer entered the public controversy in a letter from Africa to the British public in which he advocated an H-bomb test-ban. The Pope also backed the idea of a ban if it could be arranged under proper control.

Asian Prime Ministers, conferring in Colombo at the end of April, urged a suspension of H-bomb tests pending negotiation of a nuclear-weapons ban by the United Nations. The Methodist Church of New York joined the cry.

Secretary of State Dulles, in mid-May, pledged that the United States would continue to seek a "properly safeguarded" agreement. The pressures continued to build, however, especially in Britain and Japan. Scientists, church groups, unions, issued demands for a stop to tests.

The Burmese joined other Asian powers in urging an end to bomb tests before the United Nations General Assembly.

In Britain, the Lord Mayor of Coventry led a party to Stalingrad to dramatize an appeal for a weapons ban.

Marshall Islanders sent a petition to the United Nations urging an end to tests.

Imagined cases of radiation sickness multiplied, especially in Japan. Men on Japanese freighters turned up with illness said to be radiation sickness. Japanese fishing associations asked the United States $350,000 in compensation for unproved damages. Meanwhile, however, a Japanese survey ship in the Bikini area found the waters there free of contamination. A few days later Japanese officials ordered tuna caught on an expedition near Truk Island destroyed. In another two weeks, scientists on the Japanese survey ship further confused the picture by reporting they had eaten fish caught in the Eniwetok-Bikini area.

The Communist World Peace Council, on May 28, launched another campaign to stop nuclear tests.

The United Nations Disarmament Subcommittee held closed-door sessions in London and New York in May and June. The United States concentrated on the need for effective inspection and control of any disarmament. The Soviet Union virtually ignored the subject, pressing hard instead for elimination of all atomic, hydrogen, and other weapons of mass destruction. This was coupled with provisions for "simultaneous" establishment of strict international controls. But throughout the Subcommittee talks, the Soviet delegation avoided giving any precise information about what these controls would be, despite close questioning by Western representatives.

To meet the Soviet Union's demand for a ban on use of nuclear weapons under all conditions, the United Kingdom and France, supported by Canada and the United States, proposed in a memorandum of June 11, 1954, that all states agree to prohibit the use of atomic and hydrogen weapons "except in defense against aggression." The plan also provided for establishment of inspection and control in both conventional and nuclear fields before ending nuclear-weapons production. Weapon stockpiles were to be eliminated in the second phase of the disarmament process.

Soviet representatives made no immediate response, but continued to press publicly for an all-inclusive ban on all weapons of mass destruction.

Late in June, 1954, the Eisenhower Administration made its first thorough study of the test-ban idea. The President then "adopted an interdepartmental recommendation that the United States should not at that time agree to a test moratorium but that disarmament policy review should be continued and expedited." [13]

Prime Minister Churchill, under unrelenting fire from the opposition Labour Party, paid what looked like a sentimental visit on President Eisenhower in Washington in June, 1954. His main purpose, he disclosed after he returned, had been to get a first-hand report on the H-bomb's implications for British foreign policy. Shortly thereafter, he gave the order to end the British occupation of the Suez Canal area—because the H-bomb had made it futile to keep the short-cut sea route open in any big war. Whichever side did not control the waterway could deny its use to the enemy, he concluded.

President Eisenhower had held back, however, on the idea of a meeting with Soviet Premier Malenkov, as the House of Commons had suggested, to talk about banning nuclear tests.

On July 13, the Soviet Ambassador, Semyon Tsarapkin, introduced a resolution in the U.N. Trusteeship Council charging the United States with "violating its trust" by holding nuclear-weapons tests in the Marshall Islands. He added one of the first official calls by the Soviet Union to end all nuclear testing.

India's V. K. Krishna Menon, also speaking in the Trusteeship Council, proposed that the U.N. General Assembly be asked to "order" the United States to end tests pending an international court ruling on the legality of holding tests in the Marshall Islands.

Tie votes in the Trusteeship Council Petitions Committee had the effect of rejecting the Soviet and Indian resolutions, but the erosion of the United States position continued.

East German newspapers reported that nuclear-weapons tests were causing floods in East Germany in the summer of 1954.

Of the twenty-three Japanese crewmen of the "Lucky Dragon," seven were still ill in September. Aikichi Kuboyama died September 23. There was national mourning in Japan. An autopsy witnessed by an American officer reportedly showed that the fisherman had died of jaundice resulting from the radiation; but whether this hepatitis was a result of the Bravo radiation was never finally resolved.

There was a flurry of indignation against the United States in the Japanese press after the death of Kuboyama. Twelve Japanese demonstrated outside the American Embassy in Tokyo, a very small demonstration by Japanese standards. After the Japanese press furor had died down, the cry was taken up by Radio Peking in Communist China.

A public funeral for Japanese fisherman Kuboyama on October 10, touched off a new wave of anti-Americanism. Japanese authorities, meanwhile, reported that 10 per cent of a tuna haul caught 600 miles southwest of Midway Island had to be rejected because of radioactivity.

On November 4, the U.N. General Assembly called on the Disarmament Subcommittee to reconvene and consider all past and new proposals. The big powers were getting nowhere in their private negotiations. The rest of the world looked on helplessly as it saw H-bomb stockpiles multiply and an uncertain health hazard from testing mount. To keep hope alive it was important to keep the nuclear powers talking to each other.

But the United Nations resolution stated it as a principle that the world should seek "total prohibition of the use and manufacture of nuclear weapons and weapons of mass destruction of every type, together with the conversion of existing stocks of nuclear weapons for peaceful purposes." Although another principle called for effective international control, American scientists were already skeptical that it would be possible to detect hidden stockpiles. Effective control and total prohibition were becoming impossible.

In November, there were also suggestions from American scientists that the United States confine its future tests to its own continental territory. Premier Shigeru Yoshida of Japan followed this up with a statement urging the United States to conduct its future tests farther from Japan.

At the United Nations on November 19, 1954, Secretary-General Hammarskjold received Indian Prime Minister Nehru's disarmament proposals, first advanced in New Delhi in April. Nuclear testing should be halted, Mr. Nehru again proposed, full publicity should be given to the extent of destructiveness of atomic weapons, private meetings of the U.N. Disarmament Subcommittee should be resumed, and a truce in the arms race should be declared.

In the midst of the General Assembly debate, on November 23, the Communist World Peace Council proposed that the great powers reach "immediate agreement on the banning of all experimental explosions of atomic and hydrogen bombs." This was linked with a further demand that the government promise "never to use nuclear weapons whatever may be the pretext." Thus the Red campaign for a test ban was launched.

Rumors of further big tests continued to circulate. New Zealand Labour Party Leader Walter Nash charged that the United States planned an Antarctic test. The United States promptly denied it. The New Zealand Antarctic Branch Society refused to take the denial at face value, however, and urged its members to exercise vigilance for American tests in the Antarctic.

By December, 1954, Japanese sponsors of a petition for a test ban claimed 19 million signers and scheduled a world conference in Tokyo for August, 1955. The Japanese Welfare Ministry did not lift its surveillance of fish catches until the end of the year.

Reports issued in Japan at the end of the year indicated that Soviet Siberian tests were the principal source of radioactive ash that fell on the island empire, but the principal pressures for a test ban were still directed against the United States.

Later there were reports that the Soviet tests caused fallout over Chicago and other American cities. Canada reported receiving a fallout dose from Soviet tests. Korea discovered radioactive snow, presumably from Soviet tests.

Unlike other non-Communist areas, where the popular movement for a test ban did not get full government support, South Asia had its Prime Ministers leading the appeal. In their December conference, Asian Prime Ministers repeated their May demands for a world test ban. From India came suggestions from private citizens that the United States should undertake a unilateral ban as a form of pressure on the Soviet Union.

In November, the Bulletin of the Atomic Scientists had published one of the first full-fledged plans for a test ban. This was a year and a half before Governor Adlai Stevenson made a similar proposal in the Presidential election campaign.

President Eisenhower's counterpressure against the Soviet Union came in the form of demands for Soviet discussion of his Atoms for Peace proposal. Ambassador Charles E. Bohlen made frequent trips to the Soviet Foreign Ministry urging talks. The 1954 U.N. General Assembly became a principal forum for discussing the idea. Finally, the Kremlin agreed to procedural discussions in Washington in January, 1955. This was the beginning of a long series of discussions on the Atoms for Peace proposal which wound up eventually in the establishment of the International Atomic Energy Agency.

Those in charge of the development of nuclear weapons in this country were, at that time, prepared to withstand considerable popular pressure for a test ban, however. They could not be sure that the Soviet Union was behind the United States in H-bomb development. Analysis of the first Soviet test, in August, 1953, showed that Kremlin scientists possibly had struck upon a fast, cheap means of manufacture. Should the United States have accepted a test ban at that time, it might have frozen itself in an inferior position.

Leading Soviet officials reinforced such fear. In April (one month after Bravo), Deputy Premier Anastas Mikoyan reported that the Soviet Union had put the hydrogen bomb into the hands of its troops. The emerging new Soviet boss, Nikita Khrushchev, later claimed in Prague that the Soviet Union had developed the H-bomb before the United States.

As a reminder of the grim stakes in the arms race, Dr. Edward Teller warned publicly that the Soviet Union had nearly bested the United States in H-bomb development and could still take over the lead in developing refinements of the weapon.

Public suspicion, in the United States and abroad, that the full story of the Bravo accident was not being told continued to be nourished by security regulations connected with the test. The National Broadcasting Company protested late in the year that its films showing decontamination of B-36's that had monitored the radioactive clouds from the Pacific thermonuclear test series had been confiscated.

Chapter 3

1955

Wobbly rule in the Kremlin produced a confused pattern of disarmament policy in the Soviet Union early in 1955. On February 8, Marshal Nikolai Bulganin replaced Georgi Malenkov as Premier and Nikita Khrushchev, the First Secretary of the Communist Party, took over effective control of the Soviet Union.

Only six days later Khrushchev advanced officially for the first time a weapons test-ban idea. He suggested a ban, not on all tests, but only on hydrogen-bomb tests.

"We are willing to take certain partial steps—for example, to discontinue the thermonuclear weapons test . . ." he said.

In the spirit of defiance Soviet leaders often affected in times of internal stress, Deputy Premier Vyacheslav Molotov boasted that the Soviet Union led the United States in hydrogen-bomb development. Washington showed no alarm. President Eisenhower commented that he saw no proof that this was true. Defense Secretary Wilson openly expressed doubt. British Prime Minister Churchill declared flatly that the Soviet Union lagged behind the United States and had a bomb of "inferior power."

Nevertheless, Soviet H-bomb power was one of the major worries on President Eisenhower's mind as he moved early in 1955 toward "the intensified effort" to reach a disarmament agreement with the Soviet Union. Pleas to ban H-bomb tests, however, were not welcome in high government circles of Washington, where doubts about Soviet progress behind the Iron Curtain could never be honestly put aside.

On February 23, at a news conference, the President told a reporter the United States saw nothing to be gained by a separate ban on thermonuclear tests outside a decent and proper disarmament program.

In another two days, the U.N. Disarmament Subcommittee, composed of the United States, Britain, France, Canada, and the Soviet Union, resumed its meetings in London, as the United Nations General Assembly had recommended. The Subcommittee got off to a slow start, but

51

was to become an important forum for discussion of the nuclear test ban.

It had become obvious to President Eisenhower that the pace of technological advance in weapons development was increasing so fast it was sorely taxing the ability of disarmament negotiators to keep up in devising methods to control the new machines of war. Each day disarmament was delayed, the harder it became to achieve.

The only option open to him, it appeared, was to seek as quickly as possible a "mutually advantageous" halt to the arms race, before one of the new machines went off in anger or by accident. With the Soviet Union then in possession of the hydrogen bomb, it was clear that both sides could be destroyed in an all-out war. The United States openly used this two-edged prospect to persuade the Soviet Union to keep talking disarmament, even if no more than talk resulted, in the hope that eventually the Kremlin could accept a genuine halt in the arms race.

Stockpiles of nuclear weapons had been accumulating swiftly for several years, not only in American arsenals but in those of the Soviet Union, and, more recently, in Great Britain. What outsider could say where they were?

"Time and technology," the Department of State said, ". . . were bringing into question some of the foundations upon which previous U.S. disarmament policy had been based."

One of the most important of those foundations was the premise that it was possible to decree a prohibition on the use of nuclear weapons or an elimination of nuclear stockpiles.

President Eisenhower therefore decided that "a new approach" was necessary. On March 19, 1955, he appointed Harold E. Stassen as special assistant to the President for disarmament. Essentially Mr. Stassen's job was to conduct first a thorough analysis of the disarmament problem and then to chart a new course for achieving a system of international arms limitation if total disarmament was becoming impossible.[1]

Governor Stassen, who in earlier days in Minnesota had been the country's youngest state chief executive, was given responsibility "for developing, on behalf of the President and the State Department, the broad studies, investigations and conclusions, which, when concurred in by the National Security Council and approved by the President, will become basic policy toward the question of disarmament." He was instructed to seek, both in and out of government, the best brains of the nation, to provide advice.

Raising disarmament-policy review to Cabinet-level status was "unprecedented in world history."[2] So was the problem.

President Eisenhower had intended the move to dramatize before the world his interest in reaching a durable peace. It largely achieved this purpose, even in the Soviet Union. Mr. Stassen's appointment was regarded as an experiment in seeking a method to replace the increasingly hazardous "balance of terror" with a system of arms limitation based on international confidence. At the same time, of course, it would be useful in finding public positions with which to defend necessary American military policy from pacifist attack.

The White House Disarmament Staff that Governor Stassen set up was drawn from experts in the Defense and State Departments, the Atomic Energy Commission, the Central Intelligence Agency, and the foreign-aid administration with which Mr. Stassen had been closely associated earlier.

At the same time, the President established a Special Committee on Disarmament Problems, an interdepartmental instrument for coordination and review in the disarmament field. This committee, which later was to be widely split on the issue of nuclear tests, included high-ranking representatives from the State and Defense Departments, the Atomic Energy Commission, the Central Intelligence Agency, the Department of Justice (Federal Bureau of Investigation), and the United States Information Agency. Secretary of State Dulles, Defense Secretary Wilson (later McElroy), AEC Chairman Lewis L. Strauss, and John A. McCone frequently represented their own organizations in this interdepartmental committee.

As the White House Disarmament Staff went to work, the London Disarmament Subcommittee was occupying itself with the problem of phasing the reductions in conventional and nuclear weapons to satisfy both major powers. The Soviet Union, which had originally stood for *immediate* prohibition of the use and "elimination" of all nuclear weapons—a palpable impossibility—to be followed by reductions in conventional power, had somewhat modified its view. It was ready to put off the proclamation prohibiting the use of nuclear weapons until a second stage—halfway through the conventional disarmament process. The United Kingdom and France, seeking to find a compromise between United States and Soviet positions, produced a new resolution on April 19, 1955. This proposed prohibiting the use of nuclear weapons after 75 per cent of the agreed reduction in conventional armaments had taken place. Elimination of the nuclear weapons would begin at the same time that the final 25 per cent reduction in conventional armaments was undertaken. Two days later, the United States and Canada identified themselves with the United Kingdom–French proposal. Both the Soviet Union and the West still formally adhered to the idea that prohibition of the use of nuclear weapons and elimination of them was possible.

While the London Disarmament Conference ground on, the United States was conducting another series of tests at its Nevada site. Fourteen relatively small shots were exploded in Operation Teapot from February to May. In advance of the program, the AEC sent two officials on a tour of the area surrounding the Nevada test site to acquaint the public with safety precautions taken.

This was an obvious effort to avoid a flare-up like the one that followed the Bravo accident. Dr. Alvin Graves, one of the survivors of a Los Alamos radiation accident in which one man was killed, spoke before the legislature of the State of Utah on safety plans. He toured Utah and Nevada to assure residents that the hazards from radiation would be small.

Weapons effects were among the most publicized aspects of Operation Teapot. The military tested tanks and other armor. Civil Defense tested buildings. Some 9,000 servicemen maneuvered on the Nevada desert during the tests. Radiation monitoring stations were set up in the neighboring areas.

AEC Chairman Strauss joined in dramatizing the elaborate safety precautions, in a speech in Las Vegas.

Concern about fallout, of course, did not magically disappear. Charges that the Pentagon was planning to stage nuclear-weapons tests in Antarctica were advanced again, by the Communists this time, sending another thrill of fear through Southern Hemisphere peoples.

Chicago, New York, Denver, and other cities reported radioactive clouds overhead and some fallout from the spring tests in Nevada. Las Vegas was dusted with fallout after one of the shots in late March, but the careful preparations by the AEC prevented panic, and the hazard was not great. Later, it was rumored that cattle had died after being exposed to fallout at Black Lake, New Mexico, but AEC investigators found fallout levels had been too slight to harm either humans or cattle.

In the spring of 1955, the world was also awakening to the genetic effects of heavy-dose radiation. Few, however, made the important distinction between heavy- and light-dose radiation. Those eager to stop nuclear tests as an opening wedge in the quest for disarmament, quickly accepted the exaggeration of genetic hazard in global fallout as an aid to their cause.

The British Labour Party, in anticipation of an approaching election the Conservatives were expected to call to transfer power from aging Premier Churchill to British Foreign Secretary Anthony Eden, seized on the nuclear-test issue as a major point for campaign oratory. In the House of Commons, Labourites pressed the government to seek a halt to all nuclear tests by all nations until a study of the genetic effects of radiation could be conducted by a group of international scientists.

In this country, the American Federation of Scientists proposed that the United Nations sponsor a study of the effects of weapons tests, particularly of the possible genetic damage to future generations.

In April, the National Academy of Sciences, the most respected scientific group in the United States, decided to establish a panel to study fallout and other radiation effects, under a grant from the Rockefeller Foundation.

Twenty Hiroshima women who had been disfigured by burns from the 1945 A-bomb blast over their city were brought to New York for free plastic surgery in the spring of 1955. Although their visit was not directly connected with fallout effects, it was closely associated. Prominent test-ban advocates were among the principal sponsors of the project. The women were flown to New York from Japan by the U.S. Air Force.

Pope Pius XII, in his 1955 Easter message, joined in warning of the genetic effects of radiation from nuclear weapons, adding to the pressures on the big powers to end nuclear-weapons tests.

The Joint Congressional Committee on Atomic Energy called AEC Chairman Lewis Strauss before them in April to discuss the genetic-damage problem. He discounted reports not only of genetic damage but of other harmful effects from atomic tests. Dr. John Bugher, Chief of the AEC's Biology and Medicine Division, and Merrill Eisenbud, two of the first to be concerned with the fallout problem, also told the Representatives and Senators that the level of fallout radiation was not high enough to cause serious genetic damage. Mr. Strauss disclosed, however, that the AEC had ordered a $1.5-million study of genetic effects of low-level radiation. He was in the anomalous position of admitting little was known about low-level radiation effects on the genes, yet claiming that the effect really was negligible. Alarmists were in an equally anomalous position, of course, but the public was much more willing to listen to them.

The general public tended to doubt AEC protestations about the harmlessness of fallout, mainly because people had identified the AEC as the principal advocate of nuclear-weapons development. As the fears of genetic damage grew, not only in this country but around the world, the Atomic Energy Commission began a high-level counterattack to expose the exaggerations of the danger from test fallout. Commissioner Willard F. Libby was the workhorse of the group, but Chairman Strauss and others made frequent speeches emphasizing the same points Commissioner Libby developed.

Dr. Libby's learned scientific papers, however, received comparatively little circulation abroad, or even in this country. He did have effect among scientists here; increasing numbers came to understand that the dangers of world-wide fallout were not great, especially when compared with normal cosmic-ray bombardment or with the hazards of withholding tests while the arms race with the Soviet Union was still on.

Chairman Strauss, on the other hand, steered clear of the technical language, but had great difficulty convincing the public of his thesis. There was, of course, the Machiavellian image of Mr. Strauss himself, assiduously built up by his foes in this country and abroad. He was pictured as a powerful behind-the-scenes manipulator, avidly pressing for went all those dissenters who shrank from the hydrogen age. He had the development of the most destructive weapons possible, purging as he been involved, two years earlier, in the dismissal of Dr. J. Robert Oppenheimer, the scientist who led the effort to produce the A-bomb for the

United States, as a security risk. In the dramatic hearings that followed Dr. Oppenheimer's suspension, Admiral Strauss became identified as a champion of H-bomb development and as a kind of "bogey man." At the same time he was under constant attack for withholding from the public vast amounts of material on nuclear developments, which scientists insisted could be released without harm to the national security.

When Mr. Strauss said, therefore, that "Fallout won't hurt you," he sounded like General Sherman saying "War is hell." Some newsmen mockingly attributed to Admiral Strauss the slogan "Fallout is good for you."

The Soviet Union, meanwhile, launched a world-wide drive in 1955 for signatures to its World Peace Council appeal for a test-ban. Indonesian President Sukarno, Indian Prime Minister Nehru, and others among the Colombo powers pressed their favorite test-ban theme.

The Bandung Conference of April, 1955, gave the test ban a big boost throughout Asia. It had been convened at the invitation of the Prime Ministers of the Colombo powers: Burma, Ceylon, India, Indonesia, and Pakistan. Twenty-nine countries of Asia and Africa, including Red China, sent high representatives to the big event, which lasted from April 18 to 24. The nuclear-test ban was a popular subject in the conference and in the corridors. Prime Minister Nehru of India and President Sukarno of Indonesia both made formal speeches advocating an immediate ban.

The conference communiqué had a powerful impact in the uncommitted world, which was already sensitive to "the terrible consequences that would follow" a nuclear war.

"The conference considered," the Bandung communiqué said, "that disarmament and the prohibition of the production, experimentation and use of nuclear and thermonuclear weapons of war are imperative to save mankind and civilization from the fear and prospect of wholesale destruction."

Largely under the prodding of Pakistan's Prime Minister, Mohammed Ali, the Bandung conference included in their plea a demand for effective inspection. "The Conference considered," the communiqué said, "that effective international control should be established and maintained to implement such disarmament and prohibition, and that speedy and determined efforts should be made to this end."

The Bandung powers, however, came out strongly for halting not only H-bomb tests but A-bomb experiments as well. "Pending the total prohibition of the manufacture of nuclear and thermonuclear weapons, this Conference appeals to all the powers concerned to reach agreement to suspend experiments for such weapons."

Spurred on by the Bandung pronouncement, both the British Labour Party and the British Communist Party demanded a test ban in their election manifestoes in early May. Foreign Minister Anthony Eden, running for Prime Minister, rejected the idea of even an H-bomb test ban in a campaign speech May 9. Soon after he was elected, Prime Minister Eden stood off further Labour Party demands in Parliament that H-bomb tests be banned during the meetings of the U.N. Disarmament Subcommittee.

On May 10, in London, the Soviet Union tabled for the first time in postwar disarmament negotiations a provision for ending nuclear-weapons tests as part of its old total-prohibition clause.

The clause on ending nuclear tests was Point IV in the first stage of its proposed disarmament plan—for execution in 1956. The proposal stated:

> As one of the first measures for the execution of the program for the reduction of armaments and the prohibition of atomic weapons, States possessing atomic and hydrogen weapons shall undertake to discontinue tests of these weapons.
>
> With a view to supervision of the fulfillment by States of the aforementioned obligation, an international commission shall be set up which shall submit reports to the Security Council and the General Assembly.

There was no provision for action to be taken against any State violating the agreement on a nuclear-test ban. And the mention of the Security Council and the General Assembly indicated that the Soviet Union intended to maintain a veto power over any such punitive action.

When arms and armed forces of the five major powers had been cut by 50 per cent of the entire projected reduction, the Soviet proposal said, "States shall assume a solemn obligation not to use nuclear weapons, which they shall regard as prohibited to them. Exceptions to this rule may be permitted for purposes of defense against aggression, when a decision to that effect is taken by the Security Council."

This was as close as the Soviet Union ever came to accepting the Western concept that nuclear weapons should be prohibited only as aggressive instruments, not prohibited for defense. According to the Soviet Union's wording, however, any permanent Security Council member would have had a veto over the use of any nuclear weapon by any power.

Along with its May 10 proposal, the Soviet Union presented another paper, "Concerning International Control over the Reduction of Armaments and the Prohibition of Atomic Weapons." This paper was recognized immediately in the West as an important declaration on the difficulty, if not impossibility, of detecting hidden nuclear-weapons stockpiles. If the stockpiles could not be found, of course, the whole Soviet campaign for a prohibition on the use of nuclear weapons and their elimination would become meaningless. The Soviet paper declared:

> There are possibilities beyond the reach of international control for evading this control and for organizing the clandestine manufacture of atomic and hydrogen weapons, even if there is a formal agreement on international

control. In such a situation, the security of the States parties to the international convention [treaty] cannot be guaranteed, since the possibility would be open to a potential aggressor to accumulate stocks of atomic and hydrogen weapons for a surprise atomic attack on peace-loving states.

The draft document would have had the General Assembly of the United Nations recognize that "the necessary conditions for the institution of a control system which would enjoy the trust of all states and would fully meet the requirements of international security do not at present exist."

The Soviet paper continued in that incredibly candid vein:

Insofar as the necessary trust between States does not, at the present time, exist, a situation might arise in which the adoption of decisions on international control would, in reality, be reduced to a mere formality which would not achieve the objective envisaged. This is all the more inadmissible since, in present conditions, peace-loving peoples are most apprehensive with regard to the existence of atomic and hydrogen weapons, in respect of which the institution of international control is particularly difficult.

This danger is inherent in the very nature of atomic production. It is well known that the production of atomic energy for peaceful purposes can be used for the accumulation of stocks of explosive atomic materials, and moreover, in ever greater quantities. This means that States having establishments for the production of atomic energy can accumulate, in violation of the relevant agreements, large quantities of explosive materials for the production of atomic weapons. The danger of this state of affairs becomes still more apparent if account is taken of the fact that, where the corresponding quantities of explosive atomic materials exist, production of actual atomic and hydrogen bombs is technically fully feasible and can be effected on a large scale.

Thus, there are possibilities beyond the reach of international control for evading this control and for organizing the clandestine manufacture of atomic and hydrogen weapons, even if there is a formal agreement on international control. In such a situation, the security of the States parties to the international convention cannot be guaranteed, since the possibility would be open to a potential aggressor to accumulate stocks of atomic and hydrogen weapons for surprise atomic attack on peace-loving states.

Until an atmosphere of trust can be created in the relations between States, any agreement on the institution of international control can only serve to lull the vigilance of the peoples. It will create a false sense of security, while, in reality, there will be a danger of the production of atomic and hydrogen weapons and, hence, the threat of surprise attack and the unleashing of an atomic war with all its appalling consequences for the peoples.[3]

The Soviet declaration went on, then, to say that preparations for a new war would also have to include concentrations of conventional armaments—aircraft, artillery, tanks, warships, and other large land, sea, and air forces. The thrust of the argument was that any aggressor would need, in addition to atomic and hydrogen weapons, concentrations of delivery systems which could be detectable and therefore could be monitored by ground stations.

So far as the West was concerned, however, the cat was out of the bag. In this one paper, a treatise on the difficulties of controlling nuclear weapons, the Soviet Union had, in effect, destroyed its whole case for seeking the prohibition on use of nuclear weapons and the elimination of nuclear stockpiles. Neither, by the Soviet Union's own admission, was feasible. John Foster Dulles could not have stated it better.

Soviet officials repeated this theory in the next few months, in varying forms. The paper expounding this Soviet view is one of the most cherished documents in the archives of the State Department. Officials there frequently speculate that the man who wrote it is no longer with the Soviet Foreign Office and probably has been given other employment in Siberia.

The Soviet Union has to this day continued to seek the unrealistic—but globally popular—goal of prohibiting the use of nuclear weapons and eliminating stockpiles. The very May 10 proposal that discussed the control difficulties also advocated complete prohibition, an example of the contradictions with which Soviet propaganda policies frequently must contend.

The next day, May 11, Soviet Premier Bulganin, in an address before the Warsaw Conference of East European states, also conceded that nuclear control is impossible:

> Even if . . . such control were possible, it would be of an ineffectual nature, for, with the absence of mutual trust, avoidance of this control is also possible. Such a position is all the more probable because the technology of atomic production makes it possible for atomic materials to be turned from their intended peaceful uses to atomic weapons swiftly and without particular difficulty, with the aid of only certain special apparatus. Thus it is possible to have controllers, but not to exert control.[4]

Premier Bulganin indicated the admission that nuclear control would be ineffective was intended to support the Soviet thesis that ground inspection would be the crucial element in guarding against surprise attack. Nuclear weapons without large land, air, and naval forces are not sufficient to conduct a modern war, Premier Bulganin argued. It would thus be feasible to concentrate on delivery systems rather than nuclear warheads, he contended.

In the London Disarmament Subcommittee talks, the United States welcomed as "refreshing" the new candor of the Soviet Union on the impossibility of controlling nuclear-weapons stockpiles or prohibiting their use. But no alternative to the same "prohibition on use" policy, to which both the United States and the Soviet Union were committed in the 1954 U.N. General Assembly resolution, was advanced at that time.

In Washington, Mr. Stassen and his White House Disarmament Staff were wrestling with the same problem of ineffective control. The "Secretary for Peace," Mr. Stassen, presented his first comprehensive report to President Eisenhower late in May. It stressed the extreme importance of guarding against surprise attack, the necessity for effective inspection in any disarmament agreement, and the role of aerial reconnaisance with scientific instruments and photography in any effective inspection system. The nuclear age, it was decided, "had made the search for absolute solutions impossible." [5]

With the encouragement that Soviet scientists were thinking along the same lines, the Stassen report concluded that the nine-year major preoccupation of disarmament negotiators with an agreement to "eliminate" nuclear weapons had been outmoded.

Nuclear-weapons stockpiles had expanded greatly. Production technology had advanced. Great destruction was possible from a small package—a single bomb, possibly carried by a few agents with innocent-looking luggage.

As an official Government report put it later:

> The studies in 1955 thus indicated that neither our scientists nor the scientists of other countries were able by this time to devise methods which could account completely for all past production of nuclear materials, and the margin of error in known detection methods was beyond the limits we could contemplate for an acceptable inspection system. Nor was it possible to remedy this by attempting to search out any "clandestine" weapons. Scientific advances made it possible to concentrate great destructive force in a single bomb. Properly insulated, the nuclear material within a bomb defied detection by the most sensitive instruments at distances only a few yards away. Even small diversions of nuclear weapons would be sufficient to give an aggressor decisive strength in launching a great attack if the other side had fulfilled its obligation to destroy all such weapons.

The Stassen staff concluded: "We had reached the point of no return in eliminating nuclear weapons—at least until more adequate scientific detection methods were devised." [6]

Total elimination of nuclear weapons thus became a practical goal only if each side trusted the other implicitly. "But with the existing degree of international tension and hostility, no nation was prepared to gamble its national security on unverifiable commitments," an official report stated.[7]

Thus it was, that, in 1955, the United States decided to turn its attention away from the impractical goal of eliminating the bomb and concentrate instead on steps to control it. Even control would be difficult because the knowledge of making nuclear weapons was spreading. In 1955, only three nations had nuclear weapons—the United States, the Soviet Union, and Great Britain. But the United States and the Soviet Union had already agreed to cooperate in spreading the knowledge of peaceful uses of fissionable materials world-wide. The United States had opened negotiations with many countries to sign bilateral treaties for technical and material assistance in the peaceful uses of atomic energy.

The International Atomic Energy Agency was in the process of being formed, with reluctant Soviet cooperation.

It was impossible to separate knowledge of peaceful uses of atomic energy from knowledge of wartime uses. It was here that the main threat of spreading nuclear weapons to other powers would come. Fissionable material could be used either for weapons or for power plants. Atomic-power reactors, in fact, produced the very material from which atomic bombs were made. As the United States increased the number of reactors around the world it "multiplied correspondingly the opportunities for diversion of materials to weapons fabrication." [8]

Logically, the method of preventing the spread of nuclear weapons to other powers would be to seek control of the production of fissionable materials under an international authority.

The Stassen staff quickly came to another important conclusion: Nuclear weapons and intercontinental systems for delivering them had placed in the hands of a ruthless aggressor the possibility of achieving great surprise in a secret attack. One step toward security in an insecure world would be to prevent any country from achieving enough surprise to wipe out the retaliatory force of the other side.

"For these reasons, the matter of preventing great surprise attack became the dominant aspect of our first-phase disarmament policy," the State Department reported; and President Eisenhower prepared for his dramatic open-skies proposal before the Geneva summit meeting in July.[9] Tests of nuclear weapons, it should be noted, were still regarded as a peripheral issue in the disarmament field.

The Disarmament Staff, working with the President's Special Committee on Disarmament Problems, evolved at the same time in 1955 a set of guiding principles on which specific policy proposals would be based. These were the "essential" principles:

1. The United States should not accept an agreement for arms limitation or control unless provision is made for effective inspection of each phase of the agreement.

2. The United States should never agree to make any reductions or accept any controls in regard to its own armaments unless other signatory powers agree to carry out comparable reductions or controls in regard to their own armaments.

3. In the existing state of scientific knowledge, there could be no safe agreement to *eliminate* nuclear weapons. It is not possible by any known scientific or other means to account for the total previous production of nuclear weapons material. The margin of error in existing methods is sufficient to allow for clandestine fabrication or sequestering of enough nuclear weapons to constitute a devastating power advantage to the possessor.

4. The problem of controlling nuclear weapons would be complicated

enormously, if not made impossible, once the capability to produce such weapons spread to many additional countries.

5. Widespread fear of nuclear surprise attack exacerbated international tensions and was a principal motive for a continuing and accelerating competitive arms build-up.

6. The United States should never cease searching for a sound agreement and should always be willing to enter serious discussions in pursuit of such an agreement.

7. Because of the imminent development of missiles of intercontinental range and the proliferation of the means of nuclear production, the need for a solution to the armaments problem was increasingly urgent.

This was the basis on which Governor Stassen, his staff, and the interdepartmental committees set up by President Eisenhower approached the "intensified effort" to reach a disarmament agreement with the Soviet Union in 1955.

It is important to note that nuclear tests figured, at that time, neither in the decision to seek a realistic agreement for control of nuclear weapons nor in an unrealistic one to eliminate them. Nor did nuclear tests figure in countermeasures to prevent spreading of nuclear weapons to other powers. Production of nuclear weapons, not testing was considered the key. And more important than tests, of course, was the prevention of surprise attack.

At that time, the test-ban idea was generally regarded inside the Government as an ineffective disarmament measure. It would not reduce the threat of destruction, because both sides had huge stockpiles. Stopping tests would not block any nuclear power from delivering nuclear bombs on another power.

The newly-organized interagency group advising the President on disarmament, however, again considered the problem of nuclear testing in June, 1955, shortly after the Stassen staff had obtained agreement on guiding disarmament principles. The President "considered and approved" the conclusions of the interagency group, after this second review, "that a moratorium on H-bomb testing would not be in the interest of the U.S. and should not be agreed to except as a part of a comprehensive, safeguarded disarmament agreement."[10]

This was one of the key decisions that President Eisenhower made in preparation for the summit conference which was to begin July 18 in Geneva.

The Administration was already sensitive to Mr. Khrushchev's February statement suggesting an H-bomb test ban, to the pressures from some scientists in this country, to World Peace Council appeals, to the worldwide fears of fallout, and to the mounting political pressures expected in the 1955 General Assembly session in New York. Mr. Eisenhower had two other arrows in his quiver, however, in case Premier Khrushchev chose to press the test-ban issue. First, there was the atoms-for-peace

initiative of the United States, which had greatly impressed the world
and was evoking interest from most free-world countries. The United
States had already embarked on its program of bilateral arrangements for
loaning fissionable material and experimental reactors. Second, the Soviet Union had itself recognized the dangers of surprise attack, but, con-
tradictorily refused to open up its country sufficiently to give any assurance that a surprise-attack warning would be available to the West. The
opening was there for a Western move to breach the Iron Curtain. The
dramatic open-skies proposal was then in the making.

As a further indication of United States concern with the fallout problem, U.N. Ambassador Henry Cabot Lodge proposed at the 10th Anniversary Session of the United Nations, in San Francisco on June 22, that
the U.N. undertake to pool world knowledge about the effects of atomic
radiation on health. A formal American request was submitted to the
United Nations on August 4. Subsequently, the General Assembly established a U.N. Scientific Committee on Radiation. Its comprehensive
report three years later was to indicate that effects of fallout are minimal,
compared to other radiation hazards. But the panel's findings were not to
be published for another three years.

American scientists in the National Academy were to come to the
same conclusion, but their position before the world, like the AEC chairman's before the United States people, was suspect. After all, it was the
United States which needed the bomb, and minor health hazards to
other nations might easily be disregarded by policy-makers with this
outlook.

At the Geneva summit conference, the idea of the test ban was formally raised only by Soviet Premier Bulganin, and then in a perfunctory
way. He repeated his Government's proposal of May 10, that "as one of
the first measures for the execution of the program for the reduction of
armaments and the prohibition of atomic weapons, States possessing
atomic and hydrogen weapons pledge themselves to discontinue tests of
these weapons."

He also included a *pro forma* paragraph calling for "effective international control," but, as usual, gave no particulars on how this could be
achieved. Marshal Bulganin added to this proposal a statement, which he
proposed the heads of government of the Soviet Union, the United
States, the United Kingdom, and France endorse. They were to declare
solemnly that "pending the conclusion of the international convention
on the reduction of armaments and the prohibition of atomic weapons,
the Soviet Union, the United States of America, the United Kingdom,
and France undertake not to be the first to use atomic and hydrogen
weapons against any country and they call upon all other states to join
in this Declaration." [11]

This was the same old insistence on a pledge to ban the use of nuclear
weapons even in defense. It would also have prevented testing. The

West, of course, could not agree to this because the Soviet Union was still believed to possess superior conventional forces. If the West were deprived of nuclear defense, the Soviet bloc would enjoy an advantage in any conventional war.

Genetic effects of nuclear-weapons testing continued to be a hot issue in the United States. In April, Dr. H. J. Muller severely criticized Atomic Energy authorities for discounting the genetic effects of bomb tests. He conceded that the extreme view on effects of fallout was false, but charged that attempts to "whitewash" the tests weakened public morale. The AEC, he feared, was falling into the habit of exaggerating the harmlessness of fallout and thus risking loss of face in its pronouncements.

Those who were exaggerating the genetic effects of nuclear tests, he suggested, may have been instigated by Communists.

President Eisenhower, following up on the decisions of his Disarmament Staff and other interdepartmental committees, decided to concentrate at the summit meeting on inspection.

In replying to Premier Bulganin, on July 21, Mr. Eisenhower formally apprised the Soviet Union of the United States conclusion about difficulties in finding hidden nuclear-weapons stockpiles.

> We have not as yet been able to discover any scientific or other inspection method which would make certain of the elimination of nuclear weapons. So far as we are aware no other nation had made such a discovery. Our study of this problem is continuing. . . . We by no means exclude the possibility of finding useful checks in these fields.

The President's most dramatic presentation at the Summit Conference was his open-skies plan for exchange of reciprocal overflight rights to guard against surprise attack. In retrospect, the world's attention was quickly diverted from the open-skies plan when the Soviet Union greatly increased its propaganda pressure for a nuclear test ban.

The United States, in other words, was sidetracked in its campaign for open skies by the nuclear test-ban issue. A more effective promotion job by the United States Information Agency might have saved the open-skies plan from that fate.

The idea of proposing reciprocal overflights was a controversial measure inside the Eisenhower Administration before it was presented at the Geneva summit meeting.

Nelson Rockefeller, then a special assistant to the President, headed the study group that worked up the open-skies proposal. Walt W. Rostow, later to become a National Security Adviser to President Kennedy, spearheaded the drive within the Rockefeller study group for the open-skies idea.

Colonel William Kintner, an Army strategist with long experience in staff planning, and Stefan T. Possony, then an Air Force Intelligence specialist, worked with Dr. Rostow in persuading Mr. Rockefeller to take the lead within the Administration in pressing the open-skies idea.

Neither the State Department nor Governor Stassen's group were impressed with the open-skies proposal. Indeed, when the President made his presentation at Geneva, articles appeared in *The New York Times*, presumably based on State Department comments, that the proposal was "illegal."

Colonel Kintner and Dr. Possony accompanied Mr. Rockefeller to Geneva for the Summit Conference.

In preliminary meetings in Paris, Dr. Possony and Colonel Kintner wrote the first draft of the Eisenhower speech. Mr. Rockefeller presented it to a panel composed of Admiral Arthur Radford, then Chairman of the Joint Chiefs of Staff, Deputy Secretary of Defense Robertson, Governor Stassen, the United States Ambassador to NATO, and a few other officials.

There was a very heated debate. Admiral Radford ran into considerable difficulty in explaining the proposal to Governor Stassen. Later the plan was presented to General Alfred Gruenther, then NATO commander, and he enthusiastically approved the idea.

Secretary of State Dulles was not then in Paris. Admiral Radford, Mr. Rockefeller, and General Gruenther, however, sent a cable supporting the open-skies idea to Secretary Dulles.

The Dulles approval having been obtained, the Rockefeller group went to Lucerne to rewrite the speech. This draft was presented to President Eisenhower, who called in Governor Stassen to evaluate the idea.

To the consternation of the Rockefeller group, Governor Stassen persuaded the President to include in the open-skies proposal the plan for exchanging military "blueprints." There was less objection to the general idea of exchanging military information than to the unprofessional naiveté in the concept that blueprints, if they existed, would be an important factor in guarding against surprise attack.

President Eisenhower finally accepted the open-skies idea, complete with blueprints, and sprang his proposal on the startled Soviet, British, and French leaders.

Historically, however, it is incorrect to say that the open-skies proposal came out of Governor Stassen's shop. In the formative stage, Governor Stassen himself was skeptical or even negative.

Partly by Soviet design, partly because there were many detractors in the State Department and the Stassen group, partly because the conscience of the world was troubled by nuclear-weapons tests, pressure on the Soviet Union to accept the open-skies proposal was short-lived and the test ban soon became the principal issue in the disarmament field.

The Geneva heads-of-government directive to foreign ministers, dated July 23, dealt only in generalities with disarmament. It passed the ball back to the U.N. Disarmament Subcommittee, suggesting only that their representatives take account of the proposals advanced by the heads of government. They set the next meeting for August 29, 1955, in New York.

The friendly spirit in which the heads of government had rejected each others' comprehensive plans for world peace made an impression on the world, and the "spirit of Geneva" became a force in world affairs. The Atoms for Peace Conference, a conference of scientists held in Geneva from August 8 to 20, enhanced the aura of East-West cooperation. It diverted public thought away from the horrors of nuclear weapons, at least partially, and toward the benefits that nuclear energy could bring to the world.[12] The Soviet Union, nursing the spirit along, announced on August 12 that it was reducing its armed forces by 640,000 men.[13] Moscow's intention, of course, was to draw some concession from the United States in return.

Secretary of State Dulles, while welcoming the move, pointed out that the United States had reduced its own forces by about the same amount between 1953 and 1955, two years in advance of the Soviet move.

As requested by the heads of government, the London Disarmament Subcommittee reconvened on August 29, but there were no new proposals. The delegates concentrated on President Eisenhower's aerial inspection proposal, French Premier Faure's plan to disarm through budget cuts, the British plan for a pilot inspection project in the heart of Europe and similar proposals advanced during the July summit conference.

On September 6, however, the United States representative at the Disarmament Subcommittee sessions announced his country was placing a reservation on all its positions taken hitherto, "in view of new technological developments, particularly with respect to the accumulation of past nuclear production, pending the outcome of studies on inspection methods, accountability, and control arrangements."

This was a formal injection, in the disarmament negotiations, of the misgivings President Eisenhower had mentioned at the summit conference and which the American administration had been studying internally for almost a year. Mr. Stassen himself had been named United States representative on the Disarmament Subcommittee by the time the negotiators had moved on to New York in September.

President Eisenhower's heart attack of September 24 hardly interrupted disarmament negotiations or the post-summit exchange of letters with Bulganin. Scarcely three weeks after his seizure, the President was writing Marshal Bulganin again from his hospital bed in Denver, expressing hope for progress.

While the Soviet Union held staunchly to its May 10, 1955, proposals, the United States appeared before the world to have taken a step backward when it placed its reservation on all previous disarmament positions. The crucial difficulty in locating sequestered nuclear materials was not well understood. The Soviet Union, as well as other participants in the five-nation talks, agreed in the Subcommittee that accumulated materials could not be detected by any known scientific methods. But in its propaganda the Soviet Union never recognized this crucial point. United States propaganda made no effort to emphasize it.

As Secretary of State Dulles prepared for the October Foreign Ministers Conference, which had been ordered by the heads of governments, task forces set up by the White House Disarmament Staff formally registered their findings with President Eisenhower. In effect, the final report confirmed the May 26 findings on impossibility of eliminating nuclear weapons, on the danger of "fourth countries" obtaining nuclear weapons, and on the risks of great surprise attack. The same seven guiding principles were also reaffirmed.

The Soviet Union and the West returned, grimly, to their old ways of disagreement at the October-November Foreign Ministers Conference in Geneva. There was no agreement on any disarmament proposal. Foreign Minister Molotov, sticking by the old May 10 proposals, again advanced the proposition that discontinuing nuclear tests was "one of the first measures." It was a propaganda gesture, however, which produced little comment in the formal meetings.

British Foreign Secretary Macmillan, in his statement November 10, chided Foreign Minister Molotov for continuing to advance contradictory plans for complete prohibition of nuclear weapons and at the same time conceding that control was impossible. He said:

I suggest that if we are in earnest about disarmament, we cannot go on admitting on the one hand that there are possibilities of evasion beyond international control, and proposing on the other hand the total abolition of all nuclear weapons. We can retain the total abolition of nuclear weapons as our ultimate goal, but it would be misleading to pretend that it is a realizable goal in our present state of scientific knowledge . . . I cannot agree on behalf of Her Majesty's Government, and I would not expect other governments to agree, to abolish all our nuclear weapons as long as there is no assurance that every other state is doing the same. In the case of conventional weapons, one could reconcile oneself to a certain margin of error or deception in any control system. This would not be disastrous. But these thermonuclear weapons are now so deadly that the slightest margin of error or deception could be decisive for the fate of nations. The risks involved are quite unacceptable in present conditions . . . We can hope the brilliant men who ushered in the nuclear age, which is so fraught with menace and at the same time offers of many potential blessings to mankind, will not fail one day to discover ways of providing fully adequate control over all nuclear materials. But until that day comes, to accept complete nuclear disarmament would only be to contribute to that "false sense of security," of which the Soviet Union itself warned in its proposals of May 10. If we are to make progress in this complicated subject, I feel we must face these facts honestly and let a new breath of realism blow through our discussions . . . All I am suggesting now is that some of the concepts of *total* nuclear disarmament which we have been using are quite out of date in the world as it is today and that we only mislead people by clinging to them.

After becoming Prime Minister, Mr. Macmillan was less worried about lulling the world into a sense of false-security when he joined the United States in embracing Premier Khrushchev's "general and complete" disarmament—a proposal that suffered from the same lack of realism when made four years later.

In that same speech Foreign Secretary Macmillan made the first proposal for abandoning the "comprehensive" approach to disarmament in favor of a "partial" approach, which was to bemuse the world's disarmament negotiators for the next four years.[14]

The Macmillan speech was a turning point, a move toward more modest approaches to disarmament. One of these modest approaches, of which the whole world was hearing much, was to be the nuclear test-ban idea.

The test ban and the ban on use of nuclear weapons were established as priority targets of the world Communist movement at a Party Congress in Moscow where sixty-five national Parties signed a manifesto on the subject.

This statement became a directive to all Communists around the world to press for the test ban and a ban on use.

It was partly in response to the pressures generated by Communists around the world that Secretary Dulles made his bow toward the test ban in the Geneva Foreign Ministers Conference.

He sounded the opening note in a statement before the Geneva Foreign Ministers Conference on November 11. "If agreements can be reached to eliminate or limit nuclear weapons under proper safeguards," he said, "the United States would be prepared to agree to corresponding restrictions on the testing of such weapons."

At the time this was regarded as a thinly-veiled brush-off for the sweeping Soviet proposal, first advanced the preceding May, that all nuclear powers announce a discontinuation of tests. The United States would not end testing, Secretary Dulles indicated, until the immense scientific difficulties involved in assuring the elimination or limitation of nuclear weapons had been overcome. That day was not in sight on November 11, 1955, when Secretary Dulles made his statement (nor is it at this writing).

It is one of the curiosities of the diplomatic history of the nuclear test-ban idea that this statement, nevertheless, is considered by American diplomats as the first guarded expression of American willingness to talk about a nuclear test ban. Some officials have pointed to this as the first public unveiling of what later became the American "package" for nuclear disarmament.

In his speech, the Secretary had flatly rejected the Soviet demand for a ban on use of atomic weapons, noting that the United States could not "depend on pledges which cannot be relied upon and for the performance of which no adequate controls are provided." But the association between nuclear production and nuclear tests, later to be known as the "link," was contained in that significant sentence in the Dulles speech.

The phrase "limit nuclear weapons" referred not to the elimination of stockpiles or production, but to the reduction of stockpiles and to the curtailment of nuclear-weapons production. If agreement on these limitations of nuclear-weapons production and stockpiling could be reached first, Mr. Dulles was saying, the United States would be ready to limit correspondingly its testing of nuclear weapons.

At a Washington press conference on November 29, Mr. Dulles himself downgraded the importance of his November 11 statement before the Foreign Ministers Conference. He said that the question of suspension of nuclear testing had been studied for a great many months in the American administration, but no formula had been found that would be both dependable and in the interest of the United States. As he indicated, however, there were strong advocates inside the government for a nuclear-test-limitation proposal.

Governor Stassen, in the White House Disarmament Staff, was the spearhead of this group. There were other advocates in the State Department, but they did not have the President's ear. Mr. Dulles, who did, had never been impressed with the nuclear-test-ban idea as a significant disarmament measure. He preferred, wherever possible, to stress prevention of surprise attack, as he emphasized in private conversations on several occasions. This attitude underwent a gradual change, however, two and a half years later, as political costs of testing appeared to him to grow.

Atomic Energy Commissioner Thomas E. Murray, in November, reflected a previously undisclosed official doubt about dangers of test fallout. He issued warnings about strontium-90 and expressed fears of genetic harm that could result from H-bomb fallout. He also confirmed, in a New York speech, that the March, 1954, H-bomb used a new fission-fusion-fission process that produced unusual quantities of fallout.

Also in November, the Soviet Union exploded its largest weapon up to that time. It was said to be an H-bomb exploded at great height, probably to cut local fallout. Soviet Premier Khrushchev announced, in India, that a minimum of material had been used to create a maximum blast, equal to a megaton.

The height of the weapon later was estimated to have been 35,000 feet when it was exploded. Chairman Khrushchev later claimed the bomb was several megatons, not one, and boasted of its air transportability.

The 10th General Assembly, meanwhile, was attacking the nuclear-test issue from two sides. Frontally, the non-nuclear powers were seeking a moratorium. Indirectly, they were pressing for the investigation of health hazards of radioactive fallout, which they hoped would also inhibit the arms race.

The United States and seven other powers—Australia, Canada, Denmark, Iceland, Norway, Sweden, and the United Kingdom—formally proposed in the General Assembly that the United Nations undertake to pool the world's knowledge about the effects of radiation on human health. This was the fruition of a preliminary proposal first advanced by the United States at the 10th anniversary United Nations session in San Francisco the previous summer. The General Assembly accepted this proposal unanimously on December 3, 1955.

The State Department later said,

> In initiating this resolution the United States expressly recognized the widespread concern existing throughout the world over the question of atomic radiation and its possible effects on human health and safety and noted that the most competent scientists in the United States and other countries were making intensive studies on this subject.

The pressure from abroad, beginning with the demands in India, Britain, and Japan, at the Bandung Conference, and in the British election campaign earlier in that year, had borne partial fruit. But it was the confident expectation of the United States that the U.N. Scientific Committee would establish to the satisfaction of the whole world that the fallout problem had been exaggerated. What was not fully anticipated, however, was the lack of impact the report was to have in a fearful world.

The December 3 resolution set up a fifteen-nation committee to study the genetic and somatic effects of radiation on man and his environment.

At the same time, India, the Soviet Union, and other states were already pressing for a United Nations resolution calling on the big powers to suspend nuclear tests. The United States and Great Britain, however, were able to win a fifty-six-to-seven vote for a resolution merely urging states concerned, particularly the United States, the United Kingdom, France, Canada, and the Soviet Union, members of the London Disarmament Subcommittee, to reach an agreement on a comprehensive disarmament plan.

What was to become a pattern of U.N. General Assembly treatment of controversial big-power disarmament problems was evident in the final resolution, passed December 16. Initial steps recommended to the big powers in the resolution included such "confidence-building measures" as the Eisenhower open-skies plan and the Soviet plan for ground inspection. With no more real power than Afghanistan or Nepal, the United

Nations could only entreat both sides to take disarmament seriously.

The debate in the General Assembly and in its First Committee had given the West full notice, however, that additional efforts to force the United States and Britain into a nuclear test ban could be expected. In the First Committee, in early November, there had been Soviet proposals to write into the resolution a plea to all states to continue their efforts to solve the question of prohibiting nuclear weapons and, as a first step, to reach agreement on the cessation of tests. These had been rejected, but not forgotten.

The First Committee also rejected an Indonesia-Syria proposal to end tests pending a report by the scientific committee on the effects of atomic radiation.

Three days after the General Assembly had unanimously approved establishment of a fifteen-nation committee to study the fallout problem, India introduced a draft resolution in the First Committee calling for a suspension of nuclear-weapons tests and establishment of an armaments truce.

After canvassing the sentiment in the First Committee, which in actuality is the full membership of the General Assembly, the Indian delegation asked that the requests for test suspension and an armaments truce not be put to a vote. As expected, the Soviet delegation supported the proposal to discontinue atomic- and hydrogen-weapons tests as a move "of great significance."

On Christmas Eve, Pope Pius XII, in his annual Christmas message, also gave his tremendous moral backing to the nuclear-test-ban idea. He expressed support for measures, assuming adequate inspection and control, calling for first, the renunciation of experiments with nuclear weapons, second the renunciation of the use of nuclear weapons, and third, control of all armaments in general.

Throughout 1955, however, in the period when President Eisenhower intensified American efforts to seek a workable disarmament plan, the best brains in the country found that other areas than nuclear tests were much more attractive for meaningful arms-limitation measures. Stopping the spread of nuclear weapons to "fourth nations" could better be accomplished, it appeared then, through the surveillance of nuclear reactors springing up around the globe, presumably for peaceful purposes, and through inspection of the huge separation plants of the major nuclear powers, the United States, Britain, and the Soviet Union. Prevention of surprise attack, concentrating on the delivery systems of the nuclear weapons, also appeared to be a more immediate need than the stopping of nuclear-weapons tests.

These were the fundamental conclusions of the Eisenhower Administration's new look at the nuclear-disarmament problem. But the mounting pressures against the United States for curtailing its testing program had already convinced the Administration of a need to make some gesture to the nuclear-test-ban advocates. Secretary Dulles had, for the first time, indicated willingness to contribute to this cause with a lip-service concession. He had told the Big Four Foreign Ministers in Geneva in November, in carefully guarded language, that the United States might accept some limitation on its testing program if at the same time the other nuclear powers accepted a parallel limitation on the production of nuclear weapons and fissionable materials which went into them. This well-guarded contribution lay unnoticed as 1955 drew to a close.

Chapter 4

1956

The United States took public notice of the nuclear-test-ban issue in disarmament early in 1956, but only in an extremely tentative way.

Secretary of State Dulles still accented the negative early in the year. He told newsmen January 11,

We have not yet found any basis which would seem to warrant us in suspending hydrogen-bomb tests. We feel it imperative to keep to the forefront of scientific knowledge in that field, unless and until some dependable basis can be found to assure disarmament, and controlled and inspected disarmament, which would make it safe for us to cease our experimental and testing efforts which in part are designed to find ways to protect ourselves against the use of atomic weapons by others. So the situation is about where it was.[1]

Other officials of the United States, nonetheless, were then preparing for the first time to allow the nuclear-test-ban issue to creep into American nuclear-disarmament proposals, but only late in the process.

Mr. Stassen, speaking at the Disarmament Subcommittee meetings in London, produced a five-step first-stage disarmament plan which included a limitation—not ending—of nuclear-weapons tests in the fifth step.[2] It was the first small move by the United States in its long, reluctant march to a unilateral moratorium on testing.

Mr. Stassen envisaged five main elements in the first stage of a comprehensive and safeguarded disarmament plan:

First, establishment of a working system of control and inspection, embracing both Soviet and American systems for ground and air protection against surprise attack and other reciprocal inspection facilities.

Second, first-stage reduction of armaments and manpower, down to 2.5 million men for Red China, the Soviet Union, and the United States (Britain, France, and Russia were talking about cuts to 1.75 million men), with corresponding reduction in conventional armaments and in arms spending.

Third, advance notification of armed forces movements. Each side would notify the other of all projected movements by armed forces through international air, by water, or over foreign soil.

Fourth, cutoff of nuclear-weapons production. Once the air and ground inspection were operating satisfactorily the United States proposed to halt nuclear production for weapons purposes. Transferring fissionable materials from existing stockpiles would then also begin, with the proposed International Atomic Energy Agency taking custody of the released materials for peaceful purposes.

Fifth, limitation on nuclear-weapons tests. If a comprehensive inspection system were agreed to (not only for surprise attack but for a cutoff of nuclear-weapons production), nuclear-weapons tests could be limited and monitored in an agreed manner under international control.

The Administration obviously was proceeding on the basis of conclusions reached by the White House Disarmament Staff that nuclear-test suspension alone could not be effective in dealing with the problem of spreading nuclear-weapons technology to other countries. Suspending nuclear production and reducing stockpiles had been identified as the key to any real nuclear disarmament. At the same time, the fifth point took account of mounting pressure in the United States for some expression of interest by the big Western powers in ending nuclear tests.

With a full year of preparation behind him, Mr. Stassen presented on April 3, 1956, an American working paper which gave more details on the planned first phase of a comprehensive disarmament program.[3] Even limitations on nuclear-weapons tests, not a complete ban, were put off to an exceedingly remote stage—the 19th step of a very carefully inspected first-phase arms-limitation process. The first 18 steps must have been depressingly complicated even for the Russians, who were the champion sticklers for detail when they wanted to be. The steps were too tedious to be outlined here, although it is obvious from a scanning of them that each one would be fully necessary to achieve a safe partial disarmament.

This detailed new American plan, while bowing to the world pressures for a nuclear test ban, kept the moratorium far enough in the hypothetical future to satisfy those in the American administration who emphasized that United States security depended heavily on continuation of tests so long as the Soviet Union could not be carefully policed. It also convinced the Soviet Union it was not getting very far in its campaign for an uninspected ban.

On May 14, the Soviet Union angrily ended the dialogue.[4] It announced it would unilaterally reduce its armed forces by 1.2 million men within the next year. At the same time, however, the U.N. Disarmament Subcommittee was denounced as a screen to cover the armaments race. The Eisenhower open-skies plan was attacked as a proposal having no relation to reducing armaments or establishing control. Moscow called for a meeting of the parent U.N. Disarmament Commission. That was the practical end of the 1956 disarmament round.

The spring of 1956 exercise had been instructive, nonetheless. Encouraged, or misled, by vague Soviet approval of establishing an inspection network before disarmament was undertaken, the United States had taken the Soviet Union on a long walk down the road of arms limitation to show where America's best experts thought a nuclear test-ban logically fitted in the total disarmament picture. In effect, mention of ending nuclear tests had been included at the extreme end of the American first-phase plan, mainly as a bow to India, which was still pressing in the United Nations for an immediate ban; to Britain, whose Labour Party opposition was still vocal; and to influential United States public opinion, which was building up for a big effort to achieve at least a partial test-ban. The entanglement of the United States in the test-ban issue was nevertheless under way.

Clear evidence of the interest of prominent Americans had come from a hearing before Senator Hubert Humphrey's Disarmament Subcommittee as early as January 25, 1956. Mr. Stassen had told the group that the United States did not have the technical facilities to detect all test explosions, so that control of a test ban would be a problem. But the subcommittee heard others who suggested the risks of continuing the arms race exceeded the risks of stopping tests under an imperfect control system. This indirectly suggested a nuclear test ban would halt the arms race, which it would not. Production would continue; stockpiles would grow; even weapons development might proceed, although at a slower pace. The real question should have been whether the risks of continuing tests exceeded the risks of stopping them, quite aside from the much broader issue of stopping the arms race, which could not realistically have been involved.

It was no doubt unintentionally that Thomas E. Murray, then the only Democratic member of the AEC, lit the fuse of the 1956 Presidential campaign's explosion over suspending nuclear-weapons tests. He went before the Humphrey Disarmament Subcommittee of the Senate's Foreign Relations Committee on April 12 with a new plan for "rational nuclear disarmament."

The Mike thermonuclear explosion of November 1, 1952, and the spring 1954 test series, code-named Operation Castle, had shown, Mr. Murray said, that "there is no upper limit to the size of bombs that can be made."[5]

Since the bomb size was no longer a limiting factor, Commissioner Murray reasoned, military usefulness should be determining in a decision on how horrible thermonuclear weapons should be.

He then made these four proposals:

1. "An upper limit should be set on the size of thermonuclear bombs"

to be placed in the American stockpile. Bombs more powerful than those already available were unnecessary, he said. In fact, they might already be too large. (President Eisenhower made the same point at a press conference March 21, when he said there is "a practical limit" to the size of nuclear weapons. "There is an old saying: 'You do not drive a tack with a sledgehammer.' ")

2. The number of large thermonuclear bombs in stockpiles should be limited.

3. "Increasing concentration should be set on the stockpiling of a wide range of very small nuclear weapons. . . . When I speak of small weapons I mean very small weapons. When I speak of large numbers I mean tens of thousands of weapons in this range." He conceded that intensifying the small-weapons program would be costly in fissionable material. (Mr. Murray frankly admitted in the same speech that he opposed, at that time, stopping production of fissionable materials for nuclear weapons, as advocated in the London disarmament talks, mainly because of his interest in developing a larger stockpile of very small weapons.)

4. "Tests of multimegaton thermonuclear weapons should be stopped." This was a natural follow-up of his theory that weapons then in American stockpiles were already large enough for all conceivable uses, a thesis that was not necessarily shared throughout the Administration. Later, many advocated using multimegaton shots in space to defend against attacking missiles. "The testing of small weapons must of course go on, and even be greatly accelerated to keep pace with the intensified program that is necessary in this field," Mr. Murray said. "I am not recommending the cessation of these large tests on the grounds that they are dangerous to health and safety. The evidence presently available does not warrant stopping tests now for this reason."

Mr. Murray had spent six years as an Atomic Energy Commission member. Because of security restrictions, he did not feel he could be explicit. One of the things he could not then say was that the small weapons he wanted to develop would be H-bombs, not A-bombs. He warned of possible misinterpretations of his speech.

A program of "rational armament" such as he proposed, "must be publicly defined and explained on the highest possible level. There must be no misunderstanding or ignorance about the diversity of our nuclear capabilities, about our intention to use these capabilities, and about the moderate and discriminating manner in which we would use them under defined conditions."

Dr. Edward Teller, then Director of the University of California Radiation Laboratory at Livermore, later told the Senate Disarmament Subcommittee:

The Atomic Energy Commission has devoted and is devoting a very, very great deal of effort toward . . . the development of these small flexible weapons . . . We in Livermore have looked into that direction for quite a few years, and at the very time, at the very period which you are referring to [when Commissioner Murray was advocating development of small weapons] we have made big strides in this direction under full encouragement from the whole commission.[6]

Nine days later, Adlai Stevenson, heading into what was to be his second campaign for the Presidency, urged that the United States "give prompt and earnest consideration to stopping further tests of the hydrogen bomb." He apparently was the victim of a popular misconception, that all H-bombs were large, probably in the multimegaton range.

Here is the complete Stevenson statement, made April 21 in Washington before the American Society of Newspaper Editors:

I believe we should give prompt and earnest consideration to stopping further tests of the hydrogen bomb as Commissioner Murray of the Atomic Energy Commission recently proposed. As a layman I question the sense in multiplying and enlarging weapons of a destructive power already almost incomprehensible. Of course, I would call upon other nations to follow our lead, and if they don't and persist in further tests we will know about it and we can reconsider our policy.

I deeply believe that if we are to make progress toward the effective reduction and control of armaments, it will probably come a step at a time. And this is a step which, it seems to me, we might now take, a step which would reflect our determination never to plunge the world into the nuclear holocaust, a step which would reaffirm our purpose to act with humility and a decent concern for world opinion.

After writing this last week down South, I read last night in Philadelphia that the Soviet Union had protested a scheduled H-bomb test. After some reflection I concluded that I would not be intimidated by the Communists and would not alter what I had written. For this suggestion is right or wrong and should be so considered regardless of the Soviet.

In the early spring of 1956, there was already serious thought inside the Government on the need for a close study of the wisdom of seeking a separate nuclear test ban. Deputy Under Secretary of State Robert Murphy had sent a letter to the Department of Defense at that time asking that the question of a separate nuclear test ban be given a thorough study, because it could mean important political gains for the United States.

The State Department had also sent several memoranda to the AEC asking exploration of a whole range of questions on the test-ban issue: What would be the effect of limiting the numbers of tests per year? Of limiting the size of individual tests? Of limiting the total yield of weapons nations could test in the atmosphere?

Not all these memoranda were answered. Underground tests had not yet emerged as a feasible alternative, so this aspect of the problem was not being explored.

About two weeks after the National Security Council had discussed the problem and Deputy Under Secretary Murphy had sent his letter to the Department of Defense, Adlai Stevenson made his controversial proposal in Washington.

President Eisenhower was questioned about the Administration's attitude toward stopping H-bomb tests at a press conference on April 25. He responded, calmly, that the United States had no more interest in developing bigger nuclear weapons, but was proceeding with tests to develop smaller bombs, to make them useful for air defense, to reduce fallout, and to make the weapons more military, less mass-destruction, in character.

At that time the AEC and the Defense Department were in the midst of final preparations for an extremely important series of H-bomb tests at Eniwetok Proving Grounds. The Soviet Union had been testing in March and April. Soviet Premier Bulganin and Communist Party Secretary Khrushchev, on their April, 1956, visit to Great Britain, taunted the United States on its H-bomb development. In a speech in Birmingham, Mr. Khrushchev boasted that the Soviet Union was ahead of the United States in the art. He cited as proof the ability of a plane to carry the Soviet weapon. The United States, he cried derisively, had not exploded a bomb but "a hydrogen installation."

This was uncomfortably true of the first 1952 American thermonuclear shot. But, even as Adlai Stevenson spoke of stopping H-bomb tests, the United States was making final preparations for its own first drop of a thermonuclear weapon from an airplane, and for a whole new generation of "pygmy" H-bombs.

Mr. Stevenson's speech put an imprimatur of the Democratic Party on the test-ban idea that amounted to the kiss of death. Moves by career officials to meet international pressures for a test ban suddenly became a matter of monumental indifference among their Republican Administration leaders.

As one insider reported, "Everybody just walked away from it."

All copies of the letters that had been written by Mr. Murphy on the subject and all copies of the memoranda to the AEC were recalled. All mention of the subject was suppressed. "Nobody knew it existed."

This was an example, career officials said later, of "what a political campaign can do to really strangle a government."

Not only those career officials who favored making the try for a separate nuclear test ban deplored the injection of politics. Those who opposed stopping the United States weapons-testing program also had misgivings. They saw plainly the handwriting on the wall. The United States, some advised, should take its testing program underground then, with the greatest possible show of accommodation to the powers of Asia and the Labour Party in Britain which were so fearful of the nuclear-test fallout hazard.

This would have cost the United States some restrictions on testing, they acknowledged, but it was a price low enough to accept rather than to wait until the full price—a complete test ban—had to be paid.

These were cries in the bureaucratic wilderness, however, at the non-political level of government. They went for naught in the all-out political battle that was developing.

Mr. Stevenson's inspiration for the test-ban proposal probably came from scientists at the Argonne National Laboratory in Lemont, Ill. At the peak of the election campaign later, seventy-three of them issued a statement asking the United States to take the lead in an H-bomb test ban.[7] The Federation of American Scientists followed quickly with a plea for an international agreement to end "large nuclear weapons" tests.[8] Their plea may have sounded impressive, but few laymen understood that not all scientists, not even all nuclear physicists, are knowledgable in the nuclear-weapons field.

Operation Redwing, another series of American nuclear explosions in the Pacific, began May 5 as the London Disarmament Subcommission was winding up its inconclusive series of talks. The American set of tests continued until July 22.

Throughout this period, Washington was under increasing public pressure from Japan and other countries to halt the tests. Governments echoed their peoples' fears that fallout would have adverse effects on the health of living generations and might produce thousands of defective babies over many generations.

In all, there were seven known American tests in 1956, six by the British, and seven Soviet tests, at least two in the megaton range. But the United States was the lightning rod for world censure. (These test totals are based on news reports and official admissions of the three governments. It is possible that each country exploded more weapons than those publicly announced or known. Japanese scientists, for instance, reported having recorded ten tests in the Pacific area instead of the seven announced during the American series.)

The Soviet Union, meanwhile, was developing new political problems in Eastern Europe. In June, there was the Poznan uprising in Poland. Unrest was stirring elsewhere. The political conventions were the center of attention in the United States. June was also the month that President Eisenhower returned to the hospital for an ileitis operation. Still the United States nuclear-testing program was under continuous attack along a broad front.

Despite its difficulties close to home, the Soviet Union found time to introduce a resolution in the U.N. Trusteeship Council again declaring the American Pacific test series "inadmissible." India backed the idea.

A Chicago church group urged President Eisenhower to cancel the tests. Residents of the Marshall Islands sent a petition to the United

Nations Trusteeship Council expressing misgivings. A clergyman fasted in the United Nations meditation room in New York to dramatize his opposition to the new American series in the Pacific.

President Eisenhower, however, took personal responsibility for the new series of tests and described new safety precautions that would be taken to minimize fallout dangers. In the end, the Trusteeship Council voted nine to four to back the tests.

American newsmen were allowed to watch the H-bomb tests in the Pacific for the first time in 1956. When a B-52 dropped a megaton-range H-bomb over an island in the Bikini Atoll, on May 20, there was speculation that it had been the largest explosion known on earth—above 15 megatons. A new wave of apprehension swept the world. Later, officials reported, it was "only" about a 10-megaton shot. This technically conformed to President Eisenhower's earlier press conference commitment that the United States was not planning to develop any weapons bigger than the 15-megaton H-bomb previously tested. But it was still a monstrous explosion, the kind Mr. Stevenson obviously hoped could be stopped.

The London Subcommittee on Disarmament, finding itself far apart on fundamentals despite the movements in both Soviet and Western positions, had decided to accept the Soviet suggestion—that it was time to turn back to the full Disarmament Commission for fresh instructions. The Disarmament Commission met in New York from July 3 to July 16 to consider a joint draft-resolution by the United States, the United Kingdom, France, and Canada;[9] a Soviet draft declaration resuming the call for all states to end their use or threat of force and the use of atomic and hydrogen weapons;[10] a *note verbale* from the government of India pressing again for an end to nuclear-test explosions; and draft resolutions from Peru and Yugoslavia also expressing concern with nuclear-test explosions. Tests were an active issue outside the Commission, as well.

Japanese scientists reported that radioactive rain had fallen in Japan after the big airborne hydrogen-bomb blast in the Pacific. A large youth forum in New York, debating the advisability of ending tests, wound up in a split decision. The American Baptist Convention urged the United States to abandon all nuclear tests. Adlai Stevenson's call for an H-bomb-test moratorium was a lively topic of debate in the United States and in most of the world.

By mid-June, two distinguished panels, the National Academy of Sciences in this country and Britain's Medical Council had reported that the genetic and somatic effects of fallout from tests would be slight compared with natural background. But other scientists continued to give out alarmist statements to the press, most of them based on fears of nuclear war, not tests. The confusions between the wartime- and peacetime-fallout dangers persisted.

About two weeks after the British Medical Council and the National

Academy of Sciences published their reassuring findings, secret testimony of an Army general was released. He had estimated before a Senate Committee that hundreds of millions of people would be killed in the Soviet Union and neighboring nations if there were an all-out nuclear attack by the United States in Europe. When Defense Department officials and key members of military committees on Capitol Hill deplored the release of his testimony because it exaggerated the atomic peril, the public was again left with the impression that officials were seeking to hide the real dangers. Few made any distinction between nuclear tests to strengthen the American deterrent and nuclear war.

In the U.N. Disarmament Commission, the Soviet Union supported a Yugoslav draft resolution[11] calling for "the cessation of experimental explosions of nuclear weapons as well as other practicable measures in the field of nuclear armaments."

India's proposal[12] for ending tests, a formal document introduced July 12, was noteworthy for its overstatement of both the dangers of continuing and the gains in stopping. Observers wondered at the time why India's policy-makers could not be convinced their science was faulty. India said it advanced its proposal for these reasons:

a. It is universally admitted that the effects of experimental explosions are incalculable in their consequences. Many authorities are apprehensive that the continuance of these explosions would constitute a grave danger to the health and well-being of both the present and future generations. The consequences of the release of strontium-90 into the upper atmosphere are particularly menacing. They are long-lasting, uncontrollable and tend to spread even to areas remote from the scene of explosion. While there may be certain authorities who may not feel fully convinced that experimental explosions on the present scale will cause serious danger to humanity, it is evident that no risks should be taken when the health, well-being, and even survival of the human race are at stake. The responsible opinion of those who believe that nuclear tests do constitute a serious danger to human welfare and survival must, therefore, be decisive in such a context.

b. The cessation of explosions would serve as an important initial step in nuclear disarmament which might make subsequent steps less difficult.

c. The cessation of explosions would have a profound political effect and a deep impact on world opinion in general, and particularly in Asia and the Pacific area where opinion is strongly in favor of a cessation of these tests and apprehensive of the consequences of continued explosions.

d. In a measure, international tensions will thereby be relaxed and suspicions diminished.

e. Other countries would thus be prevented from acquiring the facilities for establishing, through tests, the production of nuclear weapons. The diffusion of the capabilities for testing such weapons can only increase worldwide insecurity.

f. Both international law and international morality are violated by the pollution of oceans and of the atmosphere consequent on such explosions.

g. Contrary to all past practice, these war preparations affect neutrals and consequently offend against the accepted canons of international law.

h. Since the existing stockpiles of weapons of mass destruction are sufficient to destroy the world there would seem to be no utility even from the military point of view, in further experimental explosions.

i. The prohibition of further explosions would be to a large extent self-enforcing. The question of controls and of national sovereignty would not be involved at this stage, and the available evidence indicates that with proper utilization of monitoring devices no evasion of significance would be possible.

On July 13, however, Ambassador James J. Wadsworth of the United States bluntly refused to consider ending tests under prevailing circumstances. "In the absence of agreement to eliminate or limit nuclear weapons under proper safeguards," Mr. Wadsworth said, "continuation of testing is essential for our national defense and the security of the free world." [13]

On the other hand, he acknowledged that limitations on testing should be included in a program of nuclear disarmament. The United States remained pledged, he reminded the Disarmament Commission, not to use nuclear or any other weapons in any manner inconsistent with the United Nations Charter.[14]

To preserve the chance to continue negotiations, the full Disarmament Commission adopted a Peruvian procedural resolution[15] that merely asked the Disarmament Subcommittee to give further study to both sides of the problem. Because a preamble paragraph endorsed a Western statement of principles, however, the Soviet Union opposed the resolution, and Yugoslavia abstained. The vote was ten to one.

President Eisenhower and Premier Bulganin continued their long-distance correspondence on disarmament problems in August and September, but they merely rehashed old positions inconclusively. That the United States still saw great value in nuclear testing was confirmed by the AEC's semiannual report on August 1, 1956. New principles had been confirmed in the Operation Redwing test series, it was said, and new revolutionary developments in design and construction had been made possible.

Suspicions of the world seemed merely to be fed by big-power assurances that special precautions were being taken to eliminate health hazards connected with nuclear tests. India's V.K. Krishna Menon had continued to express alarm on this count before the United Nations Disarmament Commission. American and British ambassadors' attempts to counteract the alarmist statements, however, had little effect.

After the Operation Redwing test series in the Pacific, Admiral Strauss, Chairman of the AEC, issued a statement saying the experiments had proved the feasibility of reducing fallout hazards. Instead of reassuring anyone, this had the effect, it seemed, of confirming suspicions that there was a fallout hazard of serious proportions.

Members of the Joint Atomic Energy Committee in Congress challenged the Strauss contention, thus reinforcing the general public suspicion of American Government reassurances.

Prime Minister Eden was following a parallel path of frustration in Great Britain. He tried to reassure the public that there was no danger from radiation in the planned British H-bomb tests, to be conducted high in the air over Christmas Island. His announcement only touched off a new Labour Party storm demanding a curb on nuclear testing.

The test ban was becoming a dominant political issue in this country as Adlai Stevenson pressed his campaign for some limitation on large nuclear explosions. Other Democratic party advisers apparently had steered him away from the pursuit of a flat H-bomb ban. But the Administration struck back angrily and repeatedly at what it regarded as injection into politics of a vital national-security issue about which Mr. Stevenson appeared to be poorly informed. Some Republicans whispered that the Democratic candidate was doing the Kremlin's work, which only reinforced Mr. Stevenson's determination to press his point.

Mr. Stevenson had publicly acknowledged that he was disturbed by the parallelism of Soviet Premier Bulganin's proposals on the nuclear-test issue and his own, but decided Kremlin backing for what seemed to him a worthwhile objective should be no reason to abandon it.

In a September 11 letter to the President, Premier Bulganin suggested that discontinuing tests would require no international control agreement, so that the issue could easily be separated from the general disarmament problem, not buried within it as the Republican Administration had done. No problem of inspection arises, Premier Bulganin told President Eisenhower, since "I think you will also agree" that "any explosion of an atomic or hydrogen bomb cannot in the present state of scientific knowledge be produced without being recorded in other countries." The Premier went further:

> Would not the best guarantee against the violation of such an agreement be the mere fact that secret testing of nuclear weapons is impossible and that consequently a government undertaking the solemn obligation to stop making tests could not violate it without exposing itself to the entire world as a violator of an international agreement?

This was a theory that the United States emphatically rejected, but one that had enormous appeal among the uninitiated, where fears of fallout and nuclear war ran high.

At the same time, Marshal Bulganin argued that a cutoff of nuclear-weapons production, without forbidding use of nuclear weapons or eliminating them from national armaments, would not wipe out the threat of nuclear war and "would actually mean the legalization of this weapon."

The Bulganin letter echoed an earlier statement by then-Foreign Minister Dmitri Shepilov, before the Supreme Soviet in Moscow, on July 13, stating that "the question of discontinuing tests of atomic and hydrogen weapons can be . . . settled independently" of a general disarmament agreement. At the same time, of course, the Soviet Union was pushing along with its own nuclear-test program, but making as little mention of it as possible.

Miffed that the Soviet Union was able to divert from itself all blame on the testing issue, the President decided to put the spotlight on the Kremlin's own nuclear shots for a change.

On August 26, the White House announced that the Soviet Union had exploded a nuclear device two days earlier. On August 31, President Eisenhower disclosed a second Soviet atomic explosion had occurred the previous day. The Atomic Energy Commission announced a third blast in the Soviet test series had taken place September 2.

The Soviet Union, apparently annoyed in turn, announced on September 10 that it had exploded another nuclear weapon that same day. The AEC later confirmed the report.

Mr. Stevenson, launching his second campaign for the Presidency in earnest on September 5, told an American Legion convention that he was standing by his April proposal "to halt further testing of large nuclear devices, conditioned upon adherence by the other powers to a similar policy." There were two key differences in this proposal from his earlier one, however. First, he had changed from advocating an "H-bomb" test ban to supporting the suspension of tests of "large nuclear devices." Second, he had backed away from the idea of a unilateral ban, as most people had understood his April proposal, and now stipulated that other powers must adhere to a similar policy.

On September 20, Mr. Stevenson put his proposal a third way. This country should "take the lead in promoting curtailment by all nations of hydrogen-bomb tests," he said. The three nuclear powers should act in concert, this statement implied, as the September 5 proposal had. But Mr. Stevenson once again referred to hydrogen-bomb tests, which most Democratic and Republican experts thought should be continued in the lower yields.

Candidates for political office, other politicians, newspapers in this country, had taken up the Stevenson proposal, for the most part oblivious to the "fine points," and debated it at length. A move which, as Premier Bulganin had claimed in his September 11 letter, could be "the first important step toward the unconditional prohibition of these types of weapons," was attractive politically. Many American policy-makers found the first-step argument attractive. The ban also had a strong appeal on moral grounds. The Eisenhower Administration, however, braved the political repercussions despite the election year and stood by its policy of continuing tests, to preserve what it conceived to be the nation's security.

Commissioner Thomas E. Murray of the AEC indicated in a public statement on September 21, 1956, his concern over Governor Stevenson's decision to put the test issue into the political campaign.

In this crucial area, so closely related to many problems of foreign policy, there is no place for that form of oratory, highly flavored with adjectives, that is known as "campaign talk." There is room only for a rational public argument, conducted with the utmost seriousness, on the highest possible level, and with scrupulous regard for both facts and for principles.[16]

It is meaningless, Mr. Murray said, to debate only the question of whether or not the United States should stop testing nuclear weapons. The real issue is how test cessation fits into over-all nuclear-weapons policy. He then repeated his views that the United States had enough large multimegaton thermonuclear weapons and should concentrate on making thousands of small weapons. His conclusion: "First, we should discontinue the testing of multimegaton weapons; such tests are no longer necessary. Second, we should not only continue but intensify the testing of smaller weapons; such tests are still necessary."

Democrat Murray's involvement added another dimension of confusion to the political argument. His emphasis was on pushing the nuclear-arms race in as intelligent a way as possible. Mr. Stevenson, by leaving unsaid his attitude toward testing of small nuclear weapons, gave the impression of seeking a halt to the arms race. Yet Democrat Stevenson was widely believed to have gotten his original inspiration for a large-bomb—or H-bomb—test ban from Democrat Murray.

Mr. Stevenson returned to the test-ban theme on September 29, in a Minneapolis speech. He said he had no "special pride" in his suggestions for suspending large nuclear weapons tests. But he had hoped to get some "creative thinking" started in the country about reducing the nuclear threat. He was "distressed" that President Eisenhower should dismiss his plan "out of hand." Stevenson, too, took the alarmist view of fallout.

Controlling the hydrogen bomb is an "all-important problem," Mr. Stevenson said,

for here we are talking about the actual survival of the human race itself. The testing alone of these superbombs is considered by scientists to be dangerous to man; they speak of the danger of poisoning the atmosphere; they tell us that radioactive fallout may do genetic damage with effects on unborn children which they are unable to estimate.

It is not enough to say, "Well, we have tried and failed to reach agreement with the Russians." It is not enough to throw up our hands and say it's no use to try this or that new approach. This is one time we cannot take no for an answer, for life itself depends on our ultimately finding the right yes.

Again, I have no foolish pride in my own ideas on this subject. But there must be a beginning, a starting point, a way to get off the dead center of disagreement. I have proposed a moratorium on the testing of more super–H-bombs. If the Russians don't go along, well, then at least the world will know we tried. And we will know if they don't because we can detect H-bomb explosions without inspection. . . .

The former Illinois Governor acknowledged that he knew "little or nothing" about the mechanics of the H-bomb. "But I do know this: If man is capable of creating it, he also is capable of taming it. And nothing —including Presidential frowns—can make me believe otherwise."

Former President Truman's out-and-out opposition to the Stevenson stand further muddied the waters. On October 6, in Detroit, the former President said: "We should retain our atomic advantage and if that means testing bombs, well O.K." [17]

Mr. Truman is quoted as saying: "I never had any luck with the Russians keeping an agreement. The only way to get them to keep an agreement is to force them to keep it." Two days later he was more explicit: "We can't possibly quit [nuclear tests] 'til this Russian business is under control." [18]

President Eisenhower called attention to Democratic Party confusion in an October 6 statement which he made "as President, charged under the Constitution with responsibility for the defense and security of our nation." He expressed regret that testing of large-scale nuclear weapons had been made an issue in the political campaign.

The manner in which the issue has been raised can lead only to confusion at home and misunderstanding abroad. There is no subject more difficult than this to discuss before an audience of the whole world—which must include those hostile to us. There is no subject on which the American people should have so united an understanding, free of confusion or partisan differences.

Mr. Eisenhower declared that

the testing of atomic weapons to date has been, and continues, an indispensable part of our defense program; [and that] as part of the general disarmament program, the American government, at the same time, has consistently affirmed and reaffirmed its readiness—indeed its strong will—to restrict and control both the testing and the use of nuclear weapons under specific and supervised international disarmament agreement.

The President said Mr. Stevenson's proposals "ignore some essential reasons for these tests." First, the most recent series helped develop weapons for defense of American cities against enemy air attack. Second, the latest tests helped develop weapons which reduced fallout "to a minimum" and helped develop weapons whose destructive effect could be concentrated upon military objectives.

The President advanced two other arguments for continuing tests, but they failed to survive later pressures for a test ban. The United States' "present commanding lead" in the nuclear-weapons field "could be reduced or even overtaken," President Eisenhower said, if some country made secret preparations for a test and then suddenly exploded an advanced nuclear bomb. He implied the United States would not be making similar preparations, therefore would not be ready to resume testing on short notice. This argument later fell by the wayside when the United States decided to undertake a unilateral ban itself, but continue the research and other preparations to test, as if the race were still on. In practice, however, the preparations were more imaginary than real when the Soviet Union did exactly what Mr. Eisenhower had warned against after a thirty-four-month moratorium.

Mr. Eisenhower attacked another proposition that he was later to embrace. His Administration's insistence on "perfect" or "foolproof" supervision of disarmament had been "denounced," he complained, as a "danger" imperiling any possible international disarmament agreement.

The idea was then being advanced that the United States could settle for something less than a perfect inspection system. There could be an "effective" system which need not be "foolproof," it was suggested, a deterrent rather than a completely effective prohibition.

I must solemnly disagree [President Eisenhower stated]. I shall continue this insistence for however long I am charged with chief responsibility for the security of our nation.

The danger lies in exactly the opposite direction. It lies in the direction of the vain hope that something less than secure safeguards could justify any curtailment of our power to defend ourselves, our allies, and the free world.[19]

Two years later he was to accept a test-ban control system which his military and many scientific advisers warned him was not "foolproof." Whether it would be effective was to become a matter for years of debating.

Governor Stevenson devoted an entire speech to the H-bomb-test moratorium proposal on October 15. This time he put more stress on the need to curb the questionable health hazard than he had in earlier speeches, and was frankly political in his approach.

It was the "hard, urgent need" to break the "deadly deadlock" on arms control which caused him to make his proposal, he said, and added, patching over the confusion about H-bombs and large bombs:

I proposed last spring that all countries concerned halt further tests of large-sized nuclear weapons—what we usually call the H-bombs. And I proposed that the United States take the lead in establishing this world policy. . . .

These are the reasons why I think the time is ripe and there is an insistent necessity for the world to stop at least the testing of these terrifying weapons.

First, the H-bomb is already so powerful that a single bomb could destroy the largest city in the world. If every man, woman, and child on earth were each carrying a 16-pound bundle of dynamite—enough to blow him into smithereens and then some—the destructive force in their arms would be equal to the force of one 20-megaton hydrogen bomb, which has already been exploded.[20]

Second, the testing of an H-bomb anywhere can be quickly detected. You can't hide the explosion any more than you can hide an earthquake.[21]

As the President has stated: "Tests of large weapons, by any nation, may be detected when they occur." In short, H-bomb testing requires no inspection. We will know it when it happens anywhere, and by studying the dust from that explosion we can determine what progress the other country has made.

This means that if any country broke its pledge we would know it and could promptly resume our own testing.

Third, these tests themselves may cause the human race unmeasured damage.[22]

With every explosion of a superbomb huge quantities of radioactive materials are pumped into the air currents of the world at all altitudes—later to fall to earth as dust and in rain. This radioactive "fallout" carries something called strontium-90, which is the most dreadful poison in the world. Only a tablespoon shared equally by all members of the human race would produce a dangerous level of radioactivity in the bones of every individual. In sufficient concentration it can cause bone cancer and dangerously affect the reproductive processes.

Prior to the atomic age, radioactive strontium was practically nonexistent in the world. Careful studies show that today all of us—all over the world—have some of it in our bones. It enters our body through the foodstuffs grown in soil on which the bomb dust has fallen.

I do not wish to be an alarmist and I am not asserting that the present levels of radioactivity are dangerous. Scientists do not know exactly how dangerous the threat is. But they know the threat will increase if we go on testing. And we should remember that less than half of the strontium created by past tests by Russia and the United States has as yet fallen to earth from the stratosphere.

So it seems clear to me that if it is humanly possible we should stop sending this dangerous material into the air just as soon as we can.

Fourth, the dangers of testing by three powers are ominous enough, but there is another reason why it is important to act now. Last May, Mr. Stassen, the President's disarmament assistant, said that within a year the "secret" of making a hydrogen bomb would spread around the world. Think what would happen if a maniac, another Hitler, had the hydrogen bomb. And imagine what the consequences would be if a dozen nations were conducting hydrogen bomb tests and wantonly thrusting radioactive matter into the atmosphere.

Both Russia and Britain agreed, Mr. Stevenson said, "to join us in trying to establish the kind of policy I have suggested. What are we waiting for?" (What basis existed for this claim is not clear. Publicly, Prime Minister Macmillan supported President Eisenhower's position.) If he were elected President, Governor Stevenson said,

I would count it the first order of business to follow up on the opportunity presented now by the other atomic powers; I would do this by conference or by consultation—at whatever level—in whatever place—the circumstances might suggest would be most fruitful.

In the meantime—and frankly because bitter experience has proved that we cannot rely even on the first agreement of one bloc of world powers—we will proceed both with the production of hydrogen weapons and with further research in the field.

There is little danger to national security involved because if another power conducts further tests we would know it and, as I have said, we would have no choice but to resume such tests ourselves.

Mr. Stevenson envisioned continued testing of smaller nuclear weapons, as well as research and development on guided missiles "for the defense of our cities and for use in the field." He pitched his plea on a high moral plane.

I say that America should take the initiative; that it will reassure millions all around the globe who are troubled by our rigidity, our reliance on nuclear weapons and our concepts of massive retaliation, if mighty, magnanimous America spoke up for the rescue of man from this elemental fire which we have kindled.

As the Stevenson-Eisenhower contest for the Presidency pushed toward its climax in mid-October, Marshal Bulganin dispatched another letter to President Eisenhower. The Soviet leader noted that disarmament had become an issue in the American political campaign and charged that Secretary of State Dulles, as well as other American officials, were distorting the Soviet position. Bulganin then brashly associated himself with "the opinion recently expressed by certain prominent political figures in the United States," and again proposed the prohibition of nuclear tests.

Until the necessary agreement on a prohibition of atomic weapons is attained, it would, in our opinion, be desirable to reach agreement at this time on at least the first step toward the solution of the problem of atomic weapons—the prohibition of testing atomic and hydrogen weapons . . . [the Soviet Premier wrote]. We fully share the opinion recently expressed by certain prominent public figures in the United States concerning the necessity and the possibility of concluding an agreement on the matter of prohibiting atomic-weapons tests.

It took only four days for President Eisenhower to fire back an angry reply. He charged Premier Bulganin with "interference . . . in our internal affairs, of a kind which, if indulged in by an Ambassador, would lead to his being declared persona non grata." The references to Secretary of State Dulles were "personally offensive," the President wrote. "You seem to impugn my own sincerity." He would not refuse to accept the Bulganin letter, he said, "not because I am tolerant of these departures from accepted international practice, but because I still entertain the hope that direct communications between us may serve the cause of peace." [23]

The United States had "for a long time been intensively examining, evaluating, and planning dependable means of stopping the arms race and reducing and controlling armaments," the President said. "These explorations include the constant examination and evaluation of nuclear tests. To be effective, and not simply a mirage, all these plans require systems of inspection and control, both of which your government has steadfastly refused to accept."

Senator Estes Kefauver of Tennessee struck out in another direction by suggesting that H-bomb tests could blow the earth 16° off its axis. Several scientists immediately expressed skepticism, then reached for their slide rules. Presidential Candidate Stevenson thought enough of the idea, however, to ask Mr. Eisenhower a rhetorical question in a speech on October 26 in Rock Island, Illinois: "Would President Eisenhower continue the nuclear-arms race to the point of developing 'force that can shake the earth's axis'?"

President Eisenhower did not reply, but scientists later did. After a thorough study they concluded that there actually was some shaking of the earth's axis at the time of multimegaton H-bomb explosions, but not through any angle so large as 16°. The movement was found to be so infinitesimal that it could not be noticed.

Stung by the persistence of Mr. Stevenson's drive for a nuclear test ban, and apparently genuinely worried about effects the argument might have on national security decisions, President Eisenhower, on October 26, issued another, more detailed written statement on the subject. The United States seeks "assiduously" to evolve disarmament agreeements that will promote trust and understanding, the President said. However, "at the same time, and until that international trust is firmly secured, we must—and do—make sure that the quality and quantity of our military weapons command such respect as to dissuade any other nation from the temptation of aggression. Thus do we develop weapons, not to wage war, but to prevent war."

There was "only one reason why no safe agreement had been effected to date: the refusal of the Soviet Union to accept any dependable system of mutual safeguards," the President declared. The United States, he said, has been enlarging its nuclear stockpiles and developing new types of nuclear weapons because the nuclear deterrent "could be lost if we failed to hold our superiority in these weapons."

The importance of maintaining strength in nuclear weapons "is sharply accented by the unavoidable fact of our numerical inferiority to Communist manpower."

Continued H-bomb testing, at the present rate, he reassured the world, does not imperil the health of humanity. More experiments would actually help the United States develop cleaner bombs and defensive weapons, he added. An agreement to stop H-bomb tests alone "cannot be regarded as automatically self-enforcing on the unverified assumption that such tests can instantly and surely be detected," he said. Only the large H-bomb tests can be detected with certainty, he indicated. The President then stated two conclusions:

1. We must continue—until properly safeguarded international agreements can be reached—to develop our strength in the most advanced weapons—for the sake of our own national safety, for the sake of all free nations, for the sake of peace itself.

2. We must—and we shall—continue to strive ceaselessly to achieve, not the illusion, but the reality of world disarmament. Illusion, in this case, can assume either of two forms. It can mean a reliance upon agreements without safeguards. Or it can be the suggestion that simple suspension of our nuclear tests, without sure knowledge of the action of others, signifies progress—rather than peril.

There is nothing in postwar history to justify the belief that we should—or that we could even dare—accept anything less than sound safeguards and controls for any disarmament arrangements.

President Eisenhower's election victory eleven days later slowed down the Soviet effort to achieve a nuclear-weapons test ban. On November 17, Premier Bulganin sent the United States a new set of Soviet disarmament proposals. They still contained provision for an immediate ban on testing, but the emphasis was on other items.

Russian tanks had by then rolled into Budapest to crush the Hungarian revolution. Britain, France, and Israel had struck at the Suez Canal. Disarmament had a hollow ring. So did the Bulganin suggestion for a summit meeting of the Soviet Union, the United States, England, France, and India as a preliminary to a wider convocation of heads of government from all the countries participating in NATO and the Warsaw Pact, as well as the government chiefs in Red China, India, Yugoslavia, Indonesia, and Burma.

President Eisenhower rejected the summit-conference idea, reminded the Soviet Premier of the world's indignation over Soviet conduct in Hungary, warned that NATO could defend itself against any new Soviet move into Western Europe, and pledged continued efforts to find some agreement on disarmament. He made no mention of nuclear tests.

Even then, however, the White House Disarmament Staff was well along on plans to present new disarmament proposals, giving a more prominent position for the nuclear-test-ban issue, for presentation to the U.N. Disarmament Subcommittee in 1957.

Governor Harold Stassen was widely suspected at the time to be sympathetic to Mr. Stevenson's campaign to stop H-bomb tests. A year later, however, he denied this when asked about it on a television quiz show by Mr. Stevenson's son, Borden.

Mr. Stassen told young Borden he would never speak critically of a father to his son, but thought Adlai Stevenson had been let down by his staff, "That is, I think he has been misinformed and misled and thus mistaken." [24]

"It is very important to the security of the United States," Mr. Stassen said, "that unless we have an over-all agreement to reduce the nuclear threat and to improve the prospects for peace, we do not handicap our research and our advance in this respect and I hope that as your father studies it further, that he will recognize the importance of this and will withdraw the stand he has taken."

Eugene Rabinowitch, Editor of the Bulletin of Atomic Scientists, and Professor of Biology at the University of Illinois, observed prophetically in the December issue of his magazine: "This H-bomb problem is by no means disposed of by Eisenhower's re-election. Scientists, in particular, cannot cease considering the world-wide danger of the nuclear arms race as the most important challenge to man. . . ." The campaign debate, Dr. Rabinowitch said, "clearly revealed the incapacity of the public—including most political leaders on both sides—to evaluate in a balanced way the relevant scientific and technological arguments . . . and illuminated the limitations of scientists in public life . . . . Many of them proved unable to preserve full scientific objectivity."

Chapter 5

1957

Nineteen hundred and fifty-seven was America's year of maximum hesitation and coyness about joining the world quest for a nuclear test ban. It was the year of Disarmament Adviser Harold Stassen's greatest triumph and of his greatest disappointment. The momentum he built up, however, carried into the 1960's. It also turned out to be the year when the Soviet Union was least likely to accept any real disarmament move. This the West learned when Russia first fired an intercontinental ballistic missile, then hoisted two huge sputniks into spatial orbit in October and November.

Western hopes for a "first step" toward disarmament were never higher in the summer and early fall of 1957, never lower after the sputniks. The Soviet Union, feeling its oats, turned unbearable in the General Assembly in the fall, and refused to return to the five-nation Disarmament Subcommittee with which it had worked so diligently while the launching pads were being readied. Instead, Moscow demanded absurdly that all eighty-odd members of the General Assembly participate in the actual disarmament negotiations. The United Nations rebuffed the Soviet swaggering by overwhelmingly endorsing Western proposals the Kremlin had rejected.

Through it all, the Kremlin continued to call for an uninspected, take-it-on-faith nuclear test ban. The fateful year wound up with President Eisenhower returning to his nuclear-disarmament position of the beginning of the year, which was, in effect: No end to nuclear-weapons production, no end to nuclear-weapons tests. In the era of good feeling that had built up during the summer, Mr. Eisenhower had been willing to end nuclear tests for one to two years with only paper assurance that nuclear-bomb production would be halted later.

The American policy of "no test ban without production cutoff" became known variously as "the package" and "the link" among the world's growing disarmament bureaucracy. The package had first been presented, in its bulkiest form, at the London Subcommittee on April 3, 1956.

Henry Cabot Lodge, the United States Ambassador at the United Nations, produced a somewhat more attractively wrapped package, with the same basic contents, at the Political Committee deliberations on disarmament at the General Assembly in New York in January, 1957.

In November, 1956, just after the election, President Eisenhower agreed under urging by Mr. Stassen's White House Disarmament Staff that the previous 19th-step provision for "limitation and monitoring" of nuclear tests could be broadened to "limitation and eventual elimination."

The State Department, Defense Department, AEC, and Disarmament Staff then worked out, with Mr. Lodge's United Nations advisers, a condensed five-point version of the nineteen-point proposal Mr. Stassen had presented to the Disarmament Subcommittee in London the previous April. It still packaged nuclear-production cutoff and nuclear-test suspension. President Eisenhower approved the memorandum presenting the new American position on January 12, and Mr. Lodge tabled it before the General Assembly's Political Committee two days later.

U.N. Ambassador Lodge, in presenting the American memo, stated five long-range objectives of the United States in the nuclear-disarmament field:

1. to reverse the trend toward large stockpiles of nuclear weapons and to reduce the future nuclear threat.

2. to provide against great surprise attack and thus reduce the danger of nuclear war.

3. to lessen the burden of armament and to make possible improved standards of living.

4. to insure that research and development activities concerning the propulsion of objects through outer space is devoted exclusively to scientific and peaceful purposes.

5. to ease tensions and to facilitate settlement of difficult political issues.[1]

The Lodge presentation of January, 1957, was mainly a rewrite job of the American 1956 proposals in the Disarmament Subcommittee. The one significant change from 1956 was the admission, in print, for the first time that nuclear tests could "ultimately" be eliminated completely. When "ultimately" would be was a United States secret, however. So, in a practical sense, the movement in the American position was more apparent than real.

This was confirmed later in the General Assembly's First Committee debate, when Ambassador Lodge declared:

The United States favors the limitation and ultimate elimination of nuclear-weapons testing as part of a safeguarded system of disarmament. We oppose any prohibition of weapons testing which does not at the same time strike at the heart of the problem, and that is the continued production of nuclear weapons themselves.[2]

The Federation of American Scientists' Council urged the United States to separate the nuclear test ban from the rest of its disarmament package, but the Administration was not then in the mood.

The Soviet Union had no new proposals to present at the First Committee meetings, either. Ambassador Gromyko called again for a separate ban on nuclear testing, without control. He also asked for a special session of the General Assembly to deal with disarmament; an expansion of the five-power Subcommittee to include India and Poland; and the addition of India, Poland, Egypt, and a Latin American nation to the full Disarmament Committee.

American officials hesitated to offend other nations, but they felt it would be fruitless to add to the disarmament negotiating process negotiators unsophisticated in the nuclear-weapons technology.

When the disarmament issue moved out of the First Committee and into the full General Assembly, Britain, France, and the United States had three different positions on nuclear testing. Whereas Washington wanted any limitation on testing to be part of a package including a cutoff of weapons production, London was ready to limit testing outside the context of any larger nuclear-disarmament program. France, on the other hand, would accept no limitation on testing unless there were a ban on nuclear-weapons production at the same time. The French, then preparing to test their own nuclear weapons, felt they could not accept any plan that would bar them from the "nuclear club" while the other nuclear powers were able to continue manufacturing nuclear weapons.

Canada, Japan, and Norway introduced a draft resolution that called on the states having nuclear weapons to set up a system for registering nuclear-test explosions with the United Nations—as a preliminary toward eventual prohibition of nuclear weapons through progressive stages. This was already a part of the American proposal and acceptable to the West's open societies. Conversely, it was unacceptable to the Soviet Union.

The same resolution asked the Secretary-General and the United Nations Scientific Committee on the Effects of Atomic Radiation to help set up a system for keeping world radiation hazards under constant observation.

Committee One of the General Assembly decided, however, to vote only on the procedural resolution which asked the Disarmament Commission to reconvene its Subcommittee at an early date. It was recommended that the various proposals submitted by Canada, Japan, and Norway; by the United Kingdom and France; by the United States, the Soviet Union, India, and Yugoslavia, all be given "prompt attention." This noncommittal resolution was adopted by the General Assembly on February 14, 1957. The vote was seventy-six to zero.[3]

The Disarmament Subcommittee reconvened on March 18, 1957, in London, for what the State Department looks back on as "the longest and most intensive series of negotiations in its history."[4]

The upper house of the Japanese Diet also had its eyes on the resumed negotiations. On March 15, it unanimously passed a resolution "regretting" British plans for an H-bomb experiment at Christmas Island. The resolution also called for "the total prohibition of production, use, and testing of atom and hydrogen bombs." [5]

The House of Councillors called for "solemn reflection" by the United Kingdom, the Soviet Union, and the United States, "in view of the reasonable fear that if things are left as they are today the amount of fallout from nuclear explosions may increase to the point of irremediably affecting human life." The three nuclear powers were requested to "suspend all atom- and hydrogen-bomb tests now under contemplation, regardless of whether they are to be held with previous notice or not."

Japanese Ambassador Tami, in presenting the resolution to Secretary Dulles, recalled that the Japanese people "have experienced the ravages of nuclear weapons more than any other people." Similar notes were sent to Britain and the Soviet Union.

President Eisenhower and Prime Minister Macmillan, in their Bermuda meeting in March, took note of the clamor for stopping tests but frankly stated their intention to continue. Even limitation of testing could not be effectively enforced, they said.

In the absence of an effective disarmament agreement, the two Western leaders declared "the security of the free world must continue to depend to a marked degree upon the nuclear deterrent. To maintain this effectively, continued nuclear testing is required, certainly for the present." [6]

At the time, Prime Minister Macmillan was looking forward to the first British test of the hydrogen bomb—actually a hydrogen device—which was to be exploded over Christmas Island in the Pacific in May. The comment that nuclear testing is required "certainly for the present," indicated the two leaders had in their minds that both could achieve a certain "plateau" in the foreseeable future which could permit at least a temporary suspension of testing.

Both men threw their prestige behind the proposition that fallout was not a world hazard.

We recognize, however, that there is sincere concern that continued nuclear testing may increase world radiation to levels which might be harmful [their joint statement at Bermuda acknowledged]. Studies by independent scientific organizations confirm our belief that this will not happen so long as testing is continued with due restraint. Moreover the testing program has demonstrated the feasibility of greatly reducing worldwide fallout from large nuclear explosions.

Over the past months our governments have considered various proposed methods of limiting tests. We have now concluded together that in the absence of more general nuclear control agreements of the kind which we have been and are seeking, a test limitation agreement could not today be effectively enforced for technical reasons; nor could breaches of it be surely detected. We believe nevertheless that even before a general agreement is reached self-imposed restraint can and should be exercised by nations which conduct tests.

Therefore, on behalf of our two governments, we declare our intention to continue to conduct nuclear tests only in such manner as will keep world radiation from rising to more than a small fraction of the levels that might be hazardous. We look to the Soviet Union to exercise a similar restraint.

We shall continue our general practice of publicly announcing our test series well in advance of their occurrence with information as to their location and general timing. We would be willing to register with the United Nations advance notice of our intention to conduct further nuclear tests and to permit limited international observation of such tests if the Soviet Union would do the same.

It was with this attitude of reasonable firmness that the United States and Great Britain embarked on the historic London disarmament negotiations of 1957.

Secretary of State Dulles later looked on the London Conference of 1957 as a pronounced success. "More progress toward disarmament has been made at these talks than has ever been made before in the long history of efforts toward disarmament," he said at a press conference on September 10, 1957. He also acknowledged, however, that no "real meeting of minds" necessary for any meaningful agreement had been achieved. The progress he referred to, it turned out, was in getting all the NATO powers to agree on a single plan.

Governor Stassen, in a masterful presentation of the American view on nuclear disarmament, set the tone of reasonableness and candor with which the United States went into the discussions two days after London subcommittee meetings resumed.[7] Here is an excerpt from that important statement—as valid today as then:

If we look ten years ahead it is quite evident that, in the absence of any agreement between nations, there will be more and more stockpiles of nuclear weapons, with larger and larger quantities of such weapons, with many, many bases on which nuclear forces are stationed, with added and added countries having such weapons, and with higher and higher speeds of potential delivery of such weapons by one nation upon another.

This would not mean that a modern war was inevitable. It is our view that war is never inevitable, and that it is not inevitable in the future. But it would mean that there was a greater danger of war. It would also mean that there was an increased likelihood that if war did come, the extent of the destruction would be such as mankind had never experienced before.

Just what do we propose should be done about this? The question immediately arises: Can this nuclear age be repealed? Can all such nuclear weapons be removed from the face of the earth? Can there be an elimination of every nuclear bomb from every part of the world? This idea has much attraction. But when we examine it, what do we find? We find, as I have said, that nuclear weapons are materials, plus knowledge, plus fabrication. The materials are and will be available on every continent. The knowledge exists in the minds of men; it cannot be erased. It is spreading, and it will continue to spread. The fabrication, given the knowledge and the materials, is relatively simple. We also find that when such weapons are fabricated, or when the material is available, either the weapons or the material can be very easily shielded from detection and discovery. One hundred of the most powerful multimegaton H-bombs can be placed in storage and shielded by relatively simple methods, and then the most sensitive detection apparatus thus far invented by science would give no indication of the presence of this storehouse, even if it were brought within a hundred yards of its location.

What, then, does this mean? Let us discuss it in terms not of present Governments and countries at this table—or of present Governments of any other specific countries not at this table. Thinking of the next ten years, it would be perfectly possible, even under the most effective controls, for some different and future government of some country in the world to take away and divert without the knowledge of the inspectors, a quantity of fissionable material from which twenty, forty, or even fifty multimegaton bombs could be fabricated. All of this could be carried out without discovery by inspectors, and without the knowledge of other nations, until it was completely accomplished.

Is it not clear, then, that no nation could agree that all nuclear weapons should be removed from the face of the earth if it meant that in the ten years ahead, and in the decades thereafter, some nation might suddenly have and exercise a tremendous, overpowering military force against all other nations solely by reason of having within its hands a clandestinely developed and secretively maintained storehouse of multimegaton bombs?

Thus, on the basis of present scientific knowledge, and unless and until there is some new scientific breakthrough which makes controls more effective than any one can now prescribe, the United States has reluctantly concluded that it would not be sound, that it would not serve the interests of long-term peace and that it would not be consistent with the security of the United States or of other nations to agree to the complete elimination of all nuclear weapons, and that such an agreement would be a bad agreement—a tragic mistake.

Does this conclusion mean that nothing can be done, and that we must contemplate the decade I described earlier in which there are more and more stockpiles of larger and larger numbers of weapons with more and more bases? Something can be done. What can be done is to establish a cutoff, a terminal point, a turning in the road we are now traveling. It is possible, according to the very best scientific advice we have obtained, to establish an inspection system under which each nation could be sure, on the basis of an exchange of commitments with other nations, that future production of fissionable materials would go entirely, or almost entirely, to peaceful, constructive uses. In other words, those nuclear plants which are now producing fissionable materials in countries that now have nuclear weapons would produce their materials only for nonweapons purposes of either a national or international character under the observation and accounting of an international control organ.

Similarly, as new atomic energy power plants were built—by agreement and under such an international control organ—the fissionable material involved would also be accounted for, and it would be ensured that it was used for nonweapons purposes.

Even in these instances it is not possible to guarantee 100 per cent perfection of inspection or of accountability. But so long as there does exist on various sides in the world a remaining nuclear weapons capability there would not be the incentive for relatively minor diversion into unauthorized weapons. Nor would there be the terrible consequences if there were relatively minor diversions for a few weapons; because those few weapons would be restrained, canceled out and deterred by the remaining capability in the hands of nations on various sides. . . .

We ask whether, if the point of cessation of weapons manufacture that I have described were reached under effective inspection, it might then be that the nations which had nuclear weapons would report how many kilograms of fissionable material they have previously produced and devoted to weapons purposes and then, within the first year, transfer from such previous production 8 per cent or 12 per cent for nonweapons purposes under international observation. Or should it be that in the first year the fissionable material used in the fabrication of twenty, thirty, or forty multi-megaton bombs would be taken out of such bombs, and that the bombs would be dismantled and the fissionable material turned over for nonweapons purposes under international supervision? Or, again, should it be that during the first year, when the first transfers were made to reverse the trend, there would be—with the then increased knowledge that would exist on each side on the capacity of production and of previous production—negotiations for the amounts of future transfers? It is in this range that we feel very important steps can be taken which would in fact contribute to the mutual interests not only of the nations at this table but of all nations in the world.

At the time of entering into such an agreement the United States would also be prepared to make a firm treaty commitment not to use nuclear weapons except in defense against aggression, in accordance with the decisions of the Security Council or in accordance with Article 51 of the United Nations Charter. Under such circumstances—with such agreement and with the entry into such an arrangement which would reverse the trend of nuclear threat—the United States would be prepared to stop nuclear weapons tests or, perhaps, first to limit and then to stop such tests, with reasonable and proper arrangements so that the commitment also was reciprocal and was carried out equally by all nations concerned.

Such an arrangement would result in a future where there were fewer and fewer stockpiles of nuclear weapons, a smaller and smaller number of nuclear bases, and a reduced threat and lessened tensions. At the same time no nation would have cause to feel, if the arrangement was carefully drawn up and thoroughly worked out, that its own security was at any time reduced, but, rather, could be confident that its security was improved as compared with a situation where no agreement had been reached.

Even American sentiment favoring a nuclear test ban had jumped, from 20 per cent in April, 1954, to 63 per cent in 1957, according to a nationwide survey.[8]

It was perhaps Governor Stassen's energy and drive that raised hopes in the West that some meaningful progress could be made in the 1957 London negotiations of the Subcommittee.

As the State Department put it:

> From the beginning of the session, there were signs that a genuine nego-tiation might develop—a unique atmosphere after the long weary years of deadlock. . . . This atmosphere of serious negotiation was also helped, indeed developed, by the deliberate adoption of techniques which, though procedural in nature, opened up new substantive potential for agreement.[9]

One of these procedural techniques caused some pain for the Atomic Energy Commission. The Subcommittee on Disarmament, composed of the United States, United Kingdom, Soviet Union, France, and Canada, adopted for the first time "a separable, item-by-item agenda." The French had suggested this procedure the year before, but it was not accepted until 1957. Under this technique the component elements of the large disarmament plan were considered "point by point rather than plan against plan."

For some in Washington the optimism created by this item-by-item agenda appeared synthetic. Even under the old procedures points had to be discussed individually. State Department negotiators nevertheless saw value in it. Later the Department gave this description of its ad-vantages:

> It permitted the singling out of areas of agreement, and in so doing facili-tated the serious and open exchange of views needed before further policy changes could be considered. Moreover, this approach gave time for fre-quent referrals of new concepts to the home governments without inter-rupting the continuity of negotiations. It cultivated the attitude of mind which could, without prejudice, consider a re-sorting and discarding of past elements in a new arrangement.

This was an exercise in the power of positive thinking. Governor Stas-sen explained his philosophy this way to the Subcommittee:

> Since we are here . . . to negotiate seriously and to seek after these many years of lack of agreement, an agreement that is sound and safeguarded—it would not be constructive for me to state all the points of disagreement . . . because if one emphasizes disagreement that tends to add to the rigid-ity and makes the finding of areas of agreement more difficult. . . . We are more likely to move towards agreement if we start with areas of agree-ment and then gradually and carefully expand them, move by move, point by point.[10]

The West went to the meeting with an agenda list that placed nuclear-test explosions at the bottom. Other items were conventional disarmament, nuclear disarmament, international control organs, missiles and rockets, zones of limitation and inspection, and "other matters."

The Soviet Union asked, however, that the Western four agree to place the cessation of nuclear tests at the top of the agenda.

Mr. Stassen and his State Department associates at the London Conference foresaw a long haggle, at the outset, over a point that would mean very little if there were to be a final, successful outcome to the talks. So they agreed to top the agenda with the nuclear-test discussion.

But AEC officials in Washington were aroused. They saw that putting the test issue first on the agenda would be the logical first step toward detaching it from the package. Many suspected Mr. Stassen was going all-out to get a separate test agreement, mainly to promote his domestic political ambitions. They feared that putting nuclear tests at the top of the agenda would enhance the importance of the issue, thus advancing a Soviet objective. The AEC, of course, opposed a separate suspension of nuclear tests, on the grounds that it would be difficult if not impossible to enforce and that important advances in weapons development would be prevented.

The other procedural technique which increased State Department hopes for an agreement in 1957 was the adoption of informal sessions among the Western Four and with the Soviet Union. Discussions were off the record. Propaganda statements for the record were thus rendered unnecessary for both sides. This allowed the Soviet and Western representatives to "let down their hair" without fear that their positions would later be made public, or that they would be held accountable for a chance, indiscreet remark.

The Soviet Union went along.

There was still a propaganda battle, of course, but it was waged outside the conference room by press officers—and principal negotiators—talking to newsmen. The result was a two-arena negotiation, where diplomats had to be careful to remember in which arena they were contesting. Many newsmen suspected, but could not prove, that the optimism reflected outside the London conference hall was synthetic. But they had to report what the principals told them of the atmosphere and the progress, not what they suspected.

The Kremlin followed a familiar pattern of making the first "concession" and then exploiting it propaganda-wise while the opponents figured out how to respond. If the proposal for an immediate *permanent* banning of nuclear tests was too "radical," the Soviet Government would be ready to settle for an immediate *temporary* ban, "a suspension . . . with a time limit established," Ambassador Zorin said.[11] The proposal was made public in Moscow before it was introduced in the London talks.

This move was one of the turning points of the negotiation on banning nuclear tests. It opened the way for the United States to appear to accept a ban without actually doing so, by accepting "in principle" but keeping the suspension period short. It also would give the Soviet Union a chance, once a ban were in effect, to use all its pressure techniques to make United States resumption of tests impossible. The length of the temporary period of test-suspension became the next point of discussion in London, Washington, and Moscow.

French Ambassador Jules Moch made the first veiled reference in 1957 to the technique that was to carry the test-ban issue out of the theoretical and into the actionable period the following year.

> I know quite well where the point of disagreement lies, and I shall be careful not to take sides on it. That point is whether the prohibition of test explosives can be controlled. "No," says the United States representative; "Yes," says the representative of the Soviet Union. The first thought which occurs to me is that we might gain some enlightenment from a comparison of the information on which each of these two contradictory assertions is based. Unfortunately such a comparison would lay bare certain facts which both sides are at present keeping secret; and so I do not imagine it can be made.[12]

The French Ambassador, one of the veterans in disarmament negotiations, was projecting the kind of experts conference on techniques for inspecting and controlling a nuclear test ban that was to be convened the next year.

Ambassador Moch at the same time expressed his own misgivings about inspecting a nuclear test ban. "I have said myself on a good many occasions that I did not think low-powered explosions far away from control posts, or even high-powered explosions under certain conditions, e.g., in very deep water, can be controlled."[13] His was one of the first official voices to express misgivings about test inspection.

At the same time, Ambassador Moch indicated the French government had concluded, with other leading powers, that radiation hazards from nuclear weapons fallout was not a major issue. "According to the information which is reaching me from the French atomic experts," M. Moch declared, "the question may be less urgent than certain sections of public opinion have been led to believe."

From the March 18 opening of the London talks until the adjournment for a brief Easter recess beginning April 18, delegates of the five powers had zipped through these topics in a kind of once-over-lightly aura of good will: nuclear testing, conventional armaments, nuclear disarmament, the control organ. There also had been initial discussions on missiles and zones of inspection and limitation.

Governor Stassen announced that the primary purpose of his return for the Easter recess was to visit with his son. There was time, however, for extremely important, high-level discussions with Administration leaders and President Eisenhower. Mr. Stassen was widely suspected at the time of pressing the Administration to make some further movement in the nuclear-test field to meet the new Soviet initiative for a temporary test ban.

Secretary of State Dulles indicated, however, in a note to the Japanese Chargé d'Affaires in Washington, Mr. Shimoda, that fundamental American policy had not been changed by Mr. Stassen's Easter pilgrimage.[14]

When the London talks resumed on April 30, the Soviet delegate came back with a new proposal for first-phase disarmament. In it the Soviet Union called for breaking the nuclear test ban out of the Western "package." Mr. Zorin, the Soviet delegate, still insisted upon unqualified prohibition of the use of atomic weapons, but dropped the demand for prohibition of manufacture and elimination of the nuclear weapons in a first stage of the agreement. No mention was made of the American proposals to stop the production of fissionable materials for weapons purposes or to transfer some past production of nuclear materials to nonweapons use.

On nuclear tests, the Soviet Union proposed that "discontinuation" of nuclear tests be singled out from the general problem of nuclear weapons and solved "without delay." Also included in the Soviet proposal of April 30, 1957, were items on force-level reduction, armaments control, and military expenditures, on the inspection and control system, on foreign bases, on the reduction of forces in Germany and elsewhere in Europe, and on aerial inspection. Looking at the new Soviet position as a whole, the American disarmament group, headed by Mr. Stassen, and the delegations of Canada, the United Kingdom, and France, decided that the Soviet Union was intending a serious negotiation, even though the proposals were "unacceptable as they stood." The United States decided the new Soviet paper represented "at least a willingness to move."[15]

A month later, on May 16, the Subcommittee recessed again for ten days. This time Governor Stassen reportedly had incurred the wrath of Secretary of State Dulles by presenting to the Soviet Union, in an informal session, new American thinking on zones for aerial inspection before an agreed position had been reached with America's allies. He returned to Washington for further consultations.

Mr. Stassen, for his part, came back to renew his efforts to push through the divided Administration a plan to lift out the nuclear-test issue from the rest of the disarmament package, as the Soviet Union was urging.

Besides the opposition in the AEC and the Defense Department, where the necessity for continuing tests was considered paramount, there was also opposition from France to this "break in the link."

Between May 16 and May 26, there were intensive consultations in Washington. Mr. Stassen met with the Secretary of State, other high officials in the Executive Branch, the National Security Council, and Senate leaders. On May 25, the day before Mr. Stassen returned to London, he met with President Eisenhower and Secretary of State Dulles.

One of the results of that conference was that Mr. Dulles took a more active part in subsequent disarmament negotiations because of what he considered the "fluff" Governor Stassen had committed in consulting the Soviet Union before America's allies.

Secretary of State Dulles announced at the White House after the meeting that Mr. Eisenhower had made new decisions which would be embodied in further instructions to Mr. Stassen. It was at that meeting that President Eisenhower decided that the linkage between the nuclear-test issue and a cutoff of weapons-material manufacture could be loosened. Not broken, but loosened. There was also a decision to take up the Soviet offer of a temporary suspension of nuclear tests, seeking first a ten-month suspension but accepting twelve months as a limit.

When Mr. Stassen got back to the Subcommittee, he reported, on May 27, that the United States was prepared "to move halfway" if other delegations would also move halfway to reach agreement on a first-phase disarmament plan.[16] Such a first step would embrace "reduction, limitation, control, and inspection of armament and armed forces and expenditures," he said, "the reduction of the nuclear threat with which the world is concerned, the lessening of the dangers of war, the minimizing of concern in regard to surprise attack, and the improvement of the prospects of peace . . ."

Mr. Stassen conceded that there might be differences of interpretation between the various delegations on what halfway meant. He did not, however, then mention the Administration decision that it could risk a temporary suspension of nuclear tests lasting ten to twelve months. He was working to sell the plan to the NATO Council, where France in particular was taking a dim view.

As of late May, the public American position on testing and nuclear controls was officially summarized as follows:

> Suspension or limitation of tests should commence after an inspection system to control the future production of fissionable material had been installed and was operating successfully to insure that all future production was used or stockpiled exclusively for nonweapons purposes. Pending this, tests would be made subject to advance notice and registration, with limited international observation.[17]

Almost unobtrusively, the United States had accepted the Soviet suggestion of "suspension" of tests for a fixed period rather than permanent cessation. There had been another important development.

On May 6, Britain had tabled in the Subcommittee a memorandum calling for advance registration of tests, as had been proposed by Canada, Japan, and Norway at the 11th U.N. General Assembly and endorsed by the United States.

The memorandum also proposed establishment of a committee of technical experts to consider possible methods of limitation and control of tests. This followed by about a month, French Ambassador Moch's suggestion along these lines. At that time, however, the Soviet representative rejected the proposal. He felt mere registration of the tests in advance did not go far enough. He held out for prohibition or at least a temporary cessation of tests as an immediate step, independent of disarmament and without international control.[18]

Britain and the United States objected, of course, that their scientists believed detection of tests could not be guaranteed without close control. Both Mr. Stassen and Anthony Nutting, the British representative, repeated that they could not agree to a suspension of tests except under effective control. In both the formal and informal sessions, all the Western delegates, from Canada, France, the United States, and the United Kingdom, urged the Soviet Union to accept effective inspection in all disarmament measures.

Moscow made its big move on June 14. At that day's meeting in London, the Soviet Union suddenly accepted in principle the Western demands for inspection of a nuclear-weapons test ban.[19]

Soviet Representative Zorin proposed a two- or three-year moratorium on tests, under the supervision of an International Commission, with control posts in the territories of the United States, the United Kingdom, and the Soviet Union, and in the Pacific areas. The control posts would be established "on a basis of reciprocity" and for the purpose of "supervising the fulfillment by States of their obligation to cease tests . . ." Premier Khrushchev had informally indicated Soviet acceptance of test inspection a day before.

The International Commission, the Soviet representative said, would be "answerable to the U.N. Security Council and to the General Assembly."

There was immediate excitement in the Western delegations. The built-in Soviet veto, provided by placing the inspection under the Security Council, was conveniently overlooked. The Soviet delegate had suggested an unexpectedly modest period for test suspension, and the West did not attempt to conceal its satisfaction. The two-year minimum, which Moscow must have expected would be the figure the United States would seize upon, was tempting in itself. But Mr. Zorin had "thrown in" the idea that internationally-supervised control posts could be established *inside* the Soviet Union, on what was, after all, a marginal issue only vaguely related to real disarmament. For the Soviet Union even to hold out this bait, this prospect for penetrating the Iron Curtain with international inspectors, was tantamount to a "breakthrough" for the West. Certainly it was a most uncharacteristic exhibition of charity from the Communist world. Or so it seemed.

Six days after Mr. Zorin presented his attractive new test-ban proposal, Governor Stassen began what amounted to a striptease performance, revealing bit-by-bit the new United States decisions made by President

Eisenhower on May 25. Existence of the decisions had been announced at the White House by Secretary of State Dulles the same day, but what the decisions had been was not officially disclosed. Mr. Stassen was obviously playing for time to get Allied approval and to permit more study of the Soviet initiative of June 14.

At the same time, however, he was eager to let the Soviet Union know that the United States was impressed by the latest Kremlin position. "The United States Government views this new Soviet proposal as a hopeful sign," Mr. Stassen said, "as a proposal that deserves the most earnest and sympathetic study, as a proposal on which we should ascertain all the details, and as a proposal of which we take serious consideration in our own policy and decisions in the United States Government."[20]

With that he went into a long discussion of the United States attitude toward reducing force levels, projecting possible further reductions in American forces beyond the 2.5-million-man level previously accepted, but reflecting caution for any precipitous reduction. He continued the discussion of reducing conventional forces on June 25,[21] as suspicions grew in the Subcommittee that the United States was stalling.

On July 2, the four Western delegates at the Disarmament Subcommittee meetings in London were still presenting a joint response of welcome to the Soviet pronouncement of June 14.

The Western powers wound up standing by their "package" formula, insisting that production of fissionable materials be ended, under proper inspection, before any temporary suspension of nuclear testing could be arranged. France, it appeared, had carried the day with its demands for maintaining a link between testing and other, more meaningful nuclear disarmament.

In the July 2 statement, the four Western powers proposed formally that a group of experts from the five participating nations meet to design an inspection system "to verify the suspension of testing."

The Western statement, although it kept the link, was labeled as an acceptance in principle of the Soviet proposal for a two- or three-year moratorium on tests under international control.[22]

Mr. Stassen, in his supporting statement, followed with the outline of a new United States policy in regard to timing and duration of the proposed temporary ban on nuclear tests. The United States, he reported, was willing to join in a test suspension when the first-step treaty was ratified. Test suspension, he said, would become "the first clause of the agreement that is operative."[23]

This was regarded by American officials as the most important concession of several the United States announced that day. Previously, the United States had insisted that the cutoff of nuclear-weapons production be a reality before any limitation on tests. Now, Washington was ready to accept a temporary suspension, not limitation, at a much earlier time.

As for the duration of the test-suspension, Mr. Stassen proposed a ten-month period to install inspection posts and permit other states to join in the treaty pledge. The United States would be willing to consider extending the temporary suspension for a longer period if the inspection posts were installed satisfactorily and other states joined in the program.

While nuclear testing would be the first item to become effective in the first-phase disarmament package, Mr. Stassen said, the over-all treaty should include related provisions. One of these provisions called for an agreement to cooperate in designing, installing, and maintaining an inspection system to verify a cutoff of production of fissionable material for weapons purposes. The cutoff itself, however, was to begin only after "installation of an inspection system adequate to verify compliance."

The United States had thus given way on its insistence that the inspection system for a cutoff be in place and the cutoff be operating before any nuclear-test suspension or limitation.

In a rare show of enthusiasm, the usually dour Soviet Ambassador, Mr. Zorin, said he was "gratified."[24]

The combination of the American acceptance in principle of the Soviet call for a temporary suspension of nuclear-weapons tests and Mr. Stassen's presentation of the new American proposals in London produced opposite reactions on the opposite shores of the Atlantic. Among American officialdom there was a general optimism. In London and Paris, however, there was monumental skepticism that any agreement with the Soviet Union on a nuclear test ban was in the offing.

By July 8, the Soviet Union had its answer to the new Western proposal: "No." Ambassador Zorin added an entangling link of his own. Before there could be any cutoff of nuclear-weapons production there must also be a declaration banning the use of nuclear weapons in any war or at any time, he said. He rejected the British suggestion that experts prepare a system of inspection for a test ban as "a waste of time." This was the crucial moment for a test ban in 1957. The Soviet Union appeared to be aiming for an unconditional end to tests for two to three years. Both the British and the French were plunged into deeper discouragement by the Zorin reaction. Governor Stassen, however, persisted in his never-say-die attitude. When Radio Moscow denied the Soviet Union had rejected all American proposals on July 9, American officials in London took heart.

Governor Stassen warned the Soviet Union, however, that its choice was between the short period of test suspension, say ten months, or no suspension at all. In the background of the London meeting was the continuing British popular clamor for test suspension. The powerful British Transport and General Workers' Union urged a total ban on H-bombs on July 11.

A few days later, Ambassador Zorin offered to negotiate on the period of suspension for a test ban, laying aside other matters of disagreement.

Governor Stassen viewed this as a concession, but the British delegation was not hopeful.

The talks went on for a month and a half longer, but it was already becoming clear that the Soviet Union had lost interest. Soviet Communist Party Boss Khrushchev gave the tip-off in a speech in Pilsen, Czechoslovakia on July 15. He remarked that the talks were going "badly" and blamed the West.

In London, meanwhile, Ambassador Zorin dropped the hint that the Soviet Union might be interested in a compromise on its policy, of many years standing, that all use of nuclear weapons ought to be banned. He reportedly was interested in the suggestion by the French that the use of nuclear weapons be limited to self-defense. One of the difficulties, of course, in Soviet acceptance of this formulation was its own use of the word "defense" to cloak offensive actions like that in Korea in 1950. The attack on South Korea was in "self-defense."

Secretary of State Dulles was asked about conflicting moods of optimism and pessimism at a July 16 news conference. He was neutral, but realistic.

> I do not myself have any view in terms of whether or not there is likely to be a result. The problems ahead are immense, terribly complicated. After you reach an agreement in principle, the problem of translating that principle into something that is detailed and workable presents tremendous difficulties, and we have not even approached those yet. I think it would be very premature to have come to any conclusion as to whether there is likely to be a success or a failure. I think all we can do is to keep pushing ahead as resourcefully, as determinately, as we can to try to get a result. So far there have not emerged any absolute obstructions to progress. And as long as there is not an absolute obstruction to progress, we keep working ahead.

This was a dash of cold water compared to the optimistic noises that were coming out of Governor Stassen's White House Disarmament Staff and his London group.

As for the charge that the United States might be stalling in London, Secretary Dulles virtually admitted it. He explained that it was necessary to explore fully the complete program with America's allies.

At London, Soviet Ambassador Zorin then suddenly indicated he still found some merit in the idea of an experts conference to study nuclear-test inspection.

> If the Western powers agree to an unconditional cessation of tests for a period which would really insure the suspension of the next tests planned and thereby restrain the nuclear armaments race [Mr. Zorin said], there would be real point in convening groups of experts to work out the details of control and of the other problems connected with the cessation of tests.[25]

There was a price the Soviet Union would pay, then, for a delay in the United States testing pace.

Behind the scenes in the United States, Secretary of State Dulles' doubts about Governor Stassen's conduct of the negotiations in London were increasing. He hinted at them publicly in a radio and television report to the nation on July 22.

> The United States delegation is headed by former Governor Stassen and includes diplomatic, military, and technical advisers. The delegation does not itself make United States policy. Its task is to express United States policy in accordance with guiding instructions given by the Department of State. The substantive decisions are made by President Eisenhower, after taking account of the views represented on the National Security Council. Because the negotiations might lead to a treaty, the Senate's Disarmament Subcommittee, of which Senator Humphrey is Chairman, is being kept fully informed.[26]

This was fair warning to the Soviet Union not to expect miracles of Mr. Stassen.

At another point, Mr. Dulles observed that dependable progress in the London talks could come only by "steps carefully measured and carefully taken." The free nations, he added, "are dealing with matters which gravely affect their very existence. And while it is important that we make progress, it is equally important that we be careful."

Given the feelings of many in the Washington administration that Governor Stassen was pushing so hard that he was not being careful, and was neglecting the United States allies, this sentence had added significance.

Secretary Dulles did concede, however, that the atmosphere had recently changed somewhat for the better in the London Subcommittee talks. "Whatever be the reasons, the Soviet delegation has been talking with somewhat more realism and less bombast."

In outlining the American disarmament position, Mr. Dulles had this significant comment about tests: "It is technically possible to devise a monitoring system which would detect significant nuclear tests and make evasion a highly risky business. But the possibility of concealment is such that inspection teams will have to be numerous and located near to possible test areas. *The problem is not so simple as many have believed.*"

In the same speech, Mr. Dulles explained why the United States had chosen ten months as the period for a "tentative suspension" of nuclear testing.

Mr. Dulles assured his audience that the ten-month period is not "chosen arbitrarily." He went on:

> It is designed to be the period which would not dislocate our existing scientific staffs. During this same period headway could be made on installing the inspection system in order to insure that, if the suspension of

testing were to be extended, such suspension could adequately be supervised and controlled. Also, during this same period there could be begun the inspection needed to assure that future production of fissionable material would be used only for peacetime purposes.

Until we see convincing proof that the Soviets are serious about arms limitation, our safety primarily depends on having the best weapons, large and small, that we can develop. This means continued testing. Testing makes it possible to develop even smaller weapons and to insure that larger weapons will have less radioactive fallout. President Eisenhower has alluded to the possibility of reducing the fallout of large weapons to less than one per cent of their yield. In such ways it can be insured nuclear weapons, if they had to be used, could be confined more closely to distinct military objectives. Therefore we do not separate the problem of testing from the broader issues.

During the trial suspension period that we suggest, good progress may be made in installing systems which can provide warning against surprise attack, can provide detection of subsequent testing, can insure that future production of fissionable material will not be used to enlarge existing stockpiles or to spread nuclear weapons throughout the world. Then and then only would we feel that security was sufficiently enhanced to justify considering further suspension of testing.

With the American position thus publicly stated, Secretary Dulles flew off to London to take personal charge of the United States delegation. To emphasize his considered judgment that seeking an agreement to prevent surprise attack was much more significant in the disarmament field than a nuclear test ban, Mr. Dulles immediately presented the Western working paper combining aerial and ground inspection for this purpose.[27]

It was like touching an open nerve of the Soviet Union. Ambassador Zorin angrily called for an immediate test suspension and denounced the United States for omitting overseas bases from its open-skies plan.

Further indication of waning Soviet interest in the London talks came from Premier Bulganin on July 24, when he sent a letter to Prime Minister Macmillan claiming that the Western position precluded any agreement. He complained of the linkages on which the West insisted, first the link between testing and a cutoff of nuclear-weapons manufacture, then the link between a cutoff in nuclear-weapons manufacture and political issues like German reunification.

Secretary Dulles returned to Washington on August 4, apparently convinced that the great push of 1957 had failed.

Governor Stassen apparently was the only man who had not given up hope for a test-suspension agreement. While insisting that inspection was inseparable from any test ban, he contended that an agreement was near.

President Eisenhower further emphasized the shift in control of disarmament policy from London to Washington on August 21, when a new United States concession was proclaimed. A White House statement announced that Secretary of State Dulles had "instructed" Mr. Stassen that the United States would be willing to extend the period of test suspension from ten months up to two years, given certain safeguards. The test ban was still to be part of a package. And the Soviet Union would be expected to agree that during the two-year period a permanent end of production of fissionable materials for weapons purposes would have been initiated and inspection to enforce it would have been established. Until a first-step arms control agreement comes into force, President Eisenhower said, the United States intended to conduct such nuclear testing as the security of the United States required.

In the Disarmament Subcommittee in London, Governor Stassen formally proposed the suspension of tests during a period from twelve to twenty-four months. The suspension could become a permanent ban if, at the end of two years, effective machinery to supervise the cutoff of nuclear-weapons production had gone into operation, Mr. Stassen said. He presented the proposals on behalf of Canada, France, the United Kingdom, and the United States.[28]

The nuclear-test-ban part of the first phase disarmament package was presented in these words:.

All the parties to the agreement undertake to refrain from conducting nuclear-test explosions for a period of twelve months from the date of entry into force of the convention, provided that agreement has been reached on the installation and maintenance of the necessary controls, including inspection posts with scientific instruments located within the territories of the Soviet Union, the United Kingdom, the United States, in the area of the Pacific Ocean and at such other places as may be necessary with the consent of the Governments concerned.

A group of technical experts appointed by the five governments represented in the Subcommittee will meet as soon as possible to design the inspection system to verify the suspension of testing.

Upon termination of the twelve-months period, the parties will be free to conduct tests unless they have agreed to continue the suspension for a further period under effective international inspection.

If the inspection system . . . is operating to the satisfaction of each party concerned, and if progress satisfactory to each party concerned is being achieved in the preparation of an inspection system . . . all parties to the convention undertake to refrain from conducting nuclear-test explosions for a further period of twelve months. Such an extension will be made only with the understanding that testing may, at the discretion of each party, be conducted twenty-four months after the entry into force of the convention if the inspection system . . . has not been installed to the satisfaction of each party concerned before the end of the twenty-four months, and if the cessation of production for weapons purposes has not been put into effect.

Furthermore, even under these circumstances, after twenty-four months, if tests are resumed, each party undertakes to announce and register in advance the dates of each series and the range of total energy to be released therein, to provide for limited observation of them, and to limit the amount of radioactive materials to be released into the atmosphere.

The Western willingness to enter into a nuclear test-ban agreement obviously was still carefully hedged. Governor Stassen, however, sought to put the best construction on it, telling the negotiators:

We are coming within close reach of agreement on this factor, since the first twelve-month period would merely require implementation of what had already been agreed upon. . . . Thus, these requirements for the first twelve months seem to me to be merely a matter of now applying in a sensible way and a practical manner the points already made and agreed between the parties. As a basis for extending to the full twenty-four months—which would meet the period of two years proposed by the Soviet Union—we then expect that there would be the move in relation to the cessation of production of fissionable material for weapons purposes.

But the Soviet Union was losing interest. Final preparations were under way to fire an intercontinental-range ballistic missile. Launching pads for Sputnik I and II were being readied. Mr. Zorin's mind obviously was somewhere else.

The State Department later summarized the American moves of July and August, 1957, in this way:

The United States and Western policy had thus moved more than halfway to meet the Soviet position on duration and timing of test suspension: two-years duration and the suspension to be literally the first step in a series of measures designed to move the world gradually but firmly toward safe-guarded disarmament.

Ambassador Zorin did not see it that way. On August 27, he read a 7,000-word statement denouncing the United States for presenting inspection proposals "to contribute to the preparation of aggressive war." Those who told the world that the five-month-old London talks had produced "satisfactory progress" were not speaking the truth. He raved:

In all this time the Subcommittee has not advanced one inch toward the solution of the problems referred to it. . . .
The ruling circles of the Western powers have decided to play a double game and, in order to deceive public opinion, are camouflaging their military preparations under talks of disarmament and trying to create the impression that some genuine effort is being made in the United Nations Subcommittee, whereas in fact the Subcommittee is marking time.[29]

From the Soviet point of view much of this was undoubtedly true. The United States had no intention of accepting an uninspected nuclear test ban in the summer of 1957.

Of course, which powers were using the talks to camouflage military preparations was a moot point.

Mr. Zorin's ninety-minute tirade on August 27 "slammed the door" on further Subcommittee negotiations, the State Department reported later.[30]

Ambassador Zorin complained that the United States and its Western partners were flying in the face of world opinion. "Millions of ordinary people in all the countries of the world are insistently demanding the dangerous experiments with atomic and hydrogen weapons should be stopped," Mr. Zorin complained. The Communist World Peace Council, in a recent session in Colombo, had opposed nuclear tests, he recalled. So had the parliaments of the Soviet Union, India, Japan, Yugoslavia, Indonesia, and Burma. Thousands of leading scientists, he said, in the Soviet Union, the United States, the United Kingdom, France, Germany, Japan, "and many other countries" demanded an immediate test ban. The United Nations had reflected concern about nuclear tests. Mr. Zorin then advanced the stereotyped Communist propaganda line: "It must also be borne in mind that even now the radiation resulting from nuclear explosions is a real danger to human life and health. The cessation of atomic-weapons tests would prevent the harmful consequences of nuclear explosions."

This was indeed a summary picture of the world forces impinging on the reluctant United States nuclear-test policy in mid-1957.

The Western allies finally agreed on the four-power, first-phase package disarmament plan, but the Zorin blast of August 27 indicated that they would have to hurry to present it, before the Communists walked out.

On the day after Mr. Zorin's attack, President Eisenhower expressed his concern:

> It is deeply disappointing to all true lovers of peace that the Soviet Union should have already attacked with such scornful words the proposals which Canada, France, the United Kingdom, and the United States are putting forward at the United Nations Disarmament Subcommittee in London. It is noteworthy that this attack coincides with the boastful statement by the Soviet Union that they have made advances in the development of means for bringing mass destruction to any part of the world. . . .
>
> It would be tragic if these important first-stage proposals, fraught with such significance for the peace of the world, were rejected by the Soviet Union even before they could have been seriously studied. . . .[31]

On August 29, the four-power proposals were officially presented to the Soviet Union at the London meeting. They were "unique in a decade of disarmament history," the State Department observed,[32] because they had been approved not only by the four negotiating powers but by the other eleven NATO allies. Ten interdependent beginning steps were proposed: an end to production of fissionable materials for weapons purposes; suspension of nuclear-weapons tests; reduction of nuclear stock-

piles; cut in force levels and armaments; inspection safeguards against
surprise attack; renunciation of the use of nuclear weapons except in self-
defense; beginning on control measures for outer-space missiles; regulation of armaments movements; establishment of an international control
organization; provisions for suspension of obligations in case of an important violation by another party.[33]

President Eisenhower's statement of August 28 had indicated that he
already had advance indications of the new Soviet developments in
rocketry. American radar monitors in Turkey, it later developed, had
been tracking the trajectories of Soviet missiles. The Soviet Union soon
announced publicly that it had successfully tested ballistic missiles of
intercontinental range. And on October 4, 1957, the world awakened to
the radioed beep of the Soviet Union's first earth satellite, Sputnik I.

The Subcommittee recessed September 6, after its 157th meeting, *sine
die*. The Soviet Union refused to agree to set a date for reconvening or
even to admit the possibility that there would be any further meetings.
Each side blamed the other for the breakdown.

RADIATION FEARS

As a backdrop for the London negotiations there had been a veritable
cacaphony of conflicting claims about radiation effects throughout 1957.

Public disagreements among American scientists continued unabated.
In January, for instance, there had been a report that the "mean lethal
dose" from radiation might be as low as 90 roentgens instead of 400 to
500 roentgens, as previously believed. Dr. Warren Weaver of the National Academy of Sciences told the Humphrey Subcommittee in the
Senate that 6,000 handicapped babies would be born because of past
tests. That wasn't many out of a world population of 2.5 to 5 billion, but
it was not for anyone to dispute that even one more handicapped person
in the world was a cause for concern. An AEC scientist contended that
strontium-90 levels in the bone would be small and "safe," but other
scientists, representing the Federation of American Scientists, contended
the maximum permissible levels may have already been exceeded in
some areas.

In February, a Columbia University group at the Lamont Geological
Observatory, after surveying 500 samples of human bones from 13 countries and 5 continents, found the strontium-90 concentrations to be only
1/10,000th of the then maximum permissible concentration established
by the National Committee on Radiation Protection. The team, headed
by J. Kulp, concluded that weapons tests could be continued indefinitely
at the 1956 rate without danger. Reassurance was soon offset again by
caution, however. The National Committee on Radiation Protection cut
by one-third its "maximum permissible dose" of radiation to which individuals should be exposed, thereby setting off a flurry of "I told you so's"

from those who had been warning that the genetic and somatic effects of fallout could be serious.

The Atomic Energy Commission's scientist member, Dr. W. F. Libby, continued his one-man educational program to show that the somatic and genetic dangers were much less than those to which the world's people were exposed from natural background. But he appeared to make only the smallest dent in the general world reaction.

The World Health Organization urged a curtailing of all man-made radioactivity. This was widely taken to be advice to stop tests and thus reduce fallout, rather than what the WHO clearly meant, which was to reduce X rays and other sources of much heavier doses of radiation.

Because of the world sensitivity to nuclear tests, those portions of the WHO report which referred to low-level radiation and its possible effects on the life span were lifted out for special attention. There were frequent reports of investigations by American public health agencies into the radioactivity of water, milk, shellfish, and other foods. The results, which usually confirmed AEC contentions that there was no serious danger, made little news. The general public's uneasiness about fallout, therefore, remained to nurture the advocates of a test ban.

Japan and Great Britain also continued their exchanges about nuclear tests. In early 1957, the British closed some shipping lanes in the Pacific area around Christmas Island, where a series of nuclear tests had been scheduled. Japan protested but the British went ahead with their tests anyway. Japanese shipping firms complained they would be forced to accept heavy losses because of the curtailment of their services.

Rumors of a big nuclear accident in the Soviet Union also circulated in Europe early in 1957. Soviet doctors reportedly told a West German specialist in blood diseases that over 200 persons had been treated in Moscow for overexposure to radiation.

As the Soviet testing schedule was intensified, first in 1956 and again in 1957, fallout over Japan increased markedly, but the brunt of the protests against the big powers was borne by the British Embassy, not the Soviet Embassy in Tokyo.

Officially, the Japanese Foreign Ministry sent three requests to suspend tests to the Soviet Union, the United States, and the United Kingdom. But the pressures of Japanese public opinion were concentrated on the British.

By March, there were demonstrations in Tokyo protesting the approaching Pacific test by the British. Japanese Premier Nobusuke Kishi joined with the All-Japan Seamen's Union to scotch an attempt to send a "suicide sitdown fleet" to the Christmas Island area to embarrass the British test effort.

Japan sent special missions to plead for a test ban to Washington, London, and Moscow. Ceylon took up the cry against the British, but Prime Minister Macmillan stood firm. The British Labour Party sided with the Japanese, introducing a compromise resolution in Parliament demanding a postponement of the tests.

The widespread agitation caused the British Government to issue a White Paper, stressing reliance on the bomb as a deterrent to war.

In March, a Japanese citizen named M. Hatanaka reported that Soviet Premier Khrushchev had rejected his proposal that the Soviet Union suspend nuclear tests unilaterally for one year.[34] About a year later, however, Khrushchev was to take a similar step.

Indonesia joined in the call to cancel the tests, and a Japanese group revived the idea of sending a "peace fleet" to the Christmas Island area. A Labourite censure motion in the British House of Commons was defeated in early April.

Tokyo students fought with police outside the British Embassy late in April, and over 1,000 students demonstrated at the American, Soviet, and British Embassies. The next day, a special Japanese envoy who had spent more than two months in Great Britain trying to persuade the British Government to call off the tests "apologized" to the Japanese people for his failure.

At an April symposium by the National Academy of Sciences, in Washington, the radiation from tests was compared with the dose administered by luminous watch dials, but other testimony about effects of higher levels of radiation, not associated with fallout, merely confirmed in the public mind the dangers of all types of radiation.

Dr. Albert Schweitzer sent a warning of the harmful effects of bomb tests to the Nobel Prize Committee. AEC Commissioner Libby disputed the Schweitzer view and produced later evidence to refute some of his statements, but the impact of the Schweitzer move was much greater.

Selwyn Lloyd, then Foreign Secretary in Great Britain, also sought to counteract the snowballing fear of nuclear tests by warning that those who generated fears of health perils due to tests were "nonscientific" sources with "fellow-traveling tendencies."

Dr. Linus Pauling, the American prize-winning chemist who collected thousands of scientists' signatures on a petition to end nuclear tests, reported in May, 1957, that nuclear tests up to that time would produce 10,000 leukemia victims and repeated his call for a nuclear test ban.

There were extreme statements on both sides of the issue. A Defense Department official said testing could be continued at the 1956–57 rate for forty to fifty years without any serious danger to man from fallout. Thirty thousand megatons of TNT-equivalent would have to be exploded, he said, to raise the strontium-90 level in human bones to the maximum permissible concentration.

Dr. Pauling estimated, on the other hand, in an interview on May 1, that the British H-bomb tests alone would cause at least 1,000 deaths. A few days later the British Medical Research Council rejected Dr. Pauling's view, claiming there was insufficient evidence.

A new Soviet device for keeping the spotlight on the nuclear-test issue was to appeal to the British Parliament and the American Congress through the Supreme Soviet of the Soviet Union. The Kremlin "legislators" suggested forming a committee of the three bodies to explore ways to end nuclear tests. The British Foreign Office promptly labeled the Supreme Soviet proposal "propaganda." Ambassador Malik in London retorted, however, that the Soviet Union was ready to end tests if the United States and Great Britain would. Senators Knowland and Hickenlooper both rejected the Supreme Soviet proposal.

But West Germany's Bundestag passed a resolution in May urging the United States, the Soviet Union, and Great Britain to suspend their nuclear tests. The Bundestag used the resolution mainly as a device to evade a vote on a Social Democratic resolution providing West Germany should reject nuclear arms for its armed forces.

The Soviet Union also kept up special pressures on Japan, where the fear of nuclear-weapons tests ran high. Moscow asked the Japanese Foreign Office to join in issuing an appeal to Britain and the United States to end testing. This was in early May, before the British series started. The Soviet Union was not ready to accept the British position, however, that nuclear-weapons tests should be announced in advance.

Great Britain exploded its first H-bomb in mid-May, thus bringing the British into the exclusive H-bomb club. Fallout, Prime Minister Macmillan reported to the House of Commons, was almost negligible because the device was exploded at high altitude. Some in Washington claimed the explosion indicated development of a "clean" type of H-bomb, but official secrecy prevented confirmation.

Japanese continued to demonstrate in front of the British Embassy in Tokyo in protest against the test. When the Captain of a Japanese ship, 450 miles from the aerial-test site, reported seeing the British test, 35,000 Japanese students demonstrated in Tokyo.

Labourite criticism of the Conservative Government's H-bomb policy reached a new peak after the mid-May H-bomb test. Prime Minister Macmillan conceded that after the current series of tests it might be possible to control future H-bomb tests on an international level.

A second British H-bomb, reportedly larger than the first, was exploded late in May, at a higher altitude in the Christmas Island area. This touched off another demonstration by leftist Japanese students before the British Embassy in Tokyo. Prime Minister Macmillan again indicated in the House of Commons that future tests might be curtailed to seek a nuclear disarmament treaty.

President Voroshilov of the Soviet Union, touring Indonesia, repeated his Government's demands for a test ban at every opportunity.

The AEC, apparently following a new policy of extreme caution, announced day-by-day tracking of the radioactive clouds from Nevada tests, which opened again in late May. It was emphasized that, at all stages, the radiation content of the clouds was so small as to present no hazard to the persons living below.

The second-smallest nuclear test ever reported by the United States was exploded on June 5, 1957, from a balloon anchored to the ground by cables. Its yield was listed as 0.47 ton, or 940 pounds of TNT-equivalent. The test was the third reported from the Nevada series of 1957, called Operation Plumbbob. Antitest groups continued to harass the Nevada tests in 1957. The Nonviolent Action Against Nuclear Weapons group demonstrated in Japan. Eleven pacifists were arrested for trying to enter the Nevada proving grounds in August during the Plumbbob series.

Prime Minister Nehru also was taking a new hysterical approach to the nuclear-bomb tests. In a Colombo speech in May, 1957, he urged a ban on nuclear experiments to prevent human "extinction." It was apparent from his statements that he too, either consciously or unconsciously, was confusing the effects of nuclear-war fallout with nuclear-test fallout.

With Ceylonese Prime Minister Bandaranike, Nehru later issued a communiqué urging the immediate suspension of all nuclear tests.

On May 22, the Indian Parliament passed a resolution urging a test ban.

Premier Kishi of Japan, visiting India, joined Prime Minister Nehru in urging that nuclear tests be banned.

To meet the fears of damage to health from nuclear-test fallout, AEC scientists suggested, late in May, that nuclear tests be limited, not banned, to prevent the fallout hazard.

It was obvious in mid-1957 that the United States was losing the propaganda battle on nuclear tests. But it was equally obvious that President Eisenhower was then willing to lose that battle in order to preserve the chance to continue testing if that was important to the national security, as he saw it. Whether the United States really had to lose the propaganda battle or whether it was the victim of USIA bungling is an argument that need not be pursued here.

Premier Khrushchev, in a June appearance on American television, pressed his advantage. He said he saw little value in advance registration of nuclear tests and urged an outright ban on them.

While the AEC was producing more and more information on the effects of test fallout, it was still coming under criticism for the "cult of secrecy" that allegedly kept the public from knowing the full story of the fallout danger.

Late in May and early in June, the Joint Congressional Atomic Energy Committee's Subcommittee on Fallout Hazards, under the chairmanship of Representative Chet Holifield of California, undertook a comprehensive study of the fallout problem.

In seeking to counteract the hypersensitive view that all tests should be stopped because all fallout produced an unacceptable addition to health hazards, it was perhaps inevitable that a tendency developed to take the position that "fallout is good for you." In its attempt to bring perspective to the problem, the Joint Atomic Energy Committee was able to elicit testimony from AEC officials themselves that tests could become a peril if they were greatly expanded. Dr. Wright Langham and Merrill Eisenbud told the Joint Atomic Energy Committee that tests ought to be limited to 10 megatons per year.

Sensing the need for some more-dramatic move to show the world that the United States took seriously the fears of nuclear-weapons tests, Representative Holifield urged the United States to stop testing big nuclear weapons—one of the old Stevenson positions.

Private suggestions were renewed within the Government that the United States should voluntarily take its testing program underground. To prepare for this possibility, the first underground test was scheduled for the fall, 1957, series in Nevada.

Dr. Pauling, in a TV interview, charged that each of the next 20 generations would contain 200,000 mentally or physically defective children if nuclear tests continued. He also forecast that life expectancy would be reduced from five to ten years for one million persons if tests were to continue.

Geneticists appearing before the Joint Atomic Energy Committee generally conceded that the effect of fallout would be small compared with other health hazards. But they warned that over the hundreds or thousands of generations in which fallout might be a small health hazard, the lives of hundreds of thousands or even millions of persons might be affected.

This worry with the cumulative "millenniums effect" of fallout frequently was confused with its year-by-year effect and added to the general public's exaggerated conception of the fallout menace.

A second indication that the Soviet Union was dreaming of a large propaganda coup by ending tests unilaterally "to prove its sincerity," came in the report of a letter from Premier Bulganin to Prime Minister Nehru of India. The Soviet leader asked for Indian reaction to such a move.

The Reverend Dr. Billy Graham, well-known American evangelist, had the same basic idea. He suggested that the United States should unilaterally end tests to spur world opinion to force the Soviet Union to halt testing. Quakers, Presbyterians, and others joined in urging an end to large nuclear tests.

The Soviet Union used every pressure, large and small, to keep the heat on. A Leningrad mother, for instance, wrote a letter to *The New York Times* appealing to American mothers to demand a nuclear arms ban.

Labour Party Leader Hugh Gaitskell urged the British Government to accept the Soviet offer for a two-to-three-year ban under controls in a speech at Newcastle. He opposed linking political conditions to the nuclear test ban.

Retiring AEC Commissioner Murray warned it would be reckless for the United States to agree to a test ban or the suspension of manufacturing small nuclear weapons. He again suggested ending large H-bomb tests while accelerating tests for small weapons.

The Soviet Union even brought up tests in the International Labor Organization in late June, but the ILO defeated a Soviet resolution calling for a ban, 133 to 46.

In the midst of the test-ban din, the Administration made a new effort to impress world opinion with the values of reducing radioactive fallout—producing so-called "clean" bombs. Thirty American scientists reported on June 24 that H-bomb fallout had been reduced by 95 per cent in recent tests. President Eisenhower dramatized the "clean" bomb at a news conference by reporting leading scientists' claim that they could develop a virtually nonradioactive bomb in four or five years more of testing.

The whole exercise rang hollow in the public ears. The Administration had been maintaining all along that fallout was not a hazard, had it not? Why all the fuss, then, about a clean bomb? The failure to distinguish clearly between nuclear-war fallout and nuclear-test fallout was now having another deleterious effect. Bombs with reduced radioactivity would be important in wartime as the President tried to make clear. "Clean" tests, on the other hand, were not an especially important objective.

Furthermore, the public thought, if the fallout doesn't get you the blast surely will. Why all the morality about clean bombs? H-bombs are immoral—period. Speaking of degrees of immorality, of lethality, in the case of H-bombs sounded like the Pharisee in the temple, imputing morality on himself, an obvious sinner.

Premier Khrushchev set up a hooting about the "stupidity" of the so-called clean bomb that circled the world from Vladivostok to Leningrad.

When the Asian flu epidemic swept the Far East, rumor spread that the cause had been Soviet H-bomb tests. It was one of the rare occasions when Soviet tests came in for any criticism.

The first of the Pugwash conferences, sponsored by Cyrus Eaton, the Cleveland, Ohio industrialist was held in Nova Scotia in July, 1957. Twenty scientists conferred there on the hazards of nuclear war and warned of the misuse of atomic energy, which they said might destroy man completely. Soviet scientists who attended pressed, predictably, for a test ban.

A third H-bomb had been exploded by the British on June 19, and Britain announced an end to that test series. Curbs on shipping were lifted a month in advance.

The World Council of Churches Central Committee issued a statement on August 5, circulated to all its members, urging an agreement to suspend tests or, failing that, unilateral action.

As the London Subcommittee talks were going down to failure, Premier Bulganin conferred in Moscow with a Japanese group that favored a test ban.

A new set of British tests, code-named Operation Antler, was observed by SEATO representatives in September. The explosions were set off from towers or balloons at Maralinga in South Australia. The test-ban heat was somewhat off, then, with the failure of the London disarmament talks. So the British Defense Ministry resumed its tests at Christmas Island in October, 1957.

The Soviet Union, too, reported it had completed a test series late in August, 1957.

In September, Representative Chet Holifield, Chairman of the JAEC hearings, publicly urged President Eisenhower to inform the United States completely on the fallout dangers and to explain the need for testing. He charged the AEC with neglect of its responsibilities to keep the nation informed.

Secretary of State Dulles tried to meet this criticism at a September 19 press conference. The United States, he said, is trying to develop "discriminating" nuclear weapons while the Soviet Union seeks to stigmatize all nuclear weapons as "horror weapons." [35]

In a rare reversal of form, one scientist actually made the claim that "fallout is good for you." A British doctor suggested in September that there might be a link between radioactive fallout and the rise in intelligence among British children.

In October, the Soviet Union reported the successful testing of a "mighty" warhead of a new design. Premier Khrushchev mentioned the test in an interview with *The New York Times* and said Soviet experiments would continue pending international control.

The AEC's General Advisory Council on Biology advised the President, on October 19, to continue nuclear tests as a military necessity but at a minimum rate, to keep fallout-dose rates as low as possible. Fallout was within tolerable limits, the biologists concluded. There would be no danger if tests were continued at the same rate as in the previous five years.

Shortly after the Soviet Union broke up the Disarmament Subcommittee negotiations in London, a new session of the General Assembly had opened in New York.

The Assembly's Political Committee debated the disarmament issue for a full month. Ten draft resolutions were laid before it. Two resolutions, which were rejected, pressed the test-ban idea. An Indian proposal would have set up a scientific-technical commission of experts to plan an inspection system to supervise the suspension of test explosions. The big powers were cool to the plan because it would have admitted many powers inexperienced in nuclear matters to the experts meeting. This resolution was rejected in the Committee by a vote of twenty-two to thirty-eight, with twenty abstentions.

Japan proposed a provisional one-year suspension of test explosions during which time there would be parallel discussions on other disarmament problems. This was rejected eighteen to thirty-two, with thirty-one abstentions.

Prime Minister Kishi of Japan wrote President Eisenhower about the U.N. resolution, asking that the United States give it thorough study. Mr. Eisenhower replied a week later that "for the time being and in the present circumstances, the security of the United States, and, I believe, that of the free world, depends to a great degree upon what we learn from the testing of nuclear weapons." He explained again that testing would be necessary to develop defensive uses of nuclear weapons and to reduce fallout. Mr. Eisenhower warned that suspending tests without at the same time achieving a cutoff of nuclear-weapons production would be a sacrifice which it "would be dangerous to accept." Concern for the health hazards of testing, on the other hand, was not well founded, he added.

The Soviet Union's resolution to establish a permanent disarmament commission of all U.N. members was voted down, nine to fifty-one, with twenty-one abstentions.

Two resolutions were passed from the Political Committee to the General Assembly. One was a twenty-four-nation resolution embodying the four Western powers' major proposals of August 29, which had been rejected out of hand by the Soviet Union in the Disarmament Subcommittee talks in London. The other resolution was proposed by Belgium. It provided for a world-wide information program to acquaint the world with modern armaments and the need for effective control of them.

The General Assembly passed both resolutions over Soviet objections. This action came November 14, one month and ten days after Sputnik I had been sent up by the Soviet Union.

The four-power Western proposals for a first-step disarmament agreement, advanced at London, drew support from the following twenty nations that joined in sponsoring the Assembly resolution: Argentina, Australia, Belgium, Brazil, Chile, Colombia, Cuba, the Dominican Republic, Ecuador, Honduras, Italy, Laos, Liberia, the Netherlands, Nicaragua, Panama, Paraguay, Peru, the Philippines, and Tunisia.

The approving vote was fifty-seven to nine, with fifteen abstentions. Item A in the Assembly resolution provided for "the immediate suspension of testing of nuclear weapons with prompt installation of effective international control, including inspection posts equipped with appropriate scientific instruments located within the territories of the United

States, the U.S.S.R., the United Kingdom, Pacific Ocean areas, and other points as required."

The resolution merely recommended that disarmament negotiators "give priority" to the first-step items enumerated. It was well understood that the West still considered test-suspension to be part of a package of disarmament moves.

Ending production of nuclear materials for weapons was the second item in the resolution.

The United States also succeeded in placing in the resolution a provision that technical experts should begin a joint study of inspection systems for disarmament measures at an early date.

Meanwhile, Governor Stassen's shooting star was burning out. He left the post of disarmament adviser at the end of the year. Secretary Dulles gathered back unto the State Department all the disarmament responsibilities that had been split between him and Mr. Stassen.

The United States had made extremely significant concessions during his tenure. The most important of these was that a nuclear test ban would be considered. The second concession was in expressing a readiness to go ahead with a nuclear test ban, without insisting on the prior safeguarded stoppage of nuclear-weapons production. The Soviet Union, for its part, had accepted the idea that any nuclear test ban would have to include an inspection system to verify the test suspension, and that a time limit could be set on the ban, to guard against bad faith by one of the parties.[36]

But the U.S.S.R. continued to maintain its own "link" between test suspension and another nuclear-disarmament issue: The West must agree to a complete ban on the use of nuclear weapons at the same time that it agreed to a nuclear test suspension.

The Soviet Union also rejected the idea of even a loose link between the test suspension and the cutoff in nuclear-weapons production.

Secretary of State Dulles was nevertheless encouraged by the progress made at the 1957 London disarmament talks. "I feel confident," he told a news conference, "that over the span of years the measure of agreement which was arrived at in London will prove significant and will advance the cause of limitation of armament." [37]

On October 10, in the Political Committee's discussion of the disarmament problem, U.S. Ambassador Henry Cabot Lodge presented a comprehensive statement of the American position on nuclear tests. It was one of the clearest defenses of United States policy in the nuclear-test area, but it was lost in a lengthy speech, read in a forum that got little world attention. Its contents never were picked up and played to the world—and to the United States public—to the full extent. Here, in part, is what Mr. Lodge said:

> No environmental hazard nor substance to which human beings are exposed is receiving such thorough investigation as radiation and radioactive

materials. While some leading medical and genetic authorities differ on the effects of radioactive fallout at low levels, all agree that the effects are small compared to the effects of radiation from other sources.

The present levels of radiation exposure from weapons-testing fallout are extremely low. They are but a fraction of the natural radiation to which man has always been exposed. They are far lower than the levels we customarily receive voluntarily from other man-made sources such as medical and dental X rays, and even the luminescent dials of our wrist watches. The danger to the world lies in the possible use of the nuclear weapons, not in some small addition to natural radiation because of testings. We think that that is the fundamental point—the possible use of weapons. That is the real danger.

What is seldom realized is that the tests themselves are enabling us to develop weapons with reduced fallout so that radiation hazards in the event of hostilities may be restricted to military targets. Thus if our testing program should continue at the present rate the radiation it puts into the world's atmosphere would be less in future years.

Ambassador Lodge warned that suspending tests alone would not stop the accumulation of atomic and hydrogen bombs, production of which would "go right on." But test suspension would end efforts to reduce radioactive fallout in these weapons "and consequently the weapons added to the stockpiles would contain a larger amount of radioactive fallout than they would otherwise."

He also argued that "additional nations could and probably would, without the aid of nuclear tests, nevertheless manufacture and acquire their own nuclear weapons, using techniques which are not known." [38]

This was a relatively new point which has special application even now. The world knows that France has been testing nuclear weapons and considers her the fourth nuclear power. Who is to say whether there are not already fifth and sixth nuclear powers with atomic and hydrogen bombs in their arsenals which have not been tested?

Mr. Lodge made this offer to the Soviet Union:

We will suspend nuclear tests for an initial period expected to be two years but also subject to further extension, provided you, the Soviet Union, agree on establishing an effective inspection system, air and ground; on stopping production of fissionable material for weapons purposes and reducing present stocks; on starting outer-space missile control; and on reducing armed forces.

Now we do not insist, Mr. Chairman, that all these things be done at once. An agreement that they should be done in acceptable stages is enough to get this program under way and suspension of testing would be the first thing to happen.

Influential opinion in this country was then advocating lifting the nuclear test ban completely out of the American disarmament package. Senator Hubert Humphrey of Minnesota, Chairman of the Senate Foreign Relations Committee's Subcommittee on Disarmament, had participated in weekly meetings with the Secretary of State or his deputies in the summer of 1957, during the London Disarmament Subcommittee negotiations, to follow the progress of the talks. On November 4, he wrote President Eisenhower to urge a separation of the test ban from the rest of the package.

I . . . believe that the United States has taken an unnecessarily rigid position in its insistence on combining a two-year ban on nuclear-weapons tests with a cutoff on the production of fissionable materials for weapons purposes and also with aerial and ground inspection zones to guard against surprise attack. While I understand the basis of the various parts of the present United States proposals, I do not think that their inseparableness should represent an ultimate position.

The American disarmament package "has its disadvantages," the Senator suggested, because inspection demands for each part of the package "when added together [may] be so extensive as to be impractical and unacceptable."

Senator Humphrey further suggested that

The United States, after consulting with its Allies, declare its willingness to negotiate separately on a ban on nuclear-weapons tests for a two-year period with the only condition being agreement on an effective inspection system with United Nations supervision to insure that the ban is being scrupulously observed.
It is my belief that such a proposal would be a safe and reasonable one. It would be a concrete step toward ending the arms race. It would also enable the people of this and other countries to learn more clearly whether the Soviet Union is truly ready to accept effective inspection. We cannot challenge the intentions of the Soviet Union on inspection unless we are in a position to negotiate on a test ban irrespective of the other measures in the four-power disarmament proposal.

Senator Humphrey said he had discussed this matter with Governor Stassen, and these discussions had "convinced" him that separating the test ban from the package would be in the best interest of the United States.

The implication was that Governor Stassen had privately assured his fellow Minnesotan, Senator Humphrey, that the White House Disarmament Staff was itself in favor of negotiating a test ban separate from any link to a nuclear-weapons production cutoff.

Late in November, Prime Minister Nehru addressed a personal appeal to the "great leaders" of the United States and the Soviet Union to stop tests.

Both the Prime Minister and Senator Humphrey got replies to their entreaties in President Eisenhower's sympathetic but firm cablegram answering the Indian leader. It is the Soviet Union that is barring progress on disarmament, Mr. Eisenhower said.

I know that the subject of testing of nuclear weapons is of understandable concern to many. I have given this matter long and prayerful thought. I am convinced that a cessation of nuclear-weapons tests, if it is to alleviate rather than merely to conceal the threat of nuclear war, should be undertaken as a part of a meaningful program to reduce that threat.

We are prepared to stop nuclear tests immediately in this context. However, I do not believe that we can accept a proposal to stop nuclear experiments as an isolated step, unaccompanied by any assurances that other measures—which would go to the heart of the problem—would follow. We are at a stage when testing is required, particularly for the development of important defensive uses of these weapons. To stop these tests at this time, in the absence of knowledge that we can go on and achieve effective limitations on nuclear weapons production and on other elements of armed strength, as well as a measure of assurance against surprise attack, is a sacrifice which we could not in prudence accept. To do so could increase rather than diminish the threat of aggressions and war.

I believe that bolder and more far-reaching measures are required. Specifically, I believe that any government which declares its desire to agree not to use nuclear weapons should, if they are sincere, be prepared to bring an end to their production. Agreement to devote all future production of fissionable material to peaceful uses is, as I see it, the most important step that can be taken.

The year 1957 ended with the two nuclear giants, the United States and the Soviet Union, still far apart on all disarmament measures, still on speaking terms through the letter-writing of their leaders, still importuned by the rest of the world to end nuclear-weapons tests as a first step toward more meaningful disarmament. The Soviet Union, however, announced on New Year's Eve that it would boycott the new twenty-five-nation U.N. Disarmament Commission.

In the aftermath of the Sputniks, Moscow was willing to wait for the world to come knocking at the Kremlin door.

RAINIER

Scientists like Dr. Ernest O. Lawrence and Dr. Edward Teller, who had long been associated with the United States weapons program and felt that weapons-testing must go on to help their country keep its nuclear-weapons-development lead over the Soviet Union, had watched with increasing apprehension as the pressure of world opinion and political campaigning at home pushed the United States closer and closer to suspension of testing. What was needed, it had long been clear, was some method to disarm protests about health hazards from fallout, while still permitting those tests necessary to continue nuclear-weapons development. There were two ways to reduce fallout while testing. One was to reduce the ratio of fission to fusion in a bomb, since fission produces almost all the radioactive fallout. Another method, scientists realized, would be to confine the fallout—perhaps by placing the explosions underground.

As early as November 29, 1951, a 1.2-kiloton bomb had been exploded 17 feet underground at the Nevada test site. Another 1.1-kiloton shot was exploded 67 feet underground at the Nevada test site on March 23, 1955. The 1951 shot burst through the surface. No official information has been released on the 1955 shot.

Early in 1956, however, Dr. Teller, working with The RAND Corporation's David Griggs, produced a paper proposing that the next Nevada test series include a low-yield subterranean shot "at such a depth that it will be contained." The Griggs-Teller paper argued that such tests would allow greater freedom in a test program because the time of detonation would no longer depend on the weather. The authors also suggested that tests could be held "at any time at which the test object is ready without the problem of fitting the bomb into a test series." [39]

Interruptions of airline traffic could also be avoided. And, of course, fallout would be contained.

Using data from the 1951 underground test, Dr. Griggs and Dr. Teller estimated that for a one-kiloton explosion the bomb would have to be buried to a depth of 650 feet to prevent surface craters if the tests were conducted in Yucca Flat. A slightly greater depth would be required in hard rocks such as granite.

To avoid all gas seepage the scientists estimated that a depth of 1000 feet would be sufficient for one kiloton, 2000 feet for 10 kilotons.

The cost of preparing the hole would be about $20 per foot of depth, which was said to be comparable to the cost of towers from which most of the Nevada tests were conducted. Shock arrival times and seismic signals would permit an estimate of the test's size in kilotons within an error of 5 or 10 per cent, on the basis of the 1951 experience.

One of the early worries about underground testing was the danger of setting off damaging earthquakes. However, Drs. Griggs and Teller, based on their experience with the two previous underground shots at Yucca Flat, estimated that the danger to surface structures was slight. The deep, porous "fill" that characterized the earth at Yucca Flat was "peculiarly suitable to attenuation of seismic impulses," the authors said. "In a hard-rock terrain, the attenuation would be much less. Even so, the dilational character of the atomic explosion would result in far smaller damaging effects than would an equally energetic natural earthquake."

Most earthquake damage comes from surface waves and shear waves, the "up-and-down" motions. These waves were believed to be small or completely absent in atomic explosions.

Radioactivity from the underground explosion was expected to be mixed with molten rock formed in the heat of the explosions, and "bound in the recrystallized silicates." The hazard from long-lived fission products and induced radioactivity, which might arise due to leaching of the explosion products and contamination of ground water, "is thought to be negligible," the paper said. Some feared that seepage would carry with it much of the radioactivity and cause contamination of ground water. But experiments at Oak Ridge with fission products and silicate had established that such substances were extremely resistant to leaching.

Furthermore, the amount of radioactivity produced in bombs of the size to be exploded underground would be small. But what would happen when the underground pocket of radioactivity was pierced?

"Apart from the instant of explosion itself, the only critical period [in testing nuclear explosions underground] occurs when the radioactive sampling device reaches the radioactive region," the Teller-Griggs paper said. "If this happens ten days after the explosion, the active residual activity will have substantially decayed. Even if the whole activity from an original one-kiloton event would erupt at this time [which seems inconceivable], the effect on a place like Las Vegas would be less than the one which would normally result from about a 50-ton explosion."

A trial underground shot, the scientists said, would also permit them to assess the reliability of yield estimates by seismic methods.

If the costs of underground test shots were found to be comparable to those above ground, or only slightly higher, the scientists suggested, there might be advantages to arranging a permanent test site. A number of "standby" test holes could then be drilled in advance so that a laboratory could lower a weapon and test it on short notice at any time of the year.

It is, perhaps, a commentary on the ponderous pace of decision-making in government that the Griggs-Teller recommendation did not bear fruit until nineteen months later, on September 19, 1957. The underground shot was code-named Rainier. By that time, talk of a nuclear test ban had gone so far, and American fears of evasion of a test-ban agreement had been so widely publicized, that the underground test had another important purpose: To explore the capabilities of detecting underground nuclear tests at long distances.

The nearby town of Lincoln Mine was evacuated temporarily just before the blast. Seismologists the world over were alerted for the test. Teams of geologists and other specialists were organized to move into the Yucca Flat area immediately after the test to hunt for traces of radioactivity above ground, for aftershocks and for the underground "boiling" noises that might be picked up on special listening-instruments called "geophones."

The nuclear bomb tested was deliberately kept small—1.7 kilotons—because the planners wanted to be especially careful about earthquake shocks in the surrounding area. They knew that the underground testing technique would be doomed if the surrounding citizenry suffered property losses or were frightened by the earthquake effects. All the theories were that the earth movement would be minimal.

"Nevertheless, we wanted to be safe," Atomic Energy Commission member W. F. Libby later recalled, "so we picked the softest, spongiest mountain we could find." [40]

It was not exactly a mountain, but a mesa, in which the Rainier shot was buried at a vertical depth of 900 feet. The point nearest the bomb on the slope surface of the mesa was 800 feet away. The mesa consisted of tufa or tuff, volcanic ash partly congealed and porous, like sponge. The room at the end of the tunnel approach to ground zero was six feet by six feet by seven feet. [41]

The test, when finally laid out, had three stated objectives: to develop a weapons-testing technique that would eliminate fallout; to make testing independent of weather; and to eliminate noise, flash, and shock as off-site effects. [42]

The shot was designed, weapons-development experts said, to find out the answers to these questions:

How deep would a bomb of given yield have to be buried to contain the radioactivity?

How large would the ground motions from the shot be? What would the effects be on local and offsite structures?

Would the ground water be seriously contaminated, thus risking a spread of dangerous amounts of radioactivity to wells and streams in the region?

The control point from which the shot was fired was 2.5 miles from the detonation. At that distance, a muffled explosion was heard and a few people felt a weak ground wave. Most people noticed no ground movement. That was all. The explosion caused a slight ripple which spread over the mesa's face. Some of the rocks on the crown of the mesa broke loose and rolled down the slope of the mountain.

Careful measurements later indicated that the maximum amount of upward movement as a result of the explosion was nine inches. One thousand feet from the blast point the movement was less than half an inch. A block of earth about 100 or 200 feet thick separated from the rest of the mountain, rose, and fell as a unit. [43]

Almost all the radioactive material was contained in an underground cylinder 10 feet deep with a radius of 47 to 57 feet. This pocket lay at the bottom of the underground hole carved out by the explosion.

The United States Coast and Geodetic Survey had alerted seismographs in the West—and throughout the world—to watch for the Rainier shot, to see what magnitude of signal would appear on the seismograms. Stations in the Far West picked up the test. The Coast and Geodetic Survey analysis indicated that the seismic signals from the Rainier shot corresponded to an earthquake of magnitude 4.6 on the Gutenberg-Richter scale. [44]

Ordinary earthquakes of 4.6 magnitude cause perceptible shaking of the earth as far as 60 miles from the epicenter. The Rainier shot, however, was noticed by only a few individuals who were 2.5 miles from the shot. Earthquakes released energy along "faults," where there are slippages which extend for many miles. These faults usually are located at depths far in excess of the few hundred feet at which the Rainier shot was detonated. In California, for instance, earth slippages occur most frequently at 10 miles or more depth, and over several miles in length.

Dr. Libby later told Senator Humphrey's Subcommittee this story of the firing:[45]

I was in Paris at a UNESCO meeting at that time and was broadcasting to all of the fifty-four countries there, "Please go listen. We are going to fire this bomb at six o'clock tonight." Of course, it had to be delayed three times, to the great embarrassment of us, for no reason I can figure out, because weather doesn't play any role. We were just scared, I think, and they delayed it.

Finally, on the third day, they fired it . . . on September 19. The only thing we saw [at Yucca Flat], the mountain jumped about six inches [later official reports said nine inches]. We saw that. But our Geiger counters showed no effects. We were quite worried that there might be some fissures develop so that the radioactivity might get out.

[Crews that swarmed over the mesa and its surrounding area, however, could not even locate the permanent gases, krypton and xenon.]

After waiting for a few days [to allow the radioactivity to decay somewhat] we started drilling to find this bomb. And we kept drilling.

We drilled straight down. We had in mind the notion that the bomb would have melted a glob of rock. The energy, of course, is quite sizable, and we were afraid that when we got in and hit this, that something horrible like an explosion would occur. So our drill crews were very cautious about it. But they kept drilling away, and when they got about half way down into the mountain, about 400 feet down, they found a cavity. That is, the drill machinery dropped about 50 feet, and in this cavity they found a little tiny whiff of radioactivity, the first sign. Then they kept going and they found that from here on it was impossible to keep the drilling water going, that is the drilling water seemed to just flow away to infinity. There was a porosity in the rock which was not there in the mountain before.

Well, we kept going until we got right down to ground zero, where the bomb was. And we still had not found any more except this little whiff of radioactivity that we found half or two-thirds of the way down. So the problem at that point, this was about two months after the bomb was fired, was what in goodness happened? Where was this bomb? We knew perfectly well that it had gone off and we knew the radioactivity was trapped in there, so we could not find it.

We had put the bomb in the mountain by taking a tunnel 2000 feet long into the side of it.

It isn't a mountain, it is a mesa, and so we went in the tunnel. Of course we had looked in the tunnel before. But the tunnel was closed out to about 200 feet from the bomb site, and we had rather expected that the tunnel might be closed farther out by the explosion.

The tunnel was straight for about 1600 feet and then made sort of a spiral. We put the bomb in the center of this spiral.

Well, when we couldn't find the bomb by drilling downward, then we went in the end of the tunnel and started drilling horizontally, pointed right at the bomb, where the bomb had been. Well, we got in and about 50 feet from where the bomb was known to have been located, we found a little bit of radioactivity again, quite a little bit this time. . . .

Then we kept drilling, and again we got right to ground zero. And no bomb.

Then we sat down and did the thinking that we should have done two months before, and figured out what it was. To make a long story short, what happened was that the bomb had blown itself a bubble of gasified, vaporized rock. This bubble was about 110 feet in diameter and about 55 feet in radius. The skin of this bubble was molten rock about four or five inches thick, and in this molten rock was all the radioactivity of that bomb. Even gaseous products were trapped in this molten rock. Then it cooled.

Now the shock wave had gone beyond where the bubble expanded and had broken out to 130 feet, had pulverized the mountain. So what happened was that the rock that overlay this thing had no more strength, and when the bubble cooled, when the heat cooled to the point where the pressure of the gas inside the bubble would no longer support the weight, which of course was just a few seconds afterwards, the thing collapsed of its own weight. What we were looking for in there was a broken egg, really, an egg shell which had been crushed, and so our bomb fragments were entirely in the form of sort of a bowl underlying the ground zero point.

Then we drilled from the end of the tunnel. We went down at a slant and sure enough we found the "hot" rock. Now the rock was black, dark colored. You could pick it out visually. That is, the radioactive material is entirely in rock which you can visually distinguish from the rest of the mountain. You can, of course, do it with radio instruments very easily, because it is intensely radioactive.

The Coast and Geodetic Survey received reports on the Rainier blast from forty-six seismic stations at distances ranging from 110 miles to 2,300 miles.

Six stations, all within 180 miles of the explosion, provided sufficient data to identify the disturbance as an explosion. They were at China Lake, Woody, and Tinemaha in California; Boulder City, Hoover Dam, and Eureka in Nevada.

In the first public report on the seismic detection of the Rainier shot, the records of College Station in Fairbanks, Alaska, were omitted. That station, with an extremely good seismograph, was located 2,300 miles away from Yucca Flat. It recorded a compressional wave of sufficient quality to locate the event accurately. But there were more impressive squiggles on the same seismograph—the Rainier shot almost surely would not have been noticed in Alaska had there not been a special alert.

Failure to report detection at the Alaska station became a basis for suspecting the Atomic Energy Commission of deliberately misleading the world on prospects for policing a nuclear test ban.

Admiral Strauss later told the Senate Disarmament Subcommittee that the Rainier shot had been detected as far away as Alaska's College Station only because the time of detonation had been sent in advance to all seismologists around the world. He showed the Subcommittee a seismogram of the Rainier explosion as recorded at Fairbanks. He then pointed out that the shot would have been reported as a small earthquake had not the AEC sent out advance notification of the location and probable burst time, as well as exact coordinates and time subsequent to the burst. (See Figure 3, page 585 of Notes.)

The lines on the Fairbanks seismogram are separated by about fifteen minutes in time; the width covers about one minute. Three other earthquakes were recorded on the portion shown to the Committee by Admiral Strauss. On the fourth line, there is the recording of a small disturbance in the Aleutian Islands, which occurred about three hours earlier. On the eighth line, about two hours before the Rainier blast, there was another small earthquake not identified as to source. On the second line from the bottom of the Fairbanks seismogram, about thirty minutes after the Rainier shot, there was the record of a moderate-sized earthquake in the Tonga Islands, about 6,000 miles from the Alaska station. The Tonga Islands are located between the Fiji Islands and Tahiti, almost halfway around the globe from Alaska.

The Tonga Islands earthquake also had been recorded by some foreign stations, Admiral Strauss said, and was "erroneously identified by these stations with the Rainier test."

Admiral Strauss' main point was that the Rainier shot would have been indistinguishable from the earthquakes of moderate size occurring halfway around the world at roughly the same time, had it not been for the advance notice given to the Fairbanks team of seismologists. His contention seemed to be borne out by the reproduction of the seismic signal received at Fairbanks.

Senator Anderson of the Joint Atomic Energy Committee and Admiral Strauss, figures in many past disagreements in the nuclear-policy field, clashed again in those Humphrey Subcommittee hearings over the role of the Atomic Energy Commission's management in the confusion surrounding the report of the Alaska station's detection. The original press release announcing the effectiveness of seismographs in picking up the Rainier shot had omitted the information that the Alaska seismograph had picked up the Rainier shot. The Senators eventually agreed that the AEC had not been engaged in a deliberate attempt to mislead the public by withholding the information. But this point of agreement was not reached before Admiral Strauss and Senator Anderson had another head-on clash. It was a portent of the difficulty Mr. Strauss would have if he sought reappointment to the AEC when his term expired at the end of June, 1958.

Senator Anderson later reported that the Rainier shot had also been detected in Denver, 600 miles away. Dr. Jay Orear of Columbia University told the Humphrey Subcommittee that a station in Pinedale, Wyoming, 520 miles away from the explosion also had detected the Rainier shot.

At another point, Senator Humphrey said nine seismic stations located more than 250 miles from the site of the Rainier explosion had recorded the event "in a manner sufficiently clear" to give an accurate determination of the location of the disturbance in space and time.[46] The recordings of ten other stations were "discernible but rather poor or marginal," he reported.*

Scientists concluded, after their detailed study of the data from the underground Rainier shot, that practically all of the radioactivity as well as the heat from the blast were contained, as they had expected, and in a region with a radius of only 60 feet. The explosion registered on seismographs, but the seismic effects—that is the shaking of the earth—were "negligible." [47]

Fission products were trapped in "highly insoluble fused silica," indicating that the likelihood of contaminating ground water in such an operation would be "zero."

The containment was so effective, and the seismic effects were so small, that the scientists concluded even much larger detonations could be fired safely in many locations. They estimated that what traces of strontium-90 and cesium-137 might escape from the fused, glassy, insoluble material formed in the extreme heat of the explosion would move no more than 100 feet in the twenty-eight-year half-life of strontium-90, or the thirty-year half-life of cesium-137.[48]

Drilling operations after the shot showed that about 500,000 tons of tuff had been crushed to sand and about 200,000 additional tons of broken tuff had been produced—all with the comparatively small 1.7-kiloton explosion.

Heat was held in the area of the detonation for a long time. Temperatures up to 90° C. were found three months after the detonation. Because there was a great amount of water in the porous rock, 15 to 20 per cent by the weight, the earth and rock which had first been heated to 1200° C. to 1500° C. dropped quickly to about 100° C.

It was estimated that nuclear weapons with yields two orders of magnitude greater—100 to 999 times the size of the 1.7-kiloton Rainier blast—could be safely fired at the Nevada test site without untoward seismic effects.

* See page 585 of Notes for Figure 3: Seismic Detection of Rainier.

The rock-crushing process encouraged scientists to suggest that nuclear explosives could be used in mining, to break up ore deposits, for removal or leaching, and to improve oil-extraction techniques.

Dr. Libby told the Senate Disarmament Subcommittee that the Rainier underground shot had established these things:

1. You can fire bombs in a way where the radioactivity does not come out.
2. You can crush an enormous quantity of rock.
3. We have great potentialities in nuclear explosions themselves, the possibilities of making atomic power. . . . If we have a dry mountain, we should be able to maintain the heat at a sufficient concentrated form so that we could pump water down in there and make steam.
4. We know . . . from our experiences already that we can make harbors. [H-bombs in the Pacific blasted out huge cavities in coral islands. These explosions could be placed only in remote areas] for the simple reason that the fallout is so bad that we would not dare do it, though if we used some of our cleaner bombs, the fallout is much reduced.

Continued testing, he suggested, "will allow us to clean up the smaller ones and then we may be able to move earth even in more populous areas. The cost of moving earth by this device, except for the fallout, is pretty low."

Missouri Senator Symington asked what the Rainier underground experiment showed about the difficulties in inspecting a nuclear test ban.

"As far as fallout is concerned, it took us four months to find the fallout from this little bomb when we knew exactly where we fired it," Dr. Libby replied. "Of course, we were scared and we went at it very cautiously . . . but it took us four months to the day, I believe, before we located the egg shell, the broken fragments of the bubble."

Dr. Libby expressed great skepticism about the effectiveness of an inspection system to catch a nation trying to test in secret.

Senator Symington asked him: "Let's take a one-megaton bomb—carefully prepared for cheating, with a great deal of money spent, say, in a deep mine shaft in a place like Siberia? Would you say for sure we could detect that over here, and decipher it, as against it being the result of an earthquake?"

Dr. Libby replied: "I am told it would be extremely difficult."

If a gridwork of stations could be set up worldwide, and if inspectors were given the right to examine any suspicious area, "you would have in theory the possibility of detection," Dr. Libby observed. "But suppose you localize where this thing went off? That area in which we fired this bomb is a pretty big thing, and a certain area might be five miles in diameter. As I say, it does not change the surface. It moved a few rocks, but the sagebrush is still there. If you were not watching at the instant the shot went off, you would not have known there had been a bomb fired under it."

The only way to make sure would be to drill for radioactivity, Dr.

Libby said. "That does not mean it is impossible. What I am saying is, it is very difficult."

Dr. Libby said he was not as pessimistic as Dr. Edward Teller about the possibility of detecting sneak test shots, "but I am pretty pessimistic. It is a pretty tough job." In addition, he pointed out "there will be many doubtful cases even if no one intends to cheat. It is difficult to know what we do if there is an argument."

He was referring here to the "criteria" question. What sort of signals would be required to send inspectors into the field? And what evidence above ground would be taken as sufficient proof of an underground test? An inspection system could argue for days and weeks over these points.

Dr. Libby told the Senators that the United States was well ahead of the Soviet Union in development of nuclear weapons. "Our armament is stronger and is more varied and it is more developed than theirs, by a large. factor." The question about a test ban, he said, is whether the Russians "would abide by it."

At that time Dr. Libby advocated "an intermediate position," under which the testing of nuclear weapons would be limited rather than stopped. Since it is possible to limit drastically the radioactive fallout from tests, "one could think about a type of test limitation rather than a test ban," he said. "And let the test limitation turn on the matter of the radioactive fallout which is introduced into the atmosphere as a result of the test operations." Under this procedure, Dr. Libby suggested, clean bombs would be used for any surface or aboveground shots, and the "so-called dirty bombs" would be exploded underground.

> It is probable that many people are too afraid of the amount of radiation that comes from testing, but nobody likes it, and as far as we know, it does nobody any good. So if testing were limited or there were essentially zero radioactive fallout, this would be an advancement as far as the health of the world is concerned, as far as the hazard from fallout.

Dr. Libby also stated frankly his misgivings about the test-ban idea:

> I think if we have a test ban and they violate it and we don't, they will pass us, and this is what worries me as much as anything else. So the whole thing turns on a matter of inspection, and I certainly feel completely convinced that we have to look at the matter of the suspension of production as being very very important, even though it is much more difficult to control, because the real difficult thing is after you get these bombs made, there is no detecting them.

He warned that "the psychology of banning the discovery of new things is a dangerous road to take, and we have to guard against that."

These views on control of underground testing were to gain importance in 1958, when the world's three nuclear powers really got serious about a test ban.

Chapter 6

1958

President Eisenhower took the fateful step in 1958. After the most intensive test series in United States history, he ordered a one-year moratorium on American nuclear experiments, provided that the Soviet Union also withheld further testing. The period of the moratorium began October 31. It was preceded by a phony yet persuasive Soviet "ban" undertaken unilaterally; by new pressures in the Senate for detaching the nuclear-test issue from the broader nuclear disarmament package; and by the so-called experts' conference which concluded that inspection and control of a nuclear test-ban was feasible, within certain limits never fully understood by the public.

Dr. Linus Pauling, 1954 winner of the Nobel Prize for research in molecular chemistry, filed with the United Nations in January a petition signed by 11,021 scientists from 49 countries urging "an international agreement to stop further testing of nuclear bombs." The Senate Internal Security Subcommittee later reported that 4,000 of the signatures came from Communist-bloc scientists. Dr. Pauling was a frequent supporter of Soviet policies. But the petition did show that large numbers of free-world scientists favored a test-ban and were willing to attach their names to Dr. Pauling's public petition for a separate test ban.

Detaching the nuclear-test-ban idea from the American first-stage disarmament package was still a popular idea in this country and abroad. Governor Harold Stassen, the President's disarmament adviser since 1955, disclosed that he was one of the proponents of this idea soon after he was replaced as chief disarmament negotiator for the United States. (The new man was Ambassador James J. Wadsworth, who had been serving as Deputy United States Representative to the United Nations. His appointment was announced February 27.)

Governor Stassen appeared before the Senate Disarmament Subcommittee, headed by Senator Hubert Humphrey, on February 28.

HUMPHREY SUBCOMMITTEE HEARINGS

The full airing of the pros and cons of the nuclear-disarmament issue which the Humphrey Subcommittee arranged in the first half of 1958 was an important prelude for the momentous events of the last half of the year. Most of the lions in the behind-the-scenes debate about the wisdom of a nuclear test ban appeared in the Subcommittee's arena. The issues were clearly drawn. Unfortunately, however, the public picture of the debate was clouded by considerations of military security. Testimony before the Humphrey Subcommittee was restrained when in open session and, sometimes, completely suppressed after it was given in closed sessions.

For instance, to this day, there has been no report on the testimony of Dr. Herbert Scoville of the Central Intelligence Agency, who appeared before the subcommittee on March 13. Crucial testimony by other witnesses was deleted from the public transcript of other closed sessions on the grounds that it would give important security information to potential enemies. This may have been true, but it also increased the difficulties of the general public in understanding the balances of risk and gain involved.

Because the Humphrey Subcommittee hearings did outline the issues and give the views of the principal personalities in the moulding of American policy, the testimony taken is worth reporting in some detail.

Senator Humphrey himself was already on record in 1957 as favoring the separation of the nuclear-test-ban issue from the other problems of first-stage disarmament, including stoppage of nuclear-weapons production. Senator Symington backed him in the course of the early 1958 hearings.

Stassen's Break

Late in February, 1958, President Eisenhower had told a news conference that detaching the nuclear-test-ban proposal from the rest of his disarmament package would not be supported by the NATO allies. This was a thinly-veiled reference to the position of France, which was then started on its own nuclear-weapons development. The French position, it will be recalled, was that a test ban alone would not be acceptable because it would put France in the inferior position of having to accept the permanent superiority of the three nuclear powers, the United States, Britain, and the Soviet Union. Unless there were an effective cutoff of nuclear-weapons production and a move to reduce stockpiles along with the nuclear test ban, France would not be interested in a test ban. President Eisenhower, at that point, was unwilling to go ahead with a separate nuclear test ban proposal without France's consent.

Governor Stassen made clear in his testimony before the Humphrey Subcommittee on February 28, however, that he disagreed with President Eisenhower's position. He was willing to break the link despite French resistance, apparently in the hope that France eventually would go along. "It would appear from the President's press conference that the President has been informed that NATO allies would not support this first step," Governor Stassen told the Humphrey Subcommittee. "But I believe they would."

He said he felt it "is not essential" that Britain, France, or any other nation except the United States and the Soviet Union agree to quit nuclear testing. The two nuclear giants "are far ahead" in development of nuclear weapons, Governor Stassen said.

He proposed going ahead with a four-point plan for stopping tests, regardless of the views of Britain and France. These were the four points:

1. Establish a United Nations agency to enforce the agreement by inspection and control.

2. Erect eleven or twelve inspection stations inside the Soviet Union and an equal number inside the United States, with suitable equipment to detect any attempts at cheating against the test ban.

3. End all United States and Soviet nuclear testing for two years.

4. Negotiate a follow-up disarmament agreement during the two-year period.

This plan, Governor Stassen said, could be negotiated in six months with all the nations concerned and "could come before the Senate before this session ends." [1]

Red China would eventually have to be brought into the agreement, Mr. Stassen conceded, but "at this moment, if we try to make too big a step at first, we make no step at all. The key step must be taken by the United States and the Soviet Union."

This Stassen willingness to make a deal between the United States and the Soviet Union alone was what had frightened France and Britain the year before in the London Disarmament Subcommittee negotiations. President Eisenhower had made clear at a press conference a few days before that he disagreed with his former disarmament adviser. Mr. Eisenhower told the newsmen:

> We belong to . . . NATO, and some of the nations there are . . . in different states of producing the weapons that require testing . . .
>
> We would have a difficult time, I think, under present laws, to make an agreement with them that would be binding on all of the NATO countries, and certainly we would want it to be so.[2]

Governor Stassen had suggested that the two-power agreement could be consummated at a Summit meeting within five months "if preparations started now." His main emphasis, however, was on separating the nuclear-test issue from the rest of the disarmament package. Keeping the

tie-in between nuclear tests and nuclear production "would make agreement impossible within any conceivable range of years," he testified
before the Humphrey Subcommittee, because it would require an inspection system so thorough that it would take years to establish it.
Meanwhile, he warned, nuclear weapons would be spread around the
world. "This moment in history would be gone."

On the crucial point of inspection, Governor Stassen told the Subcommittee that even the smallest shots underground could be detected
with sensitive seismographs. The source of his optimism has never been
disclosed.

Governor Stassen's testimony was a powerful boost for the advocates
of a nuclear test ban. Here was the man who had been sitting on the
inside for almost three years, listening to the secret debates of the scientists, reaching the same conclusion as those on the outside: A nuclear
test ban was a feasible objective.

Governor Stassen also questioned the validity of two claims by those
who advocated continuing nuclear tests. He denied that a two-year test
suspension would either impair or impede the program for developing
nuclear weapons with reduced radioactive fallout.

> There is no scientist that claims that they are going to have a completely
> clean weapon within two years. They speak of it as something where re-
> search and process in five or six years might prove it out. . . . But going
> on beyond, in the longer-range term, if the scientists in any country de-
> velop a completely clean nuclear explosion, that has peaceful potential to
> move great mountains of earth, to open up harbors, to dig canals, the in-
> ternational tests of such a clean explosion could be included in any future
> treaty under international participation, because then you would want
> that knowledge of a clean explosion to be known by all countries.

He attached only minimal importance to the claim that more testing
was necessary to develop small nuclear weapons for tactical use in local
conflicts. "We already have tactical weapons that are very efficient," the
Governor said.

> It of course is true that continued testing will refine and spread the weapons
> on both sides, but that specifically is a thing that should be reciprocally
> stopped in the interest of the best prospects for peace and opening up on
> both sides, so it is a matter of a restraint for two years on both sides en-
> forced by both sides.

The Senators pressed Governor Stassen repeatedly to say whether he
had recommended separating the nuclear test ban from the rest of the
disarmament package while he was a member of the Eisenhower "team."
Mr. Stassen steadfastly refused to give out this information.

In his last private letter to Secretary of State Dulles before ending his
disarmament tour, Mr. Stassen had made a strong representation for
separating the test-ban out of the package.[3] This move would be the real

test of the Soviet Union's intentions, he argued. At the same time, he noted that the United States was under considerable pressure in the United Nations to show its good faith. United States Ambassador Henry Cabot Lodge sent frequent telegrams to Washington warning of the growing discontent with American policy.

The Supreme Soviet took another dramatic step to encourage United States test-moratorium advocates, on March 31, when it approved a decree abolishing further nuclear tests in the Soviet Union, provided other countries followed suit. The Soviet Union reserved the right to resume tests if other nations did not follow the Soviet lead.

The move had been well advertised—and tested—by Soviet diplomats abroad. Soviet feelers had forecast the move in mid-March.

Premier Khrushchev had hinted obliquely at the idea on March 14 in a speech.

> The level of armaments in certain countries has reached such a stage that the time will come, and perhaps it has come already, when these countries themselves, irrespective of whether or not an agreement on the cessation of production of atomic and hydrogen arms has been reached, will have to say "enough."

The reaction, in advance of the declaration and after, was that it was a theatrical gesture. The Russians had just finished an intensive test series and would not normally have been ready for another set for many months.

The Supreme Soviet's test-ban decree laid heavy stress on the health hazards of tests:

> Today, the overwhelming majority of the earth's population is demanding that the tests should be discontinued. Although the peoples have been striving persistently for many years now to have these tests discontinued, they continue to be held, with the result that more and more new types of lethal nuclear weapons are being created, the concentration of radioactive elements in the air and soil is being increased, the human organism is being poisoned and the normal development of future generations is being threatened.

Parliaments of other states were called on to "do everything necessary to insure that test explosions of these types of weapons are discontinued by those countries also."

There was an escape clause which amounted to a negation of the whole Soviet decree on nuclear-test suspension, in view of the wide advertisement given to American intentions to test further developments of clean and defensive nuclear weapons. It stated:

> If other powers possessing atomic and hydrogen weapons continue tests of these weapons, the Government of the U.S.S.R. will naturally be free to act in the matter of the carrying out of atomic- and hydrogen-weapons tests

by the Soviet Union in accordance with the above-mentioned circumstances, having regard to the interests of its security.

The move was nevertheless an impressive step. The Soviet Union was squarely on record as willing to stop all of its own nuclear tests—all those detectable—if the United States and Great Britain would follow suit.

The State Department was ready with a counteracting announcement the same day the Supreme Soviet acted.[4]

"The Soviet statement comes on the heels of an intensive series of secret Soviet tests," the statement pointed out. While official Soviet propaganda tried to create an image of a peace-loving Soviet government, the Kremlin "openly defies the United Nations with respect to both the substance and the procedure of disarmament." It was noted that the U.N. General Assembly had approved "by an overwhelming vote" the West's comprehensive first-stage disarmament proposal and "called on the nations concerned to begin at once technical studies as to how these proposals might be carried out."

Among the studies needed would be one for supervising the suspension of nuclear testing, the State Department said. "The United States stands ready instantly to respond to that resolution. But the Soviet Union refuses to comply."

The Soviet Union also was boycotting the twenty-five-member Disarmament Commission set up by the U.N. General Assembly, it was pointed out.

"It is elemental," the State Department said, "that free nations which want to remain free will not, and should not, forego their indispensable collective capacity to deter and defend against aggression merely in reliance on a Soviet statement of intentions for which there is no system of verification, which can be evaded in secrecy and altered at will."[5]

On April 4, Khrushchev sent a letter to President Eisenhower giving formal notice of the Supreme Soviet decree and proposing that the United States and the United Kingdom also unilaterally "adopt a decision to renounce further tests." He made no mention, of course, of the intensive series of tests just concluded by the Soviet Union.

Since the Soviet Union had turned down the American proposal for ending nuclear-weapons production and reducing stockpiles, President Eisenhower replied, the United States would continue testing for defensive purposes.

Mr. Eisenhower also renewed his appeal for the Soviet Union to join in technical discussions on control measures for nuclear disarmament. This proposal had repercussions that will be explored later.

It was in this mood of bold Soviet challenge, heavy domestic pressures for a ban, and official American determination not to be stampeded by a phony ban, that the Humphrey Subcommittee conducted its hearings.

Brigadier General Alfred D. Starbird, Director of Military Applications at the Atomic Energy Commission, appeared before the Subcommittee on March 12. The session was secret, but a partial transcript was later published.[6] He presented a view almost diametrically opposed to Governor Stassen's. Testing, he declared, should continue.

The general questions posed by the Humphrey Subcommittee and General Starbird's answers were:

> QUESTION: What are the purposes that American nuclear-weapons tests are expected to serve?
>
> ANSWER: Future weapons tests will be designed to develop warheads for the more advanced weapons-systems, warheads we don't now have and don't know how to make. . . . We have learned in the last four years that we should be able to make small warheads, warheads much, much smaller than we were able to make in the past and can make today. We have learned also that we should be able to make warheads which [deleted][7] have a [deleted] greater explosive value for the weight concerned.

Since the Soviet Sputniks had proved the Russian advances in missiles with thrust enough to carry huge nuclear loads, the United States had been led to

> restudy and redefine the systems which we will use. We now require systems of smaller size, capable of being deployed in areas and with organizations that did not have them before. We require also that these be immediately ready, as we said. Nothing is immediately ready, but we mean then ready in terms of minutes instead of in terms of half-hours or hours or even days.
>
> We require systems that are much more rugged than the past systems. You can imagine that a system, for example, to go on a ballistic missile which must stand the shock of takeoff, the heat and cold of passage, must be entirely different from the type which was carried a few years ago and is now carried in a bomber that is just going through. Now each warhead designed must be tested if we are to rely on it in case of emergency. We can make minor variations on an existing warhead, but we fear making a big variant without running through a test.

General Starbird gave an example from the last American series, which had included some twenty-five shots. Some experiments failed, he said. It would be foolhardy, he implied, to stock American nuclear arsenals with weapons that had not been tested. "The best of brains with these things cannot design them so that they can be positive they will work in an emergency without some form of test."

A test-ban, the General also warned, "would cut off the introduction of many new or substantially improved systems in time into the stockpile, systems the Department of Defense desires."

Another purpose of future tests would be to develop weapons of "greatly reduced fallout." General Starbird acknowledged that scientists saw no way of making a weapon completely "clean" or without residual radioactivity. "Yet it appears entirely possible to reduce the area of fatal radioactivity to approximate the area of fatal blast and burn." In several years of research and test, the AEC was "relatively certain," he asserted, that relatively clean weapons could be produced in a variety of sizes. "It is not going to be a question of jumping right away to an optimum variety of very clean designs. We have to go forward by steps."

General Starbird addressed himself to the argument that in the next war the Soviet Union probably will not use clean weapons—so it makes no sense for the United States to develop clean weapons. Two factors make clean weapons extremely important to the United States, he declared:

> The Soviets could use high-yield, unclean weapons against the United States without undue fallout hurt to them. . . . The same, of course, is not true, would not be entirely true, of the free world in its counterattack. because there are many targets which lie close to our friends, lie close to our forces overseas. We would like very much, then, to have clean weapons in a variety of yields which we could use against those targets and use against them without hurting our friends and our own forces over there.

Furthermore, United States forces were relying more and more on nuclear weapons. For those wars involving United States troops or those brushfire wars near friendly populations, clean tactical weapons would allow the West greater flexibility.

A third purpose for future testing, General Starbird testified, would be to prove advanced weapons *systems* and establish the military and civil effects of such explosions. Air-to-air rockets, for instance, had to be tested to show that the pilot could escape safely in his launching aircraft, and to show that the nuclear rocket itself could be delivered close enough to its target to be effective.

Developing possible peaceful uses of atomic explosions, such as building harbors, canals, crushing rock underground, and so forth, would also require additional testing, the General said.

Democratic Senator Symington of Missouri suggested clean weapons would be important for antimissile defense over the United States and friendly territory. He quoted Dr. Teller as saying that the only effective defense against intercontinental ballistic missiles and intermediate-range ballistic missiles would involve nuclear warheads.

QUESTION: What would be the effect of a weapons-test ban or suspension on development of long-range missiles?

ANSWER: The nuclear test series scheduled to begin at the Eniwetok Proving Ground in April (1958) would include experiments with nuclear warheads for ballistic missiles. The aim of the tests would be to improve the efficiency of the nuclear warheads so that the weights of the warheads could be reduced or the yields increased. Soviet superiority in thrust for missiles made it possible for them to use a warhead of less sophistication yet achieve the same amount of yield on target.

QUESTION: What would be the effect of a nuclear test ban on American defense?

ANSWER: A nuclear air-to-air rocket for air defense was then (in early 1958) being deployed, the General testified. In the American stockpile there were many other types of tactical warheads—but they were of only limited usefulness because of their ungainly weight. Successive testings could greatly improve these tactical warheads and permit the use of lighter systems. The whole system was then too bulky—larger and heavier than desired to meet the dangers of surprise missile attack, the General said.

QUESTION: Were nuclear weapons yet ready for defense in local war?

ANSWER: Crude tactical weapons were already available to the Air Force, Navy, and Army. *But there were no clean tactical weapons.* Several more years of research and testing would be necessary to perfect and produce certain tactical weapons.

General Starbird also informed the Committee it was his "opinion" the United States was ahead of the Soviet Union in development of nuclear weapons. He warned that the United States would lose not only clean weapons but some other new and mysterious development if a test ban were imposed. What he referred to was stricken from the published hearings. He may have referred to the neutron bomb.[8] He argued that the United States, which would never be an aggressor, had need for more sophisticated weapons in a defense system while the Soviet Union needed only to develop an attacking system, in which clean weaponry would play less of a role. The attacking force must assume, he said, that its attack would be successful in destroying a large portion of counter-attack capability before it reached the Soviet Union. The attacker thus would have far less need for clean defensive weapons.

Senator Symington sharply challenged General Starbird's claim that the United States is ahead of the Soviet Union in nuclear-weapons development.

> The Sputnik was a great shock to the American people, because it blasted the basis of our defense planning, namely, that we could afford to pass over quantitative superiority to the Soviets because we had qualitative supremacy. We now know that is not true. When you say that you believe we are ahead of the Soviets in this field, therefore, I question that. When Defense came up for money for the satellite last August, they said that "we know we are ahead in satellites and we want this money"—that was only six months ago—"because we want to be sure to stay ahead."

Senator Symington further observed that a month after the Defense Department claimed the United States was ahead in missile development, the Soviet Union launched its first sputnik. If the Pentagon was not prepared for sputnik, it was logical to assume it might not be prepared for Soviet supremacy in nuclear weapons.

Senator Humphrey pressed publicly during the hearings for a separation of the nuclear test ban from the cutoff of nuclear-weapons production, the twinned items in previous American disarmament policy.

If either one of them could be negotiated, it would be a beginning toward a more secure inspection system and have a tendency to lead to the negotiation of the other. . . . If we could [get] . . . the test ban with inspection, you could have a setup of inspection machinery which would require some mobility and some freedom of access. . . . I believe that the main thing is to get hold of this inspection. One of the main reasons for pressing for a suspension of the bomb tests is to see whether or not the Soviet Union will ever accept a group of inspectors who have the right to monitor tests and to ascertain what is going on.

It seems to me that has political significance far greater than even a year or two years agreement on bomb-testing suspension, or even a cutoff of nuclear-materials production. I think essentially the problem with the Soviet Union is not a problem of science but a problem of politics.[9]

This pursuit of an additional intelligence base inside the Soviet Union, which the United States intelligence community sought so avidly and Moscow resisted so stoutly, was revealed eventually to be little more than an attractive mirage, because the Soviet Union made it clear that it would not permit any roaming, even moderate probing, by the inspection teams.

Dr. Harrison Brown, Professor of Geochemistry at the California Institute of Technology, told the Humphrey Subcommittee in the same series of hearings that the dangers of the spread of nuclear weapons to other countries constituted one of the main incentives for a nuclear test ban. "Today there are three nations which possess nuclear-military capabilities and a fourth will emerge shortly," he said. "It would not surprise me if fifteen nations were to possess these capabilities in another twenty-five years. In fifty years, the number may well be thirty."

As the capabilities spread, the difficulties of achieving control are multiplied many fold, he said.

"If New York, for example, were destroyed today, we would be quite sure that it was either an accident or the result of Soviet action and we would act accordingly," Dr. Brown observed. "But if New York were destroyed fifteen years from now, it might be literally impossible to determine the identity of the aggressor."

Both the United States and the Soviet Union had an interest in slowing down the rate of spread in nuclear technology, he said, and "one of the more effective approaches to this" would be a world-wide moratorium on the testing of nuclear devices.

Dr. Brown proposed a test ban that would be inspectable, but at the same time he conceded that tests below the level of notice should be permitted to continue.

Given a network of detection stations spaced at intervals of 1,000 miles "there would be a minimum cutoff, depending upon the nature of the land, below which in energy you would not be able to detect the test," Dr. Brown said. "Tests in that area should be quite permissible. If you are able, by some ingenious invention, to test some other kind of nuclear explosion of a higher energy, I would be perfectly in favor of permitting that, provided it is not detected by the detection system, for the very simple reason that there is little point in having a ban on something where you have no control over the ban."

Dr. Brown thus foresaw the possibility of decoupling the energy of an explosion from the surrounding earth. Decoupling techniques were later to become a major factor in the nuclear test-ban problem.

The threshold concept advanced by Dr. Brown was later to be adopted by President Eisenhower in the test-ban negotiations with the Soviet Union.

It was then Dr. Brown's theory that underground nuclear explosions high in the kiloton range produce visibly different wave patterns on the seismograph and could be easily distinguished from earthquakes. However, smaller nuclear explosions, on the order of one kiloton, would be "particularly difficult" to differentiate from earthquakes at long distances, he said.

He estimated there would be about 1,000 earthquakes a year worldwide that would need on-the-spot investigation. Dr. Brown said his threshold theory would have the effect of decreeing that "all tests that cannot be detected are legal. In other words, we legalize the bootlegging of tests."

The result, he conceded, would be that scientists in Livermore, Los Alamos, and other American weapons laboratories "would continue to be working, I believe, in order to find out how this network could be circumvented."

Dr. Brown suggested there be three classes of nuclear tests: the unconditionally forbidden, the unconditionally permitted, and an in-between area where the firing power could announce in advance that it was going to explode a bomb of a certain size.[10]

Dr. Brown also spoke against linking the nuclear test ban with nuclear-weapons-production cutoff. "I would avoid linking a proposal such as this with any other which would either decrease the chances of securing agreement or which would greatly increase the technological complexities," he declared.

Under Dr. Brown's plan, ten inspection stations would be installed in the Soviet Union, ten in North America. Governor Stassen had suggested eleven or twelve stations in the Soviet Union. Dr. Jay Orear, a Columbia University physicist, suggested twenty-two.

In the initial stages of an agreement it would not be "absolutely necessary" to have stations in Communist China, Dr. Brown said, but "in the long run, I think it is absolutely clear that, if we are going to make real progress in this area, China must be a part of the over-all network and control system."

Tests could be hidden in Communist China if there were no inspection stations on its territory, he believed.

Seeking a nuclear test ban is a "balancing of two risks," Dr. Brown told the Subcommittee. "No matter what decision you make, there is an element of risk in it. I am convinced, myself, as I have said, that the risks involved in stopping testing in a controlled manner, such as I have outlined, are very small compared with the risks of pursuing the status quo."

"And, of course, specifically, that is the basic big difference between your thinking and that of Dr. Teller?" Senator Symington asked.

"That is it; yes," Dr. Brown replied.[11]

By spring, it had become apparent that the American scientific community was split on the fundamental question: Could a nuclear test ban be effectively inspected and controlled?

In mid-April, the Humphrey Subcommittee brought before it the principal protagonists in this behind-the-scenes debate of the scientists.

Dr. Edward Teller, then Director of the University of California Radiation Laboratory in Livermore, California, appeared in open session on April 16. He was widely regarded as the leading foe of the nuclear test ban among the nation's most eminent scientists. He made these points:

The art of detecting tests was then already several years old, but the art of hiding tests was only a few months old. "Therefore, our knowledge of hiding tests is deficient. Even so, even matching this deficient knowledge against a well-worked-out system of detection, we already see strong possibilities, effective possibilities of hiding tests."

There was general agreement, even among the disputing scientists, Dr. Teller said, that small tests could be hidden, big tests could not.

What can be accomplished by the small tests which all scientists agree can be hidden?

First, small tests were "important in themselves," Dr. Teller testified, "because the weapons they test can perform exceedingly important roles in many military situations."

Second, "by making small tests, one can learn a very great deal about big explosions. With the help of small tests, one can improve one's big weapons." While big tests might still be necessary, the possibility that one party to an agreement might test small explosions in secret would offer the violator "a great advantage not only in the field of small weapons but in the field of the big weapons as well."

Third, small tests could be used to advance the art of hiding bigger explosions.

Dr. Teller explained that hiding small explosions need not mean that they must be kept from notice. Conducting explosions underground, where no radioactivity escapes, produces an earthquake signal. The question for one intending to hide a test would be how to make the signal from a nuclear explosion small enough and similar enough to an earthquake signal to keep it from special notice.

In a discussion on the hiding of small nuclear explosions, Dr. Teller said:

> Our knowledge is very poor. What an earthquake is, what is the cause, what is the starting point of an earthquake, slipping of layers, or whatever, is not known in detail. What a nuclear explosion underground will do, we know from one and only one shot [Rainier], and a smaller shot at that.
>
> If we had not performed this one shot, we would compare the known facts about earthquakes with a complete vacuum of knowledge. Now, we are extrapolating from a single event which we know well. This is an extremely dangerous situation.
>
> We need lots more information upon this subject. If we go into a test moratorium, with deficient knowledge, and if thereupon we do not continue to test, but the Russians experiment with small nuclear explosions which we know can be hidden, then by their experimentation, they may find out a great deal. I think they will find out more and more and clearer and clearer methods how to make these explosions disappear among the many earthquakes which occur spontaneously. A great deal can be done by hiding tests in this manner, because it is a scientific question that as yet has been hardly attacked at all.

There are many other methods for trying to hide tests, Dr. Teller warned.

> It would be a mistake to think underground tests are the only means of evasion. It is wrong to think that a net of seismic stations in the Soviet Union will make us safe. There are all kinds of other ways how a test moratorium could be circumvented. I would not like to go into this question because the subject is infinite. I should just like to assure you that the thinking along these lines has just started.

One reliable method of checking on a test moratorium, Dr. Teller said, would be sending inspection personnel into Russia in large numbers, with the right to go any place, talk to anybody without any reprisals taken against the Russians who speak with inspectors. If there is a real possibility of opening the Soviet Union to that extent, Dr. Teller said, "I am all for exploring it." He indicated that he personally did not have confidence that the Soviet Union was ready to open up to that extent.

Dr. Teller suggested an alternative approach to the test-ban problem. It was possible to reach an inspection agreement, he said, providing that future tests be held only underground, so that no radioactivity would be released. "Such an agreement would have the advantage that it could be enforced. Radioactivity released into the atmosphere can be noticed easily. Therefore, one can indeed see if no radioactivity or no substantial radioactivity is released."

While the danger of radioactive fallout has been "very, very greatly exaggerated," he added, fallout would no longer continue to increase under such a partial test ban.

Testing could be transferred underground without endangering the United States' national security, Dr. Teller estimated. There would be disadvantages, he acknowledged. Peaceful applications of nuclear explosions would be restricted and defensive measures like development of the anti-ICBM would be held back.

Another possible alternative agreement, Dr. Teller said, would be to restrict rather than stop atmospheric testing in a way that would limit fallout to a small fraction of the present levels. Under this plan, clean or small weapons would be tested in the atmosphere, the large and dirtier ones underground. Big explosions could then be conducted aboveground, provided the radioactivity they produced was not excessive. International teams could be set up to monitor the big explosions aboveground.

He warned that whereas the situation in 1958 was that large underground explosions could be detected while smaller ones could not, "future research is likely to push up the limit, in the sense that more and more explosions can be hidden as we find out more and more about this matter." Less than two years later this prophecy had been fulfilled.

Dr. Teller also warned the Subcommittee about the difficulties of on-site inspection teams proving a nuclear explosion had taken place underground.

They would have to go on the spot, look around, find where the hole had been dug originally. Surface effects from the explosion would not exist. The holes could be camouflaged very easily. "I think that inspection teams would have an extremely difficult job," he told the Senators.

The only way to check would be to bore in and find the radioactivity. In our own shot where we knew precisely where we had set it off, it took us a long time to find it. The seismographic determination of the position is not very accurate. To try to bore and find the radioactivity would be a practically hopeless procedure. I think that it is only the very big shots where you could spend a whole lot of time and research and exploration. If you would have to do that, let's say, once a year, it might be possible to resolve any doubts. But it seems to me that these inspection teams would have an exceedingly difficult time.

Dr. Teller recalled that it took four months to find the pocket of radioactivity made by the Rainier shot the year before, even though it was known where the explosion had taken place. "Our main aim was not to hurry, and if we had hurried, we could have done it faster," he told the Senators, "but we also knew where it was."

He suggested one other way of hiding nuclear explosions. The Soviet Union might carry a nuclear weapon on a submarine, explode it and blame it on the United States. "The Russians, who succeeded in convincing many people that we used germ warfare, might get away with a stunt like this," Dr. Teller observed. He declined to give further examples of methods of hiding nuclear tests because "I don't feel like saying openly how one can cheat before sitting down to a poker game."

Dr. Teller emphasized that

> the question is not to detect. The question is to discriminate this particular thing from earthquakes. Now, of this size [1.7 kilotons], there are very, very many earthquakes, and to go in and check on them, mainly on those of the earthquakes which look like a nuclear test, would be such an enormous effort that I would like to say that it is not practical. . . . I am not saying that it would not be practical for the 1.7 kilotons. I am saying that the fact that it has been detected does not say anything yet. You see, I am not saying that the line will lie below 1.7 kilotons or above 1.7 kilotons. I am merely saying that the statement that this thing has been discovered 2,300 miles away [the Rainier shot] is not the relevant statement. The relevant statement which any seismologist can tell you, is that the detection at 2,300 miles did not tell you whether it was an earthquake or whether it was a nuclear explosion.

The Humphrey Subcommittee also heard testimony of Dr. Jay Orear, member of a Columbia University task force that had studied the inspection problems involved in a nuclear test ban. He reported that a seismic system could pinpoint the location of a suspicious underground event "to within about a mile" and added:

> We would have no problem of telling that it wasn't an earthquake, once we were there, because the Atomic Energy Commission reports that that particular mountain [in which Rainier was fired] suddenly lifted itself six inches and we have seen movies . . . of how all of the rocks were disturbed. It would just be a simple problem of observation by a geologist to tell that there was an underground explosion and not an earthquake. It would be a matter of a day to locate this.

Dr. Orear also testified that inside the Soviet Union there are about 100 earthquakes per year of the power of Rainier (1.7 kilotons) or greater.

His testimony conflicted sharply with other material laid before the Humphrey Subcommittee and the Senators frankly expressed their confusion. Dr. Orear was later found to be highly optimistic on at least two points: the accuracy with which an underground explosion could be located by seismic stations; and the number of earthquakes in the Soviet Union of power equivalent to 1.7 kilotons or larger.

Dr. Orear also emphasized that nuclear weapons were so easily transportable that "the main delivery system of these smaller nations, and perhaps of all nations, will be what we call the suitcase." He did not mean the suitcase in the literal sense, he explained, but referred to the ease with which the bombs could be hand-carried across borders.

The bombs can be smuggled into a country. According to our studies, it is a simple technical problem to smuggle megaton bombs into the United States, and to plant them around in various cities, and I would predict that within a few years every major American city will contain hidden H-bombs. If I, and I am using quotation marks about "I," were in charge of Soviet espionage, the bombs would already be here.

Suppose five or ten years from now thirty nations have nuclear bombs, and suppose one of these megaton bombs should go off here in Washington, leaving us with no Administration or Pentagon. I wonder if you, Senator, have thought this out and decided just what should be our policy, just what should be done.

We might not even know with whom to retaliate. Thus our government's great hope of security, massive retaliation, is fading away, and will become meaningless and useless in a few more years.

He reported that the Columbia Inspection Committee had conjectured that an enemy might introduce a small number of espionage agents into the United States, smaller than the number of bombs that were to be planted secretly in major cities.

These agents can buy houses in various cities, and they can hide away these bombs in these houses. Then, if they wanted to completely destroy the United States, it would take really just one man going around from one city to another pushing the button. The button actuates a time-delay mechanism, gives him time to get out of the city and fly to the next city.

To the author's knowledge, no one has denied the possibility that this atomic-age nightmare could—or already has—come to pass.

Dr. Hans Bethe, Professor of Physics, Cornell University, was regarded as the principal advocate of a nuclear test ban in the scientific community and the leading defender of the inspection system. He appeared before the Humphrey Subcommittee the day after Dr. Teller's exposition of misgivings about test-ban inspection.

Underground explosions, Dr. Bethe conceded,

are a very difficult thing to detect and identify because the normal methods of detection, acoustic, electromagnetic, and radioactive, do not work at all. . . . The seismic signal is not very well known because we have had only one single underground explosion, the so-called Rainier shot of the last Nevada series, and from one example it is awfully difficult to make any conclusions on the next in other surroundings and with other yields of the nuclear weapon.

Dr. Bethe told the Senators that the seven Far West stations that had picked up the Rainier nuclear explosion could have identified it as an explosion, rather than an earthquake, even if there had been no advance notification. He explained the theory of differentiating between earthquakes and nuclear explosions by seismographs in this way:

The pressure wave which arrives [at the seismograph station] has a first impulse which corresponds to a compression of the earth, whereas if you have earthquakes, then the pressure wave, the initial pressure wave, sometimes corresponds to a compression and sometimes corresponds to an expansion of the earth. . . . If you have an earthquake, then the normal thing is that in two quadrants you get an expansion of the earth, so that if you surround the site of the earthquake on four sides by stations, then from an earthquake you will get a compression record in two directions and an expansion record in two other directions, whereas if you have an underground explosion, you will get a compression record in all four directions. This is the basis of the suggestion [deleted] for a system of seismic stations in the Soviet Union to detect tests.

The Subcommittee spent considerable time with Dr. Bethe, studying the possibilities of long-range detection of underground explosions. On March 25, 1958, there had been an underground disturbance in the Soviet Union's Ural Mountains, about 5,000 miles away. Dr. Bethe reported that the disturbance had been detected by seismographs. The data was not sufficient to judge whether the underground disturbance had been an explosion or an earthquake. But there was a strong suspicion that it was an explosion because no earthquake had occurred in that area for forty years.

Dr. Bethe made this case for an inspection network to control underground cheating on a test-ban agreement:

It is true and will remain true that we can never be 100 per cent sure from the seismic record alone that an underground explosion had taken place, and this is certainly true particularly if the test explosion were set off in a seismic region. If the Russians were to test in the Kamchatka Peninsula, or in the foothills of the Himalayas, where there are hundreds of earthquakes every year, then it would be far more difficult to tell these earthquakes from underground explosions. On the other hand, one distinguishing feature of underground explosions [deleted] is the distinguishing feature of the first signal, whether it is compression or expansion [deleted].

An individual seismic station can never tell whether there is an earthquake or an explosion from its record. . . . However, an inspection system could put a complex of stations around each possible explosion site. Thus, when you look at the signals from the entire system and find that all of them have a compressional first motion, then you would strongly suspect an explosion, and this way we could eliminate most of the earthquake signals.

Now there will still be a significant number of signals, even with this first compressional wave identification, that will be sufficiently doubtful that we will have to send inspection teams [deleted].

Let me explain just a moment what I mean by "doubtful." Earthquakes are never reasonable. They produce strange patterns of compression and rarefactions around them. It is not a clean-cut quadrant where these are all positive and these are all negative. You will find in your positive quadrants where you will have three or four out of perhaps fifteen that will be negative, and you start to worry why they were negative. Therefore, in the Rainier case, which Senator Hickenlooper mentioned, there were something in the order of eight or ten stations, I believe, I don't recall the exact number, within about 250 miles. There was one station out of step in that region.

Looking at that close-in Rainier data, you would strongly suspect that it was an explosion since, let's say, nine out of ten of the stations were compressional. But that one station would still worry you somewhat, and you would not know but what if you had had a better distribution of stations around Rainier you might have picked up a few negatives. You would strongly suspect it enough so that you would report to your headquarters, your inspection headquarters, something suspicious had occurred, and you would certainly want to investigate that spot for further confirmation.

The seismic system can never give you 100 per cent proof; but with the system involving stations relatively close in, I believe that we could eliminate a substantial majority, bring it down to a reasonable size, and inspection teams could then follow up on the questionable items.

The method of distinguishing between earthquakes and blasts from an analysis of the direction of the initial earth-motion depends on the hypothesis that earthquakes are caused by faulting, the slipping of two layers past each other. If this hypothesis is correct, earthquakes will radiate initial compressions in some directions and rarefactions in other directions. An explosion, on the other hand, will radiate initial compressions in all directions. This method of identification is not foolproof, however, for the following reasons.

First, Sutton and Berg of Columbia University have shown in a recent publication that earthquake-faulting may occur under circumstances where the rarefactions are not observable except at very small distances—of the order of 100 miles—and they conclude that the resulting earth movement may be compressional in all directions as expected from an explosion.

Second, there is also some doubt that all earthquakes are caused by faulting. Many Japanese seismologists feel that other mechanisms may be involved as well. John Hodgson of the Dominion Observatory of Canada has published a review of the results from many earthquake studies. He found that, while a high percentage of large earthquakes can be explained as being caused by faulting, it frequently happens that this explanation does not seem to be adequate.

Dr. Bethe insisted that seismic stations for detecting underground tests would have to be set up in both the Soviet Union and Red China for "a good detection capability."

He explained that detonation of the Rainier nuclear test in volcanic tuff acted somewhat as an insulation against transmission of the shock to the surrounding seismographs. Volcanic tuff is a relatively porous material which reduced the amount of energy transmitted to the earth from what the energy transfer would have been had the test been detonated in solid rock. He assumed that anyone seeking to hide an underground test would use similar insulation.

One of the problems in judging underground nuclear explosions is to translate the seismic signal into kilotons of yield. In the case of the Rainier shot, seismologists had first estimated that the magnitude of the 1.7-kiloton shot had been 4.6 on the scale universally accepted by seismologists.[12] Later, however, refined data placed the magnitude at 4.25. The medium in which the bomb was exploded would be an important factor in the magnitude of the seismic signal, of course, as Dr. Bethe pointed out. A certain uniformity in theorizing on signal size was achieved by adopting the assumption that all underground tests would be detonated in volcanic tuff such as that in the Nevada mesa where the Rainier explosion was conducted.

Seismologists then estimated the frequency of earthquakes in the Soviet Union and China of magnitudes equivalent to those produced by underground explosions of given yields. The only points of reference available were the one nuclear shot, the 1.7-kiloton Rainier shot, and the quarry blasts of TNT using 0.2 kiloton to 8 kilotons. Dr. Bethe gave these early-1958 estimates on the number and magnitudes of earthquakes in the Soviet Union and China each year:

Earthquake magnitude	Equivalent explosion (in kilotons)	Earthquakes of greater power (per year)
3.9	1	2,500
3.9–4.9	1– 5	2,150
4.9–5.3	5–10	210
5.3–6.2	10–50	120
6.2+	50+	20

Dr. Bethe explained that the estimates of the number of earthquakes of given magnitude were "rather crude," and observations of several underground nuclear explosions of various sizes would be necessary to confirm these estimates.

Nevertheless, he pointed out, it was quite certain that over 1,000 earthquakes per year in the Soviet Union and China would produce seismic signals larger than those from an explosion of the Rainier size.[13] Only a fraction of these would have to be investigated by ground teams, Dr. Bethe said, because some could be definitely identified as earthquakes from seismic evidence alone.

Dr. Bethe said further that it was not known whether rock formations other than volcanic tuff, would produce even smaller seismic signals for a given yield. He noted that Dr. Teller had used this uncertainty as an argument against a test ban. "If we have a test-cessation agreement," Dr. Bethe said, "then the inspecting agency probably should conduct experiments, further experiments, on the seismic signals which are obtainable from explosions of various sizes and various surroundings."

Dr. Teller and a number of other people who are very strongly against test cessation will argue that a country which is insistent on violation of a test agreement can defeat the inspection system by conducting underground tests in surroundings where you get a very small seismic signal.

My personal opinion is that this will be true only to a very limited extent, and if a country is intent on defeating a test-cessation agreement and violating it, then it will have to conduct a lot of experiments underground with low-yield weapons to find out whether seismic signals from these are detectable.

It is my opinion that this would be a very dangerous game for them to play and that somewhere on creeping up on the yield they would be detected.

It is Dr. Teller's opinion that they might get away with it, and this is simply a difference of opinion. Neither of us, I think, has a very firm basis for it. I am convinced that somewhere there would be a slip and the inspection system would detect the test if such a series were conducted, let's say by the Soviet Union.

Seismic signals from suspected explosions would "pinpoint" the site, Dr. Bethe said, and in most seismic areas, which are trackless, inspection teams could hunt for evidences of unusual activity. Dr. Bethe had no comment on the apprehensions of Senators Hickenlooper and Symington, that a country bent on violation might go to great lengths to camouflage its test activity.[14]

Senator Hickenlooper suggested that a cheating nation might use helicopters to approach the aboveground test site, to avoid making tracks with trucks and other vehicles. Dr. Bethe indicated, however, that he believed helicopters would also leave traces of their activity. "Quite heavy equipment" would have to be transferred to the test site, Dr. Bethe suggested, and persons working there "have at least to walk over the ground," he said. It would be important, however, to have complete and immediate access for an inspection team to any suspected area, Dr. Bethe said.

The Soviet Union's representatives are "past masters at this foot-dragging business," and might forestall immediate access, Senator Humphrey warned. Dr. Bethe responded that "whatever inspection agreement, if such an agreement were negotiated, would have to imply immediate access without further negotiations and the team would have to have the right to go to the spot, to the suspected spot right away when a seismic signal is found," [15]

(This was one of the key points on which the Soviet Union had not yielded five years later. In every formula proposed, the Soviet Union insisted on having enough control of the situation so that the classic "foot-dragging" would still be possible.)

Dr. Bethe made it clear that his principal reason for advocating an end to testing was his belief that the United States was considerably ahead of the Soviet Union. "I feel that if testing continues, then they will surely attain the same level of capability as we, and I feel that it is just a matter of simple logic that for the relative standing it is more advantageous to stop when you know that you are still ahead."

If the Soviet Union did not respect the test ban while the United States did, Dr. Bethe conceded that the Russians "would certainly catch up and overtake us." But he added that there could be no substantial improvement in their capability "without a tremendous risk of being detected."

Dr. Bethe did not explain why he thought the Soviet Union would be so eager for a test ban if it considered itself to be behind the United States in nuclear-test development.

He joined Governor Stassen, Senator Symington, and Senator Humphrey in advocating a break in the link between nuclear-test suspension and a cutoff of nuclear-weapons production.[16]

Senator Humphrey indicated again that one of his main aims was to probe the Soviet Union to see if it really intended to permit an effective international inspection system.

> I am quite convinced in my own mind that they are going to do a lot of foot-dragging, that it is going to be very difficult. But we will never find out what they are talking about, and will never really be able to give them the political litmus-paper test until we try it. They keep talking about international inspection, but the last experience we had on that was Korea, and that was anything but a heartening one.[17]

Dr. Bethe came out strongly in his Subcommittee testimony against the idea of permitting underground tests while banning others, as Dr. Harrison Brown had suggested. Dr. Bethe considered this "very dangerous" because it would not stop the development of new nuclear weapons.

Strauss Testimony

The Chairman of the AEC, Admiral Lewis L. Strauss, appeared before the Humphrey Subcommittee on April 17.

He was already well known as the leading advocate within the President's official family for continuing nuclear tests. He lived up to his reputation. He made these points:

With nuclear-weapon design in a transition from warheads delivered by large aircraft to those delivered by rockets, the United States should not rely on obsolete or obsolescent weapons systems. New systems must be "light, rugged, and instantly ready." With the Soviet capability of mounting a heavy attack on the United States, the United States had to

be sure that aggression could be deterred by assurance of effective retaliation or blunted if deterrents failed. He acknowledged that "substantial strides" had been made in developing weapons systems necessary
in the modern missile age, but further development and test was required for some warheads, "particularly those of extremely severe design
characteristics," Mr. Strauss said.

"This is particularly true with regard to weapons of greatly reduced
radioactive fallout," Mr. Strauss declared, as General Starbird had before
him. "In the interest of civil populations, we are convinced that such
weapons are a necessity in all types for both strategic and tactical use.
We know now how to make certain of the designs we need, but by no
means all. As I have indicated, it will require more development and
more tests before we will have this comprehensive arsenal."

In the face of Humphrey-Symington opposition, Mr. Strauss defended
the linkage of the nuclear test ban with the American demand for a cutoff of nuclear-weapons production. Ending tests would not reduce existing armaments, he said, it would only interrupt the development of
defense systems "which we know can be developed in time and which
we need." A test cessation would not "curtail the improvement of an
aggressor's delivery system," Mr. Strauss observed. "A future aggressor
can go right ahead perfecting the missile on which the warhead rides
and the reliability of guidance of this device."

Thus the aggressor could perfect his attacking weapons while the
defense development would be frozen, Admiral Strauss warned.

Mr. Strauss expressed grave doubts, too, on the ability of any inspection system to catch violations of a test ban. Even if the right of immediate access to a suspected area were given, "there will be no assurance
that all nuclear detonations can be identified as such," he testified. "It is
my understanding that even with a very elaborate inspection system including the right to visit suspected underground explosion sites, there
still remains a real possibility that successful clandestine tests sufficiently
large in yield to contribute materially to a weapons-development program
could be carried out by a determined violator."

The Admiral also warned that proving a violation would be "most difficult if not impossible" if the nation tested in an area where proper
detection had not been installed. He obviously referred to the possibility
that the Soviet Union might test in Communist China.

> The emphasis on the cessation of testing is a great mistake, or rather a very
> spurious argument from the point of view of its effect on disarmament or
> the security of the world. The real danger to the human race is not the
> continuance of weapons tests. The real danger to the human race is a
> nuclear war. . . . Since we are a defendant nation and cast in the role
> by the fact that we are a democracy and are not aggressors, it would be a
> tragic mistake in my opinion to cease the development of our defenses
> unless the whole threat of a surprise attack with atomic weapons were

canceled at the same time. Now this is a personal point of view, I hold it very strongly, about as strongly as any opinion that I have.

The Chairman conceded that the United States had more weapons and more efficient weapons than the Soviet Union. But it would be a great mistake, he warned, to assume that these two points of superiority alone meant that the United States could win a war with the Soviet Union, or prevent a very devastating attack.

Irrational attacks on superior forces have been made in the past, Mr. Strauss recalled, evidently having in mind the Japanese attack on Pearl Harbor. In the nuclear age, he said, "we must be prepared to protect our people from the consequences of so ill-advised an attack by an aggressor, if we can, by destroying his weapons before the impact on our cities."

The AEC Commissioner stated his reasons for opposing a separate test ban in these words:

> My belief is that a cessation of testing alone will result in an improvement of the aggressor's system and a freezing of the defender's system. An effective monitoring system to safeguard the United States interests could not be set up. I believe it would be possible to continue development with quite small weapons. I believe it will be possible for a determined violator to conduct tests in some quarter where there is no inspection net, and then it would be impossible, even when they were detected, to identify the violator.

He cited this hypothetical instance: "Suppose a submarine were to test an atomic weapon, let's say, off Cape Canaveral or off Eniwetok. I don't know how anyone could convince beyond a doubt the people of the world that that weapon had been tested by country X or Y or Z. This bothers me."

Admiral Strauss said he thought an effective monitoring system could be set up for a cutoff of nuclear-weapons production but a system to control a test-ban inspection system could not be.

"I believe that a determined violator could continue a program of testing quite small weapons without sure detection." The test-ban, he added, "would be more advantageous to the Russians" than to the United States.

Then Senator Humphrey asked how Mr. Strauss could support the total first-stage package of disarmament as presented by the Administration but find one or two items inside the package "very undesirable."

"I think the cessation of the development of our defense system would be the most important concession we would make," Mr. Strauss replied, "and to make it the first concession before anything else [as in the case of the nuclear test ban] were done would be a piece of very poor trading, from my point of view."

He could accept the full package but not the test ban alone, he explained, because the Soviet Union would then be required to pay a price for the freezing of the United States defensive development. That price would be a true beginning in nuclear disarmament.

Senator Hickenlooper of Iowa inquired what the United States would do in case a violation were discovered after a test ban went into effect. What would be the punishment for the violator?

> The only thing that has occurred to me [the Chairman responded], . . . is that we would resume our testing, but that does pose this difficulty, Senator Hickenlooper. Our laboratories would suffer. One does not know to what extent they would suffer during a period of test suspension. The Russian laboratories conceivably would remain intact, that is to say, the people who worked in those laboratories work by direction and they would be restrained to those laboratories. They certainly could not leave of their own volition, as we understand things to obtain in Russia. Our good men might feel that they would still like to work on defense projects, but there would be other projects active, and our weapons project would be suspended, and I think the laboratories would be likely to lose many good men whom we could not afford to spare, and therefore there would be a lapse of time after we wished to resume testing before the full speed could be resumed. Perhaps a year or two would be lost.

In his last days as AEC Chairman, Admiral Strauss used two other arguments against the nuclear test ban in his private meetings inside the Administration and with the President. The test-ban treaty would lead to public complacency, a belief that the need for a large defense effort was passing. Defense budgets would be harder to come by on Capitol Hill.

Also, the United States would be prevented from periodic checks of its weapons stockpile, to make sure that the bombs in it were ready for immediate use. Admiral Strauss had vivid memories of the Navy bouncing dud torpedoes off the hulls of Japanese ships at the beginning of World War II. The duds had been in the stockpile between World War I and World War II, and none of them had been test-fired.

Atomic weapons were far more complex than the old World War I torpedoes, the Admiral knew, and frequent spot checks on the effectiveness of the stockpile would be important.

Senator Humphrey's Subcommittee continued to study the problem of inspecting a nuclear test ban throughout the spring. One of the most helpful contributions to the public understanding of the problem could have been its poll of thirty-one eminent seismologists in the United States, if the poll had attracted any attention. Unfortunately it attracted very little.

The seismologists were asked to judge the risk that some country might attempt to violate a test ban by conducting experiments in secret. Senator Humphrey published optimistic conclusions on the basis of his analysis of the seismologists' reports combined with other testimony his Subcommittee heard. Others might not have been so optimistic. As it happened, the Senator's thinking coincided closely with official conclusions that were being arrived at about the same time by some experts within the Administration. Their point of view predominated and buried the misgivings of the seismologists.

These were Senator Humphrey's conclusions, not necessarily supported by others who looked at the raw data which the Senate Subcommittee provided much later for public study:

1. An inspection system to monitor suspension of nuclear-weapons tests could have a 90 per cent capability. This means that virtually 90 per cent of the significant earthquakes would be identified correctly. Furthermore, if an unauthorized nuclear weapon, i.e., one kiloton or higher, were tested underground there would be a 90 per cent chance that suspicious evidence would be recorded on scientific instruments, which in turn would call for investigation.

However, this capability could be increased through additional research and through the use of the best possible equipment stationed and operated throughout many parts of the world. An increase in the capability might also be achieved through the use of mobile inspection teams which would be permitted to investigate areas where the records of seismographs and other detection instruments were ambiguous as to whether an earthquake had occurred or a nuclear explosion had been detonated.

2. Seismographic stations manned by international inspection personnel would need to be placed at many points in the Soviet Union and surrounding areas. Such stations also have to be located in the United States and throughout the United States and British testing grounds in the Pacific, and in certain other areas.

3. There would need to be a central agency to which the seismographic records could be sent for analysis. This agency should be operated under the auspicies of the United Nations.

4. The number of seismograph stations to be placed in the Soviet Union, the United States, and elsewhere would appear to depend on (a) their location [more should be placed in areas where earthquakes occur than in nonseismic areas]; (b) the extent to which existing stations including those of the Soviet Union could be utilized; (c) how many stations of good quality could be utilized or set up in areas where tests might take place; (d) to what extent mobile inspection teams will have authority to visit areas in which ambiguous earth movements take place [this refers primarily to the ability of seismologists to distinguish correctly between earthquakes and explosions]; and (e) whether all nations will permit observers at the site of large chemical explosions [no reliable way has yet been found to differentiate between underground chemical and nuclear explosions]. The number of stations as well as other characteristics of the inspection system would also depend on whether all nuclear-weapons tests were suspended, as opposed to a limitation on certain sizes of tests, and finally, whether 90 per cent assurance is essential as opposed to a 60, 70, or 80 per cent assurance that the agreement to suspend tests cannot be violated secretly.

5. An agreement to suspend tests should be for a sufficient period of

time to allow the inspection system to be established and evaluated in terms of effective and reliable operation. Most of the seismologists estimated it would take from one to two years to complete the establishment of an adequate inspection system.

6. An international agreement to suspend tests ought to provide for continued research and testing under international supervision and registry for two purposes. One would be to check the effectiveness of the inspection system. For example, tests should be conducted in areas in which earthquakes are frequent; some should be conducted under an icecap or in the most porous material possible. Tests should be conducted in the various ways which have been suggested as possibilities for evading an agreement to suspend tests. Such a step would appear to be vital if the agreement is to cover even smaller explosions. Such explosions appear to be much more difficult to distinguish from earthquakes than those of larger yields. The other purpose to be served by continued tests under international supervision and control would be to allow for further development of nuclear explosives for peaceful uses.

These optimistic findings by Senator Humphrey and the Disarmament Subcommittee staff were subsequently to prove embarrassing. However, at the time they were written, they corresponded closely to the consensus of the wisest thinkers on nuclear-test disarmament in the State Department and some other quarters of Government eager to reach a test-ban agreement with the Soviet Union. The Humphrey Subcommittee report became an important document in the summer East-West conference of experts who studied the feasibility of an inspection system to police a nuclear test-ban.

Senator Humphrey was impressed with the potential of a nuclear test ban to become an impediment to the quest for quality rather than quantity in arms.

The arms race of today is primarily a qualitative race. Each nation is attempting to develop the most destructive weapons, or the more precise weapons, or the weapons with the longest range, or weapons with some other special quality. The quantity of armaments is important, but it is the constant improvement in quality, or even the development of entirely new weapons, which causes a nation to expend some of its best resources and energies in an effort to keep up to date. It is for this reason that a suspension of nuclear-weapons tests would constitute a meaningful disarmament measure. A suspension of tests would greatly impede, if not prohibit, the development of new types of nuclear weapons. It would also prevent the development of nuclear weapons by any nation which has not already made the tests essential to prove new weapons.[18]

The Senator warned, however, that a test suspension would not reduce the numbers of hydrogen and atomic bombs in American and Soviet stockpiles, nor would it prevent the enlargement of those stockpiles. The test suspension therefore should be regarded only as a first step, he agreed. If the suspension were for a reasonable period of time the world could decide whether the Soviet Union was really interested in reducing tensions through arms-control measures.

Senator Humphrey, aware that much of the opposition to a test suspension came from those who were opposed to impeding the arms-improvement program of the United States, observed:

> Some believe that the risks in taking this course are too great. I believe, however, that the alleged risks should be weighed against the risks and the course we are already taking—the risks of an unchecked arms race, the risks of a precarious balance of power in which both sides are so heavily armed that a minor incident could result in catastrophe for the whole world. Furthermore, a suspension of nuclear-weapons tests for a limited period with inspection would amount to a significant political breakthrough and might result in a relaxation of tension, an increase in confidence, and closer contacts between the United States and the Soviet Union as well as other countries.

These views of Senator Humphrey were published on June 23, 1958, as the Administration was moving through an important series of tests in the Pacific and as preparations were being completed for an East-West experts' meeting in Geneva to explore the feasibility of an inspection system.

Data gathered from the American seismologists, when published, became a reference work for the approaching experts' conference in Geneva, which was held from July 1 to August 22. Many of the seismologists pointed out difficulties in policing a test ban.

The Humphrey Subcommittee's questionnaire had sought information on six major points: (1) spacing of seismographs for monitoring underground explosions; (2) the ability of seismographs to distinguish underground nuclear explosions from underground chemical explosions; (3) ability to distinguish underground explosions from earthquakes; (4) estimated number of earthquakes in the Soviet Union and China each year, by size; (5) extent of inspection necessary to assure that an agreement on nuclear-test suspension was being observed; (6) the possibilities for evading a nuclear-test moratorium.

The seismologists who responded had a wide variety of experience. Some worked with the Government, some were professors, some worked in "applied seismology," as in locating oil deposits or measuring thicknesses of ice, some had worked on seismic aspects of nuclear tests.

The principal result from the Subcommittee questionnaire was a wide difference of opinion among scientists about the capabilities of seismographs to detect underground nuclear tests. It was clear that seismology was far from a precise science and would present extremely difficult problems if the test-ban inspection network depended heavily on it.

Distances: One seismologist contended it would be more difficult to differentiate earthquakes from explosions at near distances than at several thousand miles away. Among those who ventured to estimate the outer limit at which nuclear explosions could be detected, there were wide variations in calculations. For detecting a one-kiloton explosion, for instance, one seismologist set the limit at 150 miles; and one estimated 2,100 miles. For a 10-kiloton explosion, for instance, one said 460 miles; another 1,000 miles, another 1,500 to 3,000 miles, and one 4,500 miles. For detecting a 100-kiloton explosion, one said 300 miles, another 3,500 to 6,600 miles, another 9,700 miles, two said at all distances.

Distinguishing between nuclear and chemical explosions: There was almost complete agreement that seismographic evidence alone could not distinguish between nuclear and chemical explosions.

Distinguishing explosions from earthquakes: There was apparently agreement that seismograms would contain diagnostic information that would help in distinguishing earthquakes from underground explosions. The reliability of this diagnostic information, however, was open to a wide range of questions. One seismologist who had studied the records of the Rainier explosion, received only 200 miles away, said he saw nothing in the records to distinguish it from an earthquake.[19]

Many of the seismologists mentioned the "direction of first motion" of the seismic signal as a distinguishing characteristic between earthquakes and explosions. As earlier testimony before the Subcommittee had shown, explosions were thought to produce compressional waves in all directions while earthquakes were believed to produce compressions in some directions and rarefactions in others. If clear records were received by the seismic stations surrounding the site of an underground disturbance—a big "if"—it was presumed that absence of rarefactions would indicate the event may have been an explosion. Four other distinguishing characteristics were mentioned by the seismologists:

1. An explosion produces a greater percentage of surface waves compared to body waves than an earthquake; in addition, the surface waves from an explosion produce smaller signals relative to the body waves than earthquakes produce. (Surface waves or L waves from earthquakes travel around the outside of the earth instead of passing through the interior.) The principal types of body waves are the "P" (primary) waves and "S" (secondary) waves, so named for the order of their arrival on the earth's surface from the epicenter of the underground disturbance. The P wave is also called a "push," "longitudinal," or "compressional" wave. The P wave is likened to a sound wave through the earth. An S wave is also known as a "shake," "transverse," or "shear" wave. The movement of an S wave is at right angles to the direction the wave itself is traveling, like a rope that is fixed at one end and shaken at the other.[20]

2. Compressional waves or P waves from explosions are of a very high frequency compared to the P waves from earthquakes.

3. Comparing the times of arrival of signals from near and far stations indicates the depth at which the disturbance occurred. Earthquakes usu-

ally are deeper than explosions, and disturbances below a certain depth could be presumed to be earthquakes.

4. An explosion has a point source whereas earthquakes have extended sources over "fault lines" and the earthquake usually lasts a longer period of time than man-made explosions.

Some seismologists thought it would be possible immediately, others thought it was impossible ever, to make a clear differentiation between earthquakes and explosions on the basis of seismic information. Many suggested additional experience was necessary.

Most estimated, however, that 85 to 90 per cent of the earthquakes would be correctly identified. The range of estimates on correct identification was 75 to 100 per cent. One expert estimated that a twenty-six-station network in the Soviet Union could correctly identify 90 per cent of all earthquakes of magnitude 4.3 or larger and that seventy-three stations could identify 90 per cent of all earthquakes down to magnitude 3.7.

Professor Frank Press, Director of the Seismological Laboratory at the California Institute of Technology, and one of the United States government consultants who frequently advised Presidential science adviser James F. Killian, Jr., estimated that it would be possible to identify unambiguously 90 per cent of the underground blasts above 20 kilotons. With additional research this "threshold" could be lowered to 10 kilotons.

He warned, however, that "at the present time one-kiloton blasts could not be distinguished from small earthquakes. Where the crossover point occurs between 1 kiloton and 20 kilotons is questionable but could be answered by some experiments." Another seismologist estimated that anything above 10 kilotons could be distinguished from earthquakes.

There was a vast disagreement among the seismologists on the ability of a detection network to distinguish small explosions from earthquakes in seismic areas like Siberia's Kamchatka Peninsula and the base of the Himalayas in China and Tibet.

Dr. Carl F. Romney, an Air Force geophysicist who formerly had been chief seismologist for the Geotechnical Corporation of Dallas, Texas, named these areas as "particularly uncertain to me":

1. *Detectability of blasts larger than Rainier (1.7 kilotons).* While the amplitudes of the earth motion produced by Rainier are fairly well known, there does not appear to be a well established theory by which to scale up from 1.7 kilotons to 10 kilotons, or larger.

2. *Dependance of seismic wave amplitudes on materials surrounding an explosion.* There are no established relations to use in estimating the size of seismic waves from a Rainier-type bomb exploded in granite, salt, or material other than tuff.

3. *Methods of discriminating between earthquakes and blasts.* As a re-

sult of an intensive study of the seismic waves from Rainier, I have concluded that the best means for differentiating between shallow earthquakes
and underground blasts is through an analysis of the first motion in the P
waves. If the theory is accepted that earthquakes are caused by faulting,
then the first motion should be rarefactional in some locations in the case
of earthquakes, but compressional at all locations in the case of blasts.
*The theory mentioned is by no means established to be true for all earth-
quakes and particularly not for small earthquakes.* In any case, the absence of initial rarefactions is not proof of a blast because the area of the
earth where the rarefactions could be observed may be confined to a small
region near the shock or may be water-covered or otherwise inaccessible.
A seismic inspection system could thus identify many, if not most, earthquakes but there would remain a number which are totally unidentified.
I believe that an unfortunate fact, with which all seismologists will agree,
is that most characteristics of seismic waves depend chiefly on the struc-
tural and elastic properties of the earth rather than on the properties of
the source. While it is possible that new and presently unknown differences
will be observed in the case of underground explosions larger than Rainier,
I am aware of no proof for these possibilities. It must also be evident that,
if one kiloton is a realistic goal for an inspection system, the chief problem
lies in the evaluation of smaller shocks rather than large shocks because of
the rapid increase in total number as the size decreases.[21]

The comments of Dr. Romney took on special significance when he
became a key adviser on seismology to the American experts group that
negotiated with the Soviet Union on an inspection system for a nuclear
test ban. His careful delineations of the areas of doubt, unfortunately,
were not paid proper heed, as the unfolding narrative of 1958–59 will
show.

One Coast and Geodetic Survey seismologist, Leslie F. Bailey, sarcastically questioned the claim that 90 per cent of the earthquakes could
be distinguished from man-made blasts. "Over 95 per cent of the earthquakes would be correctly identified," Mr. Bailey wrote, "merely by
calling every seismic event an earthquake because the number of earthquakes in active seismic areas is much larger than the number of explosions, even during an intensive test program."

The 90-per cent identification claim was to become a familiar talking
point for test-ban advocates, but the telling Bailey remark, that this
efficiency was a function of the preponderance of earthquakes rather than
the effectiveness of the inspection, was completely lost.

Bailey expressed the opinion that even with 50 to 100 miles separation
between stations, completely-contained underground explosions could
be successfully hidden in highly seismic areas like Kamchatka in Eastern
Siberia.

There was not even agreement among the seismologists that correct
identification would improve by increasing the number of monitoring

stations, although this later became almost a maxim. Some seismologists felt that there was a "saturation point" beyond which increase of stations would not help.

Number of earthquakes in the Soviet Union and China: Estimates varied by a factor of two. The total number of earthquakes per year in the Soviet Union and China between magnitude 4.25, that of the Rainier underground shot, and magnitude 6, that of an earthquake which would be destructive of a restricted surface area, was estimated variously from 50 to 2,000. The two leading American—and world—authorities on seismology, to whom all the others looked, were Dr. Beno Gutenberg, Professor of Geophysics at the California Institute of Technology, and Dr. Charles F. Richter, Professor of Seismology at the same institute. Their book, *Seismicity of the Earth,* was regarded as the "bible" of all seismologists. The magnitude scale on which all the world's seismologists measured the size of earthquakes was named after Dr. Richter. Not even Dr. Gutenberg and Dr. Richter agreed, however, on the number of earthquakes in the Soviet Union and China. Dr. Gutenberg estimated that within the range of magnitude 4.25 to 6 there would be 200 earthquakes in the Pacific belt of the Soviet Union each year and 100 in the interior of the Soviet Union and China. He warned that the number could vary greatly from year to year. Dr. Richter, however, estimated that there would be only 45 in the interior of the Soviet Union and China between magnitudes 4.25 and 6, and 200 in the Kuriles and Kamchatka.[22]

Other seismologists estimated there would be 140 earthquakes between magnitude 4.25 and 6 in the Soviet Union and 200 in China; 300 for the Soviet Union alone; 500 to 1,000 for the Soviet Union alone; 100 in the Soviet Union and 500 in China; and 1,000 in both countries.

Some of the wide variations in the estimates may have arisen because some seismologists included earthquakes in the nearby oceans, but the range was still impressively large. How one was to estimate the number of on-site inspection teams needed to check out unidentified earthshocks, with varying predictions on earthquakes from 100 to 1,000, was a matter of importance somehow overlooked in the next three years' negotiations.

The same uncertainty appeared in the estimates for the number of earthquakes above magnitude 6 in the Soviet Union and China. The forecast ranged from 40 to 100 or more per year. The Gutenberg-Richter team agreed this time. Dr. Gutenberg estimated 20 in the Pacific belt, and 5 in the interior of the Soviet Union and China. Dr. Richter estimated 3 in the Soviet Union, 20 in the Kuriles and Kamchatka, and 1 or 2 in China. Most of the estimates were in the 10 to 25 range. There was one estimate of 50 in the Soviet Union, two of 20 to 50, and 50 to 100 in China.

Dr. Romney, the Air Force geophysicist and seismologist, emphasized the uncertainties in statistics on earth shocks in the Soviet Union and China when he wrote the Subcommittee:

Russian publications on seismicity do not indicate such large numbers (as are found in other parts of the world), but are probably not complete since they include only located earthquakes and *the Russian system of seismograph stations is least dense in the most active area near Kamchatka and the Kurile Islands*. All estimates are subject to wide variations from year to year and my belief is that a realistic inspection system must be prepared for a time of high seismic activity rather than "average" activity if the desire is to prevent weapons development.

As if these disagreements among the experts were not enough, the seismologists also indicated wide disputes on the magnitude of the signals produced by nuclear explosions, as compared to the signals from earthquakes. Dr. Richter had devised a scale, in 1935, under which earthquakes were classified by units of magnitude ranging from zero for the smallest earthquake to 8.5 for the largest. The magnitude was intended to indicate the total energy of the shock from an earthquake. By calibrating seismographs according to a strictly uniform pattern, seismologists all over the world have been able to agree on the magnitudes of specific earthquakes. Calculating the magnitudes, however, is not a precise science.

In the case of the Rainier explosion, for instance, the magnitude was first calculated as 4.6, later revised downward to 4.25.

Both Gutenberg and Richter maintained in their letters to Senator Humphrey that the magnitude scale was devised only for measuring earthquakes and could not be applied to measuring explosions. Professor Gutenberg wrote the Humphrey Subcommittee:

The magnitude scale is designed for earthquakes in which longitudinal, transverse, and surface waves are excited. In explosions most of the energy goes into longitudinal waves, so that the magnitude scale does not apply even approximately to artificial explosions. If a magnitude is given for an artificial explosion it means only that it has longitudinal waves of about the same size as an earthquake of the same magnitude.

Dr. Richter passed along a similar warning, with more details:

As the originator of the magnitude scale, I must point out that it was not devised to apply to explosions at or near the surface, but to natural earthquakes originating at depths of 10 miles or more. Assignment of magnitude to an explosion has two possible meanings:

a. The explosion produces deflection on a seismograph at a given distance from the source, equal to that produced by an earthquake of the named magnitude at a station equally distant from its epicenter: This is the significance of the magnitude 4.25 quoted in connection with the

Rainier explosion. [Note that 4.25 should be read as 4¼. Magnitudes are not assigned to hundredths.]

b. A magnitude figure may be obtained by comparing the energy of explosion with that calculated for an earthquake of given magnitude. This method is unreliable, owing to present uncertainty in the calculation of earthquake energy.

Statistics requested [on number of earthquakes] involve difficult estimation. I have used data from "Seismicity of the Earth," and from recent Russian publications. Statistics for magnitude 6 and over are fairly complete; but for lower magnitudes, they are fragmentary. Many earthquakes of magnitude as low as 4.25 probably escape attention. Some are not reported by the stations which record them. Others, while reported, are recorded so imperfectly that their location is doubtful.

In giving average annual statistics it is necessary to exclude the numerous aftershocks of large earthquakes. An earthquake of magnitude 7.5 or over is likely to be followed by 100 or more aftershocks of magnitude over 4.25 within a year.[23]

Dr. Richter explained that in his estimates of the number of earthquakes of given magnitudes in the Soviet Union and China he had excluded the aftershocks.

He did not discuss whether the aftershocks from large earthquakes should have been ignored in considering the number of events to be investigated if a nuclear test-ban agreement were signed. It would, of course, be possible, even logical, for a violator to set off a sneak explosion after a large earthquake and hope that the explosion would pass as one of the many aftershocks. For this reason, all the aftershocks would have to be investigated as well as the large earthquake itself, if an inspection system were to be effective. In that sense, the Richter and Gutenberg estimates of the number of events inside the Soviet Union and China did not meet the problem posed by the Humphrey Subcommittee.

The uncertainties in translating the power of underground explosions into earthquake magnitudes were accentuated by the wide range of estimates the seismologists submitted to the Humphrey Subcommittee. What size explosion would record a magnitude of 6? Estimates varied from 44 kilotons, to 100 kilotons, to 500 to 1,000 kilotons, even to 2,000 kilotons.

Dr. Romney took the position that the relationship between nuclear explosions underground and earthquake magnitude had not yet been established experimentally, so speculation was pointless.

Requirements of an inspection system: Seismic inspection stations would have to be distributed so that they could detect violations of one kiloton or more, it was generally agreed. Seismologists queried by the Disarmament Subcommittee were again in wide disagreement on the spacing required. Their recommendations ranged from 50 miles to 700 miles. Many pointed out that the spacing should be closer in seismic areas than is nonseismic areas. Estimates of the number of stations required in the Soviet Union ranged from about 40 to about 200. Several estimated 100 stations. This compared with Governor Stassen's recommendation to the committee that 11 or 12 stations would be sufficient. One seismologist suggested a small number of mobile stations instead of a large number of fixed stations. Professor Gutenberg proposed that the Soviet Union's own 70 seismic stations be used in the system.

Dr. Norman A. Haskell, Chief of the Wave Propagation Branch, Terrestrial Sciences Laboratory, Geophysics Research Directorate, Air Force Cambridge Research Center, gave a range of stations from 26 to 73, depending on whether one were optimistic or pessimistic about the capabilities of the system.

> If my "pessimistic" estimate of a 550-mile identification radius is accepted and it is required that all points within the U.S.S.R., including adjacent Arctic islands and China be within 550 miles of at least three seismic stations, it would require about 73 stations distributed at 550-mile intervals to give complete coverage of the area. If my "optimistic" estimate of 1,100-mile identification radius is accepted, the number of stations required would be reduced to about 26.[24]

Estimates of the number of persons needed to man the seismic stations also varied widely. One seismologist suggested that 100 to 200 3-man stations would be necessary. Another suggested 5 persons per station plus 230 analysts. Another suggestion was to have one full-time man per station plus 50 to 100 part-time employees. One respondent suggested that the world's supply of seismologists would be greatly strained to man all the seismic stations with competent personnel.

The time required to set up the inspection system was estimated at from one to two years.

Individual inspection station costs were put at $50,000, $100,000, and $150,000. Those who gave cost estimates in terms of the whole system provided figures varying from $5 million to $100 million. Between these extremes there were other estimates of $10 million, $10–$20 million, $25–$50 million, and $50–$100 million. (A year later estimates had soared to from $1 billion to $5 billion.)

Possibilities for evasion of a nuclear-test moratorium: Each of the 31 seismologists queried by the Disarmament Subcommittee estimated how many events per year would be classified "doubtful," that is, would not be identified either as an earthquake or an explosion. Estimates varied from 5 to 300. Another respondent estimated "less than 10 per cent."

Most seismologists estimated that there would be 10 to 20 per cent risk that an explosion would be identified as an earthquake. If this was based on more than intuition, no scientific basis was provided.

Dr. Thomas C. Poulter, Director of Poulter Laboratories at the Stanford Research Institute, bluntly warned that: "Unless some means is found for remotely detecting underground explosions which is more reliable than seismic, it will be surprising if most of them [sneak explosions] do not go undetected." [25]

Seismologists were asked what size areas on-the-spot investigation teams would have to cover in order to investigate seismic information about a possible underground explosion. The most frequent estimate was 10 square miles, but some estimated 25 square miles, two estimated nearly 100 square miles, and one suggested 300 square miles, although he believed this could be reduced.

The only method of verifying that a nuclear explosion had been detonated, the seismologists said, would be to find fresh radioactive debris underground. It was suggested that the permafrost might melt if the underground test were undertaken in frozen subsoil of cold areas of the world. Few expected a violator would take this chance, however. Others suggested that signs of preparations for an underground test, such as evidence of digging, drilling, and tunneling, would help localize the area where a sneak test shot had been made.

The seismologists ranged from pessimistic to extremely optimistic about chances of an on-site inspection team catching a sneak test. One optimist said that the probability of detecting a violator was so great that it would be virtually certain that no country would risk continuing tests. On the other hand, another warned that it would "be very difficult to locate an underground source if a careful attempt had been made to conceal it. . . . Our own tests proved this." [26]

Methods of camouflaging experiments were discussed in some detail by the thirty-one seismologists. The method most frequently suggested was to locate the test in a highly seismic area in the Soviet Union, such as the Kamchatka-Kuriles area. Even with stations spaced only 50 to 100 miles apart, Dr. Bailey had judged, a contained underground explosion could still be hidden in Kamchatka.

Several suggested timing the test to coincide with an earthquake, by triggering the test explosion on a strong-motion seismograph when it registered an earthquake of a size large enough to conceal the test.

Another method would be to "spoof" the seismographs in the area. Several shots could be fired simultaneously, or in rapid series, generating seismic noise. Or the firing could be conducted in a season of heavy storms. Or a non-nuclear explosion could be set off five miles away from the nuclear explosion and two seconds earlier, to mask it. Or the nuclear explosion could be "shaped" so that it would look like an earthquake. Or the experiment might be conducted at the bottom of a dry well drilled under a shallow sea.

Many seismologists suggested that small sneak explosions would be extremely hard to catch. Some mentioned possibilities for concealment in exploding the nuclear bomb in such absorbent materials as the thick ice of Antarctica or dry volcanic tuff.

To hide surface evidence of a test, some suggested that abandoned mines be used, or that excavation materials produced in placing the shot be dumped in rivers or lakes.

One seismologist estimated that only 50 per cent of the huge 50- to 100-kiloton explosions would be detected by existing stations outside the Soviet Union.

It was generally agreed that while strong suspicions of a nuclear test might be raised by seismic detection stations outside the Soviet Union, no proof would be acceptable except radioactive material from the test site itself.

Senators on the Disarmament Subcommittee had acknowledged repeatedly that they had been confused by the contradictory testimony they received. Senator Symington, for instance, burst out at one point: "What I'm worrying about is whether we can ever get a sound system. I want to try to get it. However, if it is not a sound system, then it is the American people who lose and not the Russians, because we are not going to blast Moscow off the face of the map because they cheated. The people who lose are ourselves."

There then followed this exchange with Senator Humphrey:

SENATOR HUMPHREY: That is right. What I am trying to get at all the time is this—and I'm going to be very blunt about it—why are the President and the Secretary of State talking about the cessation of tests if it is all this hazardous? I'm going to be very open about it. What are we doing? What is this?

SENATOR SYMINGTON: What is the use of packaging cessation of testing with the question of cessation of production when a person of Dr. Teller's standing comes up here [on Capitol Hill] and talks the way he did yesterday about the difficulty of detecting stockpiling? If you throw the nuclear testing in with those other two you may be really kidding the people. That is what has me worried.

SENATOR HUMPHREY: What I am worried about is if it is this hazardous, if the Soviet leaders are as sneaky, as subtle, and as clever as we always say they are, then they must have one blind spot. If it is this hazardous [for the United States], they should have bought this a long time ago. I just cannot understand how they have let us get by this long.

We have been parading around here all the time with a package in our pockets saying "sign it and we will deliver." We had a man in London for months on this basis.

Well, now, if it is this hazardous, I cannot understand why this wily Khrushchev hasn't said, "I will take that because we are going to cheat on those characters. We have got those nice noble men all tied up in the United States. They are going to be honorable, decent and truthful. We are going to be sneaks and cheats. We have got them signed up. We will cheat them while they pray."

That is just the way it adds up. So I think there must be something else to it, that is all I am saying.

Two Republican Senators seemed less confused. They gave indications at the hearings that the Eisenhower Administration was already considering entering a nuclear test ban after the summer-fall Hardtack series of tests was completed. Senator Hickenlooper, for instance, said on April 17:

> With this series of tests that is coming off now, we will learn a great deal. We will take a long step at least toward learning some of the answers that we want to know [deleted] about the chemical and physical reactions of improved weapons and explosions. I think we will have to abide these tests this summer and then take a look at it from there. Have we learned enough or do we have to go a step further? . . . I think we must go to the point where we have at least reasonable assurance from a scientific standpoint that we have adequate answers before we get into a finalized agreement of some kind.[27]

Senator Alexander Wiley of Wisconsin spoke in the same vein to Atomic Energy Commissioner Strauss:

> I understand it is your judgment and the judgment of others that the Kremlin has made undoubtedly a number of experiments [before announcing its unilateral ban], and that what we want is to make some experiments and get some knowledge which we think we should get before we go ahead, possibly, and enter into a test-suspension agreement. . . . The people would agree that we should have this next series of experiments, which would probably reach into the later part of the summer, and then go ahead with a possible agreement along the lines that have been testified to. We could see if such an agreement could be worked out.[28]

Senator Symington addressed himself on many occasions during the hearings to the problem of giving the American people enough facts to judge the nuclear test-ban issue for themselves. To Chairman Humphrey, he said:

> The American people—and I believe you will agree with me on this—are all mixed up on this subject. They want to do what is right. They do not want to ruin themselves by having these tests, if it is true that these tests are going to destroy them or change the shape and minds of future generations, etc. Everybody is mixed up on it. *We've had testimony here by so-called authorities which has been fantastically different.* Now what worries me is that the people who have access to all the information are the people who seem more prone to resist any unilateral action on our part. They also seem to be more prone to strike down the dangers of worldwide fallout at all times, and I am not talking about local fallout.

And to AEC Chairman Strauss, Senator Symington had this to say:

> The people who have given us information and warned us about the dangers of poisoning the world, and so forth, are people who are not even cleared in important cases to get the information that you have available to you and that your Commission has available to it. For example, Mr. Harrison Brown told us that he was not cleared for information, and yet

he has taken a position in all sincerity—I am sure he is a fine American—and he has taken a very definite position. Now yesterday we had Dr. Orear from Columbia University, who made some statements that were at complete variance with much of the testimony that has come from you and your advisers, and some of your own technological experts. I thought that it would be a good idea, and I suggested it to Dr. Orear, that we ought to get this thing thrashed out.

It never was, publicly. But there were many questions that needed to be "thrashed out" by the scientists too. For instance:

Should not a top-drawer panel of scientists have made a thorough study of the possibilities of hiding tests, in view of the "strong possibilities" to which Dr. Teller referred?

Should not there have been an extensive underground testing series in the whole wide spectrum of sizes and in varying media, to develop experience—where there was almost a total vacuum—on which to base detection techniques?

What countermeasures could be devised for the methods of evasion suggested by the seismologists?

These were fundamental questions to which there were no agreed American answers on June 23, the date Senator Humphrey published his report. Eight days later, however, on July 1, a panel of American experts sat down with Soviet scientists in Geneva to devise an inspection system for a test ban.

GENEVA EXPERTS' CONFERENCE

The Soviet Union's unilateral test ban and the crescendo of support on Capitol Hill for separating the nuclear test-ban issue from other first-step disarmament measures had brought increasing pressures on President Eisenhower to move in that direction in the spring of 1958.

The Kremlin's decreed ban may have been phony but it was also powerful and embarrassing to the United States.

Senator Humphrey, in a statement on the day of the Soviet announcement,[29] used the occasion to attack the Administration for dragging its feet in the whole broad disarmament field. The recent Soviet series of tests, Senator Humphrey said,

> was the most diversified and most intensified in Soviet history. I regret that our Government has not seen fit to inform the people of the United States as to the nature of these tests, even though such information is available from the scientific data which have been gathered by our detection system. . . . The United States Department of State must make it clear that the Soviet proposal is really no proposal at all. At the same time the Administration must get off dead center and press for negotiations with the Soviet Union for a suspension of tests with inspection.

Senator Humphrey then recommended that President Eisenhower "announce immediately" that the United States was prepared to break up our disarmament "package," that we are prepared to separate the matter of the testing of nuclear weapons from the production cutoff of nuclear materials for weapons purposes, and that we are prepared to meet with the Soviet Union to discuss a disarmament proposal limited to cessation of tests alone, but with inspection.

The Senator accused the Administration of spreading false information about the effectiveness of inspection:

The Administration has allowed the impression to grow that the detection of tests would be impossible even with an inspection system. This is simply not true. Our test detection measures are excellent and, if an inspection system were installed in the Soviet Union, the Soviets would have a very difficult time trying to avoid detection. In fact the consensus of those in the Executive Branch in a position to know is that our detection system would be so good that the Soviets would not dare to try to cheat.

He acknowledged that there might be some risk but the risk was so small, he said, compared to the gains of a first step in halting the arms race, that they were acceptable.

If the Administration does not soon act in this matter it will cause the United States to hand to the Kremlin the entire initiative on the question of seeking peace. We must indicate to the world the fallacy of this recent Soviet announcement but at the same time we must indicate that we are prepared to negotiate on an inspected test suspension.

In his Senate speech, Senator Humphrey said:

Mr. President, this morning our nation has been delivered a terrible propaganda blow. For months we have had the opportunity to negotiate a satisfactory test suspension, but we frittered away our time because those who were in charge of this Government have been either timid or uncertain, and the conflict in Administration circles over what should be done has left us paralyzed and immobile. Time is at hand for action, and I hope we shall not again see the specter of the Soviet Union literally keeping our nation punch-drunk from one propaganda blow after another, leaving us standing before the world in ugly nakedness, because of the sterility of our international policies on this great issue, with which the people of the world are so deeply concerned, namely, the danger of a thermonuclear war.

Three days later, Senator Humphrey delivered another stinging attack on the Administration from the Senate floor.

It is now generally agreed, even by the President and the Secretary of State, that the Soviet announcement to suspend tests of nuclear weapons has resulted in a tremendous propaganda victory for the Soviet Union. Our response to the Soviet announcement has consisted of our top officials frankly admitting that the Soviet has performed a propaganda coup. . . .[30]

We should request immediately that the United Nations appoint a special task force of scientists and technicians to prepare and design a detection and inspection system. This would not have to await the consummation of an agreement. Preliminary plans for a detection and inspection system should be in being, ready to be used and applied immediately upon the completion of negotiations and agreements.

There was in the same Humphrey pronouncement a threat that if President Eisenhower did not himself act, Congress might seek to force him.

If the Executive Branch of our Government continues to delay and hesitate, the Congress may wish to register its judgment through appropriate action on this vital matter. The responsibility, however, still rests with the Executive Branch—with the President and the Secretary of State. We have every right to expect them to lead and to act.

Khrushchev's Unexpected Acceptance

The double spur, from Capitol Hill and from Premier Khrushchev's April 4 letter, brought a prompt reply from President Eisenhower on April 8.[31]

Mr. Eisenhower suggested in a letter to Premier Khrushchev that the Soviet Union join the United States in examination of the technical requirements for inspection of a nuclear test ban. He still made it clear that he intended the nuclear-test-ban issue to be only part of a general first-step disarmament program.

The United States is also prepared, in advance of agreement upon any one or more of the outstanding "disarmament" propositions, to work with the Soviet Union, and others as appropriate, on the technical problems involved in international controls. We both recognize that international control would be necessary. Indeed, your present letter to me speaks of "the establishment of necessary international control for the discontinuance of tests."

What is "necessary"? The question raises problems of considerable complexity, given the present possibility of conducting some types of tests under conditions of secrecy.

If there is ever to be an agreed limitation or suspension of testing, and the United States hopes and believes that this will in due course come about as part of a broad disarmament agreement, plans for international control should be in instant readiness. Why should we not at once put our technicians to work to study together and advise as to what specific control measures are necessary if there is to be a dependable and agreed disarmament program?

The United Nations General Assembly has called for technical disarmament studies, in relation both to nuclear and conventional armaments. The United States says "yes." I urge, Mr. Chairman, that the Soviet Union should also say "yes." Then we can at once begin the preliminaries necessary to larger things.[32]

State Department officials look back on this April 8 letter as another turning point for United States test-ban policy. The significance of the offer for technical discussions, couched in terms which invited a Soviet reply selecting only the nuclear-test issue for study, was discussed when the letter was drafted at the home of Secretary of State Dulles on Sunday, April 6.

Mr. Dulles, few would dispute, was the Eisenhower Administration's principal policy-maker in the test-ban field. His close associates believed he drifted, rather than moved purposefully or precisely, into the test-ban entanglement. His principal worry was that the deteriorating American-propaganda position would eventually become a millstone around the country's neck.

He spoke frequently of his recollections, sometimes historically inaccurate, of the unhappy experience of the Germans in disarmament after World War I. In his opinion, Germany had taken realistic positions on the difficulties of effective disarmament. But her diplomats were so negative about it that they heaped on themselves all the blame for the failure of the disarmament conferences. While it was unjust to blame them, Mr. Dulles remembered, the world's opprobrium was nonetheless concentrated on the German nation. (Whether Secretary Dulles' recollections about world disapproval were correct is a matter for historians to argue.)

He saw parallel problems for the United States in disarmament negotiations three decades later. While the United States' insistence on inspection was vitally necessary, the Secretary also worried about the public image of "foot-dragging" on the nuclear-test-ban problem, which had caught the world's imagination. He foresaw the time when the United States might be so inhibited by world opinion that it would lose its freedom of action to use or develop nuclear weapons. This would have an extremely important bearing on the whole United States system of alliances.

The United States was in danger of appearing before the world as a military-minded nation unwilling to use its great creative talents to seek alternatives to the arms race. With this on his mind, Mr. Dulles was impressed and worried by U.S. Ambassador Henry Cabot Lodge's strong pleas from the United Nations that the United States had to do something to prove to the world its sincerity on the nuclear-test issue. Failure to do so, Ambassador Lodge warned repeatedly, might face the United States with its first defeat in a General Assembly vote. At that time the Republicans were especially proud of their record of having never been forced to move against the majority in the United Nations. The Suez experience was by then behind them. They had, with great courage and devotion to principle, favored the U.N. majority over their two greatest allies. Maintaining their perfect record in the United Nations, bought at such great cost, had taken on added importance.[33]

There was a real possibility, it appeared in the spring of 1958, that the U.N. General Assembly might someday pass a resolution calling on the

United States to stop nuclear tests.[34] Moscow's unilateral ban had impressed many unsophisticated nations. The fallout scare also put the United States in a bad spot. These were the propaganda considerations that weighed heavily on Secretary Dulles. He feared that, at some future point, the propaganda disadvantage might be translated into an inhibition on American use of its nuclear stockpiles in case of extremity, or on vital nuclear-weapons development.

Secretary Dulles never took seriously the possibility that actual agreement on a test ban could be reached. Inspection would always scare the Russians off, he was sure.[35] But to counteract the adverse propaganda effects, he took a series of what appeared to be gingerly, calculated risks to prove American willingness to reach a real disarmament agreement.

Mr. Dulles dictated the April 8 draft letter himself, as was his self-confident style. At one point, questions were raised about the possibility that the Russians might accept the challenge and go into a technical discussion of inspection of a nuclear test ban, simply to break up the American disarmament package. At the time, Mr. Dulles rated this a very limited risk, which he was willing to accept. He was completely convinced that the Soviet Union could never be persuaded to accept any kind of real disarmament controls, in any area. They would be afraid, he reasoned, that accepting technical talks would involve them too much in the whole inspection idea, would expose their aversion to it. (Events, of course, have borne him out.) If the Soviet Union unexpectedly accepted, he apparently reasoned, the United States would have a fresh opportunity to pin the Kremlin down to either accepting an effective inspection system or rejecting it. The American propaganda position would benefit either way.

President Eisenhower's natural instincts led him to encourage Secretary Dulles to pursue whatever possibilities for agreement might exist in the nuclear-test-ban issue.

After a month of hemming and hawing, during which the Soviet Union hauled the United States into the United Nations Security Council to accuse it of sending H-bomb-carrying bombers over the Arctic toward Soviet territory, Premier Khrushchev unexpectedly accepted President Eisenhower's proposal for technical talks. The letter of acceptance came May 9 and reversed a policy stated in a Soviet memorandum only four days earlier.[36] Khrushchev wrote:

Your messages indicate that you attach great importance to having experts study the technical details connected with the control of the execution of an agreement on the cessation of atomic and hydrogen weapons tests. Taking this into account, we are prepared, in spite of the serious doubts on our part, of which I have spoken above, to try even this course. The Soviet Government agrees to having both sides designate experts who would immediately begin a study of methods for detecting possible violations of an agreement on the cessation of nuclear tests with a view to having this work completed at the earliest possible date, to be determined in advance.[37]

Premier Khrushchev restated the Soviet position that test-detection methods and "pertinent equipment available to modern science" would "completely preclude" secret testing after a test ban had been proclaimed.

Governor Stassen had expressed the American eagerness for a scientific "floor" on which political negotiations could stand in the London negotiations of 1957. He had said:

> I am aware that the Soviet representative has expressed the view that it is simple to ascertain whether or not an agreement affecting nuclear testing is being carried out. We appear to have different technical advice on this subject. I think that if we could reconcile our technical advice, it might assist our program toward reconciling our political conclusions. . . . A process of getting the scientists and technicians to agree on facts is an important part, sometimes, of reaching political agreement. . . . I do not feel that we can fruitfully engage in debate about the technical advice because I do not consider myself a scientist.[38]

Throughout 1957, the Soviet Union had insisted that scientific aspects were secondary to the political considerations. This was firmly founded in historic Communist doctrine. It was for this reason, mainly, that Secretary Dulles and others did not expect the Soviet Union to allow scientific aspects to play an important part in the test-ban issue. From the Soviet point of view, of course, even the technical conference itself was mainly a political exercise. To make sure this would be the case, a high-ranking political officer, Ambassador Semyon Tsarapkin, was assigned to the talks.

Soviet acceptance of the technical conference, of course, implied real concessions on their part beyond making science an important part of a political negotiation. Implicit in the agreement was the admission of the importance of an inspection and control system. Inspection and control was the thing the Soviet Union feared most in any disarmament agreement. The Russians were not committed, of course, to accept more inspection than they wished. But the mere admission that inspection was of great importance was regarded as a long step.

Anticipation of a Soviet rejection of the President's technical-conference proposal also explains the poor American preparation for the conference. The expert group was hastily pulled together. And, of course, there had been only one underground nuclear-weapon test on which scientists could base any effective detection and identification system for this sensitive area.

It is an interesting footnote for history that what amounted to a miscalculation of Soviet intentions in April, 1958, was to lead eventually to a long-term suspension of nuclear testing, without inspection.

President Eisenhower's reply to Premier Khrushchev on May 24, drafted on May 18, at Mr. Dulles' home, stated that the United States would be ready for an experts' study of the test-ban inspection problem three weeks after arrangements were agreed upon. The President suggested Geneva as the site, provided the Swiss Government approved. To meet Premier Khrushchev's desires for a time limit, the President suggested that the experts make "an initial progress report" within thirty days and a final report within sixty days "or as soon thereafter as possible."

Premier Khrushchev answered six days later that he favored limiting the experts' conference to three or four weeks.

It was eventually agreed that the United States, the Soviet Union, the United Kingdom, France, Canada, Poland, Czechoslovakia, and Rumania should contribute experts to the technical talks, which should begin July 1.

Even after it became clear that the Soviet Union intended to go through with the technical meeting, Secretary of State Dulles could not take the prospect seriously that a nuclear test-ban negotiation would ever be entered by the Soviet Union. As the final exchanges with the Soviet Union were being handled, he quite deliberately resisted "looking down the road" beyond the technical conference to see what the consequences of agreement on an inspection system would be. This would be unnecessary, he told cautious advisers, because the Soviet Union simply could not accept an effective inspection system. He did not expect the technical conference to get past the first few items on the agenda. He was to acknowledge extreme surprise that the experts were able to arrive at an agreement.

When it became clear, in early August, that agreement could be reached, Secretary Dulles thus found himself already committed to a course that he had not thought through.

The President had made it clear that he was agreeing to the technical talks "without prejudice to our respective positions on the timing and the interdependence of various aspects of disarmament." [39]

The Secretary of State made the same point on June 10, at a press conference. [40]

> If we do come to an understanding [in the experts talks], it will facilitate an agreement to suspend testing although I would anticipate that any agreement to suspend testing, if made, would not be an isolated agreement but be a part of other arrangements and anticipate that there would be progress made in other fields.

Mr. Dulles explained that a modification of the linkage inside the package was under consideration but it involved only timing.

> There are what you might call "conditions precedent" and "conditions subsequent." Now, in the package proposal that we put up in London last

August, they were tied together in the sense that they were all to get started at the same time and all be agreed upon at the same time. The separation that is under consideration is in terms of not necessarily insisting that they should all be agreed to and get started at the same time, but that we would start perhaps at different times but with the understanding that there would be a freedom of action restored if progress was not made in some of these other fields.[41]

Thus the Administration continued to insist publicly that the first-step disarmament package would include more than nuclear test suspension alone. This public position was being eroded, however, from within.

One of the significant factors in the erosion was the gradual loss of power and influence by the Chairman of the Atomic Energy Commission, Admiral Lewis L. Strauss. His term was to expire June 30. President Eisenhower spoke frequently with Mr. Strauss about reappointment, but Mr. Strauss knew he would have to go before the Joint Atomic Energy Committee for reconfirmation. One of that committee was Senator Clinton Anderson, an old antagonist of Admiral Strauss from the days he advocated the ouster of Dr. J. Robert Oppenheimer from Government as a security risk. Senator Anderson had made it clear in many ways, since those early days of the Eisenhower Administration, that he would not permit the reappointment of Mr. Strauss, if he had it within his power to prevent it.

President Eisenhower told intimates he wanted to make the fight, but Admiral Strauss thought it would be unwise. The President finally acquiesced, and decided to appoint Mr. Strauss Secretary of Commerce. Senator Anderson, although not a member of the Senate Committee charged with confirming appointments of Commerce Secretaries, participated in those confirmation hearings. The heated proceedings confirmed Mr. Strauss' predictions. He was not confirmed. In hindsight, it appears that Senator Anderson could have blocked Admiral Strauss' reappointment to the AEC chairmanship with less exertion than was necessary to prevent his appointment as Commerce Secretary.

The meaning of the decline in influence of Admiral Strauss over the test ban was that his strong voice was no longer among the chief counsels to the President. The Strauss arguments that nuclear testing constituted no disarmament measure and would represent a net disadvantage to the United States if not accompanied by other measures, including a cutoff of nuclear-weapons production, were no longer made with the same force inside the Administration.

Another significant factor in the gradual separation of the nuclear test-ban issue from the disarmament package was the appearance on the White House scene of Dr. James F. Killian, Jr., the President's newly appointed scientific adviser. His appointment had been one of the early reactions to the waves of apprehension after the Soviet Union's launching of its first sputnik in October, 1957. To quiet fears of those who thought their President was not getting enough high-level scientific advice, Mr. Eisenhower asked Dr. Killian to come to Washington on a full-time basis. (He had been taking on several part-time jobs periodically for the President in other fields.)

Secretary of State Dulles, the main decision-maker in the nuclear-test field, was thus presented for the first time with a counterweight to AEC Chairman Strauss in the top-level strategy discussions.

The Secretary of State was quickly impressed by the fundamental disagreements that developed between Dr. Killian and Admiral Strauss. When it got down to a matter of hard fact, Dr. Killian frequently had a preponderance of the scientists on his side.

Mr. Strauss' advice, based on the thinking of scientists in the Atomic Energy Commission, was presented without precise scientific basis. He had never been challenged until the appearance of Dr. Killian. However, when the former Massachusetts Institute of Technology president cited chapter and verse, scientific facts and figures, he frequently was able to bring Secretary Dulles to his point of view.

In addition, Mr. Strauss was a strong conservative, a Republican who was probably several degrees to the right of Secretary Dulles, who was less conservative than his reputation.

It was also Dr. Killian who introduced a new scientific approach to the study of political-scientific problems which attracted Secretary Dulles' interest. A panel of scientists was posed a series of specific questions which permitted clearer thinking on the nuclear test-ban issue than had been the habit previously. Professor Hans Bethe of Cornell headed the panel that made the top-secret report on test-ban detection in the spring of 1958. The chairmanship of Dr. Bethe did not reflect any one-sided view of the panel, however. Scientists of both the pro-test-ban and anti-test-ban factions were represented.

The scientists were asked to judge the possibilities of designing an effective system to detect nuclear tests; the military advantages for the United States of continued testing; and the relative advantages or disadvantages of a test ban for the Soviet Union and the United States. Asking scientists for military judgments that could have been well beyond their competence was one of the questionable practices of the day.

Thus the technical judgment of scientists was interposed between the President and Secretary Dulles, on the one hand, and the politico-scientific judgment of Admiral Strauss and his group of scientists in the Atomic Energy Commission. The Defense Department generally favored continued testing, but was conscious of the pre-eminence of civilian control.

The Strauss judgment that tests could not be reliably detected and that a test ban would be of much greater advantage to the Soviet Union than to the United States was openly challenged. Scientists frequently marshaled conjectures disguised as facts to show that the United States would gain. And the scientists' reports had a ring of logic and authenticity. So-called scientific judgments thus were elicited from more-or-less preconceived positions. Military, intelligence, and strategic factors were confused with scientific factors throwing the picture out of perspective.

Mr. Strauss was later to be proved more right than the scientists but he did not seem so to the President or Secretary Dulles at the time. The scientists did not produce a black-and-white report, but showed that the balance could well favor the United States if a nuclear test ban were achieved.

There are many who believe that this point had more validity in 1956, when Adlai Stevenson first popularized the general idea, than in 1958.

As it turned out, Mr. Strauss was out of office less than two months before the link between the test ban and nuclear-weapons-production cutoff was effectively broken.

Mr. Strauss' last battle to protect what he considered to be the basic national-security interests of the United States in the test-ban controversy involved the appointment of the American experts for the Geneva talks.

The AEC Chairman recommended Dr. Edward Teller, the leader of that part of the American scientific community that believed an effective inspection system would be impossible without a complete opening of the Soviet Union, as one of the three members. There was such stiff resistance that Mr. Strauss withdrew this informal suggestion and named Dr. Ernest O. Lawrence, Director of the University of California Radiation Laboratories in Livermore. President Eisenhower accepted his nomination. The problem was to achieve a "balance" in the group among the various Administration viewpoints. Dr. Hans Bethe was considered the leader of the pro-test-ban group, so he was eliminated from consideration too.

Dr. Robert F. Bacher, a veteran in the nuclear-weapons field, was finally chosen instead of Dr. Bethe. The major problem was to find a "neutral" chairman. Most scientists had taken up positions either for or against a test ban.

Dr. James Brown Fisk, then Vice President of Bell Telephone Laboratories, who had headed one of the eight task forces appointed in the early Stassen period to study communications aspects of the disarmament problem, was finally named.

The Soviet Union kept the United States and its allies guessing right up until the last moment before the experts' conference. Secretary Dulles' press conference remarks indicating that agreement among the experts would not necessarily lead to a test-suspension caused the Soviet government to warn that it might not go through with the July 1 date.

In an aide memoire from the Soviet Foreign Ministry to the American Embassy, the Russians said:

If it [the Government of the United States] does not wish that the results of the meeting of experts should assure the cessation of the tests of nuclear weapons by all powers who dispose of them, then it is useless to send experts to this conference. In such a situation the Soviet Union cannot send its experts because it does not wish to be an accomplice to the deception of the peoples.[42]

Secretary Dulles finally dispatched the American team of experts to Geneva not knowing whether the Russians actually would go through with their commitment.

There were further exchanges of aide memoires between the American Embassy in Moscow and the Foreign Ministry, but neither the United States nor the Soviet Union budged from its position. Moscow insisted that an agreement would be tantamount to a forcing move for a suspension of nuclear-weapons tests. Washington said it meant no such thing and quoted again President Eisenhower's April 28 letter in which he emphasized that the studies were to be undertaken "without prejudice to our respective positions on timing and interdependence of various aspects of disarmament."

After this last flurry of hard bargaining the talks did get under way on July 1 in Geneva, as scheduled.

The American scientists went to the Geneva talks without any advance political instructions from the State Department. Secretary Dulles, ready to stand on a truly scientific assessment of the inspection possibilities, instructed Dr. Fisk and his colleagues to get agreement on a completely scientific basis.

It was intended, however, that the scientists would present their governments with a choice between several inspection systems, that is, between systems that could operate at various thresholds, probably 1, 5, and 20 kilotons, with varying degrees of reliability; or with different numbers of control posts.

It was later reported that the State Department was "not terribly pleased" when the experts, given their own heads at Geneva, produced only one system of 180 stations, designed to operate at a 5-kiloton threshold with optional and partial effectiveness down to 1 kiloton.

The Geneva experts, on the other hand, were impressed, and at times somewhat alarmed, that they went for days without hearing from Washington.

The Soviet delegation was headed by Yevgeny K. Fedorov, a corresponding member of the Academy of Sciences of the U.S.S.R.—a florid-faced, chubby figure who was to become familiar to all Western nuclear-test negotiators.

As noted earlier, the Soviet delegation list also contained the name of a veteran diplomat, S. K. Tsarapkin, Chief of the Section of International Organizations and a member of the Collegium of the Ministry of Foreign Affairs of the Soviet Union.

This injection of a high-ranking political officer into the supposedly technical conference prompted the United States to send a political officer of its own, Ronald I. Spiers, the brilliant young Disarmament Desk Officer in the State Department who had worked closely with Secretary of State Dulles in formulating American nuclear-test policy from the beginning.

The conference met in thirty official sessions at the Palais des Nations in Geneva, and completed its work August 21. All the sessions were private, but verbatim transcripts of the proceedings were released later.

The Western experts at the meeting quickly got the idea that the level of the competence of their presentations was several cuts above the Soviet presentation. Some of the Soviet-bloc scientists gave the impression of trying to do a straightforward job without getting into politics or political motivations for positions taken.

The principal exception was Dr. Fedorov, who appeared to be "very clearly politically motivated" to all the American participants. His attitude may be said to have been one of "Let's not fuss around with any of the technical details, let's just agree that this can be done, sign an agreement, and get on with the negotiation of a treaty."

While the Soviet scientists were shopping at Geneva for the cheapest possible inspection system they could buy, Soviet Premier Khrushchev was throwing out broad hints that he took little stock in the inspection idea.

> To allow one state to exercise thorough control within the boundaries of another state means to open all the doors to the other country, to admit its inspectors and control officials, to places which are forbidden even to the people of the country in question. Each church, in any case, each orthodox church, has a place in the altar where only the priests are allowed to enter. Other people, even religious believers, are not supposed to go there. In the same way, every country has its own altar and its own sacred places, where not even all friends are admitted; and if they are, they are the closest friends who have merited such trust.[43]

It was the obvious Soviet aim from the start—as Khrushchev had indicated with his suggestion that the conference last only three or four weeks—to buy a test ban for as little inspection as possible. The evidence indicates that Moscow thought it would have to pay much less than was agreed, but then Washington lowered its opening price too—by more than 50 per cent.

The conference adopted its agenda on July 4. Four main questions were to be dealt with:

First, there would be an exchange of opinions on various methods for detecting atomic explosions and other problems the conference would face.

Second, a list of "basic methods of systematic observations for phenomena indicative of an explosion" would be agreed upon.

Third, a system combining the various methods would be set up.

Fourth, the experts would draw up a report to their governments, providing conclusions and suggestions.

The Conference considered five methods of detecting and identifying nuclear explosions: recording acoustic waves; sampling radioactive debris; recording seismic waves; recording radio signals; and using instrumented earth satellites to detect nuclear explosions more than 30 to 50 kilometers above the earth.

A pattern of procedure in discussing the various methods of detecting nuclear tests quickly developed. The United States delegation presented in detail the best technical information available to it on each method of detection. The Soviet-bloc scientists presented only token studies, usually confining themselves to the basics and to theoretical possibilities for detection. The Soviet experts spent most of their time putting questions about American presentations.

One of the principal methods of detection is seismology. Here the Soviet Union is known to have extensive knowledge. Its scientific program has been far more comprehensive than anything attempted in the United States. Soviet engineers have performed more underground experiments with chemical explosives and they have done more theoretical study, according to American experts who are familiar with their work. Little of this advanced knowledge was presented at the conference.

Whatever the reason, the United States wound up contributing most of the scientific information and heavy thinking at the Geneva experts' conference. The Soviet Union sat back and accepted it all, pressing only for a quick presentation and an early agreement.

The first Soviet ploy was to get the Western technicians to agree that the purpose of the gathering was really political—to prepare for a nuclear test ban. The American chairman, Dr. Fisk, deftly demured. The job of the technical conference, he insisted, was to find out *if* a nuclear test-ban was scientifically feasible, not to affirm that it was politically desirable.

This argument took up a good part of the first four sessions and the Soviet delegation chief, Dr. Fedorov, kept trying to slip the thought into the daily communiqués for weeks thereafter.

Acoustic Waves

By the time the agenda was adopted on July 4, the group was well along into the study of the problems of acoustic detection of nuclear-weapons tests.

The Russians worked almost exclusively from American data, quoting American sources like the Joint Atomic Energy Committee hearings, science magazines, and learned journals to make their points.

Nuclear explosions produce strong acoustic or sound waves in the air over great distances. Sensitive instruments called microbarographs can pick up the inaudible sound thousands of miles away. The occurrence of an explosion probably could be noticed, therefore, at great distances. But because atmospheric and meteorological conditions would vary widely between the explosion site and the microbarograph, the size of the blast could not be judged from the strength of the acoustic signal received. The amplitude of the signal could be increased or decreased by as much as five times, depending on the atmospheric conditions along the signal path.

Both sides, of course, were wary of disclosing their prized methods of detecting the other's tests. But the Soviet scientists carried this to the point of absurdity, giving less information on their techniques than appeared in any good physics text book. It was obvious that their instructions were to avoid volunteering to accept any measure of inspection that the West did not insist on.

The Soviet side, for instance, began the discussion of acoustic detection methods by quoting an American source that underwater explosions could be detected at 14,000 kilometers.[44] No mention was made of the difficulties of locating or identifying the underwater disturbances. In the air, it was said, big explosions had been recorded at 5,000 kilometers and 11,000 kilometers. Finding the source of an acoustic signal in the air, Soviet scientists said, was "easy."

Doyle Northrup, of the American delegation, responded that the main difficulty in acoustic detection was interference from meteors and volcanoes, as well as pressure waves from earthquakes. Electrical storms and lightning also interfere, he pointed out. While it was true that megaton shots could be detected thousands of kilometers from the explosion, kiloton shots could be located only a few hundred kilometers from the site by acoustic methods.[45]

He submitted for examination by the Soviet side examples of American microbarograms, the schematic presentation of acoustic pickups, showing similarities between the signal of a meteor, of a volcanic eruption in Kamchatka Peninsula, of earthquakes, and of small nuclear explosions. He asked the Russians to produce their acoustic recordings. The Russians later did, but they presented inferior graphs made with equipment whose frequency response was unsuited to the phenomena.

Soviet data were designed to prove that control stations for the policing of a nuclear test ban by acoustic methods could be spaced as far apart as 5,000 to 10,000 kilometers. Mr. Northrup's remark that kiloton explosions could be detected only a few hundred kilometers away implied a much denser spacing. The Soviet side immediately expressed its alarm:

"There are many fewer policemen than other members of the population," a young scientist of the Soviet Union, Gubkin, remarked.[46]

The United States estimated there would be 75 to 150 natural phenomena, like meteors, volcanoes, and earthquakes, each year in the range of 1 to 10 kilotons. These would interfere with acoustic pickup of nuclear explosions. In addition there would be 4 to 8 natural disturbances in the range of 10 to 100 kilotons, it was estimated, and 1 per year greater than 100 kilotons.

Dr. Harold Brown, a young American scientist then associated with Dr. Edward Teller, produced an estimate that the acoustic method would have a 90 per cent probability of detecting a nuclear test in the kiloton range at 420 kilometers (260 miles). This was not nearly so long a range as the Soviet scientists tried to prove. Through the first seven sessions, they were maintaining that stations could be spaced as far apart as 2,000 to 5,000 kilometers (1,250 to 3,100 miles).

United States scientists also presented evidence that the acoustic method could be made much more accurate in determining signal-source direction if the microbarographs were placed at the corners of a ten-kilometer square, roughly six miles on a side. This, of course, would require a large control station. The Soviet delegates obviously had no taste for this method, and their attitude indicated that they themselves may not have thought of this refinement of the acoustic-detection technique.

When it came time to write that part of the report dealing with acoustic detection methods, Soviet Chief delegate Fedorov wanted to leave it unsaid that very high altitude tests could not be reliably detected by acoustic methods. Dr. Fisk, the American chairman, insisted it be kept in.

Dr. Fedorov also submitted a draft containing a statement that under-water detection by hydroacoustic methods was easy, up to a range of 10,000 kilometers.[47]

His draft made no mention of the key problem, identification, as Sir William Penny of Britain quickly pointed out.

Dr. Fedorov took the position the West was being unreasonable:

> It is hard for me to imagine any substantial difficulties with regard to the identification of explosions because we certainly would not have too many events which could provide a similar signal to that produced by a substantial explosion. The signals used in underwater signalization as such are very few in number. The signals which might be produced by fish, by whales, and so forth, are not numerous; I cannot think of anything, except possibly underwater eruptions which could give a signal of this type. They occur fairly rarely; they are well known, and could be detected quite easily.[48]

Dr. Fedorov, however, was more interested in a speedy conclusion to the talks than pressing endlessly for his exaggerated theories about the usefulness of the acoustic method of detection. In the end, he agreed to the cautious United States approach, which warned that both under-water and aboveground interference could paralyze acoustic detection at crucial moments. Conclusions on the applications of acoustic waves for detecting nuclear explosions were agreed upon at the Conference's eighth session on July 10, 1958.

The experts mentioned this one area of doubt about the acoustic method of detection:

> Acoustic waves which resemble in certain cases the acoustic signals of nuclear explosions may be produced by natural events [primarily meteoric, volcanic, or submarine disturbances]. In such cases the identification of the event as natural or as a nuclear explosion must be based on a comparison of acoustic data with those obtained by aid of other methods.[49]

This was compromise language that omitted, at Soviet insistence, a more precise statement about the shortcomings of the acoustic method. Later there was to be some concern among American officials that nuclear testing might be deliberately timed to coincide with the huge disturbances on the ocean floor—underwater earthquakes—so that the nuclear blast might be masked by the bigger natural disturbance.

Radioactive Debris

Sir William Penney of Great Britain gave the first conference presentation on methods of detecting nuclear tests by sampling radioactive debris from the air. Here are some important passages from the presentation:

> The equipment with which such debris may be collected is relatively simple. Filters are mounted in a device which is put on the wings or the fuselage of an aircraft which flies for several hours at selected height or heights. The design of the filter is such that several thousand cubic feet of air can be passed per minute, and all debris down to submicron sizes can be collected with high efficiency. . . .
>
> If we collect 10^8 fissions within a few days of an explosion, then with that quantity we can establish the presence of short-lived fission products, namely molybdenum-99. The very presence of such short-lived fission products as that proves that the debris has come from fission of the last few days or weeks. If we can get 10^{10} fissions, then we can begin to do an elaborate radiochemical analysis which separates the number of atoms—different species—and we can then do some [more] accurate work to determine when the event occurred. . . .
>
> We think that if the measurements are done a few days after the explosion, we can measure it within a few per cent. . . . If we get a sample three or four days after an explosion, we can tell when the explosion occurred within three or four hours.
>
> There are just two possibilities which I must mention, if only to dismiss them. The debris may come from the accident of a nuclear pile, but this radiochemistry will tell us that either it was or it was not . . . a pile acci-

dent. . . . The other possibility is that a nuclear event—a bomb—has added around it fission products from a pile in order to make the radio-chemical analysis difficult. . . .

If one has done this analysis and determined when the explosion occurred, and if one has the wind pattern from the site of the explosion to where the debris was collected, one can use meteorological arguments to say where the explosion occurred.

Sometimes the meteorological situation has been simple. If only two or three days has elapsed, the site of the explosion can perhaps be fixed within a few hundred miles. Sometimes the weather situation has been complicated, and backtracking, as we call it, backtracking in the meteorological map—tells you that there may have been two or more possible sites. You do not get a unique answer. The winds divide and go off to different centers. In the worst cases, one may be faced with a position in which there were two possible sites, and they may be a thousand miles apart, or even more. . . .

One can obtain radioactivity in rainwater. But we do not, as a rule, work with rainwater; we much prefer samples collected from the air, because it makes the chemistry much more simple and much more direct. The other point is, of course, that it does not always rain where you want it to.

Another important observation that we have made is that sometimes the debris in the air is confined to a very thin layer at any one point. Overhead there is some radioactive debris, but it may be in a layer only 1,000 feet thick—a very thin layer—so that an airplane flying on a routine patrol may miss this radioactivity if it is not just at the right height. . . .

There are some types of meteorological situation in which it is difficult to collect debris at a distance. We have had occasions with small-yield devices which gave a very low cloud, where the winds were unusual and the clouds circulated in a very small area of a very few hundred miles, and, additionally, there was very heavy rainfall. In this very unusual circumstance, it may be that a large part of the debris is washed out of the atmosphere, and one cannot be certain of getting sufficient samples at a distance to do good radiochemistry.

It is obvious, of course, that a deep underground explosion puts no debris into the atmosphere. In the case of a burst very high up, and I mean as high as an aircraft can fly, or higher—40,000 or 50,000 or 60,000 feet—the debris does go up and in time, no doubt, some of it falls down. But we have found great difficulty in getting samples when the bursts are up in the air.

I think I could summarize this by saying that, if we can get 10^{10} fissions[50] within two or three or four days of an explosion, we think we can prove that the radioactivity comes from a nuclear explosion.

If good meteorological data are available, we can identify the site of the explosion within a few hundred miles—except when the meteorological conditions are complex, in which case the site as determined may not be unique. After about four days, backtracking by meteorological methods begins to become quite unreliable. And then, as I have said, there are some types of bursts where it is very difficult to obtain debris or where debris is not put into the atmosphere.[51]

Dr. Fedorov suggested that ten-day-old fallout instead of three- or four-day-old material would be perfectly adequate for detection purposes. This would have permitted a spacing of control stations at several thousand kilometers instead of under a thousand, as Sir William's presentation suggested.

The British representative's stress on aircraft to sample the atmosphere, particularly after other detection methods had raised suspicions of an explosion, caused the Russians considerable pain. Dr. Fedorov said the Russians had at one time used large aircraft to "fish out of the atmosphere" radioactive debris, but "later we came to the conclusion that this was not a particularly valuable way of doing it." Ground stations, he said, without aircraft, would be entirely sufficient to detect radioactivity. Sticky boards that caught the radioactivity as it fell, ventilator systems that sucked the air at ground level through filters, and rain collection would be sufficient to pick up the debris, he assured the Western scientists. His aim appeared to be to avoid permitting any sampling aircraft to fly over the Soviet Union.

The United States presented evidence from its own experience in the Pacific proving grounds and Nevada tests that radioactive clouds could go for ten or fifteen days, or longer, without dropping any of their radioactivity.[52]

In an extreme case, one American again pointed out, as Sir William had earlier, the cloud could flatten out in a shape only 1,000 feet in thickness instead of mixing vertically over thousands of feet in altitude. Then it would be extremely difficult even for a plane to catch the radioactivity.

A Polish scientist sought to come to the Soviet side's aid. He reported that debris from Nevada tests in March, 1955, had been picked up in Leningrad, Moscow, and Poland five to fifteen days after the explosions. Thus, atmospheric explosions could be picked up 10,000 to 20,000 kilometers away. This kind of long-range evidence of American tests, it appeared, was the main basis for Soviet Premier Khrushchev's claims that an international control system was not necessary.

An American warning that "clean-bomb" radioactivity would be more difficult to detect gave a Soviet scientist, Dr. Leipunsky, the opportunity to deride the clean-bomb concept. He presented a mathematical "proof," using American data published by AEC Commissioner Libby and the Joint Atomic Energy Committee, that clean bombs are actually dirtier than dirty bombs, so they can be detected with ease. Dr. Fedorov followed this up with claims that stations could pick up debris 1,000 to 2,000 kilometers away (625 to 1,250 miles). This would imply a spacing of stations 1,250 to 2,500 miles apart.

At one point, Dr. Fedorov claimed the Soviet Union had picked up fallout in its ground collection system from a 10-kiloton burst ten kilometers in the air, roughly six miles up. This was interesting to the Western experts on two counts. First, it was confirmation that the Soviet

Union had exploded a 10-kiloton weapon at so high an altitude. Second, it flew in the face of all Western theory that fallout from nuclear explosions above the troposphere would stay in the stratosphere and leak out at a very slow rate which would not be picked up at ground stations immediately after an explosion. Fallout resides in the stratosphere for two to ten years. When Dr. Fedorov was asked for statistics on what amount of fallout was detected, and where, he demured. But he continued to insist that fallout had been monitored at ground stations. Americans still believe it would take months and years for fallout from such explosions to reach the ground, and then probably would first appear thousands of miles from the site of the explosion.

Until a satellite-detection system is installed, therefore, secret testing above the troposphere, especially on days of heavy cloud cover over detection stations, is probably feasible.

As the Experts' report finally made clear, there is a "blind spot" in the detection system between 10 and 50 kilometers, that is between 6 and 31 miles above the earth.

The Russians even attempted feebly to make a virtue of the delay that their sparsely spaced control-station network would entail in detecting radioactive fallout from a nuclear test. Dr. Fedorov contended that all the unfavorable meteorological phenomena that might cause a more dense network to miss an explosion in the first few days would be ironed out, according to the law of averages, over a longer period of time. Sparsely-spaced stations, he argued, would do a dependable job and remove the requirement for either so many stations or aircraft sampling.

Dr. Fedorov also claimed that if shallow underground blasts are vented they will send their radioactivity far and wide into the atmosphere. The United States contended, on the basis of its Nevada experience, that virtually all the fallout would drop in the immediate environs. Dr. Fedorov estimated that 20 per cent would go into the atmosphere.

Because there was some uncertainty, Dr. Fedorov then suggested that all mention of debris from shallow underground bursts be dropped from the report.

The Western draft stating the capabilities of radioactive-debris detection also mentioned the limitations of discovering underground pockets of debris. Dr. Fedorov suggested this be dropped, too—or at least that discussion of it be postponed for a later point in the report, when over-all systems would be discussed.

British experience, Sir John Cockcroft reported, showed that new tests were difficult to detect by the ground-sampling method after a background of previous tests had been built up. Differentiating between old and fresh radioactive debris could seldom be done effectively from ground samples alone.[53]

This background from previous tests would make ground detection of small nuclear shots of one kiloton or so almost impossible.

Depending solely on ground stations would also produce the danger of false alarm from other sources of radioactivity. Erratic dripping of fallout from the stratosphere to the troposphere might be mistaken for a new test, the Western delegation suggested. Since the Soviet delegation has not been able to demonstrate the effectiveness of the ground filter collection system, the Western scientists said, aircraft collection should be recommended to the governments concerned.

Dr. Fisk, further emphasizing the value of aircraft sampling, cited the example of a Soviet test in the vicinity of Novaya Zemlya in the Arctic on February 23, 1958, a few months before the conference. Aircraft operating over Canada collected samples of the very high yield shot, Dr. Fisk reported, six days after the test "and yet radioactivity was never picked up in ground filter units anywhere in Canada—even those filters directly under the known parts of the cloud. Similar observations were obtained on five out of ten cases on which we have data from Canada." [54]

The American scientists later also challenged the theories of Polish and Soviet scientists that they had correctly identified, by ground collections of fallout only, specific tests in Nevada. They pointed out that there was almost certainly an overlap between shots on March 1 and March 7, 1955. The Americans pointed to similar discrepancies in other Soviet claims of having detected American shots by collecting nuclear debris on the ground.

If this had been a purely diplomatic negotiation these rather bonehead Soviet "mistakes" might not have been regarded as errors but as deliberate attempts to mislead or as bargaining in bad faith. As it was, the negotiations turned into a kind of jolly game of cat and mouse, with the Soviet side openly trying to trick the West into accepting an inspection system that would leak like a sieve and with the Western scientists taking up the challenge as if it were all great sport. No warning word of the Soviet attempts at trickery was passed to the outside world, except in the verbatim records released much later.

The exercise also served to extract information on how the United States detection system worked. On July 21, two weeks after discussion of the radioactive-debris method of detection had begun, the Soviet side relented on its absurd insistence on ground stations only. Dr. Fedorov first read a lengthy justification for his previous position, that ground stations were quite enough. Then he accepted the use of home-country aircraft—along specific lanes, with a representative of the control network aboard.[55]

Although not a complete victory for the United States and its Western allies, this represented considerable movement on the part of the Soviet Union. It would have been better, from the Western viewpoint, if control-system aircraft could make the checks over the territory of the Soviet Union and the United States. But the presence of an observer in the plane partially compensated for this.

There was no stipulation, however, that the observer would have any control. As a matter of fact, the term "observer" indicated he would have no operational authority. Thus, the possible manipulation of the detection equipment in the aircraft would be beyond his control.

If any detection mission were not conducted according to the observer's idea of rigorous detection methods, of course, the matter could be reported to the control system.

The final report to which all the experts agreed provided that "representatives of the U.S.S.R., the U.S.A., and U.K., and other states participating in the operation of the control system may be on board these aircraft in the capacity of observers."

The Soviet acceptance of aircraft, in this manner, became a "breakthrough" for the American side. It was a breakthrough, however, only if one considered the Soviet Union to have been sincere from the beginning in thinking that ground stations alone could do a sufficient job of inspection. Scientific facts of the matter, however, showed so overwhelmingly that ground stations alone could not do a reliable job that many on the American delegation suspected that the Fedorov performance had been a "political" exhibition from the beginning. It was the old technique of "one upmanship" in which the Soviet Union appeared to be making a large concession. The Western experts, therefore, were under pressure to do the "decent" thing and make the next concession, perhaps on a more solid issue. Dr. Fedorov thus appeared to be introducing well-known Soviet negotiating techniques into the scientific conference.

In their agreed conclusions on the fallout-collection method of nuclear-test detection, the conference finally agreed that ground control posts spaced at 2,000 or 3,000 kilometers (1,250 to 1,875 miles) could detect explosions of one kiloton or larger, set off in the troposphere (from 0 to 10 kilometers, or 6 miles, above the surface of the earth), "with a high degree of reliability" in five to twenty days after the explosion. The place of the explosion could not be exactly determined, but the time could be set within some relatively small error. Smaller explosions could be detected if there were favorable weather conditions.

Aircraft could detect radioactive debris in two to five days, the experts agreed, if some other method of detection had localized the area where a suspected test had been conducted. The approximate point of the explosion could be established by backtracking on the trajectory of the radioactive cloud with the use of weather and wind data.

Shallow underground and shallow underwater explosions could also be identified by collecting radioactive samples, but with lesser reliability.

Over the oceans, it was suggested that aircraft be used to sample the air for radioactive debris. Existing meteorological observation craft could be used for these flights.

Flights over the United States, the Soviet Union, or Great Britain to collect air samples should be made in aircraft of the country being overflown and along routes laid down in advance. Representatives of all three nations could be aboard the aircraft as observers.

Finally, the report said, the system should be improved over a period of time, as the atmosphere was cleared of radioactive particles from previous tests, and as collection and analyzing techniques were perfected.

Seismic

By the time the scientists of East and West got to the point of discussing the seismic method of detecting nuclear tests, attitudes were hardening enough so that Dr. Fisk and Dr. Fedorov could not even agree which side should present its views first. Dr. Fisk, chairman for the day, fished a neutral Swiss coin out of his pocket and asked the Russian: "Will you please call—heads or tails?"

"Heads!" shouted Dr. Fedorov.

"It's tails," the transcript quotes Dr. Fisk. "In that event we will hear from Dr. Romney first and look forward with pleasure to his being followed by Dr. Pasechnik." [56]

The experts identified three types of waves—longitudinal, transverse, and surface—as the important ones for seismic detection of underground or underwater nuclear explosions. The longitudinal wave is the most important, they agreed, "both for detecting an explosion and for determining the place of the explosion, and also for distinguishing an earthquake from explosions. Transverse and surface waves also help to define the nature of the seismic perturbation."

Dr. Fisk had given notice on the second day of the conference, as the Soviet delegates dallied over what the purpose of the experts' talks should be, that he believed there were serious problems ahead in devising a system that could detect underground shots. [57]

He had warned that "a modest depth of burial" would be sufficient to contain completely "even quite large nuclear explosions." For instance, a 100-kiloton explosion could be contained at a depth of 1,000 meters (3,000 feet) or less. Seismic waves would be produced, he acknowledged, but "identification is extremely difficult, or *may even be impossible,* by seismic means alone."

The seriousness of the problem, he said, was demonstrated "by the fact that each year many thousands of earthquakes occur which give seismic signals which could be confused with those produced by underground explosions of a few kilotons or more."

Another uncertainty, he said, was that the seismic signal produced in various underground media had not been studied. "For example, if a nuclear explosion took place in material either natural or man-made, which is much more crushable, and, therefore, has more cushioning effect than the medium on which we have specific data for nuclear shots, seismic energy reduction or decoupling by a substantial factor could occur. Thus, a much larger explosion might be made to look as small as the Rainier shot to which I have referred."

When Dr. Carl Romney made the opening presentation for the

United States in the study of seismic-detection methods, he elaborated on the Fisk statement. The earthquake authority, Dr. Gutenberg, had estimated there are more than 6,000 earthquakes per year larger than a magnitude of 4:25, the approximate magnitude of the Rainier shot, he said.

Dr. Romney gave no estimate then of the number among these 6,000 that could definitely be identified as earthquakes. He merely stated the magnitude of the problem.

> All seismic signals look very much alike regardless of the source and this is because the primary feature of the seismic wave depends on the mechanical and structural properties of the earth.
>
> Given sufficient information, you can sometimes identify an earthquake in a positive manner. *I am not sure you could ever identify an explosion—* that is a hard statement to make; *I will say I am not sure we know how to identify an explosion in a positive manner at the present time.* I think our suspicions could be very much aroused on occasion, but *I do not know of any geophysicist who would be willing to state that the parameters of the earth are so well known that we can deduce completely the nature of the source from geophysical data.* [Author's italics.][58]

Dr. Pasechnik, in his opening statement, took the predictable position that the overwhelming majority of signals picked up on seismographs could be definitely eliminated as earthquakes. He said there would be only five or ten signals a year that would have to be investigated.[59]

Later the Soviet scientists doubled their estimate to ten to twenty unidentified events a year, but with no more scientific back-up than earlier. "The overwhelming majority of earthquakes will be excluded from discussion as a result of the use of a number of well-established factors in connection with the reading of seismograph operations by seismologists," Dr. Pasechnik claimed.

Deep underground earthquakes would be immediately excluded, he said, especially if they were of magnitude 5 or more; frequency characteristics of earthquakes were dissimilar from explosions and could eliminate large groups of earthquakes; shocks close to control stations could also be eliminated because the seismograms would be clear. Pasechnik continued: "There will perhaps remain a very small number of records, say five or ten a year, but certainly not thousands as Dr. Fisk indicated— five or ten, I say, which might raise some doubt. In order to identify these records a very careful study of the seismograms will have to be effected, of seismograms which would be contained by the network of stations."

Here was another instance where the Soviet scientists appeared to be making their science fit the amount of inspection they wanted for a nuclear test ban, rather than allowing the inspection to meet the scientifically established need.

As for decoupling, or muffling underground explosions, Dr. Pasechnik discounted the possibility of any decoupling sufficient to spoil the seismic signal. Hidden underground-explosions would cause the earth to bulge or crack on the surface, he claimed. Besides, the Rainier explosion was recorded 2,300 miles away. "Even through artificial means the soil conditions cannot be really deteriorated to that extent."

All underground nuclear explosions would produce a signal no less than magnitude 4 on the Richter scale and should be recordable over a distance of 1,250 to 1,875 miles, he estimated. Hiding nuclear explosions behind TNT explosions would be impractical, Dr. Pasechnik said. And spoofing a control station with background noise or "through an explosion" would not work, because the strange noise could be filtered out.

He also anticipated the argument that had been advanced at the Humphrey hearings—that an earthquake might be used to trigger a nuclear explosion. "An explosion against a background of an earthquake practically speaking can be identified and separated in *all* cases through combined study of all the records obtained by the several stations surrounding the epicenter," Pasechnik claimed. (Author's italics.)

A network of stations could pinpoint an explosion with an accuracy of plus or minus three miles, he claimed. The distance between stations, he proposed, should be of the order of 2,000 or 2,500 kilometers (1,250 to 1,560 miles).

Dr. Romney later showed the Soviet-bloc scientists several American seismograms of the 1.7-kiloton Rainier shot. Many of the signals, he pointed out, were too weak to be recognized. Of the College, Alaska signal he said: "I think it is quite obvious that, in spite of the fact that the Alaskan station is one of the very quietest stations we know of, this signal probably would not have been detected had we not known exactly where to look. The distance is approximately 3,700 kilometers [2,300 miles]."

Using seismograms from the Rainier explosion, Dr. Romney also tried to show Dr. Pasechnik that many of his theories were only theories—not proved in practice.

He concluded that a shot of Rainier's size is about the minimum that could be detected at "intermediate distances" of the order of 2,000 or 3,000 kilometers (1,250 to 1,875 miles). It could not be detected in the "shadow zone" of 700 to 1,100 miles. Second, Dr. Romney said, a shot producing only about half the seismic signal of Rainier could be detected only to distances of the order of 400 kilometers or 250 miles. "I should also add at this point that a shot appreciably larger than Rainier can be detected to truly great distances."

A third conclusion advanced by Dr. Romney was that the variability of the inner earth makes it difficult to distinguish between earthquakes and blasts except, possibly, at "very small distances."

The Russians suggested that the poor results from the Rainier experiment might be due to the narrow frequency-response of the American equipment. This deprecation of American equipment, which the Western experts considered far superior to that of the Russians, got to be a sore point.

Dr. Romney exclaimed with some exasperation at one point that from reading the Soviet literature it appeared Soviet seismologists do their recordings at 3 A.M., "when there is no wind." This, he said, "is hardly the basis for a year-in-year-out detection method."

Soviet TNT-shots cited were also fired in lakes "which give exceedingly efficient coupling," Dr. Romney observed. He questioned whether this evidence was "germaine" to the underground-detection problem. Ideal stations would not be possible in a world-wide network, he said. "I am afraid we would, necessarily, be saddled with a great number of average stations." [60]

The Soviet scientists repeatedly based their predictions of the efficiency of a seismic net on optimum performance, while the Americans sought to convince them that the system must be geared to operation under adverse conditions. As Dr. Romney expressed it:

> The detection which I am talking about is with instruments which also give you some diagnostic information. I have no question at all that we could detect only at greater distance than I have mentioned, with high frequency equipment, in the middle of the night, on days when there is no wind, and so on. But I do not believe that we would get from these recordings the kind of information which we would need that would prevent us from running to investigate every epicenter.

Sir Edward Bullard of the British team argued similarly with greater force. The Soviet scientists were trying to compare signals obtained under ideal conditions with the very average conditions that would pertain in an inspection system for a nuclear test ban. One of their examples, he said, had been obtained "by firing in a lake at a very quiet time in the middle of the night," using instruments with special frequency characteristics. Taking these things all together, he said, they provide an improvement factor over the norm or average of 2,000 to 20,000.

Sir Edward then suggested for the first time at the conference that the "threshold" for detecting the direction of first motion "might well be about 5 kilotons." [61]

Western scientists listened to hours of Soviet boasting about the sensitivity of their seismographs. Finally, Sir Edward asked if any Soviet stations had picked up Rainier explosions, which would have been within their capabilities if the stations had lived up to the reputation the Soviet scientists had claimed for them.

"No," Dr. Sadovski replied, "we did not obtain any records of this kind and, as far as I can remember, we did not have any report that this interesting experiment would take place."

Of course if Soviet equipment had been up to Soviet claims, there would have been no need for advance notice. Beyond this, however, Sir

Edward pointed out that the advance notices about the Rainier shot had been "in all the papers for months. It was announced in the presence of your delegation in Toronto at the International Union of the Geophysical Year." Dr. Libby had advertised it to more than fifty countries at an international conference in Paris.

Mr. Sadovski replied: "As you know, when we learn that some type of recording or registration is to take place, considerable time is required to prepare for it. In this particular case, we had no such time at our disposal."

The Soviet delegation also insisted it could get a clear indication of first motion much farther away from the epicenter than the Americans claimed. First motion of nuclear explosions could be recorded at 1,500 kilometers from the epicenter, the Russians said.[62]

It was at this point that the Soviet Union, ever eager to shut off the exchange of views before it was possible to delve too deeply into the problem, abruptly proposed that the conference adopt a conclusion on the seismic methods of detecting nuclear tests.

Dr. Fisk replied, in effect, "Not so fast." He noted that the problem of the "shadow zone" [63] was "a rather crucial question" on which there had been no agreement; second, the size of the signal from nuclear explosions had not been thoroughly explored; the accuracy with which epicenters could be determined had not been discussed; the frequency of natural events, like earthquakes, and the problems of confusing them with explosions, had not been dealt with thoroughly.[64]

American experts argued that if the spacing between stations was too great "possibly thousands of ambiguous cases can occur each year, many of which may require field inspection." [65]

The difficulties of onsite inspection were also alluded to. If the location of the epicenter could be made only within five to eight kilometers, it was pointed out, some 100 to 200 square kilometers of territory might have to be covered by an inspection team.

"Even with the use of geophysical methods, such inspection would be extremely tedious and time consuming," Frank Press, one of the United States leading seismologists said. "To avoid this, we ask for an adequate distribution of stations . . ."

To emphasize the wide gap between seismological theory and practice, Dr. Press also called the Soviet scientists' attention to experiences in Italy, where earthquakes had presented signals identical with explosions —compressional first motions in all directions. This phenomenon was said to occur frequently in Italy.[66]

After the Americans had presented seismograms showing that experience did not fit Soviet theories, the Soviet seismologists replied that since actual experience turned out to be contradictory in many cases, it would be better to rely on theory than on practical experience!

At two informal sessions, held outside the formal Palais de Nations meeting room, Soviet and American scientists finally came to agreement on the ranges at which underground nuclear tests could be detected. Compromises were frequently reached by mentioning optimum *possibilities* of detection as well as realistic *probabilities*. This had the effect of producing agreement but was misleadingly optimistic to the uninitiated.

Drs. Northrup, Romney, and Press stated the agreement on seismic detection this way:

> We are agreed that it is *possible* to register underground nuclear explosions of one kiloton at a distance of the order of 1,000 kilometer (625 miles). However, the determination of the direction of first motion may not be *possible* beyond 500 kilometers (312 miles), under average conditions or beyond 700 kilometers (472 miles) in favorable conditions, although occasionally first motion may be determined as far as 1,000 kilometer (625 miles). [Author's italics.]

That was the consensus of the American delegation of experts. In collaboration with the Soviet scientists this statement was agreed upon for inclusion in the conference report: "We believe that it is *possible* to register an underground nuclear explosion of the order of one kiloton yield at a distance of 1,000 kilometers. However, the determination of the direction of first motion will not be possible in all cases." [Author's italics.]

Thus the report stressed optimal performance, gave no indications on minimal performance.

The East-West experts' conclusions on the seismic method stated quite flatly that longitudinal seismic waves from underground nuclear explosions, set off in volcanic tuff like that at the Nevada proving ground, could not only be detected, but that the direction of first motion could be determined at distances up to 1,000 kilometers (625 miles). The "blind spot" from 600 to 1,250 miles was called the "skip distance" or "shadow zone." From 1,250 miles to about 2,200 miles, explosions could be detected and first motions could be distinguished down to one kiloton "during periods of favorable noise conditions." Blasts down to five kilotons could be "recorded" during "periods of unfavorable noise conditions." Noise levels would vary from station to station.

It would be easier to detect and identify explosions in shallow water than those underground, the report said. Subterranean detection would require relatively quiet stations using an array of seismographs to achieve this efficiency.

Coastal and island stations would be noisier than those inside continents, so that the efficiency of control posts at the noisier locations would be reduced. This would be partly compensated by the nearer inland stations, which could register the more powerful blasts at distances of from 1,250 to 2,200 miles. The quiet inland stations could catch explosions of five kilotons or more at those distances, the report said.

The experts concluded that "not less than 90 per cent of all earthquakes taking place in continents can be identified." This was later to be proved highly optimistic. Estimates bearing on the efficiency of the detection system were contained in controversial paragraph II, C, 5 of the experts' report. It said:

> The majority of earthquakes can be distinguished from explosions with a high degree of reliability if the direction of first motion of the longitudinal wave is clearly registered at five or more seismic stations on various bearings from the epicenter.[67] Thus not less than 90 per cent of all earthquakes taking place in continents can be identified.[68] The remaining 10 per cent or less of cases will require the analysis of additional seismograms where this is possible; and for this purpose use must also be made of the data of the existing network of seismic stations. If required, these supplementary stations should be further equipped with improved apparatus. In relatively aseismic areas it is sufficient merely to define the position of the epicenter. In this connection, cases of detection of seismic events will be regarded as suspicious and will require further investigation with the help of other methods. For those cases which remain unidentified, inspection of the region will be necessary.
>
> In regions where the regular disposition of seismic stations in quiet conditions is not possible, the percentage of correct identification of earthquakes will be less.
>
> With modern methods and making use of the data of several surrounding seismic stations the area within which an epicenter is localized can be assessed as approximately 100–200 square kilometers.

This meant that the control network could "pinpoint" an underground explosion inside an area of 39 to 78 square miles. Baltimore has an area of 78 square miles. San Francisco is listed as having an area of 44.6 square miles.[69]

The experts said that the range of accuracy of recording and identifying underground nuclear explosions could be improved by perfecting seismic apparatus, methods of recording seismic waves, and methods of differentiating earthquakes from explosions.

During the Geneva meetings, Dr. Romney suggested privately that additional underground nuclear tests would be necessary to perfect detection and identification techniques. He "received a tongue lashing for my immoral position in return," [70] he later reported.

The Soviet scientists gave no indication whether they had conducted any underground nuclear tests themselves, or whether they had not. And they showed little interest in small weapons.

Chairman Fisk and Dr. Romney agreed later that the Russians sincerely felt "detection and identification is easier than we thought." [71]

Dr. Romney was convinced, as well, that the Russians had conducted no underground nuclear explosions.

We beat them on the head time and time again about our Rainier experience, and I would have thought at some point they would have been provoked into saying, "We have similar experience."

I received several lectures from their seismologists on the effect of an explosion in a semi-infinite half space, and how such an explosion would be easily identifiable, and I said, "Look out the window. Does this look like a semi-infinite half space?" and of course it doesn't. The earth is very complex.

They were talking theory, we were talking practice . . . and I believe this is the fundamental difference in our beliefs.

In theory it is all very simple; in practice—and I should say in the simple theory it is all very simple—in practice it is very difficult.

The problem of "decoupling" the energy of a nuclear explosion from the surrounding earth in an underground test by placing it in a big hole came up fleetingly at the experts' conference. Dr. Hans Bethe presented the American thinking in a long, theoretical dissertation. He reached the conclusion that the maximum amount of decoupling that could be achieved by constructing a big hole would be reduction of the signal to one-half or one-third its former size. This was referred to as "decoupling by a factor of two or three."

The Soviet delegation was unanimously enthusiastic about all Dr. Bethe's presentations at the conference. There were some searching questions from the Soviet side on his decoupling presentation, however. One young physicist sought out Dr. Bethe for a further discussion of the plan in private. The Russians wound up postulating that a decoupling factor of twenty would be possible theoretically, but Dr. Bethe stuck to his estimate that a factor of two or three would be the maximum.

So far as the American scientists at the meeting could recall, there had not been any inkling at the 1958 conference that the Soviet scientists might have known more about the decoupling theory than they let on. (It was not until six months later that the expanded possibilities for hiding tests were discovered by another scientist, Dr. Albert Latter of The RAND Corporation. He found that the decoupling factor theoretically could be 300 or more.)

The Conference of Experts approved conclusions, without reference to decoupling, on the use of seismic waves as a means of detecting nuclear explosions on July 24.[72]

RADIO SIGNALS

The same pattern of debate developed in the discussion of radio signals for detecting nuclear tests in the atmosphere. The Soviet side claimed it would be easier than the American side estimated.

Soviet scientists tended to minimize the interference of lightning and other atmospheric disturbances. Dr. Richard Latter, representing the

United States, said that even after eliminating "as probably not being of nuclear origin" all but 1 or 2 per cent of the interference during a Nevada experiment, one signal every two minutes was found to be un-identifiable. That meant that suspicious signals would pile up at the rate of 30 per hour, or 720 per day.

The Nevada experience may have been "above average," Dr. Latter acknowledged, but the rate of interference would have to be reduced a great deal before the radio-signal method of detection could be considered reliable.[73]

> It appears, therefore, that within our present knowledge even kiloton explosions in the air may under certain circumstances be difficult to detect at moderate distances, if at all possible [Dr. Latter said]. However, for even quite shallow sub-surface explosions, whether in water or soil, the electromagnetic signal is negligible at any significant distances even under circumstances where there may be radiochemical, acoustic and seismic evidence.
>
> [Detecting radio signals, nevertheless,] can play a very useful, but supplementary role in those cases in which other indications of a nuclear explosion are observed.

The Soviet scientists tried, up to the end, to make as strong a conference-report statement about the inspection capabilities of radio signals as the United States would accept. The American scientists insisted, however, that mention be made of the possibility that interference would sharply reduce the effectiveness of the system. The Soviet Union finally agreed.

A big argument developed over inclusion of a statement that it was not known whether natural events in space produced particle intensities (interference from bands of natural radioactivity like the Van Allen Belt) that could confuse a monitoring satellite. This would have been an important piece of guidance for readers of the report. The Western side agreed, however, that it was not essential to be included in the final report. There was not even a discussion of the possibility that artificial signals might be produced by radio devices to confuse the picture still further.

The section on the application of electromagnetic methods for detecting nuclear explosions was approved by the conference on July 25.[74]

Very High Altitudes

Dr. Hans Bethe and Dr. Leipunski, a member of the Soviet delegation, discussed detection of nuclear tests at very high altitudes, basing their statements completely on theory since there had been no practical experience.

Dr. Bethe suggested that a system of satellites be used for these observations, at great elevation—6,000 kilometers above the earth or about

3,750 miles. "I realize this requires considerable energy of launching," Dr. Bethe said, "but I think that satellites at this altitude, especially if their weight is not too large, should be feasible in the very near future, especially if we can use the great development of satellite launching techniques of the Soviet Union."[75]

Detection of radio signals and light would be two of the main methods of catching a nuclear blast in very high altitudes and outer space.

It was estimated that interference from the sun and the stars could be minimized by focusing the detection instruments, or narrowing their field of vision, so to speak.

Dr. Leipunski estimated that the radius of detection of a satellite would be about 300,000 kilometers, 187,000 miles. "In other words, explosions conducted on the moon can be recorded quite clearly on a satellite above the earth," Dr. Leipunski claimed. Prospects for noticing a test behind the moon were not discussed.

If not only gamma rays but neutrons could be detected by equipment in a satellite, Dr. Leipunski reasoned, "It is possible even to determine the distance at which the explosion took place."

He cautioned, however, that it would not be possible to say who actually caused the explosions. The one question mark in the detection system, both sides agreed, would be the Van Allen belt of radiation that was discovered by American satellites. It was not known how this would interfere with the signal from any nuclear-test blast.

In later presentations, Dr. Leipunski estimated that five to six satellites could cover the entire earth, if they were sent into orbit at a distance of 6,000 kilometers from the surface of the earth. One satellite, he said, covered approximately one-fourth of the total surface of the earth. He further estimated that the greatest distance between an explosion and a satellite then would be 10,000 kilometers.

Dr. Fedorov, in a rare display of enthusiasm for peaceful coexistence, suggested that the Soviet Union and the United States each send up two or three satellites to comprise the nuclear-test-ban detection system in outer space.

The conference approved a set of conclusions on the effectiveness of detecting nuclear explosions at high altitudes at the July 28 session.[76]

The System

Dr. Fedorov presented the Soviet side's conception of a complete control system for world-wide detection and identification of nuclear-weapons tests on July 30.

"We consider it absolutely necessary that we should propose the simplest possible control system," Dr. Fedorov said in a predictable opening statement. Almost all nuclear-weapons tests had been detected in the past without any special international system, he claimed, and explosions of 10 kilotons and above when conducted aboveground can be detected with "the simplest control facilities."

To prove his point he reported slyly that the United States had carried out thirty-two nuclear tests in the Pacific area from the previous February 28 to July 26, "although the United States had reported only fourteen explosions." He supplied a list of the thirty-two American nuclear explosions that the Soviet Union's observation stations had detected at a distance of 3,100 to 3,700 miles.[77]

Dr. Fisk later[78] used the Soviet Union's own list to prove that remote seismic stations, without an international inspection system, would be a shaky basis on which to found a control system. Two of the nuclear explosions reported by Dr. Fedorov, on April 29 and on July 14, did not occur at the Pacific Proving Grounds, Dr. Fisk said.

> We on the Western side have no knowledge of any nuclear tests carried out anywhere at these times. Your comments to qualify these apparent errors would be useful; in particular, it would be useful to know what methods reported these particular events. We believe that further explanations about these detections, accompanied by data, would provide a most timely and valuable contribution to our present studies. Perhaps you would consider having the records sent here so that one day next week we could look at them in some detail.

Another possibility, of course, was that the Soviet Union was probing to find out if the two "errors" had been American tests. If so, the United States obliged.

Dr. Fisk offered additional comments to expose the Soviet attempt to advertise its detection capabilities from the Soviet land mass:

> The majority of the tests to which this list refers were of considerably higher yield than we had been discussing in our meetings here. The conditions under which the tests were conducted are essentially ideal conditions for tests. There was, of course, no concealment, and no attempt at concealment; none of the tests were conducted underground; the location of the test area was known; and, of course, the general time of the series of tests was announced in advance. For these reasons it seems to me that the list, as a whole, carries no particular significance as far as the work of this conference is concerned.[79]

Dr. Fedorov declined to make the Soviet detection data available to the conference. "I do not believe that they would be of particular interest to us," he said. "You have such data, we have such data. I do not think the data would introduce anything new into our discussions."[80] He made the point, however, that the United States, despite its claims of openness, had failed to report on some sixteen explosions in the Pacific series.

Dr. Fisk still had the last word. The Soviet attempt to list American explosions had raised another important problem for a control system, he said. What happens if the inspection system detects "nonexistent explosions?" It was a question that deserved much more consideration than it got.

In his general presentation on requirements for an over-all control system, Dr. Fedorov made this main point: "The special control system comprising a network of control posts distributed throughout the globe is actually necessary only for the detection of tests of relatively small magnitude, as well as the specially concealed types of explosions or bursts which might be carried out under particular conditions."

Using several methods to check on the same event would increase the efficiency of the system, he claimed. The 1-kiloton range should be the "threshold" on which the control system should be based, he said. Smaller yields could also be detected, he warned, apparently hoping to reach agreement on an all-inclusive ban. Even with this goal, however, he insisted that "the simplest possible network of control posts" could be established. Costs would be minimum and the time for setting it up would be "the shortest possible." Then he enunciated a "principle of simplicity" that raised eyebrows on the Western side:

> It would be simpler to err on the side of setting up fewer stations, because we could always establish new stations.[81]
>
> On the other hand, it would be worse to propose the establishment of an excessive number of stations. This would complicate the implementation of so cumbersome a control system. It would certainly delay the time required for its implementation and it would result in excessive expenditures by our respective governments.

Dr. Fedorov then suggested that control stations could be spaced 2,500 to 3,000 kilometers (1,500 to 1,800 miles) apart in aseismic (earthquake-free) areas,[82] which he said constituted 90 per cent of the earth's surface. In the 10 to 15 per cent of the land surface considered to be actively seismic, he said, the stations could be spaced 1,500 kilometers (900 miles) apart. This, he said, would lead to a global network of 100 to 110 control posts. Twenty of these would be scattered over the world's aseismic land areas; 10 additional ones would be necessary in the seismic areas; 40 should be posted at 1500-kilometer (900-mile) intervals along the ocean shore lines, and another 30 to 40 should be stationed on islands in the oceans or on special vessels.

The seismic stations already established throughout the world could also be used in the network, he emphasized, so that "the mean distance between seismic stations is of the order of 250 kilometers."

This arrangement, he said, would make it possible "to have every chance . . . of reliable identification of the vast majority of earthquakes simultaneously by several stations."

Equipment at all the control posts should be standardized, to simplify the training of personnel and the organization of control-post administration. High altitude detection by satellites awaited further scientific knowledge, Dr. Fedorov said.

Ever sensitive to the espionage aspects of the control system, he also permitted himself an excursion into what the Western scientists considered political aspects of the control system. Technical and scientific personnel at the control posts should be "citizens of the country on the territory of which the control post is located," Dr. Fedorov said, but "at each control post it would be necessary to have at least one or two representatives from the other side." [83] (This staffing of the control posts was to become a major stumbling block in the long negotiations for a test-ban treaty.)

Control stations established in nations not allied with either the Soviet bloc or the Western powers could be staffed by personnel of the home country, he suggested. Observers from the Soviet and Western blocs could be assigned, one or two to each station.

Dr. Fedorov also proposed an international control commission created on a "parity basis," [84] which "may, when it might become suspicious regarding the occurrence of a nuclear explosion on the basis of the control post·data . . . send to the spot of the likely explosion a visiting group to check the reliability of the suspicion of the test."

Such cases "will occur seldom," Dr. Fedorov said, because "the overwhelming majority of suspected cases can arise only as the result of the inaccurate evaluation of earthquakes as a possible underground explosion."

The Soviet conception of the casual duties of on-site inspection teams contrasted sharply with the American insistence on rigorous measures to make definite findings about possible secret testing. Dr. Fedorov had this to say about the on-site inspection teams:

> Such checking or control might be done by simultaneously appointed international control commissions, and visiting missions, if and when a need might arise for it.
>
> In the majority of cases it would be sufficient, in order to ascertain reliably that a nuclear explosion had not occurred, to send representatives to the scene with the task of carrying out the most elementary kind of observation. It would appear that only in very rare cases would it be necessary in these investigations to use methods such as geophysical surveys, and so forth.
>
> Copies of the reports on such investigations should be sent by the visiting group of this control commission to the government of the country where the investigations were carried out. The international commission should send its conclusions to the governments of all the countries participating in the agreement. The international control commission could send copies of its reports to the Security Council and the General Assembly, for their information. . . .
>
> We should not go into any detail regarding the program and form of this type of inspection; to do so at this stage would appear to be inappro-

priate. In this connection, we should again bear in mind that the obligation of governments not to conduct nuclear-weapons tests will have such a tremendous moral significance and will attract so much attention from other governments that no one assuming such an obligation will dare to violate it.[85]

Dr. Robert F. Bacher presented the Western scientists' paper laying out their general conception of a control system. He suggested a threshold of "one kiloton or more," not the one kiloton or less proposed by Dr. Fedorov.[86]

Dr. Bacher emphasized that a system effective against such small explosions would have to depend on relatively close spacing of stations or on a relatively large number of on-site inspections. In other words, the inspection-wary Soviet Union, if it was to base itself on scientific reality, had a choice between two unpalatables. It could accept a large number of control stations on its territory. Or it could reduce the number of stations and agree to a large number of on-site inspections each year. "A system with a poor capability of identifying earthquakes with a one-kiloton energy equivalent," Dr. Bacher said, "would have to be balanced with a very extensive inspection capability. In view of the inherent complications in the inspection problem, at some point an increase in the number of inspection operations required would substantially reduce the over-all capabilities of the system, if not make it inoperable." [87]

The installation of a greater number of permanent stations was considered by the Western scientists to be the preferable arrangement.

Dr. Bacher proposed a 700-kilometer (440-mile) spacing of seismic control stations in order to reduce the number of unidentified coastal seismic events to about 10 per cent of the total number for underground disturbances occurring in those areas. In narrow continental land masses, he said, the spacing should be about 300 kilometers (190 miles) to achieve the same 90 per cent effectiveness.

Dr. Bacher gave no estimate, in his first presentation, on the number of stations that the world-wide control network he suggested would require. Dr. Harold Brown and Dr. Richard Latter had calculated the total in a late-night session but the number had turned out to be so appallingly large that the delegation decided to have another look—and consult Washington the while.

Dr. Bacher envisioned an inspection administration also of greater scope than the Soviet system. Besides a central headquarters there would be continental or area headquarters and regional headquarters supervising a number of individual control posts. Instantaneous communications, continuous in some instances, would be provided among all the components of the control system. On-site inspection teams should be attached to regional headquarters and have complete freedom of access to all parts of the country. Rapid transportation, air and motor, should be available. Digital computers should be available for handling data quickly. Provisions for constant improvement of the equipment should be made.

Individual components of each control post might be located separately, for optimum performance, rather than clustered in one spot. The area required for a seismic post would be a square approximately three kilometers (almost 2 miles) on a side. Acoustical arrays should be triangular, four or five kilometers on a side (up to about three miles on a side).

Aircraft should fly the oceans routinely for radioactive-debris collections, and routine flights should be extended to the poles in a few cases. Earth satellites for very high altitude detection should be maintained continuously at heights of approximately 1,000 kilometers (625 miles), not the 6,000 kilometers (3,700 miles) mentioned by Dr. Bethe a few days before.

Dr. Bacher again paid special attention to the problem of on-site inspections:

Inspection of the suspected site of a nuclear explosion will be required in the following situations:

First, receipt by the seismic net of signals which cannot be clearly identified as belonging to an earthquake. Each year approximately 500 unidentified seismic events with energies equivalent to one kiloton or greater may be detected by the seismic net and located as occurring within an area of 100 to 200 square kilometers within the continents and their associated shelf areas.

Secondly, receipt by the acoustic net of signals which cannot clearly be established as belonging to volcanoes, meteorites, large landslides, or other natural phenomena and for which neither the aircraft nor ground sampling systems succeed in collecting radioactive debris. Each year a small number —up to about 100—of unidentified acoustic events with energies greater than one kiloton may be detected by the acoustic net and located as occurring within an area of about 10,000 square kilometers.

Although under most conditions meteorological trajectory analyses would permit collection of radioactive debris over the oceans by aircraft or over continental areas by ground sampling, circumstances may occur where radioactive debris would be expected to fall in the neighborhood of a burst point. In this case, surface inspection of a suspected location may be required to discriminate between a natural event and a nuclear explosion.

The decision to send an inspection team to the site of a suspected nuclear explosion should be taken by the control organization based on data from the control posts and criteria established in advance. The inspection team would report directly to the control organization and maintain direct communication with it.

In those cases for which the seismic net cannot discriminate between an underground explosion and an earthquake, within one to three days of the event, ground inspection will be required. A major problem will be to identify as high a proportion as possible of the small earthquakes and eliminate them as nuclear explosions. This can be accomplished in two ways: (a) by obtaining positive evidence that an earthquake occurred or (b) by assuring that necessary preparations for firing a nuclear explosion have not occurred. A combination of ingenuity, observational skill, and scientific techniques will be required to accomplish this task. Local inspection, eye-witness accounts, and local airflights at low altitudes should be most successful as a first step. Events in uninhabited areas should be the easiest to eliminate as possible nuclear tests. In more difficult situations, such as those when the event occurs in a seismic area containing caves or mining activities, geophysical techniques, including radioactivity, magnetometer, and electromagnetic surveys, may be used. Finally, in particularly difficult circumstances, deep drilling to search for radioactive debris and unusual thermogradients may be necessary. Following a deep underground explosion of one kiloton the radioactive debris will remain contained in a volume about 10 meters in radius and a measurable temperature increase will occur out to about 30 meters radius. . . .

Each inspection team must have available to it logistic support to permit rapid movement to remote areas and operation in these areas for an appreciable period. Small aircraft or helicopters should be available for low-altitude aerial inspection upon arrival at the area indicated by other elements of the detection system. The technical control organization must insure that all the instruments and equipment which may be required by the inspection team are available and maintained ready for use at suitable control stations.[88]

Aircraft and ships should also be available on short notice for monitoring in the open oceans or on other bodies of water.

Dr. Fedorov sought again to probe the attitude of the United States and its Western allies on his "self-inspection" proposal, under which home nationals would man the inspection network, with one or two observers from the outside. "Do you consider it essential to have at a control post representatives of the other side, or do you consider we could do without such representation?" he asked.

Dr. Fisk turned the question aside: "This is really not a technical question, Dr. Fedorov. I suspect that this would require some debate by others than ourselves. The real technical requirement is for scientific and technical competence."

But Dr. Fedorov pressed.

I would like to have a better idea of your opinion on this subject. I believe this point to be a quite substantive one; of course it has an organizational aspect but it is also a technical question. I will put the question in a different way. Do you consider that a control post is able to carry out observations from a technical point of view on possible nuclear explosions if it is staffed only by representatives of one side alone?

DR. FISK: This sounds to me like the same question and I'm afraid I shall have to give you the same answer.

DR. FEDOROV: Very well. May I take it then that you consider that it is not appropriate for our conference to go into this matter and to issue any recommendations on it?

DR. FISK: My feeling is that we should confine ourselves to the technical and scientific requirements and capabilities, and that this question as you phrase it is somewhat outside of our charter. . . .

DR. FEDOROV: I would like to put a further question regarding these representatives. When we adopted our conclusions on the radioactive-sampling method, and in particular when we said that it was possible in certain individual cases to use aircraft over the territories of countries, we agreed, as a matter of fact, with your proposal on this point and entered in our conclusions that in the case of such flights the aircraft should also carry a representative of the control service. So that we did look into this type of question. . . .

Dr. Fisk was trapped. He said he would seek an answer.

Next day, the Americans came in with their eagerly-awaited answer on another point: The control system, capable of identifying 90 per cent of the earthquakes in the one-kiloton range or above, would require 650 stations. Approximately 350 of these would be placed in mainland areas, 50 in ocean areas, and about 250 in seismic regions—peninsulas, islands, coastal areas, and some island mountain areas.[89]

The American control system was based on an estimate that there would be approximately 5,300 earthquakes in ocean areas of magnitude 4 or 4.1, and something like 4,700 in the continental and coastal areas, for an approximate total of 10,000 earthquakes. Magnitude 4 or 4.1 was estimated at that time to correspond to a nuclear explosion of one kiloton.

Dr. Harold Brown presented a detailed statistical analysis, based on the conference's own conclusions about individual methods of detection, which showed that spacing of stations, due to capabilities of equipment and geography, would vary from 200 kilometers to 1,200 kilometers if shots down to one kiloton were to be picked up and identified 90 per cent of the time.[90]

Even the American delegation was embarrassed about the huge number of control posts the system would require.

But the calculations had been thoroughly checked. The American scientists were sure of their ground. So sure that Dr. Fisk challenged Dr. Fedorov to prove that his 110 stations could identify one-kiloton explosions, that is, distinguish them from natural events, "without an impossible number of ground and aerial inspections." [91]

"We have studied Dr. Fedorov's presentation carefully and we are unable ourselves to answer this question," Dr. Fisk said. Soviet scientists did not immediately accept the challenge.

Dr. Fedorov noted that the 650 stations proposed by the Western side would require a large number of technicians and scientists. This led him again to inquire if the United States would agree to having Americans man detection stations in the United States and have Soviet citizens man the control stations in the Soviet Union. Dr. Fisk again declined to discuss the matter, on the grounds that it was a political rather than technical question.

> It will probably be necessary to have a suitable admixture of staff from various countries working in the control organ at its various levels, including local control posts. It may be deemed desirable that all of these personnel be direct employees of the international control organ, assigned to the various posts without worrying about nationalities. . . . I believe . . . that our governments will be concerned in judging this question not only with the technical qualifications but also with the technical objectivity of the personnel involved. Our governments will be concerned with insuring establishment of a system in which they can have absolute trust. We should, without prejudice to the final disposition of this point, agree simply to lay out the technical qualifications required regardless of nationality. Beyond this, we should not go.

Dr. Fedorov disagreed emphatically. If the United States would agree to the self-inspection provisions that he suggested, he said, the problems of the number of stations and the number of people involved and their qualifications would be greatly eased. He may have been implying that the Soviet Union could accept a much larger inspection system if it could count on "self-inspection" instead of truly international control.

How many specialists should each interested country train? Dr. Fedorov asked. "It is one thing if we have to train 500 people, but it is another if we need 50,000." In his opinion, Dr. Fedorov said, 1 or 2 foreign representatives at each control post would be sufficient.[92] Soviet Scientist Semenov called the network outlined by the West "an absolutely unimaginable number of stations."

The American presentation indicating that 650 stations would be needed to get a 90 per cent identification of earthquakes was not to be viewed as a proposal, Dr. Fisk said, but as a "conclusion." It was based on the detection data already agreed upon in the basic methods.[93] Thus the Russians were given hope the West would come down. Dr. Fedorov began pressing immediately for a firm "proposal."

Dr. Sadovski found two faults with the American system of 650 stations. First, account had not been taken of the already existing seismic stations (which the United States considered both inferior and untrustworthy in a control system intended to detect sneak one-kiloton underground tests); and second, Dr. Brown had placed main reliance on "direction of first motion" to identify suspicious underground events. The Soviet side placed greater stress on auxiliary evidence, Dr. Sadovski said.

Soviet scientists repeatedly emphasized the need to use seismic stations already operating around the world, of which there were about 700. They pointed out that in California the mean distance between stations was around 150 kilometers (94 miles), better spacing than even Dr. Brown had suggested; in central Asia the spacing was reported to be 250 kilometers (156 miles) and in the Caucasus about 200 kilometers (125 miles).

No mention was made, however, of the great American fear that the data emanating from the stations would not necessarily be as reliable as that from an internationally-staffed control station with the latest, elaborate equipment. Even if the equipment were improved, as the Soviet scientists suggested, there would still be the problem of "impartial surveillance."

Dr. Fisk said the Western scientists believed that the capability of existing stations would still be "very limited," even if improved instruments were provided. Most of the stations were not located in specially-selected quiet regions, he warned, mainly because they were placed for convenient access from population centers. "A few good stations contribute far more than many average stations," he said.[94]

To bear out his contention, he noted that forty stations had detected seismic waves from the Rainier explosion but that first motion had been detected at only ten stations at distances less than 370 kilometers (230 miles). Some of the forty stations were as close as 330 to 350 kilometers (206 to 220 miles) away.

Furthermore, Dr. Fisk recalled, when the Soviet Union set off 6- and 10-kiloton explosions underwater, producing seismic waves equivalent to 100-kiloton shots in Rainier-type terrain, "only a handful of the stations of the world reported detection."

These points would apply whether or not the issue of trust were involved—which, of course, it was. Dr. Fisk warned bluntly:

> The first motion could not be considered reliable at stations in the territory of a potential violator of a test moratorium. I state this because we must recognize that it is simple to reverse the polarity of instruments for a brief interval at a scheduled time. Thus, normal earthquakes on the same seismogram would show a normal direction on first motion so that it would be impossible to detect such a reversal of polarity. I do not make a special point of this; I simply call attention to it.

The problem of making seismographs tamperproof, even in international control posts, was to become a challenging exercise later.

Records from existing seismic stations can be used as supplements, Dr. Fisk said, but should not be fully relied upon.

It became clear in the ensuing discussion that the Soviet scientists had not made the same sort of rigorous statistical analysis of the capabilities of their system the Americans had. Their proposal of a world-wide network of 110 control stations was based on political considerations, principally the fear of inspection, rather than on technical requirements.[95]

If the 110-post system could not identify an event as an earthquake, the Russians indicated, the private seismographs could.[96] But the trouble with this, as Dr. Brown pointed out, would be that the Russian control system itself could identify only 20 to 30 per cent of the underground disturbances as definite earthquakes. This would throw a huge load onto the private system, whose equipment was unknown and whose reliability, as Dr. Fisk had pointed out, was questionable.

Even the number of stations in the Soviet Union could not be established. United States seismologists had known of only 70. The Soviet Union claimed, however, to have 120 seismic detection posts.[97]

As Dr. Richter and Dr. Gutenberg had foreseen, problems arose in translating yields of nuclear tests into magnitudes used in measuring earthquakes. The Soviet Union accepted the American measurement for the 1.7-kiloton Rainier shot as 4.25. But it did not accept the American estimate that a 5-kiloton explosion would produce only a 4.6 magnitude signal. The Soviet scientists said a seismic-signal of magnitude 5 would be obtained with a 5-kiloton explosion. This, of course, had the effect of reducing the estimate of earthquakes by which the detection system would be "confused" or bedeviled.

In addition, the Soviet scientists claimed that a 5-kiloton explosion could be detected at much greater distances—5,000 to 8,000 kilometers (up to 5,000 miles).

Dr. Romney later gave the Western estimates for correlating yield and magnitude. Magnitude 5, he estimated, corresponded to a 20-kiloton underground blast and there were about 1,400 earthquakes per year of magnitude 5 or larger. Among these would be a few of magnitude 8.

A 10-kiloton underground explosion would produce a magnitude 4.8 shot, Dr. Romney estimated. The Gutenberg estimate was that there would be 2,200 earthquakes per year world-wide, an average of six per day, equal to or larger than this.

Five kilotons would be the equivalent of magnitude 4.6. There would be 3,500 earthquakes per year, about 10 per day, of this magnitude or larger.

The 1.7-kiloton shot gave a magnitude of 4.25 and a 1-kiloton underground explosion would produce a signal with estimated magnitude of 4.1. According to Gutenberg, there were 10,000 shallow earthquakes per year greater than 4.1. "Shallow," Dr. Romney said, meant a depth of less than 60 kilometers (37 miles).

The Soviet Union's calculation that a 5-kiloton shot would produce a larger, magnitude 5 signal, was not in conformity with the basic conclusions to which the conference had already agreed a few days before.

Soviet Academician Pasechnik suggested that the Soviet system of broad spacing would require only four to five control posts in the United States, compared to the twenty to twenty-five under the American plan. In the Soviet Union, under the Pasechnik system, there would be ten to twelve control posts.

As the Russians were pressed further to show their scientific basis for claiming that a 110-station network was adequate to inspect a nuclear test ban down to the one-kiloton threshold, Soviet scientists relied more and more heavily on the 700-station world-wide network already in existence.

> I have the impression [Dr. Fisk commented], that what is now being done is to invoke the existing seismic stations of the world to establish a system and essentially to ignore the conclusions on our seismic methods on which we have all agreed in relation to the problem of identifying earthquakes. The total numbers which you arrived at, if you include the seismic stations of the world, added to the 100 or 110 stations of the control net which you have proposed, become very large indeed [800 to 810].
>
> This appears to me to be an explicit acknowledgment of the validity of our analysis which we have already presented [for 650 stations]. The crucial job of the control network, I infer from what has been said, is either a job to be done outside of the control system, or else the existing network would have to be incorporated into the control network. The former is just not a feasible system at all. The latter, namely, the incorporation of the existing network into the system, would not even make technical sense without equipment, proper site-location and the filling in of many geographic gaps.

In the absence of a Soviet evaluation of its own network, Dr. Harold Brown finally presented one of his own. He found that *the Soviet Union's 110-station network would identify as natural only 10 per cent of the seismic events of 1-kiloton equivalent occurring in inland areas, and "only a few per cent" of the events within 3,500 kilometers of a coast line, where most of the world's earthquakes occur.*

Ingenious Compromise

With the Soviet and Western positions far apart on the number of control posts necessary for an inspection system to police a nuclear test ban, the West came to the conference table on August 5 with an ingenious compromise plan that immediately attracted the Soviet side. Sir William Penney of the British delegation presented the new plan. It was no good, he said, to try to "split the difference" between the 110 control posts suggested by the Soviet Union and the 650 mentioned by the Western scientists. That would have meant a system of 380 control stations, but "we could not in any case agree that these 380 stations would have good capability with regard to 1 kiloton," Sir William said.

The solution, Sir William suggested, would be to raise the threshold from 1 kiloton to 5 kilotons. That would permit reducing the number of control stations from 650 to 170. Ninety per cent of the earthquakes in the 5-kiloton range and above could be identified, it was said, and there would still be a "residual" capability for the inspection system between 1 and 5 kilotons.

The inspection system depended on three main points, Sir William said: the minimum yield of the event to be detected and identified; the probability with which the system would detect and identify the event with that yield; and the number of recording centers throughout the world needed to provide the coverage.

He gave this tabular analysis of the control systems:

ANALYSIS OF CONTROL SYSTEMS

No. of posts	110			170			650		
Yield (kilotons)	1	5	20	1	5	20	1	5	20
Probability of Identification of Earthquakes on Land Areas	5%	50%	90%	90%	90%	90%	90%	greater than 90%	

Source: Conference of Experts, August 5, 1958, EXP/NUC/PV.26, p. 26.

The Soviet system would have a capability of less than 5 per cent in detecting and identifying events equivalent to 1 kiloton or above, Sir William repeated; but the same 100 to 110 stations would have a 50 per cent capability at a 5-kiloton threshold and a 90 per cent capability with a 20-kiloton threshold.

The 650 stations suggested by the Western side would have a 90 per cent capability at one kiloton and even greater than 90 per cent at 5 kilotons, he said. But 650 stations, it was obvious, were far too many. He then proposed a control system with four main features:

1. The posts of the control organization, in the view of both sides [are] to be capable of detecting and identifying with 90 per cent probability earthquakes with a yield of 5 kilotons or more.

2. The seismic stations now existing in the world [should be] selected according to their quality and strengthened where necessary with the best equipment to be used by the control organization in a supplemental way.

3. Where the control organization, using its own stations, detects an event in seismic areas of 5 kilotons or more which it cannot identify, arrangements must be made immediately for inspection. The system could be given a limited capability in the 1–5 kiloton range if the control organization undertakes some random inspections of unidentified events of less than 5 kilotons—some random inspections.

4. When the control organization detects an event of 1 kiloton or more in an aseismic area the event must be regarded as suspicious and inspection is required.

These 4 points could be covered with an inspection system of 170 stations, Sir William said, of which about 40 would be land-based stations in ocean areas. In addition to the 170 control posts, the system would use meteorological ships already in service, and possibly other special ships, properly equipped.

"We regard approximately 170 properly located stations, supported by effective inspection as I have summarized, as giving good probability of identification of 5-kiloton explosions or earthquakes." [98] But, Sir William warned, the system would have deficiencies.

It will not have good capability with regard to discriminating between earthquakes and underground tests—underground explosions—in an island of the seismic island chain. We should recognize that there are such defects so that our governments are aware of them.

On the other hand, the system would have a capability better than 5 kilotons in the atmosphere up to 30 kilometers, he estimated. Then he added:

There is one difficult case which I think we shall also be able to resolve—an explosion yield of a few kilotons in the troposphere located in the equatorial regions of the oceans far away from islands. The acoustic method has poor capabilities; the radio-signal method has its limitations; the debris method is the most valuable. Collection of debris by ground stations, including perhaps ships, and collections of debris by routine flights over the oceans certainly have capability, and this is the main method for discovering nuclear explosions of low yield in the atmosphere in those ocean areas. For yields of the order of 10 kilotons and above, of course, the other methods will begin to give measurements of where the event occurred and the time at which it occurred. We think that we shall be able to agree about detection and identification of this type of event over the ocean.

Of the 170 stations, Sir William estimated that 60 would be "very quiet stations," probably mostly inland in aseismic areas; 60 would be "quiet stations"; and 50 "noisy stations," most of them in coastal areas.[99]

Those who believed that one of the main gains for the United States from a nuclear test ban would be an inspection system that would, to a degree, open up the Soviet Union's closed society might have been interested in the fact that the Russians gave indications, just after Sir William spoke, of a willingness to permit as many as 300 stations world-wide. This might have meant as many as 50 stations inside the Soviet Union instead of the 20-odd eventually settled upon.

When Sir William had completed presentation of the plan for 170 stations with a 5-kiloton threshold, Soviet academician N. Semenov indicated the Soviet delegation had been thinking seriously of a 300-station network. Talking about the first American suggestion that 650 stations would be necessary for a one-kiloton capability, Dr. Semenov said:

The plan for 600 [presumably he referred to the American plan for 650 stations] does not meet the necessity of identification, even if we adopt your point of view. We could mention some further arguments in answer to Dr. Brown. However, we have checked our figures again, and we came to the conclusion that about 300 stations are sufficient for 90 per cent—or even a higher percentage—of identification, taking your assumption as the premise for underground explosions of one kiloton. Did you analyze that situation? . . . We are sure that we do not need 600 stations, but only 300 stations.[100]

This might have been an indication that if the Western delegation had withheld its 170-station plan another day or two, the Soviet Union would have presented a compromise plan providing for 300 stations.[101] But Sir William had just rejected the idea of "splitting the difference" between 110 and 650 stations.

As it went, the Chairman of the Soviet delegation, Dr. Fedorov, seized eagerly on the 170-station plan and no further mention of a possible 300-station network with a 1-kiloton capability was made by the Soviet Union.

The Americans estimated that about 104 stations in their 170-station network would be located on continental areas, about 57 on islands and 10 to 12 on ships. In the aseismic areas of the continents, the spacing would be about 1,700 kilometers (1,060 miles). In seismic and coastal regions, a spacing of about 1,000 kilometers (625 miles) would give coverage for a 5-kiloton threshold, provided that the 104 continental stations were placed as effectively as possible.[102]

It was obvious that the August 5 proposal of the Western side to institute a "sliding" threshold, anchored at 5 kilotons rather than one kiloton, had been a "breakthrough" in the deadlocked situation over the number of control stations for the nuclear test-ban network. The Soviet side was pleased and relieved. Dr. Fedorov, chairman of that day's meeting, wanted only to get out of the conference room to study the proposal closely and see if it were really as good as it sounded. If the speculation is correct that the Soviet Union had been ready to offer a 300-station network, a celebration should have been in order among the Soviet scientists in Geneva—and in Moscow as well.

The new Western proposal apparently created quite a stir in Moscow. There was not another formal meeting of the experts for six days, until Monday, August 11. During that time there were, however, three informal meetings during which draft conclusions on inspection systems were exchanged, an unexpected sign that the two sides were nearing agreement.

Dr. Brown's analysis of the new 170-station network, which he referred to as the 110-continental-station network, showed a 90 per cent capability above 5 kilotons only in inland and coastal regions on continents. The capability was "considerably less" than 90 per cent for identification of 5-kiloton events in seismic island chains, as Sir William had warned. For one-kiloton seismic events the capability would be 90 per cent if the stations were spaced 1,000 kilometers (625 miles) apart or 45 per cent if the spacing were 1,600 kilometers (1,000 miles). This would apply to interior seismic regions.

In coastal seismic regions, there would be 65 per cent identification if the stations were 900 kilometers (560 miles) apart and 15 per cent identification if they were 1,600 (1,000 miles) apart.

Mr. Northrup gave a more detailed presentation of the Western proposal for location of stations on August 11.[103]

Of the 110 continental stations, he suggested, 24 should be in North America and Greenland, 6 in Europe, 37 in Asia, 7 in Australia, 4 in Antarctica, 16 in South America, and 16 in Africa. Twenty other stations should be located on "major islands," and forty stations on small islands. In addition there should be about ten ship stations, "about the usefulness of which, again, we have some reservations." The acoustic method of detection would be difficult, he said, because of the problems of noise from the ship's engines, movements of the sea, and winds.

Spacing in aseismic areas would be about 1,500 to 2,000 kilometers (900 to 1,250 miles) and in seismic regions and coastal areas about 900 to 1,200 kilometers (560 to 750 miles). Geography would affect these spacings. In Africa, "a relatively aseismic continent," spacings of the order of 1,500 to 2,000 kilometers (900 to 1,250 miles) would appear to be adequate, Mr. Northrup said, while in North America, South America, and Asia the average spacing would be about 1,000 kilometers (625 miles).

He added that in some of the larger "ocean area poles" acoustic-detection capability might degenerate to the point where 10- to 15-kiloton explosions would not be detectable. For that reason radioactive-debris sampling would be important.

It took another ten days to iron out details. These were handled mainly in informal sessions, but the same game continued. The Soviet side tried to sweep difficulties under the rug, the American side sought to leave the difficulties in the open where they could be identified.

In the end, however, the Soviet scientists simply accepted the Western 170- to 180-station system, seeking only to put the most optimistic coloration on the conference conclusions about the system's effectiveness. The West, too, was interested enough in an agreement to cloak in vagueness many shortcomings the Soviet bloc did not wish to emphasize.

The experts stated as their general conclusion that it was possible to set up a system capable of detecting and identifying nuclear explosions, including those of low yield.

"The conference has therefore come to the conclusion," the experts agreed, "that it is technically feasible to establish, with the capabilities and limitations indicated below, a workable and effective control system to detect violations of an agreement on the world-wide suspension of nuclear weapons tests."

The conference envisioned an international control organ to supervise the functioning of the system. Technically, no specific number of stations was recommended. The system's sensitivity would depend on three things, the experts said, the minimum yield that the governments decided the system should be able to pick up; the number of control posts; and the probability of identifying natural events, particularly earthquakes. If the governments were satisfied with detecting sneak tests only down to 20 kilotons, the experts were saying in effect, the number of control stations could be reduced; but if all nuclear explosions down to the subkiloton range were important, then a great many control posts, perhaps more than 1,000 would be necessary.

The report was, in some respects, a public challenge to the Kremlin. If the Soviet Union really wanted to ban *all* tests, the only way it could be done would be with a closely spaced network of control stations and with hundreds, perhaps thousands, of on-site inspections per year. If the Soviet government would settle for a threshold, either at one kiloton or 5 kilotons or 20 kilotons, it could reduce the number of control posts and the number of sorties by on-site inspection teams into their closed society.

Events that could not be identified by the control posts or the international control organ and were suspected of being nuclear explosions, the experts said, could be investigated by "an inspection group" which would "determine whether a nuclear explosion had taken place or not." This on-site inspection group, as it came to be known, "would be provided with equipment and apparatus appropriate to its task in each case." The report did not spell out what equipment the inspection team would be allowed to carry with it. The United States had tried to interest Soviet scientists in an equipment list, without success.

What would be the capabilities of such a network of up to 180 control posts distributed world-wide, together with the use of aircraft patrolling the oceans?

The Conference of Experts estimated that "subject to certain important qualifications," the system would have a "good probability" of:

1. Not only detecting but identifying nuclear explosions of yields down to about one kiloton, taking place in the atmosphere up to 10 kilometers altitude.

2. Detecting, "but not always of identifying," explosions at altitudes of from 10 to 50 kilometers. Evidence from acoustic waves, radioactive debris, and radio signals would be used.

3. Detecting nuclear explosions of one kiloton set off deep in the open ocean. Identifying underwater explosions, the report said, "can, in comparatively rare cases, be made more difficult by natural events which give similar hydroacoustic and seismic signals." This was a reflection of the Western misgivings that upheavals on the floor of the ocean could create enough noise to mask a nuclear explosion.

4. "Recording," not necessarily detecting or identifying, "seismic signals from deep underground nuclear explosions in continents equivalent to one kiloton and above."

The report dealt at some length with the problem of identifying deep underground explosions. Distinguishing between nuclear-explosion signals and those from natural earthquakes would present the network with a problem, the report said, but the control posts "could identify as being of natural origin about 90 per cent of the continental earthquakes, whose signals are equivalent to five kilotons, and a small percentage of continental earthquakes equivalent to one kiloton."

In a footnote, the conference said that to increase the percentage of identifiable earthquakes below five kilotons "it would be appropriate to supplement the data from the control posts by trustworthy data from the best existing seismic stations."

The experts estimated that "the number of earthquakes which would be undistinguishable on the basis of their seismic signals from deep underground nuclear explosions of about five-kiloton yield could be in continental areas from twenty to a hundred a year." The unidentified events would be inspected by teams sent to the site of the explosion.

In the one- to five-kiloton yield area, the control system's capability to identify underground nuclear explosions would depend on three things: what small number could be identified from direction-of-first-motion data and other evidence gathered at the control posts alone; what earthquakes could be definitely identified with the aid of already-existing seismic stations; and what fraction still would remain unidentified—thus suspect of having been a nuclear explosion and calling for on-site inspection.

> *Although the control system would have great difficulty in obtaining positive identification of a carefully concealed deep underground nuclear explosion,* there would always be a possibility of detection of such a violation by inspection. The on-site inspection carried out by the international control organ . . . would be able to identify with good probability underwater nuclear explosions with a yield of one kiloton and above. [Author's italics.]

In effect, this italicized dependent clause was confirmation of the fears of Dr. Edward Teller and others in the United States, particularly in the AEC and Defense Department, who had warned that an effective inspection system to control a nuclear test ban could not be devised. The easy confidence that underwater shots could be identified with "good probability" was another piece of optimism that might have been hard to justify.

The conference report went on to enumerate certain other "special cases" in which the system's capability for detecting nuclear explosions would be reduced: "for instance, when explosions are set off in those areas of the ocean where the number of control posts is small and the meteorological conditions are unfavorable; in the case of shallow underground explosions; when explosions are set off on islands in seismic regions; and in some other cases when the explosion is carefully concealed."

The experts acknowledged that "in some cases it would be impossible to determine exactly the area in which a nuclear explosion that had been detected took place."

These passages were excursions in realism which had been insisted upon by the United States team of experts. They disclosed loopholes that confirmed the worst fears of those who believed the Soviet Union would be willing to go to great lengths to set up conditions for secret testing.

"However," the report said, "the conference considers that whatever the precautionary measures adopted by a violator he could not be guaranteed against exposure, particularly if account is taken of the carrying out of inspection at the site of the suspected explosion."

The lack of a 100 per cent guarantee, the conference thus concluded, would be sufficient deterrent for a potential violator of the treaty ban. This was another hair-raising conclusion for those who thought the Russians were really capable of trying to cheat.

In some cases, there was less scientific precision in the report than an unsuspecting reader might have guessed. For instance, the estimate that there would be 20 to 100 unidentified events per year at five kilotons or above was a "compromise." The United States had estimated 100; the Soviet Union estimated 20. The difference was between 2–3 on-site inspections per month to check the unidentified events, and 12–13 per month.

And if the system was to be effective against the 1- to 5-kiloton yield weapons, some of the most important yields for advanced tactical-weapons development, there would have to be many more on-site inspections to check out smaller earthquakes that could not be definitely identified.

The report gave no numerical estimate per year of these low-magnitude seismic events, but American seismologists had reported to Senator Humphrey that the number would be in the thousands.

Another hole in the experts' system was the difficulty of identifying possible nuclear explosions at altitudes of from 10 to 50 kilometers (33,000 to 165,000 feet). In addition, it was conceded that underwater blasts might be masked by natural events.

The volcanic tuff in the Nevada mesa where the Rainier 1.7-kiloton underground shot was detonated was generally regarded by the Conference of Experts as a soft medium that would tend to reduce the seismic signal more than the ordinary types of underground media. But the experts, in a little-noticed footnote in an annex to the report, indicated their belief that even more effective media for hiding nuclear weapons explosions existed.

"The underground nuclear explosion 'Rainier' with an energy of 1.7

kilotons [Nevada] was set off in unfavorable conditions for transferring energy to the ground," the footnote said. "However, even worse conditions of coupling are possible." [104]

These media were not enumerated in the formal conference sessions. But salt, marble, granite, ice—all were then believed more effective than tuff in reducing the seismic signal from explosions.

All these uncertainties, however, were concerns for the experts, not for the general public, or even for many responsible officials who might have been apprised of the hazards.

United Nations Secretary-General Dag Hammarskjold, in his congratulatory message to the Conference of Experts on its closing day, August 21, complimented the scientists for "a signal contribution in making an effective dent in the hitherto rather intractable problem of disarmament. It will hereafter be with the governments concerned and the United Nations to follow through the opening you have created."

Dr. Fisk, in his concluding statement, made special mention of the care with which the report had set forth "the capabilities and limitations of present methods of detecting nuclear explosion."

Dr. Fedorov, on the other hand, could not be expected to pass up this opportunity to overstate in public the effectiveness of the inspection system:

> What is the basic conclusion that can be drawn following the completion of our lengthy task? The conclusion is very simple and very clear. A nuclear explosion, including an explosion of small magnitude, can be detected, and the establishment of an effective control system which would make it possible to have an inspection and a checking of the maintenance of an agreement on the universal cessation of nuclear-weapons tests is a quite feasible undertaking and one which would not be particularly complicated. In certain instances, the task of detecting and identifying nuclear explosions of small yields is relatively simple; in others, specific difficulties are involved. However, no matter where a possible violator attempted to conceal his atomic explosion—under the water, on the earth, or in the cosmic space— he will not be able to succeed in concealing it.
>
> We are convinced that [if a test-ban were agreed] no single government which will undertake a commitment to cease the testing of nuclear weapons will disregard such a commitment and thus challenge the whole world.

Ambassador Spinelli, Director of the European Office of the United Nations who was the official host for the conference in Geneva, expressed what was a near-universal optimism after the successfully concluded conference:

> The whole world now knows that international control of nuclear tests is possible. You have thus demonstrated that men moved by the desire to agree and conscious of their responsibilities towards the whole of mankind can find a basis for the solution of problems which by their very nature are complex and difficult.

None of the proceedings in the conference had been officially disclosed up to that time. Misgivings of American experts about the limitations of the inspection system, not only about holes in the network but about the "well-nigh impossible" task of on-site inspection, were not reported. The impression before the world was that a nuclear test-ban inspection system was "feasible." The all-important qualifying phrase, "within the capabilities and limitations stated below," was soon dropped.

The White House was the first to drop it. Newsmen quickly followed suit. To explain each time the capabilities and limitations of the inspection system, obviously, would have filled up precious space in the newspaper and premium time on five-minute newscasts.

Before leaving this study of the 1958 Conference of Experts, it is important to the understanding of future events to pause and examine in more detail how much responsible American officials knew at that time about the possibilities of evading a nuclear test ban.

If there was a failure to alert the American public to the danger that an unscrupulous power could evade the ban, it would be important to know who failed, the President, the State Department, the scientists at the conference, or the press.

The next section will pursue further the evidence developed in formal sessions of the Conference of Experts that might have led another government or even the same government, in other circumstances, to conclude that a test ban was *not* feasible, precisely because of the same capabilities and limitations in the system.

HALF-FULL OR HALF-EMPTY?

American scientists and diplomats who negotiated the 180-station control system of 1958 brought to the conference in Geneva varying attitudes of optimism and pessimism about reaching an effective agreement. As one diplomat said of them, "They all can look at the same glass of water and some of them say it's half full and the rest say it is half empty."

In the case of a test-ban control system it might have been more accurate to compare the network to a leaky sieve. The optimists considered the sieve half full, the pessimists considered it half empty.

The Conference of Experts' verbatim records permit us to look rather closely at some of the holes in the sieve. One of the bigger holes was the on-site inspection technique, advertised as "the clincher" to catch a cheater. Seismic islands, the ocean depths, vast open areas on the Pacific ocean's surface, the stratosphere, and outer space were other holes in the sieve.

Sensing the misgivings among some American scientists, Soviet Delegation Chief Fedorov had tried to slay the dragon of on-site inspection in his first major statement to the 1958 experts' conference. His subject was the radioactive-debris method of detecting nuclear tests.[106] He suggested that the East-West experts agree that

> the radioactive products formed during an explosion can be effectively used for a later verification of the occurrence of underground or underwater explosions. In these cases the radioactive debris will spread from the source very slowly. Control drilling, with a preliminary geophysical examination of the shaft or radiometric instrument sounding of the sea, will permit *certain* identification of the fact that an explosion has taken place, in cases where data obtained by other control means might be regarded as doubtful [Author's italics].

He gave this explanation for his claim that identification would be "certain":

> Let us say that an explosion has occurred very deep in the sea, and the indications concerning the explosion are not too clear. Of course, the radioactive products in the sea will be mixed in a restricted way. In ten to twenty days after the explosion, the layer will probably extend over kilometers or scores of kilometers. Hence, if a vessel is sent to this area with simple instruments that can be dropped into the water, it will be very easy to discover what has happened.
>
> The same kind of system can be used, but with more difficulty, to verify underground explosions. When the earth's surface has not been disturbed and the explosion has occurred at great depths so that radioactive gases have not emerged, the other radioactive products will remain here [indicating] and will form an aureole, to use a geophysical term, of diffusion around the source. The longer the period after the explosion the larger will be the aureole.
>
> Thus, in these cases it is possible through control drilling to determine whether or not any radioactive products are present. Of course, the question is to locate the area itself. The area can be determined with a certain approximation to accuracy. The shaft has to be found. There are a number of prospecting methods of geophysics, as we all know, for determining this. For instance, if for mining purposes there is a shaft whose surface is covered up, a drilling operation is used to determine the existence of this hidden shaft. Control drilling will constitute an unquestionable indication of the fact that a violation has taken place in a certain area.

To balance this optimistic view, Dr. Harold Brown of the United States presented a paper on the difficulties of on-site inspection on July 21, 1958.[107]

The only way to prove an underground nuclear explosion was to obtain samples of radioactive debris, he began. To do this the site of the possible explosion had to be located very precisely by an inspection team.

The only underground nuclear blast then known, the Rainier shot of 1957, Dr. Brown pointed out, had presented "no features to help distinguish it from an earthquake except the existence of compressive first motions in many directions, and some earthquakes also give that feature." He warned that there are possibilities of producing artificial rarefactions, false first motions, at some stations, thus reducing the usefulness of what is probably our best diagnostic tool—at least at the moment—in distinguishing earthquakes from explosions by analyzing seismograms. As an example, one might expect, in order to find one-kiloton underground explosions, to have to consider as a background, that is the number of naturally occurring signals which might warrant investigation on the spot, as many as perhaps 20 per cent of the earthquakes of magnitude greater than 4, and since the best estimate of the number of such earthquakes along the lines made by Gutenberg is 10,000 a year, 20 per cent of this number is 2,000 a year over the whole world.

Dr. Brown estimated that, on the basis of the Rainier experience, a region of crushed rock and a zone of increased temperature of about 400 square meters would be produced by a 1.7-kiloton explosion. A remote seismic-detection network probably could locate the epicenter of the suspicious disturbance within 200 square kilometers, he estimated.

Inspectors thus would have to find an area of 400 square meters out of a total area of 200 square kilometers, "that is, about 2×10^{-5} of the area to be explored."

This was a mathematician's way of saying that the actual area of the explosion would be 1/200,000th of the area to which remote seismic detection would lead the inspection team.

"Clearly it will be necessary to examine this suspicious area in considerable detail before one selects specific points for drilling, where one suspects a nuclear explosion," Dr. Brown told the Soviet-bloc scientists. He outlined this set of procedures:

1. *Photo reconnaissance from small aircraft.* This would be "a very local reconnaissance covering the area within which the disturbance has been localized by the remote seismic measurements. At the same time one might make airborne magnetometer and electromagnetic induction surveys. . . . Just in case some radioactivity may have escaped through the surface of the ground—although nothing at all of that kind was observed in the Rainier explosion—one might also make a radioactivity survey from the air, again in this very local region."

2. *Search for evidence on the ground.* There would be two kinds of visible evidence: Unusual recent human activity in the area; and physical results of the explosion, like local earth movements, instrumentation of the shot, etc.

3. *Detailed magnetometer and electromagnetic surveys.* These would be conducted in "any anomalous areas" turned up by the aerial survey and ground investigations.

4. *Ground survey for radioactivity.* Soil samples probably would be collected. A vacuum pump on a tube extended into the ground might be used "to see what gases can be collected for radiochemical analysis."

5. *Local seismic noise* might be monitored.

6. *Detailed seismic profiling* might be undertaken by setting off explosions of small chemical charges, sunk into the earth, and observing their seismic signals. These might show local "anomalies" which in turn might indicate "fracturing of the rock."

This list was not to be considered "exhaustive," Dr. Brown said. He then proceeded to point out deficiencies in the methods he suggested.

We do not anticipate that the explosion itself would produce any significant permanent disturbance in the local magnetic field. So the inclusion of magnetometric and electromagnetic methods would be primarily for the purpose of locating ferromagnetic and electrically-conducting materials which might have been used in the preparations preceding the explosions and which might have been overlooked in any attempt at concealment.

[As for visual detection of explosion evidence], it may be noted that geologists and geophysicists who examined the Rainier site generally agreed that there was sufficient visible evidence at the surface of the explosion to permit a fairly good estimate of its location, a better estimate at least than somewhere within 200 square kilometers. This evidence was in the form of small fissures in the surface of the mesa, small landslides and rock slides on deep slopes and new movements on old faults and along joint planes in the rock. However, if the shot had been fired at about twice the depth or in somewhat flat terrain rather than in a mountain, *it is probable that no visible evidence of the explosions would have been found on the surface.* [Author's italics.]

Earthquakes of similar magnitude would also produce local earth movements similar to those in an explosion, it was noted, so that earth movements themselves "would produce no evidence either way" about a possible explosion. "They would tend to localize the region which would have to be carefully inspected; that is, they would reduce the area in which a suspected event might be suspected to have taken place," Dr. Brown said.

Seismic profiling would work if the area underground were of a "simple and regular geological structure," according to Dr. Brown. "However, if the area were one which already contained many faults, fissures, or cavities, the additional fracturing caused by explosion would almost certainly not be distinguished from the natural features by local seismic profiling methods."

Regarding electromagnetic methods of detecting the radioactivity, Dr. Brown went on, the variation of voltages that occur naturally "is such that surface methods of the investigation by electrical means appear quite unpromising."

Trying to measure variations in the pull of gravity would also be futile, Dr. Brown said, because natural variations exceeded the variations that would be caused by an explosion the size of Rainier by "tens, or perhaps even hundreds of times."

The use of geophones to detect microseismic noise which would result from the falling back of material, even at quite late times in the area of the explosion—this noise might be expected to be centered about the point of the disturbance—might be useful provided such noise can be differentiated from the normal microseismic noise, and provided that its source can be located accurately.[108]

If these methods of narrowing the area of suspicion were successful, Dr. Brown said, specific points could be chosen for drilling.

Even if the spot were located precisely, it is unlikely that the first hole drilled would hit the target; but each unsuccessful hole drilled, the temperature, the level of the gamma radiation, and the electrical resistivity logs should be run. In the case of a near miss such measurements would provide information which might help to locate additional drill holes.

In mid-June, 1958, Dr. Brown related, the United States had assembled a group of geophysical experts to study the Rainier case and judge the possibilities of concealing a shot (another last-minute preparation). The geophysical experts came to these conclusions:

1. The Rainier shot, which no attempt was made to hide, could have been located fairly accurately by visual and geophysical means. [Dr. Brown pointed out, however, that even knowing the position of the explosion to within a few feet, it required several months to locate the samples of solid radioactive material from the Rainier shot.]

2. A nuclear device could be detonated underground, with careful planning and execution, in such a manner that *post-shot*—that is after the explosion—*visual and geophysical inspection would probably not locate the site with sufficient accuracy to allow successful drilling for radioactive debris. Under such circumstances, proof of a violation by technical means —that is proof by technical means that a violation had taken place—would be lacking.* [Author's italics.]

The precautions and careful planning that would be necessary, Dr. Brown said, would involve "deeper burial, removal of artifacts—that is to say, tools, etc. which would indicate human activity, or else just moving them to some other place where evidence of human activity in connection with an explosion would be visible—and a number of other things of that kind."

Conversely, Dr. Brown said, a physical examination of the site of an earthquake "*probably could not, in some cases, establish that there had not been an underground nuclear explosion. In other words, in some cases, after proceeding to the site of a natural event, one might not be able to say unequivocally that it was a natural event and not an underground nuclear explosion.*" [Author's italics.]

After the Rainier shot, Dr. Brown told a questioner, and before any radioactive samples were taken, American scientists tried to find out the nature of the region surrounding the Rainier explosion by acoustic methods.

> We did this from inside the tunnel, at a distance of about 200 feet from the point at which the explosion took place. We were unable to get any significant information on reflections. They were all mixed up with local anomalies. We have subsequently carried out—and in fact are now carrying out, I believe—seismic explorations both from the tunnel and from logging wells. But I do not have the results of these surveys. . . . I can say that such surveys may not be too relevant to our important questions, because they are being made not from the surface but from underground and from a distance of a few hundred feet from the explosion. Once you are that close, drilling is not too hard, although it is still not easy to get a sample by drilling. The geophysicists who have looked at this question tell us that they think that *from the surface the chances are very poor.* It will depend very strongly on the nature of the region. *If it is completely homogeneous and flat, then the chances may be somewhat better. But there really are no such regions.* [Author's italics.][109]

Soviet scientist Pasechnik asked if any measurement of gamma-ray activity had been carried out.

"We did gamma logging in connection with our attempts to drill into the region of disturbed rock, both from the surface and horizontally from the tunnel," Dr. Brown responded. "What we found was that, until one got within a few meters of where the radioactivity was, one could see no change in the gamma level. This is what one might expect, because a few meters of rock is an exceedingly good gamma-ray shield and there appears to have been essentially no diffusion outside of the region of crushed rock."

Had the density of the underground materials been checked for variations? Dr. Brown said there had been variations up to 5 and 10 per cent in density of the area before the explosion. Samplings afterward showed no distinguishable greater variation.

No surface prospecting by the seismic method of setting off small explosions in shallow-drilled holes had been undertaken, Dr. Brown said,

> largely because all of the people to whom we have talked about this say it is completely hopeless. I would not be surprised if the seismic survey from a distance of a few hundred feet turned out to show anomalies [unexplainable variations in the underground consistency]. On the other hand, I would not be at all surprised if it resulted in there being no anomalies bigger than those existing in other places where no nuclear explosion has taken place.

He was also asked if temperature variations down to a hundredth of a degree had been taken farther out from the explosion than he indicated.

> I believe it is true that one can detect quite small temperature gradients and, as a rule, they do not occur naturally. This might extend the region of

detectability from 20 meters to 30 meters or even to 40 meters, although as one gets farther and farther away, the time required for a gradient to appear increases as the square of the distance. I cannot see this helps us very much as regards to the problem of localizing the event within a region of 200 square kilometers. It seems to me that *to try and put down drill holes every so often*—whether to find gamma activity, or increase in temperature, or to set off explosions every ten feet in order to see whether there are any anomalies detectable by seismic means—*is hopeless*, and one must try to find other means . . . of getting to a smaller distance. Once one gets to within a quite small area, perhaps an area of a 20-meter radius, then it is simple, it seems to me. One does not have to worry about finding small temperature gradients.

One of the reasons, he said, that Rainier drillers moved to the tunnels which had been bored horizontally into the mesa, rather than continuing all the way on the vertical drilling that had started from the top of the mesa, Dr. Brown said, was the increasing difficulty encountered in the vertical drilling. "Since the medium in which the device was exploded was not amenable to drilling, the drill shaft kept collapsing and drilling tools were continually being lost down the bottom of the shaft, so we finally went to the tunnel."

Once the area of suspicion has been narrowed to within a 50- or a 30-meter radius, Dr. Brown summarized, "and you know that you are within that radius, then there is probably not very much of a problem. *The difficulty is to get that close and seismographs will not do it for you, at least remote seismographs will not do it* [Author's italics]." [110]

To the knowledge of the author, the grave weaknesses in the on-site inspection method outlined by Dr. Brown were never brought to the attention of the American public, let alone the world public. It is true that in the fullness of time the verbatim records of the Conference of Experts were made public. But there is a real question whether the Eisenhower Administration acted in a responsible way by, in effect, suppressing the information that on-site inspections would be practically useless to detect a sneak nuclear shot in case a test-ban agreement were signed.

It is clear from the verbatim records of the Conference of Experts, at least from July 21, 1958, that the facts on the near-hopelessness of on-site inspection were known and accepted as official Administration judgment. Yet the on-site inspection method was permitted to become a point of principal reliance for effective control of a nuclear test ban. There was no official, responsible warning that this principal point of reliance was a mirage.

One can wonder whether President Eisenhower was ever informed of the weakness of on-site inspection as a control technique. One can be almost certain, however, that the President's scientific advisers, Dr. James F. Killian, Jr., and Dr. George Kistiakowsky, were aware of the difficulties.

Dr. Edward Teller and Senator Bourke Hickenlooper spoke publicly of these worries about the effectiveness of on-site inspection. But Dr. Teller was already branded as a super-anti-Communist scientist under suspicion of molding his science to fit his ideology. Senator Hickenlooper was not a scientist. He was a veteran Senator and influential Republican on Capitol Hill, but his warning voice was lost in the clamor of his pro-test-ban colleagues.

As a result, negotiators from the Soviet Union and the United States found themselves, in the early 1960s arguing whether there should be twenty on-site inspections or three per year, completely oblivious of the 95 per cent-plus probability that not even one on-site inspection could be properly completed within one year or even within a decade.

Using Dr. Brown's arithmetic, 200,000 drillings might be necessary to cover completely a suspicious site "pinpointed" by remote seismic detection. Even though it took four months to find the Rainier debris when the Americans knew where the explosion was detonated, let us assume that one drill hole could be completed each month,[111] or 12 per year. It would take 16,666 years to complete 200,000 drill holes at an average of one drill hole per month. Suppose one could send out 1000 drilling rigs to each suspicious site. It would still take more than sixteen years.

If it would require 16,666 "drill crew-years" to check out one unidentified event, 50,000 "drill crew-years" would be needed to complete the three on-site inspections the Soviet Union said it was willing to allow on its territory. Three hundred and fifty thousand drill crew-years would be necessary for complete coverage of the 20 on-site inspections per year the United States demanded. Of course somebody might get lucky and score a "hit" on an early probe. But one doesn't base the national security on 200,000-to-1 shots. Moreover it is entirely possible that all 200,000 would fail to produce debris—if the shot were fired exceptionally deep or if the system had been misled by a false alarm.

Add to this the 1958 estimate that there would be 100 earthquakes per year that could not be definitely labeled as earthquakes by the remote seismic method, or by other techniques the control system recommended,[112] and on-site inspection becomes more absurd. It becomes laughable when one considers the extreme sensitivity of the Soviet Union to penetration of its country by any large groups of outsiders.

Dr. Brown also warned it is possible that "in some geological environments or under specially asymmetric conditions of detonation, the signals from an explosion may have a close resemblance to an earthquake."

He referred here to the possibility of "shaped" nuclear charges which could possibly produce rarefactions in some directions, rather than compressions in all directions, and thus project seismic signals resembling those from earthquakes.

On-site inspection teams most frequently would be confronted with another problem—proving that a suspicious event was a natural disturbance.

Low-altitude local air flights and ground inspection teams could conduct visual investigations of the suspicious area. Eye-witness accounts of suspicious events might be sought from the people in inhabited areas. This, Dr. Brown said, "will provide evidence of the natural origin of many disturbances and should therefore be the first technique employed."

> [In uninhabited areas], where signs of human activity are difficult to hide, complete lack of signs of human activity will also serve to give some assurance of natural origin of seismic events. A search for surface disturbances over a large area or eye-witness accounts of motion or other effects over very large areas may help to indicate natural events, though our knowledge of underground nuclear explosions merely suggests this and does not by any means prove it.

In these remarks Dr. Brown was identifying, for the only time in the formal proceedings of the Conference of Experts, a key problem that the West would have in any inspection system inside the Soviet Union. The ability to question local inhabitants in a suspicious area might be a big aid to an on-site inspection team. But there would have to be well-advertised and credible guarantees that no reprisals would be taken against the local citizenry for informing the international inspectorate. How the inspectorate could enforce these provisions, or how they could hope to get a straight story from Soviet inhabitants in an area where the Soviet Union had carefully prepared an illicit underground test, was something that no one could tell in advance, but many could worry about.

The Soviet Union, so far as is known, has never volunteered to provide the on-site inspection teams with any special credentials that could permit free contact with the inhabitants or detailed questioning.

The Western technique at the conference was to assume that all these prerogatives would be granted the international inspection teams. Dr. Brown thus estimated:

> It will probably be possible to identify as such the large majority, *but not all*, of the natural events unresolved by the seismic records by the various means listed above [including questioning eye-witnesses], *but not all of them* either by these methods or by the more detailed inspection methods which I shall now describe. [Author's italics.]

Even granting permission for detailed questioning of local inhabitants, of course, on-site inspection could not be sure to catch an underground violation of the nuclear test-ban treaty.

"When a suspicion of a violation remains—and this presumably includes all or almost all cases where a violation would have actually occurred—it will be necessary to make a much more detailed survey of the region so as to locate the source exactly."

Where would a violator be likely to try to cheat? Dr. Brown suggested five types of places that would be "particularly difficult areas to inspect":

1. Those containing natural caves or mining activities where there would be many legitimate signs of blasting and explosions;
2. Coastal and island areas where tunneling under the water would allow the explosion to take place under such circumstances that no surface indications could be found by visual inspection, and geophysical inspection along the bottom would be very difficult;
3. Areas of extensive forest cover, such that inspection of the ground for signs of human activity could not easily be done from the air;
4. Deserts with drifting sands which might cover such evidences; and finally,
5. Areas where extensive snowfall had followed the explosions.

Dr. Brown summarized his evaluation of the possibilities of catching a sneak underground nuclear test in this way:

Although an underground nuclear test carefully planned and executed could probably be conducted in such a manner that there would be a low probability of subsequently locating it with sufficient accuracy to allow its identification by the means suggested, it should be pointed out that no amount of such care and planning could give complete assurance of escaping detection by the means of inspection which I have outlined.[113]

Put another way, this meant that the West would be accepting a 90 per cent-plus probability that on-site inspection would fail but would be "balancing" this with a 1 per cent possibility that a cheater would be caught.

The implication was that a prospective violator of the test ban would be deterred by a 1 per cent chance he would be discovered.

No study was undertaken at the Conference of Experts on what reprisals might be possible against a cheater; though it appeared that the only reprisal possible would be a resumption of testing—a possibly ineffective measure after the rival power had resumed its own experiments.

Underwater Problem

Dr. Brown was not the only "pessimist" in the Western group. Sir John Carroll, of the British delegation, presented a paper that set forth misgivings about detecting secret nuclear tests deep underwater, say at the bottoms of remote oceans.

Shallow underwater explosions that vent into the atmosphere can be observed in four ways, he said. Hydroacoustic waves propagated from the site of the explosion can be detected by hydroacoustic equipment. Radioactive debris in the water near the site of the explosion will appear for a time but will be diffused and go with the ocean currents. The seismic wave generated would be greater than that for an explosion on land involving the same amount of venting. An acoustic wave would also be sent into the air; this might be picked up. In addition, some radioactive debris might find its way into the atmosphere.

To detect these shallow underwater blasts, then, the control system would require, Sir John declared:

1. Hydrophone stations in or bordering on the oceans.

2. Measuring and sampling equipment which could be quickly dispatched to the site, in time to detect concentrations of debris before they were dissipated by the ocean currents and could no longer be measured against natural background.

3. A network of seismic stations to operate on the same general principles for locating disturbances as in the case of subterranean blasts.

4. An acoustic network to pick up that part of the signal transmitted above the surface of the water.

Suppose, however, that underwater blasts were set off so deep that little or no radioactive debris would be released into the atmosphere?

We do not know enough [Sir John warned] about the effect of local topography and oceanography on the signals generated by underwater nuclear explosions to say with any precision how often hydroacoustic signals from underwater nuclear explosions in the kiloton range will provide a signal at hydroacoustic stations indistinguishable from one generated from a natural event.

Hydroacoustic waves which resemble, in certain cases, the hydroacoustic signals from nuclear explosions, may be produced by natural events, for example, volcanic or submarine disturbances, and perhaps by meteorites.

In such cases, the identification of the event as a natural or nuclear explosion must be based on a comparison of hydroacoustical data with those obtained by aid of other methods.

The hydroacoustical method thus was not considered sufficient to distinguish a nuclear explosion from other underwater disturbances. Sir John then went on to point up other shortcomings in the hydroacoustic system:

When there is an unobstructed direct path from the source to three or more widely separated hydroacoustic stations, a location and time for the event can be deduced. But screening of direct propagation can occur by intervening islands or submarine mountains and can reduce or eliminate the signal received at some stations. *It could happen that no signal would be received from an explosion inside atolls.* On the other hand, strong signals from oceanic explosions can result from reflections off the steep submerged sides of islands or continental margins, so that the event is nevertheless observed, although such received signals may *complicate location or timing.* [Author's italics.]

Tracing the radioactive debris from underwater nuclear shots would also present special problems, Sir John observed.

There is a feature peculiar to underwater explosions, in that debris is dispersed over and in the surrounding water. This has a bearing on any inspection of a possible site that might be contemplated. The radioactive debris from a deep underwater explosion is expected to rise toward the surface and be distributed approximately as follows: one-third on or near the surface; two-thirds subsurface—that is, down below; and only a very small fraction airborne. Initially, the surface contamination will be limited to an area of less than five square miles for a one-kiloton burst. The surface radiation levels will be sufficiently high, we believe, to permit detection by low-altitude aerial survey for only a few days. Detection by ship-borne surface survey should be possible for ten days or more over an area of several hundred square miles. Detection of fresh radioactive debris by subsurface water sampling should be possible for more than a month. In most areas the ocean currents are sufficiently slow and well known to permit location of the contaminated area for considerable time after an explosion.[114]

The calculation that a deep-sunk underwater one-kiloton shot would present surface contamination over an area "less than five square miles" revealed another important hole in the world-wide detection network being planned for a nuclear test ban. In the vast reaches of the south and central Pacific Ocean, or for that matter, any other ocean, aerial surveys would be effective "for only a few days."

The inability of the control network to "pinpoint" the area of the ocean where the explosion might have taken place, combined with the brief availability of debris for aerial detection, would pose another monumental challenge to on-site inspectors. Aircraft would have only a few days to scan perhaps not hundreds of square miles but hundreds of thousands of square miles of oceans to "catch" the radioactive debris. They would have to fly low and could not cover a very wide swathe on a single pass.

If they failed, ships would have about a month after the explosion to find a patch of sea of several hundred square miles which would by then be contaminated sufficiently to allow trolling detectors to pick up the radioactive debris.

In the meantime, of course, whatever power that had arranged the underwater test could have gathered its data and moved completely out of the area, perhaps by submarine.

Thus, a third problem was posed in ocean inspection, beyond those of detection and identification. How was responsibility for the violation to be fixed on the right country?

In most situations on land, the home government would be considered responsible for an explosion on its territory. Of course this need not be the case. The Nautilus, which sailed under the Arctic ice cap, might have tested a nuclear weapon off the northern coast of Siberia. Or any other nuclear power might try to sneak a test in Antarctica.

The Soviet Union would have a hard time pinning the United States with responsibility for a nuclear explosion on the Arctic shores of Siberia. All four nuclear powers could be under suspicion for a nuclear explosion in Antarctica, but there would also be the possibility that a newly-emerging nuclear power, Israel, or West Germany, Yugoslavia, or Sweden or Belgium—might choose this method of avoiding suspicion.

Ocean Surface Possibilities

Certain ocean surfaces also might be attractive sites for a nuclear test-ban violator, the experts' conference was told, particularly around the equator. Sir William Penney explained that

> in these equatorial regions of the ocean, in the lower regions of the troposphere, the winds are slow and it may be a long time before the debris is actually collected. We, therefore, agree . . . that perhaps ships or islands must be equipped for collecting debris, but we have not persuaded ourselves that, at one kiloton, in these special regions, the debris method can have high reliability. There is a great deal of heavy rain. The slow-moving cloud means that it takes a long time to move very far; and there are other reasons of that sort.[115]

Dr. Carson Mark of Los Alamos brought up other possible ocean-surface situations in which a determined violator might evade a treaty.

> There are quite special problems presented to us by the existence of very large ocean areas, particularly in the Southern Hemisphere. There are extensive areas on the globe where one cannot establish the sort of network of geophysical stations which we have been discussing. A small island in the ocean is a poor location for an acoustic station because of the lack of space possible to establish an effective array. It is a poor location for a seismic station, although the hydroacoustic type of observation may be held to look after that aspect of things to some extent. The electromagnetic type of observation can probably be based on even small islands, provided that they are available. But it is likely that to establish the same efficiency in the Southern Hemisphere which we have been picturing in the continental areas of the Northern Hemisphere will require, for example, more reliance on aircraft for debris sampling or monitoring, and special consideration just because of its particular properties.

There was "another freak situation," Dr. Mark warned, in the Torrid Zone, referring to the same problem Sir William had mentioned.

> There is the zone from perhaps 10° or 15° north of the equator to the same distance south of the equator in which there is a fairly stable pattern of air motion, great stretches of ocean, quite heavy rainfall, and one can expect that a small explosion might be conducted at a low altitude there

at a location hard to cover by acoustic stations and under circumstances where most of the radioactive debris could be expected to rain out into the ocean before ever approaching a permanent land-based location. I mention these as kinds of problems which I think we have not taken up specifically as we have discussed the individual methods.[116]

Another possibility for conducting a small test aboveground is to conduct it during a thunderstorm. The blast might then be mistaken for lightning and a thunderclap. The fallout would be rained out immediately and in an extremely restricted area. This would be a case in which identification would be easy—because there would be considerable radioactivity on the ground—but the earlier step, detection, would be difficult.

Dr. Leslie Machta, eminent United States meteorologist, referred to this method of clandestine testing in the Conference on July 10, 1958:

> It is conceivable that almost one hundred per cent of the particulates [fallout] could be removed if a small test were conducted in a large active thunderstorm cell. The most likely case in which this would happen would seem to be a ground burst, or a shallow underground burst of a low-yield device in heavy rain and very light winds.[117]

Even in the atmosphere, generally regarded as the medium where a detection and identification system would be foolproof, there is only a 50 per cent probability that tests in the range of 1 or 2 kilotons would be detected and identified.[118]

Dr. Fedorov was not amused by all these theories for cheating. He reacted more in sorrow than in anger as he said, soothingly:

> I think there is no necessity at present to carry on a discussion on this theme. I think that I can say that neither I nor my colleagues could agree with the pessimistic deductions or the theoretical possibilities of violation which have been expressed in these statements. . . . The first point which I think should be made is that explosions can be detected underwater, on the ground, in the atmosphere, and in the air. Sometimes this will be difficult, sometimes it will be rather easy, even if they are small.

Even in the areas where Americans had special misgivings, Dr. Fedorov insisted on looking on the bright side.

> [Radioactive debris] in the air or on the surface of earth or of the oceans, [will spread] in a relatively short time over considerable distances, and provide an excellent possibility for confirming rather rapidly the fact of an explosion. In the case of an underwater explosion, and even more in the case of an underground explosion, the products will remain where they were formed, as was pointed out by the rapporteurs, and they will remain there, as it was pointed out, for about a month underwater, and for several months, many months underground. Thus they will allow, given the necessary inspection work, for a detection of these products and a determination of what has occurred; and in the case of an underwater explosion it is not difficult to find these products. By means of acoustic data, hydroacoustic

data, it is rather easy to search an area of possible explosion, and in an area of 10 or 20 kilometers [*sic!*] carry out soundings, and this might occur in a question of days or even hours. The same can be said in connection with underground explosion, which can lend itself to more difficulties than the others for detection, but the ground is a lengthy reservoir of at least two geophysical phenomena, one is great radioactivity, the other great temperature. Perhaps there are other phenomena which might allow a progressive regular approach which would provide protection.

If an explosion occurs in an inhabited area everybody knows about it, or quite a lot of people know about it—including boys aged about sixteen, they are the people who really know everything. If the explosion occurs in an abandoned steppe or in the areas of the Arctic, how can you try to hide the traces—I speak of an underground explosion—of a lengthy presence in this area of hundreds of people who had to do the drilling operations, prepare the shaft, organize the operations, bring the equipment, and all that?

One should not speak here of seeking such specific data flung out of the explosion, as seeking simply the traces of an explosion, of a large group of people during a lengthy period of time. The more uninhabited the area, the greater the desert, the greater the expanse in the Arctic, the clearer will be the traces of each individual in that area, and a group of the type that has to organize an underground explosion will not be able to hide its traces even in the most uninhabited area, given even the most careful preparations. There are many ways of checking these traces.

Dr. Fedorov was unperturbed by Dr. Carson Mark's suggestion that nuclear tests in the equatorial rains would cause all the fallout to drop locally in the ocean. The radioactivity would then be picked up in the oceans, Dr. Fedorov claimed confidently "and the rain passes and the blue skies appear again."

The American scientists were men of little faith, Dr. Fedorov suggested. "I do not think we should be afraid to that extent of the violator; the violator should be afraid of the system which you and we wish to create. He will be afraid to an even greater extent, very afraid, indeed, of the reaction of world opinion and of all humanity. The violator will not have a wonderful life at all!"

After all, there would be a large number of people in the control service. "Those people will be scientists, engineers, experts and many of them will be young, and in one, two, or three years they will invent so many things that the lives of the violators will not be worth living," Dr. Fedorov assured the Western team.[119]

Dr. Semenov suggested a change of the subject. "I . . . believe that we should stop discussing these conclusions and go on to something else. If we do not make use of the conclusion at which we have arrived after long discussions, we shall be here when winter comes."

He, too, was reassuring about the capabilities of the system. He dwelt on the 10,000-kilometer range of hydroacoustic detection of underwater explosions and concluded:

If an explosion occurs at less than 10,000 kilometers, recordings will be made at every station and there will be no difficulties with regard to detection. . . . In water, radioactivity remains for a fairly long time and can be controlled and detected. I see no problem in this connection. . . . As regards underground explosions, Dr. Brown referred to 2,000 possible events a year, but the stations can be placed at convenient depth, in a nice quiet place, proper equipment will be installed and most important—as was pointed out by Dr. Fedorov—the seismic stations' sets will be used in conjunction with this method. As the seismic areas are the suppliers, so to speak, of earthquakes, we shall be able to help the underdeveloped countries to set up seismic stations on their territories and we shall have enough stations on our territories in order to determine such recordings well enough. Out of 500 we shall have only 50 left and out of those 50 we shall be able to make a check. . . . As regards inspection, I think it is important that inspection should take place in many cases. But if at this stage we start speaking about methods and the application of inspection, I think that we shall be straying from our path. If we are to go into all these details, it would be better to organize a conference of hunters, of fishermen, of dog-sled operators and so forth. . . .

If we start going into the "ifs" of the situation, if we start referring to wind in the desert which can clear away all the traces of human presence, we shall never get down to reality. If we are going to discuss what we shall do if we find traces of a human boot in the sand or the snow, we shall simply get lost. . . .[120]

The Western team stood its ground, however. Dr. Fisk answered the soothing words of Dr. Fedorov and Dr. Semenov with a short lecture of his own on "skepticism versus optimism." It went like this:

Certainly, we all recognize that large explosions are easier to detect than small ones. We have observed that at some level of yield of a nuclear explosion—perhaps of the order of one kiloton or even less—the detection problem becomes very difficult. But we must remember that we have two problems before us. One is to detect nuclear tests, should they occur and the other—equally important—is to insure that signals from natural phenomena which would be received by a detection network are not interpreted incorrectly as tests.

Our intention was to be neither pessimistic nor unduly optimistic. The fact that we seem to have referred to difficult or pathological cases is, of course, intentional. These cases seem to us to be the ones which the control system would have to consider, *since no one would seek to violate an agreement in an obvious and detectable way*. It should, however, not be assumed that we are pessimistic or hopeless about finding an effective system. We are interested, as we should be, in making sure of what can be effective.[121]

Conversely, the Soviet concept of on-site inspection indicated no worry at all about Western cheating. Teams should not be a permanent fixture, but appointed to deal with a special circumstance at a particular time, the Russians said. The Soviet Union referred to the on-site inspection team as "a visiting inspection group," to emphasize its temporary nature.[122]

Reading the cold, verbatim transcript of the conference, it is easy to suspect that the Russians were sensitive to the shortcomings of on-site inspection and willing to play along because the teams would be ineffectual. Participants on the Western side acknowledge that the Soviet Union wanted to get away with as little inspection as possible, but claim that the Russians found themselves accepting far more than they intended. Soviet movement to accept inspection was "extremely dramatic," men with long experience in negotiation with the Soviet Union believed.

Dr. Fedorov referred again, at some length, toward the close of the conference, to American misgivings about on-site inspection. This time he seemed to be on a reconnaissance mission for the expected political conference, to find out what functions the West had in mind for on-site inspection teams.

It seems that you have some fears of interference with this inspection and this raises some questions in our mind. What kind of obstacles or difficulties are you apprehending, and what rights, what special possibilities, should be given to the inspection people in order to overcome such possible difficulties or obstacles? This is not quite clear and we would like to know more about what you mean by "unhindered inspection." Who, in your view, is likely to put hindrances in the way of this inspection and what are the measures you contemplate in order to overcome such hindrances or obstacles? At any rate we would like very much to have some clarification from you in this connection.

As regards hindrances and the like, it seems to me that governments which will participate in this control system, which will have signed the appropriate international agreements, which will have recognized the need for inspection in a number of instances for the purposes of verifying suspicions—it seems to me that these governments are unlikely then to put obstacles in the way of inspection when it is operating. We can hardly avoid recognizing that any such government would be placing itself in a very delicate and difficult situation.

The Soviet-delegation chief then raised another problem which was to remain unsettled in the next years of negotiations. It concerned "continuous and rapid communications" which would be necessary, the experts' report said, for contact between the control posts and higher echelons.

Dr. Fedorov commented: "We agree with this interpretation, but we would like to point out that this can be fully achieved with the existing means of communication, namely telegraph, telephone, and so forth. Of course, if we speak of a control post in the Arctic or Antarctic, we shall have to think of a special radio station."

Dr. Fisk replied: "We do not exclude the use of existing means of communication."

At that time it was not as clear as it later became that the Soviet Union was extremely sensitive to the use of radio communications inside its borders. Telegraph and telephone, of course, would not be secure in a closed society like the Soviet Union. Radio, on the other hand, was a suspicious instrument, by Soviet definition, in the hands of foreigners on Soviet soil.

As one of the experts at the Geneva Conference of 1958 put it later: "Mention bringing any radio transmitter with more than four or five watts output into the Soviet Union and the Russians go incoherent."

In early August, when the success of the experts' conference was almost certain, some Washington advisers suggested to high State Department and AEC officials that the United States follow the experts conference quickly with an announcement that all American tests would be conducted underground for a specified period. A declared ban or resumption of aboveground tests should be made to depend on further progress, these officials advised, such as installation of an effective inspection system, reduction of international tensions, etc.

This was close to the position the AEC was to take in a special memorandum to the Secretary of State in January, 1959.

The idea was to remove the fallout hazard and at the same time provide an incentive for the Soviet Union to accept effective inspection. It was already foreseen that if the United States completely stopped testing, the Russians could be expected to drag out negotiations to avoid participation in the objectionable inspection system as long as possible. Officials who foresaw this predicted the Soviet Union would try to keep the United States satisfied just enough in negotiations to prevent a resumption of testing, but without giving a full test ban the support it would need to be effective. If the United States had some means to continue testing, meanwhile, as, for instance, underground, the Russians would feel much more urgency in coming to agreement on a total ban.

This theory was proposed informally to high State Department and AEC officials early in August, 1958, two weeks before the final report was agreed upon.

It was also foreseen, at that time, that the Soviet Union would threaten to resume testing itself if the United States did not stop its underground testing. The United States answer, it was anticipated, should be that the United States was ready to proceed to a full ban as soon as Soviet acceptance of inspection attested to Russian sincerity. Meanwhile, underground testing would help to prove that the conclusions of the Geneva Experts' Conference were correct, help develop peaceful uses of nuclear explosives, and further geophysical studies of the earth's structure.

American scientists had concluded, even before they went into the technical talks in Geneva, that no system of instrumental measurements could positively detect and identify all nuclear bursts. There would always be some threshold, they knew. The American experts had agreed unanimously among themselves that further "proof tests" would be essential, no matter what came out of the experts' conference, to settle the technical uncertainties that remained. Consideration was given, before the Conference of Experts, to making an offer for internationally observed tests to show the difficulties of catching underground violators of a test ban.

Despite the unanimous feeling among the experts, however, Chairman Fisk asked members of the delegation at Geneva not to discuss the proof-test idea for fear it would scare off the Soviet scientists. The subject of further testing to clarify uncertainties was never raised with the Russians at any time during the experts' conference.

As the conference wore on toward its conclusion, it seemed that each side's scientists were taking positions 180 degrees out of phase with their home governments. Dr. Brown, on the United States side, was making a powerful mathematical case against inspection. He proved brilliantly that inspection of a nuclear test ban was "well nigh impossible,"[123] yet his government was heavily committed to inspection and control for any and all disarmament.

The Soviet Union, on the other hand, the country that was extremely sensitive to inspection and had on all previous occasions resisted any penetration of its country, was arguing that inspection was an effective (and, presumably, desirable) thing for controlling a nuclear test ban.

There was copious evidence that the Conference of Experts was walking with its eyes wide open into an inspection system that had important blind spots underground, underwater, on the oceans' surface, and at altitudes from ten to fifty kilometers, as well as in outer space. The outer-space problem was touched on only lightly with vague references to detectors in earth satellites. The possibility of triggering sneak subterranean tests by seismograph, as suggested to the Humphrey Subcommittee, was never even explored in the formal sessions.

To conclude that the system was feasible while pointing to the blind spots required, it seemed, a basic faith that the Soviet Union or any other party to the treaty would not try to cheat. The higher the degree of trust one put in the Soviet Union's motives, the higher the degree of feasibility one could see in the control system. The lesser trust, the lesser confidence in the system's feasibility.

The "fine print" in the report alluding in general terms to some of the blind spots, was not released until word of the "success" in the negotiations was spread around the world. The verbatim transcript on which this study has been based was not available to the public until weeks later.

Chapter 7

Optimism Unbounded

The President's enthusiastic welcoming statement the day after agreement was announced at Geneva made no mention of the "limitations" on the technical feasibility of the inspection system.

"The United States welcomes the successful conclusion of the Geneva meeting of experts who have been considering whether and how nuclear-weapons tests could be detected," the President's statement read. "Their conclusions indicate that, if there were an agreement to eliminate such tests, its effective supervision and enforcement would be technically possible."

The White House statement was noteworthy as well for two new offers it contained. The United States was ready to negotiate an agreement to suspend nuclear-weapons tests and establish an international control system on the basis of the experts' report, the President said.

The link was broken, in one swift stroke. The rationale of the past three years, developed under Stassen and refined by Strauss, was brushed aside.

The President went further. If other nuclear powers accepted in principle the proposal to negotiate a test-ban treaty, and

In order to facilitate the detailed negotiations the United States is prepared, unless testing is resumed by the Soviet Union, to withhold further testing on its part of atomic and hydrogen weapons for a period of one year from the beginning of the negotiations.

As part of the agreement to be negotiated, and on a basis of reciprocity, the United States would be further prepared to suspend the testing of nuclear weapons on a year-by-year basis subject to a determination at the beginning of each year that: (a) the agreed inspection system is installed and working effectively; and (b) satisfactory progress is being made in reaching agreement on and implementing major and substantial arms-control measures such as the United States has long sought. The agreement should also deal with the problems of detonations for peaceful purposes, as distinct from weapons tests.

(The second condition was a concession to the advocates of retaining the "link." But the State Department regarded the link as having been discarded, as did the AEC and the Defense Department.)

The United States would have test-ban negotiators instructed and ready to go by October 31, the President said, and voiced this hope:

> As the United States has frequently made clear, the suspension of testing of atomic and hydrogen weapons is not, in itself, a measure of disarmament or a limitation of armament. An agreement in this respect is significant if it leads to other and more substantial agreements relating to limitation and reduction of fissionable material for weapons and to other essential phases of disarmament. It is in this hope that the United States makes this proposal.

Ambassador Henry Cabot Lodge at the United Nations was delighted with the break in the link and credited it with having improved the world's opinion of the United States. Whereas in 1957 it had been Ambassador Lodge's task to defend all the complicated components of the disarmament package, in 1958 he could state American policy as a simple slogan. His public-relations job was made much easier. He has publicly acknowledged taking an influential part in changing American policy on the link.

> I have tried to state this [disarmament package] in as concise English as I could, and here's what it was: cessation of production of fissionable materials for weapons purposes; the reduction of nuclear weapons stocks; the reduction of forces and conventional arms; the progressive establishment of open inspection to guard against surprise attack; and the study of an effective inspection to insure the peaceful use of outer space. Effective international control was to be established throughout. . . .
>
> The Soviet Union, on the other hand, concentrated on a mere verbal exhortation to cease nuclear tests. . . .
>
> During 1958, the American position had evolved. It came to take account of the opinions expressed in the General Assembly and elsewhere, and, when the last General Assembly came into session in the autumn of 1958, I was in a position to say that the United States favored the immediate suspension of nuclear-weapons tests for one year and thereafter provided the Soviets did not test; provided a real beginning was made on an inspection system; and provided that we were progressing satisfactorily on substantial arms-control measures.
>
> I feel that the new policy certainly helped us insofar as world opinion is concerned—as I assess world opinion in my every day contacts at the United Nations. . . .[1]

In private conversations, President Eisenhower had assured many leading Administration figures that any test-suspension would be extremely short; first he had said only six months, later ten months, later one year. It is probably fair to say, however, he had not foreseen that the test negotiations would drag on to the end of his term in 1961.

John A. McCone, a Republican businessman and industrialist from Los Angeles who had succeeded Mr. Strauss as AEC Chairman, issued a two-sentence press release from the Atomic Energy Commission headquarters in Washington on the day of the President's offer to negotiate a test ban:

"Mr. John A. McCone, Chairman of the Atomic Energy Commission, stated today that he is supporting completely the position announced by the President. He stated further that the Commission was proceeding with the necessary action to complete its programmed series of tests in advance of the 31 October date."

The British Government joined President Eisenhower in taking the optimistic view of the inspection system set up by the Conference of Experts. "It is now established that effective international control over a suspension of nuclear-weapons tests is technically possible," the British statement said.[2]

Great Britain announced that it was embarking on a "short series of tests" but that it too would institute a one-year moratorium when the negotiations for a test ban were begun.

In a note delivered by the American Embassy in Moscow to the Soviet Foreign Ministry, the United States proposed formally that the negotiations toward a test ban begin in New York on October 31 and that progress be reported to the Secretary-General of the United Nations.[3]

Eight days later, the Soviet Union accepted the October 31 date for beginning negotiations toward "the permanent discontinuance" of atomic- and hydrogen-weapons tests with "appropriate" controls. But the Kremlin said it preferred Geneva for the negotiations. Again reflecting its supreme impatience, the Soviet Union suggested that the three governments concerned, the Soviet Union, the United States, and the United Kingdom, fix a two- to three-week time limit on the negotiations.[4]

Premier Khrushchev had given advance notice of the disgruntled Soviet acceptance of the October 31 date for test ban negotiations in a long, acid interview with a Pravda correspondent—who conveniently asked him all the right questions. Pledging a one-year suspension of tests, as President Eisenhower had done, was "completely meaningless," Premier Khrushchev commented, "since one year is precisely the time required for preparing the next series of tests."

At the same time, he pressed his campaign for minimum inspection. The Anglo-American condition that their moratorium would be continued beyond one year only if there were adequate progress on installing the inspection system was "artificial," the Soviet Premier said,

since it has long been known that modern science guarantees the possibility of detecting any nuclear explosions and therefore control over the observance of an agreement on the discontinuance of tests is readily feasible. If any proof is needed of the utterly contrived nature of this condition [he added], it is sufficient to recall the results of the recently concluded Conference of Experts of eight countries at Geneva.

In Mr. Khrushchev's mind, the American link between test ban and other disarmament measures had not yet been broken. He called attention with heavy-handed sarcasm, to the "rather peculiar situation" that had been created:

At first, for a long time we were told that the question of discontinuing nuclear tests could be settled only as an integral part of a broad agreement on disarmament. When the incongruity of this position of the Western powers became obvious to all, these powers retreated under the pressure of public opinion and declared that they were prepared to consider the question of discontinuing tests separately, as an independent problem. At the same time, however, they began working hard to inflate the problem of controlling the discontinuance of tests, exaggerating the difficulties of such control—contrary to the real facts of the situation—and going so far as to assert that control was impossible. Now, when it has become clear to everyone that control is completely practicable, Washington and London are again saying that the solution of the problem of discontinuing tests is possible only in conjunction with the settlement of other disarmament problems.

Thus, the vicious circle created by the opponents of an agreement on the general discontinuance of atomic- and hydrogen-weapons tests is once more complete.

Here was a reverse example of the failure of Soviet and Western governments to communicate, despite the facility of each in the other's language. The White House had intended to convey the idea that the link between nuclear tests and other disarmament measures had, for practical purposes, been broken. Premier Khrushchev did not understand it so.

He used the same interview, however, to press home his satisfaction with the conclusions of the Geneva Conference of Experts. The eagerness with which he sought to cloak the experts' inspection system with the mantle of infallibility led some to suspect that he knew and approved of its weaknesses. Here was his comment:

The significance of the Geneva Conference should be considered, first and foremost, to lie in the fact that it finally disposed of the myth that control over compliance with an agreement for the discontinuance of nuclear tests was impossible. It is well known that this myth was circulated by certain circles among the Western powers, especially in the United States of America, with the object of preventing a discontinuance of tests. The experts who met at Geneva, and they included experts from the Western powers, reached the unanimous conclusion that any nuclear explosion could be detected and that effective control of a discontinuance of nuclear weapons tests was completely feasible.[5]

We note with satisfaction that the conclusions of the Conference of Experts fully confirm the correctness of the point of view which the Soviet Government has always maintained on this question and demonstrate the falseness of the position of the Western powers. The results of the Geneva Conference compel the opponents of a general discontinuance of tests to acknowledge the utter worthlessness and antiscientific nature of their arguments.

The Soviet Government has carefully studied the results of the work of the Geneva Conference of Experts and deems it necessary to state that it agrees with all the conclusions and recommendations in the report of the conference concerning a system of control over a general discontinuance of nuclear tests.

In the light of the results of this conference, there can now be no excuses or justifications for rejecting an immediate and general discontinuance of nuclear-weapons tests, even on the part of those who previously resorted to excuses of this kind, deceiving the credulous.

In the same lengthy interview, Premier Khrushchev reported that the United States, from April 28 to July 26, had set off "over thirty" nuclear tests at the Pacific Proving Grounds. (This was the corrected count after the earlier total of thirty-two had been challenged.) The United Kingdom, he complained, had also tested H-bombs in the summer and had, on August 22, announced a new series of tests.

In view of these British and American tests, the Soviet Premier declared his Government released from its March 31 pledge of a unilateral test ban. The Soviet Union resumed testing in a month.

The United States soon accepted the Soviet suggestion that Geneva should be the site of the nuclear-weapons test-ban negotiations, but met with skepticism the Soviet hope that the negotiations could be concluded in two or three weeks.

Ambassador James J. Wadsworth, the United States representative on disarmament, was named chairman of the United States delegation to the Geneva Conference.[6]

On September 30, the State Department announced that two nuclear explosions had occurred that same day in the Soviet Union. It had been widely charged on March 31, when the Soviet Union announced its unilateral suspension, that the Soviet announcement was "primarily a propaganda exercise and that there was no real intention to suspend testing." This judgment now was confirmed, the State Department said.

Nevertheless, the United States was still expecting the Soviet Union to participate in the test-ban negotiations scheduled to open October 31 in Geneva.

"Unless the Soviet Union holds further tests after negotiations have begun," the State Department said, "the United States remains prepared to withhold further testing of atomic and hydrogen weapons for a period of one year from the beginning of the negotiations on October 31."

The President's August 22 announcement was the signal, not only for the State Department to prepare for test-ban negotiations, but also for the Defense Department and the Atomic Energy Commission to leap into action with an accelerated test-program to prove out every possible theory in the laboratories before the one-year moratorium scheduled to begin October 31. Tests continued until a few hours before the opening day of negotiations. One balloon shot scheduled by the Navy was aloft and ready for firing in the late night hours of October 30, but President Eisenhower ordered that it not be fired, for fear of creating a misunderstanding in the Kremlin, where it was already October 31, the day of the conference opening.

The results of those tests, the Hardtack II series in Nevada, were to be especially embarrassing for the experts who had boldly stated their conclusions about the effectiveness of an inspection system on the basis of only one previous underground nuclear explosion. The Hardtack II results also were to throw the negotiations for a treaty banning nuclear tests into confusion and provoke periodic Soviet outcries about the bad faith of the United States.

Chapter 8

Hardtack II

Back when the Eisenhower Administration was resolutely opposing the test-ban sallies of Adlai Stevenson, one of the arguments had been that the United States would risk its supposed lead in nuclear-weapons development if a moratorium were undertaken. The Soviet Union could suddenly break a test-ban agreement, Administration officials had warned, and it would take at least nine months, possibly two years, for the United States to get ready to test.

Mr. Stevenson's backers later recalled how conservative the nine-month to two-year estimate had been when the AEC and Defense Department sprang into action after President Eisenhower's August 22 statement that the United States would begin a one-year test moratorium on October 31.

It took only twenty-one days for the United States to open an intensive series of tests at its Nevada site. The Hardtack II series, as it was code-named, had originally been planned for the spring of 1959.

AEC officials probably knew early in August that one last test series would be ordered, but they needed less than two months to get tests under way.

The first shot, a 38-ton underground explosion, was fired September 12. Five days later there was a "tiny" 15-ton blast also underground. Both these explosions were set off at a depth of 500 feet. They produced no motion on seismographs in nearby Pasadena.

In the forty-eight days between September 12 and October 30, a total of thirty-seven tests were reported, nineteen safety experiments, seventeen full-scale weapons shots. Eleven of the thirty-seven were set off underground. The power of the subterranean shots ranged from 1.5 tons to 19.2 kilotons.

Their seismic signals were to produce important new data for the seismologists and to upset the conclusions that had just been reached at the East-West experts conference.

Here is a list of the underground explosions in the Hardtack II series:

HARDTACK II UNDERGROUND TESTS

Shot code-name	Date	Depth (feet)	Yield (tons)
Otero*	9-12-58	500	38
Bernalillo*	9-17-58	500	15
Luna*	9-21-58	500	1.5
Valencia*	9-26-58	500	2
Mars*	9-28-58	**	13.5
Colfax*	10-5-58	500	5.5
Tamalpais	10-8-58	330	72
Neptune*	10-14-58	98.5	115
Logan	10-16-58	830	5 kilotons
Evans	10-29-58	848	55
Blanca	10-30-58	835	19.2 kilotons

* Safety experiments.
** No data given.

Source: "Probing the Earth with Nuclear Explosions," by D. T. Griggs and Frank Press, Lawrence Radiation Laboratory, UCRL-6013, September 28, 1959. Based on information compiled by G. W. Johnson, for presentation to the International Union of Geodesy and Geophysics at Helsinki, 1960.

Seven of the underground shots were safety experiments, conducted to find out how weapons of various design could be prevented from going off accidentally. The four full-scale explosions were Tamalpais, Logan, Evans, and Blanca. Neptune, with its yield of 115 tons, was a safety shot, but it provided important data for nuclear-test control and to scientists developing peaceful uses of nuclear explosions. All were fired in the same Nevada mesa where the Rainier shot had been exploded in 1957.

The underground experiments confirmed generally the conclusions advanced by the United States scientists in the Conference of Experts that neither radioactivity nor temperature effects would be spread very far from the point of explosion.

The 19.2-ton Blanca shot caused a noticeable temperature rise in the surrounding earth to an average radius of some 240 feet, roughly 75 meters. Its radioactive pocket had a radius of about 130 feet, or 40-odd meters.

Logan, the 5-kiloton test, produced a radioactive pocket of 85-foot, or 25-meter, radius and a noticeable rise in temperature to an average radius of 190 feet, or 60 meters.

Tamalpais, the first full-fledged nuclear-weapons test exploded underground in the Hardtack series, was fired on October 8 at 2 P.M. It had an explosive force estimated at 72 tons. That was not enough power for persons at the firing point 2.5 miles away to notice any ground movement. The weapon had been placed in a room 20 feet by 20 feet by 17 feet high that had been lined on all sides by two feet of salt. The intention was to provide preliminary data for the planned experiment in peaceful uses of atomic energy in a deep salt bed near Carlsbad, New Mexico.

How Underground Nuclear Shots Heated Earth

Isotherm (°C.)	Approximate average radius (feet)			
	Blanca	Logan	Rainier	Tamalpais
20	240*	190*	100	—
40	120	100	80	—
60	—	80	55	—
80	—	70	30	—
R_T (feet)**	210	140	96	50

* The background temperatures for Blanca and Logan were 20°C. and 18°C., respectively.
** R_T is the radius at which temperature first rises sharply.
Source: "Underground Nuclear Detonations," UCRL-5626, pages 16–17.

The Tamalpais shot was buried 410 feet beneath the top of the mesa, but its nearest point to the side surface of the mesa was 330 feet.

Radii of Radioactive Shells

Event	Radius (feet)
Neptune	21
Blanca	130
Logan	85
Rainier	62
Tamalpais	30

Source: "Underground Nuclear Detonations," UCRL-5626, pages 16–17.

Neptune, the 115-ton "safety experiment," was exploded in a shot-room 10 feet by 17 feet by 10 feet high, located only 109.5 feet below the top of the mesa and 98.5 feet from the nearest surface point. The unexpectedly large explosion, perhaps less safe than expected, broke through the surface and 1 or 2 per cent of the radioactive material escaped. The data, however, was of special use to the peaceful-uses department of the Atomic Energy Commission, which had been studying the effects of underground explosions in cutting canals, harbors, and other large excavation projects. There was "very little radioactive contamination of the surface exposure of the broken rock produced by the explosion," the University of California Radiation Laboratory later reported, indicating that nuclear excavation might be found feasible for much larger projects. Except for one small "jet" of radioactivity which escaped, producing a radiation level of one roentgen per hour,[1] measured levels of radioactivity in and near the crater five days after the explosion were less than 100 milliroentgens per hour.[2]

The 5-kiloton Logan detonation was made at 10 P.M. on October 15. It was fired in a room 31 feet long, 9 feet high, and 9 feet wide, buried 930 feet below the top of the mesa, 830 feet away from the nearest surface point. The radioactive debris was completely contained. The ground shock was "readily felt by observers" at the control point 2.5 miles away but not at seven miles.[3]

The next important underground shot was Evans, a 55-ton explosion buried 848 feet. It was fired October 29 and produced no ground motion that was noticed.

The Evans shot later was discovered to have provided at least partial confirmation of the decoupling theory. It was fired in a room approximately 15 feet on a side. The room was at the end of a tunnel at a depth of about 830 feet. "Based on the seismic yield-amplitude curve from the other underground shots, one would say that the yield was less than 10 tons," according to a report by Kenneth Street. This amounted to a decoupling factor of five. "It is not known why Evans failed to couple seismically but a vigorous attempt should be made to try to understand and to reproduce this unexpected behavior," Mr. Street commented.[4]

The next day was the last day on which the United States tested before the moratorium took effect. Three shots were fired, one from a balloon, a tiny one from a tower, and the huge 19.2-kiloton blast, code-named Blanca, exploded 835 feet underground. Blanca was fired at 7 A.M. in a shot-room 7 feet by 8 feet by 20 feet. The distance to the top of the mesa was 988 feet, but the nearest point on the surface was 835 feet.[5]

Observers felt a strong ground shock at five miles. Automobiles were rocked violently from side to side at a distance of two miles. Others reported a rolling effect was noticeable at 16 miles. But at 20 miles there were no reports of noticeable effects, without the aid of instruments.

Because the weapon had not been buried deeply enough for complete containment, the Blanca shot vented slightly. The Lawrence Radiation Laboratory later gave this description of the event:

> On detonation the shock was clearly visible in its effect of kicking up soil as it broke through the sloping of the mountain. A large quantity of the cap rock was broken loose and fell down the sides of the mountain. About fifteen seconds after zero time a plume of dust was ejected from the mountain due to the collapse of the initial cavity to the surface. The dust rose about 1,000 feet and carried some radioactivity with it. The fraction of radioactivity which escaped is estimated to have been 0.1 per cent. There was a very small but detectable leak of radioactivity into the tunnel.[6]

Later studies indicated that radioactivity from underground nuclear explosions would contaminate ground water only within a very small radius of the explosion if placed properly. Strontium-90 would move out only about 100 feet in half its life span of twenty-eight years. "Ground water contamination does not appear to present any serious hazard, nor does the ground-water contamination problem appear to place any serious limitations on the use of nuclear explosives," the Lawrence Radiation Laboratory concluded.[7]

Induced radioactivity, produced by neutrons freed in the explosions, would not spread beyond the first 2 or 3 feet from the point of detonation.[8]

Seismographs had been alerted across the nation and world-wide to watch for the shots. Temporary seismographs, too, were specially prepared to monitor the events.

The startling and appalling results were gathered by Dr. Carl Romney in Washington around Thanksgiving Day, 1958. Signals from the far-flung system of seismographs indicated that the East-West experts had greatly overestimated the ability both to detect nuclear-weapons tests and to distinguish them from earthquakes.

Treaty negotiations were just then getting under way in Geneva, however, and the Administration was worried about the effect the new findings would have on the Soviet Union's attitude toward the talks. It was a foregone conclusion that the Soviet Union would accuse the United States of bad faith and of trying to "back out" of the test-ban negotiations if the discoveries were made known.

So the Defense Department, the Atomic Energy Commission, the President's science advisory group, all checked and rechecked their data, refined the results, tried to think up explanations for the unexpected weakness of the seismic signals.

It fell to Dr. James F. Killian, Jr., the President's science adviser, to break the bad news to Mr. Eisenhower. The President reportedly was highly disturbed to learn that the "scientific" basis on which he had launched the test-ban negotiations had melted beneath his feet so quickly.[9]

A panel of seismologists and physicists was quickly appointed by Dr. Killian to figure out what to do next. They studied the results in secret until January 5, 1959. Then the White House broke the news to the world.

Studies of the October tests in Nevada and the new data from them indicated, a White House statement said mildly, "that it is more difficult to identify underground explosions than had previously been believed." For the first time the White House took note, in some detail, of the "limitations" on inspection mentioned in the Conference of Experts report. These limitations had not been mentioned in the White House press release of the previous August, just after agreement had been reached with the Soviet scientists.

> The Geneva Conference of Experts last summer concluded that, although it is not possible to identify an underground explosion by seismic means alone, it is possible to identify a large fraction of seismic events as natural earthquakes when the direction of first motion of the seismic signal is ob-

served at several, appropriately located stations. This procedure reduces the number of seismic events which would be unidentified and could, therefore, be suspected of being underground tests. Analysis of all the available seismic data on underground tests, including the data new since last summer, has shown that this method of distinguishing earthquakes from explosions is less effective than estimated by the Geneva Conference of Experts. These analyses and new data also indicate that the seismic signals produced by explosions are smaller than had been anticipated and that there are consequently *about twice as many natural earthquakes* equivalent to an underground explosion of a given yield as had been estimated by the Geneva Conference of Experts. [Author's italics.]

These two factors mean that there will be a substantial increase in the number of earthquakes that cannot be distinguished from underground nuclear explosions by seismic means alone. For example, the total number of unidentified seismic events with energy equivalents larger than five kilotons may be increased *ten times or more* over the number previously estimated for the system recommended by the Geneva Conference of Experts. [Author's italics.]

The effect of this new analysis and data on the capabilities of the system recommended by the Geneva Conference of Experts as well as modifications of that system which could restore its originally estimated capability against underground tests are at present under study by United States scientists.[10]

The Conference of Experts, it will be remembered, had estimated that there would be 20 to 100 unidentified events with energy-equivalents larger than 5 kilotons each year. The lower estimate had been supplied by the Soviet Union, the larger by the United States, although this was not explained at the time. The estimate that these figures were wrong by a factor of ten meant that a more accurate estimate would be 200 to 1,000 unidentified events per year above 5 kilotons.

This would throw ten times as great a burden on the already hopelessly overburdened on-site inspection teams, if the control system were to have the same effectiveness as previously planned.

But this was not all. The discovery that seismic signals produced by explosions were smaller than had been anticipated would mean that larger nuclear-weapons tests underground would be lost in the seismic noise than had previously been calculated. How much larger was not then publicly stated.

The explanatory statement was prepared by the President's Science Advisory Committee with concurrence of the State and Defense Departments and the AEC.

Discovery of the drastic miscalculation of the control system's effectiveness had been met with mixed reactions inside the Administration. The attitude was generally "I told you so," in the AEC and the Defense Department. The State Department, aware of the impact the new data might have on the Soviet Union, sought diligently, but largely in vain, for some quick method of recouping the losses in effectiveness quickly enough to save the Geneva treaty negotiations.

The White House statement was a subject of prolonged bickering between the various government agencies, both before and after its release. Neither those who had favored a nuclear test ban nor those who had opposed it were satisfied with the final product.

Little was made of new and feverish efforts to improve the seismic detection network. This angered the pro-ban factions.

Not all the control-system shortcomings were fully explained. This angered the anti-ban factions.

The dilemma of the United States in the negotiations with the Soviet Union was apparent. There were three broad alternatives available: If improvements could not restore the system, the Soviet Union could be asked to reopen the technical talks so that a new control system, with many more inspection stations, could be devised; or the United States could go ahead with the Geneva experts system; or the negotiation could be terminated.

The second alternative would have risked Senate rejection of the treaty, even if it were negotiated with the Soviet Union. Members of the Joint Atomic Energy Committee had already been expressing misgivings about the wisdom of stopping tests; now that serious doubts were raised about the effectiveness of inspection, the apprehensions would increase.

There was one "out." Continuing to negotiate on the basis of a 180-station network, State Department officials pointed out, would force an extremely high number of on-site inspections. So there should have been a real incentive, not only for the United States but for the Soviet Union, to improve the equipment provided for the stations, or increase the number of stations.

The Joint Atomic Energy Committee of the Congress had been advised in advance of the new findings. Three days before the White House public statement, one member of the Committee, Representative Craig Hosmer of California, had written President Eisenhower suggesting that the nuclear-test talks be discontinued. He made no mention of the new findings beyond a comment that the "optimism expressed after last summer's scientific discussions at Geneva" had "dissipated."

Representative Hosmer was expressing the views of many other members of the Joint Committee. There were differing thoughts, however, on how far the Senate could go in pressing the President in a delicate negotiation with the Soviet Union. It was some Senators' understanding, even then, however, that the Administration would make an effort to extricate itself from the negotiations with as little pain as possible. Congressional leaders began to wonder about this, however, as the negotiations extended through two more years, until the end of the Eisenhower Administration.

One week after President Eisenhower's statement on the Hardtack findings, the Joint Committee on Atomic Energy held secret sessions with the leading scientists and policy-makers in the Administration. Members of the Committee later gave the impression that they thought it would be impossible to accept a comprehensive nuclear test ban in the face of the Hardtack material.

Although the Soviet Union was given a detailed explanation of the new Hardtack data on January 5, the American public was not given the details until January 16, when the Department of Defense released more information.

Temporary seismic stations had been set up in advance of the underground tests along a line extending eastward from the Nevada Proving Ground to Arkansas and then northeastward to Maine, the Defense Department said. The nearest station was about 100 kilometers (63 miles) from the test and the most distant station was slightly more than 4,000 kilometers (2,500 miles) away. Geologists had "carefully selected" operating sites on "suitable outcrops of hard rock remote from sources of man-made noise." Sixteen of the stations were equipped with Benioff short-vertical seismographs and with auxiliary equipment.

The Defense Department release mentioned only three shots on which the evaluations were based: the Tamalpais test of October 8, which was said to have had a yield of "about 1/10th kiloton"; the Logan explosion of October 16, with a yield of about 5 kilotons; and the Blanca event of October 30, which was then calculated to have had a yield of about 23 kilotons.

The Blanca explosion produced a signal of magnitude 4.8 and Logan 4.4. No mention was made of the signal from Tamalpais, indicating, presumably, that if one had been received it could not be distinguished from the background noise.

At the same time, the seismologists had found that the previous magnitude estimate for Rainier, the September, 1957, shot of 1.7 kilotons, was high. The revised magnitude, according to the Defense Department statement, was 4.1 rather than 4.25. Earthquakes rapidly grow more numerous as one moves down the magnitude scale. In other words an unadvertised Rainier shot would be much more difficult to pick out because it would be placed among many more natural events than previously expected.

The Hardtack data also indicated that first motion "is not usable as an identification characteristic of earthquakes which are equivalent to 20 kilotons or less when recorded at distances between 110 kilometers and 2,500 kilometers from the burst."

This was a reference to the "shadow zone" which had been explored at some length in the Conference of Experts. It was intended to indicate that the zone was 500 kilometers deeper than previously estimated.[11]

At closer range, of 200 kilometers, the Defense Department report said, "the amplitude of first motion was less than one-third of the peak amplitude in the first pulse and at 1,000 kilometers less than one-fifth. Consequently, it is now estimated that the first motion must exceed the background noise, or natural unrest of the earth, by at least a factor of three to one instead of the previous estimate of two to one if the direction of first motion is to be reliably determined."

The seismic signal, in other words, would be required to stand out 50 per cent higher against the background noise than previously thought adequate for a reliable determination of first motion. This would be true even in the closer ranges of from 125 to 625 miles, the statement said.

Delegations of the United Kingdom and the Soviet Union at the Geneva test-ban negotiations were given copies of thirty-six seismograms of the three Hardtack II underground explosions and other data, the Defense Department said.

Eleven scientists served on the panel which evaluated the Hardtack data. The chairman was Dr. Carl Romney of the United States Air Force. Other participants were Billy G. Brooks, Chief Seismologist of the Geotechnical Corporation; Perry Byerly, Director of the Seismographic Stations, University of California; Dean S. Carder, Chief Seismologist, U.S. Coast and Geodetic Survey; Frank Press, Director, Seismological Laboratory, California Institute of Technology; Jack Oliver, Professor of Geophysics, Columbia University; James T. Wilson, Chairman, Department of Geology, University of Michigan; Professor Hans A. Bethe, Cornell; Professor D. T. Griggs, University of California at Los Angeles; Dr. Kenneth Street, University of California Radiation Laboratory, and Dr. Carson Mark, of the Los Alamos Scientific Laboratory.

As expected, the Soviet Union immediately set up a clamor that the United States had lost interest in the nuclear test-ban problem and was trying to back out of the negotiations.

Reaction to the findings in this country, both inside the Administration and out, followed easily predictable lines. Those who had been in favor of a test ban continued to favor it and tended to minimize the importance of the new Hardtack findings. Those who had been opposed to a test ban cried out for an end to the negotiations, or at least a suspension, until better inspection techniques could be devised.

The decibels of the two-sided clamor were about equal, but privately many test-ban advocates were willing to acknowledge that the new discoveries had dealt a serious blow to their hopes for an early treaty.

One of the basic weaknesses of the Geneva Conference of Experts had been that it tried to calibrate its seismic inspection system on the basis of experience with only one underground nuclear shot, the 1.7-kiloton Rainier explosion. Since there were no other explosions of varying yields in the same medium, and there had been no experience at all in other media, the scientists were unable to "plot a curve" to predict how seismic signals would vary in size with variations in yield or medium.

The Hardtack II series showed that the original calibration or calculation of equivalent-yield in terms of magnitude was one-third incorrect on detection and two-thirds wrong on identification.

The Soviet Union served notice on January 20, four days after the detailed Pentagon report, that it intended to resist on a scientific level what appeared to be American efforts to raise the price of a nuclear test ban by increasing the amount of inspection required. Two Soviet "bigger guns" in seismology, Y. V. Riznichenko and L. Brekhovski, corresponding members of the Soviet Academy of Sciences, attacked the American analysis of the new data in a Pravda article. They challenged the idea, widely expressed in the United States, that the system for inspecting a nuclear test ban had been based on only one underground nuclear shot. "The experts were able to draw on many years experience in the investigation of many thousands of earth tremors as well as many hundreds of seismic registrations of large TNT explosions."

American scientists who had been at Geneva told the Senate Disarmament Subcommittee later[12] they had never claimed Rainier was the only experience on which they were basing their estimates for a nuclear test-ban control system. The difficulty was in calibrating the system, to find a suitable basis of comparison between underground nuclear explosions and earthquakes.

The rate of increase in seismic signal compared with earthquakes of a given magnitude produced a curve fairly well known. But with only one nuclear explosion no curve could be drawn to show the increasing effect of nuclear explosions on seismic signals. The scientists had to extrapolate and use data from chemical explosions as best they could. Then the two curves were compared and calibrations were made. Dr. Fisk, the leader of the American team at Geneva, told the Humphrey Subcommittee: "The calibrating point which puts our conclusion out by a factor of one-third on detection and two-thirds on identification, so far as the actual signal is concerned, rested on that one piece of evidence [Rainier]."

The Soviet scientists, in turn, accused the United States of basing all their new conclusions on only one of the Hardtack II series, the five-kiloton Logan shot.

It has to be pointed out that the data on one of these three explosions, a very small one [Tamalpais] of a power of 0.1 kiloton, are not actually quoted or utilized. . . . [The scientists] failed to consider the results of the registration of the Blanca explosion in other seismological stations of the United States, whose number exceeds ninety, as well as [the registrations] in the stations of Sweden and other countries situated at a distance of thousands of kilometers from the epicenter. Nor do the authors make allowances for the important circumstance that the Blanca explosion was accompanied by a destruction of the earth's surface and a large ejection of soil, so that the energy of its seismic effect must be smaller than is the case with a subterranean explosion of the same power.

Thus all these far-reaching conclusions are based as a matter of fact only on the data of the one new Logan explosion. Similarly, the authors do not, for some unknown reason, take the registration of the Rainier explosion, carried out in many other stations, into consideration.

Answering these charges, Dr. Romney said that the small Tamalpais explosion had been used "in a very important way" to establish the scaling law by which American scientists had estimated the seismic signals that would be produced from underground nuclear explosions. Results of close-range detection apparently were available, but were not being provided to the Russians.

The Soviet scientists' claim that Blanca should have been rated at a higher seismic magnitude because part of its energy escaped, probably was made in "the best of faith," Dr. Romney said, but it was based on a misconception:

"Blanca did not blow out; it fell in, and it fell in many seconds after the seismic effect had passed. The seismic waves were a few hundred kilometers away by the time it collapsed. So that we actually did have the shots we claim."

In their Pravda critique, the Soviet scientists also had returned to an old charge that annoyed American scientists: American equipment was not top-grade.

The U.S. note briefly described the seismological equipment used in the observations. The authors assert that it tallies with the recommendations of the Geneva Conference of Experts. This is not true. The Conference of Experts recommended the establishment by the control posts of a set of ten grouped vertical seismographs with an amplification of about a million and a maximal sensitivity for registering vibrations with a period of about one second and a sufficiently wide pass band. In addition, the establishment of several sets of equipment with a wider pass band was also recommended.

The American seismologists, however, applied equipment with a considerably lesser amplification. A narrow pass band and a maximum of sensitivity for vibrations with a period of about 0.3 second. There was no equipment with a wide pass band. To a specialist it is clear such equipment does not tally with the recommendations of the experts conference and is less sensitive in particular also in registering the amplitude of the first vibration of a longitudinal wave, which is an important factor in determining the period of the source of the seismic feature.

The scientists of the U.S.S.R. also complain that the temporary stations registered the signals of the Blanca and Logan explosions more poorly than the permanent stations.[13]

The Pravda charges telegraphed punches Soviet scientists were to throw when the second experts conference was convened ten months later. The Americans had actually claimed that the instrumentation used in the Hardtack II series had been comparable to that recommended by the Conference of Experts. They had not meant it literally, but the Soviet scientists took an ambiguously worded sentence as a claim that the Geneva system had been duplicated.

Dr. Romney denied the Soviet charge that undue weight had been given recordings at temporary stations: "The recordings at temporary stations and recordings at permanent stations, when treated separately, gave the same result. The temporary stations gave the same magnitude as the permanent stations, treated separately," he said.

Pointing out that both temporary and permanent stations gave the Logan magnitude at 4.4, Dr. Romney explained: "As a matter of fact, the temporary stations on the average gave better results than permanent stations at the same distance, and the reason is very simple. The temporary stations had better equipment than the average of the permanent stations at the same distances."

The Russians claimed that the precision of the calculations had not been high. The margin of error, plus or minus 0.4 or more for magnitudes of 4.1 to 5, was claimed to be excessive.

Earthquake magnitudes are determined to about the same margin of error, Dr. Romney countered. True, the Rainier magnitude had been overestimated originally and was reduced from 4.25 to 4.1 after further study, he acknowledged. But the 0.4 spread is "consistent," he said, with the kind of spread one gets estimating the magnitude of earthquakes.[14]

Dr. Romney summarized the problem in these two sentences: "What this new relation, based on all the data [from Rainier and Hardtack] shows is that an underground explosion produces a smaller disturbance than we had thought before. This, in turn, means that there are very many more earthquakes of the same size, because the numbers of earthquakes increase very fast as the size decreases, and this then aggravates the inspection problem."

Inability to be exact about earthquake numbers was another handicap. Dr. Romney explained that seismologists cannot give precise estimates on the numbers of earthquakes. Rather than saying there are 1,000 earthquakes of a given size, they are more likely to say there are 500 to 2,000 earthquakes; instead of 1,500 they say 700 to 3,000. "We do not know exactly," he said.

He also gave the Senate subcommittee an explanation why the size of a first-motion signal from an underground disturbance should exceed the background noise by a factor of three to one instead of two to one, as previously considered adequate.

There are many seismologists who feel now, and also felt ten years ago, that two to one was inadequate. . . . They would have required more than that. In fact, this was very explicitly stated by a number of people on our panel who evaluated this data. They said that last year[15] they did not think two to one was adequate, and this year they still do not, for earthquakes, blasts, or any other thing. This is part of the problem.

The guess of two to one was a borderline guess. This is really the minimum anyone would be willing to work with.

These were revealing remarks about the lack of caution—and absence of unanimity—among the American scientists who first established control-system requirements in 1958, before the ill-fated Conference of Experts.

The five-kiloton underground explosion, Logan, looked like an earthquake rather than an explosion, Dr. Romney said, because its first motion, which should have caused all seismograph needles to jump up, was recorded as a downward motion on some. Noise presumably had obscured some of the real first motion.

He also had an explanation for the revision of the estimated magnitude of Rainier downward from 4.25 to 4.1. There had been several stations that picked up the Rainier shot with the kind of equipment that could be used to compute magnitudes, he said. Other stations picked up the shot, but they were not equipped with apparatus adequate to compute magnitudes. Three other specific stations nearby, however, which should have picked up Rainier, did not. It seemed unreasonable to average out the magnitudes of the Rainier shot recorded at ten stations when only seven of the stations had picked up a signal at all. Three zeros "would have made the magnitude very low, and this seemed a ridiculous procedure," Dr. Romney explained. "The only average is made of the ones where you have data, and this is what was done. Now, with the experience of the next two large explosions, we found out that those seven stations gave higher than average magnitude . . ."

It was a painful exercise for the scientists who had been parties to the optimistic performance at Geneva to acknowledge that their previous estimates had been off by a factor of ten or more.

Since the Conference of Experts had estimated the annual number of unidentified continental earthquakes of 5 kilotons or more to be 20 to 100, Senator Humphrey suggested that 60 per year would have been an average.[16] Applying the factor of 10, the Senator deduced that 600 unidentifiable events would now confront the control system for a nuclear test ban. He asked how many of these 600 would occur in the Soviet Union or in Communist China.

This question uncovered another overlay of uncertainty.

Dr. Romney reported that the special panel of seismologists which had reviewed the Hardtack II data estimated the actual number of unidentified events to be 700 to 3,000, not 600. The factor of error, he pointed out, had been more nearly 15 than 10. That was the significance of the "or more" in the Pentagon and White House reports that the number had been underestimated by a factor of "10 or more."

Dr. Romney estimated that the Soviet and Chinese land mass amounted to about one-sixth of the earth's land surface. That would mean that the Soviet Union and China together each year would have on the order of 100 to 500 earthquakes indistinguishable from blasts of five kilotons, or larger.

Senator Humphrey inquired what capability the world seismographic net would have in detecting and identifying earth movements in Red China if there were no control system there. Leonard Murphy, Chief of the Seismology Branch of the United States Coast and Geodetic Survey, another witness before the subcommittee, reported that earthquakes of a magnitude 5.5 or greater could "in our normal procedure" be located in the China area. On the basis of the Hardtack II series, Dr. Romney pointed out that a 5.5 magnitude would represent about 100 kilotons.

Senator Humphrey suggested that a disarmament agreement that did not include the mainland of China would leave a huge gap there in the control system.

A nuclear explosion [Dr. Romney responded] of any size could go *unidentified* in China if we did not have inspection, and . . . this is indicated in the conclusions of the Conference of Experts or implied at least, that the only real way to be sure you have a nuclear explosion is to get a sample of radioactive debris, and seismology will never give a sample of debris.

Now, so far as detection itself is concerned, knowing that something happened, then I would accept something close to Mr. Murphy's guess as to what could be done, that we would detect events certainly of 100 kilotons, and I would also say more probably detect events less than 20 kilotons.[17]

State Department negotiators maintained an optimistic attitude toward the test talks, despite the Hardtack II findings. Philip J. Farley, Special Assistant to the Secretary of State for Disarmament and Atomic Energy, told the Humphrey Subcommittee that "the best technical advice we get is that you can recoup this technical difficulty by the kinds of improvements that will not involve having more than 180 manned stations, which is the really sensitive part. We think therefore that we have an adequate basis for continuing on our present line."

Later in the same hearings, Senator Hickenlooper brought up the on-site inspection problem.

Everybody agrees you can determine the site from any substantial distance within a space of a minimum of approximately 5 square miles. Some estimates are 10 square miles, depending on many factors.[18] Nevertheless, within that area, where are you going to look?

Suppose there is a deliberate attempt to violate the agreement and conceal a test. It would take ages to drill holes throughout the area. We have already found out that even knowing exactly where an underground explosion is, it is difficult to hit it with a drilling rig.

On Rainier we tried two or three times, and we missed the spot, even though we knew exactly within an inch where the shot had been fired.

The variations of the substructure send the drilling rig off.

How is on-site inspection going to prove anything against a real determined effort to conceal a test?

We are perfectly aware that the Soviet Union has violated understandings and agreements that it has had. These are the problems.

I am thoroughly in sympathy with the efforts, but I don't want us to get caught in an unfair trade, and that is the thing which has concerned me over the months; I, like Senator Gore, was at the Geneva meeting for a week.

If the Soviet Union is ever going to agree on anything that is realistic and workable, then I will be very surprised.

The official rationale for going ahead with the nuclear test-ban talks despite the uncertainties of on-site inspection was given by Mr. Farley:

I agree that it is always going to be possible that an underground shot might be conducted without being detected. It is very unlikely that anyone could achieve a significant new nuclear capability or a significant improvement of his existing capability without being clearly and publicly in the position of having violated or otherwise evaded the agreement.

Senator Hickenlooper interrupted: "I wish I could share a small part of your optimism on that point."

Mr. Farley said later that "while it may be that in the very small explosions you will have a kind of practical difficulty finding the thing which you mentioned, which is certainly a reality now, I would say on the other side that this matter, too, is one in which not as much positive thought and study has been given as will have been by the time we carry this through, so that I think the possibilities for improving on-the-spot inspection techniques are good also."

The Senate Disarmament Subcommittee got a new, more optimistic, slant on the Hardtack II series from Dr. Hans Bethe. He regarded the 5-kiloton Logan shot and the 20-kiloton Blanca explosion as the most important of the Hardtack II series. The magnitude of the signals from these explosions "generally were only about two-thirds of what had been expected," Dr. Bethe acknowledged.[19]

It was still important, however, Dr. Bethe said, "to get still more information," on the behavior of nuclear weapons fired underground. "We have to push, I think," he said, "for further underground tests either by ourselves or international tests under international auspices, which would teach us more closely just what you can do in the way of test detection."

He expressed optimism about the shadow zone, however, where Dr. Romney had shown pessimism a few days before.

"There was one result which was surprisingly favorable," Dr. Bethe said, "namely, it was possible to see the signal, to perceive the seismic signal in the so-called shadow region."

Signals from earthquakes received at distances from 600 to 1,400 miles are "very weak and quite anomalous," Dr. Bethe said. For this reason the Conference of Experts had decided not to pay any attention to signals received in this intervening region but to rely entirely on signals received at stations in the first 600 miles from the origin, called the first zone, or beyond 1,400 miles, which was called the second zone of detection.

"Now, it turned out in the October tests there were signals even in the shadow zone," Dr. Bethe reported. "They could be useful to detect explosions. They are, however, quite useless to identify an explosion, that is, you cannot, by means of these signals, distinguish an explosion from an earthquake."

The main result of the October tests in Nevada, Dr. Bethe said, which was more important than the reduction of the signal to about two-thirds its expected value, was that "the first motion of the earth as recorded by the seismograph is reduced to about 40 per cent of what we previously expected." [20] Dr. Bethe then launched into a valuable primer course on the importance of first motion as estimated at Geneva in 1958.

The first motion is important because this is the way we tell explosions from earthquakes. In explosions . . . the first motion is always outward. You push the earth away from the explosion, and you observe this outward motion at all seismic stations wherever you are.

In an earthquake, on the other hand, you get an outward motion in some directions and an inward motion in other directions, and therefore, if you can observe the seismic signal at many stations, then you can tell an earthquake from an explosion by observing carefully the first motion.

If you find that at all stations the first motion is positive, as we say, outward, upward, then you have an explosion.

Now the Geneva Conference of Experts did not write this conclusion down in detail, but generally agreed in the discussions that in order to identify an earthquake one should observe two negative motions: one should have at two seismic stations a clear negative signal, downward signal, where the earth first moves down and then comes back up again.

So it is the first motion which permits you to tell an explosion from an earthquake.

Now, why is that important? It is important because there are hundreds of earthquakes each year which give as big a signal as the explosions that we are concerned about, and therefore we must be able to distinguish the earthquakes from the explosions, and the best way we have found so far is this first motion. This is not the only way, but it is the best way, the most established way.

Undoubtedly, as we investigate this further, we learn more about it, we will probably learn other ways, and, for instance, Dr. [Frank] Press, who has sent you a statement but not testified to you, believes that a very good way of telling earthquakes from explosions is by looking at the surface waves, at the waves which travel along the surface of the earth instead of traveling down and coming back up again. . . .

He thinks that by looking particularly at the surface waves of very long periods, that he will be able to tell many earthquakes from explosions in the critical area of 5 to 20 kilotons.

Now this he has tried so far only in a few examples, and so we do not know yet how much you can do with this method. But both he and Dr. [Jack] Oliver of Columbia have had considerable success with this method, and it looks very promising . . . [deleted].[21]

So first motion is not the only way, but it is still the best way. And, therefore, since first motion is much less than had been anticipated, we have the result that it is more difficult to tell earthquakes from explosions in the region from 5 to 20 kilotons.

Dr. Bethe explained the basis for his hope, on which the State Department depended heavily, that new-found weaknesses in the inspection system could be overcome.

In my opinion there are a number, actually a large number, of very good methods to improve the system which was devised last summer in Geneva.

Any one of these methods has to be agreed to by the Russians. However, the Geneva Experts report already contains a very important sentence, namely, it says improvements will undoubtedly be found, and when they are found they shall be incorporated in the system. So we really have this already in the experts report that something should be done about it.[22]

What are some of the methods by which we can improve detection?

The one that I like best is that of digging a deep hole such as a dry oil well. There are lots of dry oil wells in the world, and you can dig a deep hole just like an oil well, even if you do not hope to find oil, and at the bottom of such a deep hole, maybe 6,000 feet deep, you install a seismograph.

Now, of course, you have to learn to operate a seismograph at the bottom of such a deep hole, and this will have to be studied and investigated just what you have to do . . .

The predictions of what it will do are, of course, purely theoretical at the present time, but the theoretical prediction is that you might improve your detection capability by a substantial factor.

He indicated, by choice of adjectives which apparently were intended to get around security problems, that he thought the deep-hole method could make the system good enough not only to overcome the handicaps discovered in the Hardtack II series, but to make it far better than originally expected.

You will remember that we lost a *certain* factor as a result of the Hardtack tests.

If we gain a *substantial* factor back, *then we are far better off than we were before.* [Author's italics.]

So if these theoretical predictions about the deep hole are substantiated by actual observations, then we could get a system which is actually better than we originally thought the Geneva system would be. . . .

I think it is very likely that it will be a good technique, because the trouble of observing seismic signals is that there is noise, that there are always little disturbances of the earth which are always present and which are worst near the seashore and get better inland, and it is believed that these disturbances are little waves traveling on the surface of the earth.

At the ocean, for instance, the water waves beat against the shore and they set the earth in motion and we get these little surface waves.

Dr. Bethe had this description of the size of the hole that would be needed:

We have methods to dig holes which are well known, from oil explorations, and in one oil field you have hundreds of holes. So we might easily put an extra 100 holes in the earth's surface or 200, at all the seismic stations in the system. . . . A man would not get down into it. It is the kind of a hole in which you would stick an oil pipe. Through that hole you lower your seismograph. Then you have an electric cable to bring up the signals so that you can observe the signals on top.

This has to be studied, but I think there is no great difficulty in doing this.[23]

Experiments had already been conducted in holes a few hundred feet deep, Dr. Bethe disclosed, and "there has been an improved signal a few hundred feet down. . . . They are quieter there than on the surface, but not sufficiently quiet-. . ."

He also advanced, probably for the first time in public, his theory for scattering unmanned seismograph stations around seismic areas:

Now the second method which I like very much is to put in small stations with just one seismograph, and this on the surface, but put these in not every 600 miles but every 100 miles.

Obviously you cannot do this and put observers at each of these posts. First of all, you do not have that many seismologists; and secondly, you would run into objections from the Russians.

But these stations could very well be very simple, and be unmanned. You just put them there. You put them under lock and key with a burglar alarm so people do not tamper with them, and you have some kind of system to transmit the information from the little station to the next big station so that you get a record all the time. . . .

Then every month or so you go there and fill up the gasoline tanks so that the station continues to have power, and take away the record and take it home and look at it again.

These units would be extremely powerful. Namely, at 100 miles distance the signal is 200 times as strong as it is at 600 miles distance, maybe even 400 times as strong. So that if you had these little stations, then you could easily observe a 1-kiloton explosion at something like 10 stations in each case, and this would be an enormous improvement over the system contemplated at Geneva.

Of course, again you have to reach political agreement on this, and this, I think, is where the problem lies; namely to put it to the Russians forcibly enough that we have something to improve on the Geneva experts system.

But I think there is no question that improvements are possible, and this particular improvement does not require any further study. This is already known: It is known that one can observe signals of sufficient strength; it is known that one can make very cheap and simple seismographs which will do this. And so, the only question then is to make them tamperproof, and to transmit the information.[24]

If two of the new methods, the deep hole and the unmanned-station methods, were incorporated into the Geneva Conference of Experts system, Dr. Bethe told Senator Humphrey, the detection-identification system would be better than the one originally envisioned by the scientists at Geneva.

Without improvements, Dr. Bethe said, the new threshold for identifying explosions would move from 5 to above 20 kilotons. "At 10 kilotons you already have great difficulty," Dr. Bethe said. "You maybe identify one-half of the 10-kiloton explosions and that is not enough."

Placing seismographs in batteries of 100 at each station was a third method of improving the control system, he acknowledged.

[But] I do not like this method because it is a brute force and an inelegant method. And I prefer elegant methods. But it is a possibility, and I think this possibility very likely but not certainly could bring us back to the capability of the Geneva system as originally envisaged . . . It is certain that it would improve it. It is not certain it would bring it back. It might make it even better than the original, but it is not certain that it would fully restore the Geneva capability.

The extent of the degradation of the Geneva control system was obscured in the fog of optimism and pessimism generated by pro-ban and anti-ban factions. The simple, easy-to-understand facts were never exposed to full view. These were:

Hardtack II had shown that the underground threshold for the Geneva system was 20 kilotons, not 5. That was a ceiling high enough for Nth countries to multiply and for the three nuclear powers to make dramatic new advances in weaponry.

Hardtack II had also shown that there would be 1,500 unidentified events a year, instead of 100, for on-site inspection teams to worry about.

Senator Hickenlooper's apprehensions about the effectiveness of on-site inspection lay buried in the records of the Disarmament Subcommittee hearings. Neither he nor anyone else exhumed them to warn the unsuspecting public that the last resort of an at-best shaky inspection system was totally inadequate to the task of catching a violator.

Half the experts, or more, spoke as if reality of the present would disappear and hope for the future would magically appear. Another faction of pessimists foresaw even bigger holes in the control system, but they were not yet making themselves heard.

There was available a middle ground between optimism and pessimism —to base policy on realities of the present. But each time the Eisenhower

Administration edged in that direction it was turned back, embarrassed over past errors or intimidated by humanitarians who honestly believed it was safer to talk world disarmament even when they knew they could not get it.

Chapter 9

The Big Hole

The United States Panel on Seismic Improvement had been appointed December 28, 1958 by the President's Special Assistant for Science and Technology, Dr. James V. Killian, Jr., at the request of the State Department.

Lloyd V. Berkner, President of Associated Universities, Inc., was named chairman. The seismologists' mission was to find methods of improving the 1958 control system.

The panel included a "Who's Who" of American seismologists, many of them the same men who had responded to the Humphrey Subcommittee's questionnaire the previous summer. Besides Dr. Berkner the other 13 members of the panel were: Professor Hugo Benioff, California Institute of Technology, designer of the Benioff seismograph; Professor Hans Bethe, Cornell University; Professor W. Maurice Ewing, Columbia University; Dr. John Gerrard, Texas Instruments, Inc.; Professor David T. Griggs, University of California at Los Angeles; Jack H. Hamilton, the Geotechnical Corporation; Dr. Julius P. Molnar, Sandia Corporation; Dr. Walter H. Munk, Scripps Institute of Oceanography; Dr. Jack E. Oliver, Columbia University; Professor Frank Press, California Institute of Technology; Dr. Carl F. Romney, Department of Defense; Dr. Kenneth Street, Jr., Lawrence Radiation Laboratory, University of California; and Professor John W. Tukey, Princeton University. In addition there were three consultants: Dr. Warren Heckrott, Lawrence Radiation Laboratory, University of California; Dr. Montgomery Johnson, Aeroneutronic Systems, Inc.; and Dr. Albert Latter, The RAND Corporation.

It took only about two months for the Panel on Seismic Improvement to complete its work but the results were not made public until June 12. The panel's final report on its findings was submitted to the Government on March 16, 1959.

The results of the seismologists' study were explosive enough to touch off a huge tug of war between the pro-test-ban and anti-test-ban advocates inside the Administration. Who was responsible, however, for

tor." It alone meant that a 300-kiloton underground explosion, fully tamped, would appear as what formerly would have been taken to be a 200-kiloton explosion.

The Latter theory showed that a 200-kiloton underground shot could be made to look like a two-thirds kiloton shot. So small an explosion would be lost in the noise.

On the other hand, the "big hole" to conceal the explosion would really have to be monstrous. Spherical holes the diameter of the Washington Monument would be necessary to achieve such decoupling factors as 300. The difficulty in digging such big holes in secret quickly became one of the chief points of argument among those who wanted to go on negotiating for a test ban.

Although Dr. Bethe had learned of the big-hole theory for decoupling nuclear tests on his trip to California in January, 1959, apparently he did not mention it a few days later, on February 2, 1959, when he appeared before the Senate Disarmament Subcommittee.[4] He spoke instead of glowing hopes for recouping fully all the "losses" in effectiveness of the Geneva control system and even of improving it.[5]

He left the Subcommittee with the feeling of all-round confidence to judge from Senator Humphrey's closing remarks: "Gentlemen, we could have Dr. Bethe here all day. It is like sitting at the table with Socrates."

Dr. Bethe had appeared before the Humphrey Subcommittee on February 2. His testimony was released March 12.

At that time Senator Humphrey issued an optimistic statement disregarding, in effect, the cautious testimony he had heard from other scientists:

It is clear from Dr. Bethe's testimony that technical problems are not the main obstacles to an agreement on the stopping of nuclear-weapons tests. The main problem is political, and if the world is to see a first small step toward halting the arms race, the nuclear powers must resolve the political questions which are now impeding the Geneva negotiations for a test-ban treaty. . . . As a consultant to several agencies in the executive branch directly involved in the detection and evaluation of nuclear-weapons tests, Dr. Bethe has helped put in perspective the new data on detection of underground nuclear tests obtained from the Hardtack II series.

It is interesting to note the different judgment made by Senator Humphrey on the basis of Dr. Bethe's testimony from that made by Senators and Representatives in the Joint Committee on Atomic Energy at their hearings a few weeks before.

So far, of course, the general public knew nothing of the big-hole theory. It was obvious from some of the comments by the Senators on the Disarmament Subcommittee that they either had not heard of the theory or put no stock in it.

PANEL ON IMPROVEMENT

The pattern of delay in publishing material on the test ban was repeating itself. The results of the Hardtack II series had been known by Thanksgiving but were not published until January 5, in general terms, and January 12, in more detail.

Dr. Killian's panel of seismologists, which had been studying both the Hardtack II series and Dr. Latter's big-hole theory, submitted its report March 16. Its findings were not made public until June 12. Even then there was mention only of decoupling by a factor of "10 or more" or, possibly, "by a much greater factor."

That was the first inkling the general public got of the startling Latter theory, which hangs to this day as a huge question mark over the whole nuclear test-ban idea. Taken together with the bleak prospects for effective on-site inspection, another aspect of the problem left largely unexplained, decoupling possibilities left little hope for an effective ban.

The RAND study by Latter, made available to the panel of seismologists on a classified basis in March, was declassified October 20, 1959, to permit its use at the Geneva talks. But it was not made known to the general public until December 22, 1959, almost a year after the theory had been developed. The Russians knew about the 300–1 decoupling factor, then, two months before the American public.

Advocates of the test ban were indignant, meanwhile, because more stress was not being placed, in policy statements, on the prospects for improving seismic detection methods. The March 16 report of the Panel for Seismic Improvement dealt with both problems. Three basic questions were considered:

1. How could the Geneva control system be improved within existing technology?

2. How could the Geneva system be improved further through a program of research in seismology?

3. Could the capability of the Geneva system be reduced by concealment of underground tests?

A summary of the panel's conclusions was prepared by the Killian Committee staff in the White House, in consultation with Panel Chairman Berkner.

In its introductory paragraphs, the summary again took an attitude toward the accomplishments of the Geneva Conference of Experts that contrasted sharply with the White House-prepared statement issued by President Eisenhower the day after the conference ended. This time the emphasis was much stronger on the negative.

The experts had concluded, the March 16, 1959, report said, that "although it was not possible to identify an underground explosion by seismic means alone, it would be possible to identify a large fraction of seismic events as natural earthquakes when the direction of first motion of the seismic signal was observed at several, appropriately located stations."

The previous August there had been no mention of the impossibility of identifying underground explosions by seismic means alone. Nor had it been deemed necessary to go into the "first motion" problem. The old Geneva system, the panel confirmed, would have a capability only above 20 kilotons, not 5 kilotons as originally estimated.

The seismic-improvement panel concluded that a "partial recovery" of the originally estimated capabilities of the Geneva system could be achieved. The net of 180 stations could identify about the same proportion of underground disturbances above 10 kilotons as had been previously claimed for subterranean shots above 5-kiloton equivalents.

This partial recovery could be obtained with two improvements, it was suggested: Increasing the number of seismometers in the arrays at each station from 10 to 100, and analysis of long-period surface waves. The peak frequency of explosions was found to be twice that for earthquakes, thus permitting a distinction between explosions and earthquakes.

The second improvement could "probably identify about 50 per cent of earthquakes equivalent to 5 kilotons or more," the panel concluded.

The panel produced this table comparing capabilities of three test-ban control systems:

ESTIMATED NUMBER OF UNIDENTIFIED WORLD-WIDE CONTINENTAL EARTHQUAKES

	5 kt and greater	10 kt and greater	20 kt and greater
Geneva Conference of Experts, August, 1958	20–100	—	—
Geneva Network and Equipment on basis of Hardtack data, January, 1959	1500	400	60
Geneva Network with Improvements within the present state of technology on basis of Hardtack data, April, 1959	300	40	15

These estimates were presented with warnings about "the limited nature of the data on which all estimates of seismic detection capabilities depend." There had been only a few underground nuclear shots, and all of these in the same type of rock in a single location.

The type of rock, the location, and the design of the chamber in which the shot is fired could all have "major effects" on the strength of seismic waves produced by nuclear tests, it was warned.

In constructing the table it was assumed, the panel said, that the de-

gree of coupling nuclear energy to seismic waves in the Rainier shot had
been used as a standard on which to estimate the number of unidentified
earthquakes.

Vigorous research could bring "important improvements" in detection
and identification of small earthquakes, the panel said. Boldly, the
seismologists predicted that their recommended research program "would
in 3 years probably result in further improvements which could achieve
the same capability in the Geneva net of 180 stations as was originally
estimated by the Geneva Conference of Experts." [6]

The panel singled out for special attention as an improvement "of
particular promise" the same "deep-hole" technique Dr. Bethe had been
so enthusiastic about in his appearance before the Senate Disarmament
Subcommittee. Since seismic noise is transmitted along the earth's surface, it was reasoned, placing seismographs in 6,000-foot holes would
largely eliminate noise as an interference factor.

"Seismometers located in holes thousands of feet below the earth's
surface may be able to detect 'first motion' with much greater sensitivity
than instruments on the surface," the Panel said. Placing seismometers
on ocean bottoms, where "extremely low-noise levels" could be found,
also was recommended, despite engineering difficulties.

Dr. Carl Romney, Defense Department seismologist, estimated later
that drilling a 10,000-foot "well" for experimentation with the "deep-
hole" method for improving detection and identification of seismic
events would cost $100,000 to $150,000. The cost of a 10,000-foot well
in granite would be about $500,000 to $1 million. [7]

Dr. Bethe's February 2 suggestion for an auxiliary network of unmanned seismic stations was also an important method suggested by the
Panel. If such unmanned stations were spaced at 170-kilometer intervals
in seismic areas of the world, "about 98 per cent of the events as small
as 1-kiloton equivalent, located within the network, would be identified
by this system," the Panel claimed. "This capability would be reduced
to about 75 per cent for events located at the peripheries of continents.
The capability of such a net would depend primarily upon the degree of
reliability of equipment that could be achieved."

In this mild last sentence the White House summary of the Panel
report was reflecting the violent opposition of some experts in the field,
primarily in the military, to the unmanned stations idea because they
could see no way to make the stations "tamperproof."

Considerable effort was made to find a tamperproof system. But the
experts always came up against the problem of guaranteeing secure communications with the control posts and headquarters.

No estimate of the number of stations required world-wide was made,
nor was there any hint that the Soviet Union might consider such tight
spacing excessive.

Since all of the nuclear tests conducted so far had been exploded at the

Nevada test site, in a single medium, the seismologists recognized that "it is entirely possible that some natural conditions will yield seismic signals much smaller for a given size shot than those from shots in the volcanic rock of the Nevada test site. The Panel recommended that, in order to resolve the uncertainty on this question, an experimental test program involving many high explosives and some nuclear shots be undertaken as soon as feasible."

No estimate of the decoupling factor attainable merely by moving the site of explosions from the Nevada tuff to some other, perhaps harder rock, was reported.

The same technique of reporting in generalities was used in the Panel's public discussion of decoupling. The idea of using a big hole was not even mentioned.

> In considering the possibility that the capabilities, now or in the future, of the Geneva system might be reduced by the intentional concealment of underground tests, the Panel concluded that decoupling techniques existed which could reduce the seismic signal by a factor of 10 or more. Moreover, preliminary theoretical studies have shown that it is possible in principle to reduce the seismic signal from an explosion by a much greater factor than this. Nevertheless, in view of the many complexities involved, it is necessary that these ideas be tested with appropriately designed experiments to determine how large a decoupling factor can actually be realized in practice. While many of these tests can be carried out with high explosives, complete evaluation of the theory probably cannot be made without nuclear explosions. Such tests may also disclose some characteristics which might allow long-range detection of such decoupled underground tests.

This was the first inkling the general public got of the big-hole theory. It came not on March 16, when the panel report was presented formally to the President and other Administration officials, but on June 12.

Several reporters, including this one, were misled by the mention of a factor of "10 or more," followed by the vague references to possibilities that a much greater factor might be achieved.

It will be recalled that Dr. Latter had obtained agreement of both Dr. Teller and Dr. Bethe as early as March that the 300 factor was theoretically possible. To report in the first public document on the big-hole theory that the decoupling factor was "10 or more" looked in retrospect like a deliberate attempt to mislead. Even in Dr. Latter's January preliminary calculations there was no thought of so small a decoupling factor—it had been 100 to 200.

Officials who had helped write the summary explained that there was still controversy among scientists about the theory and it was decided to use this terminology until the theory was more firmly established. Who these scientists were who disputed the Latter figures and what their standing was remains something of a mystery. Moreover what happened to convince them in the interval between June and December has never been explained.

Dr. Bethe was the authority who, at the 1958 Experts' Conference, had presented the theory that decoupling would not work. He had subsequently accepted the theory and was to present it in his own way at a later conference with Russian experts. It appeared unlikely, therefore, that it was Dr. Bethe who had raised questions about the validity of the theory. There was no indication what other scientist in the fourteen-man panel would have challenged the theory. Dr. Albert Latter himself was one of the panel participants.

By March 30, Dr. Latter and his three associates, R. E. LeLevier, E. A. Martinelli, and W. G. McMillan, had produced a printed, classified report entitled "A Method of Concealing Underground Nuclear Explosions." [8] It mentioned the 300–1 decoupling factor. This report was declassified (for the Russians and British) October 20, 1959, but not brought to the notice of the American public until December 22, 1959. Until December 22, the American public was allowed to think that decoupling might be only one-thirtieth of the problem it really was. ·

For five months—until June—the Latter theory was completely suppressed. And it was not until nine months had passed that the Eisenhower Administration disclosed the existence of a cheating possibility of such staggering proportions that it made the test-ban idea virtually moribund. Here was a case of vital information being withheld in a crucial negotiation which freedom-of-information committees have never investigated.

Test-resumption advocates fumed privately over the toned-down public report on the possibilities of decoupling. Foes of the big-hole theory, meanwhile, ridiculed the idea of building underground caverns the diameter of the Washington Monument. Those who took the big hole seriously warned, however, that "what is impractical today is routine tomorrow." Limestone and salt deposits underground could be dissolved and pumped out, they suggested.

The Administration decision to make only vague references to the big-hole theory, either in public announcements or to the Soviet Union, might well have been based on apprehension that the United States might find itself teaching the Soviet Union how to cheat. This explains, unsatisfactorily for many, why the information was held up until October, 1959, according to one knowledgeable official. It does not explain the last two months' delay in notifying the American public. Nor does it take into account the risk that the Russians had already discovered the big-hole decoupling theory for themselves, or would eventually, and defeat the control system after it had been established.

The RAND scientists actually suggested that decoupling factors greater than 300 could be obtained by introducing into the big hole thin foils to absorb the blast energy in the form of heat; another possibility would be to introduce lampblack. "Some of the energy they absorb goes into non-pressure forms such as latent heats of melting and vaporization."

Theoretically it would be possible, using these refinements, to achieve decoupling factors of 1,000, the RAND report said.

The Panel on Seismic Improvement also proposed that the United States construct a complete prototype experimental station including all of the seismic features of the control system recommended by the Geneva Conference of Experts. Studying the operations of such a station would provide experimental evidence on the capability of a station to detect and identify earthquakes, the Panel said, and would help in working out installation and operational problems to be encountered when the control network was to be established. Eventually, such a station could be expanded to embrace new facilities proposed by the Panel.

Two weeks after they had submitted their summary report on the possibilities for improving seismic detection and also on the suddenly-improved prospects for decoupling, the Panel on Seismic Improvement produced a report entitled "The Need for Fundamental Research in Seismology."

Contributing scientists outlined programs that would cost $23 million the first year and $30 million the second. These costs, they said, did not include "implementation." The money would go for research projects and system development, which would constitute about half the total cost, and for the nuclear and high-explosive detonations, which would account for the other half.

The Soviet Union in recent years had emphasized seismological research to the point where "the Soviets enjoy a position superior in many respects to our own," the Panel warned. The Soviet Union was spending an estimated $1 million on exploring the earth's crust by means of small explosions, the Panel reported, compared to about $100,000 for similar crustal studies in the United States. The greater effort showed in "the resulting higher level of Soviet work" in recent Soviet publications when compared with American journals, the Panel said.

The scientists suggested that studies be expanded on source-phenomena, on effects of transmission of signals through the earth, on instrumentation for recording seismic signals, and on certain suggestions for more sophisticated processing of the recorded data.

Once the quality of instrumentation in seismic areas was improved and intensive studies of earthquakes were undertaken, it would be possible to re-evaluate techniques of assigning magnitudes to seismic disturbances, the report said.

"It is distressing that, as a result of present instrumental limitations, seismologists are unable to fix such a fundamental physical quantity as the seismic energy released in an earthquake within a factor of ten or more." [9]

The closely-related difficulty in translating earthquake power into nuclear-test power had caused the high priests of seismology, Gutenberg and Richter, to issue warnings before the 1958 Conference of Experts met. This problem caused difficulty at that meeting, when the results of Hardtack II became known, and at the second experts' conference late in 1959.

The seismologists poured out their hearts in the Panel report, disclosing publicly for the first time some of the misgivings they felt, even after the Hardtack II series, about designing a control system for a nuclear test ban on a "scientific" basis:

Our knowledge of seismic wave generation by large explosions, particularly nuclear explosions, is very limited. Only three completely contained underground explosions with yields greater than one-kiloton have been fired, all under very similar environmental conditions. The parameters that can significantly affect the magnitude and type of seismic effects produced by nuclear explosions should be experimentally explored so that theories can be developed which will permit reasonable confidence in our understanding of these parameters and deductions about them. The following parameters require study: (a) dependence of spectrum of body and surface waves on yield of explosion; (b) dependence of seismic wave excitation on the medium surrounding the shot; (c) effect of depth of burial; (d) effect of local environment such as shot-cavities size and shape, etc.; (e) effect of local geology and topography.

This was a lament that few, if any, seismologists had sung publicly before the Conference of Experts in 1958, when their knowledge was even more meager. Many had had an opportunity to speak before Senator Humphrey's Subcommittee on Disarmament. There was as a result some quietly unfavorable reaction among scientists without government contracts that the seismologists had not spoken out more effectively before.

All Administration officials and most scientists acknowledged, on the other hand, that seismologists were under tremendous pressure to do "their best" with inadequate knowledge, in the hope of saving the world from a nuclear war. They were asked to gamble with their own science, against great odds. It was, of course, a widely voiced criticism of both sides in the nuclear test-ban controversy that the scientists paid all too little attention to their science and all too much attention to their political preferences.

The Berkner Panel suggested four additional nuclear shots "as soon as feasible," to advance the art of nuclear detection:

1. A 5-kiloton shot in granite for information on the effect of shooting in another medium.

2. "A shot in an environmental situation designed to decouple explosion energy from seismic energy."

3. "Two 5-kiloton shots near the Rainier site but at appreciably greater depths."

Decoupling, the Panel said, "should also be experimentally tested as soon as feasible." The intention apparently was that these tests should be with TNT as well as nuclear shots.

The seismologists recommended that 100 to 200 of the 500 existing seismic stations in the world be equipped with modern instrumentation "as soon as possible," without obligating the "grantee" beyond a commitment that the station would be maintained and operated at his expense. The Panel observed that traditions in seismology provide for "access to records by qualified investigators."

The first step would be to equip existing American stations with the best instruments now available and to establish new stations in the United States.

The Panel also went into the problem of developing tamperproof unmanned stations capable of operating for thirty to sixty days without servicing. It also suggested development of a second, special-purpose instrument called a "throw-away" or portable seismic detector. It would be designed for rapid deployment in suspicious areas and "could be used both for research purposes and by inspection groups for investigating unidentified events."

The Panel's appeal for setting up a complete experimental station patterned on the Geneva Conference of Experts model suggested that "for maximum effectiveness" the station should be installed in a seismic region "where the data collected would assist in more general research problems." The main seismic region in the United States is in southern California, but the station eventually was set up in Oklahoma.

High-speed computers were said to be essential for a Geneva-type monitoring system. The tremendous amount of data passing through stations for analysis would require some mechanical assistance. "A single station, as supplemented by certain possible equipment for improving the capability beyond that of the Geneva-type stations, might have an input-data rate of as much as 2,000 samples per second," the Panel estimated.

Here was a new feature of the Geneva system that had not been fully explored in the 1958 Conference:

This data must be analyzed, filtered, and combined in different ways to take full advantage of the array, and possibly of outlying remote seismometers before it will be possible to make a decision as to whether any seismic event is a natural earthquake or whether it justifies further investigation. Since there are many thousands of events recorded per year at some seismic stations, to perform this analysis adequately by manual methods will require a large skilled staff. The use of computers should be investigated as a means of performing at an adequate rate the tasks and filtering and decision-making that are required of the Geneva system.

The research program outlined by the Panel of Seismologists was admittedly a big job, taxing the facilities of universities, government, and industry. To collate and evaluate the program, it was suggested that the National Academy of Sciences establish a special advisory panel. The whole project should be considered "a package," centrally funded and directed.

To ensure proper coordination it was suggested that plans be set up immediately for "system development." This new group would plan details of the complete world-wide seismic-detection system. At first the system "will probably resemble closely that envisaged in the Geneva proposal (and it will not likely be possible to develop anything more sophisticated in the time available)," the Panel observed optimistically. But there should be planning beyond this early stage.

While the individual methods of seismic improvement should be entrusted to individual scientists and private or government laboratories, the system development should be assigned to a "single, well-organized central laboratory," the Panel suggested. They had in mind a Manhattan Project approach.

It was to be a point of major disappointment to the seismologists that the Administration was slow in implementing its recommendations. Senator Humphrey applied periodic prods, but without noticeable effect. The Defense Department's Advanced Research Projects Agency was entrusted with the responsibility for setting up the entire system.

However, it took more than two years before the experimental seismic station modeled on the Geneva experts pattern had been put into operation. The equipping of other stations in the United States and abroad had barely got underway.

The findings of the Panel on Seismic Improvement, submitted to the Conference in Geneva on June 12, 1959, can be summarized as follows:

1. Retaining a network of 180 control posts, the originally estimated capability of the Geneva control system could be partially restored by equipping each post with 100 instead of 10 long-period seismographs.

2. A vigorous research and development program in seismology could within three years regain the original capability that had been ascribed to the Geneva control system.

3. Significant improvements in the efficiency of the detection system could be achieved by an auxiliary network of unmanned seismic stations.

4. All these uphill battles might be lost, however, against the downhill charge of the science of concealment.

Chapter 10

Treaty Conference

The opening days of the "Conference on the Discontinuance of Nuclear Weapons Tests" at Geneva, from October 31 to November 3, 1958, marked another important watershed in the history of the nuclear test ban. In these days the three nuclear powers embarked on unilateral test suspensions without inspection or control, which were to last until September, 1961, if one could believe unverified pronouncements.

President Eisenhower had announced August 22, 1958, that the United States would withhold testing for one year beginning October 31, provided that the Soviet Union did not test after that time. The Soviet Union did shoot off two more blasts on November 1 and 3, however. As far as was known these were the last Soviet nuclear tests for more than two and a half years.[1]

Because the Soviet Union had conducted tests after the American deadline and since there was no way of knowing whether she would resume later, President Eisenhower announced on November 7 that the United States was relieved of any obligation to continue its one-year ban. Nevertheless, Mr. Eisenhower said, the voluntary suspension would be continued for the time being.

The United Kingdom had undertaken a similar test suspension at the beginning of the nuclear test-ban negotiations, October 31. Because of the Soviet tests the United Kingdom also considered itself relieved of its pledge. Later, however, London took the position it would not resume nuclear-weapons testing as long as the Geneva discussions were useful.

President Eisenhower, to encourage the Geneva negotiations, was to announce just before the expiration of the first one-year period in the American test suspension that the United States would continue its unilateral ban through the calendar year of 1959.[2]

A few days later, the Soviet Union announced it would not resume tests unless the Western powers did. In a statement by the Soviet Government it was announced:

The Council of Ministers of the U.S.S.R. has resolved not to resume nuclear tests in the Soviet Union if the Western powers did not resume the testing of atomic and hydrogen weapons. Only in case of resumption by them of nuclear-weapons tests will the Soviet Union be free from this pledge. The Soviet Union will continue the struggle for the complete cessation of nuclear weapons, regarding this as an important step toward stopping the nuclear-arms race and averting the threat to the life and health of millions of people.[3]

Whether the Soviet Union was keeping its pledge became a matter of concern a few years later, when the Geneva negotiations dragged on and on without agreement.

The Soviet Union had set off at least fourteen nuclear-test explosions between September 30 and October 28, 1958, and was showing no sign of stopping as the scheduled opening of test-ban talks drew near.[4]

On the day before the opening of the conference, the Soviet Union issued a defiant statement declaring that American and British resumption of tests had forced the Soviet Union to "resume nuclear testing to insure its security." The Kremlin claimed its "right" to continue nuclear tests until it had made as many as the United States and the United Kingdom, since the March 31, 1958, opening of the Soviet unilateral ban. Moscow was still ready to end all testing "for all time" if the United States and Britain would join the agreement.

The Soviet Union was presenting an image of hair-trigger readiness to move in either direction, to a full resumption of the arms race or toward a nuclear test-ban treaty. There may also have been misgivings inside the Soviet hierarchy about the suspension of nuclear tests. American officials speculated that this may have been responsible for the bellicose public attitude of Soviet Premier Khrushchev at this crucial time.

After the Geneva Conference had been launched, the United Nations General Assembly passed a resolution urging the parties in the test-ban negotiations "not to undertake further testing of nuclear weapons while these negotiations are in progress." [5]

Little noticed at the time, this was to be an important consideration for the Eisenhower Administration as the question of resuming tests came to the fore in the later years of the Republican tenure. Had the United States resumed testing, it would have been in the position of defying a United Nations resolution. The Republican Administration was proud of its record of never having been on the side of the minority in a United Nations vote. When the question of resuming tests came up, this General Assembly resolution was always cited as a major stumbling block.

Despite the inhibiting effect on the United States, the Soviet Union considered the General Assembly action a defeat. Soviet representatives had sought a General Assembly resolution that would have called for an immediate cessation for all time of nuclear tests. "As a result of improper maneuvering," however, the Soviet news agency Tass reported later, this became impossible. "When it came to the vote, latent pressure and blackmail by the United States compelled a number of states dependent on that country to vote for the United States and the United Kingdom proposal," Tass said, "which was designed to hamstring any agreement on the cessation of atomic weapons tests and to secure the continuance of these tests." [6]

This outward eagerness for a nuclear test ban was not matched, characteristically, by the Soviet negotiators in the private sessions of the treaty conference at Geneva. With the United States and the United Kingdom "on the hook," the Soviet Union spent the first two months of the conference insisting that agreement on a permanent end to testing should be reached before controls were ever discussed.[7]

The Soviet representative, Ambassador Semyon Tsarapkin, therefore tabled at the first meeting a short draft treaty providing only that the three negotiating states cease forever all tests of nuclear weapons and accept a system of verification based on the report of the Conference of Experts. The Soviet draft contained no provisions for establishing control machinery under international supervision.

Before the treaty negotiations opened in Geneva, there were already strong indications in the hands of American officialdom that the 1958 Experts inspection system had been highly overrated. Senator Gore of Tennessee later reported that he had been briefed on the Hardtack II results by responsible officials in Washington before the negotiations began. He knew about the ineffectiveness of the control system recommended by the 1958 Experts and was bemused by the unreality of it all when he attended the opening-day session in Geneva. The Hardtack data were then still in a preliminary state, of course. There was no public evidence, however, that the government even considered postponing the negotiations until the data could be refined.

Senator Gore later commented charitably that he had come to realize that "although I was briefed on it, the careful calculation and analysis of the data were not possible before the conference had begun and, therefore, I do not believe that our government had abandoned its goal or has changed its position." [8]

The negotiators fell into an immediate wrangle over the agenda. The United States and the United Kingdom maintained that control measures should be the first item to be discussed while the drafting of an agreement should be second. Ambassador Tsarapkin's position was that the important thing for the Geneva Conference to agree on was an end to tests. "Details" like international control could be agreed upon at a later meeting and included as a protocol to be attached to the treaty on discontinuing tests. There was no assurance, of course, that the Soviet Union would ever get around to attaching any protocols once the agreement on a test ban had been completed.

So the United States and the United Kingdom insisted that detailed provisions for establishment and operation of the international control organization must be contained in the treaty proper.

It took all November to budge the Soviet Union on this point. The Soviet delegate finally relented on November 29, and early in December the three-power conference began writing the first articles of a test-ban treaty. When the conference took its first recess on December 19, 1958, however, the American delegation went home with a definite impression that the Soviet Union was "extremely reluctant to get down to cases on a control system which could effectively police" a ban.[9]

One of the Soviet causes for concern was the growing realization that the Hardtack II series had raised new doubts among the Americans about the efficiency of the control system set up in Geneva in July and August. Presumably, the Soviet negotiators were made aware of the new findings in general terms before the December 19 recess. By that time, there had been more than two weeks of discussion at the political level in the United States on the consequences of the findings. Scientists had reported initially to the White House and the State Department around Thanksgiving. There were many factors working against public disclosure of the problems, however:

First, it would be difficult for the scientists to admit their mistake.

Second, it would be difficult politically for the Republican Administration to admit its part in the fundamental error.

Third, world sentiment would certainly turn bitterly against the United States if Washington were to announce new findings showing inspection to be nearly impossible. It would look like Washington was inviting a break-off in the nuclear test-ban talks, negotiations which the uncommitted world suspected the United States never wanted in the first place.

On the other hand, opposition to the test ban inside the Administration was strong enough to prevent complete suppression of the new findings.

After consultation with his science adviser, James F. Killian, Jr., President Eisenhower decided to hold up official disclosure of the Hardtack II results, however, in a move for time to draw up some statement of hope on the possibility of recouping the losses.

A panel of seismologists, organized under Dr. Killian's direction, worked intensively on a program to improve seismic-detection methods.

The Soviet Union, as anticipated, treated the American release of the new data as evidence the United States was not sincere in its negotiations for a treaty. To help offset this position, and also to focus world attention on the Soviet Union's own reluctance to accept controls, the Western delegations to the talks announced a modification of their position on January 19.[10] President Eisenhower had made continued suspension of tests dependent on year-to-year findings: first, that effective control had been installed and operating; and second, that progress was being made on other disarmament issues. On January 19, the United States and the United Kingdom dropped the second condition. Continuation of the test-suspension no longer would be contingent on progress in other disarmament areas, only on effective control.

This January 19 move was really the formal, black-on-white break in "the link" on which the Eisenhower Administration had insisted so stubbornly in the past. But, in a 1960 report on this point the State Department made no mention of the broken link. Instead it mentioned the strategy of putting all stress on control measures for a nuclear test ban. "In this manner *control* became the key to agreement and the core to the negotiations," the State Department said. (State Department italics.) [11]

As previously noted, State Department officials considered the President's August 22 statement to have marked the *de facto* break in the link. The January 19 move was the *de jure* break.

On January 22, Radio Moscow broadcast a statement by the Soviet Government claiming Washington and London "are obviously looking for an excuse to torpedo the current Geneva talks. . . . The means available at the present time for the detection of nuclear explosions, together with on-site inspection of unidentified phenomena, suspected of being nuclear blasts, make it possible to detect and identify nuclear explosions *wherever they might be staged,* including those set off underground." (Author's italics.) [12]

The Soviet Union obviously intended to hold the United States and the United Kingdom to their 1958 agreement on the feasibility of control, and then some, despite the new data.

Two days later, the Department of State issued a denial that it was seeking to torpedo the talks. At the same time it mentioned three major issues on which the Soviet Union was dragging its own feet: the veto, staffing of control posts, and freedom of movement for on-site inspections. [13]

The statement put the three major issues of the test-ban conference this way:

1. Will the Soviet Union be able to veto and obstruct every action of the Control Commission, as it now demands, or will it be possible for the Control Commission to act without this obstacle? The United States believes that any control system which could be frustrated in its day-to-day operations by the veto power in the hands of a single party would be worse than useless.

2. Will the control posts be manned by an international staff, or, as the Soviet Union demands, by nationals of the government on whose territory the control posts are located, with only one or two outside "observers"? The Soviet position would amount to self-inspection and as such cannot be the basis for an agreement in which all parties can have confidence.

3. Will international inspection groups be organized and ready to move quickly to the site of an event which could be suspected of being an explosion? Or will sending of such a group be subject to weeks of debate and a veto? The Soviet approach would entangle this key provision in miles of red tape.

These same issues were unresolved in 1962.

The new Hardtack II data had given the State Department a political weapon that the Department used publicly for the first time in its January 24 statement. The Soviet Union could stick by the old Conference of Experts control system, but this would merely mean a burdensome number of on-site inspections, which would be the principal remaining tool to identify possible underground nuclear explosions. Change the system, in other words, or accept enough inspection sorties per year to identify 700 to 3,000 suspected underground events.

The State Department maintained an optimistic outlook throughout the period during which the Soviet Union refused to countenance the new Hardtack II data. Four days after the State Department had called on the Soviet Union to pay attention to the real problems, the veto, self-inspection, and preventing delays in on-site inspection, Philip J. Farley, Special Assistant to the Secretary of State for Disarmament and Atomic Energy, told the Senate Subcommittee on Disarmament:

> This new information on the problem of detecting and identifying underground nuclear explosions has not had a significant impact on the negotiations as yet. It bears, of course, only on a limited part of the control system described last summer by the Geneva Experts, and prospects are encouraging that ways will be found to maintain the full effectiveness of that system.

Whatever suspicions the Soviet Union may have had could be regarded as "understandable," Mr. Farley said.

> We need only ask ourselves how we would have reacted had the Soviet Union come up with such new information and proposed reopening the Geneva report. The Soviet Union does not readily grasp the conviction of our Government that it has a responsibility to inform the public of the United States of such important developments, nor does it appreciate the sense of fair play that led us to bring these data promptly to the attention of the Soviets. When our continuing studies of possible ways of overcoming these technical difficulties have reached the state when they can be communicated in their turn to the Soviet Union, this may help persuade them of the probity of our intentions.
>
> In the meanwhile, the Soviet Union finds this U.S. action a convenient propaganda weapon to replace the one we have just deprived them of by our recent decision not to insist on a treaty link between disarmament progress and nuclear testing.
>
> Hard facts should in the end persuade the Soviet Union that the problem here is one of direct concern to them also.[14]

Mr. Farley, evaluating the first three months of the Geneva treaty negotiations, took the view that the matters of basic importance were then just being reached. "The shifts in the Soviet position have, while numerous, not been significant," he reported.

On this point he differed with Dr. Hans Bethe, who testified before the same committee a few days later. Dr. Bethe believed Kremlin officials "have gone a long way already" toward installing an effective inspection system.

[They agreed, first of all,] that there be one treaty embodying both the control system and the test cessation. This was a very difficult part of the negotiations, as you may know.

They have agreed that there be a considerable number of foreign scientists at each observation post. Originally they wanted one controller.

They have agreed in principle to inspection, but there our opinions are still miles apart, because they want to be able to veto an inspection, and this we cannot tolerate.

They have agreed now to peaceful explosions as part of the general agreement. They have agreed to a whole list of things, and I am quite hopeful, but it is much too early to say whether we can really come to an agreement that we can honestly subscribe to, and this we must have.[15]

Mr. Farley had found only "one real change" in the Soviet position. This was acceptance of nuclear explosions for peaceful purposes under appropriate restrictions. "This does represent a shift from the initial hostile Soviet propaganda line," Mr. Farley reported.[16]

The other Soviet concessions [on the other hand] have no real substance. They could hardly have believed seriously, for example, that their original proposal for a simple treaty leaving the details of the control system for subsequent negotiations would be accepted by the United States and the United Kingdom. Similarly their charges, both in the meeting and in their public statements, that we do not want a lasting treaty should probably be taken not as reflections of real concern but as efforts to apply propaganda pressure. From our point of view what has gone on so far has been to clear out of the way various false issues raised by the Soviet Union. We are now down to the issues of real substance.

He referred to the three points mentioned in the State Department release of January 24.

Preventing a veto, avoiding self-inspection, and providing for swift on-site inspections of unidentified events "are crucial not only to the present negotiation but to any subsequent disarmament negotiations," Mr. Farley said.[17] Three years later American officials were still citing the same three fundamentals and the Soviet Union was still holding out.

By January, 1959, the Soviet Union apparently sensed that it could prolong the then three-month-old test-suspension without inspection if she handled the Geneva political negotiations skillfully. There was no incentive for her to conclude a treaty; on the contrary, her fear of inspection gave her an incentive not to conclude a treaty, but keep the talks going without letting them get anywhere.

Soviet Premier Khrushchev could not be accused of hiding his rejection of inspection. Three days after Mr. Farley testified, Khrushchev told a Communist Party Congress:

> Judge for yourselves. Here's what they want: They want all the control posts created for the detection of explosions to be manned only by foreign personnel and for the foreign inspectors to travel unhindered all over the territory of signatory states. They also want to create a situation in which the control commission to which these posts and inspectors are subordinated could by a mechanical majority and the votes of Western representatives impose decisions that affect the interests of the security of the Soviet Union. . . .
>
> Now that they have encircled us with their military bases, the Western powers want to establish bases on our territory for military reconnaissance, to obtain the right to fly over Soviet territory in order to be able, with the aid of that reconnaissance, to select the moment to put their military bases into action against our country. And they want us to help them in realization of these plans. Is not that a bit too much, gentlemen? [18]

Mr. Farley did not mention in his Senate testimony how long the negotiations could be allowed to continue before the United States would conclude that the Soviet Union was shying away from inspection.

Rather than become too deeply involved in a review of the tedious Geneva negotiations, this book will deal with the major developments in the treaty conference chronologically as they affected fundamental issues.

Macmillan's Quota

Although the diplomats and technicians were writing the actual test-ban treaty in Geneva, the major moves were handled in Washington, Moscow, and London by President Eisenhower, Premier Khrushchev, and Prime Minister Macmillan.

In Washington, late in January, 1959, AEC Chairman McCone formally submitted to Secretary of State Dulles a new plan for a "phased" agreement. In the first phase, he suggested the nuclear powers should stop detectable atmospheric tests. Tests underground and beyond the atmosphere should be continued while more effective detection systems were developed. The formal proposal was presented after long deliberations of the five members of the AEC.

Two and a half months later, President Eisenhower was to present what was essentially this same idea to the Russians.

Before this plan had waded through the Washington bureaucracy, however, British Prime Minister Macmillan made the first major diplomatic move of 1959. In February, he went to Moscow to sell Premier Khrushchev on a totally different compromise to save the Geneva talks from what looked like the gathering doom. The Hardtack II series' degradation of the inspection was bad enough, but the big-hole theory looked from the eastern shores of the Atlantic like an ill-concealed plot to scuttle the whole test-ban idea.

The British Government had gone to the great expense of buying a ticket to the private arena in which the Soviet Union and the United States were conducting their tug of war over the nuclear test ban. By her costly development of the atomic bomb and thermonuclear weapons, Britain had gained admittance to the exclusive "nuclear club." But at the same time she developed a much deeper respect for the awesome weapons' power than either of the other two members. Both the Soviet Union and the United States covered large land masses but Great Britain was referred to by Premier Khrushchev as a "floating aircraft carrier." The British people generally, not only the Labour Party and the pacifists, were sensitive to their vulnerability to huge thermonuclear weapons.

In time, the British came to realize they had a bigger stake than either of the other two members of the nuclear club in making some start toward nuclear disarmament. The test ban had been made to look like the only first step in sight.

Dr. Carl Romney had told the Senate Disarmament Subcommittee, however, that the number of earthquakes in the world per year which could not be definitely identified and thus would be eligible for on-site inspection should be 700 to 3,000 per year. In the Soviet Union and China, there would be an estimated 116 to 500 of these. It was a fantastic thought, dismissed at the very instant it arose, that the Soviet Union and Red China would accept even 100 on-site inspections, let alone 500.

The danger, therefore, as seen from London, was that the nuclear test-ban talks would break down on the United States insistence that control measures be based on science and kept free from Soviet veto.

It was presumably with thoughts like these running through his mind that Prime Minister Macmillan flew to Moscow on February 21 for personal talks with Soviet Premier Khrushchev. The Soviet Premier administered an arrogant snub, keeping the Prime Minister waiting in Moscow while he went out of town "on business," but Mr. Khrushchev did accept for study Prime Minister Macmillan's "compromise" plan for test-ban inspection to bridge the wide gulf between the Soviet Union and the United States.

The three negotiating powers should agree in advance on a limited annual quota of on-site inspections to be permitted each side, Mr. Macmillan proposed. Within this number, the inspecting side could choose for investigation whatever suspected events it wished. If Prime Minister Macmillan mentioned the quota he had in mind, it was not made public.

In return for this concession on on-site inspections, Premier Khrushchev should give up his veto demands, the Prime Minister proposed.

Two days after Mr. Macmillan's February 21–March 3 visit to Moscow, Senator Humphrey offered a similar proposal to President Eisenhower. There was no provision in the Senator's plan, however, for an exchange of concessions. Prime Minister Macmillan had sought to use the quota idea to get the Soviet Union to move on the veto question.

> When one tries to visualize just how the inspection and control system would work in practice [Senator Humphrey wrote President Eisenhower on March 5], the conclusion seems obvious that only a limited number of on-site inspections could take place. An event which the control posts are unable to identify could lead to an inspection and this fundamental right would in itself act as a deterrent to a potential violator. If all tests were banned, obviously not every unidentified event could be inspected. All such events occurring in areas in which earthquakes do not usually occur would probably be inspected . . . but inspections of unidentified events in earthquake areas would need to be on a spotcheck basis. If a limit were placed on the number of inspections per year, for example, it would be necessary that the control organ never exhaust all of its inspections before the end of the period.
>
> Would not a limit on the number of inspections on the territory of each of the nuclear powers and in the areas in which tests might take place preserve the interests of the United States and at the same time clearly indicate to the Soviet Union that we would not, as Mr. Khrushchev maintains, be inspecting all "mines, quarries, woods, ravines, and all the rest?"[19]

President Eisenhower sent back a noncommittal reply. He merely said the suggestions would be studied. Whether the British government and Senator Humphrey got their ideas independently or exchanged views beforehand, neither side said.

In the 1958 Experts Conference the United States had mentioned that spot-checking 20 per cent of the unidentified events would provide a sufficient deterrent for a would-be violator. When news of the new Macmillan proposal first leaked out in March, American officials pointed to this formula. Using the seismologists' estimate that there would be 100 unidentified underground events above the 20-kiloton detection threshold, they arrived at a tentative quota of 20 on-site inspections per year inside the Soviet Union.

But the State Department, Prime Minister Macmillan, and Senator Humphrey were either forgetting or deliberately ignoring the best scientific advice that on-site inspection had only 1 per cent chance of succeeding.

PHASED AGREEMENT

Prime Minister Macmillan traveled to Washington March 19–24, to report to President Eisenhower on his Moscow talks. The new proposal for limiting on-site inspection under a quota system was laid before the President. Mr. Eisenhower indicated in a subsequent press conference that he was cool to the idea.

He also managed to convey that impression to Soviet Premier Khru-shchev in an important letter on April 13.[20] The President proposed the "phased" approach to a test-ban suggested in January by the AEC com-missioners. Prime Minister Macmillan sent a letter to the Soviet Premier the same day, supporting the Eisenhower view.[21]

As an alternative to a complete ban, Mr. Eisenhower proposed that the Soviet Union accept a "phased" agreement in which a prohibition of nuclear-weapons tests in the atmosphere up to 50 kilometers could be proclaimed immediately. Meanwhile, negotiations could continue to resolve the political and technical problems of control of underground, underwater, and outer-space tests.

This would have left the way open for a resumption of testing under-ground, underwater, or in outer space. The proposal was met with satis-faction, of course, by Defense Department and Atomic Energy Com-mission officials who felt that important things could be gained by a resumption of testing.

The President mentioned in his letter to Khrushchev that he had talked with Prime Minister Macmillan, "who reported to me of his frank discussions on this matter with you." He pointedly made no men-tion of the Macmillan quota plan. Mr. Eisenhower repeated that the United States strongly favors a lasting agreement banning nuclear-weapons tests as an important step toward reducing international ten-sions and toward further agreement on disarmament.

But the test ban must be "subject to fully effective safeguards to in-sure the security interests of all parties, and we believe that present pro-posals of the Soviet Union fall short of providing assurance of the type of effective control in which all parties can have confidence. . . ."

In his view, the President declared, however, "these negotiations must not be permitted *completely* to fail." (Author's italics.)

"Could we not, Mr. Chairman, put the agreement into effect in phases beginning with the prohibition of nuclear-weapons tests in the atmos-phere? A simplified control system for atmospheric tests up to 50 kilo-meters could be readily derived from the Geneva experts' report and would not require the automatic on-site inspection which has created the major stumbling block in the negotiations so far."

The idea in limiting the agreement to tests up to 50 kilometers was to re-emphasize to the Soviet Union the United States interest in further exploration, on a technical basis, of the possibility of policing a ban on high-altitude tests. The 1958 Conference of Experts had only touched on the problem and a further study was considered necessary. American negotiators had pressed this point with the Soviet Union in the Geneva treaty negotiations without success.

President Eisenhower required movement by the Soviet Union on three points in order to proceed with negotiations toward a comprehen-sive agreement on test-suspension. "If you are prepared to change your present position on the veto, on procedures for on-site inspection, and on early discussion of concrete measures for high-altitude detection," Mr. Eisenhower wrote Premier Khrushchev, "we can of course proceed promptly in the hope of concluding the negotiation of a comprehensive agreement for suspension of nuclear-weapons tests."

The alternative, the President said, could be "the first and readily attainable step" of a ban on tests in the atmosphere, which after all, was the "most important" phase. "Meanwhile, fears of unrestricted resumption of nuclear weapons testing with attendant additions to levels of radioactivity would be allayed, and we would be gaining practical experience and confidence in the operation of an international control system."

Mr. Eisenhower was again tilting at that old propaganda windmill, the fallout hazard. His aim now was to put the onus on the Soviet Union for a change. The United States was offering, in effect, to rid the world of its worries that the fallout hazard would be increased by atmospheric testing. If the Soviet Union now refused to join in an immediate ban on atmospheric testing, Moscow would bear the responsibility for any increase there might be in the world-wide fallout hazard.

Test-ban moves had been pushed backstage, however, while the crisis over Berlin and upset over the slow death by cancer of his trusted Secretary of State, John Foster Dulles, occupied most of the President's attention. All White House business was being conducted in an atmosphere of sadness and grim determination to stand up to cruel Soviet threats against the isolated, plucky people of free Berlin. There was also a certain vacillation as General Eisenhower sought to steady his own hand on the wheel Mr. Dulles had helped him to guide with such a sure grip for the previous six years.

While preparations were being made for the Big Four foreign ministers to meet in Geneva on the German question, it was something of a surprise to find the Soviet Premier taking only ten days to get off an answer to President Eisenhower's giant step backward from a comprehensive test ban.

Premier Khrushchev replied to both President Eisenhower and Prime Minister Macmillan on April 23.[22] In his letter to Mr. Eisenhower, the Soviet leader rejected the proposal for an immediate agreement on banning atmospheric testing, dodged the attempt to make him responsible in the future for fallout and, somewhat amazingly, took the initiative in advancing Prime Minister Macmillan's proposal for limiting the number of on-site inspections in any comprehensive test-ban agreement. The proposal was amazing only in that Premier Khrushchev publicly identified an outsider, Prime Minister Macmillan, as the originator of an idea he espoused. It was not, of course, surprising that the Soviet Premier would be eager to limit the number of on-site inspections in the Soviet Union.

An atmospheric test ban "would only be misleading the public," Premier Khrushchev wrote the President, "since in fact the tests would continue to be carried out underground and at high altitudes. Thus the aim which is before us—that of preventing the production of new and ever more destructive types of nuclear weapons—would not be attained."

Nuclear tests above 50 kilometers "would also poison the atmosphere and the earth, contaminating with radioactive fallout the vegetation which finds its way into the foods of animals and into the human organism, just as is occurring at the present time," Premier Khrushchev wrote. "I think that you will agree with me that, from the viewpoint of concern for human health, it does not make any difference whether radioactive fallout originates in an explosion carried out at an altitude of 40 or, let us say, 60 kilometers." Such a first-phase treaty would be "a dishonest deal," Premier Khrushchev wrote. This was a sharp phrase which fit the tone of his shrill threats against the West on Berlin.

This "dishonest deal" could be concluded "only if there were assumed a lack of awareness on the part of the public at large. This is something that is not possible at the present time, for scientists would immediately understand the meaning of such a treaty and make it clear that it would not solve the problem but would leave the situation just as it was before the conclusion of the treaty."

Scientifically, Premier Khrushchev was about half right. How much radioactive debris would be returned to the surface of the earth after an explosion above 50 kilometers depended entirely on how far out the explosion occurred. Close in, at 60 kilometers as Premier Khrushchev mentioned, it would be possible that as much as half of the total debris would return, the other half being propelled into outer space. At hundreds of thousands of miles away, however, most of the debris would sail through space and if it ever settled anywhere, it would likely settle on some other planet or some other star in some other galaxy.

There had been just enough fallacy in the Eisenhower proposal to help Premier Khrushchev avoid the transfer of the fallout-monkey from President Eisenhower's back to his own.

Premier Khrushchev then returned to his favorite theme, the need for an all-inclusive ban. He also noted in his letter that the "most serious difference between us" concerned the dispatch of on-site inspection teams to suspicious sites:

As you know, during his stay in Moscow, Prime Minister Macmillan of Great Britain expressed the opinion that it would be possible to agree to carry out each year a certain previously determined number of inspections on the territory of the Soviet Union as well as on the territories of the U.S.A., Great Britain, and their possessions, if the reports of control posts would indicate the existence of phenomena that might be suspected of being nuclear explosions. It is understood that such inspections would not be numerous. I consider that, strictly speaking, it would not be necessary for many trips to be made to each country.

Having been presented, presumably, with a generalized proposal by Prime Minister Macmillan, the Soviet Union was carefully circumscribing it to conform to its own conceptions of the extreme limitations that should be placed on any inspection system inside the Soviet Union. Premier Khrushchev was setting two conditions: first, the evidence of a suspected event would have to meet certain pre-arranged criteria; second, the number of on-site inspections should not be "numerous."

He explained in his letter to Prime Minister Macmillan what he had in mind on the necessity for unidentified events to meet certain criteria before the dispatch of on-site inspection teams would be permitted. He was also very clear on keeping the annual number of inspections at a minimum.

"The number of annual trips by inspection teams should not be great," the Premier wrote Mr. Macmillan.[23] "Indeed, there is no need for many groups to travel to each of the countries concerned." The Soviet Premier's requirement for specific criteria before the dispatch of on-site teams was interwoven with his argument that the mere possibility of investigation would be enough to deter governments from cheating.

> The possibility of control being effected in areas where according to instrument readings nuclear explosions are expected will inevitably restrain the states from violating their obligations, since they will have to reckon with the fact that inspection teams might detect the violation of their obligations. *It goes without saying that suspicions concerning explosions must be based on objective readings of instruments and not on conclusions drawn by staff members of the control agency.* [Author's italics.]

This insistence on criteria was to become a major stumbling block later in the treaty negotiations. But it was many months before the Soviet Union spelled out either the number of on-site inspections it would permit or what criteria it would ask for dispatching of investigating teams.

In the letter to President Eisenhower, Premier Khrushchev used similar language: "Naturally such suspicions must be based, not on conclusions on the part of persons working in the control organization but on objective readings of instruments."

There was also a notable omission in Premier Khrushchev's embrace of the Macmillan proposal for a limitation on the annual number of on-site inspections. He made no mention of the other half of the bargain which Prime Minister Macmillan had suggested in Moscow in February, that the Soviet Union should modify its position on the veto. In his letter to the Prime Minister, Premier Khrushchev merely referred vaguely to "a favorable attitude toward your proposal . . ."

Besides parrying President Eisenhower's thrust on the fallout hazard, Premier Khrushchev had succeeded in relegating the Eisenhower initiative for an atmospheric test ban to a secondary position. By "accepting" the Macmillan proposal for an annual quota of on-site inspections, the

Soviet Premier was ignoring the Eisenhower phased approach. He was threatening to drive a wedge between the British and Americans at a time when unity would be important, not only for the test-ban talks, but also for the Geneva Foreign Ministers Conference on Germany. There too, the British were taking a compromise attitude which neither the United States nor its other two Western allies, France and West Germany, could fully approve. The United States was not keen on limiting the number of on-site inspections at this point in the negotiations, although it had been clearly recognized at the 1958 Geneva Conference of Experts that the mere physical difficulties of the on-site inspection process would preclude very many sorties per year. A single on-site inspection might take decades. Premier Khrushchev could hardly have been unaware of Dr. Brown's devastating remarks on the ineffectiveness of on-site inspection.

British Foreign Secretary Selwyn Lloyd a few days later confirmed his Government's awareness of this ineffectiveness:

> *In any case, every suspicious seismological incident cannot be investigated for purely physical and practical reasons. There are not sufficient resources to do it and not enough scientists available to investigate every suspicious seismological incident.* But the risk of inspection and discovery would be a deterrent against breach of the treaty. [Author's italics.] [24]

The British, pursuing their own plan for limiting the number of on-site inspections, helped the Soviet Union bury the Eisenhower proposal of April 13, calling for a ban on atmospheric testing only. White House Press Secretary James C. Hagerty issued a statement April 27, saying the President and Secretary of State both were "disappointed" that Premier Khrushchev had not been willing to "take the practical and immediately feasible measure of nuclear test suspension" in the atmosphere. The tone of the statement was defensive. Regardless of what Mr. Khrushchev says, the Press Secretary said, the United States "does want a complete test ban." But the Soviet Union so far had been unwilling to accept the controls which would make it possible, he added.

As for the new "Soviet suggestion," apparently referring to the idea borrowed from Prime Minister Macmillan, Mr. Hagerty said, it "does not address itself to the key point—the veto—which has thus far blocked agreement. The President and the Secretary of State hope, that when clarified, the Soviet position may reflect a change in attitude on this question so that progress can be achieved."

The failure to press the April 13 proposal for a ban on atmospheric testing has frequently been mentioned with regret by Administration officials who had seen in it a way out of the nuclear dilemma. In their view, it could at least have been used, despite the Khrushchev-Macmillan emphasis on the quota system, to end world criticism of the United States for adding to the fallout hazard. It also could have put responsibility on the Soviet Union, and opened the way earlier for nuclear-weapons development in underground and outer-space tests.

Pressures for renewing the April 13 proposal were strong inside the Administration. There were counterpressures, however, from those who predicted such a move would provoke the Soviet Union to walk out of the negotiations.

With President Eisenhower showing signs of uncertainty and with the Soviet Union refusing to listen to American scientists' new findings on the difficulties of control, the view from Capitol Hill still looked like a possible prelude to break-up.

Under the leadership of Senator Hubert Humphrey of Minnesota, the Senate therefore passed its Resolution 96 on April 30, stating the determination of its members to "support the efforts of the United States to continue to negotiate for international agreement for the suspension of nuclear-weapons tests. . . ." How many Senators knew what they were voting for we can only guess.

Little noticed in this country or abroad, this resolution had a strong effect on White House thinking. For the President to have broken off the talks, or even to have recessed them at this point, would have placed him in near-defiance of the Senate. President Eisenhower, who throughout his two terms insisted on having Congressional backing on major matters of foreign policy, took due note.

At this crucial point in the test-ban negotiations the Senate thus shared significantly the responsibility for United States policy on nuclear testing with President Eisenhower. He sent a second letter to Premier Khrushchev on May 5,[25] dealing first with the Macmillan suggestion for limiting on-site inspections. Mr. Eisenhower said the United States would "explore" the idea, but he did not support it. He thus indicated the continuing American coolness toward the British initiative in the nuclear test-ban field.

> In keeping with our desire to consider all possible approaches which could lead to agreement for discontinuance of nuclear-weapons tests with effective control, the United States is prepared to explore this proposal through our representatives in the negotiations at Geneva. In particular it will be necessary to explore the views of the Soviet government on the voting arrangements under which this and other essential elements of control will be carried out, the criteria which will afford the basis for inspection, and the arrangements which you would be prepared to accept to assure timely access to the site of unidentified events that could be suspected of being nuclear explosions. It will be necessary to know, also, the scientific basis upon which any such number of inspections would be determined and how it would be related to the detection capabilities of the control system. I have noted your understanding that these inspections would not be numerous. The United States has not envisaged an unlimited number of inspections, but adheres to the concept that the number should be in appropriate relationship to scientific facts and detection capabilities.

The President stated publicly for the first time the American position that the number of inspections per year should be based on scientific estimates of the unidentified events likely to occur each year. He also restated his three conditions for continuing negotiations toward a comprehensive ban: first, the Soviet Union must change its position on the veto; second, the Soviet Union must modify its on-site inspection policies; and third, the Soviet Union should agree to early discussion of high-altitude detection techniques. Mr. Eisenhower mentioned that Ambassador Tsarapkin in Geneva had given some reason for thinking that the Soviet Union might be ready to make changes on these points.

If no change were forthcoming, however, the President wrote, he would renew his proposal for a phased agreement beginning with an atmospheric-test ban.

No deadlines for Soviet movement were set, but the way was now prepared for a unilateral declaration by the United States that it was withholding all tests in the atmosphere. This was a line of action that was still being pressed with vigor by the advocates of continued testing despite the Senate resolution or United States sentiment.

The President attacked from two angles the unreasonable Soviet position "in principle" that Moscow would engage in no further technical talks while the political conference was meeting to write a test-ban treaty. The Soviet position had been that a sufficient technical basis for the political negotiations had been laid down at Geneva in 1958. The United States position was that new data had made that technical basis insufficient. To bolster its case the United States made frequent references in the Geneva negotiations to the sketchy character of the provisions for policing a test ban at high altitudes and the implication that later scientific data would be necessary before such a system could be devised. Obviously more technical talks on the high-altitude question would be in order, particularly with the rapidly expanding satellite-gathered knowledge about cosmic phenomena. If the Soviet Union were to agree to technical talks on high-altitude test detection this would amount to an acceptance, in principle, of the American position that further technical talks were necessary before any treaty banning tests could be agreed or signed. This principle could then be applied to the underground situation.

Premier Khrushchev made the acceptance in principle in the answering letter to President Eisenhower on May 14, 1959.[26]

At the same time, he performed one of his clever sleight-of-hand tricks which took the Soviet veto from view, so far as it applied to the on-site inspection problem, without actually renouncing it. Noting with satisfaction that President Eisenhower had agreed to study the Anglo-Soviet proposal for limiting the number of on-site inspections per year, Premier Khrushchev said that the question of veto need not come up in the dispatch of the teams to the site of a suspicious event.

We consider that agreement on a previously-determined number of visits
of inspection teams precludes the necessity of voting or of obtaining agreement on that question within the control commission or within any other
organization. The sense of our proposal consists precisely in such an elimination of the question of a so-called "veto" in regard to sending inspection
teams on the spot. Inspection teams could, for instance, be sent, within
the limitations of the agreed number of visits, upon the request of any of
the initial parties to the agreement on the cessation of nuclear weapons
tests, that is to say: The U.S.A., the U.S.S.R., and Great Britain, *in those
cases where the indications of the instruments of control posts provide a
basis for suspecting a phenomenon of being a nuclear explosion.* We are
ready to accept the obligation guaranteeing opportune and unhampered
access of the inspection teams to the area within the territory of the
Soviet Union in which there are observed phenomena suspected of being
an atomic explosion, and to which an appropriate party expresses a desire
to send such teams.

The Soviet Premier made no further explanation of how the criteria
for dispatching of the on-site inspection teams would be determined.
Who would decide what the instruments said? He had merely palmed the
veto behind the criteria question, like a magician palming the ace of
spades.

Premier Khrushchev held firmly, however, to his contention that "no
large number of inspection visits would be necessary, of course. . . . As
far as the Soviet government is concerned, we have solemnly stated and
do state that even in advance we shall strictly adhere to the agreement
and shall not violate the agreement concerning the cessation of tests,
which will be signed by us." The number of on-site inspections could be
revised once every two years, he suggested.

Vetoes on other questions, besides on-site inspection, Premier Khrushchev said, would not be an obstacle. Appointing an administrator for
the control organization "would be undertaken by agreement between the
initial treaty members in the control commission, and you do not object
to this either," the Soviet Premier noted. "We might be guided by the
same principle in appointing the personnel of the control posts, inspection groups, and so forth."

This was an extension, not an abandonment, of the veto idea. It was
true that the West had accepted the idea that the Administrator of the
control organization must be acceptable to both sides, a principle well-
established in the United Nations where the Secretary-General had been
accepted by all the leading power-blocs. Mr. Khrushchev was now suggesting that this principle of appointment by agreement apply not only
to the Administrator, but to all the personnel of the control posts, the
inspection groups, "and so forth."

Senator Humphrey was either fooled by the Soviet sleight of hand on
the veto or preferred to emphasize the positive in the hopes it would

encourage the Soviet Union to give a little more. In a speech on the Senate floor he declared:

> The Soviet Union, in indicating its willingness to give up the veto on the dispatch of inspection teams, has taken a significant step which could bring us closer to agreement on a treaty. The Soviet move offers a real possibility that an effective agreement can be reached, for the problem of the veto has plagued the test ban conference from the beginning. Now that it appears to have been removed the conference may go forward to try to deal with the other questions that remain.

At the State Department, the center of interest was Mr. Khrushchev's acceptance of technical talks on high-altitude detection.

Following a pattern that was becoming well-established by that time, the Soviet Premier's letter had advanced one comparatively tiny step, by agreeing to a high-altitude conference, but left open all the other questions in the West's mind. There was no indication how many on-site inspections the Soviet Union would settle for, no answer to questions about what criteria would be used for the automatic dispatch of on-site inspection, no indication on what basis the Soviet Union wanted to select the annual quota of on-site inspections.

One of the three Eisenhower conditions for continuing negotiations for a comprehensive ban had been met, however, and the President was ready to settle for that. Technical Working Group I on high-altitude detection began meeting in Geneva on June 22.

High Altitude Conference

A nuclear power seeking to test a weapon in space would send a rocket carrying the device to the outer-space region, then discharge from the main vehicle a set of "test pods" which would travel about 10 miles from the device. These test pods would be equipped with detection equipment to telemeter signals from the explosion back to earth.[27]

Scientists have decided on the basis of theory and limited experience that this space-testing procedure would be practical. But difficulties increase with the distance into space that the test is attempted. The farther out one goes, the heavier the test pods must be in order to carry telemetry equipment strong enough to send information about the test back to earth.

The Joint Atomic Energy Committee accepted 200 million miles as a practical, outside limit for a potential violator. Testing beyond this range "would require, with present-day rocket propulsion technology, that the violator wait for about one year after launch of a nuclear-test vehicle before the vehicle reached its scheduled detonation point and test data was telemetered back to earth," the Committee observed. "From a practical point of view such a test program would be extremely lengthy and uneconomical." [28]

There would be some limitations on the number of test observations that could be made of explosions in space. But scientists concluded that, in principle, the conditions would be "entirely adequate for weapons development." [29]

The only United States experience with high-altitude tests was in the Hardtack I series of 1958, the shots code-named Teak and Orange in the Pacific, and in three Operation Argus blasts over the South Atlantic, also in 1958. Only a small fraction of this experience, however, would apply to the general high-altitude test-detection problem.

The Hardtack I weapons were tested in the vicinity of Johnston Island, about 700 miles southwest of Honolulu. The first shot, named Teak, was exploded just before midnight, July 31, after having been carried aloft by a missile. It was ignited at an altitude above 200,000 feet. The Orange shot was exploded at about 100,000 feet at 11:30 A.M., August 11. It was also lifted by missile. Both tests were huge megaton blasts.

They were, "by far the most spectacular shots ever fired by the United States," according to an Atomic Energy Commission–Defense Department report.[30]

In the rarefied air the force of the explosion spread quickly and the 200,000-foot Teak shot rapidly produced an aurora which spread north. The Orange shot, more than 100,000 feet lower in the atmosphere, developed more slowly and its aurora was smaller than that from Teak.

The megaton shot exploded at above 200,000 feet, roughly 38 miles, produced some heat that could be measured on the earth's surface at Johnston Island but not sufficient to produce first-degree burns in human beings.

The Teak shot also caused serious absorption of radio communications and radar waves in the ionosphere. The same effects were observed to a lesser degree at stations farther from the blast than Johnston Island.

High-frequency communication was blacked out by the higher-placed Teak shot but not all channels were completely disabled. Radar operations were also hampered by the "clutter" on the radar screens caused by the aurora from the Teak shot. The clutter lasted for as long as half an hour.

An area of 3,000 miles diameter was sufficiently affected by the Teak explosions that some communications were disturbed, more severely in the ground zero area.

Radars that observed the Teak and Orange shots were found to respond better at the lower frequencies. They received little or no return in the first minute after the explosion. Thereafter, the signal built rapidly to strong interference over a wide area, in an oval shape, with the long axis in the north-south direction. This "saturation" signal lasted several minutes. In the third period the interference pattern again faded, however.

There was relatively little experience with detection methods at high altitudes. Radiation detectors had been flown in satellites, however, and results had been telemetered over long distances. On the basis of this limited experience, scientists concluded that detection problems could be solved. But no actual equipment had been tested up to the time the United States submitted its full draft treaty, calling for a complete ban on outer-space testing, in the spring of 1961.

Nuclear explosions emit many kinds of radiations that travel thousands and millions of kilometers in the vacuum of outer space. The earth's atmosphere, however, absorbs all but a small fraction of the radiations propelled in its direction. For this reason, detection of explosions in outer space requires not only a ground-based system, but one in satellites above the atmosphere.

Of the five principal types of radiation emitted by nuclear explosions in space, only one, visible light, reaches down to the ground. The others, X rays, prompt gamma rays, delayed gamma rays, and neutrons, are absorbed in the upper layer of the atmosphere. And in some cases the emission pulse is extremely short, measured in microseconds (millionths of a second).

X rays, for instance, are emitted because of the extremely high temperature of the nuclear device right after its detonation. These emissions last only from 0.1 to 1 microsecond. Prompt gamma rays are emitted for only 0.03 microsecond; delayed gamma rays from radioactive-fission fragments last for about 1 second.

Neutrons are emitted in two groups, prompt and delayed. The delayed neutrons have an effective time of emission on the order of minutes. But neutrons do not travel at the speed of light. They would arrive at a detector, for instance one placed in a satellite, over a comparatively long period of time.

Visible light is emitted for 0.1 to 1 microsecond and is due to the incandescence of the nuclear device. In addition visible light would be produced by the X rays when they came in contact with the upper atmosphere and caused it to fluoresce. Both the flash and the fluorescence might be picked up from the ground if there were no cloud cover or natural phenomena like lightning or auroras to confuse the system.

Another secondary effect of a nuclear explosion in space that might be detected would be the change in the ionosphere when it absorbed the energy from the nuclear explosion. This change would affect the absorption and reflection of radio waves from earth and would be detectable by two methods—the so-called ionospheric radar method and the cosmic-noise receiver. The cosmic-noise receiver would detect variations in radio signals received on earth from outer space when the resistance of the ionosphere changed with the advent of test radiations.

A third phenomenon caused by nuclear explosions is the so-called

"Argus effect." Electrons emitted in the radioactive decay of fission fragments from a nuclear explosion were found to be trapped in certain regions of the earth's magnetic field, above the atmosphere. Measuring the changes in the numbers of electrons in the earth's magnetic field might also be considered as a method of detecting an outer-space nuclear blast. It would have to be assumed, of course, that man-made nuclear explosions were the only other source of variations in the electron count.

One of the problems with all the types of radiation to be detected would be the already existing background radiation. This paralleled the "noise" problem that interfered with reception of underground seismic signals.

Designers of satellite systems to detect outer-space nuclear explosions would have to have extremely accurate information on the natural background signals before they could "read" the signals from an explosion and say with any confidence whether they were natural or artificial.

At the Geneva Conference of Experts in 1958, the high-altitude area had been the only one in which no set of agreed conclusions was produced. In accepting the Eisenhower proposal for technical discussion of high-altitude test detection, Soviet Premier Khrushchev had again stressed the need for quick agreement. Experts from the United States, the United Kingdom, and the Soviet Union met from June 22 until July 10, 1959, at Geneva on the high-altitude detection problem. On the final day they presented to the parent body, the Conference on the Discontinuance of Nuclear Weapons Tests, their agreed report.

It was the American scientists' theory that because no single method of detection of outer-space nuclear blasts would be reliable, as many types of signals should be collected for study as possible.[31] This was all the more important because there was no possibility for "on-site inspection" in space.

The Conference considered eleven methods of detecting high-altitude and space explosions, six of them to be carried in satellite systems, five to be based on the ground.

The Soviet Union eventually accepted ten of the methods, but balked at the ground-based radar method because it could produce incidental intelligence on Soviet missile development.[32]

The State Department later gave this summary of the general recommendations by the East-West experts, called Technical Working Group I:

> That five to six earth satellites, to be equipped with counters for the detection of neutrons, prompt gamma rays, delayed gamma rays and soft X rays, be placed in orbits at altitudes of more than 30,000 kilometers so as to insure complete surveillance of the earth and outer space;
>
> That if it were thought necessary for technical or economic reasons to establish an earth-satellite system at low altitudes, such a system could be set up as an alternative to the above;

That a satellite be placed into an appropriate elliptical orbit around the earth to provide maximum coverage of the region in the earth's magnetic field in which electron trapping occurs;

That, if it were thought necessary to expand the capabilities of the system to provide increased coverage of the regions behind the moon and the sun, a system of four satellites be placed in appropriate solar orbit;

That ground control posts be equipped with instruments for observing direct visible light, for observing fluorescence in the upper atmosphere, for measuring the absorption of cosmic-radio noise in the ionosphere and for measuring radio signals.[33]

Ground-Based Methods

The United States proposed five methods of ground detection: Direct optical; indirect optical or fluorescence; "backscatter" radar observations of the ionosphere; measurement of ionospheric absorption of cosmic noise; and electromagnetic.

Not any one of these systems would be totally reliable, however. Cloud cover could blind the two optical methods. The probability that all ground stations would be socked-in by clouds at the same time would be small, however.

Fluorescence can be produced by naturally-occurring events—sun storms, for instance. Photoelectric cells would hardly be able to distinguish an aurora from a nuclear explosion's fluorescence. And small nuclear shots produce little fluorescence in the first place. Shielding could cut down on the fluorescent effect.

> The difficulty in relying on the absorption method [fluorescence] only in observing ionospheric disturbances [those at altitudes from 30–50 up to 1,000 kilometers] is the fact that the method is very sensitive to the local noise conditions, and the result, as has been verified in the American observations, is that the method does not lend itself to the observation of weapons of low yield.[34]

Lightning might spoof the electromagnetic detection method.

Soviet scientists at the Technical Working Group I conference again exaggerated the capabilities of some detection methods to cut the amount of inspection. The backscatter-radar method proposed by the United States was intended to fill in the gaps where direct optical observations were impossible. But the Russians simply refused to allow it. Other methods would suffice, they claimed.

By refusing to accept the backscatter-radar method for detecting tests below 1,000 kilometers, Dr. Wolfgang Panofsky told the Soviet scientists:

> They were restricting ground stations to a relatively small coverage . . . that . . . does not provide coverage for small weapons at a low altitude. Although the electromagnetic signal is a very valuable method and re-

quires no additional equipment or personnel at control posts, it does not by itself constitute a means of identification because of problems involved with lightning and disturbances. . . .

I realize that an answer to this is that the coverage of satellites reaches down to altitudes of approximately 100 kilometers. . . . However, we believe that the ground systems fulfill a very important function quite independently of the satellites . . . the problem of identification rather than detection is a very difficult one and, hence, confirming evidence is most desirable. Secondly, the satellites—in particular the satellites we visualize for the earth system—are very complicated devices and what concerns us most is that there is a certain problem of what to do in case one or two of these satellites cease to function—which, after all, has been known to happen in any kind of equipment. In that case a violator would know of this and he would also know the orbit of the satellites. Therefore, if we were to rely on satellite coverage only there would be a fair amount of time in which no coverage existed in certain conditions which could easily be made use of.[35]

Dr. Panofsky discussed the cloud-cover problem with the Russians in these terms:

I should also point out that the direct optical method becomes completely useless in the presence of cloud cover. However, at high altitudes—and this is where I would like to emphasize the method—the cloud cover is not present over all stations, or at least the probability of this being so is exceedingly low. We have made an analysis on this question. We have looked at the meteorological tables. If a violator wished to make use of the fact that cloud cover did exist over all stations he would have to wait for a very long time before he could carry out his tests. So, although we admit completely—in fact we have it documented . . . the decrease in range of the fluorescence method due to cloud cover, we do feel that it has its value. We also admit that the fluorescence method is subject to concealment by shields in the same way as any method based on thermal radiation. The direct optical method is not subject to this because shields, in general, will degenerate the energy, but this amount of energy in the optical region will not be very greatly modified. . . . So it is just the complementary property of the direct optical and fluorescence methods on the one hand and both ionospheric methods (backscatter-radar and cosmic noise), which leads us to make this suggestion. We simply believe that without these complementary methods we would not have a very satisfactory system.[36]

The Soviet delegation claimed the backscatter-radar method was both unnecessary and undesirable. "Backscatter-radar installations established at control posts could enable alien staff to spy upon military objectives in the territory of sovereign states. The first radar stations that provided backscatter intelligence during World War II operated on the very frequency range now contemplated."

The United States delegation felt that the inspection system without radar had two "holes." First, in the area from 50 kilometers above the earth to 100 kilometers, there was no method sufficiently reliable for detecting sneak shots.

Second, in the area from 100 kilometers to 1,000 kilometers, there were two systems, optical and cosmic-noise detection, but they operated with only a low level of reliability. Dr. Panofsky referred to this region as a "half-hole." Main difficulties would be false alarms. Thunderstorms could mask explosions. Sudden ionospheric disturbances, solar noise, and aurora would look like nuclear explosions.[37]

These weak points in the detection system at the lower altitudes were considered especially dangerous by the United States delegation, because it was in just this area where capabilities already existed for boosting heavy shielding apparatus to "muffle" nuclear-explosion signals.[38]

Satellite-Based Methods

Six techniques were approved at the Geneva conference on high-altitude test-detection: Thermal X rays, prompt gamma rays, delayed gamma rays, prompt neutrons, delayed neutrons, and trapped electrons.[39]

At the outset of this discussion it is important to adjust to cosmic distances. Three hundred thousand miles sounds like a lot of range; it is greater than the distance between earth and moon. But both the Soviet Union and the United States have already fired rockets to the vicinity of the sun, 93 *million* miles away. These are the ranges—in millions of miles—that will be important in the years ahead. Both the Soviet Union and the United States may already have the capability to test nuclear weapons in the vicinity of the sun.

Of the six satellite-borne methods recommended by the Geneva Conference, however, only one had earth-to-sun range—thermal X rays. Prompt and delayed gamma rays could be picked up 300,000 miles out; prompt neutrons 100,000 miles; delayed neutrons 10,000 miles; trapped electrons, 30,000 miles. All these ranges apply to explosions of 1–10 kiloton yield.

American experts insisted from the outset that there should be maximum coverage in all regions of space out to the sun, a distance of 93 million miles. The five "short-range" detectors were included, however, to compensate for the uncertain reliability of individual methods. And in the early years of the space age, there was some possibility a potential violator might try evasion of the ban in relatively-near space.

The trapped-electrons method was a direct outgrowth of Operation Argus. Electrons emitted from fission fragments of the Argus nuclear explosions were trapped in the earth's magnetic field. A single satellite traveling in an orbit below the Van Allen belts of radiation would quickly notice a sharp increase in the trapped electrons even from a relatively small detonation if it were set off only a few hundred miles out.

Far-earth satellites would be the most desirable system for space detection. If the individual satellites could be boosted up to 20,000 or 30,000 kilometers they would achieve almost complete coverage with about six satellites. The only blind spots would be behind the moon and behind the sun.

Near-earth satellites would be the next best thing. But more satellites would be required, about ten, and there would be several blind spots, especially if a few of the orbits were wobbly. There would be less requirement for a big thrust, however; the orbit would be only 700 kilometers from the earth, and it would be a more economical system, even though more satellites would be required. This system also would be unable to see behind the moon or the sun.

Seven hundred kilometers was the minimum height needed to avoid background interference. But an impractical total of sixty satellites would be needed to provide full coverage. At 1,000 kilometers, the number of satellites necessary for full coverage would be thirty-six.[40]

Ten carefully placed satellites at the same height could keep the blind spots to tolerable limits, however, the American scientists judged.

Solar-orbit satellites, circling the sun at radii approximating that of the earth's orbit, were believed also to be necessary by the United States scientists, to check behind the sun and the moon and also to force potential violators into a more difficult shielding process. Four satellites in solar orbit could do the job, the Americans calculated. The Russians scoffed at the whole idea of hiding tests behind the sun or the moon.

Formidable ground support of the various satellite systems would also be required. First there would have to be launching sites, with standby satellites ready for action the moment one of the orbiting satellites was discovered to be defective. Second, there would have to be an elaborate world-wide tracking network and facilities to receive and process the radio reports from the satellites.

Persuading the Soviet scientists to accept a workable system was difficult, as could have been expected. In meeting Chief Delegate Fedorov's easy confidence that a minimum of surveillance would provide a completely reliable system, American and British scientists expressed their own misgivings. At one point a British participant had this to say:

I was commenting on his [Dr. Fedorov's] statement that we can have a wholly reliable satellite program. My comment was that we were not yet in a position to decide that, because we have no experience of such a complicated satellite. We hope it will be wholly reliable, and I for one am satisfied that the detection from satellites has very considerable advantages over the detection from a ground station, but I am not convinced in advance that the satellite program can here and now be stated to be wholly reliable. So I do not think it is a question of deciding now if it is or is not reliable; that would be a most unscientific thing to do. I merely wish to point out that because we cannot guarantee that it will be wholly reliable, therefore it is desirable to add other methods—and here I think is the important point—using apparatus which can be maintained, tested and looked after constantly. I have no desire to come categorically one way or the other on the reliability of satellites, because that I think would be most unscientific.[41]

The American chairman, Dr. Panofsky, commented on the same point:

My feeling in the matter is that the term "reliability" cannot be used in a quite undefined way. One can talk about instrumental reliability, which is the main concern voiced by Mr. Hulme. One can talk about reliability of identification, one can talk about many such things, but we feel very strongly that ground systems are necessary and also that satellite systems are necessary. . . . If there is a failure of satellites it will be known to everybody, and such a failure may persist for a fair amount of time and until they can be replenished—unless we recommend to the commission that there should be a very large excess of satellites. But in that case if one does worry about costs, although this is not the province of this meeting, I believe one will find that the cost will greatly exceed what we are talking about here in backing things up with ground stations. So I am afraid that our position remains the same, namely, that we would feel that these ground stations as given in the draft submitted are both necessary and barely sufficient.[42]

Dr. Panofsky then turned to another problem, the "false alarm":

The methods suggested—and this includes the methods suggested by you and the methods suggested by us—do not permit us to make a very quantitative assessment of the false-alarm rate. There does not exist enough geophysical experience and experience of lightning and sudden ionospheric disturbances—auroral phenomena and so forth—to permit us to specify very precisely what the number of ambiguous cases might be with the ground system, even the ground system proposed by us, at this time.[43]

The reason we are not satisfied with the ground stations alone in the region up to 100,000 kilometers is that, on the basis of the studies we have made of the ionospheric disturbances and the lightning disturbances, we cannot make a completely secure assessment concerning incorrect signals which may be received by the ground system. We may be able to do that in the future, but we cannot do so now. Therefore, we feel that it is necessary to have this multiple coverage in the lower region.[44]

The uncertainty about maintaining far-off satellites in working condition was a related worry:

The satellite . . . has problems all its own. It would be quite independent and it does not have the property of maintenance which is possible in the case of ground stations. It has the property that it moves in an environment which, though I believe it is basically simple, is very much less explored. For that reason, it may bring surprises in the future.

In short, both systems [ground and satellite] are subject to some unknowns. We may be experts, but we are not prophets, and for that reason I feel it is necessary, in the interest of proposing a system that can do the job to be assigned to it, to propose the use of both these systems in the region up to 100,000 kilometers.[45]

I would like to mention again that mechanical failure is only one of the sources of unreliability. I believe the chances of failure of a mechanical nature are greater in the initial operation of the satellite than they are of components of a ground system. However, this may improve in time.[46] On the other hand, we cannot assess in a quantitative way the other causes of lack of reliability. But one thing we can be very sure about is that the sources of failure of a physical nature imposed upon us by natural phenomena are quite independent, and therefore we have a very much greater chance of reliability of the system as a whole if we adopt both methods.[47]

I fear that the question whether we are recommending a maximum or a minimum system—which were the words used by Mr. Fedorov—is really a rather peculiar one. Clearly there is not such a thing as a maximum system. In discussing the number of satellites, as an example, the number could be increased, but we are obviously trying to discuss a minimum system which we would consider to be necessary and sufficient to fulfill our mission.

At one point, the Russian scientists suggested that solar orbits were far beyond the capabilities of the day. Dr. Panofsky half agreed:

Earth satellites in the 10,000-kilometer to 30,000-kilometer range [present a problem] in rocketry and propulsion and guidance which is involved, is more difficult in the case of earth satellites than in the case of solar satellites . . . the reasons for this are manifold. One is concerned with the simple laws of classical mechanics of putting satellites into high orbits and the propulsion requirements. This is a matter of ordinary mechanics, which we can easily demonstrate, but I am sure we agree on. The second is concerned with the fact that the earth satellites must not be permitted to be all in the same place; they must be distributed in a controlled way over a surface of a sphere at a certain distance from the earth, because otherwise they will bunch together and develop holes of viewing so that they will lose effectiveness, because it will be very easy to predict when these holes will occur and the control system will lose its effectiveness.[48]

British Delegation Chairman Hulme also expressed misgivings about the day-to-day operations of the system:

We feel that to have a satellite which is continuously relaying signals— and, moreover, signals which must be correct, which must not falsely indicate that an explosion has occurred, and which must do this without care or maintenance for a whole year—is a technical undertaking that is, to say the least, a difficult one. It is for that reason that we feel that the satellite program cannot be regarded as wholly reliable. For that reason—there may be others, but certainly for that reason—we are most anxious to support this with the ground stations.[49]

The Soviet scientists took the position that it was absurd and "science fictional" to consider seriously the possibility of detecting nuclear explosions millions of kilometers from the earth. The detection system was to be installed soon, not in a matter of decades, the Soviet Chairman, Dr. Fedorov declared.[50]

Dr. Panofsky, Chairman of the American Delegation, explained, however:

> The thrust requirements of the vehicle which would be in a test program do not vary by very large amounts as you go from 100,000 [kilometers] to large distances, and therefore the problems in going farther away are not really quite as fantastic or science-fiction-like as Mr. Fedorov mentioned. It is for that reason that these numbers appear to be worthy of serious consideration by this group, and the larger ranges are of considerable interest in particular when combined with the shield considerations.[51]

The Soviet Union at first resisted the idea that shielding would be used on outer-space nuclear tests, on the grounds it would be too complicated. Russian scientists finally were brought to accept the idea, however, and the possibility of shielding was mentioned in the final report.

It was estimated that shielding could reduce the ranges of detection by an order of magnitude. That would apply even to explosions as large as half a megaton.

Thus the range of soft X ray detectors listed as 200 million miles, could be cut to 20 million miles if there were shielding for the apparatus being tested.

System Evaluation

The Joint Committee on Atomic Energy later found the Technical Working Group's system unimpressive. The combination of ground-based and satellite-based methods had the range and "redundancy," the Joint Committee's analysis found, to pick up tests out to the moon's orbit.[52]

But in special areas beyond 300,000 miles and inside 100 million miles from the earth, only X ray detectors in satellites had the necessary range, the Committee observed. By inference rather than explicit statement, it was indicated that the necessary "redundancy" to compensate for unexpected difficulties was not available.

The area beyond 300,000 miles contained "over 99.99 per cent of the total volume of space available to a violator," the Committee analysis observed.

The X ray technique intended to cover this area is "vulnerable to shielding" which could cut the range of detection by a factor of ten or more on large-yield devices and by a factor of 100 or more on smaller yields, the Joint Committee said:

> It is with this limitation in present space detection system design in mind, that scientists believe that an intensive program of research and develop-

ment should be carried out in the next three to five years. Hopefully such a program would provide more reliable possibilities for detecting explosions in that region of space beyond the moon where present theoretical system capability appears marginal.[53]

This was hardly a statement of confidence in outer-space detection. There was even a noticeable reserve about what three to five years of research could do. And the program undertaken after the report could hardly be described as "intensive."

The Committee also cautioned that the world had only scanty knowledge about the natural radiation that might interfere with satellite detection networks:

Very little is known about the natural radiation of gamma rays, neutrons, and X rays in regions where satellites would be installed. The effectiveness and reliability of the satellite system will therefore depend greatly upon the degree to which pulses of radiation similar to those produced by nuclear explosions in space might be produced naturally.

Technical Working Group I did not consider many of the key problems that would be involved in detecting outer-space nuclear explosions. For instance: How would decisions be made, after suspicious signals had been received, that a violation had or had not occurred? How would the satellite-detection system be financed?

How would the detective-satellite launchings be handled? Once launched, what would be the procedures for determining that the satellites were operating properly? How would technicians be recruited?

All these questions, which were appearing in a parallel form in the test-ban treaty negotiations, would have to be ironed out before a satellite system could be launched. Presumably the ground components of the space system would come under the rules of the 180-control posts being established under the treaty. But the satellites would present a different set of problems.

In addition, a whole new complex of equipment would have to be designed and developed. For instance, to observe the light flashes from nuclear explosions in outer space a group of detectors looking out into space would have to be developed, tested, and installed. This would take about two years, with a "very large effort." [54]

Once the equipment was developed there would also have to be a period of operation to evaluate the performance.

As a rough estimate, American experts predicted that the near-earth satellites could be put in orbit in two to three years, the far-earth or satellite orbits would take two years longer. So the total time span would be about five years from the decision to begin development. These would be the "technical lead times," only. A period of operational testing would have to follow. Dr. Panofsky had mentioned the need to the Russians in

Geneva: "One of the problems confronting us, of course, in our discussions is the fact that *confirmation in practice* exists only for very few of the devices we are discussing here. Really, almost all the devices we are discussing, including all those carried in satellites, have not been confirmed in practice." [55]

Neither the Russians nor the United States had placed a satellite in orbit that could perform at the level required by Technical Working Group I for high-orbit satellites.

If the Soviet Union could find enough to argue about for upwards of twenty sessions in Geneva in the general area of criteria for sending out on-site inspection teams on the relatively easily defined characteristics of earthquakes, it would be logical to assume that the Soviet Union could argue much longer on how to read a single short pulse of X rays—lasting one millionth of a second or less—and signaled across thousands of miles of space to some ground receiver.[56]

The attention given to shielding outer-space explosions was, in the opinion of some officials well acquainted with the problem, an unnecessary exercise. Representative Craig Hosmer, for instance, asked Dr. Panofsky in the Joint Atomic Energy Committee hearings on test-ban controls, "What would be the sense of going to shielding, because if an outer-space explosion were detected, who could say who caused it?"

Dr. Panofsky's reply stated succinctly the near-futility of the outer-space detection idea:

> This is the significant point here. There is no way unless information was available on vehicle launchings. Of course, each party would know what launching they had undertaken. *But there is no means in space surveillance to connect a given violation with a particular party.*
>
> REPRESENTATIVE HOSMER: In other words, the actual violator could just blame it on somebody else and there is no way to prove he's lying?
>
> DR. PANOFSKY: However, there is the point to consider here that this treaty provides no specific sanctions of any kind, as the matter stands now if a violation occurs, beyond the voiding of the treaty.

How does one define "identification" of an outer-space nuclear explosion? How many signals from how many ground stations and how many satellites are necessary to make the conclusion that there has been a nuclear explosion in space?

Because there were not enough statistics to go on, the East-West experts made no attempt to estimate the number of false alarms that the high-altitude detection system would encounter. Nor was there any effort made to prescribe how the detection system would operate to distinguish false alarms from sneak explosions.

It was conceded, however, that the control system would have to rely entirely on the instrumentation, and there would be no opportunity for "on-site inspection" in the case of high-altitude testing.

Thus this important part of the control system had the built-in handicap that proof of a nuclear test would be practically impossible. Dr. Panofsky told the Technical Working Group I:

> Nobody would ever believe an identification if the light signal, say, gave an indication and then, when one looked at the records of the ionospheric methods—I do not wish to discuss which of the ionospheric methods—for corroborating signals—[they gave no indication]. The chances are that one would find corroborating signals, because there are always signals of various kinds in the ionospheric methods. We have not evaluated this. We do not know how to evaluate it. This is a problem.[57]

The spectacle of competition between Livermore and Los Alamos laboratories over the space-detection problem was brought to light in the 1960 Joint Atomic Energy Committee hearings. Los Alamos had been assigned the job of developing the detection system. But Livermore scientists, generally more interested in continuing weapons development than the Los Alamos group, raised the possibility of shielding outer-space tests, which had not been considered at Los Alamos. The Livermore scientists developed on their own initiative elaborate theories for shielding nuclear shots in space, painfully complicating Los Alamos' job. This "butting in" was resented at Los Alamos, but at the same time it saved the United States from at least one false opening step in the high-altitude talks like the seismologists made at the 1958 Geneva Experts Conference.

The Technical Working Group I conference had shown that effective policing of an outer-space test-ban would be out of reach for many years.

SENATOR HUMPHREY'S CRUSADE

The time was approaching, in the summer of 1959, for President Eisenhower to decide whether to extend the United States voluntary test-ban past October 31 or resume experiments.

As the time for decision approached, Senator Hubert Humphrey, the Chairman of the Senate Disarmament Subcommittee, made a major speech on the subject on the Senate floor. It was entitled "Shall We Resume Nuclear Tests?"

His answer was, "Emphatically, no."

His long speech was representative of the thinking by proponents of pressing forward for a test-ban.

The Senator took a much more hopeful view of prospects than even the State Department. Of the remaining undecided issues, he said, "only one [the number of on-site inspections] really stands in the way of an agreement among the three nuclear powers." The State Department still regarded the veto and the staffing of control posts as companion stumbling blocks of major proportions.

Neither of the big powers had a negotiating position on this on-site inspection issue, Senator Humphrey complained. In the case of the

United States, this was because the Government was divided on basic aspects of the problem:

> It is divided between those who are concerned about the risks involved in a continuing arms race—those who think it is important to take a real step toward arms control—and those who feel that we have more to gain than to lose by continuing tests and that we cannot afford to stop testing our nuclear weapons in the face of a control system that is less than perfect.
>
> [The State Department's negotiators] are burdened by obstacles which have been built primarily by the Atomic Energy Commission and to a lesser extent by the Defense Department. The AEC seems to have difficulty in remembering that it was not created to be a policy-making body in the area of foreign relations. Although I think the AEC has overstepped the bounds of its functions in this instance, nevertheless, I cannot dispute its right to argue its case. The AEC is allowed to continue to oppose the official position of the United States and to inject its own views on foreign policy due to a lack of leadership at the top.

Senator Humphrey charged that President Eisenhower had "failed to assert the leadership necessary to reconcile conflicting views. Our position is being determined by an interdepartmental committee which can decide only when it is unanimous. In effect, every department has a veto over the State Department's role in the negotiations in the absence of active Presidential participation."

Fallout, he said, is still an immense concern.

> I personally think that if tests resume before we know the outcome of the test-ban negotiations the United States will be inviting an outburst of indignation and criticism by the people of other nations. Furthermore, our own people are immensely concerned about the possible harmful effects of radioactive fallout. Scientists are still studying this problem so we as yet do not have all the answers we need. The results of studies conducted thus far, however, continue to give cause for alarm.

The judgments were already in by then, of course, that fallout presented considerably less than 10 per cent the amount of hazard that natural background radiation caused.

> We could conceivably claim that tests should be resumed because there are no harmful effects of fallout and that the test-ban talks are not making progress, two of the lines of argument being advanced by the AEC, [Senator Humphrey observed]. The facts of the former are uncertain, as I have said, and the facts on the latter are to the contrary. The facts of this situation must be made known. Otherwise the public will be fooled and decisions will be made behind closed doors without the kind of public discussion and knowledge which the people of a democracy must have in our system if our system is to survive and endure.

His arguments for more public discussion of the problem were shared by the AEC, the Defense Department, and others who opposed Senator Humphrey's views.

As for the claim that progress had been made in the test-ban talks in Geneva, this depended on the reference point one used. If one started at the beginning of the negotiations in October, it could be claimed that some of the less important articles had been agreed upon by the end of March. But beyond March, in the second five-month period immediately preceding Senator Humphrey's speech, not one other article had been approved.

The Senator listed six points on which the three nuclear powers had "not yet agreed."

1. Staffing of control posts. Whereas the Soviet Union claimed that no more than one-third of the staff should be foreigners, the United States argued that no more than one-third should be home-country nationals. "Translated into terms of actual numbers, the difference between the two sides is approximately a difference between ten and twenty-five, a difference which," Senator Humphrey said, "I expect, can be resolved if negotiations continue."

2. Composition of the control commission. This "should not provoke fundamental differences," the Senator judged. He suggested a compromise composition of two Western nations, the United States, and the United Kingdom; two members of the Sino-Soviet bloc, the Soviet Union, and one other country; and three countries not allied with either of the two sides.

3. Control system for high-altitude tests. Recommendations of East-West scientists had not been incorporated into the treaty and this was not expected to involve political problems. Here, there were "some engineering problems, however," including "the means by which satellites will be sent into space so as to assure that no nuclear tests are being conducted there," the Senator said. He had no solution to recommend here.

4. Budget. The Soviet Union wanted a veto on the budget, he said, but the United States and the United Kingdom wanted it voted on by all members of the treaty with a majority determining the final budget. Agreeing on adoption of a budget should present no insurmountable obstacle, the Senator said.

5. Equipment at control posts. "If the United States should raise the question as one of improving the equipment at the control posts instead of asking a reconsideration of the entire question of the detection and identification of underground tests by seismic means, I should think that the Soviets would see the merits of our proposal," Senator Humphrey suggested. "In any case, improvement of equipment should not be a major obstacle to agreement."

The Senator was apparently assuming that the equipment would bring improvements that would restore the system to a satisfactory effectiveness. This was an assumption that others did not make. They saw the problem as a broader one.

6. The number of on-site inspections. This was "the main and only major area of difference," the Senator said. "This must be emphasized so that the public can know that, except for one major problem, the probabilities are that an agreement could be reached."

The Senator undertook, for the first time in public, an examination of what the on-site inspection problem had grown to be as a result of the Hardtack II series. He recalled that the United States had recommended to the Soviet Union and Great Britain a formula for determining how many unidentified events to inspect. All of them above five-kilotons equivalent power should be inspected, according to the formula, and 20 per cent of all events below five kilotons should be inspected as well. Before the results of the Hardtack II series were made known, it was estimated that this would result in roughly 85 inspections a year in the Soviet Union, Senator Humphrey reported.[58]

After the Hardtack series, and after the improvements in the seismic system recommended by the Berkner Panel, Senator Humphrey estimated that the new figures for total inspections inside the Soviet Union would be 366, about 1 per day. AEC Chairman John A. McCone reportedly had been using the same figure as his estimate for the number of on-site inspections per year in the Soviet Union.

This amusingly precise estimate of 366 on-site inspections per year in the Soviet Union was apparently based on a new estimate, in the summer of 1959, that there would be about 1,700 earthquakes a year in the Soviet Union between a half-kiloton and 5-kiloton equivalent power, of which 20 per cent would be 340. Seismologists estimated there would also be about 140 earthquakes per year in the Soviet Union above 5 kilotons of which about 110 could be identified. That would leave an additional 30 for on-site investigation. The total of 370 comes reasonably close to the Humphrey-McCone figure of 366.

There were two pieces of optimism in this figure. First, it seemed extremely optimistic to expect that 110 of the 140 events above 5 kilotons, or 79 per cent of them, could be identified. In the second place, seismographs, especially in "noisy" areas, are not capable of even detecting all the half-kiloton earthquakes. Aspiring to a system capable of detecting secret shots down to one-half kiloton was unrealistic, of course, in a sense more optimistic than the 1958 Geneva experts had been.

The suggestion that there would be a requirement for 366 on-site inspections per year in the Soviet Union, using the American formula, appeared extremely high to Senator Humphrey.

These numbers give the impression that the inspection problem is so huge that the negotiators might just as well pack up their bags and go home because it is almost absurd to suggest that such a large number of inspections should take place [the Senator told his colleagues]. I would like to show in a few ways that the inspection numbers game must be subjected to more thorough analysis.

First, earthquake specialists tell us that at least two-thirds of all earthquakes in the Soviet Union occur in the Kamchatka Peninsula, which is a very small part of the entire Soviet Union. Furthermore, they tell us that another 25 per cent occur along part of the southern periphery of the Soviet Union. This would mean, using the above figures, that 242 inspections would take place in the Kamchatka Peninsula; 91 would take place along the southern periphery; and this would leave 33 for the rest of the country. I am reasonably certain that it would not be necessary to conduct 242 inspections in the Kamchatka Peninsula to satisfy ourselves that the Soviets were not sneaking tests in that area. A mobile inspection team might check on several earthquakes during one visit. Other means also exist to determine whether tests have taken place in addition to the reading of instruments and the conducting of mobile inspection teams. I am referring here to a variety of intelligence measures which would be available to the United States and which would have nothing to do with the operations of the control system.

Senator Humphrey had access to the verbatim records of the 1958 Geneva Conference of Experts. He apparently had not read, or was not impressed by, the presentations of Dr. Harold Brown—official statements of United States judgments—which had shown the difficulties in the on-site inspection method and the official, scientific estimates of the amount of time that could be taken up in only one inspection.

Second, most of our able seismologists say that once the control posts are established and operating, many events will be identified as a result of close observance of earthquake activity from a given region. In other words, we will learn more about earthquake patterns which make the identification problem less complicated. [As the seismological records were examined, new opportunities for deceiving the system presumably would also appear.]

Third, one of the recommendations of the Conference of Experts is being completely ignored by our Government scientists and consultants. That is the possibility of using and re-equipping existing seismograph stations throughout the world, and devising means to help assure that the data from them will be reliable. There are some 650 stations now in existence of which only a fifth or a fourth are probably located in spots that can be used. However, the recommendation of the experts is ignored by the Executive Branch and thus kept out of any discussion from improving the control system.

Senator Humphrey suggested that the United States should ask the United Nations for help in improving the seismograph stations around the world. A special working group should be established to assist other nations in improving their stations, and, if necessary, erecting new ones, he suggested. Since the United States was the only country with the capacity and will to help other countries with a crash program, it sounded more like a plan for the United States to subsidize the United Nations in setting up the seismograph network.

Having accepted in theory but not in practice the estimate that 366 on-site inspections—one per day—probably would be required in the Soviet Union each year, Senator Humphrey addressed himself to the need for establishing "the principle of deterrents" to master the control problem. The same principle of deterrents was being used, he said, in the armaments race.

We should apply the principle of deterrents to the control problem. We live by the concept of deterrents in our defense policy. We know that we cannot necessarily stop the Soviet Union from sneaking some missiles with nuclear warheads through our warning system to bomb our people and the people of nations allied with us. But we operate on the principle that if we have enough defense so we can strike back, then the Soviets will be deterred from launching a surprise attack.

The same principle ought to apply in a control system. We must accept the fact that we cannot cover every little unidentified event in the Soviet Union to see whether it is an earthquake or a nuclear test. We can, however, demand the right to inspect a certain number of cases on the assumption that such inspections will constitute a spot-check system of random sampling which will have a high probability of accuracy and which will deter a nation from thinking a few sneak tests can be held without being caught.

At the present time there is no known perfect system for any arms-control measure. There is a certain percentage of risk. But there is also a certain percentage of risk involved in doing nothing. If we let the present test-ban talks die, then what do we think we can accomplish by starting new arms-control discussions? If the test-ban talks succeed, then new arms-control discussions become imperative.

The suggestion that the United States agree to a "spot-check system of random sampling" seemed to indicate that the United States could get by with much less than 366 inspections per year. But the 366 inspections per year already constituted a random sampling system—based on about a 20 per cent sample. If the number were further reduced to make the total of on-site inspections "more manageable," this would amount to spot-checking the spot-check system. The sampling would become so thin it would become ineffective; the deterrent the Senator sought would evaporate.

The President's science advisers had decided on the modified 20 per cent random-sampling deterrent. Degrading the deterrent to 10 per cent random sampling would still require 183 inspections; a 5 per cent sampling would call for 91 inspections; a 2 per cent sample would get it down to 37 inspections per year in the Soviet Union. But then the Kremlin would have 49 chances in 50 of getting away with a sneak test. Senator Humphrey did not say how far down the road of degrading the inspection deterrent he wished to go. Nor did he mention an alternative method of reducing the number of on-site inspections: raising the threshold from one-half kiloton to, say, 5 kilotons. This, of course, would have opened up the problem of decoupling.

I want to state flatly that new data do not preclude a workable control system from being realized [Senator Humphrey told the Senate]. The scientific problems that have been discovered during the course of the negotiations are not substantially or fundamentally different from those the scientists and the negotiators faced when the negotiations began. *We knew then that we would never be able to explore for each and every unidentified earthquake. We knew then that in inspecting the site of an unidentified event it would be immensely difficult to determine whether it had been an earthquake or a nuclear explosion.* We knew then that although our techniques of detecting and identifying tests would improve with increased research and knowledge we would also discover a larger number of natural phenomena with this newer and more scientific equipment.

Nothing has changed since last October that justifies our giving up.

Neither Senator Humphrey nor President Eisenhower nor anyone else in a position of responsibility had warned in 1958 that it would be "immensely difficult" to distinguish an earthquake from a nuclear explosion. This was a fine-print proviso in the body of the Geneva experts' report which everyone, including Senator Humphrey, chose to accept without comment at the time.

Senator Humphrey included another interesting concept in his important August 18 speech. "If the total inspections [of a prescribed quota] were used up and another inspection appeared necessary and if the Soviet Union vetoed it, then the agreement could be called off," Senator Humphrey declared. "It is my opinion we would seldom want to use the maximum number of inspections allowed us. But if and when we did, any use of the veto would be a warning signal at the least and the end of the agreement at the most."

If the United States had previously agreed to a limit on the number of on-site inspections, to break the agreement on these grounds would be tantamount to imitating one of the worst features of the Soviet system, that is, breaking a solemn covenant.

Senator Humphrey also included in his speech an appeal for funds to conduct the program of research which the Berkner panel had recommended. Not only had the Executive Department not recommended a program, Senator Humphrey complained, but three of his attempts to persuade Congress to appropriate money for this purpose had also failed.

He then gave this summary of his own position—which could be taken as an authoritative representation of the general sentiments of most pro-test-ban groups in the country:

1. Nuclear-weapons tests should not be resumed on the part of the United States unless the nuclear test-ban negotiations collapse. I recog-

nize that the military officers and AEC scientists want to start testing again but the civilian authority of our government and the overriding dictates of foreign policy and national security must be upheld.

2. The United States must not allow the talks to collapse through a failure to achieve a reasonable negotiating position on the most important remaining issue in the negotiations—the number of on-site inspections. The number of inspections must not be the few suggested by the Soviets and it need not be 366 suggested by Mr. McCone of the AEC. And, in arriving at a reasonable position in the negotiations, we must keep in mind that if the Soviets ever use the veto when the control organization wants to investigate a truly suspicious event that is the warning signal that cheating may be going on. That is the warning signal which could mean the end of the agreement.

3. The United States should seek the assistance of the United Nations in modernizing existing seismograph stations around the world. We should look to them for assistance in reaching a successful test-ban agreement, an agreement, may I add, that eventually and in agreed-upon stages, must include other nations.

4. The Executive Branch should immediately embark on a vastly expanded research program to improve our knowledge, methods, and equipment of control. The Berkner Panel on Seismic Improvement revealed extensive Soviet advances in seismological research. It also recommended several important programs but the President has asked for no funds from the Congress for any of them.

I want to urge my colleagues in the Senate and my fellow Americans everywhere to ask themselves these questions: Do we want to be responsible for terminating the test-ban talks before we have determined whether the Soviets will accept adequate controls? Do we really think our defense demands resuming tests the moment the gong strikes on November 1 [the expiration of the United States one-year voluntary moratorium]? Do we want to face the prospect that the arms race cannot be held back?

I think every member of this body would answer these questions in the negative. Let us pray that the President will have the wisdom and the courage to pursue the right course.

Eight days later, the President announced the United States would extend its unilateral moratorium for two months, until the end of 1959. His decision was made in a growing atmosphere of *détente*.

In July, Premier Khrushchev had been quietly invited to the United States. No agreement was reached on Berlin or any other important issue. But the crisis abated. In August there was public announcement of a projected exchange of visits between Premier Khrushchev and President Eisenhower.

The nuclear test-ban negotiations ground on at Geneva from June 8 through August 28, then recessed while Premier Khrushchev made his tour of the United States. On August 26, however, President Eisenhower announced he was extending the voluntary unilateral moratorium on nuclear-weapons tests until the end of 1959.

"As far as can be determined," the State Department said in announcing the President's decision, "the Soviet Union has conducted no [nuclear] tests since November 3, 1958." On that basis it was indicated the United States could continue its own suspension.

"In continuing its voluntary suspension of atomic- and hydrogen-weapons tests to December 31, 1959, the United States wishes to allow a reasonable period of time for the negotiations to proceed following their resumption on October 12, 1959," the State Department said.

Pressures were building in the United States for a resumption of tests. The President, personally, however, was taking a greater interest in making one last try in the remaining eighteen months of his Administration to set the world on the road to a more stable peace. His decision, after years of fruitless prodding from Soviet Premier Khrushchev, to invite the Soviet leader here and to pay a return visit to Moscow the following year was part of this plan. The pressures from the Defense Department and the AEC for a resumption of tests ran head on into this general ambition of the President.

It was in this spirit that the United States extended its voluntary test ban. But the brevity of the extension, only two months beyond the old October 30, 1959, deadline, emphasized that even President Eisenhower's patience could be exhausted. Two months more, after twelve months behind them, the President reasoned, would be "a reasonable period of time" for the Soviet Union to show a genuine interest in reaching agreement.

A spokesman for the British Foreign Office announced at a press conference, August 27, that the British Government had a different formula for extension of its own voluntary test ban. The British government would not resume nuclear-weapons tests as long as useful discussions were under way at the three-power Geneva Conference.

The next day the Soviet Government put the blame for the delays in reaching agreement on the Western powers. At the same time it announced readiness to agree immediately to a complete end of all nuclear tests. Going the Americans and British one better, the Soviet Union announced it would not resume nuclear tests in the Soviet Union if the Western powers did not resume. "Only in case of resumption by them of nuclear-weapons tests will the Soviet Union be free from this pledge." [59]

The U.N. General Assembly, meanwhile, kept up the pressure in 1959 for the nuclear powers to continue their supposed suspension of testing and directed special attention to France, which was known to be preparing a test series.[60]

Senator Humphrey was being mentioned as a contender for the Democratic nomination to the Presidency in October when he made yet another proposal to try to break the continuing deadlock in the nuclear-test talks in Geneva. He perhaps reflected the anguish of most advocates of the test-ban, who had placed all their faith in the hope that the arms race could be reversed, and none of their faith in the idea that a balance of terror might, in the long run, be safer than an imbalance of disarmament. He would accept an atmospheric ban alone as "better than no agreement," he told a political meeting in Pontiac, Michigan, on October 30, 1959, but he believed there would be better alternatives if the attempt for a comprehensive ban failed:

> If the Soviet Union is unwilling to discuss the technical complications of a comprehensive agreement and if the United States is unwilling to reach a negotiating position regarding the number of annual inspections it believes would be both safe and reasonable, then some other way out of the impasse must be found. For we must *not* let the Geneva negotiations fail.

If the control organization for a test-ban had to inspect only for explosions of about 5 kilotons or more, Senator Humphrey said, the number of inspections needed in the Soviet Union would be somewhere in the range of twenty-five to fifty. "Such a range does not appear to me to be too high, either from a practical point of view or from the viewpoint of the Soviet Union with its suspicious outlook toward any inspection or control," Senator Humphrey said.

He then presented this 5-kiloton threshold proposal:

1. Let the United States extend its general moratorium on all nuclear tests, now scheduled to end on December 31, for a maximum of one year. This would give the nuclear powers ample chance to reach agreement. I would not extend this moratorium more than one year; if the Soviets stall longer than that, it is a sign they are trying to get a test-ban with no controls whatsoever. I think the United States must not allow this to happen.[61]

2. We should be prepared to enter into an agreement banning nuclear tests equal to and above 5-kiloton explosions. The agreement would specify that all unidentified events with a signal equal to and above a 5-kiloton explosion would be subject to inspection. The ceiling on the number of mobile inspections would be somewhere between twenty-five to fifty. In this way I believe we could arrive at a number of mobile inspections that would correspond to our present best educated guesses from a scientific point of view as to what is necessary.[62]

3. We should be prepared to join with the other countries for two years from the time the agreement goes into effect in a moratorium on tests below 5 kilotons. At the end of that time we shall know two things: (1) whether the Soviet Union and other countries are cooperating in installing the control posts; and (2) whether by observation and further research the control posts can be improved to detect and identify most of the unidentified events below a size of 5 kilotons.

4. During the two-year period in which the control posts and inspection system for the 5-kiloton-threshold agreement were being established we should conduct a comprehensive research program in cooperation with the Soviets, with the United Nations, and also by ourselves. Such a program would be designed to find ways of improving the control systems so that all suspicious events would be subject to inspection within a reasonable ceiling.

5. The agreement should specify that if the international control posts

or our own detection gave evidence that the Soviet Union was not cooperating in the moratorium on tests below 5 kilotons—those not subject for two years to mobile inspection—then we would be free ourselves to test in this range. We would present our evidence to the international control commission to show that the moratorium had been violated. And if the Soviets did not agree to install appropriate and reasonable controls for tests below 5 kilotons we should be free to test in this range if our defense requires it.

A new voice on the nuclear-test issue was heard in the fall of 1959, as the warm-ups for the 1960 political campaign began. Governor Nelson Rockefeller of New York startled his Republican colleagues on October 25 when he suggested in a television interview that the United States should resume nuclear tests. "I think that we cannot afford to fall behind in the advanced techniques of the use of nuclear material," the Governor said. "I think those testings should be carried on, for instance, underground, where there would be no fallout or strontium-90 in the air."

This provided an opportunity for Senator Kennedy of Massachusetts, another hopeful for the Presidency, to comment again on the nuclear test-ban issue. Speaking before students at the University of California at Los Angeles on November 2, 1959, Senator Kennedy registered "my own emphatic disagreement" with the suggestion of Governor Rockefeller. The Senator accused the Governor of damaging the American image abroad at a time when the Russians had unilaterally suspended their tests and when most of the peoples of the world "are fearful of continued fallout." His speech was one of those uncanny mixtures of naïveté with popular appeal that carried many a politician to success.

Just before the reopening of the recessed negotiations with Great Britain and the Soviet Union at Geneva, Senator Kennedy said, it was "unwise" to suggest a resumption of tests. He acknowledged that Mr. Rockefeller had proposed resuming the tests only underground, which would have prevented fallout, but scored the Governor for discounting the harmful effects of fallout. This, Senator Kennedy said, is something "I am unwilling to do."

The Senator acknowledged "many competent scientists agree that there had been no great harm done to mankind as a whole from the amount of radiation created by bomb tests so far." On the other hand, he emphasized that "it is also true that there is no amount of radiation so small that it has no ill effects at all on anybody."

There is, he said, "actually no such thing as a minimum permissible dose." [63] This was literally true, but the Senator had confused minimum with maximum. The common term, and the only issue in dispute among scientists, was the concept of "*maximum* permissible dose," not "minimum." A minimum permissible dose is illogical. If anyone endorsed the concept they would have to contend that at least a certain measure of fallout is good for you.

Senator Kennedy took the humanist approach followed by many geneticists and supporters of the nuclear test ban:

> Perhaps we are talking about only a very small number of individual trage-
> dies—the number of atomic-age children with cancer, the new victims of
> leukemia, the damage to skin tissues here and reproductive systems there—
> perhaps these are too small to measure with statistics. But they neverthe-
> less loom very large indeed in human and moral terms. Moreover, there is
> still much we do not know—and too often in the past we have minimized
> these perils and shrugged aside these dangers, only to find that our esti-
> mates were faulty and the real dangers were worse than we knew.

There was the additional hazard, he said, that the resumption of tests would provoke the Russians to return to testing in the atmosphere and "the kind of long, feverish testing period which all scientists agree would threaten the very existence of man himself" would ensue.

It was to be one of many ironic moments for Senator Kennedy when, as President, he would face the decision of resuming tests and of pre-cipitating the very kind of Soviet action he had dreaded.

Senator Kennedy indicated without saying so that he, too, believed a nuclear test ban would inhibit the spread of nuclear weapons to other powers. "Once China, or France, or Sweden, or half a dozen other na-tions successfully test an atomic bomb," he said, "then the security of both Russians and Americans is dangerously weakened."

In the cautious manner of the Kennedy campaign, the Senator bal-anced his pro-test-ban remarks with statements on the other side. He conceded, for example, that there were powerful arguments on the side of resuming tests. He acknowledged that the need for weapons develop-ment was "not to be dismissed lightly."

He agreed the United States needed small technical nuclear weapons and the so-called "clean" nuclear weapons, as well as increased flexibility and range of weapons already in the American arsenal.

Weapons-development programs cannot be suspended indefinitely, the Senator acknowledged, without scientists and technicians scattering to other positions in other laboratories. But he concluded that it was more important to find a way out of "the present menacing military situation."

He accepted the unsubstantiated theory that the Soviet Union was also withholding tests. On this basis, and assuming that the United States was ahead of the Soviet Union in development of atomic warheads of all sizes, he concluded that "for both sides to resume atomic tests today might well turn out to be more of a disadvantage to the West militarily than a help."

The Soviet Union, the Senator concluded, had apparently made great progress in its 1958 tests. The danger, as he then saw it, was that the Soviet Union could, in any new test, "score a breakthrough with some new means of destruction which will make all the more delicate the present balance of terror."

Senator Kennedy acknowledged, however, that he would not favor giving the Soviet Union an indefinite test-ban without inspection.

> If our best efforts do not succeed [however] the negotiations collapse, the Russians resume testing, and then it becomes necessary for our tests to resume, even then, they should be confined to underground and outer-space explosions, and to the testing of certain small weapons in the upper atmosphere, in order to prevent a further increase in the fallout menace—and in the hope, moreover, that the Russians and others will be forced by worldwide opinion to follow our example.

AEC Chairman McCone declared in a television interview on November 22, 1959, that the United States should be ready to extend its fourteen-month ban on testing "only on a week-to-week basis." A year's extension would be too long, he said.

Asked if the United States had good information that the Soviet Union had not been conducting secret tests underground, Chairman McCone replied "We do not know of any tests that they have conducted nor do we have any monitoring devices which could disclose small tests up to five or ten kilotons, if they had chosen to conduct them in a clandestine manner. I am inclined to believe that they have not done so."

On the other hand, he warned, "I think it would be impossible" to detect Soviet underground nuclear explosions if they had held some.

Mr. McCone's public plea for a week-to-week extension of the ban beyond the end of 1959 was an indication of the depth of feeling in the AEC about the dangers of too long a ban. It was, of course, known to Mr. McCone that President Eisenhower's freedom of action for a test-resumption was being circumscribed by a combination of "Camp David spirit" and "election-year protocol."

By November, 1959, it had become apparent the United States would not be able to test throughout 1960. Influential American officials acknowledged this at the time—privately—and their views were reported, without naming the sources, in the *Washington Star*. By then, it was clear that the President was preparing to go to a summit conference with Premier Khrushchev the next spring. This was to be followed in the early summer by President Eisenhower's visit to the Soviet Union. The Eisenhower Administration would not upset world relations in advance of these meetings with a resumption of nuclear tests. In July, 1960, the political conventions would be held and President Eisenhower would become a "lame duck." His principal advisers were conceding that the President could not then take upon himself the responsibility of committing his successor to the kind of unsettled world that would follow a United States resumption of testing.

Chapter 11

Technical Working Group II

Ten months after the United States had started prodding the Soviet Union for a reopening of the Experts conference to study the discouraging Hardtack II series data, the Soviet Union proposed formation of a three-power technical working group to draft "objective criteria" for the dispatch of on-site inspection teams to unidentified underground events. At the same time, the Soviet Union indicated informally that the experts could consider other data bearing on the underground detection problem, which the United States took to mean the Hardtack II findings. Soviet Delegate Tsarapkin said his government was prepared to do this in order to eliminate the "artificial obstacle" the United States had placed in the path of the negotiations. The break came November 3.

Technical Working Group II met officially twenty-one times from November 25 to December 18, 1959, and ended in wide disagreement.

The snail's pace at which disarmament negotiations in general have moved, nuclear test-ban negotiations in particular, could hardly be better illustrated than in the year-long American attempt to bring the Soviet Union to the abortive discussion of new data from the 1958 Hardtack II series.

Unexpectedly ambiguous signals from Hardtack shots began accumulating in September and October, 1958.

Evaluation of the information was far enough along around Thanksgiving, 1958, for the United States to know that a revision of the control system—a drastic one—would be necessary if all nuclear tests of 5 kilotons or more were to be effectively banned. But the information was not refined enough to present to the Soviet Union until January 5, 1959. At that time, the United States asked the Soviet Union to join with other experts in re-evaluating the Geneva control system.

The Soviet Union flatly refused. Technical talks were behind them, the Russians said, and there would be no further ones until the political negotiations setting up a test-ban and a control commission had been completed. Then it would be the job of the control commission to look at the new scientific data.

The United States kept pressing for a reconvening of the technical talks, however. In April, 1959, President Eisenhower stated formally he could not agree to ban underground tests or those in outer space unless the Soviet Union agreed to further technical talks on the control systems that would be necessary in those two environments. After two exchanges of letters the Soviet Union made its first move—"in principle"—away from the idea that there could be no more technical talks until the political conference had completed writing a treaty. Moscow agreed to technical talks, not on the more sensitive underground problem with which the Hardtack II series had dealt, but on policing a ban on high-altitude and space tests.

This conference was held, broad if imprecise agreements were reached, and the principle was firmly established that the Soviet Union was indeed ready to engage in more technical talks. The principle stood, however, without the Kremlin taking the next logical step of accepting new technical talks on underground control, for six months.

It was not until November, 1959, that the Soviet Union agreed obliquely to take into consideration the new Hardtack II data. When the Soviet scientists finally did get around to looking at these data, two months of wrangling were required to satisfy the Americans that the Russians had no intention of recognizing the material's import: that the 1958 control system would have to be drastically revised if it were to maintain its previously hoped-for capabilities.

Merely getting the scientists back together took a year. Meanwhile, the whole technological picture was changing still more.

This is an important practical demonstration that the art of diplomacy, too, has been a victim of the swift pace of science. Science is moving so fast in so many directions that diplomacy, intended to tame the science of war, has been falling further and further behind.

The day before the conference opened, the State Department listed fourteen experts to make up the United States team:

Dr. James Brown Fisk, Chairman; Dr. Hans Bethe; Dr. Harold Brown, Associate Director, Livermore Laboratories; Dr. Richard Foose, Stanford Research Institute; Richard L. Garwin, IBM; Spurgeon Keeny, Jr., Office of the Special Assistant to the President for Science and Technology; Dr. Albert Latter; Dr. J. Carson Mark, Los Alamos Scientific Laboratory; Jack E. Oliver, Lamont Geological Observatory; Dr. Wolfgang K. H. Panofsky, Stanford University; Dr. Frank Press, California Institute of Technology; Carl F. Romney, Department of Defense; John Tukey, Princeton; and Dr. Anthony L. Turkevich, University of Chicago.

The return of Dr. Fisk as chairman was intended to indicate President Eisenhower's continuing confidence in him and the other members of the 1958 Conference of Experts who had overestimated the effectiveness of seismology in detecting underground tests.

The Russian scientists again were led by Dr. Fedorov. They came to the conference table on November 25 worried that the United States would try to draw them into an agreement that the 1958 experts' control system had been found to be greatly inferior to their earlier estimates. At the beginning there was a long debate on the terms of reference for the working group. The United States wanted to provide for a re-evaluation of the Geneva system's capabilities, after a study of the new data. The Soviet Union wanted to permit only presentation of the new data and suggestions for improving the system—no re-evaluation of the old 1958 system. As a compromise, it was decided that the new data would be discussed, suggestions for improving the system would be made and criteria for dispatching on-site inspection teams would be considered.

The evaluation of the system was by-passed, but the United States took the position that in discussing the new data and the criteria for on-site inspection there would be a *de facto* evaluation of the old system.

From the opening day, the Russians made periodic speeches that they saw no need to revise the 1958 experts' agreement as a result of the new seismic data which the United States had given them months before.[1]

They agreed, however, to listen to the presentation of the data. In the opening statement by Dr. Romney, the United States gave this basic information on the Hardtack II tests:

Shot	Yield (kilotons)	Date
Evans	.55	10-29-58
Tamalpais	.72	10-8-58
Neptune	.90	10-14-58
Rainier	1.7	9-19-57
Logan	5	10-16-58
Blanca	19	10-30-58

Rainier was monitored by about forty stations but was not detected by all of them. The Hardtack II series was monitored by more than ninety stations, including some in Sweden and Japan. "We would be pleased," Dr. Romney told the Russians, "to see any similar information which our Soviet colleagues may have on these explosions."

He expressed the view that large explosions, of the order of about 20 kilotons, would produce larger signals than the 1958 Conference of Experts had expected but that small explosions would produce smaller signals than expected.

Even the 20-kiloton Blanca shot, however, produced first-motion rarefactions, the downward signals which had been thought to be characteristic only of earthquakes. The rarefactions appeared at distances beyond 900 to 1,000 kilometers.

The United States delegation proved, in the seismograms turned over to the Soviet delegation, that the first motion of explosions was recorded as a rarefaction on both sides of the "shadow zone" (1,100 kilometers and to 2,500 kilometers from the event). There were numerous rarefactions recorded on vertical-component seismograms monitoring the Hard-tack operation. In the "shadow zone" itself the first-motion signals were also found to be unreliable. First motion, therefore, would be useful only at "substantially higher equivalent yields than was concluded by the Conference of Experts," the American delegation said.

This had been one of the stunning discoveries of the Hardtack II series. The first-motion criterion was not a reliable earthquake indicator even at so high a yield as 20 kilotons. Dr. Romney gave this table of magnitudes, according to the Richter and Richter-Gutenberg scales, for the American underground shots:

Shot	Yield (kilotons)	Magnitude
Blanca	19	4.8 ± 0.1
Logan	5	4.4 ± 0.1
Rainier	1.7	4.1
Neptune	.09	2.4
Tamalpais	.072	2.6

The Evans test apparently could not be assigned a magnitude. Dr. Romney merely reported that "nature was not kind to us." The Rainier shot had earlier been estimated to have produced a signal of 4.25. The smaller Tamalpais shot, curiously, produced a larger earthquake signal than Neptune.

How many earthquakes would look like Rainier? Using the Gutenberg estimate of world earthquakes per year, Dr. Romney presented Technical Working Group II with this drastically revised calculation:

	Estimates	
Size	Original (1958)	Revised (1959)
1 kiloton	10,000	25,000
10 kilotons	2,400	3,000

At 20 kilotons there was expected to be no difference in the estimates from the 1958 Experts conference. Dr. Romney emphasized that the new data were based on six times as much information as was available at the time of the 1958 Conference of Experts. There were, however, significant deficiencies still in the amount of scientific knowledge available. All the shots had been exploded in the same medium, at the same location, and at about the same depth.

As soon as Dr. Romney had finished his opening presentation, the Soviet delegation attacked the American position in a harsh manner that set the mood for the whole conference. D. R. Pasechnik, one of the higher-ranking Soviet seismologists, and the Russian chairman, Dr. Fedorov, made opening statements heavily overlaid with sarcasm. Pasechnik inquired patronizingly why the Americans had not used the magnitude-calculating methods he had recommended in a letter to Washington.

Dr. Romney explained that instruments at many of the stations picking up the Hardtack II series were not calibrated. The whole Russian delegation was outraged.[2] They wanted to know what kind of slipshod procedure this was.

As the Soviet scientists warmed to their task, Dr. Fedorov implied that the United States was withholding data on the Hardtack series.[3]

Dr. Romney replied indignantly that the United States had given the Russians 250 seismograms and more from the Hardtack series. The Russians, he observed, had not given the United States any of their data on the Hardtack explosions. Who was withholding data?

On the second day of the conference, the Soviet scientists took another tack, criticizing the United States for not equipping the seismograph stations with the ten-unit arrays recommended by the 1958 Conference of Experts. They strongly implied that the Americans had falsified the Hardtack seismographic data.

"What are the reasons for consistently minimizing magnitudes obtained at the Woody, Barrett, and Riverside stations?" the Russians asked. Their intent obviously was to plant in the record of the meeting their suspicions, or professed suspicions, that the United States had juggled the Hardtack results to discredit the test-ban control system.

Dr. Romney answered that the three stations in question were among the best in the United States. Heterogeneities in the geological structure of the western United States were responsible for the spotty readings, he conjectured. When the Russians observed caustically that there had been no trouble for far-away Swedish and Japanese stations in observing the Hardtack series, Dr. Romney replied that these stations' recordings had been small, the noise levels had been high, and the data were not reliable.

The Americans claimed that the only difference resulting from the use of large arrays at the seismic stations would have been an increased signal-to-noise ratio in the recording. This would not have changed the conclusions about yield-to-magnitude correlations or first-motion clarity.

Dr. Sadovski complained that the Barrett, Riverside, and Woody stations were "not satisfactory from the geological point of view." He drew the conclusion that the data from these stations "logically also [are] not satisfactory." His aim was to throw out the unexpectedly low signals from these stations. This would have tended to raise the average magnitude and minimize the difficulties that the Americans had discovered as a result of the Hardtack series.

Dr. Frank Press, a member of the American delegation familiar with the California stations, commented indignantly: "Woody is the very best station we have—it is a station on solid granite [a choice base]. . . . Barrett is also on granite. Riverside is on recent but compacted rock." [4]

Throughout the conference there were Soviet attempts to impugn American motives, mixed with extremely harsh criticism of American scientific methods. The Hardtack data, the Russians said, contained a "flagrant inconsistency" between the quality and completeness of the data and the "categoric conclusions" arrived at by the United States delegation. Dr. Fedorov ventured the observation that the Hardtack data added "only insignificantly" to knowledge of underground nuclear explosions. Not a single station had been equipped as the Geneva experts suggested. The "deluded reader" of the American reports on the Hardtack data was led to believe the equipment used was similar and that this equipment had yielded poor results, Dr. Fedorov charged, while in reality the data presented was carefully selected to produce a result desired by the United States.[5]

Dr. Fisk pressed for Soviet scientific data which would refute the American conclusions. "We would like to know . . . what data you may have from any of these experiments in the Hardtack series, such as the large Blanca underground explosion, which would lead you to conclusions other than those which we have presented," he told the Soviet delegation.[6]

Dr. Fedorov dodged an answer but promised to produce "comments" later.

Magnitudes

During that same session, Y. V. Reznichenko did produce Soviet seismograms from the big Blanca shot, picked up from "distances above 6,000 kilometers." At the same time Reznichenko pressed the American delegation to drop the signals from the Barrett and Woody stations, suggesting that Blanca then would be registered at magnitude 5 in the first zone and 5.1 in the third zone. These magnitudes would then correspond to the 1958 Conference of Experts conclusions, he said.

Hardtack results, in reality, showed not a twofold increase in the number of earthquakes similar in effect to 5 kilotons, he contended, but a decrease of about 10 per cent. He achieved this result by juggling the weights accorded to selected signals in arriving at magnitude averages.

The Russians suggested that Rainier, instead of being magnitude 4.1 was 4.3; Logan instead of 4.4 was 4.8; and Blanca instead of 4.8 was 5.1.

Thus the Soviet scientists were claiming that it would take only a 5-kiloton explosion to produce a 4.8 signal, while the United States claimed it would take a 20-kiloton explosion. Reznichenko also claimed that "more detailed calculation leads not to an increase in the number of earthquakes from 1 to 20 kilotons, but to a reduction of the order of 1.5," on the basis of his analysis of the Hardtack series data. He suggested that there would only be 1,600 earthquakes of 10-kiloton equivalent or larger each year, not 3,000 as the United States estimated. And above 1 kiloton, he said, there would only be 7,000 earthquakes per year, not 25,000, as the Americans estimated.[7]

On December 7, Dr. W. D. H. Panofsky presented a new set of American estimates on the number of small earthquakes per year.[8]

There would be 2,000 shallow earthquakes per year with an equivalent power of 20 kilotons or more, Dr. Panofsky suggested; 5,000 per year of 5 kilotons or more; 15,000 per year of 1 kiloton or more. Earlier the estimate had been 25,000 a year above 1 kiloton.

"However, our knowledge of frequency of occurrence is uncertain by at least a factor of two either way," Dr. Panofsky said.

Dr. Pasechnik reacted with a wry joke: "I remember that, in the old days, when a puppy was given for transport to the baggage department at a railway station, by some error the person who was to receive it ended up with a large dog and it was explained that the puppy had grown in transit. Here again we see that the data has grown significantly over the initial readings in the material."

After the Russians later agreed to meet the American scientists in informal sessions to discuss the magnitude problem, Dr. Romney presented them with what should have been a clinching argument. The Russians claimed that the Hardtack underground nuclear shots had really produced much greater magnitude signals than the United States was willing to admit, he said. Thus, they claimed that a 5-kiloton shot would make as big a signal as the United States said was made with a 20-kiloton shot. Dr. Romney showed them, however, that if this theory were carried through to the Russians' own chemical explosions underground, the shots that the Soviet Union claimed were only 2 kilotons could have been as much as 40 or 50 kilotons. The Soviet explosions registered such signals abroad. The idea that 40 or 50 kilotons of chemical explosives would be used underground is absurd, or at least unlikely because of the huge volumes involved. Great underground cavities would have to be constructed.

The Soviet scientists, however, stuck by their inconsistency. In the informal sessions the American scientists came to believe that the Russians knew they were presenting specious arguments but had to stick to them for reasons that were not stated.

Dr. Romney later commented that "the Soviet criticisms of our [magnitude-calculating] procedures, in my view, are dishonest."

They took the point of view that we should reject all data which tended to indicate there would be more earthquakes. In other words, they said let us forget about all the low determinations of magnitude and consider only the high ones. They followed this procedure with as many technical and pseudo-technical arguments as they could through the whole proceedings.

Their final paper, their final report, contains information which, I believe, is incorrect and which I believe they know is incorrect.

They have computed the numbers of earthquakes or the size of earthquakes on one magnitude scale, and the size of explosions on another magnitude scale.

This is kind of like measuring the height of a man in feet, and then saying he is 6 yards tall. The result is to make the numbers of inspections appear smaller, and I think clearly this was their objective.[9]

The Soviet scientists first looked down their noses at improvements in the Geneva system which the Americans recommended in the fourth meeting. The Americans were trying to show that they sincerely intended to recoup the losses in effectiveness of the control system which had been discovered in the Hardtack II series. The Russians were far from accommodating, and there were frequent clashes about the methods of procedure.[10]

Dr. Fedorov singled out Dr. Tukey for a kind of playful mockery. At one point he exclaimed: "I give the floor to Professor Tukey, and with our hearts beating we await what he has to say." At another: "In the name of the Soviet delegation, I would like to tell Dr. Tukey that we have noted the remarkable way in which he played with the black boxes. We hope that he will remain in good health and not fall into the box that he has so well described." [11]

The Americans finally retaliated. In the fifth session they attacked the scientific methods of Reznichenko. Dr. Tukey charged him with "errors in statistical techniques," and claimed the Soviet scientist had "distorted the true probabilities by a factor of more than 50." He had dropped significant data from his calculations, they charged, to arrive at his inflated magnitudes for the Hardtack shots.[12]

Eventually the Soviet delegation produced seismograms from five points where the 19-kiloton Blanca explosion had been picked up, three of them inside the Soviet Union, one in Antarctica, and one in Czechoslovakia. These were the only stations among the more than one hundred inside the Soviet Union and many others in the Soviet-bloc area which had picked up Blanca or any other Hardtack shots. American officials regarded the recordings as undistinguished.

The closest station, at Tiksi, 6,890 kilometers (4,300 miles) from the epicenter, *showed the Blanca shot as a rarefaction.* Thus, the Soviet Union also would have mistaken the largest of the Hardtack underground nuclear shots, the 19-kiloton Blanca explosion, as an earthquake.

The Soviet Union used single, vertical seismographs, not arrays of instruments.

Dr. Pasechnik was pressed for an answer on why the Tiksi station gave a rarefaction as first motion. He replied lamely that this was maybe for the same reason that the Palo Alto station had given a rarefaction.

The United Kingdom delegation chided the Soviet Union into acknowledging that many other stations inside the Soviet Union had completely missed both the 19-kiloton and 5-kiloton Hardtack shots. Thus, the perennial Kremlin claim that control of a test ban would be unnecessary was exposed as a canard. But the exposition was in a small room of the Palais des Nations in Geneva, not over Radio Moscow. The

United States Information Agency apparently never read the verbatim records.

The Russians continued during the conference to develop their theme that the American scientists had deliberately revised downward the estimated amplitudes from all nuclear shots. Dr. Fedorov complained, for instance, that the Rainier magnitude had been changed from 4.6 in February, 1958, to 4.3 in the summer of 1958, to 4.1 in January, 1959.

"Such changes of basic data with which we have to deal and which are put before us by the American side give rise to bewilderment on our part," Dr. Fedorov exclaimed. "We try to have maximum respect and confidence in all the matter you put before us but such changes of basic data do not serve to strengthen our confidence." [13]

Dr. Fisk replied: "It seems to me the fact the seismograph centers all over the world can agree among themselves concerning the magnitude of well-recorded events suggests that we should be able to clear this matter up." He suggested that the Russians join in informal meetings to iron out disagreements, but Dr. Fedorov declined.[14]

First Motion

Despite the evidence from their own stations that first motion was a dubious criterion on which to make a distinction between earthquakes and explosions underground, the Russians continued to contend that first motion was reliable. Difficulties, the eminent Dr. Keilis-Borok explained, arise from "peculiarities of the stations, or questions of random errors."

As the daily wrangles continued, it became clear to the American delegation that any control commission for a nuclear test-ban could bog down for days over the simplest problems if a treaty were ever signed and control were put into effect. The public was never forcefully warned of this, either.

Dr. Fisk struck back hard at some of the Soviet claims, calling the conclusions on first motion "naïve misinterpretations." He also accused the Russians of making "totally meaningless" presentations about earthquake signals, particularly first motions, because the problem of noise had been "completely ignored." Soviet instruments, about which the Russians had boasted, Dr. Fisk said, "will lead to excessive noise." The new system recommended by the Soviet Union "appears to us to be a deterioration rather than an improvement," he declared. Dr. Pasechnik, the American chairman said, had introduced ideas which ignored "the elementary principles of signal and noise in the analysis . . . in order to produce conclusions pointing in one direction only."

Dr. Frank Press accused Dr. Keilis-Borok of trying to pawn off a huge 7.25 earthquake on the Western delegations to prove that first motion was still an important criterion for distinguishing earthquakes from explosions. The Soviet scientist should have had the courage to conclude, Dr. Press suggested, that the control system needed more stations in the first, or inner, zone to identify a nineteen-kiloton explosion.

After Dr. Keilis-Borok had made another suggestion for using frequency ratios to help distinguish between earthquake and explosion signals, Dr. Press declared: "I believe this suggestion shows that Dr. Keilis-Borok has not often read seismograms of magnitude 4 to 5 earthquakes or explosions. . . . Now, I consider Dr. Keilis-Borok a personal friend, and I rank him among the three outstanding theoretical seismologists of the whole world, so I regret exceedingly that I must tell him that his talk is irrelevant to the problem at hand. . . ." [15]

Dr. Hans Bethe made his first appearance at the sixth session of the Technical Working Group II conference. He told the Soviet delegation that "first motion is valueless beyond the first zone." Furthermore, he said, in the first zone—out to 625 miles—there would have to be five to six or possibly eight stations to use first motion as a criterion for distinguishing earthquakes from explosions. The Geneva system had provided only about three stations.

"From Dr. Keilis-Borok's table we can draw precisely the same conclusion we have drawn from the data," Dr. Bethe declared, "namely that the Geneva system provides an insufficient number of stations to be sure of first motion, and that first motion is valueless beyond the first zone, except of course for very large shots, which we have not been considering."

Dr. Bethe's use of the highly regarded Soviet expert's own figures to prove the new difficulties that arose from the Hardtack data was an effective technique. Dr. Bethe had always commanded the deep respect of the entire Soviet delegation.

Dr. Fedorov intervened after the Bethe presentation, promising that Dr. Keilis-Borok would reply later. Then he covered Soviet embarrassment with invective. "It's not the Geneva system," Dr. Fedorov shouted, "but your statement that is wrong, and your data, your experiments, do not give you grounds for saying whether the Geneva system is good or bad."

At the same sixth meeting the Soviet Union presented seismograms showing signals from a 3.5-kiloton TNT explosion in granite. It was claimed that the surface-wave frequency of both the TNT and nuclear explosions would be two or three times higher than for earthquakes of the same energy value. The suggestion was that frequency-analysis of surface waves could be an important factor in distinguishing earthquakes from explosions.

The Russians returned again and again to the scattergun attack on the Hardtack series data. On December 2, Dr. Fisk tried to shut it off. After a typical exchange, he declared:

I have just listened with great interest, but without pleasure to Dr. Fedorov's remarks. It seems to us that nothing will be gained by insinuations regarding motives of delegations or by loose and easy statements tending to cast doubt on the ability or integrity of their scientists. It would be a matter of regret if overtones of this character were to detract from the scientific nature of our deliberations and thus to hamper us in reaching satisfactory conclusions. . . . I hope that we can return to discussing the important technical matters before us and no longer hang our arguments on what I consider to be quibbles.[16]

Dr. Bethe estimated at a later session that 12 or 15 per cent of the first motions from underground explosions would be registered as rarefactions because the actual first motion would be lost in the noise.

"We want to draw the conclusion," he said, "that if rarefactions are indicated by instruments as first motions this does not exclude the possibility that the event was an explosion."

Dr. Fedorov responded optimistically that some day instrumentation might be better so that the first motions could be properly detected. In any case, he said, this was a matter for the control organ. As for the estimate of 12 to 15 per cent, this was "guesswork."

Dr. Fedorov's optimistic repetition of his faith in science to find the true first motion drew a blunt response from Dr. Bethe. "You say that there will always be some apparatus which is well-enough designed to determine the true motion. This is not correct."

Dr. Fedorov replied: "I regret to cause dissatisfaction from time to time to our distinguished American colleagues."

Dr. Fisk retaliated that Dr. Fedorov's "argument is largely formalistic. It contains neither logic nor substance." [17] The Soviet argument was "not logical," and "not straightforward."

The Soviet chairman retorted: "After all there are three delegations to this Technical Working Group. We are not here to have a lesson read to us by you."

Dr. Fisk challenged the Soviet delegation to informal debate on the problem of first motion, but Dr. Sadovski came back with an insult: "We believe that if today we are going to be guided by the very low level of technique which was applied to the Hardtack data we shall certainly not get very far."

The session seemed to be heading for a walkout by one side or the other when Dr. Fisk suggested the discussion be advanced to the next item on the agenda. Dr. Fedorov immediately agreed and a break was avoided.

Decoupling

The Americans undertook on the same day to begin their discussion on decoupling, or the big-hole theory. First Dr. Fedorov tried to filibuster them out of it. The problem of "camouflage" of explosions could probably be "more appropriately put on the agenda of the conference of those who do not want to respect the agreement," he declared sarcastically.

Dr. Bethe was finally allowed to speak. He presented the basic theoretical development of the decoupling theory to indicate

under certain conditions the signal amplitude from an underground explosion can be a few hundred times smaller than that from an explosion of the same yield in our usual underground surroundings in Nevada.

[Decoupling would occur] if the explosion is set off in the middle of a large cavity in the rock, so large that the walls of the cavity are only deformed elastically by the explosion and suffer no permanent, plastic deformation.

Once the hole has been made large enough to insure elastic behavior of its walls, the seismic signal is no longer changed by further increase of the hole's size. This result, that the signal in an elastic medium is independent of the hole size, was known to the U.S. delegation to the Conference of Experts, 1958, but led us then to the erroneous conclusion that an explosion in a large hole would give the same signal as the same explosion closely tamped with rock. [He concluded, conservatively, that a decoupling factor of 250 would be possible in a large hole whose walls behaved elastically.]

If an explosion is set off in a big hole in hard rock, the signal from it is theoretically predicted to be about 300 times smaller than that from an explosion of the same yield in the usual Nevada surroundings.[18]

Dr. Albert Latter, the discoverer of the decoupling theory, followed Dr. Bethe to sketch in more of the details. The decoupling factor in a Rainier-type medium would be 40, he estimated, but in hard rock, such as salt, it would be more than 300. This means, he said, "that a 100-kiloton explosion would not even be detected and located by the experts control system."

In developing his theory, Dr. Latter said, the size of the cavity had been intentionally overestimated.

Additional decoupling factors were also possible, he told the experts of the Soviet Union:

The pressure spike could be greatly reduced in strength by filling the cavity with a light gas, such as hydrogen or helium, instead of air, or else by partially evacuating the cavity down to a pressure of about 0.01 of normal sea-level pressure. The result . . . might be that the size of the cavity could be reduced, but there is also the possibility that the decoupling factor could be further increased.

The latter possibility requires, in addition to eliminating the pressure spike, that a large amount of material, such as lamp black or powdered graphite, be added to the cavity.

[If this substance were distributed in capsules more or less uniformly throughout the cavity, so that the] mass of material in tons would occupy a volume of only 0.5 per cent of the total volume of the cavity . . . such a small volume of obstacles would not impede the flow of energy throughout the cavity. Now the important point is this:

The energy required to vaporize such a mass of material is more than ten times greater than the total energy of the explosion. If the energy from the explosion could be shared rapidly with all of this material, then most of the energy would be wasted in the non-pressure-producing form.

[To be effective this energy absorption ought to take place in about one second, and this might not be possible.] We believe, however, that it is important to mention this method in an incidental way since our analysis so far suggests that another factor of 10 in the decoupling might be achieved, leading to an *over-all decoupling factor of perhaps several thousand.*

Cavities already exist which could accommodate a yield of several kilotons. Moreover, the most experienced construction engineers in our country have given their opinion that cavities of the required volume are quite feasible for yields as large as 50 to 100 kilotons. It is also believed that it might be possible to use the same cavity for repeated shots.

These last comments were directed not only to suspicious Russians but to the complaints by Dr. Bethe and others that it was impractical to build holes of the size that would be necessary to decouple nuclear explosions effectively. This was a favorite theory of State Department negotiators who could not, for more than ten months, take the big-hole theory seriously without deserting their most basic theories.

Dr. Latter said his calculations showed that the underground cavity must have a volume of 70,000 cubic meters per kiloton and that the average pressure from the blast must not exceed one-half the overburden pressure. He indicated that it was a "real possibility" that the size of the hole could be substantially reduced without losing all decoupling.[19]

A 100-kiloton explosion in a big enough cavity would give a seismic signal corresponding to only one-third of a kiloton with Rainier coupling, Dr. Latter calculated. The decoupling factor could be increased by another factor of 10, or the size of the hole might be reduced by the same factor, he suggested, if heat-absorbing materials were introduced into the cavity.

Soviet scientists sneered at the Bethe and Latter presentations but promised to study them.

In the conference room, the decoupling theory quickly became taboo. The American chairman, Dr. Fisk, could not get the Russians to discuss it "on the record." He made frequent references to it, chiding them with the observation that the theory "has not in any sense been refuted." His pleas for informal talks to discuss not only the decoupling theory but also first motion and other outstanding scientific issues were ignored. Dr. Fedorov turned aside the talk of decoupling with self-righteous comments like, "We have not had underground explosions, we have not carried out such experiments." Sprinkled through the proceedings was a persistent Fedorov hostility. "I thank you very much for your very imprecise reply," he told Dr. Fisk at one point.[20]

The Soviet Union made its first substantive response to the Latter decoupling theory at the tenth meeting. Dr. Fedorov announced dramatically that his side would demolish the Latter-Bethe theories. "We have comments to make which show how and why we do not agree with the conclusions of the two speakers," Dr. Fedorov said.[21]

The young Soviet scientist, Dr. Gubkin, who had shown interest in the decoupling theory at the 1958 conference, presented the "refutation." He claimed that "solids and liquids comport themselves differently," and that "matter after decompression remains compressed; the formation is irreversible." The elastic effect that Dr. Latter expected, Dr. Gubkin suggested, would not occur. The "refutation" was too scientific for discussion at length here. Some of young Dr. Gubkin's barbs aimed at Dr. Bethe had little to do with science, however. The eminent European-born physicist who had always commanded such great respect from the Soviet scientists now was accused of "mixing oranges with bananas," or experimental and theoretical data.[22]

The decoupling factor of about 250 "we cannot accept," Dr. Gubkin declared. "In the case of an earlier-built cavity, a prefabricated cavity, there would be no decoupling." The theoretical assumptions made by Drs. Bethe and Latter did not "flow logically from theoretical consideration," he said, and were "highly contestable."

"We think that there is no difference between the effects of an explosion in a prefabricated cavity and an explosion in a tamped surrounding medium. This is a finding that we come to on the basis of our theoretical considerations," Dr. Gubkin declared. He dismissed Dr. Latter's suggestion that an additional decoupling factor of 10 could be obtained with carbon as an idea "put forward as a hypothesis, so that I do not think we should really try to criticize this seriously since the subject matter does not exist."

"We also seriously doubt the feasibility of building such a large cavity," Dr. Gubkin said. "At any rate, we are sure that the cavity would not give rise to the effects described by Dr. Bethe." [23]

After Dr. Gubkin's presentation, Dr. Sadovski dropped what amounted to a minor bombshell. He reported that *the Soviet Union had been experimenting with the decoupling theory*, thus contradicting Dr. Fedorov. The result, Dr. Sadovski reported, had been to prove that the seismic effect of an explosion "*can be increased* if it takes place in an underground cavity."

Soviet experiments had been conducted with chemical explosives, he reported, in underground cavities, where the ratio of cavity volume to volume of the explosives was 8,000 to 1.4. (According to Dr. Latter's calculations, this was too small by a factor of 10.) These experiments "did not give any result from the point of view we have mentioned," Dr.

Sadovski said. "We did not observe any increase in seismic propagation nor did we see any decrease in that factor," he added, thereby contradicting his earlier claim that the signal had been increased.

He added: "If you remember that ratio of volume to explosion was 1.4 to 8,000 you will see that this ratio is similar to the one mentioned by Dr. Latter in his statement." [24]

The series of Soviet experiments was conducted with chemical explosives of different energy-producing capacities, Dr. Sadovski reported. There had also been a "concrete experiment," he disclosed, with "dust." Presumably this was to test the Latter carbon-black theory. He reported that

> the charge was surrounded by a substance which produced dust, and the mass of this surrounding part was superior by 120 times to the volume of the explosive load. We measured the strength of first arrival in the first and in the second case, and there was no difference in the arrival of the first wave and the shock waves. The dust which was produced worked as well as a gas and transmitted its energy to the gas that surrounded it without any significant loss.

Other experiments were also conducted, Dr. Sadovski said, in such a way that the shock wave had to go through the dust screen. With great difficulty, he reported, the Soviet engineers succeeded in diminishing the energy coupled into the shock wave by a factor of 2.

He wound up with this parting shot: "To conclude, we would like to give our view that if we had half the government's budget to prepare the appropriate cavity we could obtain the result that no measurable seismic effect will be transmitted or obtained on the existing instruments, but I do not think that we should study such far-fetched cases." It could have been a confession of inferiority, but it was not intended to be.

Dr. Pasechnik followed with a discussion of chemical explosions the Soviet Union had undertaken in various mountain drillings in different rock species for seismic experimentation.

He reported that the volume of the chambers that had been used for the Soviet experiments with the decoupling theory had been about 15 to 30 cubic meters, sometimes a little larger. The actual shot was about 0.1–0.3 kilograms of explosive, sometimes larger.

He too claimed that the relation between the shot and the volume of the chamber was the same as prescribed in the Latter theory, although it obviously was not. Dr. Pasechnik repeated that signals at "some hundreds of meters from the region of the explosion did not fall but rather the amplitudes rose." Inexplicably, the United States had at that time conducted no underground decoupling experiments of its own so the Soviet data enjoyed a certain brief standing at the talks, by default.

> It appears to us [Dr. Pasechnik pontificated] that underground nuclear explosions in prefabricated underground chambers would be no less well re-

corded than explosions carried out in small-sized chambers; in fact, they would be better recorded, because when you have explosions taking place in large chambers, spectrally speaking, better oscillations will be generated; they will be lower-frequency oscillations than oscillations coming from small-chamber explosions.

During their dramatized presentations, the Russians illustrated their lectures on the "impossibility" of decoupling with equations written on the blackboard. At the end of that day's meeting, December 7, Dr. Latter copied the Soviet equations.

The next day he used the Russians' own equations to prove that decoupling was not impossible, as claimed, but indeed possible. Eye witnesses later reported that Dr. Fedorov literally turned gray and almost fainted when he understood the Americans were right and his Soviet experts were wrong. Some of the men at the table thought Dr. Fedorov, an excitable man at quiet moments, was about to have a heart attack.

The stakes were exceedingly high. If the Soviet Union had succeeded in proving that underground decoupling was not possible, the United States could be accused of having been caught in a "monstrous plot" to wreck the nuclear test-ban talks. American scientists would have been discredited. The pressures would have built quickly for the United States to accept a test ban.

If it were true, as the Americans at the conference sincerely believed, that the Russians genuinely believed they had caught the American scientists in a monumental error, the Soviet delegation must have sensed a golden opportunity to score another victory for Soviet science.

When the opposite result occurred, the Russian scientists' appalled reaction was understandable. Presumably Moscow would be wanting a report on the dramatic confrontation. It would be extremely embarrassing to admit that American scientists had defeated the Soviet scientists, the leaders of the world in sputniks. More than that, it would set back the Soviet hopes for a speedy conclusion of a test-ban treaty.

The American scientists later were closely questioned as to whether the Soviet team had been "playing possum" and had hoped to steer the American side off from suspicions that the Soviet Union was preparing a fruitful area for cheating.

Americans at the conference table did not believe this was possible. The Russians were too gleeful in announcing beforehand they would "demolish" the Latter theory, it was said. They came in with too obvious an anticipation of victory in the great scientific debate, the Americans said. "Scientists aren't that good actors."

Nor did they believe that Dr. Keilis-Borok and the others would walk into the trap of writing their equations on the board for Dr. Latter to copy and use against them.[25]

After the senior Soviet scientists had been shown the Latter proof, using Russian equations, Dr. Latter and Dr. Bethe held several informal sessions with Soviet scientists to give them the "freshman version" of the decoupling theory. In these meetings, the Americans were satisfied that they had convinced the Soviet scientists of the validity of the decoupling theory.

Nevertheless, in the later formal sessions, the Soviet scientists backed off their acceptance, if that is what it was—either on orders from Moscow or to ward off criticisms from Moscow for accepting the American thesis.

Both Dr. Latter and Dr. Bethe appealed to the Soviet scientists to accept the Rainier measurements as proof of the decoupling theory. It had been found that at distances of 110 meters and 140 meters from the explosion the Nevada tuff in which the bomb was fired underwent a peak displacement of about 15 centimeters. Only about 5 centimeters of this displacement was permanent. The rest was "elastic."

"We believe," Dr. Latter told the Soviet scientists, "that there is no logical way to question this result once the measurement of a 15-centimeter displacement at 110 meters from the Rainier explosion has been accepted. Moreover, we have examined this experiment with considerable care and find no reason to doubt its validity."

Professor Bethe, a gifted teacher, approached the problem as he believed the Soviet scientists approached it:

> Before the Rainier experiment, one might well have assumed that the porous tuff around the explosion would compact under the pressure applied; in other words, that its volume would decrease permanently due to the shock. . . . Actually . . . the experimental data from the Rainier explosion show that this was not the case. The indication is that there was no permanent compression of the rock in between. . . . I find this very strange, just as strange as you do, and it is obviously very strange when you remember that the Nevada tuff had about 10 per cent porosity. It is somewhat less strange if you take into account that these pores were mostly filled with water and the water could not be compressed. [He said that the hole had transmitted only 1 or 2 per cent of the energy of the blast at a few kilometers.]
>
> I think it is difficult to find any fault in the theory of the elastic behavior; in fact, I think we all agree on that. So what we are asking you to believe is the measurements we have made on the Rainier explosion and, according to these measurements, the Rainier signal was about four times what you would get in a large elastic cavity in the same medium and about 300 times what you would get in a large cavity in very hard rock.[26]

The British delegation, aware for some months of the decoupling theory, had viewed it with deep reservations. The prospect that the theory might lead to a break-up of the nuclear-test negotiations was not a happy one for British policy-makers. Sir William Penney, the Chairman of the British delegation to the technical conference, expressed one of the fears that had haunted American scientists and policy-makers both, and had been partly responsible for the reticence about discussing it with the Russians or presenting it to the American public:

"Certainly, here we have prepared a textbook on the violation in a hole."

Sir William had other more hopeful comments about the big hole. It would be very expensive and it might not work in practice, he said. "There would be quite a high cost in scientific effort in getting ready in order to be sure that the hole-cheating was not going to fail because we had the wrong ideas." The theory was based, he observed, on "an idealized situation. . . . I am not sure how far reality would differ from this theoretical model."

There would have to be an entrance to the hole and the stress would be "quite different" from that of a perfect sphere. The effect of gravity had not been taken into account, Sir William suggested. Dr. Bethe's theory, he said, is that the roof would not fall in, but in a real hole "one just does not know." As for achieving an additional decoupling factor by sprinkling graphite in the hole, "I am very doubtful whether it is in fact possible to distribute graphite powder uniformly in a cavity in the way [Dr. Latter] assumes for his calculations." Sir William observed that "fine powders have a way of binding together when you try to distribute them quickly. . . . I therefore do not really accept the graphite calculation, although it may have a small factor which I do not think is important."

The theory was probably reliable, Sir William said, but "it has in it certain unknowns on the practical side." [27]

Having expressed these doubts, the British disclosed that they too had conducted their own experiments in decoupling. Unlike the Russians, *they succeeded in proving the theory*, although they were not ready to accept 300–1 as the correct decoupling factor.

Dr. I. Maddock described the experiment, conducted in a limestone medium. Thirty kilograms of high explosives were fired in the center of a chamber 6 by 4 by 3 meters. There had been 18 meters of overburden over the chamber, produced by blocking an already existing tunnel that joined two quarries. The tunnel was blocked with 1 meter of concrete followed by 6 meters of rubble. Another charge, this time closely coupled, was exploded in the same medium. This was a 3.6-kilogram chemical charge.

The closely coupled charge, roughly one-tenth the size of the decoupled charge, produced seismic signals that were "if anything, larger" than the decoupled explosion, Dr. Maddock reported. The Americans had compared tuff with hard rock to achieve their 300-to-1 decoupling, Dr. Maddock pointed out, while the British experiment had been in the same medium, limestone. In addition, the British experiment was conducted in a chamber that had not been spherical. Two of the walls were concrete, backed by loose filling, not the compact mediums the Latter theory foresaw.

"This simple experiment demonstrates," Dr. Maddock informed the Russians, "that with only a crude chamber and using conditions which are a long way removed from those postulated by Professor Bethe and Dr. Latter, it is possible to achieve a decoupling factor of about one order of magnitude for explosions of the order of 30 kilograms of high explosives under the conditions stated."

It was another telling blow against the Soviet argumentation at the conference. Dr. Fedorov, seldom at a loss for words, suggested that "perhaps, for the sake of economizing time, we could waive the debate on this." [28]

For the next week, decoupling was not discussed in the formal sessions.

At the December 14 formal meeting, however, the Soviet delegation abruptly returned to its attack on the decoupling theory. Since Soviet scientists had apparently been convinced in informal sessions that the theory was correct, this was a strange performance.

Dr. Sadovski noted in the on-the-record meeting that the British decoupling factor was much smaller than Dr. Latter's and that the Soviet Union, in its experiments, had found no decoupling factor at all. Besides the 3.1-kiloton chemical explosion in granite, which the Russians had mentioned previously, Dr. Sadovski now reported another 1-kiloton explosion in clay where the volume of the chamber was 300 to 400 times the volume of the explosive charge. This was a cavity, of course, not nearly large enough to fit the Latter decoupling theory either.

Dr. Sadovski charged that the Rainier measurements on which the United States based its experimental proof were not reliable, that the Hardtack series had produced no data on decoupling, and that Dr. Bethe, who was wrong in 1958 about the decoupling theory, could be wrong again. [29]

Dr. Latter expressed surprise that Dr. Sadovski still disagreed. "I thought that in our informal meeting we had agreed on some very important points," Dr. Latter said, for the record. Soviet and American scientists had agreed on the correlations between the Rainier data and the Soviet high explosives, he recalled. The big-hole theory conformed to both Soviet and American experiments, not only to mathematical formulas, Dr. Latter said. In the Soviet experiments where there had been no decoupling, the size and depth requirements for the cavity had not been met, Dr. Latter noted, "and we are not surprised that the decoupling was not observed."

As for the British experiment, Dr. Latter noted that "the size of the cavity was small by a factor of almost four relative to the condition we stipulated." In fact, Dr. Latter suggested, the British experiment "may have a very important consequence on the practicability of constructing large cavities." The size of the hole possibly could be reduced considerably without degrading the decoupling completely, Dr. Latter suggested.[30]

Apparently on instructions from Moscow, Dr. Sadovski then read this official Soviet attitude toward the decoupling theory into the record:

> We consider that now, in the present state of knowledge, it would be premature to come to practical conclusions on the basis of the material put before us by Drs. Bethe and Latter, no matter how intelligent and elegantly formulated the conclusions and assertions may appear.

The United States, for its part, kept the record clear on what had gone on in the unrecorded informal meetings. Dr. Fisk said:

> I have to admit that I'm mildly astonished by Dr. Sadovski's statements, particularly in view of the rather lengthy discussion I had with Professor Bethe following their two informal meetings. Professor Bethe's impression, and the one that he conveyed to me, was that our Soviet colleagues understood and agreed with the theory of the coupling and decoupling in the big hole. I believe there was some debate on the question of whether or not the measurements of Rainier had given an overestimate.

As to the feasibility of building the huge underground caverns that would be necessary to decouple nuclear explosions, Dr. Fisk said, "Actually it turns out to be rather easier in salt formations than I, at least, had expected."

Dr. Sadovski then retreated part way:

> We really do not harbor any objections to the theoretical construction put forward by Dr. Latter and Dr. Bethe. . . . Our view [is that] at the present the decoupling theory is speculative in nature and not confirmed by facts. Consequently, the Soviet delegation finds further discussion of it within this technical group premature. We have no proposal to make which would merit being given a place in the final report of the group.[31]

In view of the previous Soviet reports of experimental disproof of the Latter theory, this was another strangely unscientific position to take.

On-Site Inspection

At this conference, it was Dr. Fisk, the Chairman of the American delegation, who voiced the deep misgivings of United States scientists, which had prevailed for more than a year, about the effectiveness of the on-site inspection method. In a formal statement, Dr. Fisk said:

> Our present evaluation of on-site inspection would not be inconsistent with the 1958 [Experts] statement, *though it would emphasize that the probability of identification may be very small.* . . .
> The various geophysical techniques, such as radiation, magnetic, gravity, electrical, and electromagnetic surveys, seismic profiling, post-shock listening with geophones, and so on, *appear to be less useful in locating sites of*

underground nuclear explosions than had been thought, although several of these techniques warrant further study.[32]

Next day the Soviet chairman, Dr. Fedorov, sought to pour soothing syrup on the previous day's worries expressed by the United States:

> If a nuclear explosion takes place, let us say, in the ocean, and if the inspection vessel arrives late, a certain period of time after the explosion, then the chances of finding out what occurred and of determining whether there was a nuclear explosion are smaller in view of the fact that the radioactive material will have mixed in the waters of the ocean and will have traveled over great distances.

As for underground nuclear tests, Dr. Federov said, the radioactive material would remain where it was confined for years. "In certain cases we need more time and in other cases less time," but as the 1958 experts' report had said, "With the help of the inspection, a deep underground explosion will always be detected." Keep hunting long enough, in other words, and the evidence is bound to be discovered.

Dr. Fisk responded skeptically. Radioactive debris might last for years, he acknowledged, "but the inspection presumably would not. Particularly if the event were located within an area of 100 square miles *it might, indeed, be very problematical that the actual event would ever be discovered,"* Dr. Fisk warned.

Dr. Fedorov may have been suggesting that a Soviet on-site inspection team might be ready to stay for years in a suspected area to check out every possibility of a nuclear explosion. Dr. Fisk, on the other hand, indicated no such desire on the part of the United States.

Dr. Bethe was unexpectedly nettled by the extravagant Fedorov claim. Knowing as well as he did the arguments of his rival, Dr. Edward Teller, and others who were deeply worried about the ineffectiveness of on-site inspection, he told Dr. Fedorov:

> You probably remember that in the Rainier explosion the debris was located in the region of 55 feet from the center of the explosion, and if my arithmetic is correct, and if the area in which the seismic evidence locates the explosion is 100 square kilometers, this requires 500,000 drillings, each taking a month or so. Since I believe your delegation will permit 2 or 3 inspectors to go to the place, we can calculate how long that will take them.[33]

Dr. Fedorov was full of scorn. "The result which you will get will not be equal to infinity," he said, somewhat incongruously. Geophysical knowledge would restrict the area where drilling would be necessary. "You would not have to drill through the whole area."

Dr. Bethe shot back that geophysical evidence is "not very useful."

Dr. Fisk then made a curious comment. It typified the failure of the American scientists to discuss the ineffectiveness of on-site inspection publicly and indicated that this was, perhaps, deliberate.

"Mr. Chairman," he said, addressing Dr. Fedorov, "we do not intend to make any great issue of this." [34]

He suggested a joint research program on the difficulties of on-site inspection. Further papers would be presented pointing out the need for more research, Dr. Fisk said, but he did not intend to present the material orally or discuss it in great detail. He did not say why. These papers are not a matter of public record.

A few days later, Dr. Fedorov returned to the problem of on-site inspection. He did not accept the Fisk evaluation that geophones were not helpful in locating an underground nuclear explosion. The American findings "gave only preliminary, provisional results," Dr. Fedorov remarked, "that could not lead us to a conclusion." The Soviet chairman said he believed the cavity of an underground nuclear explosion would be a "permanent source of noise or other seismic signals." [35]

In any event, Dr. Fedorov said, all this discussion of the effectiveness of on-site inspection was something that the future control organ should deal with, not Technical Working Group II.

Dr. Fisk responded that "geophones were used after some of these explosions [Hardtack] and, at least after a few minutes, did not give signals."

At the thirteenth session, Dr. Fisk put on the record, in the most forceful terms ever used in an official paper, United States Government misgivings about the technique of on-site inspection.

The Soviet chairman seemed to assign "a 100 per cent probability of success to identification by inspection," Dr. Fisk observed. "We can't understand how he could make such a statement. While we do not disagree with the conclusion of the 1958 Conference which states that there will always be a possibility of detection, it is our opinion *the probability may be very small.*"

The important "parameters," Dr. Fisk said, would be topography, vegetative cover, climatic conditions, geologic environment, location with respect to seismic zones, population, and human activity.

"The important thing to note," Dr. Fisk said, "is that *there is no assurance that initiation of an on-site inspection will, in fact, result in accurate identification of a seismic cause.*"

An ocean shot would be easy to detect, he observed, leaving open the problem of identification of the guilty party.

As for an underground shot, however, Dr. Fisk said, "*if it were ever the purpose of a violator to attempt to hide such an event the task of an on-site inspection group might be so great and so difficult that the probability of success would be close to zero.*"

Dr. Fisk agreed there should be on-site inspections and that it would be "an important deterrent." He did not explain how important the deterrent would be if the violator knew that on-site inspection possibilities of success would be "*close to zero.*"

Criteria

The Soviet delegation introduced its concept of superstrict criteria for the dispatch of on-site inspection teams at the eighth meeting. The criteria, the Russians had been contending for a long time, should be based on "objective readings of instruments and conditions which would give the right to dispatch inspection teams to the site of an event suspected of being a nuclear explosion."

Professor Ustyumenko presented the formal Soviet proposal. It set out such carefully contrived criteria that the dispatch of the on-site inspection teams would have been a rare event. He began by proposing to exclude all suspicious events "in densely populated areas" or with "a depth of origin beyond the modern possibilities open to mankind."

He did not explain either of these exclusions. Presumably he thought that no violator would try to set off an explosion in a densely populated area for fear of being caught. Any attempt to establish a floor below which, by definition, nuclear tests could not be held, could become an incentive to a violator unless the floor were set so low as to be meaningless.

The Ustyumenko criteria were a formula for frustration of any on-site inspections at all, whatever the quotas that might be set in advance. First, he suggested, first-motion compressions, the previously-agreed "trade-mark" of explosions, should be recorded at five stations on various azimuthal bearings, he said. The Hardtack series had demolished all hope on the American side that this many stations in the Geneva system would record compressions.

And the vibration frequency in "Rayleigh waves" from nuclear tests should be four times greater than the typical Rayleigh waves from earthquakes, Ustyumenko said. This was a brand new criterion, which assumed it had been proved that the frequency of explosions' signals was always much greater than the frequency from natural earthquakes. This was far from established, in the American view.

"If, in one or two control posts within a radius of 3,500 kilometers from the epicenter, the first motion of longitudinal waves shows rarefaction," the formal Soviet proposal read, "the suspicion that a nuclear event has occurred is eliminated and the event is classed an earthquake."

This totally disregarded the Hardtack II findings that nuclear explosions, contrary to expectations, frequently produce first-motion rarefactions. American seismologists could not think of any set of circumstances under which two rarefactions would not appear among the stations within 3,500 kilometers from the epicenter. Under the Russians' own criterion the Blanca shot would have been "classed an earthquake" and no on-site inspection would have been permitted.

The Soviet proposal also made what could have become official provisions for decoys and jamming:

"Seismic events for which it is not possible with an accuracy up to 200 square kilometers to determine the position of the epicenter should also not be subject to on-site inspection," the formal Soviet proposal suggested.

This could have become an open invitation to a would-be violator to jam control-station seismographs or set up decoys which would prevent the stations from locating a suspicious event.

In order to dispatch an on-site inspection team, the Soviet delegation suggested, the control system would have to record compressions at five stations, no more than one rarefaction within a radius of 3,500 kilometers, *and*, if the event in question could not be explained as an earthquake, "then the party concerned can if it deems fit carry out within the quota agreed upon a *stage-by-stage* inspection on the national territory of the other party in accordance with the procedure laid down in the treaty on the discontinuance of nuclear-weapons tests."

This was another formula for frustration of on-site inspection. Compressions would likely appear only at close stations and the chances were that five would never be that close. More than one rarefaction would be routine. The stages prescribed would become a "backstop" against effective inspection.

The Soviet Union explained what it meant by stage-by-stage inspection:

1. Over-all survey of the region of the suspected event by a relatively small group of inspectors (two to three persons);

2. A geophysical survey of the region;

3. Boring on the site of the underground nuclear explosion for the purpose of obtaining radioactive samples.

"If during the first stage of inspection the event is identified as a natural one, the subsequent stages of inspection shall not be carried out," the Soviet proposal stated.[36]

How a quick comprehensive survey of 200 square kilometers could have been conducted by only two or three persons was not explained. No provision was made for aerial surveys.

Dr. Fisk presented the critique of Russian criteria at the twelfth meeting. He found them "inflexible," he said, and no allowances were made for the many indeterminate cases that were bound to arise. The Soviet paper also had assumed a precision of seismology, Dr. Fisk declared, "which present-day techniques have not achieved." [37]

He then listed seven points of dispute on the Soviet criteria:

1. No allowance had been made for spurious rarefactions.

2. A proposal that occurrence of surface waves with dominant or predominant periods of more than five seconds should be taken to be earthquakes would "literally" have caused both the Blanca and Logan underground nuclear tests to have been categorized as earthquakes.

3. The Soviet criteria contained no mention of how to decide the

initial direction of a given seismic reading. (This would require a discussion of noise and the relation of first motion to the noise levels, a discussion the Russians had been eager to evade.)

4. The proposal to exclude from inspection seismic events that could not be located within an accuracy of 200 square kilometers would seriously restrict the on-site inspection teams. "In dealing with seismic events in the Rainier-Logan class we may reasonably expect uncertainty in location which exceeds this figure," Dr. Fisk said. Under the Soviet criteria, Dr. Fisk declared, the Rainier shot would not have been subject to inspection. He indicated that the seismic detection of the Rainier explosion, even though it had been picked up 2,300 miles away in Alaska, had not been accurately located by stations at distances provided for in the 1958 Experts Conference.

5. The Soviet proposal that focal depth of an underground disturbance be used as a criterion in identifying earthquakes was "appropriate" but there were "uncertainties," Dr. Fisk said. He suggested that the "floor" below which all disturbances would be considered as earthquakes should be about 60 kilometers.

6. The Soviet proposal had again elevated to full status the data that might be obtained from national observatories. This would presuppose that the staff, the equipment, and the reliability of all national observatories would be on a par with the control posts. Since the performance at most national observatories would not be up to control-post standards, it would be more prudent to consider their data as supplementary only.

7. The Soviet proposal made no provision for the swift gathering of data on a suspected event. It was important to emphasize that the materials from the various stations should be gathered "with the utmost dispatch, preferably by modern communication methods," Dr. Fisk said. He suggested that the Soviet experience in telemetering seismograms would be "very useful" in that connection.

The Soviet scientists still wanted to admit data from national stations. Dr. Fedorov remarked indignantly: We took your Hardtack data from national observatories. Why don't you take other data from the same sources? Dr. Fisk had a ready answer: Yes, you did, and you also complained that some signals were not calibrated. Moreover, *Izvestia* criticized the Soviet Union's own seismic stations in the Caucasus.[38]

The American proposal for criteria to initiate on-site inspection was presented on December 11. All seismic events occurring in aseismic areas should be considered eligible for inspection. Aseismic areas were defined as those areas "at a distance of more than 100 kilometers from the epicenter of a located earthquake of magnitude 4.4 or greater."

To locate seismic events there should be at least four clearly measurable arrival times, including longitudinal waves from three control posts, the United States stipulated. The area eligible for inspection would be 500 square kilometers (not 200 as the Soviet Union proposed).

If there were good data in all four 90° quadrants around an epicenter, the American criteria stated, the area eligible for inspection could be confined to 200 square kilometers.

In the process of identifying earthquakes, the United States suggested that a located seismic event could be ruled ineligible for inspection "if, and only if," it fulfilled one or more of the following five criteria:

1. Depth of focus was below 60 kilometers.

2. The epicenter was in the deep open ocean and there was no corresponding hydroacoustic signal.

3. The event was established within forty-eight hours to be a fore-shock by the occurrence of a larger underground event with a magnitude of at least 6. The eligibility of the second event would be determined separately.

4. The directions of first motion on clearly-recorded seismograms strongly indicated an earthquake. First motions recorded in the shadow zone between 1,100 kilometers and 2,500 kilometers should not be used. First motions beyond 3,500 kilometers should not be used for events of magnitude 5.5 or smaller. In addition, the "apparent direction of first motion" should also meet these other minimum conditions to be considered "clearly recorded":

a. The amplitude of first motion should be twice as large as any noise in the preceding few minutes.

b. The amplitudes of subsequent motions from the shock should be twenty times larger than the noise at epicentral distances less than 700 kilometers and forty times larger beyond 700 kilometers.

c. At least four rarefactions should be recorded in two opposite quadrants and these same two quadrants should contain not more than 15 per cent compressions among the clearly recorded first motions of the event in order "strongly" to indicate an earthquake.

5. It is established to be an aftershock of a seismic event of at least magnitude 6, clearly identified as an earthquake. The aftershock must occur less than a week after the main shock and must have an epicenter within 10 kilometers of the main shock.

The United States plan called for using only control-post data as basic information, relegating the recordings from independent seismic stations to a "supplementary" category.

Several techniques for using auxiliary seismological information were also listed in the American paper to decide whether an on-site inspection should be made.

Sir William Penney suggested at the thirteenth meeting that the problem of criteria for dispatching on-site inspection teams should be divided into two parts: first, that part dealing with firm criteria; second, that part dealing with "suggestive phenomena" where the data was not firm.

The suggestive phenomena, he said, should be used only after an event had been declared eligible for inspection but before on-site inspectors were dispatched.

Dr. Fedorov defended all the Soviet criteria. On the plan to except heavily populated areas from inspection, he declared: "No one is likely to carry out an underground explosion in a large city; I think this just does not make sense. . . . I think San Francisco would suffer more than any other town" if this exception were not made.

Dr. Fisk responded: "I, myself, think it rather unlikely that San Francisco would be a proper scene for such an activity. In fact, both Dr. Brown and Dr. Panofsky, who are natives of San Francisco, extend to you an invitation to visit them in that city, with safe conduct."

"After the conclusion of the agreement," Dr. Fedorov replied, "we entirely accept."

After the chuckles had subsided, however, disagreement on the Soviet proposal to except large, heavily populated areas still stood.

In the case of ambiguous signals of an underground event, Dr. Fedorov suggested, it would be better to avoid controversy by looking the other way. "There can be cases when nothing can be obtained from the readings of the control posts," he noted. "In order to do away with the possible discussions and controversy that might occur on the subject, we believe that . . . this should not be considered as an event that will be further studied. . . . We do not consider that there is such an event if the event is not sufficiently accurately determined." [39]

Dr. Fedorov later complained that the American plan for considering as suspicious everything that cannot be identified as an earthquake "is a rather exotic approach to the problem." [40]

In the discussions on first-motion criteria, Dr. Panofsky listed three ways that a reversal of first motion could happen: first, because of a bad signal-to-noise ratio; second, by "physical processes"; and third, by error, incorrect observation, reversing leads, and so forth. Reversal by noise would be the dominant problem, Dr. Panofsky predicted, apparently unwilling to suggest that any power might deliberately try to cheat.

Dr. Fedorov approached the inspection problem from the standpoint of the number of likely violations, rather than from the standpoint of the number of unidentified events which would mask them. "The number of explosions [after a ban] will necessarily be very small," Dr. Fedorov said. "We cannot count them in thousands, or in hundreds, even if the violators were to work very hard indeed, with great zeal, and without taking into account the danger of being caught. We believe that the chances are that there will be no explosions, but perhaps there will be a few." [41]

The Case of the Ambiguous Seismometer

The argument that developed over the Benioff seismometer, the American instrument discussed in the 1958 conference, was another example of the incredible wrangles that lay ahead if a nuclear-test-ban control system were ever set up.

The Conference of Experts had described a seismometer that was to be used at the 180 control stations. The wording of the report, it was discovered during the Technical Working Group II conference, had been ambiguous in English but not in the Russian translation. In the Russian version, it was prescribed that the seismometer should have a natural period or frequency of one second. In the English version, it was stated that there should be maximum amplification of the instrument at a period of one second. The English version left open the question of whether the maximum amplification should be only at one second or whether the maximum could apply to a whole band of frequencies.

Soviet scientists apparently understood the Russian version to mean that their own seismometer, with a one-second period, was the prescribed instrument for the control system. The United States and Britain, on the other hand, understood that the broader-band Benioff seismometer, which had been the instrument used to monitor the Rainier nuclear blast, and was discussed at Geneva in 1958 as if it were accepted as the "official" instrument, should be the control system's basic seismometer.

In the American view, the Russian version of the 1958 report was improbable, to put it charitably. It described an instrument that had not been used at all in the Rainier monitoring. But the wording of the experts report was clearly open to the Russian interpretation. It was partly on this tenuous basis that the Russians criticized the Americans for not using instrumentation prescribed by the 1958 experts report in monitoring the Hardtack II series. There may have been trickery on this point in the 1958 experts conference, but the Americans were stuck with it.

At the 1959 conference, the American experts knew that the one-second-period seismometer favored by the Russians would not perform as well as the one-third-second period Benioff seismometer. First the Americans confirmed their beliefs with theoretical analyses. Then the Americans arranged to have a one-second-period seismometer built to Russian specification in the United States. It was operated alongside a Benioff seismometer. On December 9, the two machines picked up an earthquake. The Benioff instrument recorded the first motion much more clearly than the instrument built according to Russian specification.

On December 15, the American delegation sprang its surprise in Geneva. The Soviet-design, American-built seismometer had been operated in Oklahoma from December 9 to December 15, Dr. Romney reported. As luck would have it, he said, there was a large-enough earthquake on December 9 to test the apparatus. *The American seismometer installed at the same site produced a signal five times the noise level while the Soviet-favored instrument produced a signal only half as large as the noise.*[42]

The Benioff apparatus was shown to be ten times as good as the Russian instrument, at least in this one case.

Dr. Sadovski responded magnanimously. He welcomed evidence that the United States side "has tackled seriously the elaboration of new instruments which I think would be superior to the present Benioff [American] one." Dr. Fisk asked if the Russian was trying to be funny. "I was serious," Dr. Sadovski replied as the Americans threw up their hands.[43]

The Russians never did recognize the superiority of the Benioff seismometer. They did inquire cutely whether the United States would like to introduce the Benioff machine as a possible improvement to the system. The United States was then in the laughable position of being offered an opportunity to introduce as an improvement the very seismometer on which the 1958 control system was based.

The American scientists went along with the gag. They would be glad to introduce the Benioff instrument as an "improvement" for the system, they responded, but it should be made clear that it was this instrument that had produced both the Rainier and Hardtack data. The Russians would have had to admit, then, that the Hardtack data had been based on the "improved" system. They could not bring themselves to admit this. It was the Russians' move next, but they made none. The matter was left unsolved. In the final report, however, the Russians stuck by their charge that the instrumentation to monitor the Hardtack series had not conformed to the experts' specifications.

The ambiguity about the prescribed seismometer for the control system still stands. It would seem likely, if the Soviet Union follows through on its past policy of obtaining as little inspection as possible, that the Soviet Union would continue to insist on the inferior Russian instrument, the one-second-period seismometer.

This was another bridge left to be crossed before an inspection system for a nuclear test-ban could be installed and operated.

Prelude to Breakup

The Soviet scientists persisted to the end in their efforts to revise American estimates of explosion magnitudes. The long debates usually degenerated into exercises in name-calling. The Russians spoke patronizingly of "the main error made by Dr. Romney and Dr. Brown" and told the parable of "an unobjective seismologist who was trying to get the lowest possible readings of magnitude." Dr. Romney spoke of "the incredibly complicated distortion of the magnitude scales" by the Russians.[44]

The failure to agree on magnitudes of signals and the correlation between earthquakes and nuclear explosions was becoming the rock on which the conference was to fail. Dr. Panofsky warned on December 16 that it was "extremely serious" that the United States and Russian experts disagreed "on the simple measurements of primary data." For one thing, writing criteria for identifying earthquakes could hardly be discussed "with the basic measurements in doubt," Dr. Panofsky observed.

But there was a second reason, he added, that the impasse was extremely serious: "It introduces a new fact into the assessment of the system, namely, the probability that the various representatives of the control organ will not read the same amplitudes out of the same data."

This was perhaps the single most important lesson of the Technical Working Group II conference. Even if the Soviet Union could be brought to agree to a written prescription for "effective" inspection, the actions of the inspection groups would still be subject to a frustration-by-wrangling of which the Russians were giving the West a preview at Geneva.

Dr. Riznichenko, answering Dr. Panofsky, obligingly pantomimed a Soviet inspector in action. He was embittered about being "treated as a child." He complained of the "trick" the United States was using in "manipulating" magnitudes. The American performance was like stating the equality that a person who is half alive is equal to one who is half dead, Dr. Riznichenko said. "If one multiplies both sides of the equation by two, one gets a result that a man who is alive equals a man who is dead."

At the December 16 meeting, Dr. Fedorov made a formal complaint of "manipulation" against the American scientists:

> We must state, and here I am being quite sincere, that the manipulations made with the same identical data, giving the same values with different significance, the different interpretations that you yourself placed on the same operations, the misstatements that we find in the documents concerning the instruments used for the Hardtack operation, and—in our view —the erroneous provisions that we find in a number of your documents, all this, of course, obliges us more and more frequently to consider your data as being somewhat tendentious information.

Tempers were getting shorter and shorter on both sides.

On December 17, Dr. Fedorov introduced another charge that the United States had introduced new data. He referred to a new analysis of the Hardtack data to prove in another way the validity of the American view. Dr. Romney retorted that the Soviet Union could have derived the same data from seismograms presented to the Soviet Union at the beginning of the conference.

Dr. Fisk intervened a little later to observe:

> It seems to me that in a certain sense Professor Fedorov is making a circus of this operation. No new data were presented this morning by Dr. Romney, for reasons which you, Professor Fedorov, very well know, and I think that it is wrong for you to insinuate that Dr. Romney either is being dishonest or has said something he should not have said.

Dr. Fedorov complained sarcastically that Dr. Romney had not provided all his measurements immediately.

In his "synthetic indignation," Dr. Fisk charged, Professor Fedorov "has taken my colleagues to task in an unjustifiable way it seems to me. . . . Why did you ask on the first day for the seismograms, of which we gave you 250 within a short time of your request, if you did not put them to any use? What did you want to do with them?" The Chairman of the American delegation complained that Dr. Fedorov had "turned this into largely a political meeting rather than keeping it on a strictly technical plane."

Dr. Fedorov replied with a diversionary attack on Dr. Albert Latter, recalling that he had been one of the builders of the atomic bomb.

The next day, Dr. Latter was chosen by the Americans to present a new paper. It suggested that identifying earthquakes be attempted with an analysis of second motion instead of the first motion. This would have the advantage, he said, that a second-motion signal is roughly ten times as great as the first.[45] Dr. Latter estimated that the new theory would identify earthquakes with a 50 per cent certainty above 30 kilotons approximately. Dr. Fedorov sneered.

Tensions continued to rise and it became clear that little would be agreed at the meeting. In a morning session, December 18, the participants composed their agreements on improvements in the system. The Soviet Union was willing to accept most of the American suggestions. Beyond that, however, the delegations were able to agree only that it would be up to the political committee whether the experts should reconvene. They were on the verge of break-off. During the noon recess it was decided to continue long enough to wind up their work on the details of the improvement section. Language for the improvement section even became difficult and the conference erupted into a new argument. Dr. Fedorov complained "your stubbornness only confirms our suspicions."

After a twenty-minute informal conference outside the room, beyond earshot of the recorders, Dr. Fisk came back to suggest that the conference produce three separate reports, one by the British delegation, one by the Soviet delegation, and the third by the United States. "I would like to ask you to adopt a serious attitude toward what we are doing," Dr. Fedorov told Dr. Fisk in the closing minutes of the final session.[46] "I am quite serious," Dr. Fisk replied. It was that afternoon that the Technical Working Group II conference ended in a final "compromise." They agreed to disagree on everything except system improvements, to produce three separate reports to the political committee, and to end the technical discussions.

On December 19, Technical Working Group II reported to the Conference on the Discontinuance of Nuclear Weapons Tests that it had met in twenty-one sessions, agreed on an agenda and on possible improvements of the technique and instrumentation in detecting tests, but disagreed on everything else.

Technical Working Group II made three recommendations for improvements in the 1958 control system. Control posts should install three-component, long-period seismometers of periods greater than ten seconds, the group said, the numbers of short-period vertical seismometers at control stations should be raised from ten to 100, and optimum short-period seismometers should be chosen for best registering first motion in the presence of noise.

Each delegation then made its own comment on the conference, presenting its own rationale for the disagreements that developed.

Soviet Statement

The Soviet statement criticized the instrumentation used in the Hardtack tests, the American methods of deriving magnitudes, the United States conclusions on the usefulness of first motion, the significance of the new seismic data, and American criteria for initiating on-site inspections.

In monitoring the Hardtack II series, the Soviet report said, "not one of the stations situated in the United States used the array of seismic instruments recommended in the experts report." The assertion in the United States statement of January 5, 1959, that all stations were equipped as recommended at Geneva, thus was exposed as "a misrepresentation, as the United States delegation itself has virtually admitted."

The American scientists had not admitted this. They argued that there had been no claim the stations had been equipped as described by the Geneva conference of 1958. They pointed out, however, that the instrumentation was good enough to prove the 1958 experts conference had overestimated detection and identification possibilities of a control system.

> The document of 5 January and the report to the conference give the impression of a large-scale, well-conducted experiment [the Soviet experts said in their report]. In actual fact, the situation was quite different. It was ascertained during the meetings of the group that of the dozens of seismic stations in the United States, only a small proportion possessed instruments that satisfy, if not the recommendations of the Conference of Experts, even the elementary conditions demanded by any scientific instrument. For example the Logan explosion was registered by fifty-four seismic stations in the United States. However, only about one-half of them [twenty-eight] had properly calibrated instruments and, in the opinion of the United States seismologists themselves, seismograms from only sixteen of these twenty-eight could be used for analysis. It is indeed surprising that the instrumentation was not calibrated at least for the period during which these unique experiments were to be conducted.

The Soviet experts also charged that American scientists had "repeatedly modified the primary data submitted by them in support of various conclusions." They mentioned the example of the Rainier explosion's magnitude, which was revised from 4.6 to 4.25 and later to 4.07–4.06. They complained that the magnitude of the Tamalpais explosion had also "undergone similar perturbation," from 3.1 down to 2.6.

The Soviets, Dr. Fedorov said, had tried to approach the material presented them "with the utmost confidence in its reliability, on the assumption that it was the result of careful scientific work.

[But the] manipulations of the primary data, the erroneous findings in the documents presented by the United States experts and the fact that the instrumentation used for the observing of the tests was not in conformity with the 1958 Geneva recommendations have compelled the Soviet scientists to adopt a more cautious attitude toward the quality and objectivity of the figures that were supplied by the Americans.

This was strong language, even for the Soviet Union, and could have been intended as justification for Soviet refusal to participate any further in scientific examination of disarmament problems. The technical conferences had been an experiment for Moscow, too, in the potentialities of achieving political objectives by scientific conferences. The first one, in 1958, may have turned out satisfactorily, but the 1959 effort obviously had not, from the Soviet viewpoint.

The Soviet scientists charged flatly that their American counterparts did not know how to figure magnitude, even though Americans had invented the methods the Soviet Union was using. By mixing up different scales in figuring average magnitudes, they claimed, the American scientists had produced "meaningless" figures. The magnitudes for Rainier, Logan, and Blanca explosions were "greatly undervalued," the Soviet experts said. They themselves knew how to do it better. Instead of 4.07, the Rainier-shot magnitude should have been 4.7; instead of 4.4, the Logan shot should have been 4.95; and instead of 4.8, the Blanca shot should have been 5.2, the Soviet scientists said.

Their method was to exclude signals from the shadow zone, where the signals were not as large. This was contrary to accepted international practice. The omission of these relatively low readings in figuring the averages accounted for the "corrected" magnitude derived by the Soviet Union. It was a classic example of the old saying that figures don't lie, but liars can figure.

By inflating the magnitudes produced by the Hardtack underground nuclear shots the Soviet scientists were able to claim that there would be many fewer unidentified earthquakes and thus a much smaller problem of inspection. There would be not 25,000 but only 3,000 earthquakes equivalent to or bigger than explosions of 1 kiloton. Instead of 5,800 above 5 kilotons, there would be only 1,500, the Russians said; instead of 3,000 at 10 kilotons, there would only be 1,000; instead of 1,600 at 20 kilotons, there would only be 800.

The Soviet experts thus were able to "prove" that "the annual numbers of earthquakes throughout the world equivalent to explosions of given yield are, if anything, smaller than the numbers estimated at Geneva in 1958 and not one and a half or two times greater, as is asserted in the United States documents." [47]

And in computing continental earthquakes, the Soviet Union's team declared, the estimates could be cut in half. By their own manipulation of figures, the Soviet experts thus had justified their political estimate that the number of on-site inspections required would not be nearly so great as the Americans contended.

To throw another block in the way of on-site inspections, the Soviet experts produced their own science on the problem of first motion. The United States delegation's conclusion that determining the direction of first motion in a nuclear explosion was more difficult than anticipated had "not been sufficiently substantiated," the Soviet experts declared.

If the instrumentation used to monitor a Hardtack series had been up to the standard set by the 1958 Conference of Experts, the Soviet scientists said, the 5-kiloton and 19-kiloton explosions would have produced first-motion signals of compression at distances up to 3,500 kilometers. The Soviet experts concluded the 1958 estimate that 90 per cent of all earthquakes in continents could be identified if there were five clear registrations of first motion at stations surrounding the event "is by no means refuted but rather confirmed by the measurements taken during the Hardtack experiments, if the quality and characteristics of the instruments used are duly and objectively taken into account."

The Hardtack data should be studied carefully by the control organization to be set up by the test-ban-treaty powers, the Soviet experts said; but the conclusions derived by the Americans from their data should not be accepted.

The Russians repudiated "categorically" the conclusions by the American delegation:

> Having uncovered many errors as mentioned above, and even some misrepresentation, in the United States statements and documents, the Soviet experts note that they all tend in a single direction—toward reducing the estimates of the control system's effectiveness. The Soviet experts therefore cannot regard these shortcomings as resulting from carelessness and coincidence, and have come to the conclusion that there has been tendentious use of one-sidedly developed material for the purpose of undermining confidence in the control system whose basic characteristics were determined by the 1958 Geneva Conference of Experts.

The time to improve the inspection system would be after it was put into operation, the Soviet group declared.

There was also a comment on the decoupling theory. The American idea was only a theory, the Russians said:

Even from the theoretical point of view, the earth's crust is a very complex medium. Therefore, a combination of formal mathematical solutions for the problems involved in the dissimilation of underground explosions does not as yet offer a sound basis for any findings relating to the possible amplitude of the seismic signal generated by an explosion in a deep underground cavity or to the technical feasibility of carrying out vast underground construction operations at a depth of the order of one kilometer.

The American delegation later reported to the treaty conference:

Cavities are known to exist in salt formations which would satisfy the volume and depth requirement for explosions of several kilotons. Engineering studies indicate that it is feasible to construct cavities which would satisfy the volume requirement for explosions at least as large as 70 kilotons. The total construction time for a cavity of this size in a salt dome is estimated to be from two to four years.[48]

If one were to assume that the United States had taught the Soviet Union the big-hole method for secret testing underground, and one were using the time scale foreseen in the American experts' report, a potential violator could have been ready by the end of 1961 for underground nuclear tests as large as 70 kilotons. And tests up to "several kilotons" could have been going on since January, 1960.

As to the criteria for narrowing the number of on-site inspections, the Soviet Union found that the United States delegation had suggested

a system of criteria which virtually rejects the very idea of selecting suspicious events from the events recorded by the control system. As a result of analysis, it became clear, for example, that if the United States criteria were used, the determination of first motion could be considered basically reliable only in the case of explosions with yields of hundreds or thousands of kilotons. Obviously, such a formulation of criteria is challenged even by the United States interpretation of the Hardtack measurements. According to the United States scientists themselves, their criteria would leave under suspicion the overwhelming majority of the earthquakes registered by the control system.

The Soviet experts submit that here their United States colleagues are on the brink of absurdity.

The State Department later referred to the Soviet reports as "intemperate and technically unsupportable." At the time, when Soviet Chairman Fedorov read the report into the record of the Conference on Discontinuance of Nuclear Weapons Tests, on December 19, Dr. James B. Fisk answered briefly but with indignation:

Since Dr. Fedorov has read his incorrect, distorted and misleading statement, I feel that the record would be lopsided if I did not make a few moderate comments on behalf of the United States delegation. [The Soviet complaint that the Hardtack data did not provide a test of the 1958 experts' system was] irrelevant. The instruments which were used in the Hard-

tack experiments have been conclusively shown, in the course of the meetings of the Technical Working Group, to be superior to those which we
understand were recommended by the Conference of Experts. Mr. Fedorov
challenges us because not every one of the total number of seismographs
used in the Hardtack experiments were used in every experiment. This has
no essential bearing on the results. I would simply observe that sixteen
seismographs, well calibrated and well placed, for any one of these underground explosions, are a rather unusually large number and the data from
them are good, relevant, and complete.

Responding to the charge that the American scientists had manipu-
lated source data, Dr. Fisk said:

I should like to remind him [Dr. Fedorov] that the source data are the
seismograms themselves. Many of them have been available to the Soviet
delegation for a number of months. In the first few meetings of the Technical Working Group, 250 were made available to the Soviet delegation.
Those are the source data. If the Soviet scientists are willing to do their
own homework, they have available every bit of data that we have labored
on for so long.

It was "absurd" to charge, Dr. Fisk said, that the United States had
introduced new data at the nineteenth meeting of the Technical Working Group; all the data presented had been obtained by measuring "the
very seismograms that had been made available to the Soviet delegation
earlier." It was only at the nineteenth meeting, just before the end of
the conference, that the Soviet delegation could be brought to discuss on
a technical basis the problem of first motion.

Dr. Fisk conceded that scientifically based criteria could classify "only
a small fraction of the seismic events as natural earthquakes, leaving a
large number eligible for inspection."

While the Soviet delegation wanted to remove a large fraction of the
seismic events from eligibility for inspection, Dr. Fisk observed, the
United States believed "this is impossible within present technical
knowledge." The criteria suggested by the Soviet Union, Dr. Fisk told
the political conference,

would have classified such events as the recent underground nuclear-test
explosions, which ranged up to 19 kilotons in yield, as natural earthquakes
and thus would have made them ineligible for inspection. It is the United
States delegation's view that as scientific knowledge progresses more useful
criteria can be formulated in the future.
[Forming criteria for on-site inspections is a strictly technical problem,
Dr. Fisk said.] If technical knowledge permits one to identify a large fraction of seismic events as earthquakes, then it is clearly a great advantage to
the control system. If technical knowledge does not permit that, then
seismic events must remain eligible for inspection. Determination of the
means of selecting events to be inspected must be left for further consideration by the main conference.

Impotence of on-site inspection was not mentioned by Dr. Fisk.

United Kingdom experts, in their comments on the conference, made four points. First, the Hardtack series had shown the 1958 experts' report had been too optimistic in its estimate of the value of first motion as a criterion for the identification of earthquakes. Second, it was not possible "at the present time" to construct criteria that would identify a large proportion of earthquakes as such. "In our opinion, the best that can be done in the present state of knowledge is to define the criteria which will identify a modest proportion of earthquakes. The remaining events must be regarded as eligible for inspection, even though the number of events will, for a few years, be far too large for all to be inspected." [49]

Third, world research on seismology could "materially increase" the percentage of earthquakes that could be identified after "a few years."

Fourth, the three participants in the test-ban negotiations had no common understanding of the problems existing in the underground environment, no agreed criteria for inspection, and no common assessment of the capabilities of the control system outlined in 1958.

Addition of unmanned stations to the control system might have been of some help. But they were not suggested by the United States, despite the feelings of some American scientists, Dr. Bethe prominent among them, that the system could be improved markedly by including them.

Dr. Fisk later explained that the United States worried about the reliability of the information that would come from the unmanned stations. "The security of the system, the engineering estimates, the economics, the political implications, and so on," Dr. Fisk later explained, ". . . we felt would have to be studied through before we could make a positive presentation to say we must consider this."

At the time of the Technical Working Group II conference this work had not been completed.[50]

Summary

In the four weeks of meetings in Geneva, the Soviet Union had agreed with the American scientists on all propositions which implied that the detection and identification problems of a control system would be either as easy or easier than indicated in the 1958 experts' conference. Communist scientists would not agree on anything that appeared to show the 1958 system had deteriorated. They accepted all the proposed improvements to the Geneva system. Additional seismic instruments could be sent to control posts, they agreed, and there could even be changes in classifications of instruments proposed by the 1958 conference.

But the Technical Working Group II conference uncovered six major areas of disagreement among Soviet and Western scientists:

1. They disagreed on the estimated number of earthquakes equivalent to explosions of a given yield.

2. They disagreed on measurements of first motion.

3. The Russians disputed the validity of the decoupling calculations, as well as the feasibility of constructing the big hole.

4. The teams of scientists disagreed about unexpected surface phenomena which were observed in the Hardtack tests.

5. They disagreed on the adequacy of the seismographs used in monitoring the Hardtack series.

6. They disagreed on the principles which would be the foundation for criteria on dispatching on-site inspection teams.

The Russians took the position that science should conform to their political aim, which was to reduce the number of events eligible for outside inspection to a small fraction of the total number of eligible events. The Soviet criteria were so stringent that, as the American team showed at the conference, nuclear explosions of the Hardtack series would have been classified as earthquakes. They would have been ineligible for on-site inspection.

American officials later took it as significant that the Soviet delegation did not include in its final report to the treaty conference its proposed criteria.[51] This may have been an indication, it was speculated, that the Soviet Union recognized its criteria would not stand examination.

The United States approached the problem of criteria with the intention of including a large fraction or all, if possible, of the unidentified underground events among those eligible for inspection.

The Russians insisted, quite openly, that scientific facts had to be found which would serve the political necessity of reducing on-site inspections to a few per year. The American delegation looked hard for scientific facts which could produce these results, but insisted that the scientific facts be found first.

Despite the stringent Soviet requirements, there was no contribution to the science of seismology from the Communist side.

Dr. Fisk later acknowledged that the Soviet scientists had contributed very little original information at the Technical Working Group II conference:

> Dr. Fisk: Their direct contribution in terms of new data, measurements, studies, was quite minimal, quite small.
> Senator Hickenlooper: Did they get down to the point of a scintilla?
> Dr. Fisk: A semiscintilla.
> Senator Hickenlooper: Well, that is pretty small. It approaches deminimis.[52]

The total Soviet performance at the Technical Working Group II conference had been an eye-opener in many respects. A wide range of methods for procrastination was clearly open to the Soviet side and it was already testing them.

From Moscow's point of view, the conference could have been a kind of "dry run" for frustrating a test-ban control system. The world knew little of this, however, because the whole exercise occurred behind closed doors. Later the transcript of the conference proceedings was made public, but the attention paid it was almost nil. Summary statements of American and Soviet positions sounded like the same old propaganda battles and made no impact.

The result was world-wide indifference to mounting evidence of the total ineffectiveness of inspection—while the negotiations toward a test-ban proceeded with the same old zeal and determination.

Dr. Fisk returned to the United States after the abortive conference and reported to President Eisenhower at his vacation headquarters in Augusta, Georgia. The President then issued a blunt and angry statement from Augusta on December 29:

> The prospects for such an agreement [on a nuclear-test ban] have been injured by the recent unwillingness on the part of the politically-guided Soviet experts to give serious scientific consideration to the effectiveness of seismic techniques for the detection of underground nuclear explosions. Indeed the atmosphere of the talks has been clouded by the intemperate and technically unsupportable Soviet annex to the report of the technical experts. The distinguished American group of scientists who composed the United States delegation will make public from the verbatim records of the conference the facts which will completely refute this Soviet document.

The President expressed the judgment that "no satisfactory agreement is yet in sight." Nevertheless, he said, the United States would return to the negotiating table "in a continuing spirit of seeking to reach a safeguarded agreement."

But the United States would feel free to resume nuclear tests, he warned. In noting that "the voluntary moratorium on testing will expire on December 31," he said:

> Although we consider ourselves free to resume nuclear-weapons testing, we shall not resume nuclear-weapons tests without announcing our intention in advance of any resumption. During the period of voluntary suspension of nuclear-weapons tests the United States will continue its active program of weapons research, development, and laboratory-type experimentation.

President Eisenhower, however, filled out his term in office without ever giving any notice of intention to resume nuclear testing.

The Eisenhower statement did contain one interesting reference, to "laboratory-type experimentation," which was to be "continued." This brought up a question that had not been discussed in the Geneva negotiations: When is a test a test? Would the test-ban that the three powers were trying to negotiate apply to laboratory-type experimentation? The precedent set by the Eisenhower statement would seem to indicate that the United States intended laboratory-type experimentation would be exempted from a nuclear-test ban. At least the United States considered laboratory tests to be outside the scope of its voluntary moratorium.

Next question: How big a bang is necessary before one passes from "laboratory-type experimentation" to a full-scale test? These problems were never elaborated on in public.

OPERATION COWBOY

There has never been an adequate explanation why the United States was not able to mount an experiment to prove out the decoupling theory between January 1959, when Dr. Albert Latter invented it, and November 1959, when the Technical Working Group II conference opened.

As has already been noted, it was left to the British, with an extremely crude facsimile of a "big hole," to present the Russians with proof that the Latter theory held up in practice. The Americans did not arrange an experiment of their own with the decoupling theory until the second Geneva technical conference was almost ended.

Seventeen high explosive shots were fired in salt cavities near Winnfield, Louisiana, between mid-December 1959 and mid-March 1960. The "Operation Cowboy" charges ranged from 20 to 2,000 pounds. The decoupled shots were exploded in two spherical cavities of 12 and 30 feet in diameter. Both had been cut out of salt domes at a depth of 800 feet. Seismographs were placed at twenty-three locations, some as far out as 60 miles from the epicenter. Measurements were taken on the surface and underground.

Seismic signals produced by explosions in the cavities were compared directly with signals from closely tamped shots of comparable yield—in the same medium and at the same depth.

The theory of decoupling was completely verified. The decoupling factor in the single medium of salt was shown to be 120. Dr. Latter's decoupling ratio of 300 to 1 had compared a tamped explosion in Nevada tuff with a big-hole explosion in rock. But the Latter factor was found to be conservative—350 to 1 would be more nearly accurate.

The ratio between 350 and 120 assumed an approximate decoupling factor of 3 merely by transferring explosions from Nevada tuff to salt. That is, a tamped explosion in salt would produce one-third the signal of a tamped explosion in tuff. If the decoupling factor derived from transferring a chemical explosive of given charge from Nevada tuff to salt has been experimentally determined, it has not been reported.

The Cowboy series produced another result suspected but not verified. A large decoupling factor was found to be attainable even if the size of the underground cavity were well below the optimum volume specified in the Latter theory. Exactly how the decoupling factor would decline as cavity-size was reduced was a matter of dispute.

Dr. Latter, who had invented the decoupling theory, estimated that a decoupling factor of 30 could be achieved even if the volume of the hole were reduced to one-thirtieth of the optimum value. Dr. Hans Bethe predicted on the basis of the Cowboy tests that a reduction in the volume of the cavity to one-thirtieth of the optimum value would produce a decoupling factor of only 10. The proof depended on nuclear experiments, proscribed under the voluntary American ban.

It was calculated that the high explosives used in the Winnfield salt mines had produced greater pressures proportionally than nuclear explosives. In other words, nuclear explosions of the same power could be expected to produce relatively smaller signals than chemical explosions. The decoupling factor of 120 for chemical explosions in salt possibly could be increased.

Additional decoupling factors would be possible, theories showed, by increasing the depth of the big hole or by using other geological materials as the medium for the decoupling. Full-scale tests probably would be required to prove out these points.

As Dr. Latter mentioned in Geneva, it is theoretically possible to place heat-absorbing materials in the cavity to absorb the energy that otherwise would go into pounding the walls. Not all scientists think this would work. Dr. Teller mentioned possibilities of increasing the decoupling factors to 3,000 or more using this method. Dr. Bethe believed the heat-absorbers probably would not work. Further experiments with nuclear explosives would be required to see which scientist was right.

The practical experience of Louisiana encouraged some scientists to predict that existing cavities could accommodate explosions much larger than the several kilotons that had originally been predicted and still produce significant decoupling factors. Explosions of about 20 kilotons, for instance, would produce seismic signals equivalent to about 1 kiloton, under Rainier decoupling, or even less, in medium-sized cavities.

In addition, those who conducted the experiments were encouraged to believe that the same hole could be used over and over again for nuclear experiments. This was another point on which the skeptics had raised doubts. There was no assurance, they said, that each large cavity, costing millions of dollars and requiring two to four years to construct, would not be damaged so by the first nuclear shot that it could not be used again. The Cowboy evidence showed this was not true.

THE THRESHOLD

Under the cloud of pessimism generated by the Technical Work-Group II conference, negotiators at Geneva made little headway until

February 11, when the United States presented a new major proposal for a phased treaty. The year before, the Eisenhower concept of a phased treaty was to eliminate underground tests entirely from the first-phase ban. This was, in effect, setting the threshold for a ban at ground level.

In 1960, President Eisenhower offered to lower the threshold below ground, to include all underground tests that produced seismic signals of 4.75 or greater on the universal magnitude scale. This was the threshold, or limit of detection and identification, for seismology in 1960, according to the best judgment of American scientists. President Eisenhower announced the significant American move at a press conference. U.S. Ambassador James J. Wadsworth presented the detailed proposal at the Geneva negotiations.

The President said the United States move was made "to end the apparent deadlock in the negotiations." While he was still committed to a complete ban, his new proposal was designed to stop these nuclear-weapons tests that could be effectively controlled. It would, he said, end "forthwith" and "under assured controls" all nuclear-weapons tests in the atmosphere, in the oceans, in those regions in space where effective controls could then be agreed to, and beneath the surface of the earth which could be monitored.

His proposal would also permit, "through a coordinated program of research and development, a systematic extension of the ban to the remaining areas, especially those involving underground tests, for which adequate control measures appear not to be possible now." These moves would prevent increases in the level of radioactivity in the atmosphere, he said, "and so allay world-wide concern."

At the same time, they would "offer an opportunity to consolidate the important progress made in negotiations thus far." In setting the underground threshold, an accompanying White House statement explained, an effort was being made "to find ways around the significant disagreements that remain unresolved in the Technical Working Group which reported to the Conference in December."

Magnitude 4.75 is the level that "can now be adequately monitored," the President asserted. "We proposed to express the level in terms of signal strength since the Soviet and Western scientists are in substantial agreement as to the measurement of signals but not on the equivalent kiloton yields of seismic disturbances."

The White House statement made it official, for the first time, that the new Hardtack II series were considered to have blocked chances for a comprehensive ban. "With the failure to reach agreement after the technical conference which ended on December 19, 1959," the White House statement said, "it became clear that a controlled, comprehensive agreement could not, at this time, be achieved without great improvement in instrumentation or a degree of on-site inspection which would be impractical to attempt."

Newsmen questioned President Eisenhower about his new proposal. Would the United States resume underground testing if the Soviet Union accepted the threshold plan? No decision had been made, Mr. Eisenhower replied. "But I have already told you that laboratory testing —not of weapons testing, but of just nuclear science—goes on all the time. But when it comes down to weapons testing, that is something that we would have to decide with our own allies."[53]

Ambassador Wadsworth's more detailed presentation at the Geneva negotiations gave a slightly different impression of the American idea. The United States did not intend its threshold to be rigidly fixed at magnitude 4.75. It was a "sliding threshold" that could move up or down depending on the amount of inspection the Soviet Union was pre-pared to accept. The 4.75-magnitude threshold envisioned the 180-station control network. If more stations were accepted, or more on-site inspections, the threshold presumably could have been lowered immediately. Also if research paid off, the threshold could come down.

The general outlines of the new American threshold approach had been reported in advance in the press.[54]

Soviet Ambassador Tsarapkin was ready, therefore, with preliminary comments and questions when the plan was presented at Geneva. He said he found little new, and "in order to find out if there is anything new" he asked two questions:

Would nuclear explosions below the 4.75 threshold be permitted underground?

Is it intended to accompany the treaty with a "moratorium" to be ap-plied below the threshold?

All three nuclear powers would be free to conduct tests below the threshold, Ambassador Wadsworth replied, during the first phase of the agreement, and there would be no provision in the treaty for a mora-torium. "The moratorium which has been in effect over the past year and several months is one which is unilateral and voluntary in nature, and the United States does not propose to include such a procedure in the treaty," Mr. Wadsworth said. According to American calculations, about twenty on-site inspections per year would be needed to check unidenti-fied events above the threshold, he indicated.

Ambassador Tsarapkin had further questions about the 4.75 threshold.

Who is going to define that magnitude and on what basis?

I ask this question because, when the matter of magnitude was being dis-cussed in December last year, our scientists assimilated the magnitude of, say, 4.75 to an explosion of a yield of about 5 kilotons, whereas the United States experts assimilated the same magnitude to the yield of an explosion of about 19 kilotons, so even on this point there was a colossal discrepancy between the calculations of Soviet experts and the calculations of United States experts. The one side insisted that they were right and the other side that they were right. How do you propose to achieve agreement on the question of magnitude if, say, a magnitude were laid down in the treaty?

Ambassador Wadsworth explained that switching to seismic magnitude had been proposed to avoid the argument about what size nuclear explosion produces what seismic signal.

It is our opinion that the instrument readings could give us the magnitude, whereas we might not agree on the kiloton yield of a device which had given such readings. Thus, in our view, we would overcome the difficulty over translation by using the instrument readings on the commonly-accepted scale in seismology.

Ambassador Tsarapkin retorted:

As far as I know, when the experts discussed the question of magnitude—let us say the Blanca explosion which had been carried out in the United States—the Soviet experts equated it with a magnitude of 5.3, while the United States experts estimated the Blanca magnitude at 4.8. Therefore, the problem of magnitude readings is not one that is noncontroversial for both sides.

In this the Soviet ambassador was correct. There was every reason to expect, on the basis of the long wrangles among Soviet and American experts in Technical Working Group II, that Soviet and American technicians in any control mission would fall into bitter arguments over whether a given seismic signal, read from several control posts, represented a magnitude more than 4.75 or less.

The earlier technical conference had shown clearly that what Ambassador Wadsworth had referred to as the "unified magnitude scale in common use by seismologists," and the "commonly-accepted scale in seismology," was not accepted by the Soviet Union.

Ambassador Wadsworth had no satisfactory answer. He explained that he was not a technician.

In Washington, reporters who received briefings on the new American proposal found that high State Department officials could not explain how Soviet and American differences on magnitude calculation were to be resolved, either. One high official indicated he understood that there was no chance for dispute, since it was merely a matter of measuring signal sizes. He clearly did not understand that selection of individual readings for inclusion in the averaging had led to disputes that had gone on for days and weeks between Soviet and American technicians in Geneva. Ambassador Tsarapkin made another revealing point in his early reaction to the American proposal. The Soviet Union had paid for a comprehensive nuclear test-ban with a certain level of inspection, he said. Now the United States was asking that the Soviet Union pay the same amount of inspection for a less than comprehensive ban on nuclear-weapons tests.

As a matter of fact, Mr. Tsarapkin claimed, no international inspection system would be needed at all to monitor a test-ban that excluded underground explosions producing signals smaller than 4.75. All the monitoring necessary, he claimed, could be done by national systems and there would be no need for an international net. He apparently forgot that only three stations in the Soviet Union picked up the 4.75 Blanca nuclear shot and even those would have classed it as an earthquake.

This could have been a subtle threat to withdraw all Soviet offers of inspection inside the Iron Curtain if a threshold plan were insisted upon. In 1961, the Soviet Union made just such a move.

Ambassador Tsarapkin brought up the effects of the new Eisenhower proposal on the spread of nuclear weapons to other powers. "Is this an invitation to other states to start nuclear explosions and to develop nuclear weapons?" he sneered.

"The answer to that question is a very definite 'No,'" Ambassador Wadsworth replied. "It is felt that a threshold of 4.75 would in fact be a deterrent to fourth, fifth, and Nth countries against starting a program, because we believe that the smaller and more sophisticated devices which might be developed under our proposal would generally not be within the capability of countries which had not had experience in these matters."

The ingenious American proposal to set a test-ban threshold stated in terms of seismic magnitude of 4.75 was not easy to understand. Neither the American administration, the scientists, nor the press kept the meaning in proper perspective, mainly because it took several hundred words of explanation each time it was mentioned.

Magnitude 4.75 corresponds to the seismic signal produced by about a 20-kiloton nuclear explosion, closely tamped, and fired under the conditions of the Nevada test site. Because the magnitude of 4.75 was not widely understood, it became a widely used shorthand to refer to the threshold as a "20-kiloton threshold." But it was not by any means a 20-kiloton threshold.

If a testing power were to explode its nuclear weapons in salt, limestone, granite, or marble—closely "tamped" and without digging a big hole—it might test up to 40 or 60 kilotons before producing a 4.75 signal.

The experts had estimated that a decoupling factor of two or three could be achieved merely by transferring the nuclear shots from the Nevada tuff to some other medium, such as granite or salt.

If, on the other hand, the testing power were willing to go to the added trouble of digging a big hole, underground nuclear-weapons tests up to the megaton range would be legal. The excavation could even be conducted in the open; at least it would not be illegal.

We can go one step further. If Dr. Latter's theories about sprinkling lampblack in a large cavity underground would achieve another decoupling factor of 10, the threshold theory really could legalize under-

ground testing up to 60 megatons. The largest known test of the hydrogen bomb then was 15 megatons, by the United States in 1954. President
Eisenhower subsequently announced that there was no further need for
testing weapons of this size.

Thus, the real meaning of the 4.75 threshold, having cranked-in the
decoupling techniques developed between August 1958 and February
1960, was that all conceivable sizes of nuclear weapons could be tested
underground. The suggestion that the 4.75 threshold would be 20 kilotons was really a mirage. *The threshold was variable, depending on the
coupling, from 20 kilotons up to 6 megatons, and possibly as high as 60
megatons.*

Up until the last minute before the American threshold proposal was
presented at Geneva, the British pressed for the United States to include
with the threshold proposal a two-year extension of the entire nuclear-
test moratorium. It was the position of the British that the threshold
principle, rejected in advance by the Soviet delegate to the Geneva talks,
would meet a quick rebuff and get nowhere, leaving the United States and
Britain again on the short end of the propaganda stick.

The United States decided against advancing the moratorium idea,
however, to be consistent with President Eisenhower's often-stated principle that no disarmament would be accepted or offered that could not
be inspected.[55]

The British delegate to the nuclear test-ban negotiations, Sir Michael
Wright, who was chairman on the day the American threshold proposal
was made, pointed to another important American concession—the
formal acceptance of the quota principle for conducting on-site inspections. It was true that the two-part formula suggesting a quota of
twenty on-site inspections per year did accept, in the conference room, a
principle previously accepted only outside the negotiations.

Ambassador Tsarapkin seized on another comment of Mr. Wadsworth to put the new American proposal in a bad light. The American
Ambassador had said that the threshold approach would inhibit the
spread of nuclear weapons to other powers because they could not
develop the small and more sophisticated weapons to be tested underground.

> The United States would appear to be striving to gain for itself some kind
> of military advantage in proposing the resumption of underground nuclear-
> weapons tests; namely to give an opportunity of carrying out tests only to
> itself, the United States, because it considers that it will be difficult from
> the technical standpoint for other states to make weapons of such low
> yield. Would it be correct to understand those to be the true motives of
> the United States in this approach?

Ambassador Tsarapkin also repeated his government's threat to resume unrestricted nuclear testing if the United States resumed re-

stricted testing underground. "If the United States were to resume nuclear-weapons tests, by that very fact an impulse would be given to the resumption of an utterly unrestricted nuclear arms race in testing weapons of any yield and in any environment."[56]

The Tsarapkin reply actually represented a rejection of the American proposal out of hand. But from past experience the United States did not accept his *Nyet* as final. During the next month, the Soviet Union did come to accept the idea of a phased approach, at least with respect to the criteria for determining which underground events would be eligible for inspection.

The Soviet Union proposed, in fact, that, until more sophistication was acquired in actual practice, virtually all events that produced a seismic signal and were located by the control system would be eligible for inspection. This was a significant shift for the Soviet Union, because up to that time Soviet scientists and diplomats alike had insisted that the criteria should greatly restrict the number of events eligible for inspection.

Apparently the way for this concession had been opened up by the Wadsworth proposal of February 11. At that time the United States had said it was prepared either to consider 20 per cent of all located events for annual on-site inspections or 30 per cent of those that remained unidentified. This was acceptance of an on-site inspection quota, in principle. The Soviet Union, in turn, was accepting the principle that deciding which underground events were eligible for inspection should be up to the suspicious powers, not the suspected, so long as an announced quota of inspections were agreed.

A good deal of the hard bargaining that went on in the context of the Geneva negotiations was conducted outside the conference room. On March 16, the Atomic Energy Commission announced ominous plans to prepare for an underground nuclear test in New Mexico in 1961. The AEC said the project, code-named "Gnome," would be a step in a program aimed at using atomic explosives for peaceful purposes, including the production of electric power. President Eisenhower, however, would have to issue final authorization for the actual detonation, expected to be a 10-kiloton shot.

Senator Anderson, Democrat of New Mexico, Chairman of the Senate-House Atomic Energy Committee, said he understood the shot was planned for January, 1961. The locale of the underground shot would be 25 miles southeast of Carlsbad, N.M., in salt beds there. The AEC, in making the announcement, said: "During the current nuclear-test suspension negotiations in Geneva, the United Kingdom, the United States, and [Russia] have agreed in principle on the use of nuclear explosions for peaceful purposes."

Scientific results of the experiment would be made available "worldwide," the AEC said, and observers from the United Nations or any of its member countries would be welcomed. The cost of the construction project for the experiment was estimated at about $1 million. A shaft 1,200 feet deep would be dug. Leading off from the bottom of the shaft would be a tunnel 1,100 feet long to the site of the nuclear detonation. The AEC listed four objectives for the project:

1. To explore the feasibility of converting the energy from the nuclear shot into heat for the production of electric power.

2. To investigate the practicability of recovering useful radioisotopes for scientific and industrial applications by "mining" them from the site of the blast.

3. To expand information on characteristics of underground detonations—presumably to check further on possibilities of detecting sneak tests of weapons.

4. To make measurements which might contribute to the further development of reactors for power and other purposes.

In the context of the Geneva negotiations for a test ban, the third purpose of Project Gnome had the effect of a needle. If the Soviet Union were indeed stalling in the Geneva negotiations, this would be an incentive to make a counterproposal. If the United States were to prove, for instance, that the decoupling theory was valid, or that there would be significant decoupling even in tamped explosions when they were transferred out of the Nevada tuff into salt, the concept of a control system advanced by the 1958 Conference of Experts would undergo a further degradation.

Three days later, on March 19, the Soviet Union called a special Saturday session of the Geneva negotiations to present its counterproposal to the American February 11 position.

The Soviet Union was ready to agree to a treaty banning all tests in the atmosphere, in the oceans, in cosmic space, and underground above seismic magnitude 4.75. It also would be ready to participate in a research program as the United States suggested. But this treaty should be accompanied by a simultaneous obligation not to test below the seismic "threshold" of 4.75 during the period required to conduct a research program. This was the moratorium about which Ambassador Tsarapkin had inquired.

By its move the Soviet Union had accepted, conditionally, the State Department considered, a phased-treaty approach banning tests in most environments but not below 4.75 magnitude underground. The Soviet Union also accepted the idea of a joint-research program. In principle, the Kremlin had conceded that small underground tests were uninspectable.

But the proviso that the United States must at the same time declare a moratorium on testing below the threshold in effect brought the negotiations back to where they had been before. The Soviet Union still wanted a comprehensive treaty—now, however, in two treaties, not in one.

The semantic trick of calling the one part of the agreement a treaty and the other part a moratorium for some reason had great weight in the diplomatic community as well as outside. The Soviet Union said that the agreement not to test below the 4.75 "threshold" should be an integral part of the treaty. This made the distinction between a treaty and a moratorium completely artificial.

At the same time the moratorium period should run four to five years, Ambassador Tsarapkin said, and at the end of that period, the United States, the United Kingdom, and the Soviet Union should decide whether or not to extend the moratorium. The Soviet Union still refused to name a number for the annual quota of on-site inspections but did indicate that any quota could be applied either above or below the threshold. Establishing the on-site inspection quota would be a purely political decision, not dependent on science, the Soviet Union insisted.

Ambassador Tsarapkin made it clear that Moscow did not intend to go back on its main principle:

> The treaty must be comprehensive without any exceptions or reservations, otherwise it will have no meaning and will not achieve the purpose for which it is intended. Agreement on the cessation of all nuclear-weapons tests would be a dam barring the way to the further development and spread of nuclear weapons, and would deliver mankind from the terrible threat associated with this dangerous sequence of events. For this reason the treaty on the cessation of nuclear-weapons tests should provide for the prohibition of all atomic- and hydrogen-weapon tests for all time without exception. No loophole should be left in this treaty for any kind of nuclear-weapon tests.[57]

In the same speech, Ambassador Tsarapkin called the United States' attention to the attitudes of neutrals and even some of America's allies like Canada, that all nuclear tests should be stopped. The Ambassador mentioned the United Nations resolution of 1959 calling on all the states to conclude a comprehensive ban and withhold testing until it was concluded.

> [Soviet scientists] do not agree with the opinion of some United States and United Kingdom experts that there exists some sort of a threshold in the matter of detection and identification of underground nuclear explosions. In this respect we entirely hold the position formulated in the report of the 1958 Geneva Conference of Experts. Since, however, the United States and the United Kingdom have turned the question of the so-called threshold into a serious impediment holding back the progress of our conference, in order to remove this new barrier to negotiations the Soviet Union government has instructed me to submit for the consideration of the conference the following [treaty plus moratorium] proposal, which opens the

door wide to a rapid settlement of all questions not yet decided at our conference.

[The form to be taken by the moratorium] should be reflected—in one way or another—in the treaty, and should form some part of the treaty. We consider that this is a very important part of the agreement, and this is the essential point of our proposal. We consider that this agreement should be part of the treaty. I do not want to predetermine its form. Whether it will be in the form of an article, or whether it will be contained in an annex, or perhaps it will be a separate protocol—that we can decide later. I do not think it should be very difficult to agree on the form. But it should be part of the treaty.[58]

In developing American questions on the Soviet counterproposal on March 21, Ambassador Wadsworth returned to the question of magnitude, this time better prepared to discuss the problem. "Our proposal was that we adopt the unified magnitude scale, which could provide the most noncontroversial basis for applying the threshold concept," Ambassador Wadsworth said. "My question is: Does the Soviet delegation feel that this scale can be adopted?"[59]

Ambassador Wadsworth asked also about the number of on-site inspections the Soviet Union was prepared to accept. In this same area, also, it was unclear how the threshold would affect the on-site inspection problem: "Do we have a quota above the threshold, or do we have a quota below the threshold, or do we attempt to negotiate a quota for the entire range?"

The Soviet proposal had also been couched in terms assuming that all high-altitude explosions could be banned because there was adequate control. Since the control measures for high-altitude testing would be difficult to install immediately, Ambassador Wadsworth noted, there was need for clarification of the Soviet position.

The last American question: "In the event that effective control of small underground explosions proved impossible and if the proposed temporary prohibition against such explosions lapsed, would the remainder of the treaty continue in effect?"

As for the period of the joint research program, Ambassador Tsarapkin told the Geneva negotiators:

We feel that five years or four years, for example, would be roughly the suitable length for this program. [If the research program should not be completed successfully], I do not know what will happen. This is a purely hypothetical question. We consider that, if for any reason, it so happens that your specialists and our specialists, working together within the control organization or control system—we do not admit the possibility, but if we took as pessimistic a view of the matter as you do—failed after four or five years to work out together improved methods of detecting and identifying seismic events below the United States figure of threshold magnitude, that fact should not automatically release the parties to the treaty from their obligations regarding the moratorium and should not mean that the treaty would terminate or be liquidated. No. If such a situation even did arise—and we consider it highly unlikely—then the governments concerned would have to discuss the situation created and agree on further measures in connection with it.

This was tantamount to saying that both the "moratorium" and the "treaty" would last indefinitely. While this was clear to the negotiators, it was not to the general public. The West speculated for months on this point.

The Soviet delegate maintained his position that the number of on-site inspections should be set by "a political decision, a political compromise," and in that respect "it is absolutely firm, and we cannot agree about the inspection quota on any other basis."[60]

Ambassador Tsarapkin also expounded a "doctrine of circumvention" of his own, to avoid the disputes about magnitude of earthquakes:

Regarding the different evaluations of magnitude to which I have referred, we propose—at least, we shall assume—that no threshold should be fixed with regard to inspection. We consider that events both above and below the so-called threshold of magnitude will be subject to inspections within the limits of the agreed quota. Thus questions concerning the disputes which different approaches to the determination of magnitude may produce are eliminated and have no meaning whatever.

Here was the core of the Soviet meaning: "No *threshold should be fixed with regard to inspection.*"

But the only reason the United States introduced the threshold idea was to draw the line between inspectable and uninspectable events. The Russians were merely erasing the line with a new moratorium gimmick.

To this day, there has been no explanation why neither the State Department nor the President nor his scientific advisers nor anyone in the Executive Branch of the government has pointed out forcefully to the American public that the Soviet "response" to the February 11, 1960, American proposal was merely a repetition of their old demand for a comprehensive ban. The above-quoted paragraph was the key. It was never quoted by the Americans.

Ambassador Tsarapkin made this statement on March 21, 1960, eight days before Prime Minister Macmillan began new discussions with President Eisenhower at Camp David.

On Capitol Hill, in press rooms, in the Defense Department, in the Atomic Energy Commission, there was suspicion—but no verification—that the Soviet Union was making, in fact, no new proposal. The speech of Ambassador Tsarapkin on March 19, and his amplifications on March 21, made this abundantly clear. But they were made behind closed doors. No responsible official of the American Government warned the American public or explained the nature of the Soviet proposal.

The Soviet initiative was instead rated officially to be "an important statement," to use Ambassador Wadsworth's phrase, also behind closed doors, on March 19. "I merely wish to say that it is an important statement and I believe it has been made in a serious attempt to see our conference make some progress," Ambassador Wadsworth declared in the greatest cordiality.

The British Ambassador, Mr. David Ormsby Gore, was equally cordial: "I agree with my United States colleague that we have heard a very important statement this morning which we shall naturally study with very great care."

A few days later, the Department of State announced publicly that it considered the Soviet move "an important and serious document meriting minute consideration and study."[61]

In view of Ambassador Tsarapkin's replies explaining the treaty-moratorium proposal, the British delegate, Sir Michael Wright, made what was in many respects an incredible speech at the end of the March 21 meeting. His principal object, it was clear, was to pin down the fact of the Soviet acceptance "in principle" of the threshold concept. But in so doing he closed his eyes to Ambassador Tsarapkin's clear and precise rejection of that very threshold idea:

> It appears to us that the essence of the Soviet proposal consists in the acceptance by the Soviet Union of the principle that in the initial phase of a comprehensive treaty it will be necessary to apply different treatment to underground tests above the threshold from the treatment applied to such tests below the threshold.
>
> In essence, the Soviet representative has now, as we understand it, accepted this proposition which both Western delegations have been urging upon him for reasons amply explained, and in accepting it he has made the condition that no testing of any kind by the parties shall be permitted in the initial phase.
>
> At the same time, of course, the Soviet representative has also accepted the specific threshold level proposed by the United States, as well as the United States proposal for joint research aimed at improvement of underground controls and at the consequent lowering and eventual elimination of the threshold.
>
> It appears to us, I repeat, that the Soviet delegation has been concerned primarily to put forward these determining principles or characteristics of the solution which the Soviet government is prepared to accept.
>
> From the comments of our Soviet colleague today, as well as from his statements at our last meeting, it appears to me that he is suggesting that if these principles are found mutually acceptable the actual treaty provisions and the details will be matters for discussion or negotiation between us. If I am wrong in this understanding of the Soviet representative's approach, no doubt he will correct me; but that is how I understand his position.

As I say, my government will certainly be prepared to examine the Soviet proposal in this light. We shall be prepared to examine it as a proposal of principles aimed at enabling the conference to circumvent the technical disagreements which still exist and to reach a practical solution which takes account of those disagreements. In this sense the Soviet proposal seems to us quite in accord with the spirit in which we have been trying to negotiate a way out of our difficulties since January of this year. . . .

The Soviet Government has now accepted the principle of a phased approach with a distinction initially between tests above and below the underground threshold and with a program of research covering, if I understand rightly, the whole question of underground controls. The successive advances in the Soviet position have seemed to us important steps forward in the right direction, and we welcome them as such. Other questions, of course, remain, but it does seem to us that our negotiations are now on a more hopeful path.

The Soviet Ambassador in the Geneva negotiations had specifically rejected, not accepted, the threshold concept. On the day he made his proposal, March 19, Ambassador Tsarapkin had said: "Our scientists do not agree with the opinion of some United States and United Kingdom experts that there exists some sort of threshold in the matter of detection and identification of underground nuclear explosions. In this respect we entirely hold the position formulated in the report of the 1958 Geneva Conference of Experts."

And two days later, in answering further American questions, the Soviet Ambassador was even more emphatic: "Regarding the different evaluations of magnitude to which I have referred, we propose—at least, we shall assume—that no threshold should be fixed with regard to inspection. We consider that events both above and below the so-called threshold of magnitude will be subject to inspections within the limits of the agreed quota."

The State Department, too, somehow missed the point. In a press release on April 8, the Department issued a "summary of the clarification made by the Soviet representative in response to questions by the United States representative on the Soviet proposal of March 19, 1960." This was a summary of the March 21 proceedings, reported above.

In the Tsarapkin comments on inspection, the State Department reported no rejection of the idea of a threshold. "On the matter of inspection and whether this could be applied to events both above and below the threshold," the State Department told the public, "it was made clear that the Soviet Union had not changed its position which based any quota on a purely political decision, and it indicated that any quota agreed upon this basis could be used both above and below the threshold."

The technique of releasing verbatim transcripts of the daily meetings of the nuclear test-ban negotiations months after they occurred gave the State Department an opportunity to put its own construction on the proceedings. By the time the transcripts were made public, the chances to catch up with the distortions had passed.

Democrats Bestir Themselves

As the Presidential-election year progressed, the Democratic Party took an increasing interest in the disarmament problem. Senator John F. Kennedy, speaking at the University of New Hampshire in Durham on March 7, 1960, had declared that "the most gaping hole in American foreign policy is our lack of a concrete plan for disarmament."

He offered an estimate that the world nuclear stockpile on that day contained the equivalent of 30 billion tons of TNT, "about 10 tons of TNT for every human being on the globe." He quoted scientists as saying that "the radioactive fallout from a single bomb can wipe out all higher forms of life in an area of 10,000 square miles."

The United States conferees on nuclear testing, as on other disarmament measures, "have in every instance been ill prepared and inadequately instructed," he charged.

The Senator expressed the same aspirations as the Eisenhower Administration and its predecessors. They were that a small first step, such as an agreement on nuclear tests, "can lead the way, once the Russians learn that international control and inspection are not necessarily to be feared, once Americans learn that accommodations are not necessarily appeasement, and once both sides learn that agreements can be made, and kept." He acknowledged the need for an inspection system "as reliable and thorough as modern science and technology can devise."

But he indicated a readiness to take risks:

> Peace programs involve risks as do arms programs, but the risks of arms are even more dangerous. Those who talk about the risks and dangers of any arms-control proposal ought to weigh—in the scales of national security— the risks and dangers inherent in our present course. The only alternative to pursuit of an effective disarmament agreement is reckless pursuit of our present course—the arms race, the gap, the new weapons, the development of ever higher orders of mutual terror, all of which not only reflect tensions but obviously aggravate them.

These were the thoughts, if not the words, of Professor Jerome Wiesner, of the Massachusetts Institute of Technology, who was to become White House science adviser the next year.

Senator Kennedy had specific criticism for the Eisenhower Administration's conduct of the Geneva Conference on a nuclear test ban.

> When . . . the Russians finally agreed to veto-free, on-site inspection on a quota basis—a major concession—we were not ready to state what a realistic quota would be. The technical data we presented on frequency response and grid-spacing—the distance between monitoring stations— turned out to be wrong. Our own new data on underground testing baffled

our negotiators. Even today, as that conference continues under our threat to resume testing, it is difficult to say what represents a single, clear-cut, well-defined, realistic American inspection proposal.

This was an indictment of scientists and negotiators that could have been soundly based, but the Senator gave no facts, only judgments.

It appeared, however, that Senator Kennedy had misjudged as had many others, the Soviet "sleight-of-hand" proposal to "drop" its veto on one phase of the on-site inspection problem only to insert it into another phase. True, Soviet Premier Khrushchev had announced with much fanfare that acceptance of a quota of annual on-site inspections by the West would be compensated by a withdrawal of the Soviet demand for a veto. But at the same time an effective veto reappeared in the criteria for dispatching on-site inspection teams.

Senator Kennedy's reference to incorrect technical data is somewhat obscure. Presumably the reference to grid-spacing was intended to criticize the 1958 Conference of Experts for having recommended too few control stations. What errors had been made in the field of "frequency response" was not clear. He could have meant that a closer spacing of stations would require seismometers capable of responding to higher frequencies, which traveled relatively short distances.

At another point, Senator Kennedy declared:

> Development of a workable plan to halt weapons testing requires detailed studies in seismology, atmospherics, acoustics, and geophysics. Detection and monitoring systems are even more complex than the expensive weapons they are designed to replace. New techniques of aerial reconnaissance, radar surveillance, and atmospheric sampling, new ways to denature plutonium, inspect power reactors, and measure air and water pollution—these are among the research projects that we need to complete before an effective arms control agreement can go into operation. . . .

To get these projects under way, Senator Kennedy said he was introducing a bill in the Senate to establish an "arms-control research institute." This institute would be a "considerably modified version" of the National Peace Agency proposed by the Democratic Advisory Council's Science and Technology Committee.

On March 12, Senator Kennedy's foreign-policy adviser, Democratic Congressman Chester Bowles of Connecticut, indicated a keen sensitivity to the world-wide uproar that would follow any American decision to resume nuclear tests. He noted that President Eisenhower had announced that the United States considered itself free to resume testing.

"But are we really free to do so?" Mr. Bowles asked in a speech before the Modern Forum in Los Angeles. He quoted a February 16 column of Walter Lippmann that

> there would be an uproar around the world. Quite competent and cool observers believe that the uproar would bring about a special meeting of

the General Assembly of the United Nations to protest against our action, and that if the question were put to a vote, we would be lucky to get ten votes out of the eighty.

Mr. Lippmann may overstate the uproar [said Mr. Bowles], but I doubt if he exaggerates by a wide margin. Unquestionably the damage to our moral position would be enormous if we resumed tests.

Thus we are facing another real dilemma. If we break off negotiations and resume testing, we bear the full brunt of world opinion. If we allow the test-ban negotiations to drag on, month after month, the Russians will get what they have wanted all along, an informal, *de facto* suspension of tests without any means available for the rest of the world to determine whether the U.S.S.R. is behaving.

No one who really hopes for the successful conclusion of the test negotiations will readily agree that nuclear tests, however small, should be resumed as long as there remains a chance, however small, that agreement will be reached. At the same time we know that an indefinite suspension of tests without controls could damage our military capability. This is especially true when we have no way of assuring that the U.S.S.R. has refrained from secret tests.

Like Senator Humphrey and other Democrats who favored an inspectable test-ban, Mr. Bowles suggested that "more reliable scientific preparation, in depth, might already have saved us much time, uncertainty, and embarrassment" on the inspection question.

To the degree that forces within the governments involved desire to test regardless of the verifiability of testing, a solution for the detection problem would not end this controversy. But it would end the source of tremendous confusion and obstruction at Geneva.

In a field in which progress on all sides is difficult, it would be prudent not to neglect those areas where more accurate scientific information might tip the scales of policy. One obvious area for effort is to improve the scientific underpinning of the controversy over detection of underground tests. Since we have not moved ahead with vigor to close this major technical gap in the past, it is essential that we do so now.

This was the same theme pursued by Senator Humphrey in the Senate Disarmament Subcommittee, where he had pressed State Department and Defense Department officials for prompt initiation of a multi-million-dollar research program in seismology and other fields to improve inspection techniques.

On March 14, the Democratic Advisory Council issued a report by seventeen scientists on its Committee on Science and Technology, dealing with "nuclear tests and national security."

On the committee were some of the best-known advocates of a nuclear test-ban, including Dr. Harrison Brown, Professor of Geochemistry at the California Institute of Technology, and Dr. Harold C. Urey, of the Institute of Technology and Engineering at the University of California in La Jolla. Another member was Trevor Gardner, then Chairman and President of Hycon Manufacturing Company, and formerly Assistant Secretary of Defense, who had resigned in protest against Eisenhower Administration economies at the expense of air power.

The committee recommended that the United States ask the Soviet Union to junk the 180-station control network for the nuclear test-ban as entirely inadequate, and accept in its place a grid with spacing between stations of only 250 miles. Instead of the 21 stations envisioned for the Soviet Union, this would have required some 400 stations, either manned or unmanned, and presumably more than 2,000 world-wide.

The new system, they claimed, would permit adequate monitoring down to a level of three kilotons, even if the explosions were muffled in deep underground cavities. At the same time the system could locate suspicious events within an area of roughly three square miles, "thus greatly facilitating on-site inspection."

In essence, the proposal of the seventeen scientists was a severe indictment of the Conference of Experts of 1958 and of the Eisenhower Administration for risking the nation's security with an entirely inadequate control system. But the remedy they suggested was so radical, so far from what State Department negotiators or even the public in general considered would be accepted by the Soviet Union that the proposal died very quickly.[62]

Dr. Hans Bethe later presented a similar proposal before the 1960 Joint Atomic Energy Committee hearings on test-ban control, calling for 600 stations inside the Soviet Union, all but 20 or 30 of them unmanned. But Ambassador James J. Wadsworth had inquired on two occasions at the Geneva test-ban talks if the Soviet Union would consider expanding the 180-station control network to include robot stations. On both occasions he had got an emphatic "No." [63]

American scientists on Technical Working Group II had considered the installation of unmanned stations to recoup some of the optimism on control that the 1958 Conference of Experts had generated. But most of them decided against it because they were not convinced that the unmanned stations would be tamper-proof or that the Soviet Union would be likely to accept them. Such stations would require periodic maintenance and this, it was reasoned, would lead the Russians to believe again that the West was trying to increase the amount of intelligence-gathering from the control network.

Split on Capitol Hill

On Capitol Hill there was some anxious waiting for a reaction from the Administration that would expose the latest Soviet treaty-moratorium proposal as the same old Soviet package, a comprehensive ban, in a different wrapping. But it did not come.

Senator Clinton P. Anderson, Democrat of New Mexico, and one of the most influential members of the Joint Committee on Atomic Energy, raised his voice to warn of the Soviet proposal on March 22:

> It is again an attempt to secure U.S. agreement binding the U.S. against all testing regardless of whether the agreement can be inspected. . . .
> Again the U.S. is asked to buy a "pig in the poke." We are asked to forego testing and to accept a totally inadequate inspection system. We are asked again to agree to a system based largely on trust of the Soviets rather than the real controls.

As far back as December 29, 1959, Senator Anderson recalled, he had expressed the opinion:

> It would be unwise to devote additional weeks to fruitless conference. This is still my strong opinion. To continue discussions on such a basis merely allows them to have the moratorium they want, and with no inspection. They have through procrastination and maneuvering succeeded in dragging on negotiations and securing a moratorium for sixteen critical months, with no controls. If the Soviets will not approach test negotiations realistically, we should terminate the conference. We should not allow them to prolong this delay month after month by successive "new proposals" which differ only insignificantly one from the other.

Here was a strong warning from a man who had as much power as any single person on Capitol Hill to block any treaty that the President might present to the Senate for advice and consent. It was especially significant that Senator Anderson chose to speak out publicly. Senator Humphrey, another Democrat, had operated publicly in supporting the test-ban negotiations. Senator Anderson, in worrying about the disarmament effort, had expressed most of his worries privately to the Executive Branch. Here, however, was evidence of a new-level alarm that the new Soviet proposal was not being viewed with the skepticism that Senator Anderson thought it deserved.

Lest the idea spread to the other end of Pennsylvania Avenue that the entire Senate was skeptical of the new Soviet proposal, Senator Hubert Humphrey, Chairman of the Senate Disarmament Sub-committee and at the time a prominent candidate for the Democratic Presidential-nomination, made a speech on the Senate floor the next day, March 23.

"My conclusion is that a comprehensive treaty is in sight," Senator Humphrey told the Senate. "The remaining differences can be solved. We may still have to wait for the outcome, but the ingredients for the solution of the remaining problems are now before us."

He referred to the projected summit conference then being scheduled for July in Paris. As the unofficial spokesman for the pro-test-ban elements in both the Executive and Legislative Branches, Senator Humphrey was speaking at a moment of high optimism. His views, as carefully stated in his Senate speech, therefore represented a significant body of opinion in both the Democratic and Republican leadership in Washington. The Senator began with a résumé of his four-point program:

1. A test-ban treaty should cover a permanent ban on all tests in the atmosphere, underwater, in outer space, and underground down to a certain threshold. In these categories detection and control are fairly simple. Last fall figures issued by the government indicated that between twenty-five and fifty on-site inspections would be needed to inspect all unidentified events equal to five kilotons and above. Below the threshold, no on-site inspection was to take place for a limited and specified period. It was in this category that the distinction between earthquakes and tests was so difficult that inspection of all unidentified events was either impractical or politically unacceptable.

2. A moratorium on weapons tests below the threshold should be declared and agreed to by the nuclear powers for two years.

3. During the period of the moratorium the United States, the Soviet Union, and the United Kingdom should conduct a high-priority research program to improve the capabilities for detecting small-yield underground tests and distinguishing them from small earthquakes.

4. If the research program indicated positive results, then the permanent ban should be extended to cover, with on-site inspection, all tests.

If no improvements in the inspection system were made or the Soviet Union did not cooperate, the moratorium should end and weapons tests should be permitted below the threshold "if military security required it," Senator Humphrey said. Also, if the Soviet Union were suspected of testing below the threshold, the United States should be free to resume its tests.

Even though on-site inspections would not be allowed below the threshold, the United States would have three ways of checking on Soviet tests below the threshold, he suggested. Control posts being established for the above-threshold network would at least detect, if not identify, many signals in the lower ranges; the United States would have its national system to rely upon; and "our regular intelligence sources would furnish information on whether suspicious activity was going on in certain areas."

President Eisenhower's February 11 proposal to the Soviet Union had accepted three of the Senator's general points, the concept of the threshold, a joint research program, and provisions for extending the permanent ban below the threshold as soon as science permitted. Mr. Eisenhower had been silent, however, on the moratorium on small tests.

The Soviet counterproposal, the Senator said, was similar to his own with the exception that the number of on-site inspections per year was not specified. "I might add," Senator Humphrey said, "that particular inspection is an important key point, because it is the number of on-site inspections which will really lend validity to an inspection and control program." He, too, credited on-site inspections with improved effectiveness.

According to the Humphrey analysis, there were two big differences between the United States and Soviet proposals:

First, the United States had not indicated whether it would agree to a moratorium on tests below the threshold, while the Soviet Union asked for a four- or five-year moratorium.

Second, the United States asked twenty on-site inspections above the threshold and the Soviet Union had not yet stated how many on-site inspections would be allowed.

Senator Humphrey pointed the obvious way to a compromise: The Soviet Union should be willing to accept at least twenty inspections a year and the United States should be willing to accept a moratorium on small underground tests "for a designated period pending the outcome of the research program."

He acknowledged that there might be some opposition to this proposed solution. "It may be argued that the Soviet Union might try to sneak a few tests beneath the threshold which would go unnoticed; that is, detected but unidentified and uninspected. Is this possibility too great a risk to take for a two-year period? This is the question to answer."

His answer, of course, was that accepting the uninspected moratorium was not too great a risk to run, especially since international control posts, the United States own detection system, and regular intelligence sources would still be available for keeping an eye on Soviet cheating.

There were others in Washington, represented by Senator Anderson, members of the Atomic Energy Commission, and high officials in the Defense Department, who disagreed with Senator Humphrey. Mr. Humphrey had much greater faith, for instance, in the Central Intelligence Agency's ability to compensate for whatever weaknesses there might be in the control system.

It appeared to many that the Soviet Union would have a comparatively free hand to "sneak a few tests beneath the threshold which would go unnoticed," as Senator Humphrey suggested.

And if they went unnoticed, there would be strong pressures to renew the moratorium indefinitely until the Soviet Union had overtaken the alleged United States lead in nuclear-weapons development.

Senator Humphrey made one more point: If there was a "real indication" that the Soviet Union had tried to test secretly during the moratorium period, he said, "then I believe we should ask for the right to inspect the suspected area. In other words, we may have to insist on the right to have the quota on inspections applied below as well as above the threshold, if necessary."

The State Department was unenthusiastic about this because it would paper over the threshold concept Moscow was allegedly accepting. It wasn't the United States which would have to insist, either. Moscow had already offered to apply on-site inspections above and below the threshold.

Soviet Premier Khrushchev, answering questions of members of the French Peace Council, also took the view that the stage had been set for a nuclear test-ban. He also accepted Western ideas about the threshold. In a remarkable admission of the threshold theory which his negotiators in Geneva never permitted themselves, Premier Khrushchev said:

> Now there are differences only on the most insignificant range of problems: underground explosions which cannot be recorded by any instruments. What is our attitude to such explosions? We accepted the proposal of the United Kingdom and the United States and said: let us work together to identify such explosions, but as long as there is no method of distinguishing these explosions from natural volcanic tremors, let 'us act in this way: Each side undertakes not to stage such small explosions. We never stage underground explosions, and we are not preparing for them. If this solution is adopted, all issues will be settled, and a protocol can be signed. We have already agreed on all other questions.[64]

Here was another reference to "volcanic" tremors, a particular kind of earthquake which, for some reason, fascinated the Soviet Premier.

Both sides in the nuclear test-ban controversy in the United States, on Capitol Hill and in the Administration, knew that the Soviet counterproposal had set the stage for crucial decisions. So did London. Britain's Prime Minister Macmillan hastily arranged to come to Washington at the end of March to confer with President Eisenhower on concerting a reply to the Soviet proposal.

On March 25, AEC Chairman John A. McCone, whose interests were not the same as Britain's, spoke out in Los Angeles. He was alarmed:

> We seek and insist upon safeguards that will foreclose beyond reasonable doubt the possibility of one party continuing weapons development in secrecy and thus gaining an important military advantage.
>
> [After 17 months and almost 200 meetings, he observed with delicate sarcasm], the safeguards we seek, and must have, hinge on the important issues yet to be resolved.
>
> [Although the United States and Britain have] faithfully [adhered to their promise not to test], we are told, but have no way of verifying, that the Soviets have also stopped their tests.
>
> [Testing underground would be an attractive objective for a violator.] It is relatively easy, produces the desired scientific data, and if properly done, releases no radioactivity into the atmosphere. Hence, the public fear of fallout, a serious concern of the United States government, is not an issue. The question is raised as to the value of underground tests. It is a new technique and not widely understood. However, I can say with assurance that weapons, large and small, can be developed and improved by testing in this medium. It follows, therefore, that any decision to suspend nuclear testing must be accompanied by a control arrangement which will assure us that this type of testing has been stopped by all parties.
>
> [With decoupling, a 100-kiloton test] might escape identification altogether. This we have known and have demonstrated repeatedly to the

Russian scientists. It seems to be their penchant for security to ignore these facts.

[The latest Soviet proposal, of the week before, at first had appeared] on the surface to accept our principle of appropriate controls.

When examined closely, however, the Soviets were doing quite the reverse. They were calling for a complete suspension of all tests for a period that could stretch to five years or possibly indefinitely. Furthermore they insisted that in the most critical area of tests, under the threshold of which I have spoken, we accept them on faith.

Thus, the United States and its allies, according to Soviet plan, would hold our nuclear experimentation idle for at least five years, or more, and during this long interval we would have no way of telling whether the Russians, let alone their Chinese partners, were observing a similar restraint.

The Soviet proposal has been widely hailed as a concession. It is not.

It concedes that we have been right in our position that there is a lower limit on the seismic capabilities of the detection system we have been talking about.

But their proposition failed to deal with the problem. Instead it sets forth in language designed to deceive the people of the world that a plan for adequate control finally was being offered by the Soviets.

Nothing could be further from the truth.

This was an unusual public position taken by one of the most responsible members of the Eisenhower Administration on the eve of the President's important decision-making conference with Prime Minister Macmillan. Mr. McCone had never been so blunt before.

What the Soviet Union was asking, Mr. McCone said, was that the United States "forego for an indefinite period the safeguards that President Eisenhower said are 'indispensible prerequisites' to an agreement."

Chairman McCone was thus seeking, in a delicate way, to pin the President to his earlier conclusion that whatever arms-control measures were agreed upon must be accompanied by the "indispensible prerequisites" of adequate inspection.

On the issue of secrecy, Mr. McCone declared, it was the Soviet Union, not the United States, that must change: "The hope rests in a change on their side. Are they now willing to drop the wall of secrecy, draw back the Iron Curtain and present to the world a frankness and action commensurate with their word, so often and so recently repeated?"

It was obvious from the tone of his remarks that the AEC Chairman strongly advocated standing pat on the President's February 11 proposal, not moving in the direction that Senator Humphrey, Soviet Premier Khrushchev, and, it soon became clear, Prime Minister Macmillan, advocated.

If President Eisenhower was to remain consistent with his determined news-conference statements of February 11, it was clear to Prime Minister Macmillan that a favorable response to the Soviet offer would be difficult to formulate. At the news conference the President had said "We are not going to make an agreement when we can't know—and we cannot have any information as to whether or not it will be carried out by the other fellow as well as ourselves. . . ."

What the Soviet Union had asked for was an uninspected ban below the 4.75 threshold. An experienced diplomat like Mr. Macmillan would not have put it this way, but his mission was to talk the President out of his rigid demand for adequate inspection.

The Federation of American Scientists, the group of physicists, biologists, and other scholars long active in the support of nuclear test-ban proposals, was bent on the same mission. It welcomed as "an important step" what it called Soviet "conditional acceptance of President Eisenhower's February 11 proposal to ban all nuclear tests except small underground tests."

Putting scientific weight behind the optimism of Senator Humphrey, the Federation declared:

[The proposed detection network,] if supplemented by about twenty on-site inspections per year in Russia, would disclose not only all blasts in excess of earthquake magnitude 4.75, but would be sufficiently effective to discourage clandestine testing below that level as well. At the least, the risk of evasion would be far less than under the present unmonitored suspension of tests.

[Inspection would be] really quite effective at the upper limit of small tests, because there is no line distinctly dividing the large from the small blasts. A violator would risk detection in all but the very small end of this small-test group. Even the small-test moratorium will thus not be entirely "on the honor system," as has been erroneously implied but, to an important degree, will be monitored, thereby discouraging evasion. The risk of evasion, or of the Soviet's learning something significant, should there be evasion, is much less than with the present unmonitored moratorium on all sizes.

Nuclear explosions for peaceful purposes should be postponed, the Federation said, rather than allow such events to upset the nuclear test-ban talks.

Even before President Eisenhower and Prime Minister Macmillan of Great Britain flew to Camp David for their hush-hush conferences on the latest Soviet proposal, it was clear in Washington that the President did not intend to be drawn into a soft, compromise proposal. The British also had let it be known in advance that Prime Minister Macmillan would not try to persuade Washington the Soviet proposal could be accepted outright. The idea would be to find some middle ground between acceptance and rejection.

After a day and a half of conversations at the Camp David mountain retreat, the President and Prime Minister issued a communiqué expressing their general view of the Soviet counteroffer. It was favorable, but clearly intended to encourage the Soviet Union to move toward the Western viewpoint.

First, the treaty barring tests above the 4.75 threshold underground and in other environments should be signed, the two leaders said, and arrangements should be made for a coordinated research program. Once this had been done, the two free-world leaders declared, they would be ready to institute a voluntary moratorium "of agreed duration" below the threshold, "to be accomplished by unilateral declaration of each of the three powers."

The timing was the most significant point. First the threshold treaty should be signed, the President and Prime Minister said, and the joint research program should be arranged. After that, there could be a voluntary moratorium of "agreed duration"—but not written into the treaty, only proclaimed in unilateral declarations.

The sooner the research program could start, the better, they said. President Eisenhower was standing his ground, without inviting a break-off.

Here was the important paragraph from the Camp David joint declaration:

> Meanwhile, the President and the Prime Minister believed that progress can be made toward their ultimate objective of a comprehensive agreement. They have agreed that much has been accomplished in these Geneva negotiations toward this objective. They point out that in the effort to achieve the early conclusion of a treaty there are a number of important specific problems to be resolved. These include the questions of an adequate quota of on-site inspections, the composition of the control commission, control post staffing, and voting matters, as well as arrangements for peaceful purposes detonations. They believe that negotiation on these points should be speeded up and completed at the earliest possible time. The Prime Minister and the President have agreed that as soon as this treaty has been signed and arrangements made for a coordinated research program for the purpose of progressively improving control methods for events below a seismic magnitude of 4.75, they will be ready to institute a voluntary moratorium of agreed duration on nuclear weapons tests below that threshold, to be accomplished by unilateral declaration of each of the three powers. In order to expedite progress, the President and the Prime Minister have agreed to invite the Soviet government to join at once with their two governments in making arrangements for such a coordinated research program and putting it into operation.[65]

Once the treaty was signed, it was understood, each country would institute its own ratification processes.

Officials later indicated that the United States was thinking of an "agreed duration" of only one year for the voluntary moratorium.

In effect, the President and Prime Minister had placed five conditions on their joining in a comprehensive test-ban, even for one year. Five important articles in the first-phase treaty would have to be agreed to: the quota for on-site inspections, the composition of the control commission, the staffing of control posts, "voting matters," and peaceful-purposes detonations.

There would have to be inspections both above and below the threshold, as well, officials said in explanation of the communiqué.

Besides the twenty or twenty-one on-site inspections the United States wanted above the threshold, there should be another "X number," an official said—to cover suspicious events below the threshold.

By speaking of the need for inspection below the threshold, the United States was weakening its position that all on-site inspections should be based on scientific considerations. There would be so many unidentified events below the threshold that there could be no hope of making any scientific determination of how many should be inspected. It would be only a random check.

The joint Anglo-American position actually was the asking price for a nuclear test-ban that the British and American leaders expected to present at the Geneva summit conference, then set for May 16, 1960.

President Eisenhower met the press the day after his Camp David talks with Prime Minister Macmillan ended. He narrowed even further the significance of the Anglo-American concession on a voluntary moratorium below the threshold by conceding that his successor in the White House would have the right to end any short-term moratorium on small, underground weapons tests that might be agreed on with the Soviet Union during his term.

The four- or five-year period for a small-test moratorium, as the Soviet Union had suggested, would be "just excessive," the President told newsmen.

At the same time, Mr. Eisenhower paid tribute to the Soviet Union for having come a long way toward the Western position on the test-ban inspection issue. "All signs," he said, had indicated that the Kremlin really wanted a degree of disarmament and a test-ban.

"The driving force behind me," Mr. Eisenhower said, was his desire to head off expansion of the number of world nuclear powers from the then-four members. The chance that other countries would join Britain, the Soviet Union, the United States, and France in the nuclear club "ought to be stopped," he said.

The general expectation was that the number of on-site inspections to be allowed each year would be a matter for settlement at the summit conference.

Secretary of State Christian Herter expressed the opinion on April 4 that the United States and the United Kingdom had by their joint response to the latest Soviet offer "brought within reach" an agreement that "could well be an historic turning point in the quest for the agreed arms-control measures which would lead to a far greater degree of international peace and security."

Now, the Secretary added, "it is up to the Soviet Union. It is their move."

The Eisenhower-Macmillan pronouncement, which represented conditional acceptance of the Soviet proposal for a new-type comprehensive nuclear test ban, was received with misgivings by test-ban foes and with satisfaction by test-ban advocates.

In the Joint Congressional Committee on Atomic Energy, there was consternation and worry that the public had not been properly warned about the inadequacies of the inspection system envisaged in the test ban. The Soviet Union, the United States, and Britain were maneuvering for a summit deal on the nuclear test-ban problem. It was in this atmosphere that the Joint Committee scheduled a series of dramatic hearings on test-ban controls.

Part III

THE 1960 JOINT COMMITTEE HEARINGS

Chapter 12

Probability Almost Zero

It was not until a year and a half after the Geneva Conference of Experts had produced its misleading results that the American scientists who had participated in the technical conference with the Russians were "surfaced." On April 19, 1960, the Joint Committee on Atomic Energy began four days of hearings to explore "the technical aspects of detection and inspection controls of a nuclear-weapons test ban."

In the first hour of the first day's hearing, Dr. Harold Brown, of the Lawrence Radiation Laboratory in Livermore, one of the participants in the 1958 Conference of Experts, gave enough testimony to scuttle the whole test-ban negotiation. But an indifferent nation paid little heed. There would be about 500 earthquakes equivalent to 1 kiloton or larger (with Rainier coupling) in the Soviet Union each year, he said. The American side in the Geneva treaty negotiations was at that time demanding twenty on-site inspections per year. Representative Jack Westland, Republican of Washington, suggested that even with this number of inspections the odds would be twenty-five to one against catching a violator.

Dr. Brown replied:

You would have one chance in twenty-five of inspecting a nuclear explosion if somebody had been foolish enough to set off a nuclear explosion with a seismic signal that was easily detected. I think if somebody is going to carry out a nuclear explosion he is going to take rather extreme precautions. *It would only be an accident, I think, if it were detected.* If it were detected then there would be according to this arithmetic 20 out of 500 or one out of 25 chances that you would have an on-site inspection, not allowing for any additional selection you might hope to be able to make either on the basis of the seismic signals or on the basis of likelihood figured some other way. This would still leave the question of whether you would find the event even if you inspected it. . . .

Suppose, then, one were inspecting on-site an event which had actually been a nuclear explosion, what would be the probability that one would be able to localize it sufficiently so that drilling would allow it to be identified as such? The Conference of Experts was unable to answer that question and that is not surprising. Though further studies have taken place since then, the question can still not be answered today. If one reads what the Conference of Experts had to say about this question and its conclusion on the capability of the system, one finds the statement that there would always be some probability of on-site inspection establishing a violation if one had occurred. This is equivalent to saying that the probability is not zero.

Senator Hickenlooper, who had explored this same question in the Humphrey subcommittee hearings, asked if the probability of establishing a violation would not be "almost zero." Dr. Brown cautioned that this was a matter of opinion not based completely on technical knowledge because not enough facts were available.

> [But], *I think it can be made very close to zero.* . . . It depends so much on the circumstances. It depends a great deal on how well someone is able to anticipate what effects may be, although he could of course start off with small explosions which nobody could find and then scale up. It depends on the degree of success. It depends on what one is able to find out in other ways. One may be able to know something about activities in various areas which would enable one to localize things. I think that is something that one might have to depend upon. I myself would prefer not to depend on it very much. But then I think—here again it is a personal opinion—*it is fairly important to have more than a rather slim chance of catching someone. The fact that he is anxious for you not to catch him is likely to result in a very small chance of your catching him.* [Author's italics.]
>
> [Dr. Brown observed that] *there is always some level below which a violator can test with essentially complete immunity. I think if a violator is willing to go to a little trouble, one kiloton is well within that limit. It will be undetected and unidentified by any system which I have heard proposed.* [Author's emphasis.]

Several experts appearing before the Joint Committee quickly established that the chances for a violator to get away with a sneak nuclear shot would be good. Whether a nation would avail itself of the opportunity to violate the treaty, however, was a matter of judgment about which scientists disagreed. This judgment was based on four factors in the view of one of the participants: first, the importance of continuing weapons-development; second, the mechanical effort required on the part of a violator to carry out this violation; third, opportunities that might be passed up in other areas if this effort were carried through; and fourth, evaluation of what chance a detection system had to provide an adequate deterrent.

The incentive to cheat would be high, Dr. Brown said, thereby taking issue with others who claimed underground shots would have little use. In pointing out that for the development of small nuclear weapons underground tests would be, in general, just as valuable as if they were held above ground, he said:

I think the military effectiveness of nuclear explosions in the atmosphere has now been determined many, many times in various tests in the atmosphere, and that problem is quite well covered by now. The underground tests really would be aimed at something different. These tests would be aimed at determining the energy yield and characteristics of a new design of explosion. . . . There's one exception to this that I perhaps should point out, and that is, the effects in the upper atmosphere which may go to determine some military applications [that] are not completely understood. Those could not easily be determined underground.

Dr. Brown specified that his remarks on the capabilities of the system were directed at the 180-station network set up by the 1958 Conference of Experts. The system did not take into account seismic improvements.

It does not take into account decoupling or subsequent observations which may have shown that the system had less capability than thought, nor does it take into account that some of the equipment which was discussed at the time of the Conference of Experts and subsequently does not, in fact, exist nor did it exist then. In other words, it was a hypothetical system with probably better equipment than had existed until that time or than exists now.

The second scientist to appear before the Joint Committee, Dr. Wolfgang Panofsky, testified with the same revealing candor about this high-altitude test detection systems that Technical Working Group I had examined in Geneva the summer before.

"From the purely technical point of view, it appears likely, given arbitrarily high incentives on the part of the violator, it will always be possible to devise an essentially undetectable means of carrying out the violation," he said.

By incorporating shields into the test device, he observed, the violator could reduce the chances of detection or force the detection network to a more expansive level of efficiency.

"I believe, however, that before that point [of devising undetectable means of violation] is reached, there is a question of whether there really is sufficient incentive either for the violator to carry out tests under these extreme conditions or for the detecting system to be expanded to the maximum possible degree."

Thus Dr. Panofsky rated the incentive to cheat at high altitudes lower than did Dr. Brown underground.

Dr. Brown estimated that "in almost all cases" one could be sure that any tactical weapon could be manufactured on the basis of tests as low as one kiloton. Dr. Alvin Graves, of the Los Alamos Weapons Laboratory, made much the same point.

Dr. Hans Bethe warned, however, that this would apply only to countries "already very sophisticated in weapon design. It will not be possible for a new power entering the field."

He also questioned whether there was "the overriding necessity" of getting still more types of tactical weapons. "We have already a very large number of tactical weapons," Dr. Bethe declared. This judgment, shared by White House science advisers, was the principal reason that President Eisenhower decided to go on with the unilateral moratorium. He took the advice of scientists who said that the tactical weapons already being made were satisfactory, although admittedly not ideal.

Among the questions the scientists posed themselves in the Joint Committee hearings were these: What happens if one country cheats and another one does not? What kind of relative advance can the first one make? How important is such an answer?

These three questions raised the problem of what the experts in weapons development could do with explosions in the range of 10, 20, or 30 kilotons. Dr. Brown believed:

> One can make many advances in design of strategic weapons of very much larger yield. I will not make exactly the same statement as I made about one kiloton relative to tactical weapons—namely that one can make all the advances one can think of. I think this is a somewhat different situation. I think one is rather more limited in the advances that one can make in strategic weapons with concealed explosions in the 10- or 20-kiloton range. However, I think a very substantial fraction of the advances that a country developing nuclear weapons might want to make in the strategic field could be made with such explosions. These two figures—1 kiloton and 20 kilotons, I think—are fairly significant ones to examine, because . . . there will always be a threshold.
>
> Actually there are two kinds of thresholds. There is the detection threshold, below which one can, in fact, not locate an event at all. There is another threshold higher than the detection threshold for any given system station spacing and given kind of instruments—which we can call the identification threshold. It is characterized by being the yield below which the system is swamped by the number of inspections.

In a panel discussion between a group of the testifying scientists and the Joint Committee, Dr. Dean S. Carder, Chief Seismologist of the United States Coast Guard and Geodetic Survey in Washington, pointed to another "variable" in the inspection system: the reader of the seismograms. He illustrated how he would have read the first motion of one signature of the 19-kiloton Blanca shot as an "up" motion, but most other people would have read it as a "down" motion. The down motion would have indicated an earthquake. "I am not the one who will read those records. Someone else will read them. What I see in them does not matter," Dr. Carder said.[1]

Chairman Holifield inquired: "So we have a little variable factor in the interpretation of the reader also to consider?"

"This is correct," Dr. Carder responded. "I would say there is quite a bit of intuition involved."

Decoupling

Dr. Albert L. Latter, originator of the big-hole theory, opened the discussion of decoupling in the Joint Committee. The strength of the seismic signal, Dr. Latter said, depends on five factors: the yield of the explosion, its depth, the medium in which it is exploded, the local geology, and characteristics of the explosion chamber, particularly its size:

"All these factors can be controlled, and we must assume that anyone wishing to violate the agreement would choose that combination of conditions which gives a minimum signal."

Four of the five factors which influence the size of the seismic signal were the same for all six American underground nuclear shots. The depth, the medium, the local geology and the size of the explosion chamber were unchanged. Only the yield was changed. But the size of the shot chamber "is now known to be particularly important and is the basis of the so-called big-hole method of decoupling," Dr. Latter said.

He then gave this explanation of how the big-hole decoupling method works:

To give a quantitative understanding of the big hole requires the use of a lot of mathematics. However, the essential physical idea is a very simple one. If the explosion occurs in a small hole—as is the case for a tamped explosion—the pressure which acts on the surrounding medium is very great and the medium is not strong enough to stand the pressure. As a result, the hole must expand and this causes a large motion of the surrounding earth. It is this motion, this large motion, in the immediate neighborhood of the explosion which shows up at great distances as a tiny seismic signal.

On the other hand, if the explosion is made in a big hole, the pressure which the surrounding medium experiences is not very great and the medium can stand the pressure. As a result, there is very little expansion of the hole and essentially no motion of the surrounding earth.

I think you can see from this description that there is not really any question as to whether the big hole works in principle; it does. The only question is: how big does the hole have to be to insure that the pressure from the surrounding medium is not too great?

Before turning to this question of how big the hole must be, and if it is big enough, what sort of reduction in signal will occur, I want to mention a rather curious fact: namely, that once the hole is big enough, the signal will not be further reduced by making the hole any bigger. This happens because of an accidental cancellation of two opposite effects. One is, that as the hole gets bigger, less energy goes into the earth's motion, which tends to decrease the signal. On the other hand, it turns out that the energy which does go into the signal has a longer wave length as the hole gets bigger, and this longer wave length signal is more easily propagated to great distances through the earth, which tends to increase the signal. The net effect is that the seismic signal which occurs at great distance from the scene of the explosion is independent of the size of the hole—provided the hole is big enough. As a matter of historical interest, this fact that the distant signal does not depend upon the hole size was known to United States scientists prior to the first Conference of Experts in 1958, but at that time they did not realize that this is true only provided the hole is big enough and as a result they came to the erroneous conclusion that a big hole is no different from a little hole and hence a big hole will not decouple the signal. It was not until the early part of 1959 that we came to understand the importance of making the hole bigger than some critical size to insure that the pressure would not be too great on the surrounding medium.

I turn now to the question: How large is the seismic signal from an explosion in a big hole compared to the signal from the same yield explosion fully tamped in Nevada tuff? In other words, what is the big-hole decoupling factor?

The answer to this question is based upon measurements, which were made of the earth motion in the neighborhood of one of our underground nuclear explosions, in conjunction with some theoretical analysis which employs the well-understood laws of elasticity. The result is that the seismic signal will be reduced by a factor of about 300 if the hole is in a hard-rock medium such as salt or granite. . . .[2]

The analysis which is used to make this estimate has been carefully scrutinized by many scientists for more than a year, and we may be quite confident that the decoupling factor of 300 is solidly founded. . . . I would like to point out that not all of the factor of 300 is due to the action of the hole. Part of the effect is due to the medium in which the hole is made. If the hole is made in a soft medium like Nevada tuff, the signal would be reduced by a factor of about 50 instead of 300. The further factor of 6 comes from making the hole in salt or granite, which are stronger media.

The difficulty imposed on the control system by such large decoupling factors is of course obvious. To use a by-now-familiar example, a 100-kiloton explosion in a big hole looks seismically like an explosion of only one-third kiloton under ordinary tamped conditions. Such a weak seismic signal would not even be noticed by the proposed Geneva control system against the natural background of seismic noise.

Turning now to the crucial question of how big the hole must be to produce such a large decoupling, I would like to recall to you the figure which we presented in Geneva to the Technical Working Group II, 70,000 cubic meters per kiloton of yield for roughly spherical holes at a depth of about 1 kilometer. To be a little more graphic, this means that for a 20-kiloton explosion the hole must have a diameter of 140 meters. Still more graphic perhaps—450 feet. This is a very large hole compared to holes that we are used to. But, the only meaningful way to judge the size of the hole in the present context is to ask can such a hole be made? How much does it cost? And how long will it take? These are questions which fall outside my competence, but I have understood that the most expert construction engineers in our country say that such holes are feasible and indeed could be made to accommodate yields all the way up to 100 kilotons, and possibly greater, at a reasonable cost and in a reasonable time. . . .

Also I want to remind you that such a large size for the hole was stipulated in order to be absolutely sure that the full decoupling factor of 300 would be achieved. In other words, this criterion for the big-hole size was a conservative one which was laid down prior to any experiments. Experiments were needed to determine how the decoupling factor might be reduced if the size of the hole were made smaller than the safe size. This was one of the principal reasons for the so-called Cowboy series of tests held recently in Louisiana. . . .

The experiments were a complete success, and from them we obtained all the information that we had hoped to obtain. The experiments demonstrated beyond any doubt that the big-hole principle of decoupling is correct. Specifically, the experiments showed that the seismic signal from a fully tamped explosion in the salt was about 120 times bigger than that from the same yield explosion in one of the cavities.[3] This figure of 120 results from the analysis not just of a single piece of data but of many measurements made for yields of explosion and at various distances from the point of the explosion.

We must now ask the question: Why does this value of 120 differ from the decoupling factor of 300 previously mentioned? The answer to this question is that the Cowboy experiment compares the signal from a hole in salt with the signal from a fully tamped explosion in salt, whereas the factor of 300 refers to the signal from a hole in salt compared to fully tamped explosion in Nevada tuff. The latter comparison is the one which is relevant for the Geneva detection system. The best estimate of this decoupling factor is still 300. The ratio of 300 to 120, namely 2.5, is interpreted as the amount of decoupling which can be achieved simply by exploding the bomb in salt rather than tuff, without making use of a big hole at all. This is a very important by-product result which has come from the Cowboy experiments. It says that the seismic signal from an underground explosion can be reduced by a factor of two or three simply by changing the medium, and it raises the question whether other media might give even smaller signals. This question remains to be answered by further experiments.

Now let me come to the question: What happens to the decoupling factor if the hole size is made smaller than the critical size? The results of the Cowboy experiments in this connection were very surprising. The best theoretical judgment prior to the experiment was that the hole would behave exactly like a boiler, which when subjected to too large a pressure loses its effectiveness in an abrupt and violent way. The Cowboy experiments, however, showed that the hole does not behave in this way. Rather it is possible to reduce the hole size by a large factor and at the same time maintain an appreciable amount of decoupling. In one case, the hole was too small for a yield of the explosion by a factor of 15; but the decoupling was degraded only by a factor of 4 or 5. Furthermore, the damage to the cavity was slight and it was possible to use it again. This time the yield of the explosion was doubled. The decoupling was further reduced but only by another factor of 2. These experiments indicate that it would be possible to reduce the size of the hole from the safe volume we had stipulated, namely 70,000 cubic meters per kiloton, to a size only one-thirtieth as great, and still achieve a very appreciable decoupling factor, perhaps of the order of 30.

Of course, all these results are based upon experiments with conventional rather than nuclear explosives. It is proper to ask whether our conclusions would have been different if nuclear explosives had been used. Here we have only theoretical analysis to rely upon. Theory says that for two explosions of the same yield, one conventional and the other nuclear, in the same size cavity, the conventional explosive creates a much more severe pressure on the cavity wall than the nuclear explosive does. That is, theory says that the decoupling factor which would be obtained with a nuclear explosive is, if anything, greater than the decoupling factor obtained with a conventional explosive. I think we can be quite confident of this result, but I also believe it is important to demonstrate it experimentally with nuclear explosions.

By way of summary let me now enumerate what are the important conclusions from the Cowboy tests:

1. The decoupling principle is correct.

2. The decoupling factor for a hole in salt relative to a tamped shot in salt is about 120.

3. The decoupling factor which is relevant for the Geneva system is for a hole in salt relative to a tamped shot in the Nevada tuff. The best estimate of this quantity is still 300.

4. The difference between the factor of 300 and the factor 120 is explained as due to a medium effect for tamped explosions. In other words a decoupling factor of two or three results simply by using salt rather than Nevada tuff as the explosion medium.

5. A violator of the test ban would not have to build a cavity with a large margin of safety. The decoupling factor is reduced by exceeding the safe limit but only in a gradual way.

6. For explosions of the order of 10 or 20 kilotons, which is a militarily significant yield, it is not necessary to achieve the full decoupling factor of 300. For such explosions a decoupling factor of 30 or 40 would be ample to insure that they would not be detected by the proposed Geneva system. This smaller amount of decoupling can be obtained by using relatively small holes, in fact a size in which holes are customarily made for storing petroleum products. In other words it appears possible with existing holes to conceal explosions of the order of ten or twenty kilotons from the proposed Geneva system.

This last conclusion, I think, is of particular importance, and it would be desirable to provide further confirmation of this conclusion with explosions of greater yield and of a nuclear rather than a conventional type.

To make a 300-kiloton nuclear weapon look like a 10-kiloton shot, Dr. Latter estimated, the hole in salt should have a diameter of 360 feet. The diameter of the hole in salt should be 250 feet to reduce a 100-kiloton shot to three kilotons; a 195-foot-diameter hole could make a 50-kiloton shot look like less than 2 kilotons.

Nuclear yield (kilotons)	Diameter of hole to decouple in salt (feet)	
	Factor of 300*	Factor of 30†
10	360	115
20	450	145
50	610	195
100	770	250
300	1,100	360

* Or 50 in tuff.
† Possibly 5 in tuff.

Note: The apparent yield as measured on distant seismographs is the nuclear yield divided by the decoupling factor. For example, a 100-kiloton explosion in a 250-foot-diameter hole in salt would have an apparent yield of about 3 kilotons.

Dr. Latter also cautioned that changing the depth of the explosion could also influence the signal but there were no experiments to show how. "We need such experiments," he told the Joint Committee. Effects of local geology also were unexplored, he noted.

He mentioned again other possibilities for refining the big-hole technique, pumping out a large portion of the air in the big hole, or introducing into the cavity heat-absorbing materials like finely divided carbon.

Preliminary calculations indicated, Dr. Latter said, that the decoupling factor could be raised to several thousand by introducing divided carbon. "In short, I believe there are still many advances to be made in the art of concealing underground nuclear explosions."

The committee next heard from L. P. Meade, an engineer of the Phillips Petroleum Company. He reported the United States already has around 300 underground holes, most of them about 300 feet in diameter but a few of them up to 500 feet in diameter, mostly along the Gulf Coast in Texas and Louisiana.

Most of these would be able to produce a decoupling factor of 30, compared with Nevada tuff, for nuclear explosions up to 300 kilotons. In other words, holes already exist in the Texas and Louisiana underground for making a 300-kiloton nuclear explosion look like a 10-kiloton explosion, a 100-kiloton explosion look like a 3-kiloton explosion and a 50-kiloton explosion look like less than 2 kilotons.

Besides these holes, used by petroleum companies for storage and by salt companies for producing salt, Mr. Meade showed the Joint Committee how to build 500-foot diameter holes—they could go up to 750 feet in diameter, he said—from scratch, in salt domes which exist in Texas, Louisiana, and to a lesser extent in Kansas, New York state, and Ontario (Canada).

If the aim were to keep the cost down, it would take an estimated four years to hollow out a salt dome and build a 500-foot-diameter spherical hole, Mr. Meade said. The cost would be about $3.5 million.[4]

If the aim, on the other hand, were to build the underground cavern quickly, the same job could be done in sixteen months at a cost of about $12.5 million.

Mr. Meade described in detail the methods for drilling into the salt dome, pumping water into a small area and gradually washing out the salt, pumping out the brine.

A larger hole, on the order of 750 feet in diameter, would take two years and cost about $14.5 million. This cavity could produce a 300 decoupling factor for 90- or 100-kiloton explosions.

These cost and time factors involved in the building of decoupling holes would be feasible or unfeasible, of course, depending on who was the judge. It was entirely predictable, then, that the advocates of a test ban found the cost and time factors so great that they would discourage a violator; and the foes of the test ban found the cost and time factors would not deter a violator.

There are some large man-made caverns, not in use, filled with brine and owned by salt companies, Mr. Meade told the committee. Presumably these would be available at even less cost.

Representative Van Zandt, of Pennsylvania, stated it as a "fact" that a nuclear shot in outer space would cost about $20 million. Underground cavities, he observed, would provide far better instrumentation and could be prepared "at much more reasonable cost."

In both environments, of course, the radiation hazard from atmospheric tests could be eliminated.

Mr. Meade said that a brief search of geological literature had uncovered about 50 references to salt domes in the Soviet Union. One which he cited mentioned 100 salt domes in the area of the Soviet Union between the south end of the Ural Mountains and the north shore of the Caspian Sea. It was expected that "future discoveries" in the same area would bring the total to more than 300 salt domes, "including the deep ones."[5]

In addition, Mr. Meade observed, "the salt mines of Siberia are legendary."

Representative Van Zandt and several of his colleagues on the Joint Committee were impressed by Mr. Meade's testimony showing the ease with which large underground caverns could be constructed. "From your statement you convince me," Mr. Van Zandt declared, "it is really possible to do some cheating when using these salt domes. If the Russians have them, there may be some cheating going on."

Mr. Meade was asked how difficult it would be to find evidence that brine had been pumped out of such salt domes, perhaps in a gulf or a body of water nearby.

It would depend on what efforts were made to dispose of the brine [Mr. Meade said]. In producing a salt cavity we do not leave any traces of our brine. There are various governmental agencies that don't like brine dumped loosely in the rivers. We usually use disposal wells. We drill a well down to another formation which has salt water in it and inject the brine into that. A lot of the Gulf Coast cavities have the brine dumped into the Gulf of Mexico. You ask is it possible to detect it. It probably would be if you instrumented and searched for it. However, it apparently has not upset the equilibrium of the Gulf enough so that anybody has noticed it so far. You must also remember that a lot of brine is produced with oil. That brine, too, is dumped into the ocean.

The problem for an on-site inspection team, in catching the evidence of an underground cavity in salt, it appeared, would be to prove deposits of brine that might be found, at considerable difficulty, had come not from oil exploration or petroleum-storage activities, but from nuclear testing operations.

The bayou country of southern Louisiana, Mr. Meade said,

seems to me [to be] the easiest place in the world to go ahead and build a cavity without detection. You would move in . . . on a salt dome that didn't have any oil and sulphur. You would set up a drilling rig that for all the world is an oil drilling rig. People know there are lots of oil wells in that country. After having completed it the rig is taken down, you have left there some pumps and other things that are often associated with oil wells. You might lay a pipe out into the Gulf for several miles and lay the brine down on the bottom of the Gulf, 50 or 60 feet below the surface. Due to the fact that it has a specific gravity of about 1.2 as contrasted to slightly over one for sea water, which is roughly one-tenth of saline, it would stratify and lay on the bottom of the Gulf, in my estimation. We know of cases in coastal rivers which are tidal where the top layer may be 8 or 10,000 parts per million of salt and the bottom will be up to 25,000 parts per million of salt, which is sea water.[6]

In their presentations Dr. Latter and Mr. Meade had developed, to a considerable extent, one ingenious method of evading the inspection system for a nuclear test ban. It remained, however, for Dr. Edward Teller to impress upon the Committee that even this painstaking, detailed, and proved method of decoupling had only scratched the surface of evasion possibilities.

As Dr. Latter had indicated, there were other methods to get more decoupling out of the big hole. Dr. Teller explained several more of these:

This [decoupling] factor of 300 is greatly in excess of any improvements which had been suggested and which it will take a long time to carry into practice. Dr. Latter has also emphasized that the decoupling by a factor of 300 is not necessarily the strongest decoupling which could be accomplished. It is merely the simplest kind of decoupling, that kind of decoupling for which a purely theoretical estimate could be carried out and about which everybody is in full agreement.

There are other possible procedures of decoupling, all of them based in one way or another on the presence of some sort of cavity. Therefore, the testimony which you have just heard from Mr. Meade continues to be relevant for the things that I am saying.

What causes the earth movement which seismographs detect at a great distance is the pressure-pulse which arises in the volume of the cavity. The cavity may have been there originally or it may have been produced by the nuclear explosion itself.

There is an extremely simple relation, simple and not quite correct, but for a point of reference I will quote it. You take the pressure in this cavity and multiply it with the volume of the cavity and you get roughly the energy released by the nuclear explosive. Now it is not the energy really which causes the earth's motion, but the pressure which is related to the earth's motion. There are other things that energy can do apart from causing pressure in a gas. Energy can also evaporate substances that one has put into the cavity. Energy can also heat substances without evaporating them. There exists a suggestion, a very old one which several of us made from time to time and on which some crude calculations are in progress. This suggestion is that we put into the cavity some substance which can be evaporated and in so evaporating will use up some of the energy. Thus a smaller fraction of the energy will be left over to make pressure and thereby to move the walls of the cavity.

The latest proposal is to evaporate a substance which is rather hard to evaporate; namely graphite. It is entirely likely, although not proven, that by this means *the decoupling factor can be increased from a factor of* 300 *to a factor of* 1000 *or* 3000, *or conceivably more.*

Furthermore, this absorption of energy into evaporating substances also makes it possible to use smaller cavities. It will reduce the critical size of the cavity at which the cavity is big enough. Therefore, we can get more decoupling without excessive expense. Instead of evaporating the substances we may merely heat them and possibly melt them. If one has the cavity filled with some sort of iron filings, one could lead the energy into the iron. The energy which is absorbed in heating and melting this iron will not appear as pressure. One has to see how quickly the heating can be accomplished and how long the pressure will persist before the iron takes up the excess heat. What really causes the earth's motion is not just the pressure but the pressure times the time during which this pressure has been acting. This is again only approximation, but by letting the pressure act only for a short time and then dumping it into some heat sink, one again can reduce the size of the signal.

All of this is hard to calculate and I cannot tell you here that thereby it will be possible to increase the decoupling factor threefold or tenfold or more. I suspect so, and I think the only reliable procedure is to find out by experiment. Unfortunately, in this case nuclear experiments are greatly preferable to high-explosive experiments. The best heat-absorbing substances seem to be those which need the highest temperatures and which will not be evaporated by high explosives. Also when you try to use iron filings as an energy sink, the problem is to get the energy from the explosive to the metal, to the heat sink. This can be accomplished in the case of nuclear explosives more expeditiously than . . . in the case of high explosives. Therefore, to see whether these future improvements in decoupling will or will not work, nuclear experimentation will be necessary.

Dr. Teller then turned to other decoupling methods:

This does not exhaust by any means the list of possible methods of concealment. It does not even exhaust the more limited list of methods of which
I know, or of which I hear. There is the possibility of multiple explosions
which are not aimed at decreasing the strength of the earth's shock, but
which are aimed at changing the characteristic shape of the earth's movement, so that it should be more easily confused with genuine earthquakes.
Or one can so arrange the explosions that it will be more difficult to locate
the nuclear explosion.

By placing several nuclear explosives around a central point and then
detonating them simultaneously, one obtains a shorter travel time from
each to the periphery. The result will be that the explosion seems to come
from the center, but the signal has arrived in a shorter time than expected.
Earthquake waves are faster when they are moving in the lower layers of
the earth and therefore this arrangement might give the impression that
the explosions happened deeper down. We always have agreed that an
explosion that appears to happen at a greater depth than 10 or 20 miles is
not likely to be man-made.

You have heard that nuclear explosions, and generally explosions, are
apt to give an earth movement outward as the first phase. This phase is
then followed by an inward movement, the inward movement being quite
a bit stronger than the first outward movement has been. One can precede
a decoupled nuclear explosion with a much smaller explosion, decoupled or
undecoupled, in such a way that this much smaller explosion will make a
positive outward-going signal which is too small to detect. But its bigger
inward-going signal can coincide with the outward-going signal of the
nuclear explosive and compensate it or overcompensate it. In this way it
can wipe out the characteristic signature of a nuclear explosion. It is
therefore by no means clear whether or not nuclear explosions can be
identified as such even if lots more work is done on the subject and even if
we have a very closely spaced net.

[Study of underground nuclear explosions is a new technical subject, Dr.
Teller warned.] This is the reason and not our ingenuity which has made
it possible to find out more about the behavior of nuclear explosions and
in particular about the possibilities of decoupling than it has been possible to find out about better seismological methods.

My hunch is that further developments may continue to go in the direction that we shall learn even more about concealment, and that it will
be quite difficult for methods of detection to catch up with methods of
concealment.

I should, however, like to make one point quite explicitly. If you want
to be optimistic, and if you want to believe that methods of detection can
be worked out so that tests can be really controlled and checked and
policed, I dare not say that this is impossible. Very few things in science
are impossible. But I dare say that we shall have to improve presently available methods very many fold, and this will take a lot of money and it will
take a lot of time. *I do not believe that there is any great likelihood that in
two years from now, or even in four or five years from now, there will be a
really foolproof method of checking underground explosions down to, let*

us say, 1 kiloton. If we should be successful in this very different enterprise, it will take a time of many years and an amount of money of very many millions of dollars.

Up to this point Dr. Teller had been exploring the prospects for progress in the art of concealment and the art of detection in underground nuclear testing. He was also concerned about testing in space:

I am convinced from studies which have been pursued that space testing is entirely feasible. It is more expensive than underground testing, but *not necessarily more expensive than the kind of test operations which we performed in the Pacific.* Because of the great number of precautions which we had to take, these tests ran into many millions of dollars. Space testing could be extremely important when we try to test big explosions. The fact that you perform tests in a vacuum gives rise to some difficulties, but can also give rise to some advantages. There is no doubt that in space testing the lifting power of rockets is a very essential point, and the Russians clearly are ahead of us in the lifting power of rockets.

I would like, however, to end here with a word of caution. I wholeheartedly agree with the possibilities of space testing that have been laid before this committee. I agree with the possibilities of observations of space testing, and with the possibilities of evasion of these observations which Dr. Panofsky and Dr. Richard Latter explained to you in great detail.

With all of that I agree. They have done work which is outstanding and which is done as well as it could be done. But such work cannot be done satisfactorily. Today we know as much about space testing as we had known about underground testing before 1957 when the first underground shot was fired. Since that time we have made many pitfalls, we have corrected some of our errors, and we have a little perspective how much more can be learned by experimentation.

I think if we talk seriously and conscientiously about policed disarmament then a great deal of experimentation, underground and in space, remains to be performed before a decent technical judgment can be delivered.

Dr. Teller warned that "with our present setup" the United States could detect "nothing" in space. *"The Russians may be testing in space at any size right now."*

Representative Carl Durham, a former Chairman of the Joint Committee on Atomic Energy, asked Dr. Teller: "Is it your opinion [that] at the present time science has advanced or provided the adequate means to identify nuclear tests under present conditions?"

Dr. Teller answered:

I think that science has not advanced to that point. With respect to this treaty, from the point of view of a technical person, I would like to make this much of a recommendation. If the United States signs a treaty in which there are adequate safeguards against cheating, this I think is a clear-cut situation with which I certainly would feel that as a scientist I ought to agree. If we want to sign a treaty in which it is clearly stated that there is an attempt at control but this attempt is and will remain for the next decade in all likelihood open to extremely serious doubt, so that actually now and for the next decade we will not have policing, if for reasons of politics into which I should not and cannot enter, this is deemed to be right, as a scientist and as a technical expert again I cannot comment and I cannot object to it. *But if we enter into a treaty where the pretense is made that we can be checking, where the fact that there are really great loopholes and possibilities of evasion, where these facts are not put clearly before the American people, then I feel that I must raise my voice as a scientist in protest.*

Dr. Bethe expressed the opinion that only sophisticated nations could profit from small, kiloton-range underground tests, extrapolating the results and using it as a basis for manufacture of larger weapons. The 1960 Joint Atomic Energy Committee noted, however, that France had moved promptly from the blunderbuss stage into a low-yield test on its second shot.

The Joint Committee, in its evaluation of the hearings, decided that "it was definitely established by the testimony that it is feasible to construct cavities in salt domes of the required depth, size, and shape to decouple nuclear explosions up to about 100 kilotons."

The Committee also tended to accept the advice of Mr. Meade, rather than the skepticism of Dr. Bethe, on the possibilities of concealing the evidence that a cavity in salt has been constructed.

"For concealment purposes," the Committee's summary-analysis later said, "the brine pumped out of the cavity can be disposed of by injecting it into another formation already containing salt water. Brine produced in oil-storage operations, for example, in some cases is dumped into the ocean. Thus, washing operations would not necessarily be detectable by salinity measurements in oceans or seas."[7]

On-site Inspection

The Joint Committee devoted the better part of an afternoon to a study of the on-site inspection problem. These questions were examined:

How might a violator try to cheat?

How would the on-site inspection team try to catch him?

How much would on-site inspections cost and how long would they last?

Curiously, the Senators and Congressmen spent little time verifying the probability that an on-site inspection could catch a determined cheater. Apparently they were willing to accept the testimony of Dr. Harold Brown on the opening day that the probability could be made "very close to zero."

To answer the first question the Committee had called on Dr. Gerald

Johnson, of the Lawrence Radiation Laboratory in Livermore, California. Since he was unable to attend, his prepared statement was read by an associate at the Livermore Laboratory, Dr. C. E. Violet.

Dr. Violet permitted himself the observation that if drilling were the only method of locating radioactive debris underground from a one-kiloton explosion, the probability would be one part in 100,000 of hitting the debris with the first hole. He said to make the probability one, there would have to be 100,000 holes drilled.

"Is it being ridiculous," Chairman Holifield asked, "if there are 500 unidentified events that you wish to explore that you might have to drill many thousands of holes in order to locate them?"

Dr. Violet pleaded lack of qualification to answer. "Presumably," he said, "we are armed with more than drilling instruments as a tool. We have other tools to reduce this or to improve our inspection capabilities."

It was theoretically correct, however, Dr. Violet told Representative Hosmer, that evidences of the explosion could be minimized or eliminated completely in advance, and "really would not be available in a smart cheating job."

He also agreed with Senator Bennett of Utah that a violator "also might put a few of those [misleading evidences] around to pull you off and start you drilling places where you were bound to fail." Nobody mentioned how deep one would drill before accepting failure.

Dr. Johnson's paper speculated that the nation intent on conducting a secret nuclear-weapons test would:

1. Give strong support to the group carrying out the operation. The best technicians would be involved and adequate means, legal and administrative, would be provided to minimize the chances that the sneak shot would be detected or that the intention to cheat would be detected.

2. Carry out the operation so that, under the treaty provisions, no inspection would be expected. Yields of the test shots would be kept below the threshold of detection and decoupling techniques would be used—whatever was necessary to avoid on-site inspection.

3. As insurance, in case the system did demand an on-site inspection, keep field operations to a minimum, conducted quietly and as quickly as possible in a way to reduce the chances that evidences of the shot could be found.

A national decision would have to be taken that the operation would provide enough of an advantage to warrant the risk of being caught.

Typical weights of devices to be tested would be 2,000 pounds, Dr. Johnson's statement suggested. Greater weights would not be too burdensome for a violator, however, he said. A major complex would be necessary to design and build the devices to be tested, Dr. Johnson estimated. Large laboratory facilities would be required, including provisions for high-explosive experiments and a supporting industry. The complete designing and building job could be done within a secret area, he said.

The laboratory would also develop a special firing and monitoring system of minimum weight and high reliability which would require little attention in the field. It would be developed and completely checked out at the laboratory before being shipped to the test site. Firing orders would be sent to the device by radio, not by cable, he suggested, because of the time it would take for cables to be laid and because cables might be discovered.

Radio firing systems have already been developed, Dr. Johnson reported, and some were planned to be used for peaceful-purposes nuclear shots. The Alaskan harbor-excavation test was planned for firing by radio from an airplane, he said. For a secret test, of course, a special radio firing system would have to be designed.

Test data, like the firing orders, would be sent out of the test area either by radio or by light, according to the Johnson plan. Such telemetry systems have been used successfully already. Detectors to "view" the test would be placed a few hundred feet from the device, but still within the underground area which would collapse after the explosion. A recording system outside would receive the information outside the damaged area.

Dr. Johnson estimated that the whole operation would take only four days in the field by ten or fifteen people. If there were access to the site by water, it would greatly enhance the secrecy, Dr. Johnson observed. "The shot point itself would be in a drilled hole, or a washed-out cavity at the bottom of a drilled hole for decoupled shots, either in the water off shore or on the shore line," he said. "Such a drill hole could be provided using standard oil-well drilling equipment and could be located in a shallow sea, a river, or a lake. After construction was finished the test team could approach the site by small boat, lower the device, and fire it. The total time in the field for preparation, firing and recovering the data would be four or five days. The staging port could be located several hundred miles from the test site."

One of the greatest risks of detection, he estimated, would be leakage of radioactivity. But, Dr. Violet told the Committee this was actually "a very small risk." It was clear from the Johnson-Violet presentation that Dr. Johnson's group believed it would be fairly easy to pull off a secret nuclear test underground.

It was estimated that a 3°C. temperature rise in the surrounding area, due to the nuclear explosion, would be detectable at 30 feet from a 100-ton explosion; at 100 feet radius for a 1.7 kiloton explosion; 320 feet for 20 kilotons; and 390 feet radius for 100 kilotons.

The detectable area underground could be reduced still further, it was suggested, by setting off the nuclear explosion in other kinds of rock, rather than in the Nevada tuff.

Representative Hosmer suggested that there probably would be no visible above-ground manifestations of a sneak shot if the hole were drilled from the inside of a building in the middle of a city, and if the test were conducted "in the middle of a May Day parade."

"That is correct," Dr. Violet responded.

"It probably would not be suspected, either," Representative Hosmer said.

"That is right," Dr. Violet replied. "Personally I believe this would be very simple to hide on the basis of visual surface observation."

Dr. Richard M. Foose, Chief of the Department of Earth Sciences at Stanford Research Institute, outlined the methods for pursuing an on-site inspection. He cautioned at the outset, however, that "even if it were known that a nuclear explosion had occurred, if through decoupling or any other means a seismic signal were not received, then there would be no basis for inspection as the present system is conceived."

His point, which was not elaborated or discussed, was that the concept of requiring criteria before the dispatch of on-site inspection teams would very likely preclude the use of the independent intelligence which many of the American scientists frequently mentioned as an added aid in on-site inspection.

Dr. Foose estimated the area within which a nuclear explosion could be confined at 40 to 200 square miles. The maximum size was only half the figure quoted by Dr. Brown earlier. No one, however, inquired about the basis for either set of figures.

A three-phase procedure of on-site inspection was outlined by Dr. Foose, who was an optimist, judging from his testimony. First there would be aerial reconnaissance, second a low-flying inspection by air and investigations on the ground to locate the event within 500 feet of the epicenter. The third phase would consist of drilling to locate a radioactive sample.

Out of the first-phase aerial reconnaissance four alternative findings might emerge, Dr. Foose suggested. First, there could be definite evidence of an earthquake. Second, there could be definite evidence of an underground explosion. Third, there might be no conclusive evidence, but clues to human activity in the area. Fourth, there might be neither evidence of a seismic cause nor signs of human activity. He left open whether the inspection team should quit or keep looking if it were confronted with the fourth alternative.

Quickly turning to phase two, he assumed that the first phase would have narrowed the search down to areas of one to five square miles. He did not say how many such areas, nor what the prospects were of successfully narrowing the search. Phase two could result in a finding that there had been an earthquake, that there had been an underground explosion which needed further investigation, or that the evidence was "inconclusive"—which might be followed by a finding of "no event" or might spur further investigation, Dr. Foose said.

The more detailed inspection techniques of phase two would be used in the small areas of one-half to one square mile, in the hope of confining the area of the explosion to a radius of 500 feet.

Drilling would not commence until phase three had been entered. The Foose paper thus moved quickly into the optimistic area where the epicenter of the explosion had been narrowed to a circle of 500-foot radius. No convincing techniques were presented to confine the area so drastically. It might take months or years to reach phase three—if one were to accept other scientists' testimony.

Even under his remarkably optimistic assumptions, Dr. Foose estimated that *it would take almost three years* to check a 500-foot area for a 1.7-kiloton shot, using three shifts of drillers per day. The cost was estimated at $378,000 for one inspection.

If it were a 20-kiloton explosion that was being sought in the ridiculously small 500-foot area, it would still take 3 shifts a day 360 days to cover the area. The cost would be $135,000. If the sneak test had been as large as 100 kilotons, Dr. Foose estimated, 3 shifts could "drill out the area" in 251 days at a cost of $94,000. In other words, a shot 5 times the size of the Hiroshima bomb might take 8 months to find—if it were accurately located.

These costs, however, were for only one on-site inspection. Of course, another assumption was that the radioactivity would not be found until the last hole was drilled.

If the drill teams were to use special patterns to spot-check the areas, Dr. Foose said, the probability of discovering the radioactive zone from a 1.7-kiloton explosion would be 3 per cent for five holes, 12 per cent for ten holes. In the case of a 20-kiloton explosion confined to the same 500-foot-radius circle, the probability of finding the debris in the first five holes would be 26 per cent, in ten holes 94 per cent. Five holes would be sufficient to make a 100 per cent probability of discovery of a 100-kiloton explosion in the same 500-foot radius, Dr. Foose said. An effective evaluation of on-site inspection could not be made until a simulated or real clandestine nuclear test was undertaken, he told the committee.

Representative Durham, tongue in cheek, observed: "If you have about ten seismic disturbances and had to inspect them on the basis of what you told us here, you would probably have full employment in most of the country if we tried to find them."

The hope would be that many earthquakes could be identified because they produced effects over a larger area than a nuclear blast. Most of the earthquakes that produced surface evidence would be above the 4.75 threshold.

The problem of positively identifying a violator would exist even if radioactive evidence of an underground blast were found. As Representative Craig Hosmer of California pointed out, finding radioactive debris in a mine, for instance, might merely provoke the nation in whose country the debris was found to remark: "Well, I'll be darned, some dirty foreigners must have come in there and blown off a bomb."

As in the case of detection devices, there was a plea for extensive research to improve on-site inspection. Continental versus marine locations for secret tests should be investigated, it was suggested. Other "major environmental variables" like climate, topography, vegetation, the type of rocks, and the kinds of surface features that cover the bedrock (sand dunes, glaciers, etc.) should be investigated, Dr. Foose suggested.

But 60 to 80 per cent of the research, he estimated, would have to be geared to realistic, nuclear testing.

Dr. Foose optimistically estimated that phase one could be completed within a day, phase two would be of indefinite duration but might be as short as a day, and phase three would take days or months—or even years. All his estimates about the drilling time, however, were based on the unsubstantiated premise that the epicenter could be located within a 500-foot radius.

Drilling teams and their equipment would be transported to the site by helicopter, he said. They would use not oil drilling rigs but diamond drilling equipment. The Congressmen did not even explore how much time might be required for an on-site inspection if it were not possible to confine the epicentral area to a 500-foot radius.

One of the appendixes accompanying the presentation by Dr. Foose came closer to realism on the impotence of on-site inspection than his main presentation:

> Unless these [first] two phases result in selecting a reasonably small target area, preferably less than 500 feet radius, little success can be expected from the drilling phase.
>
> Drilling will be the most expensive and logistically difficult of the three phases. Indiscriminate drilling with the hope of intersecting a target appears to be out of the question because of the time and expense involved. It has been estimated that to insure the discovery of a cavity or shattered zone produced by a 20-kiloton explosion within a circular area of about three square miles, more than 250 holes would have to be drilled. If all 250 holes were drilled to scale to depth, it would involve about 275,000 feet of drilling. The estimated cost would be $1.5 million under the best conditions and would take two years to complete.

Even this paper did not face what the problem would be if, instead of a 20-kiloton explosion, the target had been a 1.7-kiloton explosion. Using the ratios from other materials presented by Dr. Foose, the cost would rise to $4.2 million and the time would jump to six years. And these estimates were still based on the notion that somehow the area of drilling operations could be confined to only three square miles. There was no assurance, as American scientists had indicated to the Soviet

Union in the two Geneva technical conferences, that the area could be confined to anything like so small an area. In Geneva the areas mentioned were 40 to 80 square miles; Dr. Brown mentioned 400 square miles in his presentation to the Joint Atomic Energy Committee.

The other problems, of establishing that a violation of the treaty had occurred underwater and then of fixing the blame on the violator, were only briefly alluded to in the Joint Atomic Energy Committee hearings.

Dr. Roland Beers, a consultant on seismic techniques, explained to the Joint Committee the use of "seismic profiling" in seeking the cavities from underground nuclear explosions. According to the theory, a line of temporary seismographs would be set up to record the waves reflected from shallow chemical explosions near the surface.

It was a system widely used by petroleum prospectors to seek out oil wells. Dr. Beers was optimistic that the system would also contribute significantly to the "prospecting" for underground cavities produced by nuclear explosions.

He conceded, however, that natural variations in geology might frequently mislead the seismic-profiling method. (Dr. Brown had indicated this factor would nullify the usefulness of the process.)

It appeared likely that anomalies occurring in nature would sharply reduce the effectiveness of the method. Once the area of a nuclear explosion had definitely been narrowed to, say, a circle of 500 feet radius, however, the seismic profiling method probably could be of real value.

Dr. Beers estimated that ten men operating two drills and other equipment carried on five trucks could complete 200 profiles per month. He suggested that a two-and-a-half-month exercise, including 500 profiles, would cost a maximum of $125,000 when conducted over land. Over water, the same survey might be performed in one month and should cost only about $60,000.

Without first finding the 500-foot-radius circle, however, the profiling of a vast area would be impractical.

On the last day of the hearings, in a prepared statement submitted for the record, the Joint Committee received the most profoundly pessimistic appraisal of the on-site inspection method. It came from Dr. Carl Romney, the Defense Department seismologist who had been prominent in the Geneva technical conferences. Dr. Romney told the Committee:

> A typical on-site inspection can be expected to result only in the conclusion that it has not been proved that an explosion occurred. The degree of confidence with which it could be stated that the questionable event was probably natural will depend critically on the vigor of the inspectors and the thoroughness of their investigation.

Dr. Romney later presented the Joint Committee with the Air Force Technical Application Center's revised, January, 1960, estimates of the number of earthquakes in the Soviet Union which would be detected but unidentified in the first period of the control system's establishment. In the first period of a test ban, posts would be installed only in the Soviet Union, the United States, and the United Kingdom.

By cranking into the calculations the 100-detector arrays at the control stations, AFTAC estimated, one could regain the effectiveness assumed in 1958—above 19 kilotons. That is, no more than seventy events above 19 kilotons would remain unidentified. But there would be more than twice as many above 5 kilotons, even with 100-detector arrays.

EARTHQUAKES IN THE U.S.S.R. DETECTED BUT UNIDENTIFIED BY CONTROL POSTS IN THE U.S.S.R., U.S., AND U.K.

Total earthquakes recorded	Magnitude	Equivalent yield (kilotons)	Number of unidentified earthquakes 100-detector array	10-detector array
620	4.0	2	560	590
320	4.3	4	260	290
170	4.6	11	110	140
123	4.75	19	70	100
72	5.0	40	35	45
47	5.2	80	20	24

Source: 1960 Joint Atomic Energy Committee Hearings, "Technical Aspects of Detection and Inspection Controls of a Nuclear Weapons Test Ban," Part I, April 19–22, 1960, p. 92.

Under revised estimates there would be 123 earthquakes instead of 100 above 19 kilotons. But the improved arrays would identify 43 per cent of these, instead of the previously calculated 30 per cent—leaving only 70 unidentified.[8]

The table was interesting in another respect, because it indicated in a crude way the odds against being caught which a violator would face if he chose to test above 19 kilotons—or miscalculated in a decoupling effort.

There would be seventy-two Soviet earthquakes a year equivalent in power to 40 kilotons, and thirty-five of these would be unidentified even by 100-detector arrays. A Soviet violator would have one 40-kiloton earthquake every five days—one unidentified 40-kiloton event every ten days —to screen a coupled shot of 40 kilotons or a decoupled shot of 4 megatons (assuming feasibility of a 100–1 decoupling hole).

In the Joint Committee's summary-analysis of its hearings there was such an effort to be "objective" and to restrict the discussion to the "technical" aspects of the nuclear test-ban, that there was little guidance as to the meaning of the testimony on on-site inspection.

The objective of the first two phases of on-site inspection, aerial and ground reconnaissance, the Committee report said, "would be to attempt to locate, hopefully within a circle of about 500 feet in diameter, the spot directly over the suspected underground nuclear explosion." There was no advice that this objective was completely unrealistic, except for the single adverb "hopefully."

The drilling phase, the Committee report said, "would not be started until the successful conclusion of the second phase. By successful conclusion is meant that one or more areas equivalent to a circle of the order of 500 feet radius can be selected for drilling operations."

Another opportunity was passed up here to sound the alarm that "one or more areas" probably would turn out to be a composite area of anywhere from 5 to 400 square miles, depending on the "expert" making the estimate.

The closest the Committee report came to stating the hopeless picture was in this passage:

> It was variously estimated by scientific witnesses that the over-all probability of success of an on-site inspection in locating and identifying a single underground nuclear explosion varies from "very nearly zero" to a probability of 100 per cent success if the inspection were conducted in an exhaustive manner for a period of several years at a cost of tens of millions of dollars.

Considering that the responsible officials of the American government were negotiating with the Soviet Union to use on-site inspection as the key method of pinning down any violation of a nuclear test-ban treaty, most readers of that statement would be likely to conclude that the probability of success would usually be 100 per cent. What the public needed here was the guidance, which the Joint Atomic Energy Committee could have given, that the probability of success in almost all cases of on-site inspection would be "very nearly zero," as American experts had advised the Soviet Union. No mention was made, either, of the need for speedy arrival of the inspection team in the suspected area.

The Committee report also stopped short of saying that aerial reconnaissance would be virtually helpless in on-site inspections. It said:

> In aerial employment visual and photographic methods can identify and differentiate between unconcealed nuclear explosions and major earthquakes but not between a contained nuclear explosion and an earthquake of a comparable magnitude. Aerial surveys for gamma radiation from surface sources would be useful only if the nuclear explosion vented slightly to the atmosphere but could never identify an event as an earthquake. Airborne magnetic surveys would be useful for the detection of ferromagnetic objects which might be associated with human activity. Airborne electromagnetic surveys would be used to detect nonmagnetic conducting materials. Infrared detectors to measure temperature variations on the surface are not likely to detect the heat generated by a nuclear explosion at containment depth but may detect the heat from poorly concealed small sources.

This was backing into an evaluation which was never stated explicitly. Apparently the Committee wished to go no farther than imply that aerial reconnaissance would be next to useless unless a bungler were trying to cheat.

The Committee also avoided over-all evaluation of the surface-inspection method for restricting the suspect area. These were the Committee observations:

> Visual examination on the ground would be limited by rugged terrain, snow and ice, and heavy vegetation. Most earthquakes, except small ones, will produce surface alterations which can be detected by a trained observer; however, a deeply buried explosion will not produce noticeable changes in surface appearance. Ground surveys to detect the vertical motion of the earth's surface may be a potential method for identifying a seismic event but may be limited by rough topography in the area. Measurements of horizontal motions are only useful in the case of major earthquakes. Radiation surveys are useful if the nuclear explosion vents. Surface magnetic and electromagnetic surveys have limited usefulness in the detection of artifacts. Seismic refraction and reflection techniques might be used to detect cavities produced by nuclear explosions and warrant further evaluation. Recording of aftershocks following an explosion has potential value although it may be limited by natural microseisms; but, in any case, an extensive research program on aftershocks from natural and artificial seismic events would be required to evaluate any locally-recorded seismic signal as due to an aftershock. Geochemical analysis of soil would be useful if the explosion vented, while geochemical analysis of ground water has low potential usefulness except where there is rapid movement of water. Biochemical analysis of plant life for absorbed radioactive fission products does not appear promising.

The Committee also considered the problems an inspection team might encounter in entering a mine or in seeking underwater evidence:

> Techniques useful for inspection underground or in a marine environment differ only in detail from those used in land surface detection. In the underground environment, human activities would be more closely confined and geological features more readily recognizable because of better exposures. In an operating mine, activities associated with setting off a nuclear explosion may be difficult to distinguish from normal and legitimate mining operations. In marine areas the fluid nature of the environment would almost immediately erase surface manifestations of the seismic disturbance whether from an earthquake or a nuclear explosion. Detection of artifacts such as drill-casing and marine cable required in conducting the explosion offers the best potential.

What were the prospects of pinpointing the suspicious area to a circle of 500 feet radius? There was no Committee judgment.

Chapter 13

The Network

If the Joint Committee's treatment of the on-site inspection problem had been comparatively gentle, the study of the problems involved in installing twenty-one stations inside the Soviet Union was, by contrast, brutal.

Dr. Raymond Peterson, Vice President and Director of Research for the United Geophysical Corporation, of Pasadena, California, told the Committee of a sixty-day study; "under rather intense conditions," evaluating the feasibility of installing a network of twenty-two seismic arrays in the Soviet Union one more than the usually accepted number.

Dr. Peterson's group concluded that arrays of seismometers, instead of single seismometers, could improve the detection capabilities of the Geneva system, as conceived in 1958, only by a factor of 4 or 5, not 10 or 20, as theoreticians had earlier predicted before the Joint Committee.

To install the network in the Soviet Union alone would require three to five years and cost $1 billion, Dr. Peterson told the Committee.

If similar systems were installed on a world-wide basis, "the costs could well amount to five billion dollars," Dr. Peterson said, adding that the cost figures were his "personal estate." [1]

He had more astounding information:

As we became engaged in the project, the farther we got into the thing the more I became impressed that we are dealing with a project of the magnitude of the DEW [distant early warning] line.[2]

I have not a very detailed knowledge but I understand after a very rush crash program of six months in which a prototype station was tried out to furnish actual practical knowledge, with a crash program and the expenditures of multibillion dollars, the network was completed in something like thirty-two months, and probably did not come into full operating effectiveness for some time thereafter. I do believe that time is an exceedingly important element when we talk about all these matters. It is strictly not a "honeymoon" operation. If we attempt to operate it on that

419

basis we will have many "unhappy wives" returning to their mothers. This is going to take very rugged he-men out there to do this job. It will cover a continent [Eurasia] which spans one-fifth the circumference of the globe. It covers something like nine million square miles of area. It will involve the particular feature of installing arrays. It will involve something between 6,000 and 21,000 miles of cable, tens of thousands of telephone poles, hundreds of tractors, earthmovers, steam jets, ice breakers. It is like a military operation, like a war.

Dr. Peterson explained that he was not speaking of installing the seismic arrays alone. The network of 22 seismic stations and associated arrays in the Soviet Union would cost about $250 million, Dr. Peterson said in a supplemental statement. There would be another estimated $750 million in support costs:

Item	Cost (in millions of dollars)
Roads, airports, and other transportation facilities required in construction and operation of this system	100
Construction and testing of network data communications system	150
Numerous indirect hidden costs involved in expenditures for logistical support and transportation by military facilities	150
Station operating costs while the over-all system is being tested and put into final operation	50
Costs involved in acquisition of land, rerouting of local roads, and possible relocation of farms from array areas	50
Preparation of base map of U.S.S.R. of sufficient precision for detection purposes	50
Costs of adequately testing the performance of the completed over-all system by a series of controlled underground test explosions	200

Note: The items listed above represent an aggregate sum of approximately $1 billion and could well require three to five years for accomplishment. These estimates cover the U.S.S.R. alone. If similar systems are installed on a world-wide basis, the costs could well amount to $5 billion.

Dr. Peterson told the Committee:

The magnitude of the task was a rather surprising conclusion to us because in commercial prospecting for oil it is quite common and simple for us to "throw out" a number of seismometer groups. Instead of using one seismometer, we use on the order of 30 or 50. It is rather a routine thing to "pick them up and lay them down" several times a day.

[The seismic stations in the Soviet Union, however, present] a completely different order of magnitude of difficulty. We are talking about putting out groups of anywhere from 30 to 100 seismometers over a circular area about 2 miles in diameter. This greatly complicates the problem.

Furthermore, we are talking about doing this over thousands of miles, in wild, remote, and inaccessible regions, many of them north of the Arctic circle where temperatures go 50°, 60°, 70°, 80° below zero, where transportation is virtually nil, where you have every known difficulty to overcome. In the construction of the DEW line this was done on home soil, friendly soil, with friendly allies along the Arctic shores where maritime transportation could be had once a year. If this is to be done under less favorable circumstances with unenthusiastic partners, it will greatly compound the difficulties of realizing a successful network.

Dr. Peterson had another blockbuster for the advocates of augmenting the control system from 21 to 600 stations. *The limit of good locations for seismic stations, he estimated, was 25.*

The conditions of topography and geography in Russia are such that it is extremely difficult under stipulated conditions to pick many more than 25 good locations. One of the determining factors is that one of the major topographic features in Russia is the Ural mountain range. To the east of the Ural mountain range there are millions of square miles of wasteland which is nearly inaccessible even to fur trappers. So when you start with the Ural range as an anchor point and build outward in a network, you end up essentially with the kind of network that was proposed. *When you locate 22 stations you use up many of the "good" locations in Russia. When you speak of 600 stations you are speaking of geologically low and poorly situated stations.*

Enough of the topography and geography of Russia was known, Dr. Peterson convinced the Committee, to ascertain the exact location of the twenty-two stations. World aeronautical charts were used as base maps. These charts, he speculated, had "become available" during World War II and shortly thereafter, when American planes were over-flying Siberia. While the charts were "in many ways surprisingly good," he said, they had two deficiencies: They were generalized and the contour intervals were often 500 to 1,000 feet, whereas intervals of 100 feet were required for satisfactory location of the stations.

Dr. Peterson also had available to him what he described as "rather extensive geological information" about the Soviet Union. He said that he had heard that thousands of geologists had been put to work in "big lines" and that they "swept" the country, doing a modern job of geological mapping "in a relatively short time."

The Russians, Dr. Peterson reported, had done intensive investigation of certain aspects of seismology:

They have been very much interested in the distribution of earthquakes in highly active regions. Around the margins of Russia in the high Hindu Kush area, which rises to 15,000 to 20,000 feet, along the Kurile Island chain, and Kamchatka, there are very active mountain-building activities now taking place. I think some of the most seismic areas in the world are located in these areas. There are recent publications on detailed studies in Southern Russia which show the locations of literally thousands of earthquakes. The maps look like a shotgun pattern at short range. They have done this by concentrating a number of seismological stations in these very active areas.

Bombshell number three from Dr. Peterson was his conclusion that the number of seismometers in the arrays should be cut from 100 to 31. This was mainly on the basis that the area of the control station should be limited to a circle two miles in diameter.[3]

Frank Coker, Director of Research of the United Electrodynamics Corporation, of Pasadena, elaborated on the problem of finding suitable locations for seismometers:

First, it is a matter of finding large basement outcrop areas on which a 3-kilometer circle can be drawn and which are properly spaced at 1,700 kilometers and 1,000 kilometers as previously mentioned. Secondly, within each circle, it is necessary to find isolated locations, a few thousand feet apart, and numbered perhaps 30 or as high as 100, on which individual seismometers can be placed. In the first category, we studied 22 major areas, each 250 kilometers in diameter, in an attempt to find whether or not the large 3-kilometer-diameter basic granite outcrops were available. Of the 22 areas, each larger in diameter than the distances from here to Philadelphia, we concluded that in some cases *there were no "optimum" geological positions available for these arrays.* But to sum it up, from the geology maps, about 75 per cent looked reasonable.

The remaining 25 per cent fell on poor geology, which would presumably degrade the detection capability of that station, or on very poor geology in some cases. So it boils down to this: to obtain 75 per cent out of 22 in these enormous circles, we in several cases had to go outside of the circles by more than 100 kilometers to find anything suitable. In addition for the remaining 25 per cent, nothing really desirable appeared to be present unless very inaccessible locations were selected.

Dr. Peterson's study showed that of the twenty-two control posts likely to be placed in the Soviet Union under the 1958 Experts prescription, sixteen stations could be located in good geology, but six would have to be placed on fair, poor, or very poor geology.

As the Committee later pointed out, "six of the twenty-two stations of an actual Geneva system of seismic arrays in the U.S.S.R. can be expected to have a capability lower than that theoretically expected by the experts."[4]

Dr. Peterson raised other problems that would be as difficult, if not more difficult, to solve in the United States than in the Soviet Union.

Once having found the quiet site and the right kind of rock, "what if selected areas fall where there are farmers? Will you evacuate the farmers, will you rerun the roads to avoid noise? You can anticipate more problems in populated zones."

The two witnesses also warned of the effect wind would have on the performance of the detection network.

During a gale, they said, the efficiency of a particular station might be reduced to only 20 per cent of its normal value.

The cumulative effect of the Peterson-Coker testimony can be estimated from this exclamation by Representative Hosmer:

"This is a startling bit of testimony here. The best indication is that we are negotiating on the basis of a sham seismological system. The principal value would be to delude ourselves."

This outburst prompted Mr. Coker to elaborate:

Theoretical calculations have been made which suggest very large improvements for such arrays (of 100 or more seismometers). But these have been done on paper. They suggest improvements of 10 or 20 or more times in the detection capability, but 100 or 200 or so seismometers.

On the other hand, our study is based on what we believe it is practical to put into the field. How many seismometers can physically be located on high rock? Can they be maintained in Northern Siberia? What are the manpower requirements and that sort of thing?

Our general conclusion is that, first, *some of the mathematically predicted improvements in detection capability of large arrays will probably not be found in actual practice.* One of the reasons is that as you put seismometers out on the ground you cannot always place them at the mathematically ideal positions because you do not find rock outcrops there, for example, or they end up on rocks of differing elevations. These practical factors tend to degrade the performance of an actual array somewhat compared to a theoretical mathematical ideal. It should be noted that the practical over-all result of fivefold or sixfold improvement for an array of 100 elements confirms the figures used earlier by Dr. Richard Latter in his testimony.

However, combining all practical field factors, we believe that arrays of 100 seismometers may not be the most optimum to use. We certainly believe that arrays of larger than 100 tend to be impractical. In summary an array of perhaps 30 or 50 seismometers may be an optimum value producing an increase in detection capability of about fourfold.

REPRESENTATIVE HOSMER: As a practical matter, is the whole thing practical or impractical?

DR. PETERSON: It is a matter of the effort put in. I think it will take a major crash program and major support to make the thing work and function. It will take great effort. If it is carried out in a wishwashy fashion it will be a complete "flop."

If each of the arrays were confined to thirty-one individual seismometers, Mr. Coker estimated, 6,600 miles of electric cable would be required for the twenty-two stations, or about 300 miles of electric cable per station. If ninety-seven-element arrays were used, 21,000 miles of cable would be required, about 1,000 miles of cable per station.

All the cable would be subject to sabotage, under the cost estimates they presented, Mr. Coker said. The problem of security was not dealt with.

Dr. Peterson was unimpressed with theories that enough of the stations in the network his group had designed could be confused by noise alone to paralyze the system. He did observe, however, that "the more practical means or the more real danger would occur if the explosion were deliberately set off in the wake of a fairly good-sized natural earthquake, of which there are a substantial number occurring every year. That would be another way of attempting concealment." The sneak shot, Dr. Peterson suggested, would be set off "within a half minute or so after you have identified" the earthquake.

Even with the tremendous effort envisaged, Mr. Peterson said, "you end up with a very low probability of detection if there is an intent to conceal. You have very little chance of detection." [5]

> REPRESENTATIVE HOSMER: With this system that you have described here, if you were calculating whether or not to try a clandestine test, and you used your best efforts at concealment, what chance do you think you have of beating the system?
>
> DR. PETERSON: I hesitate to put numbers *but maybe 99 chances out of 100 if you went at it in a competent fashion . . . by evasion, by using proper decoupling and timing.*

The Peterson-Coker team made two more stunning points before they left the committee room. Accurate knowledge of the geographical location of each station in the network would be exceedingly difficult to establish, Mr. Coker said:

> If you place a station at some spot out in the U.S.S.R., all of the readings that station makes and all of its predictions of the locations of earthquakes or bomb tests are not better than the accuracy of the station location. . . .
>
> First, you must accurately survey the precise location of each of the twenty-two stations so that they are precisely known on a global longitude and latitude network.
>
> Secondly, in order to direct an inspection team to the spot on the physical ground they desire to inspect, you must have sufficient local mapping so that when they get there, they know how far to go and in which direction and where to stop and where to start looking. . . .
>
> There are two kinds of different problems. One is that you have to make twenty-two accurate surveys, and this may be relatively simple. The other one is, that you must be able, by more accurate topographic maps or portable surveying apparatus or by some other means, to direct the inspection teams so that they can find the area on the ground that all the detection stations located.

The key would be the condition of the Soviet triangulation net. "Bench marks" have been set up all over the United States by government engineers. Precise locating is thus possible. What would one be likely to find in the Soviet Union, or India, or Africa, or the Western Hemisphere? Or Red China?

"I am not aware of the degree of accuracy of surveying in the U.S.S.R.," Mr. Coker observed. "We understand there is a fine triangulation net over certain areas, but the question of local surveying accuracy should be an understood limitation of the system."

As Dr. Peterson pointed out, many inaccessible areas of the world had not been accurately mapped. They had been located in a general sense, merely by taking astronomical observations.

"We have not made a thorough study, but we suspect that the locations of many of these spots are not known within 25 miles at the present time," Dr. Peterson declared. "It would take a very all-out method to get a good base map on which to work out the area. There is a major job there involving many man-years of effort."

Thus even if the twenty-two stations were accurately located in latitude and longitude, the rest of the country would have to be carefully mapped, locations of towns, roads and other things carefully located as to longitude and latitude, or the on-site inspection teams would be in constant danger of "missing the mark."

Dr. Peterson put the problem this way: "You might get out there and you might be 10 miles farther than you think you are. You would be no closer than the map accuracy."

His estimate that chances for getting away with a sneak shot were 99 out of 100 had not taken into account these added difficulties in accurately locating the area of a disturbance.

The Defense Department's Advanced Research Projects Agency estimated the cost of the complete Geneva control system, not only the seismic detection network, but the other paraphernalia for acoustic, electromagnetic, and radioactivity-sampling methods, to be $1 billion in round numbers, with an annual operating cost of about $250 million.[6] This was only one-fifth the Peterson estimate, although still fifteen times the annual U.N. budget, for installation costs alone, and four times the annual operating cost of the U.N.

Carleton M. Beyer, of the Advanced Research Projects Agency in the Defense Department, told the Committee that about 20,000 people would be required to establish and operate the control system envisioned at Geneva.

Technicians were not then available to fill all these posts, Mr. Beyer said. He agreed that setting up the control system would "involve a very extensive training program in the field of seismology and electromagnetic readings of devices, maintenance of devices."

There would be "some difficulty," Mr. Beyer said, in recruiting people to work in places like the Antarctic, Siberia, remote areas of Red China, Mongolia, Australia, and South Africa. An added drawback, from the recruitment point of view, might be that the teams would have to be international.

The costs, no doubt, would vary considerably between a remote post in the Arctic and one in Westchester County.

Establishing the system would take about six years, Mr. Beyer estimated. He suggested that all the costs "'would be shared by the participating countries." [7]

Under questioning, Mr. Beyer indicated that the ARPA estimate of $1-billion cost for a world-wide system was based on only 10 seismometers in each array. Under the Technical Working Group II recommendations, each control post was to be equipped with 100 seismometers.

The ARPA system, it was apparent, was not directly comparable with the United Electrodynamics system presented by Mr. Coker. The hundred-array seismic stations, it had been estimated, would cost $250 million in the Soviet Union alone. Much of the cost would be directly attributable to the increase in the number of seismometers and communication cable.

The Joint Committee, in its summary analysis of the hearings, made no attempt to give guidance on which figure might be the more correct, the ARPA figure of $1 billion or the $5 billion figure of Dr. Peterson and Mr. Coker.

The failure to debunk the Peterson-Coker analysis, however, was evidence that the Joint Committee believed the higher figure to have some standing. The seismic arrays, of course, would be the highest-priced part of the control system. The Peterson-Coker calculation included road-building, access, and communications which, to some extent, would be usable by the other elements of the system. If the usual experience with ballooning of costs in spectacular projects like the DEW line were to be repeated, the over-all cost of installing the complete system could be expected to exceed $5 billion. The operating cost per year would depend on how accurate the $0.25 billion ARPA estimate had been.

After the hearings, the Joint Committee staff itself took a close look at the United Electrodynamic Corporation's work in selecting preferred areas for an array at station nine in the Soviet Union.

A circle 200 miles in diameter was drawn on the world aeronautical chart in the area of the Soviet Union assigned for Station Nine. A detailed study of noise sources was conducted within this circle. The study group looked for roads, railroads, and other areas which would be likely to cause background noise that would disturb a seismometer. Having discarded all the noisy areas as unsuitable, the study group then scrutinized the remaining area on a geological map for suitable granite outcroppings on which the seismometers could be placed. Only three circular areas of

6 miles in diameter were found. It would then remain for actual inspection on the ground, the Committee reported, to find a specific 2-mile circular area within one of the three larger 6-mile circles.

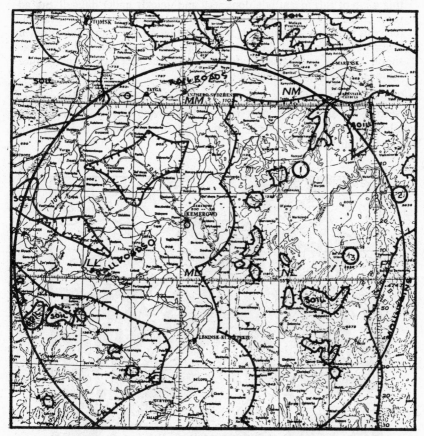

FIGURE 1

Station Nine was considered to be more accessible than most of the Soviet Union's stations. It was much better from this standpoint than the posts in Northern Siberia. But the difficult problems that would be posed were already evident. Local farm roads, potential sources of noise, traversed the preferred areas. The Soviet Union would have to be asked to reroute the roads to avoid local traffic noise at the seismic station. The "right of eminent domain" would have to be invoked against several Soviet collectives. Most Soviet roads aren't in condition for year-round operations. The Soviet Union would have to be asked to hard-surface many miles of roads.

The Committee was impressed by the difficulties the inspection teams would encounter from the Soviet Union:

A seismograph network in the U.S.S.R. would presumably be built with "partners" who might not be imbued with the feeling to finish the job as soon as possible. Motivation is a tremendously important factor in getting a job of this magnitude done well and quickly under difficult and adverse conditions. Without this motivation, construction could drag out for years with low priorities on transportation facilities and difficulties in "clearing" supplies and shipments through customs. Even such seemingly simple matters as language differences and lack of effective communications can cause serious difficulties.[8]

The committee was also impressed with the weather problems posed in setting up an inspection system in the Soviet Union. Four stations would have to be located in the Arctic zone, four in the central zone, and five in the southern zone.

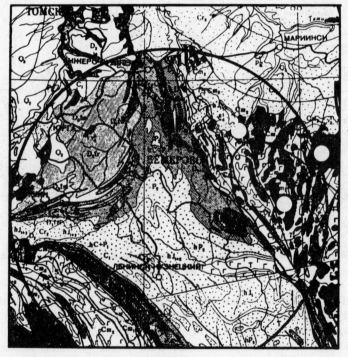

FIGURE 2

In the Arctic zone the weather would be like northern Canada or Alaska, with short summer seasons, long dark winters, temperatures down to —70° F.—"nearly impossible transportation problems during spring thaw and fall rains, permafrost soil conditions [which would have special effects on seismic arrays] and general inaccessibility."[9]

The central zone stations would still have bitter cold winters, on the order of Alberta, Canada, although they would not be "unbearable," as the Committee report put it. All the stations in the central zone would be located close to the Trans-Siberian railroad, except for stations 20 and 21 on Kamchatka Peninsula and in the Kurile Islands.

In the southern zone, the stations would be set up on the flanks of high mountain ranges. Four out of the five would be established in desert. The station in the mountains would encounter heavy snowfalls, those in the desert would face dry and very hot summers but might be called on to investigate events in snow-covered ranges.

The Committee elaborated on the picture presented by Dr. Peterson and Mr. Coker on the logistics and living problems: tens of thousands of telephone poles and hundreds of miles of steel messenger cable must be installed and hundreds of miles of roads and trails must be constructed and maintained. One or two thousand seismometers must be carefully placed at well-chosen locations, trees must be cut down, many miles of fences must be built. Many miles of roads must be rerouted, airfields must be constructed, farms and farmers must be relocated. Power plants, power lines, water supply, and sewage facilities must be constructed, an extensive communications system must be provided, heating and air conditioning depending on the locations of stations must also be provided. Thousands of barrels of fuel will be required, many trucks, vehicles, bulldozers, cable handlers, augers, steam jets, trucks and tractor-trailer trains, and ice-breakers must be provided and maintained.[10]

And who could say that Soviet leaders would even allow such a program? If they did, would they insist that the Soviet Union should build the system? That would give them broad new vistas for skulduggery.

Richard Latter's Irregular Grid

Those who did not take the decoupling theory seriously and tended to discount the difficulties anticipated in obtaining proof of underground nuclear tests with on-site inspection teams have come to take the 1960 Joint Committee presentation of Dr. Richard Latter on improving the Geneva control system *without increasing the number of stations* as an article of faith.

Dr. Richard Latter, like his brother a RAND Corporation scientist, devised a special system for spacing control stations inside the Soviet Union. It would significantly increase the capacity to detect and locate underground events—although the identification problem would remain. If the decoupling phenomenon had not been discovered, and many wishful advocates of the test ban succeeded in putting it from their minds as if it had never been, the Latter system would have gone far to recoup the degradations in the 1958 control system discovered in the Hardtack series.

Dr. Richard Latter's ingenious spacing of stations was first brought to public notice in the 1960 Joint Atomic Energy Committee hearings. He himself did not fall into the trap of lifting his plan out of perspective. At the outset of his presentation he warned of "two vital points":

[First,] seismic signals from an underground nuclear explosion can by deliberate effort be reduced by a factor of three hundred or more. [Therefore even very large explosions might go undetected.] Against these explosions the control system has no capability whatsoever and cannot provide a technical safeguard.

[Second,] nuclear explosions cannot be identified by their seismic signals alone. A control system can only identify earthquakes. Inspection of the site of an unidentified event, and therefore a suspected event, is required for the purpose of obtaining positive proof of the cause of the event. To prove that a nuclear explosion has taken place it is necessary to obtain a sample of radioactive debris.[11]

Dr. Richard Latter mentioned other serious limitations on the science of explosion seismology. Only six underground nuclear explosions had been undertaken by the United States. "These experiments have several possibly vital limitations," he said. All were undertaken in the same environment, at the same depth and in essentially the same geological conditions. Since the amplitude of first ground motion to be recorded from a nuclear explosion may depend on these three parameters, namely environment, depth, and geological conditions, Dr. Latter said, these limitations loomed large. The three parameters were also important in applying the diagnostic aids which were discussed at Technical Working Group II for discriminating earthquakes from nuclear explosions.

It could not be known, therefore, whether the seismic "signatures" from the Nevada explosions were characteristic of all unconcealed shots or whether they were "a very special type of signal which will be different from explosions under other conditions."

This uncertainty could be of overriding importance in evaluating the capability of a control system. For in using the characteristics of the Nevada signals as a basis to discriminate earthquakes from nuclear explosions, *the possibility exists that our conclusions will be proved wrong at some later time.* Nevertheless, for the present that is all we can do and that is what we have done.

The American criterion for identifying earthquakes, Dr. Latter said, was that the *peak* seismic signal should be twenty to forty times the noise background and that *first-motion* rarefactions (to identify earthquakes) should be observed at four stations at least. (Peak seismic signal is not the same as the first motion; it is almost always a later cycle.)

The RAND Corporation undertook several studies of the Geneva control system, Dr. Latter explained. In the first study it was assumed that control stations would be located in three countries only, which would be the situation in the first stage of a nuclear test-ban. This would mean that fourteen control stations would be located in the United States, one in the United Kingdom, and twenty-one in the Soviet Union. All, it was assumed, would be equipped with the improved instrumentation prescribed by Technical Working Group II. This would include the 100-seismograph arrays which Dr. Peterson found impractical.

More than three times as many earthquakes above the 4.75 threshold would be recorded but unidentified in the United States as in the Soviet Union, under this kind of control system, the study showed. There would be 175 unidentified earthquakes above 4.75 magnitude in the United States each year, 53 *per year in the Soviet Union.* If the Geneva system were installed world-wide, the numbers of unidentified earthquakes would be reduced to 143 per year in the United States, 28 *in the Soviet Union.* This was as far as Dr. Latter went. But the import of his new figures was revolutionary.

If 30 per cent of the unidentified events were to be inspected, as the American formula provided, there would be fifty-two on-site inspections per year in the United States when the control system was established in the three original-signatory countries, and forty-three when the control system was established world-wide. In the Soviet Union, on the other hand, *there would be only sixteen inspections per year under the three-country control system, only eight per year with a world-wide system.*

This was a startling result. It was incompatible with the demands of the United States in the Geneva negotiations for twenty or twenty-one inspections per year above the threshold. Even in the early stages of the nuclear test ban, only sixteen inspections per year would be needed, according to Dr. Latter's figures, and later, when the system was spread world-wide, only eight per year would be needed.

The RAND figures were also out of line with the estimated number of earthquakes, detected and unidentified both, which Ambassador Wadsworth had predicted in the Geneva negotiations.

Ambassador Wadsworth had told the Geneva Conference: "Our scientists believe that roughly speaking about 100 seismic events above a threshold magnitude 4.75 are likely to occur each year in the area of the Soviet Union and that about 70 of them are likely to remain unidentified by the original control net."

This calculation was made by the Air Force Technical Applications Center and accepted by the office of the Special Assistant to the President for Science and Technology, then under Dr. George Kistiakovsky. The calculation was based on "the best information available at the time," which was January 6, 1960.[12]

The President's scientific adviser and his associates also developed the formula for determining a quota of on-site inspections: 20 per cent of all estimated earthquakes above magnitude 4.75; or 30 per cent of the estimated unidentified events above magnitude 4.75. Twenty per cent of the estimated 100 earthquakes above 4.75 would be 20 on-site inspections. Thirty per cent of the 70 unidentified events above 4.75 would be 21. Thus, about 20 on-site inspections were settled upon as the United States figure, presented to the Soviet Union on February 11, 1960.[13]

Latter estimated that there would be only fifty-three unidentified earthquakes per year in the Soviet Union.

If The RAND Corporation calculations were valid, then the United States was missing an important propaganda advantage as well. It would be well for the world to know, for instance, that the United States might ask only sixteen inspections per year in the Soviet Union, compared with fifty-two in the United States in the early stages of the nuclear test-ban agreement, and only eight per year in the Soviet Union, compared with forty-three in the United States once the system were established worldwide. Thus, the United States might have been willing to accept five times as many on-site inspections per year as the Soviet Union, handing the Kremlin another intelligence bonanza in return for only a marginal opening of the Soviet Union.

One of the great difficulties, of course, was the uncertainty of world knowledge about the frequency of earthquakes. But it was curious that the scientists on whom the United States government was depending for its technical advice should produce an entirely different set of figures than Washington's chief negotiator was using at the Geneva test-ban talks.

The observer from the Soviet Embassy, who sat through the entire four days of the Joint Committee hearings, could also be expected to have an interest in a calculation which showed that, once a world-wide control net were established, American scientists estimated there would have to be only eight on-site inspections per year in the Soviet Union above the 4.75 threshold, not twenty or twenty-one, as the United States was demanding.

The results of Dr. Latter's second study were as startling as those of the first. In re-examining the criterion for identifying earthquakes, the RAND group "were not able to convince ourselves that the [United States] criterion of Technical Working Group II is a valid criterion." The main reason: it depended "almost entirely" on detecting first motions at great distances like 2,500 to 3,500 kilometers, the far zone. "Unfortunately the Hardtack seismic data do not provide reliable confirmation of this capability."

On the basis of the Hardtack data, however, Dr. Latter said, the RAND group did find that "the first motion can be reliably detected within the so-called near zone, out to about 1,100 kilometers."

The near-zone criterion could require a peak signal of only ten to twenty times the noise level instead of twenty to forty, and only two rarefactions instead of four, Dr. Latter said. His third disclosure was that the new, easier criterion produced a capability for the Geneva system which was substantially the same as that calculated for the Technical Working Group II criterion. It had the advantage, however, of being better supported experimentally.

Richard Latter's estimate of only fifty-three unidentified events in the Soviet Union above 4.75 threshold was based on what was later called "less rigorous criteria for identification of earthquakes." [14]

But Dr. Latter claimed, and he was never challenged, that the improved spacing justified using the "less rigorous" criteria. There was also a question whether "less rigorous" correctly described the new analysis. It is true that he proposed working with a smaller signal-to-noise ratio, but the signals could be considered more reliable because they would be recorded at short distance.

Having thus re-evaluated the criteria, the RAND group searched for "some minor changes" in the system that might improve it. It was found that by increasing the number of stations inside the Soviet Union from twenty-one to twenty-five, the number of unidentified events per year above the threshold could be reduced from fifty-three to about twenty. Instead of sixteen inspections, only six would be required in the early phase.

"This is a big improvement for a small cost," Dr. Latter declared. Adding four additional stations, it was calculated, would cut the number of on-site inspections per year by more than 50 per cent.

Adding another five stations, increasing the total number of control posts in the Soviet Union from twenty-five to thirty, Dr. Latter reported, could reduce the number of unidentified earthquakes above magnitude 4.75 to only nine per year. And if the threshold were lowered to magnitude 4.36, above 5 kilotons for Nevada-tuff coupling, the number of unidentified earthquakes would be only thirty-six per year. This was essentially back to the capability originally calculated for the 1958 Geneva experts' system.

Thus an addition of nine stations in the Soviet Union would restore the Geneva system to its formerly-estimated capability, *excepting that even the 30-station network would have no capability against muffled explosions that went undetected*, and the problem of obtaining positive proof of a nuclear explosion would still remain.

The pro-test-ban enthusiasts did not pick up Richard Latter's presentation and run with it, as might have been expected. Perhaps they were caught in a dilemma. One of the principal reasons they favored a test-ban was to crack the Iron Curtain and open up the closed Soviet society. But the effect of the Latter testimony with its reduction in on-site inspections would have been to patch over some of the chinks in the Iron Curtain that had been opened in the 1958 Conference of Experts.

Foes of the test ban could afford to look down their noses at the new RAND data, because it had done nothing to remove the twin paralyses of the decoupling theory and the on-site-inspection weakness.

Dr. Richard Latter completely demolished the Democratic Advisory

Council's scheme for a network of stations spaced at 400 kilometers when he was asked for comment in the Joint Committee. He assumed, optimistically as the Peterson-Coker testimony showed, that all the stations would be exceedingly quiet, and that all could be equipped with 100-seismograph arrays of the most improved kind.

In the Soviet Union, the 400-kilometer spacing would require approximately 190 stations, as compared with the 20 prescribed by the 1958 Conference of Experts, Dr. Latter estimated.

The lower limit of detection for the 400-kilometer grid would be an amazing 18 tons. "But at this level of detection," Dr. Latter said, "there are possibly 19,000 events which will be observed by the system in the Soviet Union alone. Of these events, 13,000 are unidentified. That is a very large number to be faced with when trying to make a feasible detection system."

Using the standard American formula that 30 per cent of the unidentified events should be inspected, this would mean 3,900 on-site inspections per year—in the Soviet Union alone.

In such a large system, with 190 stations inside the Soviet Union and 100 seismographs at each of them, the problem of cost would also enter the picture. Nineteen thousand seismographs would be required in the Soviet Union alone. In retrospect, it is surprising that these analyses by Richard Latter did not have a greater effect on the test-ban debate. Most of the world was still playing deaf.

In addition to adding stations to the system, other methods of improvement were discussed by Dr. Romney. One would be to get better response characteristics out of seismographs in the presence of noise. This could be done by developing better high frequency seismographs, those which record earth tremors of 10 cycles per second, and better seismographs at the very low frequencies, at 0.1 and 0.01 cycles per second.

More work was also necessary with arrays, Dr. Romney said:

> The effect of an array is to reduce the response to incoherent noise relative to the response to coherent signals. What this means in simple language is that with the seismometers spaced at intervals along the ground, you would expect that the noise present in the ground will cause one seismometer to be moving up at the same time another one is moving down. On the average there will be some cancellation, therefore, to the noise. . . . On the other hand, a signal will arrive virtually simultaneously at all of the detectors and in that case all the detectors will move up at the same time or down at the same time.

The third improvement under study, he said, was the "deep wells several thousand feet below the surface of the earth," where seismic noise would be less troublesome. Dr. Romney said a program operating seismographs of low-frequency response at depths of 9,700 feet and shallower had been going on since 1954. "The results to date are encouraging, but there are still major engineering problems to overcome." Signal cables capable of withstanding the pressures and temperatures and corrosive chemical reactions of the fluids in the wells had not yet been developed, Dr. Romney said. Another problem was connecting the seismometer to the wall of the hole. "If the seismometer is simply floating in the mud in the bottom of the well it does not respond to earth motion the way it should."

Dr. Bethe's Counterattack

Dr. Hans A. Bethe undertook at the Committee hearings the main job of recouping the full effectiveness anticipated for the inspection system in 1958.

Decoupling factors of 300 could be neutralized, Dr. Bethe declared, by closer spacing of the control stations. Moving to the blackboard, the Cornell professor wrote down two numbers, 5 and 3,000. At 1,000 kilometers from the 19-kiloton Blanca explosion, he said, the seismic signal had measured 5 millimicrons. Moving closer to the epicenter at 400 kilometers the corresponding signal was 400 millimicrons; and at 200 kilometers, the number was over 3,000 millimicrons.

"You will see that going from 1,000 kilometers to 200 kilometers you get an improvement by a factor of about 600," Dr. Bethe declared. "This is more than the decoupling factor. Therefore, I want to submit that at least technically it is possible to overcome the large factors for decoupling which we have learned about."

It was an important point which the advocates of a resumption of testing and the scientists who had explored the decoupling theory had mentioned only in passing. If the Soviet Union would accept enough stations, and enough suitable sites could be found, there was no doubt that the inspection system could be effective. Having established the "coupling factor" of 600, Dr. Bethe considered its use in a situation of "complete" decoupling—by the full factor of 300—of a 20-kiloton explosion. The complete decoupling, he said, would be possible in a hole of 500 feet diameter, such as the petroleum company engineer, Mr. Meade, had mentioned.

The 20-kiloton explosion, Dr. Bethe said, would produce a signal of about 25 millimicrons at 200 kilometers, and about 3 millimicrons at 400 kilometers. Since the noise at an average station is about 5 millimicrons, Dr. Bethe explained, and with the introduction of 100 seismographs in array, the noise becomes 0.8 millimicron at the 200-kilometer station, one gets "a very big signal (25 millimicrons), which is more than thirty times the noise," at the 200-kilometer station.

At the station 400 kilometers away, one gets a signal four times the size of the noise, Dr. Bethe said, "but not more."

The decoupled explosion is characterized, however, by a signal propagated mainly in the high frequencies. Since high frequencies die out very quickly with distance, "the signal which is propagated in the earth will be one that starts and very soon dies out," Dr. Bethe told the Committee.

"Therefore, you will have a much better chance of observing a signal from a decoupled explosion if you use higher frequency" in the seismic detection instrumentation, Dr. Bethe said. High frequencies had received little attention before because they were not detectable at long ranges.

The Geneva system has to rely on seismographs of relatively long periods and of low frequency because the high frequency signal will not go very far. But if we could have a system in which the stations are closer to the event, then we are free to choose higher frequencies which we know are generated in much larger intensity by the decoupled explosion.

If you go to a ten-cycle-per-second detection, then the energy which is fed into the signal increases about *thirtyfold* over that which we are recording with our present system, and at the same time—and this is very fortunate—on the average, the noise energy—that is, the energy of the wiggles which exist anywhere in the earth—decreases as we go to higher frequency, at least on the average, and under average conditions.

Dr. Bethe was building a powerful case for a closely spaced grid based on detection of higher frequencies. He acknowledged, after a question from Chairman Holifield, that the science of high-frequency waves in seismology was "in a very early stage." The problem would require "a good deal of research," he said, "I think it is not very difficult research, but a good deal of research."

Dr. Bethe proposed a system, based on a ten-cycle-per-second frequency at stations with average noise, that would produce a signal ten times the noise. "That is an easily recognizable signal, which is obvious to anyone at eight stations from a *fully decoupled* 20-kiloton shot, and this system will require that I have a station at every 200 kilometers."

Two hundred kilometers is about 125 miles.

"I think everybody realizes that 200 kilometers is a small spacing," Dr. Bethe acknowledged.

The 1958 Conference of Experts had provided for 600-mile spacing. Dr. Bethe told the Committee that it would take about 600 stations, 30 times as many as had been proposed in the 1958 system, to cover the Soviet Union under his new plan.

"Of course, by saying this number, it is clear that something has to be done to make this number acceptable," Dr. Bethe said. "This is a political question and no longer a technical question. The stations have to be made acceptable to the Russians and to ourselves."

He quickly added that most of the additional stations should be un-manned and tamper-proof, so that "you cannot easily reverse the polarity in a station." Such a system could be developed, Dr. Bethe estimated, in one or two years. "I would think that by the end of the period which we would need to install the big stations, we would probably know about the small stations. Maybe a little earlier."

His one-to-two-year estimate, he said, referred only to research and development. After this, he said, an experimental station should be set up somewhere in the United States to test the idea. Attempts should be made, he said, to reverse the polarity of the unmanned stations or to confuse the stations with noise. "One would have to learn from such experiments just what one can do and what one cannot do against such spoofing."

Under the 600-station Bethe system, the number of unidentified events per year was estimated to be about 500. This did not, however, contemplate further improvements in the decoupling factor, which then stood at 300.

Dr. Brown later told the Joint Committee that "some calculations done at my laboratory [Livermore] would indicate that one can get a factor of three increase in decoupling factor merely by stacking a lot of graphite in solid blocks, which are known to exist, around the explosive. So it may be possible to get another factor of three in decoupling that way. I think eventually it might be possible to get a factor of ten."

This meant there was some theoretical basis then for expecting the decoupling factor to go to 900 rather than 300. Presumably that would force the Bethe system of 600 stations to be augmented again, Dr. Brown commented half in jest.

"One would then probably have to increase the number of stations by another factor of three (if the decoupling increases by a factor of three) according to some calculations that Dr. Richard Latter made," he suggested.

Dr. Bethe agreed with Dr. Teller that the research program for improving seismic detection was "by no means" adequate: "It has taken a very long time since the Berkner report, which was issued about a year ago, before anything was done for implementation of the research program which was recommended."

As to cost, Dr. Bethe estimated, with Dr. Romney, that it would amount to $100,000 per station, or about $80 million in the Soviet Union alone. This, Dr. Bethe suggested, "is not a small sum, but also it is not a large sum. It is a small sum compared to the requirements for a detection system in space."

Dr. Bethe moved next against the Latter-Teller argument that a closely spaced grid of seismic stations would produce thousands of unidentified signals which could not be checked out:

Supposing we had such a system, what would we do with the information? You will recall that I required that the signal be ten times the noise, I required such a large signal in order to be able to see first motion in addition to just seeing the signal. We know from the experience of the Hardtack series that the first motion increases relatively much more if you go to small distances than does the signal afterwards. So that we should really be quite well off in regard to first motion.

Dr. Richard Latter mentioned in his testimony this morning that there would be some 18,000 events above an equivalent yield of 18 tons—tons, not kilotons. What I am aiming at in my exercise here is a somewhat more modest goal. I am aiming at 20-kilotons divided by 300, which is about 70 tons. That is, I want to detect a normal explosion, a coupled explosion of 70 tons, or an uncoupled or decoupled explosion of 20 kilotons. . . . This would be 20 kilotons decoupled in salt, which is equivalent to 70 tons coupled in tuff. . . . At this level I estimate that the number of earthquakes in Soviet Russia would be about 5,000. I would hope that with a rather good system of detecting first motion we could identify 90 per cent of these, which would leave about 500. Five hundred is still a very large number. However, you would obviously not try to inspect 500 seismic events. After all, we are interested in the decoupled 20-kiloton explosions, and these decoupled 20-kiloton explosions can be easily performed only in salt. Only in salt beds can we easily use Mr. Meade's method of solution mining. Therefore, one would inspect first of all only those events which happen to originate from a place where there are salt beds.

Now, although salt domes are widespread and there are hundreds of them in the Soviet Union, as we hear, they are not all over the place. I don't know what fraction. We once made an estimate which was that it was quite a lot less than 1 per cent of the Soviet Union which would be eligible for such excavations. Hopefully saying 1 per cent, this would leave you with only five events. You might in addition have some evidence other than the seismogram which tells you that somebody has done a major operation (after all, this excavating of the salt is a major operation) in such and such an area. If they wanted to excavate these cavities near the Caspian Sea, let us say, this further restricts the area in which we need to look. If they excavate somewhere else, then it won't be so easily possible to put the brine into the sea. So I believe that it is quite possible to select by other evidence than just the seismic signal those signals which originate from places where there might possibly be a fully decoupled shot. When you come down to ten or twenty events a year of this type for which signals have been set and which are in regions where you could have a salt cavity, then you get a perfectly manageable problem of inspection.[15]

Other scientists did not accept Dr. Bethe's assumption that all salt beds in the Soviet Union are known. Nor was it necessarily true that none of the salt deposits were located in seismic areas.

It was neither the economics nor the science of the problem which had deterred other scientists from suggesting as many as 600 stations inside the Soviet Union. It was the Soviet fear of inspection. As a matter of fact, American scientists at the 1958 Conference of Experts had suggested 650 stations to get down to a 1-kiloton threshold. But this was never made a formal proposal, mainly because it was well understood that the Soviet Union could not accept such a large network of stations.[16]

Dr. Bethe, however, had another point of dispute with the decoupling experts. In order to acquire a decoupling factor of thirty, Dr. Bethe declared, one could reduce the optimum size of the big underground hole to only one-tenth the total volume, not to one-thirtieth as Dr. Albert Latter calculated. "This," he observed, "is still a very big volume."

While acknowledging the big-hole decoupling theory as valid, Dr. Bethe attacked the other theories presented by Dr. Latter and Dr. Teller:

When the big hole theory was first advanced by Dr. Albert Latter, I immediately recognized that this was a sound theory. I did my own calculations and confirmed his results. I do not feel at all the same way about the further decoupling possibilities. They depend on rather complicated schemes. One of the schemes that Dr. Teller mentioned is to distribute graphite dust in the big hole. This method was presented at the Geneva Conference. It didn't draw any particular fire from the Russians. But unofficially our friend, Dr. Penney, the head of the British delegation, pointed out to us that he had done experiments on very similar devices for quite different purposes and that they did not work at all. The difficulty is that this carbon dust must not be present before the nuclear explosion because if it is present then it is just swept by the nuclear explosion to the wall. It is thereby rendered ineffective. In addition it increases the initial pressure spike which you always get when the shot from the air hits the wall. So you must not have the carbon dust before the nuclear explosion. So you are asked to suspend little balls of carbon dust, let us say, at quite frequent intervals in a big cavity, explode them all simultaneously, and explode them at a time after the nuclear explosion passes them, but still early enough to absorb the heat from the nuclear explosion. What Dr. Penney pointed out is that he had tried to explode little balls of carbon dust, and instead of being nicely distributed in a space he found that it all came together and was therefore useless. That doesn't mean that all these schemes will not work. I only want to leave with you the impression that these further decoupling schemes are by no means as simple as appears on the surface and by no means as sure. It is my opinion that the next round ought to go to the detection rather than to the concealment.

In a supplementary statement Dr. Bethe presented to the Committee after the hearings had concluded, he suggested indirectly that he would be willing to accept as few as 10 on-site inspections per year to police a 4.75-threshold agreement: "I believe that even 10 per cent inspection would be a very strong deterrent against the Russians' conducting clandestine tests in violation of a treaty." He indicated these 10 per cent would be based on the estimates of 100 earthquakes of this magnitude per year in the Soviet Union.

The thrust of Dr. Bethe's supplementary testimony was to ignore, in important cases, the effect of decoupling in an over-all treaty. Dr. Richard Latter's scheme to increase the number of stations from twenty-one to thirty, Dr. Bethe said, for instance, would, with twenty inspections, deter "clandestine tests down to well below 5 kilotons under Nevada conditions." And with "two to three years of intensive research" the ability to identify earthquakes could be improved "by at least a factor of 5." Then, he said, the Latter system of thirty stations "could monitor explosions down to 1 kiloton in standard conditions. Already now, the Geneva system of twenty-one stations can detect and locate (though not identify) explosions down to well below one standard kiloton."

Dr. Bethe staunchly refused to be intimidated by the big hole. Existing cavities in salt domes are big enough to fully decouple nuclear explosions of only two to three kilotons, he wrote the Committee. The agreed Geneva system could detect and locate a 30 kiloton bomb exploded in such a cavity, he calculated, even though it would be made to look like a one-kiloton shot:

In spite of the testimony of Mr. Meade, I still maintain that the construction of a large cavity in salt, of 2 million cubic meters volume, is a major undertaking. A violator would have to be afraid that such a construction job would be detected by other means than seismographs, e.g., by photography from satellites. The disposal of the brine alone seems a formidable problem. The volume of the brine will be many times the volume of the salt. It may be estimated at perhaps 100 million barrels.

a. To dump this into an old oil field requires a major field, and a lot of pipes which would be visible. Moreover, this would greatly limit the geographical areas where big cavities might be suspected to be constructed, and hence would reduce the number of seismograph recordings which would require on-site inspection to very few.

b. Mr. Meade suggested dumping the brine directly into the sea. I suppose this would be the Caspian Sea. This restricts construction of cavities to the shores of the Caspian, again a very limited geographical region.

c. If the cavity were constructed elsewhere, it would probably be necessary to dump the salt into a river. If this were done in one of the very large rivers in North America—the Ohio, the Columbia, or the St. Lawrence—it would at least double their natural salt content over a period of two years. Chemical analysis of river water would be a very simple safeguard against digging of salt cavities.

Constructing large cavities in limestone, as proposed by Dr. Teller, "seems far more difficult than in salt," Dr. Bethe observed:

I discussed this problem with some chemists. The limestone would first have to be heated to about 1,000° C. and decomposed, at considerable expense in power. Then it would have to be cooled to room temperature, at considerable expense of cooling water, in order to have the lime dissolve. More important is the fact that lime is almost insoluble in water: It would require the entire water supply of New York City over a year to dissolve the lime in a cavity of the size discussed by Mr. Meade. Direct mining operation, at great expense, would probably be more feasible. It is also questionable whether the walls of a limestone cavity would have the desirable elastic properties of a salt cavity.

Nor was Dr. Bethe impressed with the suggestion that a big hole could be used for more than one test:

It would be most suspicious if two signals were recorded by the detection stations which originate from the same source. It would therefore be very dangerous for a violator to use the same location for two or more tests. This goes especially for decoupled tests in large cavities if they can be detected by a system of unmanned stations. This greatly adds to complications, cost, and time required for testing.

Dr. Bethe was especially sensitive to the criticisms that his 125-mile spacing for an unmanned supplementary net of seismic stations in the Soviet Union would be politically unacceptable to the Kremlin. By using the tight spacing only in seismic areas, Dr. Bethe suggested in his supplementary paper, the total of unmanned stations in the Soviet Union could be reduced to about 200. This would be a tenfold increase over the 21 full-fledged control stations envisioned in the 1958 experts' report. He accepted cost estimates by the Sandia Corporation of Albuquerque, New Mexico, that the unmanned stations would cost about $100,000 each, and communications cables for the Soviet Union would add another $50 million to $100 million.

This would mean a cost of $70 million to $120 million in the Soviet Union alone. It would provide only the stations and communications. The other expenses mentioned in the Peterson-Coker presentation would still have to be faced.

The unmanned-station network, Dr. Bethe claimed again, would "greatly reduce the number of on-site inspections required" by increasing the capacity of the system to distinguish explosions from earthquakes.

If the Russians could be persuaded to accept the closer spacing, Dr. Bethe suggested, high frequency seismographs should be included and this would open up a whole new field for improving the chances to identify more earthquakes. The closely spaced net also would permit more accurate determination of the depth of the source and thus further increase the number of identifiable earthquakes. The unmanned network also would make more difficult the circular spoofing suggested by Dr. Teller, he said.

As for Dr. Harold Brown's statement that one-kiloton tests would permit either the United States or the Soviet Union to develop efficient higher-yield tactical weapons, Dr. Bethe declared: "I do not agree." The minimum yield required for such tests "is more likely to be three to five kilotons. This is also the opinion of the Los Alamos Laboratory."

Dr. Bethe also managed, as had Dr. Teller before him, to inject his

political views into the technical hearings. He told the Committee he did
not believe the Russians wanted to violate a test ban. They broke a moratorium in September, 1961, but Dr. Bethe was right when he conjectured
that the Russians did not want particularly to develop small weapons.
"Even a very imperfect" inspection system would "greatly impede" the Soviet Union's progress and "slow it down to a snail's pace," Dr. Bethe said.

He came out strongly for a moratorium below the 4.75 threshold. "If
testing were resumed below magnitude 4.75, they (the Russians) could
operate openly, easily and quickly and could soon catch up to our present
position in tactical weapons. On the other hand, we already have tactical
weapons of many yields and sizes, and it would be difficult (though not
entirely impossible) for us to make further progress of real military significance."

Dr. Bethe indicated in a still later letter, dated April 29, that he would
favor extending the moratorium below the 4.75 threshold to a period of
two to three years. Mr. Meade indicated it would take two and a half
years to construct a cavity in salt to decouple fully a 30-kiloton explosion.
If the Russians began construction at the moment a limited test ban was
put into effect, Dr. Bethe reasoned, they "could not reap the fruits of
such construction during the moratorium." Others questioned, however,
whether it was safe to assume that the Russians would wait to build an
underground cavity until the limited test ban went into effect.

Dr. Bethe argued that "even if the Russians want to construct such a
cavity, which I do not believe, they could not well have started to do so
until recently."

The Teller Rebuttal

Dr. Teller, continuing his dramatic debate with Dr. Bethe, later made
these comments before the Committee about the Bethe 600-station network for the Soviet Union:

This procedure, if it is implemented with 600 stations, could indeed be
worked out to detect explosions down to 20 kilotons. Below 20 kilotons
no capability has been claimed, and if you want to claim for it a capability
below 20 kilotons then I believe the difficulties in that case, too, will have
to be considered quite seriously.

Here, therefore, we have a system requiring 600 stations in the Soviet
Union alone, and many thousands of stations throughout the world, if
you want to make it a really international system, which will then have,
according to our present knowledge, a threshold of 20 kilotons.

This threshold can then change in the future downward if, as Dr.
Bethe hopes, the methods of detection will be improved. It can change
upward if some of those admittedly hypothetical decoupling methods I
mentioned yesterday, should work out.

In that case, the same network will still be usable, but not down to 20
kilotons, but only 50 kilotons. In particular, the number of inspections is,

again, a very bothersome question. There are 5,000 events of which Dr. Bethe hopes to eliminate by direct observation 90 per cent, and then to eliminate many more by looking only in the areas in which there are salt domes.

It is by no means clear that only the salt dome areas have to be looked at. Furthermore, the system of elimination is based on the idea that the first arrival has a positive phase. I have tried to indicate . . . that research on several simultaneous explosions will quite possibly—in fact, I would almost say probably—confuse the signal sufficiently so as to make a nuclear explosion look more complicated and uncharacteristic.

I think you should have clearly in mind the difference between an earthquake and a nuclear explosion. The principle of the difference is that the nuclear explosion is something simple, which starts from one point and goes outward. An earthquake, instead, is a relatively complicated effect. By making more than one nuclear explosion, or more than one explosion —for instance, one decoupled nuclear explosion and then another normal explosion or two other normal explosions—you can confuse the picture to an extent where untangling it will become more difficult. Of this I am sure.

Whether untangling it in that case will be possible or not is something which research will have to show, and . . . such research should indeed be carried out.

Was the art of concealment or the art of detection advancing faster? Dr. Romney, in reply to Senator Jackson of Washington, said:

The art of concealment in the past couple of years certainly has advanced far faster than the detection improvements. Many people feel that this could well continue for some time. On balance, I find it difficult, myself, to forecast results. . . .

In terms of a specific, fixed network of stations, I believe the concealment can proceed at least as fast as the improvement techniques. However, if you will allow, as a means of improvement, the addition of new stations to the detection system, then I am not sure what the answer is.

Dr. Richard Latter, discussing the same point, observed that there is a technical reason for believing that the capability to conceal will increase more rapidly than the capability to detect.

Suppose, he said, that concealment methods improved by a factor of ten, so that by concealment a 10-kiloton explosion could be made to look like a 1-kiloton explosion. This advance in concealment art confronts the detection side with two problems, not one. First the detection system must develop the capability of detecting events at 1 kiloton.

Second, the detection side would have to cope with ten times as many events at the 1-kiloton level as at the 10-kiloton level.

The old Geneva system, for instance, was estimated to have a capability of identifying 90 per cent of the earthquakes, leaving 10 per cent unidentified. If at the 10-kiloton level there were a total of 100 events, 10 would be unidentified. If the detection capability were improved by a factor of 10, 90 per cent of the events at 1 kiloton could be correctly identified.

But there are 1,000 events at the 1-kiloton level. With a 90 per cent capability of identification, that would leave 100 events, instead of 10, requiring identification.

So the detection system needs improvement by another factor of 10 to get back to the same number of unidentified events as there were at the 10-kiloton level.

You are . . . facing the problem that at the lower yields . . . there are a greater number of confusing signals. Not only must you for a given capability of the system change the yield at which you achieve that capability, but you must increase the capability.

So a factor of 10 improvement in concealment would require a factor of 100 improvement in detection capability.

Another limiting factor on improvement, Dr. Latter said, was the fact that the system did not improve proportionally as the number of stations was increased. As he had pointed out earlier, adding only a few stations would make a relatively large improvement, but then no further improvement would come until there was an exceedingly large number of stations added.

For these two reasons, detection and identification improvements would have to be made much more rapidly than concealment improvements—merely to stand still.

PROJECT VELA

On April 23, 1959, in a memorandum of agreement signed by Dr. Killian, AEC Chairman McCone, and Deputy Defense Secretary Donald Quarles, the Defense Department had been given the assignment of developing better detection techniques in a project to be called Vela. But Advanced Research Projects Agency was not officially assigned responsibility until September 2, 1959—six months after the Presidentially appointed board of seismologists had outlined the program.

ARPA divided the problem into three parts: (1) Project Vela Uniform for the detection of underground tests; (2) Project Vela Sierra for the ground detection of high-altitude detonations; and (3) Project Vela Hotel for space detection of high-altitude detonations.

The Coast and Geodetic Survey worked with the Defense Department in Project Vela Uniform. They developed a plan for providing the seismological research stations of the world with standard, calibrated instruments which were to be maintained and operated by the individual stations as part of their normal routine. It was stipulated that data accumulated at these stations would be exchanged freely among seismologists throughout the world. The National Academy of Sciences established a committee of seismologists to standardize the equipment to be provided. The Coast and Geodetic Survey, a division of the Department of Commerce, was to procure the equipment and distribute it.

Another part of Project Vela Uniform was to establish a large-scale basic research program in universities and other areas to study the generation and propagation of seismic waves. At the same time, new types of seismic instruments were to be investigated and new techniques like deep-hole seismic listening posts were to be developed.

A third project under Vela Uniform, to hasten the development process, was to build and operate two prototype detection stations, one based on the recommendations of the Geneva Conference of Experts, another on the improvements suggested by the Berkner Panel. The new stations would serve two purposes, as prototypes for a control system but also as experimental stations.

Project Vela Uniform was to have a fourth task: the supervision of a series of underground nuclear and high-explosive detonations to provide more basic scientific knowledge and to test components of the control system as they developed. The plan was to conduct the experiments in a variety of geological environments.

Also envisioned were several short-term studies to include: (1) a review of the feasibility of unmanned stations; (2) a systematic review of earthquake statistics in the hope of developing distinguishing characteristics between earthquakes and explosions; and (3) a study of the feasibility of using large arrays of seismographs.

The 1960 Vela Uniform program was budgeted for $8.7 million, including $2.3 million for nonnuclear test shots.

Project Vela Sierra, for ground-based detection of high-altitude shots, was stalled while additional research and development programs were planned. Funds for the Vela Sierra program were not made available until April, 1960. They then amounted only to $1 million.

Project Vela obviously was not being pushed full speed ahead. Chairman Holifield of the Joint Atomic Energy Committee expressed his displeasure.

"Yesterday Dr. Bethe indicated some disappointment in that not much progress had been made in the last year," Mr. Holifield observed. "I want to emphasize that I feel the same way as Dr. Bethe on that point."

Dr. Teller agreed. He told the Joint Committee:

I believe the Berkner report's recommendation of $30 million has been too modest. It has also been much more than we have actually spent. . . . I think we have here an issue on which our national security may well depend. I think that the support of this program is woefully inadequate. . . .[17]

I feel that there should be a higher priority program in seismology, in methods of detection, and also in methods of evasion. Because if you restrict yourself to one, then you are instructing me to play chess, but to move the white pieces only.

Back in February, the Humphrey Disarmament Subcommittee in the Senate had also urged the Administration to take a deeper interest in improving the detection and identification systems.

Faced with these two Senate committees' strong initiatives, President Eisenhower reacted on May 7, less than two weeks after the Joint Committee hearings had ended. There would be "a major expansion of the present research and development," the White House announced. From an expenditure of about $10 million in the fiscal year that ended June 30, 1960, Mr. Eisenhower announced, the next year's budget would jump to about $66 million.

At the same time, the President kept the pressure on the Soviet Union with the threat to resume nuclear testing for research purposes. Project Vela, he said, called for, among other things, "an experimental program of underground detonations encompassing both high-explosive and where necessary nuclear explosions."

Such nuclear explosions as are essential to a full understanding of both the capabilities of the presently proposed detection system and the potential for improvements in this system would be carried out under fully contained conditions and would produce no radioactive fallout. In order to develop sufficient reliable data from the program, it is anticipated that it will be necessary to conduct a series of explosions of various sizes, in differing types of geological formations.

Recently, the Soviet negotiators at Geneva concurred with the proposal that underground nuclear explosions should be conducted to improve the capability of the proposed control network to detect and identify underground explosions.

They have also indicated a willingness to discuss research and development in the seismic-detection area with the United States and the United Kingdom. Agreement has been reached to convene a group of U.S.S.R., U.K., and U.S. scientists in Geneva on May 11, to exchange information on the seismic-research activities of the three nations as a basis for future determination of the areas in which coordinated or joint research would be most fruitful.

The Defense, Commerce, and Interior Departments would work with the AEC, universities, and private organizations in carrying out the research and development program, the President said.

In addition to responding to the "advice" of the Senate, President Eisenhower was obviously moving swiftly in an effort to encourage the Soviet Union to a full research effort.

On May 3, the Soviet Union had indicated its willingness to engage "at once" in a seismic-research program. The Soviet move was framed as an answer to the United States late-March acceptance by the United States and Britain of the idea of a short-term moratorium on tests below the 4.75 threshold if a research program could be undertaken immediately.

Moving with unusual speed, the three powers were able to convene another technical meeting in Geneva on May 11. The United States went to the meeting with the hope that joint research, including the use of nuclear detonations, could be undertaken by all three nations.

Each of the three delegations—the United States, the United Kingdom, and the Soviet Union—outlined their separate plans for extensive seismic research, including plans for chemical explosions underground. The United States experts, in addition, presented plans for American nuclear detonations.

Soviet scientists sounded unusually cooperative, but when the three technical delegations reported separately to the political conference in Geneva, Soviet Ambassador Tsarapkin repudiated his scientists. The Soviet Union would not participate in the joint research program, he said. Failure of the Paris summit conference may have had some effect on the Soviet attitude.

Despite the inconclusive results of the three-power meeting on joint research, the United States went ahead with its own program. On October 11, 1960, the Defense Department was able to announce that a new seismic-research station, designed especially to meet all the requirements set up by the 1958 Geneva Conference of Experts, had been completed at Fort Sill, Oklahoma.

The station, to be called the Wichita Mountains Seismological Observatory, was part of the Project Vela Uniform effort for improving detection of underground nuclear tests.

Although the station began operation in the fall of 1960, no date was set for initiating the program of experimental underground nuclear explosions. The site in the Wichita Mountains, about fifteen miles northwest of Lawton, Oklahoma, had been selected because seismic noise was at a minimum in that area. The Geotechnical Corporation of Garland, Texas, developed the seismological observatory and would operate it, the Defense Department announced, under the supervision of the Air Force Technical Applications Center.

No spectacular successes emerged quickly from the station, however. AFTAC scientists indicated in 1961 that the faster pace of the concealment art was producing the difficulties scientists like Richard Latter and Carl Romney had foreseen in their Joint Committee testimony.

TESTING IN SPACE

Dr. Byron P. Leonard, of the Space Technology Laboratories, Inc., a subcontractor working with the Advanced Research Project Agency of the Department of Defense, told the April 1960 Joint Committee that the United States could conduct a nuclear test in space in "less than two years" with then-existing technology. The explosion could take place at distances up to tens of millions of miles, he said, with little danger that the nuclear explosion would take place prematurely. Instrumentation sent up with the satellite would send back not only information that the device had been exploded but its yield and some other data, Dr. Leonard advised.

He read the prepared testimony of Allen F. Donovan, Vice President of Space Technology Laboratories, and a member of the American team at the Technical Working Group I conference. The Soviet attitude toward satellite systems was especially significant, Mr. Leonard indicated. The Soviet delegation to the high-altitude conference objected to the system of solar satellites, which could look behind the moon, the sun, and the other planets, "in spite of the fact that Soviet luniks demonstrated the capability of reaching this region." [18]

Soviet objections were that the cost of launching solar satellites would be excessive and the communications problem would be too severe, Dr. Leonard recalled.

> Nevertheless they were willing to accept the far-earth satellites [system] in orbit at 50,000 kilometers [31,000 miles]. Strange as it may seem to those of you who have not been involved in the peculiarities of space vehicles, it takes a more powerful rocket system to put a satellite in orbit at 50,000 kilometers altitude than it does to launch one above the speed of escape into orbit around the sun. In either case, it requires a powerful multistage rocket system beginning with an Atlas or large-size booster.

A satellite detection system for nuclear explosions in outer space would be available, Dr. Leonard reported, as soon as nuclear signal detectors and the signal analyzer had been built (no government order had then been placed), and as soon as the system could be integrated into a total satellite vehicle. By the time these things were done, he said, the launching vehicles would be ready. He added, however, words of caution about catching a possible violator of the nuclear test-ban:

> There are important questions as to the effectiveness of satellite-based systems for the detection of nuclear explosions at high altitude which can only finally be resolved by measurements of the natural radiation in space and testing detection system components in this radiation environment.
>
> I wish to make it clear that our present concept of the satellite detection system assumes certain things about this natural radiation. Only after this background is known and experience is gained from testing detection equipment in it can we accurately assess the effectiveness of any satellite system proposed. Hence, my statements on the ability to create and launch satellite vehicles of the presently conceived type, while certainly encouraging, do not automatically insure that doing so will give us an adequate capability for detecting nuclear explosions in space.

Dr. Leonard ran a mock nuclear test in outer space for the Committee, assuming a one-megaton device would be used. He chose that yield because it appeared logical a potential violator would go to outer space, rather than underground or near the earth's surface, to test large-yield weapons during a test ban.

The gamma-ray detector could see a megaton shot out to 5 million nautical miles; a neutron detector out to 2 million nautical miles; and the X-ray detector, between 600 million miles and 5 billion miles.

The X-ray device, according to theoretical predictions, would be able to see a nuclear explosion at distances as great as three to thirty times the diameter of the earth's orbit around the sun, Dr. Leonard estimated. So the X-ray technique was rated several orders of magnitude stronger than the other techniques of detecting outer-space nuclear explosions.

One could use Pioneer V, the American satellite now circling the sun, as an example of a test vehicle that a potential violator might use, he suggested. Its orbit took it about 4 million nautical miles from the earth three weeks after it was launched.

At seven weeks, Pioneer V was 8 million miles away; at eleven weeks, 18 million; and finally, at about half a year after launching, it was to have reached a point 85 million nautical miles away.

Dr. Leonard concluded from his example that

while many different detection techniques have been proposed for detecting high-altitude nuclear explosions, the present space technology implies that a potential violator need wait only a matter of a few weeks [after launching his test vehicle] before he has to contend with only one type of detector, namely, the X-ray detector.

Furthermore, a limited amount of shielding studies, where one postulates placing a shield around the nuclear device, indicates that only a special type of X-ray detector can function reasonably well against a shielded explosion. *That type of X-ray detector has not yet been built [or] flown in the environment in which it must operate.*

Shielding would not reduce the amount of information a potential violator could get out of a test in outer space. The shield would be oriented, Dr. Leonard said, so that radiation was reduced only in the direction of the detection system; and if the test-monitoring equipment were placed on the other side, the amount of information being sent back to the violator would not be affected.

The required X-ray detector awaited "some basic research and development," Dr. Leonard continued. It would be a period of years before it would be ready. Thus, there would be the same period of years when a violator could test in space without detection. Or, as Congressman Hosmer put it, "with a 100 per cent chance of being undetected."

DR. LEONARD: That is right. It is really no trick at all to run tests outside of the X-ray detection circle shown in the figure.

REPRESENTATIVE HOSMER: Yesterday we had testimony that you could do it underground with a 99 per cent chance of not being detected. This is an even more loose area.

DR. LEONARD: That is right. I think, however, that was predicated upon getting a certain capability in these ground networks.

REPRESENTATIVE HOSMER: They would have to improve tremendously to get that one-in-a-hundred chance.

DR. LEONARD: I would like to conclude my remarks by simply stating that it is clear that in the area of space, detection systems are in much the same situation that we have been previously on underground shots, namely, we are relying upon the development of a new device to detect nuclear explosions at great distances from the earth.

The uncertainties in just what the ultimate effectiveness of this detector will be are such that *it is not clear what the final capability of a space detection system will be.* The only way we can make it clear is through a vigorous research and development program.

The Committee next heard from a designer of detection instruments for satellites, Dr. Richard Taschek, of the Los Alamos scientific laboratory in Los Alamos, New Mexico.

Dr. Taschek estimated that with "due deliberation," it would take two years of development to make ready for the first satellite-launch in an experimental program to develop a satellite detection system for outer-space explosions. He believed that another two years, roughly, would be required for "full definition of a prototype operational unit."

Most of this time would be devoted to developing the electronic decision-making elements of the system. Installation of an operational system might require about two more years, making a total of six years before a completely operational system could be in orbit.

Meanwhile, however, Dr. Taschek pointed out, a limited capability for detecting outer-space tests could be obtained through ground-based detection of Argus effects or possibly other, less understood phenomena. Also some of the neutron detectors then in satellites might also provide limited surveillance against nuclear explosions.

He estimated that by using space communications networks now in existence a limited satellite detection capability might be achieved in as short a time as six months. Its range, however, would only be out to "moon distances" or 189,000 miles for a nominal 10-kiloton nuclear detonation. As Dr. Leonard warned, capabilities for testing beyond such ranges already existed in both the United States and the Soviet Union.

Dr. Taschek pointed out that the six-satellite system proposed by Technical Working Group I, for a far-earth orbit, would require the launching of twenty-four satellites per year "provided we cannot improve reliability." He indicated that reliability might be improved most easily by increasing the amount of weight, but this again awaited development of suitable thrust.

Dr. Taschek presented a $25-million, five-year program intended to support three successful launchings (eleven payloads) to obtain the necessary data on which to base a complete satellite system for detecting outer-space explosions.

Chapter 14

Judgment Withheld

The Joint Committee on Atomic Energy of the Congress of the United States is empowered to deal with both the political and technical aspects of atomic energy.

The four-day hearings on the control system for a nuclear test ban were carefully confined to the technical aspects of the problem. As in the Joint Committee's fallout hearings, a full exposition of the technical picture was made. But much of the technical material was complicated and took more than a few minutes casual study to understand. What was needed after this exposition of the technical material was a similar set of hearings on the political conclusions that could be drawn from the technical facts. This the Joint Committee did not do. In another compartment on Capitol Hill, the Senate Disarmament Subcommittee was considering the political side of the problem without careful study of the technical facts. And never the twain did meet.

A little sniffing of the Washington atmosphere would indicate that the Senate Disarmament Subcommittee favored a test ban and that the Joint Committee, in general, disapproved the test ban because it was technically unsound.

But the Joint Committee did not permit itself to express a public, collective judgment that the test-ban agreement would be technically unsound.

At the risk of discouraging a committee that has filled a vital need in America's democratic society, it should be made clear that the Joint Atomic Energy Committee, despite its good intentions, stopped just short of performing the public service that was required of it.

As Senator Humphrey pointed out in one of his hearings after the Technical Working Group II conference, the business of the Senate, as outlined in the Constitution, is to provide its advice and consent in the making of treaties. The nuclear-test-ban treaty would come before the Joint Committee and the Senate Foreign Relations Committee for consent, once the Executive signed it. The Joint Committee thus would be called upon to exercise political judgment as well as technical judgment on the feasibility of a test-ban.

451

Some of the members of the Joint Committee may have been giving their political advice to President Eisenhower—and President Kennedy after him—in private. To this extent they were fulfilling their constitutional obligations. But in a matter that was of important public interest, the Joint Committee, like the Executive Branch, withheld important political judgments from the public.

The Joint Committee's summary analysis of the hearings on the technical aspects of the test-ban control system was a prime example of a scrupulously technical assessment carefully contrived to avoid all political judgment. The result was a unanimous report by the Joint Committee members participating that read like a technical catalogue. It had practically no impact on the general public.

The summary analysis reported "general agreement" among the experts interviewed on five points:

1. The Geneva Control system of 180 stations will require augmentation and improvement to restore the capability for detection and identification of underground seismic events to the value of 5 kilotons estimated by the 1958 Conference of Experts.

2. It is possible to increase the difficulty of detection and identification of underground seismic events by decoupling nuclear explosions by a factor of up to 300.

3. To establish a capability for the Geneva control system to detect and identify underground seismic events of yield equivalent to that of a 20-kiloton fully decoupled explosion, it will be necessary to increase greatly the number of stations and to improve the instruments and techniques of seismic detection.

4. A vigorous and sustained program of research and development is necessary to improve our instruments and our techniques of detection, identification, and inspection of underground nuclear explosion tests.

5. An increase in the number of stations in the Geneva control system, in order to lower the threshold of underground seismic events which it can detect and identify, will result in a considerable increase in the number of unidentified events which may require inspection.

Only the experts and a few disarmament buffs around the country could understand what these five points meant. It would have taken a reading of the 478-page hearings, or at least of the 77-page summary-analysis, to judge how to add them up.

What was the Committee's judgment? Did the United States dare to sign a nuclear test-ban agreement along the lines proposed by President Eisenhower? On the basis of its investigation of the technical aspects of control, would the Committee give its consent to a treaty along the lines the United States proposed? What value as a disarmament measure would there be in a test-ban with a 4.75 threshold?

The Committee provided no judgment on these points.

Its summary-analysis noted that there were "certain differences as to scientific facts and judgments" that had been brought out on these points in the hearings:

1. The degree and practicality of decoupling by means of large cavities;
2. The extent and practicality of further improvements in detection networks and devices;
3. The significance of further weapons development through clandestine tests.

In the last paragraph of its introduction to the summary-analysis, the Committee came as close as anywhere to making a political judgment:

> The Subcommittees [two participated in the hearings] were also impressed by the importance of the time factor in relation to nuclear test cessation. The United States has not tested any nuclear weapons since its Hardtack II series in the fall of 1958. It appears from the testimony that at least for the next several years it will not be possible to identify underground events whose seismic signals record the equivalent of a nonmuffled nuclear explosion of 20 kilotons or less, although they may be detected. Further, it appears that for this same time period it will not be possible to detect muffled tests of 100 kilotons or more set off deep underground in large cavities. Therefore, it seems for the next several years and possibly thereafter, there could be a race between improved means of detection and identification as against improved means of concealing and muffling nuclear tests.

Skepticism was in those words. But they raised more questions than they answered. What was the significance of the time factor? Was it that the moratorium below the threshold, which President Eisenhower and Prime Minister Macmillan had accepted, would permit indiscriminate cheating for the next several years? What was the significance of the distinction between nonmuffled and muffled tests? Did the Committee think that a treaty violator could make significant gains in weapons development by nonmuffled explosions? By muffled explosions?

And what were the prospects in the race between detection and concealment sciences? Was the detection science at a serious disadvantage bordering on complete hopelessness to catch up on the concealment-art?

The summary answered none of these. In the body of the analysis, some isolated paragraphs came closer to the point:

> With the present state of knowledge, detection of an underground low-yield test by a violator attempting to conceal it will be extremely difficult if not impossible. Similarly, it was agreed that clandestine testing of high-yield weapons in space could be conducted within the present scope of missile and satellite technology.

The Committee report then sifted the testimony of the experts on the significance of clandestine tests. Where there was agreement the summary-analysis made clear statements:

> In the opinion of the scientists who testified at the hearings, further under-

ground tests at yields smaller than 20 kilotons would permit development of new weapons in the low-kiloton range. They also agreed that further testing in space would permit full-scale tests of weapons developed by underground scaled-down tests, as well as permit development of improved models of high-yield nuclear weapons.

Where the witnesses differed, however, the Joint Committee took no sides. One of the key points of difference was on the military significance of small underground tests or big outer-space tests.

The witnesses differed, however, on the relative military significance of such developments compared to the stockpile of the sophisticated weapons presently available to the three principal nuclear powers, the United States, the United Kingdom, and the U.S.S.R. For example, Dr. Teller considers such developments of very great importance, while Dr. Bethe considers they would be of only nominal importance.

The Committee explained its reasons for not expressing a judgment of its own:

The importance to the United States of future development of low-yield nuclear weapons, as well as improvements in high-yield weapons, is determined by military requirements—strategic and tactical. These are the responsibility of various agencies in the Executive Branch, including the Office of the President, the Department of Defense, and the AEC, as well as designated Congressional Committees in the Legislative Branch. However, the military significance to the United States of possible future nuclear weapons must also be considered and assessed in relationship to the over-all diplomatic and foreign policies of the United States. While these hearings were concerned primarily with the technical problems of a nuclear test ban, it is recognized that diplomatic and policy matters of great importance must also be considered in the final evaluation. The latter, however, were not within the scope of these hearings.

If the test-ban control system were unsound, of course, exposing its weakness might embarrass the United States in "diplomatic and policy matters." But if the cost of avoiding embarrassment would be risking the national security, the higher duty clearly would be to expose the control system's weakness.

Noting a disagreement among the experts on the importance of improvements in weapons development for the three nuclear powers, the committee report observed: "The experts did not discuss in detail the possibility that further testing might result in major technological breakthroughs which would give that nation achieving such breakthroughs a major military advantage over the other nuclear powers."

The Committee report was also delicate in judging the on-site inspection capability. Further knowledge was needed in the field, it observed:

It was apparent from information presented at the hearings that the state of the art of on-site inspection is not very far advanced. Although many scientific techniques have been suggested for a possible application to this problem, it appears that most are limited to very short distances from the site. This puts a heavy responsibility on the methods of aerial surveillance and observations of recent human activity.[1]

Could we rely on aerial surveillance? No guidance was provided.

The cynic would come away with the strong impression that the Joint Atomic Energy Committee's report on the on-site inspection problem deliberately sought to avoid exposing its weakness.

There were gaping holes in the on-site inspection system which must have been obvious to every member of the Committee. Representative Durham indicated recognition of the obvious in his remark: "If you have about ten seismic disturbances and had to inspect them on the basis of what you told us here, you would probably have full employment in most of the country if we tried to find them."

But Dr. Foose's unwarrantedly super-optimistic assumption that aerial and ground inspection, in a day or two, could narrow the area of search to a circle of 500 feet went unchallenged. As it was, Dr. Foose had showed that one drilling rig operating twenty-four hours a day could take almost three years to search out fully even a dinky 500-foot radius circle. If fifteen highly skilled drilling crews could be spared, five rigs could be kept going twenty-four hours a day, and the time could be cut to six or seven months.

It was logical to assume, after Dr. Harold Brown's statements before the 1958 Conference of Experts and Dr. James Brown Fisk's comments at the Technical Working Group II conference, that leaders of both the United States and the Soviet Union knew of the on-site inspection system's ineffectiveness. Why did they go on with the charade?

One explanation could have been that on-site inspection, for which read intelligence, was regarded as the currency in which the Soviet Union would pay for a halt in American nuclear-weapons development.

If this were the case, the general public was being allowed to believe that on-site inspection would be the focus of the system to control a nuclear test-ban, when indeed it was the farthest thing from an effective instrument. It has become commonplace for the world to expect the Soviet Union to delude its own people. It is not commonplace—yet—for the United States government to permit its people to be deluded.

If, as appeared obvious, the Joint Atomic Energy Committee shared the Executive Branch's quiet knowledge of the complete ineffectiveness of on-site inspection, there was, to some extent, an acquiescence in the charade by the so-called "watchdog" Joint Committee.

It was the theory of one eminent member of the Committee, who confided privately in this reporter, that the Administration knew since December, 1959, that the nuclear test-ban agreement was a bad one, could not be signed, and that a graceful way had to be found to back out. The eminent member, recognizing fully the weaknesses of the inspection system, decided to let the government back out with as little embarrassment as possible.

Part IV

THE KENNEDY YEARS

Chapter 15

One More Try Fails . . .

During the 1960 election campaign, Presidential Candidate John F. Kennedy had written former AEC Commissioner Thomas E. Murray that if he were elected he would first "exhaust all reasonable opportunity to conclude an effective international agreement banning all tests—with effective international inspection and controls—before ordering a resumption of tests."

Shortly after Mr. Kennedy was elected, two of his principal campaign advisers, Dr. Jerome Wiesner of Massachusetts Institute of Technology and Dr. Walt W. Rostow of MIT's Center of International Studies, joined a group of American scientists in Moscow for the latest in the Pugwash series of exchanges with Soviet scientists. This one dealt with disarmament, and the Americans came away with the idea that the Soviet Union might still be ready for a nuclear test ban.

President Kennedy then called in John J. McCloy, a former Undersecretary of War, to examine the twin problems of a nuclear test ban and general disarmament.

Mr. McCloy's review of the test-ban situation caused a postponement of resumption of the Geneva test-ban talks from February 7 until March 21. By that time, the Kennedy Administration had agreed on a test-ban package. Policy-makers in the State Department made much of the new accomplishment. It was the first time that a United States Administration had agreed within its own house on a complete program for ending nuclear tests.

Ambassador Arthur Dean, appointed as chief disarmament negotiator by President Kennedy, presented the Soviet Union with a list of seven concessions soon after the Geneva negotiations resumed. These were the offers:

1. To reduce the annual number of on-site inspections in the nuclear countries from the previously proposed twenty to a possible twelve, depending on the number of suspicious seismic events that occurred.

2. To reduce the number of control posts on Soviet territory from twenty-one to nineteen.

3. To extend from twenty-seven months to three years the proposed moratorium on the smaller underground tests and the associated research program.

4. To establish means for banning all nuclear-weapons tests at high altitudes and in outer space.

5. To ask Congress for legislative approval permitting Soviet inspection of internal mechanisms of the nuclear devices to be used in seismic research and peaceful uses programs.

6. To accept the Soviet demand for a veto on the annual budget of the control organization.

7. To agree with the Soviet demand for parity among the Western and Soviet blocs on the Control Commission, thus giving the Soviet Union itself power equal to that of the United States and the United Kingdom combined in setting control-system policy.

This ought to have gotten the conference off on the right foot, but Soviet Ambassador Tsarapkin did not respond in kind. Instead of concessions, he recanted earlier reasonableness. Particularly, he introduced into the Geneva test-ban negotiations the veto-ridden "troika," proposing that the already-agreed single administrator for the control organization should now be replaced by a tripartite board representing the Soviet Union, the Western allies, and the neutrals. The board should act only in unanimity.

It was immediately recognized that the troika would destroy whatever effectiveness the control organization might have, given its technical handicaps.

In retrospect, it appeared that the sudden hardening of the Soviet position was intended to provoke a break-off in the talks. At the time this was suspected but not known.

The Soviet Union itself occasionally dropped hints that it was looking forward to the day when nuclear tests could be resumed. For instance, on March 31, the Communist Youth newspaper *Komsomolskaya Pravda* reported that Russia would use nuclear and thermonuclear processes to melt the water frozen in Soviet glaciers. The time that this would be done was "not far off," according to a summary of the article by Soviet news agency Tass. The biggest glaciers were said to be in Central Asia and the northern Caucasus, areas which badly needed water, it was said, and each contained millions of gallons of water.

President Kennedy did not oblige by breaking off the test-ban negotiations.

Ambassador Dean first spent several days explaining in full the seven American concessions. On April 16, he tabled a complete draft treaty on behalf of the United States and British delegations. He said both nations were ready to sign the treaty immediately. The United States was thus on record before the world that it was ready to go the "full mile" in getting a test-ban treaty.

To this day, the draft treaty tabled by Ambassador Dean stands ready for Soviet acceptance.

The Kennedy Administration claimed that there was complete agreement among the three principal interested agencies in the Executive Branch of the American government, the Atomic Energy Commission, the State Department, and the Defense Department, and certainly this was true of the Secretaries of State and Defense and the Chairman of the AEC. Below those levels, however, there was considerable apprehension that the Soviet Union might reverse itself once again and accept the treaty. Then the West would have been stuck with a control system good enough to bind itself but leave the Soviet Union a wide field for maneuver.

For the reasons which have been already outlined, Soviet acceptance could have completely frozen American nuclear-weapons development while permitting the Soviet Union to race on.

The draft treaty was not even presented on a take-it-or-leave-it basis. Ambassador Dean told the Soviet representative that the Western delegations were ready to give careful consideration to any Soviet suggestions for revision.

The Soviet Union showed little interest in the draft treaty, attacking it in terms which amounted to outright rejection. But Ambassador Semyon Tsarapkin let drop one interesting observation on April 19. The Soviet suggestion for a quota of three inspections per year, he said, was "very close" to one of the numbers mentioned by Prime Minister Macmillan when he visited Moscow in February, 1959, to sell the idea of a quota for on-site inspections to Soviet Premier Khrushchev.[1]

This was the first known time that anyone had indicated, on the record, even vaguely, how many inspections per year Prime Minister Macmillan had proposed. The Soviet insistence on only three inspections is more understandable if Prime Minister Macmillan had, as early as 1959, encouraged Soviet Premier Khrushchev to think that the Western powers were ready to accept an annual quota "very close" to three.

Ambassador David Ormsby Gore responded that the idea of a quota had arisen originally in a conversation between him and Professor Fedorov. The Soviet chairman of the technical conferences on nuclear test-ban control had suggested, Ambassador Ormsby Gore recalled, that it was difficult for the Soviet Union to open its territory for an unlimited number of inspections each year. Professor Fedorov reportedly suggested that a limit should be set.

"I can also tell our Soviet colleague that the figure proposed by the United States and the United Kingdom was not the highest mentioned by Professor Fedorov for the possible number of inspections that would be needed each year in the Soviet Union," Ambassador Ormsby Gore said.[2]

The synthetic quality of Soviet abandonment of the veto over on-site

inspections, offered if a suitable quota could be agreed upon, was emphasized again in the spring of 1961 by Soviet insistence that only those
events which could be located within 200 square kilometers could be inspected.

This would have required the widely spaced control posts to pinpoint
any event within a radius of 5 kilometers and would have ruled out inspection of a great proportion of the annual seismic events that could
not be located so precisely.

Despite the obvious impasse, American negotiators expressed hope
that Soviet Premier Khrushchev and President Kennedy could break
their deadlock at their Vienna "little summit" on June 3 and 4.

The President reported a few days after the Vienna meetings that it
was "a very somber two days" in which Premier Khrushchev refused to
reconsider the Soviet position on any test-ban issue. He presented the
President with a long memorandum on the test-ban problem, but it contained no new proposals. The deadlock persisted, agitation for American
test-resumption increased, but President Kennedy still was not to be hurried.

Representative Chet Holifield, Chairman of the Joint Committee on
Atomic Energy, was the first leading figure in the nuclear test-ban issue
on Capitol Hill to bring public pressure to bear on President Kennedy
for the renewal of United States testing. On June 14, Mr. Holifield mentioned four principal obstacles at the Geneva test-ban conference, which
he visited in the spring of 1961:

1. The Soviet troika proposal, which "would be entirely unworkable."

2. The disagreement on the number of on-site inspections to be per-
mitted on Soviet territory: from twelve to twenty proposed by the United
States and the United Kingdom; only three proposed by the Soviet
Union.

3. "There are important problems as to whether an adequate detection
system can be developed to control tests which register below 4.75 magnitude. . . ."

4. Considering that the voluntary moratorium had then gone on for
thirty-two months, and adding to this the three more years required to
install an inspection system, this would mean that the Soviet Union
could obtain a test ban without controls for five and a half years or more.

The third point was one that never was made by the Executive Branch.
Throughout the long negotiations, no doubt in the interests of consist-
ency, neither the State Department nor the Atomic Energy Commission
nor the Defense Department publicly stressed the obvious inadequacies
of the proposed detection system.

On the other hand, Congressman Holifield mentioned four gains the
United States could make by resumption of testing: (1) getting lighter
weight-to-yield ratios for warheads on American missiles; (2) developing
an antimissile missile; (3) developing improved small-yield weapons; and
(4) improving safety features of weapons.

But more important, in my judgment, is the ultimate general effect on weapons technology of a continuing test ban. It will inevitably stifle developments undreamed of at the present time. Concepts are now being considered by our scientists which could be as revolutionary as the H-bomb [was] in 1949.

And had the Soviet Union been testing secretly?

It seems to me that we must assume that the Soviets have tested, or will test, if they think they can get away with it. And since our detection system is not adequate to detect and/or identify small underground disturbances it is quite possible for the Soviets to conclude that they could get away with clandestine tests.

Thus in reappraising our position on the test-ban, I believe the United States must assume the possibility or probability that the Soviets have been testing or will be shortly. In any event we cannot continue to gamble our destiny, when we base such a gamble on ignorance of our opponent's actions.

The United States, Mr. Holifield said, should continue to negotiate with the Soviet Union but should get ready to resume underground tests "whenever the President determines that our national defense requires it."[3]

Senator Thomas Dodd, Democrat of Connecticut, also called for a resumption of nuclear tests on the same day as did Congressman Holifield.

The test moratorium, Senator Dodd said, had been the most fatuous blunder ever committed in the field of American foreign policy.

The moratorium was wrong, because we were staking our security as a nation on preposterous assumptions that an organization of conspirators and murderers and liars, which has violated virtually every agreement into which it has entered, would for some strange reason, respect its commitment to a reciprocal moratorium. What was worse, we assumed that it would do so even though there was no system of inspection and no way of detecting sneak tests.

Soviet Premier Khrushchev, noting the stirrings in the fringes of American policy-making circles, publicly vowed that his scientists would also resume nuclear tests if the West did.[4]

As the deadlock at Geneva persisted into July, the United States and the United Kingdom took the test-ban problem to the United Nations. On July 15, they asked Secretary-General Hammarskjold to inscribe on the agenda of the Sixteenth General Assembly, scheduled to open in mid-September, an item entitled "The Urgent Need for a Treaty to Ban Nuclear Weapons Tests Under Effective International Control."

The United States was orchestrating a propaganda campaign of its own, this time to show the world that the Soviet Union, not the United States, was the real obstacle to a test-ban. Inviting General Assembly comment, however, virtually admitted President Kennedy's willingness to withhold tests until the United Nations debate ended, which would likely be the end of 1961. It would be very difficult for the United States or the United Kingdom, which had brought up the test-ban problem, to return to testing while advocating before the United Nations the signature of an effectively controlled nuclear test ban.

Obviously disturbed by the continuing delay in a Presidential decision to resume testing, Chairman Holifield called the Joint Atomic Energy Committee into session late in July to hear a new report on progress made in methods of detecting and identifying underground and high-altitude nuclear explosions.

Dr. Richard Latter, the RAND Corporation scientist who had been one of the advisers on the inspection system for a test-ban from the very beginning, was almost contemptuous of the control system still being sought so diligently by the United States at Geneva.

His own four-paragraph summary of his testimony, on the first day of the hearings, reflected in general terms the conclusions of eminent scientists who followed him:

> The control system currently being negotiated at the Geneva test-ban conference has a very limited capability to monitor nuclear weapons tests. For atmospheric and underwater tests it has a good capability of detecting and identifying nuclear tests above about 1 kiloton. For underground tests, large tamped explosions are detectable but large decoupled explosions are not. For space tests, unshielded explosions are detectable at great distances but large shielded explosions are not.
>
> To improve detection, extensive research is needed. The most important problems for research are means to make decoupled underground explosions and shielded space explosions more detectable and means to carry out on-site inspection of suspected underground events.
>
> Research requires underground nuclear explosions and an extensive satellite program for measuring space radiation.
>
> At present, minor improvements in a Geneva control system are foreseen—but no solution to the problems of shielded space explosions or decoupled underground explosions.

Once more, this was fair warning. There were few who heeded it, however, beyond Congressman Holifield and his Committee. The Latter appraisal received little notice in the press. Instead, attention was focused on President Kennedy's determined optimism in the face of ever more gross Soviet obstructionism at Geneva.

Dr. Latter made these more specific points in his main presentation:

> 1. The Geneva system could not identify, although it could detect, nuclear explosions as small as one kiloton carried out at altitudes between six and thirty miles [Author's paraphrase].
> 2. Underwater nuclear explosions might require difficult-to-execute inspection at the site to accomplish identification, because underwater chemical explosions and some natural events produce similar signals [Author's paraphrase].

3. In some large areas of the oceans, particularly in the Southern Hemisphere, the capability of the system is degraded as a result of the great distances between control posts.

4. Underground tests could not be identified, although there would be a good probability that they could be detected and located, down to one-half or one kiloton if exploded under the same conditions as the Rainier explosion [Author's paraphrase].

5. [For] fully decoupled explosions in salt, *locating* requires a yield greater than 150 to 300 kilotons.

6. For underground explosions above magnitude 4.75, that is for explosions above about 20 kilotons conducted under the same conditions as the Rainier explosion, approximately 50 to 70 seismic events per year out of a total of 100 to 140 per year in the U.S.S.R. will not be identified by the Geneva system.

These numbers of unidentified events vary from year to year due to variations in the annual number of earthquakes. The same numbers apply to fully decoupled explosions of 6,000 *kilotons in a salt medium*. Unidentified seismic events require on-site inspection to determine what caused them. Since explosions of magnitude smaller than 4.75 are not subject to inspection according to the U.S. proposed treaty, these explosions—which can have yields from 20 kilotons under Rainier conditions to thousands of kilotons fully decoupled—cannot be identified and cannot be controlled.

Dr. Latter explained that a monstrous hole, 3,000 feet in diameter, would be necessary to decouple a 6,000-kiloton (6-megaton) explosion. He said scientists did not know whether such a large cavity could be built. It was already agreed, however, that a decoupling hole 800 feet in diameter, which could accommodate 100 kilotons, would be feasible.

For space explosions, Dr. Latter expressed the belief that the Geneva system probably could detect *unshielded* nuclear explosions above about 10 kilotons up to distances of a few hundred million miles, but that knowledge of background radiation in space was so limited that suitable detection instruments could not be designed "at present."

More realistically, it is estimated that the system will be unable to detect unshielded explosions of about 10 kilotons at distances greater than a few million to a few tens of millions of miles—distances currently accessible by rockets. Moreover, shielded explosions of as much as tens to hundreds of kilotons are not detectable at these same distances. Since natural events may produce signals similar to space explosions, space nuclear explosions cannot be identified.

Dr. Latter also examined the possibility for improvement of the detection system.

These improvements [however], all require major changes of the Geneva system and considerably greater access to the Soviet Union than [that] contemplated in the current political negotiations. They require many more control stations and many more inspections than are considered politically acceptable at the present time.

Finding some politically acceptable system "is by no means an easy job," Dr. Latter warned. "And its success is uncertain."

He then went through the inventory of possible improvements and concluded that none of them had a lively prospect for overcoming the shortcomings of the Geneva system.

Aside from the concealment problem, possibilities for which would be nearly infinite, Dr. Latter put his finger on the problem of on-site inspection as the most difficult faced by the control system:

> Locating the site is possible at the present time only to within a few hundred square miles. When in such a large area it would be exceedingly difficult to locate the small regions, a few tens to a few hundreds of yards in diameter, containing the radioactive debris left by a nuclear explosion.

Finally, Dr. Latter observed:

> Although minor improvements by research are foreseen, research has as yet given no clue as to means for improving the Geneva system sufficiently to permit detection and identification of shielded tests in space or decoupled tests underground and certainly no clue how to detect and identify any underground or space tests without a control system. An agreement to ban all nuclear weapons tests would have to rely therefore not upon control by the Geneva system but rather upon the self control of the potential violator and on such unevaluable factors as motivation, need, and intent.

Another RAND scientist indicated that further experiments with decoupling established that a cavity, one-tenth the volume required for full decoupling, still reduced seismic signal strength by about one-fifth compared to tamped shots in salt. At greater depths, the one-tenth volume could probably decouple by about one-fifth to two-fifths relative to tuff, it was found. Thus the art of concealment had made another gain: reducing the required size of underground-testing cavities.

Ambassador Arthur Dean, a prominent New York lawyer named to negotiate the test-ban treaty as the President's representative, testified before the Holifield group at the end of its deliberations: "Contrary to some of the testimony you have heard here, our scientific advice, both British and American, was that the control systems set forth in our treaty would provide reasonably adequate control over those regions which the treaty purported to control." He did not cite his advisers or set them up in opposition to Dr. Latter and the others appearing before the Committee.

Chairman Holifield was impressed with the size of explosions that could be sufficiently muffled by decoupling techniques to produce signals below 4.75 magnitude and thus avoid control in the threshold-type treaty.

"From the scientific standpoint it makes our position completely unrealistic," he told the hearing. "This makes it a dangerous formula."

At another point, Chairman Holifield said the United States was "leaning on a broken crutch" if it relied on the Geneva system to indicate whether the United States' foes were testing or not.

In a panel discussion among the leading scientists of the country who were gathered for the Holifield hearings, it was agreed that to improve the detection and identification system a scientific breakthrough would be necessary.

One problem that was not dealt with adequately, according to Dr. Hugh Benioff and other leading seismologists who participated, was the shattering effect on detection that aftershocks from earthquakes would have. Large earthquakes produce a series of postquake signals around the world. These could partially or fully mask small underground nuclear explosions—"small" in the sense that they could have the power of 100 to 150 kilotons but produce signals below 4.75 magnitude.

Dr. Benioff noted at one point that the Chile earthquake in 1960, with a magnitude of 6.5, was followed by 4,000 aftershocks of a magnitude between 5 and 6, well up on the scale for concealing large nuclear explosions.

A large earthquake in Kamchatka had 3,000 aftershocks in the first month following the disturbance.

John J. McCloy, President Kennedy's adviser on disarmament and nuclear tests, met with Premier Khrushchev in Sochi on July 27, as the Holifield hearings were winding up. The Soviet leader told Mr. McCloy that Soviet scientists and military leaders were urging the testing of a 100-megaton bomb that could be carried in a rocket. The nuclear moratorium was still on. Mr. Khrushchev did not then indicate his government had decided to test his new weapon. But he obviously had it very much on his mind.

This was the first hint to the outside world of the momentous intimidation offense then being planned in the Kremlin. Like the Holifield hearings, the Khrushchev warning itself went largely unheeded in Washington.

There was a brief burst of curiosity, but no one took the 100-megaton threat seriously. American scientists themselves had dismissed the idea of building such huge bombs from their minds. Few took the trouble to examine what Soviet Premier Khrushchev's aims may have been in developing a 100-megaton bomb. Suggestions by experts, later to be proved correct, that the Russians may have found a way to reduce the weight and size per megaton of their warheads went unheeded until the Soviet testing program was well along.

President Kennedy reacted in two directions at once. He announced, on August 10, that he had been made to feel "more urgently than ever that, without an inspection system of the kind proposed by the United States and the United Kingdom at Geneva, no country in the world can ever be sure that a nation with a closed society is not conducting secret nuclear tests." This suggested that he was thinking of resuming tests himself.

But, at the same time, he sent Ambassador Dean back to Geneva on August 24 to make another attempt for a test-ban agreement. Meanwhile he withheld tests. The Geneva conference actually got under way again on August 28. Ambassador Dean offered four more concessions, chief of which was to lower or possibly eliminate the threshold on underground tests. The Soviet representative would not even discuss the American offers.

Radio Moscow made it all academic in a broadcast on the night of August 30, 1961, announcing that the Soviet Union was renewing nuclear-weapons tests. France's earlier tests became one excuse. She was testing for the West, it was suggested. At the same time, Moscow said it was reacting to American attempts to step up the arms race in Germany. The Berlin crisis, of course, had been whipped up by Khrushchev himself.

A Soviet series of some fifty-odd tests began September 1. It contained the largest man-made explosions in history, one of them 30 megatons, another 55–60 megatons, as closely as could be calculated by American and Allied detection devices.

Dr. Hans Bethe headed a panel of scientists that sifted data collected in the world-wide network that observed the Soviet series. They found the Russians had made impressive improvements in the efficiency of their nuclear weapons. Officials were guarded in their comments, but they used adjectives like "impressive" and "substantial" to describe the amount of explosive power the Russians were now able to pack into each pound of weapon.

The increase in efficiency, an area where the United States had been ahead previously, would give the Soviet Union two options, either to pack more destructive power on missiles of the old size, or to develop smaller, more mobile nuclear missiles and weapons for battlefield use.

Soviet Premier Khrushchev could make good on his boast that he could fire 100-megaton rockets, officials now were convinced. In fact he could pack more devastation into a single warhead than he claimed.

The Soviet test series concentrated mainly on strategic weapons. Objectives were to develop new weapons, study weapons-effects, and to test fully assembled missiles with nuclear warheads.

The Bethe group was particularly struck with the remarkably small size of the fission trigger used to set off the big 55–60 megaton shot of October 30. The Russians apparently had discovered a way to prolong the fission reaction in the A-bomb trigger for the big H-bomb, thus holding down the size of the fission device and permitting unusual economies in costly fissionable material. They now could revamp their whole stockpile, using less fissionable material per bomb.

One of the principal weapons-effects areas believed to have been studied in the series was that for anti-missile missiles. Some of the Soviet shots reportedly were designed to direct the blast upward, as would be expected in a missile-defense device.

In another phase of the Soviet series, "full assemblies" were fired. The Russians reportedly launched and exploded rockets equipped with nuclear warheads.

As a result of their test series, the Soviet Union reportedly pushed into the lead in the efficiency area, but the United States expected to wipe out the lead as soon as it could test in the atmosphere itself. American scientists had also improved the efficiency of American weapons, officials said, but actual tests of the new designs had not been conducted.

It was obvious that the Soviet Union had been preparing for the big September-October test series while its negotiators continued to talk at Geneva. The performance was similar to that of the Japanese at the time of Pearl Harbor, when Japanese diplomats were talking of peace in Washington while Japanese aircraft carriers were sailing into range of Oahu. The difference, however, was that few had predicted Pearl Harbor; many had predicted a Soviet "surprise" in the test negotiations.

Many, including Dr. Edward Teller, were convinced that the Soviet Union could not have made its great leap forward without prior secret testing during the moratorium. Premier Khrushchev and other Soviet officials could confidently mention 100-megaton weapons that were rocket-transportable—that is remarkably light for so powerful a warhead —months *before* the September, 1961, open resumption of testing. How could they be so confident unless they had made small-scale tests in advance?

Blasts below 1 kiloton, some of the most interesting, could easily have been concealed by any of several methods of which American policymakers should have been fully warned. It is quite possible, in fact, that the Soviet Union used the nearly three-year American moratorium to forge into a big lead in nuclear-weapons development.

Two days after the Soviet series started, President Kennedy and Prime Minister Macmillan appealed to Premier Khrushchev to agree immediately "not to conduct nuclear tests which take place in the atmosphere and produce radioactive fallout." No inspection system was demanded. The deadline for the offer was September 9. But the Soviet Union rejected the offer out of hand.

The rejection actually brought a private sigh of relief from many American officials who feared the Soviet Union stood to gain even by this limited agreement. The United States would be forced to withhold all atmospheric tests, while there could be no assurance that the Soviet Union would have to do the same.

President Kennedy still did not break off the talks at Geneva. He only recessed them. He then announced the resumption of American tests—underground—on September 5. The first announced explosion took place in Nevada on September 15.

But the rate of underground testing was slow. President Kennedy withheld all atmospheric tests for the rest of the year, milking the Soviet display of defiance for all the propaganda gains possible. He had to go easy on blaming Moscow for contaminating the atmosphere, however. First there was little health hazard; second, the United States itself might eventually want to resume atmospheric tests.

At the United Nations, the neutral nations were finally persuaded to denounce the Soviet tests after an unusually timid initial response at the Belgrade conference of uncommitted powers in early September. Moscow responded by renouncing all international inspection.

Early in 1962, President Kennedy agreed with a proposal the Soviet Union had been pushing since he took office, namely that the nuclear test-ban talks become part of general disarmament negotiations. Then the Russians balked, however, and indicated they did not want to talk about tests at all.

During the Geneva charade, the Soviet Union had achieved a three-year suspension of American nuclear testing, not by force but by persuasion. The effects of their persuasion lingered.

Advocates of the test ban, for instance, took the Soviet resumption of atmospheric testing as proof that the Soviet Union thought it was behind the United States and had to resume testing to catch up.

Throughout the three years of the negotiations toward a test-ban treaty, the United States and Britain had derived what many times appeared to be artificial and contrived satisfaction from synthetic "progress" in the Geneva talks. Agreements were reached on seventeen relatively unimportant articles of a treaty. But all the basic points that could have led to effective control were always frustrated by the Soviet negotiators. They always blocked the road to effective inspection.

The test-ban negotiations had been like a long contest between two evenly matched wrestlers. Holds were occasionally broken after long periods of fruitless grunting and groaning, but the new holds were just as evenly matched and unproductive of a decision.

At one point in the negotiations, in March, 1960, the American delegation listed twenty-five points of East-West disagreement on treaty issues. There were at least that many at the end of 1962.

A State Department analysis[5] of the long negotiation listed four fundamental issues unresolved: on-site inspection, criteria for on-site inspection, the number of control posts, and the installation schedule for the control system.

Besides these fundamental differences there were many more specific points. But all these problems of inspection and control were on the *negotiating* level.

The difficulties that could be expected at the operational level, once the treaty went into force, were never actually encountered. These prospective frustrations, clearly foreseen in 1958, certainly should have been the real reason for a United States withdrawal from the nuclear-test-ban charade long before 1962, long before the Kennedy Administration ever came on the scene.

The United States resumed testing underground, at the Nevada testing site, in mid-September, 1961. In the next six months, some twenty underground shots were announced, most in the "nominal" range of 20 kilotons or below, and at least one as small as 20 tons.

British politicians had a brief second honeymoon with the test-ban idea when they claimed to have found big new improvements in the detection and identification of underground shots. British Prime Minister Macmillan and the new British Ambassador in Washington, Sir David Ormsby Gore, pressed the United States for a liberalization of the inspection system.

While Secretary of State Rusk and the director of the new Arms Control and Disarmament Agency, William C. Foster, were in Geneva listening to the sharp rejections by the Soviet Union of all international inspection for a nuclear test ban, the British dispatched two of their top scientists, Sir William Penney and Sir Solly Zuckerman, to Washington with "new data," which, it was hoped, would convince the United States it would be safe to depend on national detection systems outside the Soviet Union to detect nuclear tests.

They went away empty-handed, having only impressed American scientists with some ingenious new ways for processing data, mainly using mathematical techniques that had already been foreseen.

Leading American scientists said they had reached an agreement with the British that there was "nothing new" in the detection and identification problem. The weaknesses of on-site inspection, in other words, were about as bad in 1962, as they had been in 1958, when the incredible test-ban fantasy opened to the orchestration of world-wide Soviet propaganda.

The British effort did manage to wipe out some of the safeguards the United States had previously insisted upon. Later, Secretary of State Rusk agreed to eliminate the 4.75 threshold and sign a comprehensive test ban, even though there had been no improvement in the detection and identification techniques disclosed.

There were growing indications, meanwhile, that American scientists were dissatisfied with the results of underground testing and saw new need for atmospheric testing, especially in the area of judging effects of nuclear blasts at high altitudes.

On March 2, 1962, less than two weeks before the opening of the Geneva Foreign Ministers Conference on general disarmament, President Kennedy announced his decision to resume nuclear tests in the atmosphere unless the Soviet Union were to agree, by late April, to sign the draft treaty Britain and the United States had tabled in April, 1961.

His repetition of the offer to sign a test-ban treaty was based on the same questionable estimate of on-site inspection as before, but no voice was raised in protest. Presumably the Senators and Congressmen who had been told of the uselessness of on-site inspection, and the scientists who had long been aware of it, were counting on the Soviet Union to turn down the whole test-ban idea and save the United States from embarrassment or, possibly, even future catastrophe.

President Kennedy told his nationwide radio and television audience on March 2 that "no single decision of this administration has been more thoroughly or more thoughtfully weighed."

Those who knew the pitfalls of detection, even with nineteen control posts within the Soviet Union, and of identification, even with the on-site inspection the United States and Britain proposed, winced at the President's renewed offer to sign the April, 1961, draft treaty, before tests were to be resumed the latter part of April.

It was true that the chances for Soviet acceptance looked slim, but it was also true that if the Soviet Union were to reverse itself and agree to sign the Anglo-American treaty, American nuclear-weapons development would be much more seriously hampered than the Soviet Union's.

Secretary of State Rusk presented to Soviet Foreign Minister Gromyko "new modifications" for the draft test-ban treaty in an informal meeting in Geneva on March 15. Mr. Rusk offered to drop the 4.75 threshold and make the treaty comprehensive, this without increasing the number of on-site inspections or the number of control posts in the Soviet Union. He said the United States also would seek to restrict on-site inspections to the seismic areas of the Soviet Union, mainly the east Siberian and south-central Siberian area, agreeing that "only a few would be allowable in a large region in the heart of the Soviet Union where there are normally few seismic noises which would require investigation."

Because the Soviet Union had sprung its 1961 test series on the United States and Britain while they were negotiating in good faith toward a test ban, Secretary Rusk demanded some small treaty modification to safeguard other states against preparations for testing. These were token demands, however, seeking merely periodic declarations from the heads of state "that there will be no preparations for testing," Mr. Rusk said, "and agreed rights to inspect a certain number of times per year, equal numbers of declared sites on each side." The American Secretary also asked that the four-to-six-year period for installing the inspection system should be speeded up "by all possible means," including establishment of temporary control posts.

Still, the United States would be willing to sign the unrevised treaty of April 16, 1961, Secretary Rusk promised, plus the amendments proposed later in 1961.

As Mr. Rusk himself acknowledged, "the United States and United Kingdom have been willing to accept a very considerable degree of risk."

For those who had studied the potentialities of on-site inspection—the crucial area that came to be called "international verification"—this was an understatement.

In his important statement to the Geneva Conference on general disarmament, when the "final, final" deadlock between the Soviet Union and the United States was being announced, Mr. Rusk spent considerable time explaining to the Soviet Union's representative that on-site inspection teams would be "devoid of espionage possibilities," and control posts could be so closely circumscribed by Soviet authorities that they could not become spy centers.

In his presentation, the Secretary, probably unintentionally, emphasized some of the weaknesses of on-site inspection. "To get to the site of the inspection," he told the conference, "the teams would have to use transport furnished by the Soviet Government. They could only carry specified equipment related to their immediate job. Although there would not be any Soviet national members of the inspection team, half of the team would be nationals of nonaligned countries, and the Soviet Union would be invited to assign as many Soviet observers as it wished to verify the activities of the inspection team."

From the standpoint of those who were impressed by the "needle in the haystack" problem that would face each on-site inspection, the Secretary of State completely missed the point in emphasizing, before the inspection-sensitive Soviet Union, the "small" area the on-site inspection teams would probe.

"Even if there were twenty inspections per year in the U.S.S.R.," Secretary Rusk declared, "and even if each of these inspections operated within a 500-square-kilometer area, less than one-twentieth of 1 per cent of Soviet territory, i.e., less than one part in 2,000, could ever be subject to inspection in any one year."

Secretary Rusk did not mention, and presumably did not even know, that one on-site inspection might take years and that twenty inspections per year would impose a ludicrous strain on the inspection facilities of any international authority.

Mr. Rusk's speech was obviously intended to be the last American appeal, for the record, to the Soviet Union to let down its bars against inspection. The prompt rejection that the Rusk appeal provoked from the Soviet Union could well have saved the day for the United States.

The United States resumed atmospheric testing at Christmas Island in the Pacific with British cooperation, on April 25.

In July President Kennedy went ahead with high-altitude testing from

Johnston Island in the Pacific. Both plane-dropped weapons and nuclear-tipped missiles were used. The aim was to study weapons' effects against incoming missiles and against ground and air communications systems.

The Nevada test site quickly developed into a "when needed" facility so that any time a new device was developed in the laboratory it could be tested promptly without waiting for an elaborately-planned series. The tests in the Pacific had their ups and downs but it was clear that the United States had put together a testing program impressive not only in numbers but in results.

On the other hand the validity of the demands, during the test moratorium, for proof testing weapons systems also appeared to be confirmed by the repeated false starts on some of the shots.

The United States made no announcement of the results of its test series but it was logical to assume that the efficiency of nuclear weapons, the amount of bang that could be packed into each pound, had been significantly improved and some of the ungainliness in both intercontinental and battlefield weapons had been removed.

It was also logical to expect that the long-mooted "neutron bomb" had been launched along a development program. What new surprises may have been tested was for Moscow to find out.

Except for a stunt Soviet test on February 2, 1962, there were no known Soviet tests between November 1961 and the early fall of 1962, when the Kremlin launched a second series of thunderous atmospheric tests, many of them in the range of tens of megatons.[6]

Estimates of the relative positions of the two rival nuclear powers varied. Some American officials reported our scientists were supremely confident—that the Soviet Union had been left far behind.

But Dr. Edward Teller was publicly pessimistic. In a speech to San Francisco editors and publishers of the United Press International in the fall of 1962, Dr. Teller said: "It is my guess, and it is only a guess, that the Russians are ahead of us in the nuclear race today." The United States' efforts since the resumption of testing "have not been quite satisfactory," he said.

President Kennedy gave no hint of his own evaluation. Instead he pressed whatever propaganda advantage he could find out of the Geneva test-ban negotiations, which by then were engaging the energies of 17 diplomatic delegations.

At the same time the President gradually whittled down the Western demands for inspection facilities inside the Soviet Union, moving still closer to the Soviet position which held firm for a system without inspection at all inside the Soviet Union.

The President's concessions were based on inspection improvements achieved in some three years' research and development work in the test detection field under Project Vela.

Using improved techniques and equipment to monitor the American underground and atmospheric tests in 1961 and 1962, Project Vela scientists had reportedly been able to achieve two things:

First, "a substantially better capability to detect, i.e. record, seismic events at long range, as compared to short range, than had been predicted in the past."[7]

Second, the estimated "number of earthquakes occurring in certain areas of interest comparable to an underground nuclear test of a given magnitude has been substantially reduced from the previous estimate."[8]

On the basis of these improvements, the United States and Britain presented a revised draft treaty on August 27, 1962, holding out prospects for some important additional concessions:

1. Control posts required worldwide and inside the Soviet Union would be cut "substantially."

2. On-site inspections would be reduced from the 12-to-20 annual quota previously proposed. No specific numbers were mentioned but it was understood the United States would settle for from three to eight on-site inspections per year inside the Soviet Union.

3. Control posts could be manned by nationals of the home country, operating under international supervision. Previously the United States had demanded that home nationals' roles be restricted to observation, without any operational responsibility. Thus the United States appeared to be ready to accept a greater risk of "self inspection."

Specific fine print in the treaty on all three points was left to further negotiations, which the Soviet Union did not quickly accept.

As an alternative to this treaty, which would ban tests in all environments, the United States and Britain also offered to sign immediately a test-ban agreement ending shots in the atmosphere, under water and in outer space.

This "threshold" treaty, permitting continued testing underground, would not require the on-site inspection which the Soviet Union so consistently opposed. It would also end periodic increases in radioactive fallout to which the world had become so sensitive. It was a close approximation of President Eisenhower's treaty proposal of April 13, 1959.

The new pair of treaties also opened up again some of the questions left unresolved in earlier treaty negotiations, some of them mentioned, some unmentioned.

Sites for newly-constructed control stations would be "agreed upon by the parties to the treaty." [9]

The size of the area to be inspected in case of an unidentified event would be designated in the treaty.

"States would assume an obligation to facilitate and to cooperate in any on-site inspection undertaken under the treaty."[10]

Conditions under which a party could withdraw from the treaty were spelled out:

A. If the offended party judged a treaty had been violated.

B. If the obligation to facilitate an on-site inspection had not been fulfilled by a country under suspicion.

C. If a nuclear explosion by an identified state not a party to the treaty was judged to jeopardize a signatory's security.

D. If a nuclear explosion by an unidentified state was judged to jeopardize a state's security.

Definition of what constitutes a nuclear explosion was identified as another point to be included in the treaty.

"The United States wishes to make it abundantly clear," Ambassador Dean informed the 17-nation conference in Geneva on August 27, 1962, "that no party is precluded under any test-ban treaty from conducting laboratory tests and other work preparatory to tests."

Almost any one of these items could keep treaty negotiators talking years longer without results, if past experience were a reliable guide.

These August 27, 1962, draft treaties thus were not intended to be signed immediately—as had been the case with the April 1961 "package" which President Kennedy presented to the Russians soon after he came to office.

The Geneva talks continued throughout the fall of 1962 despite the United Nations General Assembly debate of the test-ban issue in New York. So did Soviet and American testing.

It was anybody's guess whether Western inspection demands would be lowered enough or Soviet insistence on secrecy could be sufficiently modified to get an accommodation. Even if there were a treaty, however, the record made it obvious that neither the nuclear arms race nor world tensions would become any the less dangerous.

Chapter 16

But the Quest Goes On

The public generally, and the Soviet Union in particular, had taken little notice of the rather radical changes the United States had made in its position on an inspection system for the test ban when the new proposals were advanced in the summer of 1962. At the treaty negotiations in Geneva, the Soviet Union steadfastly refused even to discuss either the comprehensive ban or the partial treaty proposed by the United States on August 27, 1962.

Nevertheless the test-ban talks went on, even when the principal negotiators went to New York to duplicate the barren dialogue at the United Nations. Both the Soviet Union and the United States continued to test. President Kennedy announced the end of the current American series on November 4. The Soviet Union continued its atmospheric series further into November.

Private hearings before two Congressional committees in the summer of 1962 were kept secret until 1963. So was a secret, year-end exchange of letters between President Kennedy and Soviet Premier Khrushchev. They triggered new waves of hope and fear when they were released early in 1963.

From the Soviet viewpoint, the test-ban conference seemed to have narrowed down to a case where Moscow might get the treaty it wanted, relying only on national systems to inspect a test ban, if she would only recognize the validity of the United States-sponsored principle of on-site inspection.

Premier Khrushchev made that precise move in a secret letter to President Kennedy on December 19, 1962. He returned to the old Soviet position, held before Soviet test resumption in September 1961, accepting two or three on-site inspections on Soviet territory. He combined this offer with a bonus. The Soviet Union would also accept three unmanned seismic stations at specifically designated points in the Soviet Union.

He still insisted, however, that the national inspection stations should be manned completely by Soviet nationals inside the Soviet Union. The

477

August 1962 position of the United States, backing off to primary reliance on long-distance detection, then provided for "internationally supervised" stations inside the Soviet Union, manned by Soviet citizens.

Chairman Khrushchev refused to admit there was any real necessity for on-site inspection. Nevertheless he offered the United States and the United Kingdom two or three on-site investigations per year anyway. He suggested the automatic seismic stations, unmanned, be placed in Central Asia, Altai and the Far East.

He acknowledged in his letter that there were two other seismic zones in the Soviet Union, in the Caucasus and in Carpathia.

"However these zones are so densely populated that conducting nuclear tests there is practically excluded," the Premier said.[1]

Premier Khrushchev said foreign personnel could participate in delivering the equipment to and from the automatic seismic stations. This element of international control, he said, "is a major act of good will on the part of the Soviet Union."

As his reason for offering two or three on-site inspections, Chairman Khrushchev gave the argument frequently mentioned in private Soviet-American conversations in Geneva: "You will not manage to persuade the U.S. Senate to ratify an agreement . . ."

Ambassador Dean, Premier Khrushchev wrote the President, had told Soviet First Deputy Foreign Minister Vasily Kuznetsov that "in the opinion of the United States government, it would be sufficient to carry on two-four on-site inspections each year in the territory of the Soviet Union." Mr. Dean made no such offer, the President later claimed.

The Soviet Union, said the Soviet leader, "in order to overcome the deadlock and to arrive at last at a mutually acceptable agreement . . . would agree, in those cases when it would be considered necessary, to two-three inspections a year on the territory of each of the nuclear powers in the seismic areas where some suspicious earth's tremors might occur."

This was again a carefully circumscribed offer: He had no suggestions on how it would be decided, or by whom, when an on-site inspection "would be considered necessary." He also undertook to confine the inspections to seismic areas on the nuclear powers' territory. This would preclude investigation at the United States' Pacific Proving Grounds but not in Nevada, where there have been earthquakes. The Semipalatinsk area in Central Asia, one of the Soviet nuclear testing grounds, is near a seismic area but Novaya Zemlya is not.

"We believe that now the road to agreement is straight and clear," Premier Khrushchev said, with grand disdain for all the fine print his generalities had omitted. By January 1, 1963, he said, "the world can be relieved of the roar of nuclear explosions."

President Kennedy answered cordially only nine days later. He asked that the "black boxes," or unmanned seismic stations, be placed in areas of higher seismicity, like Kamchatka and Tashkent. He rejected the suggestion that on-site inspections be permitted only in seismic areas. The President suggested that Premier Khrushchev designate a negotiator who could meet with William C. Foster, Director of the Arms Control and Disarmament Agency, to pursue the discussions. "After talks have been held we will then be in a position to evaluate where we stand and continue our work together for an effective agreement ending all nuclear tests," Mr. Kennedy wrote.[2]

Premier Khrushchev sent a second letter on January 7, 1963. The Soviet Union would not object, he said, to placing two of the unmanned stations in Tashkent and Kamchatka even though Soviet seismologists believed that "functioning of automatic stations will be seriously handicapped by seismic hindrances" in those areas.[3]

He proposed plots near the city of Samarkand in Tashkent and Seimchan in Kamchatka.

Mr. Khrushchev also suggested that location of the three automatic seismic stations should be considered "agreed upon." The President, he added, should now designate three areas in the United States for setting up Soviet "black boxes." (Or, as one wag suggested, red boxes).

As for on-site inspections, the Soviet Premier stuck by his annual quota of two to three, but insisted the American negotiators had been giving figures "practically equaling the quota proposed by us." Mr. Khrushchev agreed that on-site inspections could be carried out in non-seismic areas "provided such inspections are conducted within the annual quota indicated by us."

If there were a defense installation in the area designated for inspection, however, Premier Khrushchev said, "naturally, in such a case it will be necessary to take appropriate measures which would exclude a possibility to cause damage to the interests of security of the state of the territory of which inspection is carried out."

This would leave open the possibility, it appeared to some, that the Soviet Union could test underground, as it had on February 2, 1962 at Semipalatinsk, or underground in the Novaya Zemlya proving grounds, with immunity from on-site inspection.

Premier Khrushchev named N. T. Fedorenko, the new Soviet representative to the United Nations, and S. K. Tsarapkin, the Soviet representative at the 18-nation Disarmament Committee in Geneva, to meet with Mr. Foster in New York early in January to pursue the increasingly intriguing test-ban negotiations.

In secret talks in New York and Washington, Mr. Foster indicated to the Soviet representatives that the United States wanted at least seven automatic seismic stations inside the Soviet Union. But he could not get the Soviet Union to explain what sort of on-site inspections or automatic seismic stations they had in mind.

Apparently seeing that quick agreement on its proposed terms would not be possible, the Soviet Union broke off the talks as suddenly as they had been started and the discussions were resumed in the old context in Geneva. Mr. Foster went there in February to lead the American delegation and continue the exploration.

The Kennedy-Khrushchev exchange, part of an increasingly secret traffic between the two world leaders since the Cuban crisis, also triggered new interest in Washington.

REPUBLICAN CRITICS

Senators and Representatives of the Armed Services Committees, the Joint Atomic Energy Committee and the Foreign Relations Committees suddenly revived the nuclear-test-ban issue, which had been relatively dormant in Congress since testing was resumed in 1961.

Representative Craig Hosmer of California, a Republican member of the Joint Atomic Energy Committee, quickly emerged as the Republican spokesman for a partisan critique of the dangers of accepting a long-range detection system, the core of the Kennedy Administration's new proposal. The Republicans named him chairman of their Conference Committee on Nuclear Testing. One of his first moves was to gather the views of test-ban friends and foes, then publicize them with critical comments of his own about the "relatively unsafe" inspection system the United States was proposing. He struck responsive chords among both Republicans and Democrats in Congress, and many other Democrats had misgivings which they kept to themselves for reasons of party solidarity.

There was considerable apprehension by January 26, when President Kennedy announced postponement of American underground nuclear shots in Nevada, an obvious attempt to "butter up" the Kremlin during the New York-Washington talks.

When the Soviet Union, apparently unimpressed by these blandishments, broke off the talks, President Kennedy promptly announced resumption of testing, a week after his postponement.

Soon after the negotiations resumed in Geneva, Mr. Foster mentioned informally to the Soviet delegation that the United States was willing to accept as few as seven on-site inspections—not the eight to ten annual quota previously demanded by the United States—provided the investigating teams for the Soviet Union were composed mainly of Americans and British.

During the Kennedy years the number of on-site inspections sought by the United States and the United Kingdom had moved steadily downward from 20 to 7, reportedly because the science of detecting tests was improving. Some suspected, however, that the new scientists in the Administration, with a greater interest in a test ban than the former scientific advisers in the Eisenhower Administration, were willing to take greater risks to get a test ban treaty.

The first Kennedy move downward in the annual ceiling for on-site inspections was the switch to a sliding-scale formula under which the United States asked for at least 12 on-site inspections per year, with one on-site inspection for each five unidentified events in the Soviet Union above 60.

Thus, in 1961, the Kennedy Administration still accepted the theory that a 20-percent sample of puzzling earth tremors would be the proper deterrent for an effective treaty inspection system to maintain.

In 1962, however, the United States began reaping the first fruits of its research program under Project Vela. New seismological observatories, featuring arrays of seismometers, were found to have brought the threshold of detection down from magnitude 4.75 to about magnitude 4. This confronted the system with more earthquakes at the lower ranges, but the identification capabilities were also slightly improved. More important, however, a closer look at the number of earthquakes in the Soviet Union equivalent to a given yield indicated that there would be fewer natural events at a given yield than had been previously expected. The Soviet Union had maintained this for a number of years, but American seismologists could not verify it until 1962.

With the detection threshold lowered and the number of earthquakes at any given yield reduced, the Kennedy Administration decided in the fall of 1962 to lower its requirements for on-site inspection to eight to ten visits per year.

This was the level at which the inspection quota stood until early 1963, when Mr. Foster reduced it to seven.

Before 1962, the United States believed there would be about 100 unidentified shallow earthquakes above magnitude 4.75 in the Soviet Union. Magnitude 4.75 is the equivalent of 19 kilotons in tuff. At the same time it was expected there would be some 600 shallow earthquakes above magnitude 4.0, the equivalent of two kilotons in tuff.

By July 1962, however, the estimates of unidentified shallow earthquakes in the Soviet Union above magnitude 4.75 had shrunk from 100 to about 40 and above magnitude 4.0 from 600 to 170.

Looking at these changes from the standpoint of the work on-site inspection teams would face, the actual number of unidentified events had risen from 100 to 170, because the threshold had been lowered and more small earthquakes were brought into the equation. But the number of inspections had been lowered to seven, providing a sample in 1963 of only five percent.

At the same time, the 1962 comprehensive treaty attempted to cover all events and claimed some capability all the way down to magnitude

3, of which there would be 1,000 events per year against which the seven on-site inspections might be set.

Foster's Defense

William C. Foster, the disarmament agency director, presented the first public statement defending the reduction in inspection requirements made by the Kennedy Administration in a February 1, 1963 statement for the Republican Conference Committee on Nuclear Testing.

A test-ban treaty continued to be in the national interest, Mr. Foster argued, because it would give the United States these advantages:

Weapons development—With continued unlimited testing, the United States' lead in small-weight, high-yield weapons "would probably diminish." He reasoned that both sides would improve their weapons technology and the Soviet Union "would eventually be able to match our diversified and numerous arsenal" of tactical weapons. "Overall," he said, "the trend would be toward equality between the United States and the USSR." With a test ban, Mr. Foster said, improvements by both the Soviet Union and the United States in weapons efficiency, that is, yield-to-weight ratios, would come more slowly because only laboratory work would be possible. "The United States' advantage in smaller weapons would persist over a longer time." He predicted that some weapons effects phenomena would remain "unsettled or undiscovered by both sides" and that anti-missile systems development would be slowed down on both sides. "In general," Mr. Foster said, a test-ban treaty would preserve the United States' present nuclear advantages for "a considerably longer period" than unlimited testing.

Spread of nuclear weapons to other countries—In the Administration's judgment, it was in the United States' interest to prevent or slow the rate of diffusion of nuclear weapons, Mr. Foster said. He conceded that "a test ban as such would not alone prevent other nations from acquiring nuclear weapons." But continued testing would "certainly" invite other nations to acquire nuclear weapons. He claimed "the rate and motivation for diffusion would be dampened considerably by a test-ban treaty."

Introducing an inspection system in the Soviet Union—This would have "potential significance" in other areas of arms control and disarmament being negotiated with the Soviet Union, Mr. Foster contended. Both sides would get experience with inspection. The United States could appraise Soviet cooperation and use the experience as an indicator of how far it could go in other disarmament verification projects with the Soviet Union. Mr. Foster also repeated the claim that the treaty might serve to open the Soviet Union to some extent and reduce Soviet fears of inspection "espionage."

Elimination of fallout—"Whatever danger exists from fallout from the United States and Soviet nuclear weapon tests" would be eliminated.

Mr. Foster set against these four claimed advantages these two disadvantages:

Risk of secret preparations and surprise abrogation of the treaty—The Soviet Union might gain as much as 18 months on the United States if it were able to pull off a surprise resumption of tests, some years after a test-ban treaty had been in operation. For this reason, Mr. Foster assured the Republicans, the Administration would make it a matter of national policy to maintain its readiness to test and would provide incentives for scientists to continue nuclear weapons research. This would minimize any possibility of a long Soviet head start in preparing tests, Mr. Foster contended.

Risks from possible cheating—Many important scientific principles involved in nuclear weapons can be studied with nuclear explosions of less than three kilotons, he told the Republican committee. He chose three kilotons because this was the threshold of detection for tests conducted in alluvium, a soft kind of earth plentiful in both the United States and the Soviet Union. Included in the possible advances that could be made with tests of three kilotons or less would be development of "pure fusion weapons" and reduction in weight-yield rations, Mr. Foster said. He also acknowledged that "artificial decoupling" by the big-hole technique "might permit considerably larger-yield explosions without detection."

Mr. Foster argued, however, that secret underground testing would be "unsatisfactory" for making the kind of progress which might substantially change the military balance. He also advanced the theory that science was reaching some sort of ceiling in the development of nuclear weapons. "The point of diminishing returns in improving weight-yield ratios is fast approaching," Mr. Foster said. Moreover, "pure fusion weapons would not be of great advantage to us because they would constitute primarily a cheaper substitute for the explosive components in our already large stockpile of nuclear weapons."

He drew from this the conclusion that "any inhibitions on the development of these weapons would appear to our net advantage." This was the view of the Executive branch, he said. A treaty violator would risk leaving tell-tale surface craters behind if he tried testing in alluvium, Mr. Foster said. Furthermore, the evader "could not be sure of evading" because of the wide variability in size of seismic signals that could be produced in the unpredictable earth.

Big-hole decoupling was "both time consuming and expensive," Mr. Foster said. Preparation of the large cavities necessary for muffled shots might be detected "during the construction phase." (This hinted that the United States had a new surveillance capability, possibly satellite-based if not U-2 based. Mr. Foster was not counting here on on-site inspection but on observation, by other means, of the construction in process.)

He also advanced the theory that this form of decoupling "has never been tried on any practical scale so far as we know," indicating a willingness to trust the quality of American intelligence in catching the Soviet Union in such an attempt. A potential violator, he said, would be unsure he could escape detection.

At the same time Mr. Foster introduced the single test versus series theory. "While single tests might sometimes escape detection by seismic means," Mr. Foster acknowledged, "a test series would be far more difficult to hide. Yet, little progress can ordinarily be made with individual, isolated tests."

In balancing the risks of unlimited testing versus the imperfect effectiveness of a test-ban treaty, Mr. Foster said, the entire Administration had chosen the treaty as a lesser risk.

Secretary of State Rusk, Defense Secretary McNamara, Atomic Energy Commission Chairman Seabory, General Maxwell D. Taylor, Chairman of the Joint Chiefs of Staff, and Central Intelligence Agency Director John McCone, as well as Presidential Assistants Bundy and Wiesner had decided unanimously with him, Mr. Foster reported, that the test-ban treaty would be the lesser risk.

"The risks of secret evasion and surprise abrogation were outweighed by the risks of continued unlimited testing on both sides," he said. Others familiar with the methods of operation in the so-called Committee of Principals, later objected privately that the Arms Control and Disarmament Agency frequently "took silence for approval" when it was not so intended.

The Joint Chiefs of Staff were reliably reported to have objected to many of the major concessions made by the United States in 1962-63.

(The disarmament agency disputed those who regarded the 1962-63 changes in the American position as "concessions." They were merely "concessions to science," not to the Russians, Ambassador Jacob Beam, assistant director of the agency, said later in a Rochester, New York speech.)

Since the Kennedy Administration came to power, Mr. Foster said, long-distance detection of earth tremors had improved so much that a simpler and much more economical system could be proposed, relying on United States-operated stations for the detection of tremors in the Soviet Union. This permitted the United States to accept Soviet-manned stations only as "auxiliary tools," while placing primary reliance on the American-British system, Mr. Foster explained. The result: "We need be much less concerned about the possibilities for cheating at these (Soviet) stations." At the same time, the size, efficiency and use of the system would be under the United States' direct control, instead of under international authority. A great reduction in cost would be possible.

A second significant reassessment was the reduction in the number of earth tremors in the Soviet Union which might be confused with shocks from nuclear explosions. For one thing, the number had been overestimated by two and a half times, Mr. Foster reported. Also, identification at long range had improved so much, he said, that first-motion readings at the United States' stations watching tremors inside the Soviet Union had been able to eliminate half the tremor signals as earthquakes, Mr. Foster said. Another third, he added, "were found to be unlikely possibilities for nuclear tests based on non-siesmic criteria such as their general geographic location and the detailed characteristics of the area of the tremor's origin."

This was the first public indication that the Arms Control and Disarmament Agency was cranking in a new factor, "non-seismic criteria," to help reduce the number of unidentified earthquakes.

The disarmament agency's predecessors had resisted the temptation to do this on the grounds it was unscientific. They could not know what areas would be remote or unacceptable for test sites, they reasoned. Now, however, the disarmament agency was willing to classify as earthquakes events that took place in remote regions, appeared to have happened off shore or in other places the American second-guessers considered unlikely.

Mr. Foster acknowledged a certain risk of cheating or surprise abrogation but claimed that "the gains to the United States far outweigh these risks" in the nuclear test ban. He also claimed that "the changes in our requirements for verifying compliance with a test-ban treaty would not significantly alter the deterrent effect of such a treaty on the Soviet Union." An even smaller number of on-site inspections would constitute an adequate deterrent, Mr. Foster told the Republicans. A few days later, in a luncheon conversation with the Soviet Union's First Deputy Foreign Minister, Vasily Kuznetsov, he said seven on-site inspections would be acceptable under certain conditions.

Mr. Foster concluded his paper with an appeal for "continuing bipartisan effort in this crucial area of the United States foreign policy."

He went to the unusual length of assuring the Republican Committee that "no test-ban treaty will be placed into effect without either the advice and consent of the Senate to its ratification or the approval of both houses of Congress."

This was an extension of the usual practice in ratification of treaties. Only the Senate would ordinarily be involved. The new procedure was patterned after President Eisenhower's precedent of getting joint-resolution support from both houses of Congress.

Teller's Dissent

Dr. Edward Teller led the attack against the proposed test-ban system.[4] The proposed ban would be "virtually unpoliced," he charged and "it would endanger our security and help the Soviet Union in its plan to conquer the world."

He made three principal points:

1. *The test ban would prevent vital improvements of our atomic explosives*—The Russians have announced that they have solved the problem of missile defense. Our missile defense is unsatisfactory. In the absence of testing our defense will not improve because we need more knowledge concerning the use of nuclear explosives in missile defense and in the penetration of such defense. If the Russians install a satisfactory defense system while we are unable to do so, this will put us at the mercy of Soviet blackmail and aggression.

We have started the development of clean and cheap nuclear explosives. We need more tests to complete this development. Clean and cheap explosives are needed for battlefield use, for peaceful applications, and for missile defense.

Testing has frequently stimulated the invention of new approaches in the development of nuclear explosives. Past advances of this kind are classified; future advances are unpredictable. Nevertheless these advances are real and important. Without them our weapons laboratories will lose their competence in weapons research.

2. *The test ban will not interfere with Russian progress*—The difficulty to police small underground explosions has been pointed out. The present Russian concessions will certainly not permit the control of small underground tests. Tests of small explosives are helpful in all branches of weapons development. Even bigger tests can be carried out secretly in space. This fact has been jointly asserted by American, British and Russian experts meeting in Geneva in June and July 1959. The Russians have prepared an effective test series while negotiating with us. They have executed their series in the fall of 1961. In the closed Russian society such a maneuver is possible. In the open American society it is not. Repetition of the 1961 tactics may place the Soviet Union into a position of commanding leadership. Only great and comprehensive openness could guarantee the observance of a test ban.

3. *A test ban may endanger the NATO alliance*—The avowed purpose of the test ban is to halt the arms race and to set limits to the proliferation of nuclear weapons. It is hoped that a test ban will be applied in a universal manner. It is unlikely that the ban will restrain the Chinese. But it is highly probable that the ban will be resisted by the French and we shall be expected to exert pressure on them. This may strain NATO to the

breaking point. The Russians may desire a ban for this very reason. In 1938 the Western allies abandoned Czechoslovakia. This led to World War II. Had the Munich agreement prohibited fighter planes and radar, the consequences would have been the fall of Britain. The Russians want us to sign a Munich-type agreement and in this they are supported by widespread public clamor. I hope that patriotic Congressmen of both parties will resist the pressure of a public frightened by crises and misled by the mirage of peace.

Dr. John A. Wheeler, of the Physics Department of Princeton University, who had worked on the atom bomb project during World War II, told the Republican Conference Committee he saw "the decisive loss to national security from a test ban."

He objected principally because it would prevent the United States from developing "a technology of pure hydrogen devices free of fission fallout."

Present nuclear weapons would be outdated in three to ten years, he warned. The new technology, he claimed, would not only have important peacetime applications in mining and earthmoving, because of their fallout-free nature, but "will revolutionize ground warfare."

Others will take the scientific leadership if the United States does not keep it, he warned. "Second-level nations will be able to make these ultimately inexpensive devices," Dr. Wheeler warned. "No responsible proponent of any detection system has claimed ability to detect a minuscule pure hydrogen detonation underground."

He charged "it is unconscionable to renounce for the free world a revolutionary device which others will then make without our knowledge."

On February 10, the Republican Conference Committee called on President Kennedy to "declassify and disseminate all data necessary for informed and widespread public discussion" of the test-ban problem. The Committee also urged the President to give his pledge not to try any more moratoriums.

In Geneva, Mr. Foster was making other concessions beside the reduction of on-site inspection requirements to seven per year. He also abandoned the provision for international supervision of the national stations inside the Soviet Union. A new draft treaty under preparation in the Arms Control and Disarmament Agency dropped all provision for international supervision of the verification system, contemplated only an international "clearing house" to pass messages back and forth between accused and accuser powers.

Thus the Soviet Union had finally achieved the objective it had set out to get at the Conference of Experts in Geneva in 1958: A test ban that left its closed society virtually closed.

Dodd Speaks

The pure fusion bomb, sometimes called the neutron bomb, was believed to be a major Soviet objective but was discounted publicly by Mr. Foster—even though it would also be extremely useful to the United States as an anti-missile warhead. Senator Thomas Dodd, Democrat of Connecticut, in a long Senate speech on February 21, 1963, indicated the potential worth of the pure fusion bomb as a tactical weapon. He posed the problem of a possible Soviet blockade of Berlin. Suppose, the Senator said, the Soviet Union had developed the neutron bomb and the United States had not. If the United States tried to break through the blockade with a military convoy the Russians could "detonate a number of neutron bombs at crucial heights above our concentrations of armor. In an instant, our units are rendered useless. The armored vehicles are still intact, but their crews have been immediately incapacitated, doomed to quick death by an intense flux of neutrons.

"If we do not ourselves possess the neutron bomb, what, then, would our reaction be?

"To continue to wage war with conventional weapons would be to invite a crushing military defeat."

If the United States were to resort to stockpiled tactical nuclear weapons, large amounts of radioactivity would be released on friendly peoples, but even then the Americans would be at a disadvantage. As Soviet military experts have written in their journals, tactical fission weapons would have only a fraction of the effectiveness of the pure fusion weapon, Senator Dodd said. The neutron bomb could be just as effective against personnel as a fission bomb 330 times more powerful.

"If the Soviets possess the neutron bomb in quantity, its far greater effectiveness, its relative cheapness, and its freedom from widespread devastation and from fallout, would give them an advantage of critical proportions," Senator Dodd said.

The Senator then posed the frightening question: If American tactical fission weapons were no match for the Soviet neutron bomb, would the President go to all-out thermonuclear warfare? This cruel dilemma could be avoided if the United States had its own stockpile of pure fusion weapons, the Senator suggested.

On the basis of this kind of tactical evaluation, Senator Dodd claimed, the neutron bomb could "breathe new life and confidence into NATO, even with its present manpower."

Republican and Democratic static was causing the Administration's disarmament planners to mount a campaign of defense.

In an important policy speech on February 28, Ambassador Jacob D. Beam, assistant director of the disarmament agency, acknowledged before a Rochester, New York audience that a determined cheater could on occasion outsmart the proposed inspection system for a test ban. If he used a "very large cave underground," or if he sent a nuclear warhead millions of miles into space, "he might detonate a nuclear bomb without being caught."

Such isolated success "would not give the Soviet Union a chance to make any substantial inroads into the United States nuclear lead," Mr. Beam claimed. "The chances of the Soviet Union conducting a series of tests which would remain undetected are vanishingly small. The probability that the advantages to be gained from a single test would be sufficient to make an attempted evasion worthwhile, is also vanishingly small."

Both these statements were to be challenged by some of the most respected scientists in the government at new hearings before the Joint Atomic Energy Committee.

Before those hearings began, however, another disarmament agency official, Deputy Director Adrian S. Fisher, carried Ambassador Beam's thesis a step farther:

It is true that if the USSR were able to test small devices clandestinely underground for an indefinite period, they could make significant advances in the general field of small nuclear weapons. However, every analysis conducted by the Executive Branch in recent years has reached the conclusion that the strategic military balance between the U.S. and the USSR could not be altered in any major way by such developments.[5]

This was confirmation of test-ban foes' worst fears. Advocates of a ban had convinced themselves that even if the Soviet Union could pull off a series of small tests the American nuclear lead could not be seriously challenged.

It was tantamount to saying that there was no reason the United States should not accept whatever inspection provisions the Soviet Union cared to provide. The Russians, Mr. Fisher concluded, could not cheat enough to wipe out the American lead anyway.

This assessment, that the Soviet Union could pull off a series only in the small nuclear range, overlooked the possibility of extrapolating technical information from little tests for development of large tactical weapons. It also completely discounted the possibility the Soviet Union might use the space or big-hole techniques to test strategic weapons.

Republican Representative Hosmer immediately jumped on Mr. Fisher's statement. It was an invitation to the Soviet Union, he charged, to sit tight and wait for the United States to make more concessions on inspection. He also claimed the Fisher theory, that a series of small tests would not affect the strategic military balance, "flies in the face" of all the advice of American scientists available to the Joint Committee on Atomic Energy.

Two days later President Kennedy repudiated Mr. Fisher's extension of the cautious Foster-Beam theory that occasional Soviet cheating would be tolerable.

Stewart Hensley, United Press International's diplomatic correspondent, put the question:

Mr. President, on Monday Adrian Fisher of the disarmament agency said even if the Russians were able to test underground indefinitely, this would not alter the strategic military balance between the United States and the Soviet Union. He said this was the Executive assessment. Given that assessment, can you tell us what considerations then would prevent accepting the test ban on the terms set by Russia?

The President replied:

I don't think, if I may say so, in my opinion, that is not what is the Administration's position. We have suggested that we would not accept a test ban which would permit indefinite underground testing by the Soviet Union. We would not accept a test ban which did not give us every insurance that we could detect a series of tests underground.

That is the Administration's position. We would not submit a treaty which did not provide that assurance to the United States Senate. Nor would the Senate approve it.

Did that mean the United States would stand on its demand for seven on-site inspections, Mr. Hensley asked.

"I believe we will insist on a test-ban treaty which gives us assurance that if any country conducted a series of clandestine underground tests, that series would be detected." He thus claimed more than Administration scientists who expected to catch only one test in the series, not the whole series.

The President added that he expected there was still a "good deal of distance in securing an agreement with the Soviet Union" because so many questions remained about the number of inspections, the kind of inspections, circumstances under which they would be carried out. The area to which an on-site inspection would be confined was another problem, Mr. Kennedy pointed out.

Across town from where the President spoke at the State Department auditorium, the Joint Atomic Energy Committee was getting different advice about the abilities of the President's inspection system to pick up a series of small Soviet tests underground.

JOINT COMMITTEE'S 1963 HEARINGS

In the six days' testimony from March 5 to March 12, Defense Department scientists, who had been leaders in the search for improvements in the United States' verification system for a test ban, revived all the serious doubts of 1960 and 1961 about the wisdom of the United States' entering a test ban. Lead-off scientists were Dr. Carl F. Romney, a veteran in the field, and Dr. Jack Ruina, Chief of the Advanced Research Projects Agency, which directed the Project Vela program to improve test detection.

On *detection* of nuclear tests in the Soviet Union, Dr. Romney testified that the United States' pullback to primary reliance on a long-range surveillance system outside the Soviet Union had produced a system then rated "less capable" than the old 1958 Geneva system was believed to be in noticing underground nuclear shots as powerful as 70 to 150 kilotons.

The Latter decoupling theory still stood, the Committee was told, and was expected to reduce signals to 1/250th to 1/300th their actual size.

The disarmament agency's chief scientist later acknowledged that even an ideal system of more than a hundred stations along the Soviet Union's entire borders could not, on the average, detect coupled, three-kiloton shots in alluvium or comparable material if they were exploded in the 2.5-million-square-mile area in the interior of the Soviet land mass. Most of the Soviet borderland is inaccessible to Western monitors because it lies in the Arctic or is shielded by Communist China or Soviet satellites in Europe. Only 15 stations were planned by the Administration, not a hundred or more.

On *identification* by on-site inspection, Dr. Ruina acknowledged "We have no assurance on-site inspection will succeed."

He mentioned these "promising methods" for narrowing the suspected area once an on-site inspection had begun: Detection of minute traces of gaseous fission products which tend to vent through the earth's crust; visual and photographic inspection of suspect areas for evidence of human activity or other surface clues; probing for "solid state" effects on rocks in the vicinity of the explosion; and aftershock variations between earthquakes and explosions.

Dr. Ruina said other methods mentioned at previous hearings—seismic profiling; searching for unusual concentrations of subsurface gases; seeking variations in soil density and for anomalies in the resistivity of the earth's crust—all "did not work."[6]

By 1963 Pentagon officials had also reinforced their respect for the hopelessness of drilling for the only proof recognized, pockets of radioactivity, if the area were not carefully limited in advance. It would be a major construction job, they reported.

"Deep drilling is an expensive and difficult operation and it involves movement of much heavy equipment," Theodore A. George told the Committee.[7]

> Conducting such an operation in a remote region of the world, far removed from roads and airfields would require considerable logistics planning and preparation. We have tried to estimate weight of equipment required for deep-hole drilling and have come up with some figures which may interest you. In order to reach a depth of 5,000 feet, the rig, casing and other equipment would weigh approximately 100 tons. For a 10,000-foot hole the weight increases to about 200 tons. A U.S. company is known to have developed an air-transportable drill rig. The main feature is that no single item of this rig weighs more than two tons. Helicopter transport could therefore be used, unless the region was high in the mountains. Time-wise, we estimate that it would take no less than 30 days to reach a depth of 10,000 feet after assembly of the rig on site. As you can see, drilling probably would not be undertaken as part of on-site inspection unless there was some extremely strong evidence that drilling would probably hit gold or a nuclear explosion cavity.

If two tons is an average haul for a helicopter, 50 trips would be necessary to bring enough equipment to go to 5000 feet, 100 trips to go to 10,000 feet. The reaction of the Soviet Union to such a milk run is not known, but quite predictable.

On *location* of a suspicious event for subsequent on-site inspection, the system had been startlingly degraded, Dr. Ruina indicated, from the old capability of around 120 square miles to 1000 square miles. Dr. Romney, later in the hearings, put the new range for locating an event with the new system at 300 square miles to 3000 square miles for small underground shots inside the Soviet Union.

The Gnome peaceful-uses shot in New Mexico had produced miscalculations in surface location and depth that startled the whole seismology community. Instead of getting within 6¼ miles of the shot by seismic location, monitors were 19 miles off, making the circle of error 10 times greater than expected: 1,100 square miles instead of 120 square miles.

What no one reported to the Committee was that another anomaly had appeared in the monitoring of the Gnome shot. Its depth, which had been 1200 feet, was calculated by seismic methods to have been about 80 miles. This gross overestimate of the depth by a factor of over 300, would have caused a long-range detection network, even the short-range detection network in the United States, to conclude that the Gnome explosion had been a deep underground earthquake. One of the basic assumptions in identifying earthquakes is that all underground disturbances below 60 kilometers, roughly 40 miles, can be considered earthquakes because man cannot begin to dig that deep.

In the face of this inadequacy of science, disarmament officials were still hoping to eliminate as earthquakes all underground events calculated to have been 15 to 60 kilometers deep.

Black boxes, the Committee discovered, were "mythical." Representative Holifield of California interjected, "We are talking about a very elaborate underground vault." Each would cost $350,000 to $425,000, require 18 months to develop a prototype. Their purpose, to help identify at short range events picked up at long range, could be frustrated by clever spoofing, scientists acknowledged. Some said the unmanned observatories could definitely identify half the suspected tremors; others said, only 15 to 20 percent of them. Mr. Holifield said the Soviet Union would never allow such huge vaults to be installed or to be effectively used.

On *high altitude* test detection, "Nothing has transpired since the last open hearings before this Committee which should cause a revision of our estimates of the satellite detection capability," the Joint Committee on Atomic Energy was told by Dr. Alois W. Schardt, Deputy Director of the Nuclear Test Detection Office of the Advanced Research Projects Agency. Cost estimates had been reduced, however, because other space technology was being advanced to the point that test-detection satellites could be expected to last three to five years in orbit, a much longer period than previously expected. Ground-based detection techniques were also proving capable of detecting tests conducted in the earth/moon space, Dr. Schardt reported, thus leaving for the satellites the main job of covering deep space. Fewer than the six far satellites previously planned for the system would be required in 1963 because the "geometric constraints are less severe."

Dr. Schardt estimated that the annual operation cost of a complete high-altitude and space monitoring system would be $100 million per year. Eventually the cost could be lowered to only $20 to $30 million per year "but it is not yet clear when this point can be reached." Initial costs for establishing a system were not included in those figures.

Needless to say, neither ground nor satellite systems were installed, and testing of component prototypes would not be begun until mid-1963.

Republican Senator Hickenlooper of Iowa spent less than a half hour in the hearing room, but that was enough to confirm his old suspicions about the improbability that the United States system could catch a determined cheater.

Given the much wider expanse in hostile Soviet territory which an on-site inspection team would have to roam under the new system, Senator Hickenlooper observed, the chance of finding evidence of a treaty violation underground would be "fantastically impossible."

What was the significance of nuclear testing below this new threshold of notice? Dr. Ruina pointed out that half the United States' weapons tested underground in Nevada since 1961 had been under 3½ kilotons.

Later Major General A. W. Betts, the AEC's top weapons developer, told the Committee, it is "as true today" as when Dr. Harold Brown told the Committee in 1960, that tests as small as one kiloton would permit development of "almost any tactical weapon that one had in mind up to quite a lot larger yield."

Dr. Brown had also testified that with explosions in the 10, 20 or 30-kiloton range, "one can make many advances in design of strategic weapons of very much larger yield." This estimate also still stood, General Betts said.

To feel secure against detection, however, Dr. Ruina estimated in 1963, a treaty violator would have to confine his nuclear tests to one kiloton or less if he were to imbed the weapons in tuff, but could test single, isolated shots as high as seven to ten kilotons in alluvium.

If the violator were to use large underground cavities to decouple, testing up to 40 kilotons would be practical, Dr. Ruina estimated.

Both Dr. Romney and Dr. Ruina later agreed that a complete series of secret Soviet nuclear tests could go undetected with the seismic system then proposed. Dr. Ruina, however, set the ceiling for the secret testing at one kiloton while Dr. Romney set it at three kilotons. Dr. Ruina is an engineer, Dr. Romney is a seismologist. Dr. Romney went farther. He said the opportunity to catch a three-kiloton series in alluvium in Nevada would be available only "on exceptionally quiet days." The Soviet Union could hardly be expected to oblige.

Dr. Franklin A. Long, Assistant Director of the Arms Control and Disarmament Agency for Science and Technology, appeared before the Joint Atomic Energy Committee on March 8 and 12, 1963. He gave great weight to "national intelligence" in helping to catch a violation.

A cheater nation would have to contend with the possibility of "windfall" information from a defector, he suggested, possibly one with knowledge in the military or scientific field. This was taken at the time as a threat that an American agent in the Soviet Union might be "surfaced" to help prove a test-ban violation.

Dr. Long's principal reliance on catching a cheater, however, rested on locating events in areas he considered impractical for cheating. He apparently was unimpressed by Dr. Romney's worries about inaccuracies in locating events. "A large fraction of the epicenters would, we know, fall in areas characterized by remoteness, inaccessability or close proximity to international waters or borders," Dr. Long said.

Other factors, on the other hand, might enhance suspicion, Dr. Long added, "such as geological maps and past seismic records which might indicate the presence of mines, underground caverns, good logistic support, or an aseismic area."

He estimated 55 percent of the 170 unidentified events could be eliminated by signal-reading as events of natural origin.

That alone would cut to 75 the troubling events. But about 30 of these occur in areas "which are quite unlikely for clandestine underground tests," Dr. Long estimated. He attributed a 75 percent or greater probability that these 30 events would lie "more than ten kilometers across the borders of adjoining countries, or more than ten kilometers into the sea from the coastline of the USSR."

In a typical year, Dr. Long contended, another 15 unidentified events would be "in areas in which testing is more conceivable but which are either so remote as to make the technical problem of clandestine underground testing difficult or sufficiently close to the outside world—on the Kuriles or the eastern coast of Kamchatka—as to present severe inhibitions to clandestine operation."

So far Dr. Long had eliminated 45 events, leaving about 30. "A vast majority of these would be in central Kamchatka or the Pamir mountain area," Dr. Long reported. Automatic recording stations would be relied on to help identify these, he said.

Thus Dr. Long, by his optimistic appraisal, had cut the most difficult 75 events to something like 15 or 20. Senator Humphrey put it at an even dozen.

It was this subjective and essentially non-scientific appraisal of the 75 "most unidentifiable" events in the Soviet Union which permitted the disarmament agency to advocate so few on-site inspections.

Seven investigations against 30 events would represent a 23 percent probability of inspecting a violation. Dr. Long introduced another deterrent effect, of undoubted value. He emphasized that it would be important for the United States to keep secret part of its capability to detect and identify nuclear explosions in the Soviet Union. For a number of years, the United States had relied mainly on a secret system developed by the Air Force Technical Applications Center, based not only on United States soil but on friendly ground around the Soviet periphery.

Dr. Long leaned more heavily on seismology, however, than some seismologists found comfortable.

"If there is reason for optimism, that a general solution to the underground detection and identification problem is possible and applicable to explosions in this low-kiloton range, I believe it lies in the fact that we know so little and thus have so much to learn about the earth, rather than what we now understand. . ."[8] These were the opinions of Dr. Romney, the Defense Department's leading seismologist, as expressed in a symposium of scientists at Detroit, Michigan, in October 1962.

The President's science adviser, Dr. Jerome Wiesner, a communications engineer, frankly disclosed the wishful philosophy of the Administration in seeking a test ban, in an appearance on the Voice of America program, "Press Conference U.S.A." on January 22, 1963. Dr. Wiesner said:

I think you ought to look at this thing from a different point of view. And that is, if you say to yourself that it's unlikely that either side is going to carry on clandestine nuclear tests and the purpose of the system is really to provide reassurance, in other words to build confidence, you want enough inspection so that there aren't unassessed seismic events that could have been nuclear explosions, so with passing time you get more and more confidence in each other rather than less and less. And if there are too many unresolved events, the danger is that with passing time suspicion will increase rather than decrease. I think what you are looking for is the number that is large enough to provide the assurance I am talking about.

Dr. Wiesner's colleague, Dr. Long, had shown how to reduce the number of unresolved events. He apparently used the Wiesner technique of convincing himself that "it's unlikely that either side is going to carry on clandestine nuclear tests."

This was the power of positive thinking that had carried the United States closer to the Soviet position on a nuclear test ban in March 1963 than it had ever been before.

Part V

AN APPRAISAL

Each man who looks at the nuclear test-ban issue takes with him a basic preconception of the intentions of the Soviet Union. Curiously enough, there is a wide difference of opinion in this country on what the true intentions of the Soviet Union are, and it is from these varying basic assessments that most attitudes toward the test ban originate.

One would have thought that a $40–$50-billion-a-year defense budget, supported by Republican and Democratic administrations alike, would have been unmistakable evidence that all Americans have a profound distrust of the Soviet Union. Americans pay the highest taxes in the world, mostly for defense, under the stimulus of but one potential threat—from the Sino-Soviet bloc. America as a nation has a $50-billion-a-year suspicion of the Soviet Union's intentions toward the United States.

Below this level of mass suspicion, however, there flows a contradictory eagerness to trust. The eagerness is so strong that, at times, the same people who are spending $50 billion-plus to emphasize their distrust take long chances experimenting in exercises of trust with the Soviet Union.

The basic division in world opinion on the nuclear test-ban issue is over this judgment of how far the Soviet Union is to be trusted.

Those who favor a test ban believe the Soviet-American arms race is getting so dangerous that we must trust the Russians. Opponents of the test ban believe it would be more dangerous to trust the Russians and stop racing.

Between these two "hard-core" opinions there ranges a great mass of people, leaders and followers alike, who think part of the time the Soviet Union can or must be trusted, and part of the time that she cannot be. Many find it hard to conquer intermittent waves of forlorn hope. The Soviet Union has administered too many periodic setbacks to the world's hope to say that even test-ban advocates have more than a forlorn hope. Some cling to it, others turn away and look for alternatives.

When one batch of hopefuls are disillusioned, a new batch comes to Washington to replace them.

Any cold analysis of the postwar history of Soviet-American relations must conclude that there can be no basis for trusting the Soviet Union's intentions toward this country. When we disarmed, they did not; while we were marking time self-consciously, the Soviet Union worked feverishly to build its own nuclear weapons; later Moscow launched a war in Korea that challenged our nuclear superiority; she raced to develop the hydrogen bomb ahead of us; she secretly developed her military rocketry and did not reveal it until she was ahead of us, then carried the race into space. The Soviet Union has broken treaties, propagated monstrous lies against us, sought to subvert our friends, stolen our secrets. In 1962, the Kremlin tried to sneak a check-mate on American nuclear power by secretly installing nuclear missiles in Cuba. But President Kennedy blocked her.

All this time the United States has been holding out to the Soviet Union the opportunity to end the quickening arms race. It is as true today as it was in 1945 that the United States would be willing to end the arms race and start scrapping its military power if it could be assured that the Soviet Union and the rest of the world were doing the same. The Soviet Union has steadfastly refused to give such assurances. Because she has not, and because she has been intensely hostile throughout the globe, we have come to distrust her to the extent of spending $40–$50 billion a year on defense.

The history of the nuclear test-ban, however, is proof that this distrust is not limitless. President Eisenhower approved the flights of the U-2 over the Soviet Union out of distrust. But the same man permitted a unilateral, self-denying test ban to drag on indefinitely because he had trust that the Soviet Union was withholding tests. Anyone who doubted the unilateral ban was doing us harm should have been convinced by the 1961 Soviet test series, in which Moscow gained noticeably in relation to the United States.

The President's offer of a unilateral moratorium on testing in all environments, made the day after the Geneva "experts" reached their misleading agreement on control, also deprived the Soviet Union of whatever incentive it might have had to open up its country to international inspection.

But the United States repeatedly acknowledged its concern over trusting Russia. Washington had no evidence whether the Soviet Union was or was not testing behind its Iron Curtain. It was entirely possible that the Soviet Union had been conducting a whole series of tests—underground, in outer space, or even in the atmosphere in remote parts of the world—without our knowledge.

In the curious mode of double-think that the Soviet Union somehow persuaded a lot of people to adopt, Moscow propagandists made it a virtue of the Kremlin that the United States can be trusted and a crime of the United States that the Soviet Union cannot be trusted. There were a surprising number of guilty consciences in the United States, among officials and private citizens, because the United States could not see its way clear to trust the Soviet Union. Some compassionate leader was forever rising to parade his humanitarianism and despair for the future if nuclear war could not be outlawed. He usually indicated it was the United States' fault nuclear war still threatened the world.

Before the world is overcome with guilt for having produced the atomic age's brilliant mushroom cloud, it would do well to reflect how much more of this globe would be under the Communist cloud today were it not for the United States' nuclear capacity.

It would hardly be too much to say that the more than two hundred American explosions of nuclear devices, in Japan, in the Pacific, and in Nevada, since 1945 have ended one war and preserved this country and all her allies, including former enemies, and neutrals, from Red pressures, bullying, or even conquest. Certainly, American nuclear power has saved western Europe from Communist takeover. Sir Winston Churchill is not the only world leader who believes this; obviously there have been others —in the Kremlin.

For the United States, it matters only to a minor degree—it is not even morally defensible—if neutrals complain about our sprinkling them with radioactive fallout that may possibly harm a very few of their people. Dysentery and influenza which the complainers export to us more than balance the grievance lists. If the safety of all America is at stake, however, one takes the risk of harming a few people, foreigners or fellow citizens. We can regret the injury—perhaps try to compensate in some way for it. But we cannot sacrifice our whole nation's safety or our own very lives, out of deference to a vague fear that is more mystic than scientific.

Since World War II, testing nuclear weapons has been of fundamental importance to the defense not only of America but of its allies and of its nonallied friends, prominent among them, India. The great question today is: Is testing still that important?

Americans must judge the nuclear test-ban issue in the framework of United States military requirements.

The starting point in building that framework is an ugly fact that cannot be erased no matter how hard we wish it. Nuclear weapons are here to stay. We cannot uninvent them; too many men and too many countries know how to make them. We cannot destroy them all; so many have been made and they are so easy to hide we could not find them all. Even if we could destroy them all, a stockpile could be accumulated again—in secret.

All this applies even if the world were somehow able to agree on the best possible inspection and control system of global scope. American defenses, therefore, must be built on the assumption that nuclear weapons may be used in any future war. Every major power must in prudence maintain at least the *capability* to use nuclear weapons, even if it has no *intention* to use them.[1]

The two major nuclear powers, the United States and the Soviet Union, both maintain a formidable *capability* to use nuclear weapons. We do not know what the Soviet *intentions* are about using nuclear weapons; we suspect, however, that in the face of America's massive nuclear power, the Soviet Union would try to confine future wars to the use of conventional weapons, with which the Sino-Soviet bloc has a better chance to win against the West. Soviet nuclear weapons most logically would be used as "backup" and as a deterrent against nuclear attack from other powers.

On the other hand, if the Kremlin thought it could wipe out most of the United States nuclear capability in a first strike, thus preventing any effective United States retaliation, our vulnerability might tempt her to try initiating all-out nuclear aggression.

If our suspicions about Soviet intentions are correct, the United States needs nuclear-weapons capabilities to deal with two situations. First, we must retain an invulnerable striking force obvious enough for the Soviet Union to respect it, strong enough to absorb a first strike by the Soviet Union and retaliate devastatingly. Second, we must retain a precise nuclear capacity to compensate—but not overcompensate—for our conventional forces' inferiority. Here, the United States may some day be confronted with a second ugly fact: We may be forced into a position where we must use nuclear weapons first to protect our security interests from being overwhelmed by enemy conventional power.

This so-called doctrine of first use is still debated in this country. George Kennan, United States Ambassador to Yugoslavia, advocates abandonment of the doctrine of first use. So does the Federation of American Scientists. But until a Western will, strong enough to offset Sino-Soviet bloc conventional power, can be clearly demonstrated, it would seem the better part of prudence to accept the doctrine of first use of nuclear weapons. All our nuclear-age Presidents have.

United States *intentions* thus include determination to use nuclear weapons first, if necessary, even in limited war. This is not as immoral as it sounds to some. The initial act of aggression will not be made by the United States. This country traditionally shuns both "preventive" and "pre-emptive" strikes, nuclear or non-nuclear.[2] Potential aggressors are on notice, however, that any conventional attack on the United States or its allies may be met with nuclear weapons in defense.

Thus, the United States has two broad sets of *intentions* involving nuclear weapons: To meet all-out nuclear war only after the enemy has struck the first blow, and to meet so-called limited wars with the first nuclear-weapons blow if necessary. The Kennedy Administration has differed with the Eisenhower Administration on the so-called "threshold" at which a conventional war would be escalated to a nuclear war. But it is not necessary to get into this controversy here to establish the point that United States *intentions* to use nuclear weapons in both all-out and limited war impose on policy-makers the obligation to provide their armed forces with a broad range of nuclear weapons.

The nuclear test-ban idea, however, has had important effects on both our capabilities and our intentions. United States *capabilities* to deal with all types of Soviet-bloc attack, from small to all-out war, with the least loss of life and property on both sides, had not been fully provided when President Eisenhower announced the unilateral moratorium on testing nuclear weapons on October 31, 1958.

And the very act of suspending tests raised doubts about the *intention* of American presidents to use nuclear weapons in case of need. The United States, by remaining at the test-ban conference table for months in 1961, after the Soviet Union made it clear that it would not accept inspection without full veto powers, reinforced the image of timidity in handling nuclear weapons. It may also have given the Soviet Union the impression that the United States had no intention of using nuclear weapons except *in extremis*, an attitude which may have been tested in Cuba in October, 1962.

From the Soviet standpoint, the nuclear test-ban negotiation, and the world propaganda buildup that preceded it, was intended both to restrict the capabilities and to redirect or confuse the intentions of the United States to defend itself and its allies.

The Soviet Union was able to mask its own aims with propaganda that sounded plausible to far too many intelligent people. The two-pronged Soviet assault on United States capabilities and intentions was made to appear as a great humanitarian campaign to save the world from radioactive fallout and to lead the globe at least "one step" away from devastating nuclear war. A companion piece of "humanitarianism," a campaign to ban all use of nuclear weapons, was actually a bid to disarm the West of the weapon principally responsible for preventing Soviet expansion into Europe and Asia since 1945.

In fact the Soviet Union was enticing the United States into a cleverly camouflaged ambush. By a massive propaganda effort of its own, and with the aid of many in the non-Communist world who did not view the testing problem in the context of American national security requirements, the Soviet Union made these gains after the 1958 moratorium started:

1. It interrupted development of high-yield warheads in small enough weights and diameters to make United States rockets widely dispersible and invulnerable to a Soviet first strike.

2. It hampered the United States missile-defense technology in its infancy, thereby restricting efforts to whittle down the invulnerability of the Soviet missile offense, once launched.

3. It interrupted the development of small, clean tactical weapons usable on the ground at close range without "overkilling" or endangering friendly troops.

4. It nearly froze United States basic science in the nuclear-weapons field without the assurance that the Soviet Union had also frozen its basic-science development to a similar extent. Penicillin and radar are two examples of quantum-jump scientific developments discovered by accident, while looking for something else. What unknown developments the Soviet Union might have been making could not be introduced into the strategic equation as a definite measurable quantity. But this one-sided freeze was probably the most significant gain the Soviet Union achieved.

In short, the United States requirement for its defense strategy had not been fulfilled when President Eisenhower ordered the unilateral test moratorium in 1958. The test ban was a bad idea on broad strategic grounds.

Even if the freeze on nuclear-weapons development could have been reciprocal, it was disadvantageous to the United States because it left this country without a second-strike capability, while the Soviet Union had already achieved its own much less sophisticated first-strike capability.

The United States entry into the unilateral nuclear test ban was tragically ill-advised for other reasons. It would not work; it could not work. An effective ban was impossible to enforce from the start and it got more impossible as scientists began thinking about methods that might conceal nuclear tests.

Cataloguing the errors of the United States in science, diplomacy, and intelligence as it grappled with the nuclear-testing issue is painful, but if we profit from these mistakes the exercise will be worth the pain.

Instead of unstigmatizing nuclear weapons, our most important weapon against the Sino-Soviet bloc, we helped to stigmatize them.

Although we knew that effective control of a nuclear test ban was impossible, we entered negotiations to achieve one. We set as one of our principal aims in the nuclear test-ban exercise an opening of the Soviet Union, then proceeded to circumscribe the movements of the inspection apparatus to such an extent that the inspectors would have had to rely on our own intelligence network to do their job.

We attempted to defy one of the fundamental laws of human nature, by attempting to stop the spread of knowledge and to abolish an idea, to uninvent nuclear weapons to arrest technological advance.

In the face of clear evidence that France and Red China would not join in a test-ban agreement, we listed as one of its principal advantages its influence to prevent the spread of nuclear weapons to other nations.

In the face of repeated intelligence underestimates of Soviet capabilities, we accepted it as a fact that the United States was far ahead of the Soviet Union in nuclear-weapons development.

We contended that tensions would be eased by a nuclear test ban, although the Western unilateral moratoria were less than a month old before Soviet Premier Khrushchev precipitated the Berlin crisis, then went on to stir up trouble in the Congo, and build up Communist forces for a takeover in Laos.

We touted the nuclear test ban as the first step toward saving money by disarmament, then discovered the test-ban inspection paraphernalia alone could cost as much as the continuation of tests.

When Is a Test a Test?

Neither the 1958 Conference of Experts, nor the treaty negotiators at Geneva, nor the writers of the American draft treaty that was tabled in April, 1961, defined what a nuclear test was.

One way would have been to state the number of fissions or fusions per microsecond required to constitute a test. In the threshold concept alone, this problem of a small test would not arise. With a comprehension treaty, however, we might be confronted with the problem of how many fusions or fissions made a test.

Furthermore, suppose an attempt were made to shoot off a nuclear weapon and it didn't "go off." Would that be a test? Suppose one made a nuclear weapon too small to go off. When this test "misfires," has there been a test? Somebody might claim as much.

And suppose a nuclear power reactor blew up? Would that be a test? Who is to judge?

In the summer of 1952, when the H-bomb was a lively topic of discussion but no country was known to have tested one, a former pupil of Professor Enrico Fermi was reported to have achieved a thermonuclear explosion in an Italian laboratory. The Italian scientist, U. Losthi, later denied he had exploded the first H-bomb, although he claimed to have succeeded in fusing hydrogen nuclei into helium.[3]

If there had been an H-bomb test ban, as Dr. Vannevar Bush was then suggesting, would the laboratory experiment have violated the ban? And what about laboratory experiments in general?

The AEC, in reporting to the Joint Congressional Committee on methods of protecting personnel against radiation, has mentioned that "experimentation with critical assemblies of radioactive materials, although done with great caution, cannot always be done without some unpredictable brief exposures in excess of the described weekly or quarterly limits. There are also weapons-related research projects, which involve continuous low-level exposures in situations where the experiment cannot be performed with complete shielding."[4]

If a test-ban were to set some limit on laboratory experiments for so many fissions or fusions per microsecond, this would not only complicate the detection problem, but also invite violations by an unscrupulous power.

What good would laboratory experiments be in developing weapons? The Alamagordo bomb of July, 1945, was an extrapolation from laboratory experiments and tests with high explosives. The first shot worked. The Hiroshima bomb was a weapon of an untried design, different from the Alamagordo and Nagasaki shots.

FIXING RESPONSIBILITY

Any reader of whodunits knows that it is as important to know who committed the murder as that one has actually been committed. Fixing responsibility for a nuclear test is a comparable problem.

The oceans cover two-thirds of the surface of the globe. Patrolling them for surface evidence of underwater nuclear explosions on a regular, comprehensive basis would be too big a job. With torpedoes, submarine-launched missiles, and helicopter-dropped depth charges, there might be little to dissuade a clever violator from "planting" an underwater test, say between the Panama Canal and the Marshall Islands, collecting his test results, and absconding from the area long before inspection apparatus could get to the scene. Chances are the control system would detect the underwater bang; but because of the echoes off deep undersea mountain ranges and other phenomena, chances are not so good that it would locate the event accurately. But the radioactivity would be dispersed over a comparatively wide area. One can be optimistic and assume that underwater nuclear explosions would not only be detected but also identified. Would we know which country to blame, however?

The violator could easily complicate the fixing of responsibility by participating in the search, or even by making the first announcement of detection.

No matter where it is found, radioactivity does not carry dog tags. Innocent nuclear powers could quickly be accused of the crime, whether discovered in the oceans, underground, or aboveground. In such circumstances, the tensions in the world might well increase instead of decrease.

Consider for a moment an explosion in the Sahara at a point far removed from the French testing-sites. How would we know that the radioactive debris was French? Might it not have been Israeli or Egyptian or Yugoslav? Or Russian or American or British?

Or suppose that an on-site inspection team were sent to investigate a suspicious event in the Grand Tetons in Wyoming and, to our great surprise, located an undermountain pocket of radioactivity. Suppose the President of the United States denied his government had made the test. Who would believe him?

Suppose, on the other hand, an on-site inspection team located an under-ice pocket of radioactivity in Northern Siberia. The American submarine "Nautilus" is known to have traversed the general area. Soviet denials of any involvement could be expected. Who should be blamed?

What would happen if the identity of a violator could not be established? Would this be grounds for ending the nuclear test-ban agreement? Probably. Since it is unlikely that any action in violation of a treaty would be admitted, there probably would be some sort of international effort to fix blame. Unless it were a crude violation, however, no competent court, national or international, could claim to know who was responsible.

The argument was frequently made, in parrying suggestions that on-site inspection would be ineffective, that other techniques such as questioning the population and using independent intelligence would help to catch a violator. But the Western experience with another kind of on-site inspection, in Korea and Indochina, showed that the Communists were ready to go to great lengths to mislead on-site inspection teams.

In Korea, for instance, after the 1953 armistice, a four-power control commission composed of Sweden, Switzerland, Poland, and Czechoslovakia, known as the Neutral Nations Supervisory Commission, was charged under the armistice agreement with responsibility for checking that armaments on both sides were not increased or modernized.

But the Swiss and Swedish members of the Commission were obstructed by the Communist Polish and Czech members of the Commission from doing an honest job. In a memorandum to the Military Armistice Commission in Korea on May 7, 1954, the Swiss and Swedish members said:

> The Korean Peoples Army and Chinese Peoples Volunteers' side, on the other hand, adopted a rigid procedure. . . . It never submitted any other documents for inspection than prior notification reports. Beyond inspection of duly reported combat materiél, the inspection teams were unable to check off efficiently on other movements and this because of the stand taken by their Czechoslovak and Polish members. . . . All efforts under-

taken by the Swedish and Swiss members of the inspection teams in order to increase the scope and frequency of the spot-check controls have been constantly and persistently frustrated. The way these spot-check controls are carried out they have merely become a face-saving device devoid of any real significance. The inspection teams in the north [of Korea] have therefore never gained the insight in movements of materiél as have the inspection teams in the south.

The Communist side in North Korea removed or hid aircraft before the Neutral Nations commission arrived. Witnesses were elaborately prepared to give false testimony in response to questions posed by members of the inspection teams. There was deliberate deceit and obstructionism on every hand.

The Polish and Czech members of the Neutral Nations Supervisory Commission also found loopholes in the Korean armistice agreement by which it was possible to evade the control measures.[5]

After the armistice in Indochina, Communist China supplied large quantities of arms to the North Vietnamese, in complete disregard of the provisions of the Geneva accords to which she was a party. The International Commission for Supervision and Control in Vietnam, composed of representatives of India, Poland, and Canada, found itself unable to obtain proof of the violations, however.[6]

The terms of reference for the International Control Commission were broad. Teams were set up in ports of entry and exit, but they were confined to that area. Other mobile teams were established to operate in "zones of action" near land and sea frontiers and along the demarcation line between North and South Vietnam. The mobile teams were supposed to have the right to move freely and to receive from local authorities the facilities they would require. Transportation and communication were to be supplied. Outside the "zones of action" the mobile teams were to move only after agreement with the military command in charge.

But the Control Commission was unable to function because of the unwillingness of the Red North Vietnamese regime to grant the teams freedom of action. The so-called zones of action for mobile teams were restricted to 10 kilometers in width. Numerous points of entry went unwatched because inspection teams were not allowed.

Outside the zones of action transport facilities were dependent on local authorities. These local authorities could prevent investigation by claiming they were unable to guarantee the security of the team or furnish accommodations. The control teams were kept from military areas or warehouses, even at points of entry, and movements of personnel and materiél were not under international control.

In 1960–62, the Soviet Union mounted an airlift carrying military supplies and arms to Laotian rebels from a main base in Hanoi, North Vietnam, under the very noses of the Control Commission, which made no protest.

The North Vietnamese army, it is reported, increased its firepower about 600 per cent after the 1954 armistice, in violation of the agreement.[7] Where the Communists *can* cheat on an inspection system, it seems rather well established, even on recent experience, they *will*.

Now let us assume the unbelievable. Assume that the test-ban violating nation kept such loose tabs on persons connected with the secret tests that one of them defected and "spilled the beans." Suppose, too, that somehow he could bring proof that he was telling a true story, such convincing proof that the world believed his story. Suppose, in other words, responsibility for the violation were pinned beyond doubt on country A.

How would country A be penalized for the violation? War would be no answer. The violator could be a nuclear power, possibly one of the principal nuclear powers. Economic sanctions might be effective against a small power, although a new nuclear power might not look so small as it had before.

The only other reprisal that persons who have made a close study of the problem can think of would be to break off the agreement and resume the arms race.

Test-ban advocates put great reliance on the pressures of world opinion to deal with an established violation. The violator would lose prestige around the world, they say. Premier Khrushchev himself referred to the "shame" that would be heaped on the violator's head. But in September, 1961, he bore the shame and resumed tests in a big way.

How would world opinion shame a violator? No doubt there would be action in the United Nations, speeches and resolutions; most of the other governments of the world would issue indignant statements of condemnation. But this would hardly deter a violator, or even impress him very much.

We have the example of the violations of the Korean armistice terms by the Communists. There were speeches and resolutions in the United Nations; there were outraged cries from the United States and its associates in the U.N. Command; there were indignant editorials in the press. All in all, however, it was a pretty anemic performance. The Soviet Union and its Chinese Communist associates went ahead with their buildup of the North Korean Army. The war was not resumed. The U.N. Command did not even initiate a counterbuildup for four years.

World opinion was much more aroused by the Soviet suppression of the Hungarian Revolution. But it could not be said that world opinion was very effective in staying the hand of the Soviet Army. There was outrage after outrage, in full view of the world. Imre Nagy and General Maleter were tricked into surrendering to the Soviet forces—then executed. World opinion stood aghast. Hungary's new puppet leader, Janos Kadar, the successor to Nagy, was seated in the General Assembly's summit meeting at the United Nations four years later.

Red China embarked on a campaign closely resembling genocide in Tibet. World opinion was briefly aroused. But Red China ignored it.

Mr. Khrushchev broke the test moratorium in September, 1961, and the Belgrade conference of neutrals was so cowed it even avoided condemning the act. Would violations of a test-ban treaty draw stronger reaction?

Violations could be made to look extremely ambiguous. World opinion could be made to doubt there had been a clear-cut case of violation. Accusations against the innocent would be inevitable. World opinion, ineffective in clear-cut cases of violation, could not be expected to be more effective against ambiguous transgressions.

Violations could be further confused, in the classical Soviet pattern, by preceding them with accusations and trumped-up evidence of breaches on the other side.

Khrushchev's emphasis on the power of public opinion in shaming test-ban violators contrasts markedly with his contempt for public opinion in the Hungarian case. Here is what he said:

"International reactionary circles are still trying to discuss the so-called 'Hungarian question' in the United Nations. Let them keep it as a souvenir if this consoles them."[8]

His defiance of world opinion in the September, 1961, resumption of multimegaton testing probably effectively demolishes the argument that a treaty to ban tests would produce a climate that would inhibit the Soviet Union.

Not only world opinion, but even the governments most directly threatened by the violation might well find themselves impotent. Democracies especially are difficult to arouse with ambiguous evidence that old agreements may have been broken. England's sleepy response to Germany's rearmament after World War I is a classic example. For political reasons, the party in power even toned down the evidence of Hitler's buildup. Winston Churchill accused the Baldwin Government of "watering down or whittling down of the facts" on German rearmament in the 1930's.[9]

The decision to expose a test-ban violation and act on it would not be easy for a democratic government. The reaction probably would involve increasing free-world defense budgets, at the least, and losing votes in the next election, at the most.

Far from covering the violator with "shame," as Mr. Khrushchev suggested, public opinion in the affronted countries could conceivably put a damper on sanctions against a violator. The experience of British Prime Minister Baldwin, at the time of Hitler's defiance of the Versailles Treaty, illustrates the point. In 1936, Mr. Baldwin gave this explanation:

You will remember at that time [1932–33] the disarmament conference was sitting in Geneva. You will remember at that time there was probably a stronger pacifist feeling running through this country than at any time since the war. You will remember the election at Fulham in the autumn of 1933, when a seat which the National Government had held was lost by about 7,000 votes on no issue but the pacifist. . . . I asked myself what chance was there . . . within the next year or two of that feeling being so changed that the country would give a mandate for rearmament? Supposing I had gone to the country and said that Germany was rearming and that we must rearm, does anybody think that this pacific democracy would have rallied to that cry at that moment? I cannot think of anything that would have made the loss of the election from my point of view more certain.[10]

In the 1959–62 period, Prime Minister Macmillan was in much the same situation as Mr. Baldwin. Mr. Macmillan made frequent trips to Washington to prove to his own pacifist factions that he was working eagerly for a test-ban. Under the provisions for full NATO consultation, it appeared that any Western reaction to a violation of the nuclear test-ban treaty would have to be preceded by agreement from all powers. The British influence might inhibit sharp reaction to a violation.

If, contrary to expectations, the injured governments were to resume the arms race at an accelerated pace, they would in fact be penalizing themselves at least as much as the violator. If there were a $30-billion increase, say, in defense spending as a result of a violation of the test-ban agreement, it could be expected that the violator would be fully prepared to match this increase, no doubt one jump ahead of his rival.

The United States really had no inspection system, no plan for detection *and identification* on which it could rely, even if one were to accept the theory that a "foolproof" system was impossible and a "deterrent" would be acceptable. By the United States' own definition, a deterrent should present a possible violator with a 20 to 30 per cent chance of being caught. For the next decade or more, science could not claim that any violator would be confronted with a 20 or 30 per cent chance of being caught.

The simple, overriding fact about the inspection system for a nuclear test ban is that nobody knows enough about it to construct one.

From the time the Soviet Union began testing her nuclear weapons she had a built-in incentive to conceal them. Military power is the most secret item in her secret society. She also had a good chance to maintain military security by conducting tests deep inside her own vast territory. This reporter, for one, is not convinced that we detected the first Soviet test. To avoid the problem of local fallout, many of the Soviet tests were held high above the ground. This, of course, might have made detection easier for the United States, if acoustic and electromagnetic sensors were on the job early enough. At any rate, Moscow was soon made aware of the United States detection network when President Truman announced the detection of the Russian experiment in September, 1949.

From that time on, at least, inability to conceal nuclear experiments in the atmosphere must have appeared to the secrecy-prone Communists to be a serious flaw in their armor. It would be logical to expect the Soviet Union to try hard to develop methods of concealment, beginning well before 1949. American scientists did little thinking about concealment before 1956.

Thus, it could be that the Soviet Union was at least seven years ahead of the United States in techniques of concealing nuclear tests at the time of the 1958 Conference of Experts.

The question frequently was raised why the Soviet Union would go to such lengths to get a test ban if it intended to go on testing secretly. If the Western development of nuclear weaponry could be stopped while the Soviet Union's continued to improve, even at a slow pace, this would be an advantage the Soviet Union would work hard to get.

American officials who live with the nuclear-test-detection problem day in and day out are amused, however, by the frequent flurries of excitement when the Soviet Union announces suspicious-sounding "chemical explosions for peaceful purposes." They point out that there are 300 to 400 earthquakes per year in the seismic regions of the Soviet Union, each one of which could mask a nuclear test without the United States being any the wiser. There was no control system, inadequate as it would have been, nor were there any on-site inspections, inadequate as they would have been, during the long unilateral moratoriums.

Did the Soviet Union test during the period of the unilateral moratorium?

Spokesmen of American intelligence agencies let it be known there was no positive evidence she had or had not. This was very ambiguous phrasing, however, and papered over at the top level some contradictory findings at lower levels in the American intelligence community. There were extremely competent evaluators down the line who thought they had enough data to indicate a very high probability that the Soviet Union had been testing.

After discussions and delays the agencies in the Defense Department finally recognized that clandestine testing probably had been occurring in the Soviet Union. Some had a higher, some a lower degree of conviction; some played their apprehensions down, some others emphasized them.

Test-ban proponents always claimed the evidence was not conclusive. But obviously the evidence could not be conclusive in the case of underground testing. American intelligence is good but it can hardly be expected to get hold of encapsuled radioactive samples from underground cavities. Yet in the absence of such proof, it was claimed that the evidence was inconclusive.

The nature of intelligence is that one very rarely has such a thing as conclusive intelligence. Yet American agencies had more intelligence on the probability, or if one prefers, the possibility, of clandestine Soviet testing than on many other developments in the Soviet Union.

Because of the appeal of the test-ban idea, however, there was insistence on more convincing evidence in the case of possible underground testing than in almost any other field involving the Soviet Union.

For a long time after the undeclared moratorium of November, 1958, few were looking for intelligence that the Soviet Union might be cheating. Then one Air Force group, assisted by a few lone wolves in other agencies, got busy. The very idea that one should look for indicators of Soviet cheating was considered to be sacrilegious by some of the faithful of the test-ban religion. The project was strongly resisted. It was an uphill fight to turn intelligence resources to the job of seeking evidence of clandestine Soviet testing, or for that matter, prove on a sound evidential basis, that they were not.

Once data were collected, interpretations varied widely, according to the attitude toward nuclear testing. Nevertheless, the evidence was sufficiently strong so that most evaluators in the Pentagon agreed it was ominous enough to force resumption of testing.

When this intelligence was passed up the line, to the secretarial and Presidential science adviser levels, it was always discovered that the evidence was not conclusive. Which, of course, it couldn't be.

The CIA continued to argue that there was no evidence either way as to whether the Soviet Union was or was not testing. To the inexperienced, in and out of government, this was a loophole big enough to delay a decision on test resumption.

There are several lessons in this. One might be that one gets intelligence only if he is really searching to get it; he certainly won't get it so long as he doesn't want to receive it.

Another lesson has been that intelligence can easily be ignored if it doesn't fit into the popular political scheme. It is always extremely easy to ignore intelligence because of its uncertain character. (Cuba is a recent example.)

"Conclusive evidence" is so rare as to be mostly impossible to attain. Much intelligence is in the nature of estimates, a great deal is projection of future events.

Intelligence indicators of clandestine Soviet testing were pooh-poohed frequently on the grounds that the Kremlin would not dare to test because its cheating might be found out and then the Soviet Union would have world public opinion trouble. This type of estimating should have been discredited when the Russians resumed testing in September, 1961, and almost deliberately flouted the public opinion of the world—and yet did not get an overly negative reaction.

At one point it was argued that the Soviet Union really needed no additional nuclear progress. The September-October series in 1961 unmasked this wishful interpretation as well.

Amateurishness? To some extent, yes. Infiltration? Hardly. The most plausible interpretation is that wishful thinking beclouded the minds of many who were supposed to give the warning. Others who had advocated the ban fell victim to the most common failing of man: to rationalize away one's mistakes.

The decision maker, whoever the President may be, is at the mercy of his top intelligence co-ordinators, as Mr. Kennedy found at the time of the abortive Cuban invasion. Down the line he might have found rawer and less polished but better information on both Cuba and Soviet testing.

Whether President Kennedy was told, for instance, of the indicators suggesting that secret tests were under way is open to excruciating doubt among intelligence professionals.

Those who banked on American intelligence to detect and identify nuclear explosions, however, were in an anomolous position. These were the same people who supported the need for 21 elaborate control stations, each with arrays of 100 seismometers, inside the Soviet Union to detect explosions. There were no such stations. If these people felt that the American intelligence network was reliable enough to conclude Russia was not testing, why did they want the control stations?

Soviet science had decided in 1956 that large, non-nuclear explosions underground cost at least fifteen times as much as nuclear explosions of equivalent power.[11] If there is some measure of doubt whether the Soviet Union has conducted secret nuclear explosions since 1958, there is certainly much less reason to doubt that the Soviet Union would like to use nuclear explosives for mining, dam building, and canal construction.

If one adds to the economy motive the prospect that the Soviet Union could use newly developed nuclear weapons in these "peaceful" projects, one has a better circumstantial case that the Soviet Union may have been secretly testing in the moratorium period.

All this circumstantial evidence—and much more—of course was known to the United States from intelligence not divulged.

American officials whose job it was to keep track of information on possible Soviet cheating believed that the "big hole" for decoupling such shots had been "overglamorized." There was a much easier way for the Soviet Union to cheat, these officials said, so long as there was no control system operating. All that would be necessary would be to dig a small tamped hole in the mountains of a seismic area, where there are many natural earthquakes. The shot could then be completely contained underground, but triggered on a natural event. The big engineering job of hollowing out underground cavities thus could be avoided. And, if the underground shots were started small enough, that is below the 1-kiloton range, they would not even be picked up. These American officials think that there could be no serious worry about detection, let alone identification, up to 5 kilotons. American scientists told the Holifield Subcommittee in 1960 that such tests would be large enough to develop all the tactical weapons and most of the strategic weapons conceivably needed.

The big China explosion of 9 kilotons, in 1956, was picked up by the United States detection network, for instance, but the remote system could not identify it as an explosion. The shot could have passed as an earthquake if the Communists had not made announcements themselves. There would have been suspicions, of course, because the epicenter was in what was believed to have been an aseismic area.[12]

No suspicions would have been aroused, however, if the same signal had originated in Kamchatka Peninsula or some other seismic area.

Late in 1960, Moscow radio reported that Soviet scientists had created artificial earthquakes in central Asia that had enabled them to sketch the structure of the earth's core to a depth of about 62 miles.[13]

The Moscow radio reported that charges had been exploded on the bed of Lake Balkhash and in the Nura River near Temir-Tau. Seismographs picked up the blasts up to 250 miles away, it was reported. The explosion would help geologists prospect for minerals with greater accuracy, Radio Moscow observed.

CHINA: 3.4-MILLION-SQUARE-MILE HOLE

There was another hole in the nuclear test-ban inspection system as it was being negotiated—the 3.4-million-square-mile hole of Red China.

Bringing Peking into the treaty was a bridge the Administration preferred to cross after the Soviet Union had signed on the dotted line. Some seventeen inspection stations were planned for Red China. Without them, control would be more difficult in the Soviet Union. Without them, it would be impossible to check on suspicious underground events inside Red China. The Peking regime itself, or, through special arrangements the Soviet Union, thus would have a ready-made "sanctuary" for clandestine testing while the West would be effectively prevented from testing.

The West's idea was to get the three nuclear powers signed up in the nuclear test-ban treaty first. Then it would take some time to install the inspection system. During this time, it would be up to the Soviet Union to work on Red China to get her to join up. More than that, Red China would have to accept the whole inspection network, including the possibility of on-site inspections, at a time when forced industrialization and starvation inside the country were reaching appalling proportions. Only the most fanciful would expect that Red China would join the test-banning powers, especially after the split over Communist ideology widened.

Without Red China the test ban would not be meaningless. It would effectively cut off testing by the United States, Britain, and any other democracies that joined.

Putting the Red China issue on the shelf was thus another case of wishful eye-shutting to the impossibility of getting an effective test ban.

NTH-COUNTRY PROBLEM

One of the mysteries of United States diplomacy has been the tenacity with which American negotiators have stuck to the disproved theory that a nuclear test-ban treaty would stop, or delay, the spread of nuclear weapons to Nth countries.

Nuclear weapons are inherently the great equalizer in war, consequently at least as important to small nations as to big nations. A small nation can deter big-nation attack if it has a small stockpile of nuclear weapons. The British understood this first and developed their own nuclear capability in the first postwar years. France followed this course in the mid-1950's and joined the nuclear club in 1960. Intelligence reports indicated Red China was driving hard to develop a nuclear capability of its own.

In 1960, also, it was disclosed that Israel had been working with France in the nuclear-reactor field. The disclosures created enough of a sensation in Egypt to cause President Nasser to warn that he was prepared to seek nuclear weapons for Egypt as well.[14] Most signs pointed to a proliferation of nuclear weapons in the sixties.

Back in 1957, and in the earlier disarmament negotiations, there had been some difference between the Soviet Union and the United States on what measures would be necessary to inhibit the spread of nuclear weapons to other powers. The Soviet Union had claimed that a test ban alone would have this effect. The United States claimed that the test ban was of secondary importance, that an inspected cutoff of nuclear-weapons production, agreed to "by all other essential states in the world," was indispensable before there was any hope that the spread could be halted.[15]

When the test-ban was lifted out of the American disarmament package, however, the United States adopted the Soviet view.

Small powers also doubted the theory that the nuclear test ban would retard the spread. Irish Foreign Minister Akin, in the 1959 U.N. General Assembly, had this to say:

> It is sometimes asserted, for example, that an agreement on the cessation of tests will serve the same purpose [of stopping the spread]. My delegation finds it hard to accept this. It is true that universal agreement on test

cessation, which is most earnestly to be desired, would be a long step in the right direction. Such an agreement would, of course, require participation of all nations, including nonmembers of this organization, and the setting up of a world-wide system of inspection machinery. Granted that an agreement at Geneva were followed by world agreement not to test, it would still do little to check the actual dissemination, as distinct from the testing, of the weapons. They could still be manufactured and be transferred from one country to another without in any way infringing international law or breaking any agreements. For these reasons, we do not believe the test suspension would in itself be an adequate check on the wider dissemination of nuclear weapons.

The second objection, which was indeed advanced against the proposals when we made them last year, is that inspection and control may not be possible. Here the problem falls into two parts: secret production of nuclear weapons by non-nuclear states, and secret transfer of nuclear weapons by the nuclear powers. It is, we understand, relatively simple and cheap to install an effective system of accounting to insure that the entire production of a given reactor goes to peaceful uses, from the date of installation of the accounting system. The point about the date is important and underlines the need for urgent action before further reactors are installed in non-nuclear states. Agreement on inspection and control against manufacture of nuclear weapons in new countries would in itself be an advance, but their advance is unlikely to be achieved unless there can also be an agreement against transfer of the weapons.[16]

Stopping the spread of nuclear weapons, then, would more logically be the task of a vast inspectorate, which would guarantee that nuclear power reactors outside Britain, the Soviet Union, and the United States were not producing plutonium for bomb production and which would guard against the transfer of nuclear weapons from the then-nuclear powers to other nations.

It could be argued that the spread of nuclear weapons gave the Soviet Union more to worry about than the United States and Britain. Moscow had to worry not only about its potential enemies but its friends. Not only would a nuclear-armed France and West Germany be formidable opponents of the Soviet Union, but Red China or Poland would be dangerous allies if they, too, were to have nuclear weapons.

The United States, on the other hand, had less to fear from French or West German acquisition of nuclear weapons, although just as much if not more from Red China's entry into the nuclear "club."

The Soviet Union first announced its plan to aid nuclear development in Communist China, Poland, Czechoslovakia, Rumania, and East Germany on January 18, 1955. The beneficiaries were to exchange materials, equipment, and data for processing raw materials.

At the Atoms for Peace Conference in Geneva in August, 1955, the Soviet Union disclosed it was designing an experimental reactor for

China. Czechoslovakia subsequently acquired an experimental reactor, which reportedly went into operation in September, 1957.[17]

Red China's first nuclear reactor became critical on June 16, 1960, according to a report of the New China News Agency. It was reported to be a 10,000-kilowatt, heavy-water research reactor, built with the Soviet Union's help, located near Peking at the Institute of Atomic Energy of the Chinese Academy of Sciences.

On May 11, 1960, Premier Chou En-lai told a Rangoon press conference of an interesting Red Chinese condition that would have to be met before his government would even participate in disarmament negotiations: diplomatic recognition. "If China is invited to take part in the big-power disarmament conference while the People's Republic of China is not recognized, we, of course, cannot consider the matter. How can one who is not recognized go to attend a conference with those who do not recognize him? This is inconceivable." [18]

Official Red Chinese pronouncements indicate, therefore, that the Peking regime fully expected to become a nuclear power and refused to be bound by disarmament agreements in which she had not participated from the beginning.

How seriously the Russians take the hope of stopping the spread of nuclear weapons is not known, of course. But there have been some hints of skepticism. Scientist Leo Szilard reports, for instance, that a Russian scientist agreed with him at a 1957 Pugwash conference that there was little validity in the idea.[19] Dr. Szilard also was skeptical about Red China's interest in acceding to a test ban.[20]

People's Daily in Peking stated the Communist Chinese position on September 12, 1962:

> The reason U.S. ruling circles are so interested in preventing what they call nuclear proliferation is no secret. The Western papers have recently more than once disclosed that Washington is anxious to tie China's hands in developing nuclear weapons, and have even openly stated that this is one of the objectives of the limited ban draft treaty recently put forward by the United States. In the eyes of the U.S. rulers, it would assure U.S. nuclear superiority and make it easier for Washington to use nuclear blackmail if it can prevent China and other socialist countries from possessing nuclear weapons. The basis of U.S. disarmament and test-ban policy is to assure U.S. nuclear superiority.
>
> However, this is only U.S. wishful thinking. China's policy on disarmament is known to all. We have always advocated the cessation of the arms race, realization of armaments reduction, and, particularly, prohibition of nuclear weapons. We maintain that only a complete ban of nuclear weapons and the unconditional destruction of all existing nuclear weapons can prevent a nuclear war.
>
> On the other hand, as long as the imperialist powers refuse to ban nuclear weapons, the socialist camp must possess a powerful military potential to

check effectively the U.S. imperialists' nuclear blackmail and aggressive activities and to promote the cause of world peace. The discontinuation of nuclear tests should be the first step toward a complete banning of nuclear weapons. It should under no circumstances become a means by which the United States may achieve and maintain nuclear superiority. The people of the world are clear-sighted. This trick of the United States can deceive nobody.[21]

Sweden

Swedish officials predicted, meanwhile, that Sweden could have a "small number" of tactical atomic weapons by 1970.[22] Official Swedish policy, as outlined by Premier Tage Erlander, was to await the outcome of the Geneva test-ban negotiations. "My whole policy has been to give the Swedish people all the possibilities to decide whether to make atomic weapons without being stopped for technical reasons," Dr. Erlander said.[23]

Twelve Candidates

A study group of scientists rated twelve nations to be ready in January, 1960, to embark on "a successful nuclear-weapons program in the near future." [24] The countries were Belgium, Canada, Red China, Czechoslovakia, France, West Germany, East Germany, India, Italy, Japan, Sweden, and Switzerland.

"Most of these countries are highly industrialized and either have operating reactors or have already made plans and arrangements for obtaining reactors. A number of these countries have already talked about embarking on a nuclear-weapons program," the scientists said. A month after their report, France joined the nuclear club by exploding her first nuclear device in the Sahara.

A second group of eight countries, the scientists estimated, were "economically capable, fairly competent technically, although perhaps somewhat more limited in scientific manpower" than the twelve countries to become nuclear powers. These nations were Australia, Austria, Denmark, Finland, Hungary, Netherlands, Poland, and Yugoslavia.

A third group of six nations had the economic capability to become nuclear powers but more severe limitations on industrial resources and scientific manpower, the group found. "It is not too likely that any of these countries could presently achieve a successful nuclear-weapons program within five years." The nations were Argentina, Brazil, Mexico, Norway, Spain, and the Union of South Africa.[25]

Scientists in many countries were also working on cheaper ways of producing weapons-grade fissionable materials. If the "gas-centrifuge" technique for separating-out Uranium-235, a process based on the principle of the cream separator, could be developed, there were predictions that nuclear weapons would be put within the reach of twenty-odd nations. Costs of producing the fissionable material would be much lower. There was no assurance that the gas-centrifuge process would be cheap from the outset, but laboratories were pressing in this direction.

The very existence of the possibility that a cheaper method of producing fissionable materials was at hand also militated against signing a nuclear test-ban treaty by non-nuclear powers, or, if the treaty were signed, against long-term adherence.

West Germany and the Netherlands were reported working on the new centrifuge process in 1960. At Washington's request, both countries were keeping the results of their research secret, presumably in the hope that this would prevent the spread of the knowledge.

In the meantime, to become a nuclear power a nation needed mining and milling facilities; refining, fuel element, and fabrication plants; operation of nuclear reactors or isotope-separation plants; facilities for chemical and metallurgical processing of intensely radioactive materials; and bomb-assembly plants. The scientists concluded that manufacture of a few "nominal" atomic devices, meaning those of a yield of about 20 kilotons, would require an outlay of about $100 million before a single bomb could be produced.[26] In achieving operational nuclear-power reactors, countries simultaneously move more than half way toward an operational plutonium bomb, the scientists said. They pointed out that forty-two countries were in the process of setting up nuclear power reactors.

A rapid rise in the number of atomic powers was expected by the mid-1960's. "By 1970, most nations with appreciable military strength will have in their arsenals nuclear weapons—strategic, tactical, or both," the National Planning Association estimated.[27] The NPA did not discuss the influence of the test ban on the spread of nuclear weapons.

There were four main ways that a nation could obtain nuclear-weapons capabilities. It could develop a bomb out of its own resources. A test ban could but need not have impeded this development.

The second method would be to get a nuclear reactor as part of a bilateral or multilateral assistance program and use it to produce weapons material.[28] Again a test ban could but need not be an impediment.

The third method would be through direct military assistance from a friendly country. This aid could take the form either of production facilities or finished weapons. The United States' NATO allies fit into this category; they would get finished weapons in time of war. The test ban need not be any impediment against this method.

The fourth possibility would be that nuclear bombs might eventually be sold on the world market. If this sounded absurd at the time, it should have been remembered that nuclear reactors already had been bought and sold on the world market. The test ban would be no impediment here, either.

As Fred Charles Iklé, a RAND Corporation expert has noted, there were four limitations on the effectiveness of test-suspension as a curb for the spread of nuclear weapons: potential Nth countries simply might not accede to the treaty; nations might join the nuclear club without testing; others might join with secret tests that would not be detectable; a country could always sign up for the test ban, and, once there was a change in administration, or even without this, might test openly anyway.[29]

Economy was one of the factors, aside from prestige, that encouraged some countries to develop a nuclear-weapons capability. Some leaders in Great Britain, for instance, argued that the most effective use they could make of their limited economic resources was to produce nuclear weapons and reduce conventional forces. France, however, found that costs of basic installations were a serious strain on the national budget.

Another point of pressure for some nations to develop their own nuclear capacity was the fear that allies with nuclear capability would not come to their defense effectively. French leaders, in particular, feared the United States would not come to France's aid with nuclear weapons as quickly as necessary.

Tensions Eased?

Another wishful prediction by test-ban advocates was that such an agreement would relax tensions around the world. While the 1958 Conference of Experts was still in session, the Chinese Communists launched the Quemoy-Matsu crisis.

Before the political negotiations for a test ban were a month old, Soviet Premier Khrushchev threatened to squeeze the West out of Berlin. While the negotiations continued, Castro came into power; the Congo crisis brought Soviet and American armed forces into brief confrontation in Africa, Laos slipped farther behind the Iron Curtain; Vietnam appeared on the verge of explosion.

It was said, of course, that the relaxation of tensions could not be expected until the nuclear test ban was signed. Why things would be any better under a declared moratorium than they had been under the undeclared moratorium was unclear. The anticipated occasion of Red China's first test was not likely to produce a less tense situation, whether or not there was a nuclear test ban. Quite probably the tensions would be worse if there were a test ban. With the faulty inspection system, false alarms would multiply. The Soviet Union would have constant opportunities to accuse the West of cheating, perhaps as a cover for its own secret operations.

It was even debatable whether a relaxation of tensions was healthy. Tensions were relaxed between the first and second world wars when Britain and the United States disarmed. The trouble was that the Germans and Japanese rearmed and World War II was under way before the imbalance in arms could be righted.

President Truman tried to reduce tensions by setting a disarmament example from 1945 to 1950. But then Stalin struck in Korea.

WHO LEADS WHOM?

According to the informed guesses of American intelligence, the United States nuclear-weapons-development program was three to four years ahead of the Soviet Union in November, 1958, when the testing of the two countries presumably stopped.

This estimate deserves to be regarded with a considerable measure of reserve in view of the consistent underestimation of Soviet capabilities—or overestimation of American capabilities—regarding the atomic bomb, the H-bomb, heavy bombers, rockets, Sputniks, and space.

As a matter of fact, the United States got a slow start in the nuclear-weapons field. When the AEC came into being after the war, a three-month survey of the American atomic-energy program was undertaken. The five new commissioners found

> there were serious weaknesses in the operation from the standpoint of national defense and security. The number of bombs was disappointing, and those we had were not assembled. The highly skilled civilians who had been trained to do the assemblying had scattered to better-paying jobs in private employment. The training of military personnel to perform the assembly operation was not yet completed.
>
> While there had been some test explosions at Bikini during 1946 for strategic purposes, the more advanced type of bomb on hand had yet to be tested. Furthermore, there were serious questions about the supply of raw uranium. Most of it at that time came from the Belgian Congo, and the demand exceeded the supply.[30]

When British-American cooperation in the atomic field broke down, the Belgian supply of raw uranium was divided about equally between the United Kingdom and the United States. This imposed a shortage on the United States but left the British with a glut. It was not until January 7, 1948, that Britain and the United States reached a new agreement under which all the uranium produced in the Belgian Congo during 1948 and 1949 would go to the United States. In addition, the United States got an option on a portion of the British stockpile.[31]

In early 1947, the General Advisory Committee to the AEC had found the American atomic program in "an unsatisfactory state."[32] They reported:

We very soon learned that in none of the technical areas vital to the common defense and security, nor in those looking toward the beneficial applications of atomic energy, was the state of development adequate. Important questions of technical policy were undecided, and in many cases unformulated. Giant installations and laboratories were operating with confused purposes and with inadequate understanding of importance and relevance of the technical problems before them. Our atomic armament was inadequate, both quantitatively and qualitatively, and *the tempo of progress was throughout dangerously slow*. This state of affairs can in large measure be attributed to the long delays in setting up an atomic authority, and to the inevitable confusions of policy and of purpose which followed the termination of the war. The difficulties were increased by the fact that the wartime installations and laboratories, which served so well their primary function of developing atomic weapons for early military use were in most cases not suited to continue the work as the nature of the technical problems altered, and as the transition from wartime to peacetime operations changed the conditions under which rapid progress might be possible.

The Advisory Committee reported "great progress" in 1947. But there apparently had been an eighteen-month doldrum:

We shared with the Commission an understanding of how dangerous complacency could be with regard to our work in this field. We have been much gratified at the establishment of the Pacific Proving Grounds, where the performance of altered and improved weapons can be put to the test of actual proof and measurements. While much remains to be done, and while the long-term program of atomic armament is only in its earliest beginning, we nevertheless believe that steps already taken to improve our situation, and others which will follow as time makes them appropriate, have gone very far toward establishing this activity on a sound basis.

President Truman was not satisfied that the "kinks" had been removed from the atomic program until early 1949.[33]

In July, 1949, President Truman's special committee of the National Security Council, composed of Secretary of State Dean Acheson, Defense Secretary Louis Johnson, and AEC Chairman David Lilienthal recommended a step-up in production of atomic weapons, another indication that there was still dissatisfaction with the program as late as mid-1949.

There were only two American tests of nuclear weapons from the summer of 1945 to the spring of 1948. These were the Bikini Able and Baker shots of 1946. Even here there was no advance of nuclear design. The tests were merely to inform the military more precisely on the effects of nuclear weapons on ships and in ocean environments.

The 1948 tests, code-named "Operation Sandstone," emphasized efficiency. Senator Edwin C. Johnson of Colorado was quoted as saying four nuclear devices had produced a bomb six times as effective as the Nagasaki weapon. Presumably this meant that one of the explosions had a yield of 120 kilotons, since the Nagasaki weapon was 20 kilotons.[34]

Dr. Edward Teller told a special congressional committee that the H-bomb might have been achieved four years earlier if the Administration had gone after it in 1945.

In the early 1950's, when the H-bomb was being developed, Dr. Teller told the Oppenheimer committee that "the influence of the General Advisory Committee at the time was to the best of my understanding in the direction of go slow, explore all, completely all, the designs before looking into new designs, do not spend too much on test programs, all of which advice I consider somewhat in the nature as a brake rather than encouragement." [35]

The Oppenheimer hearings also disclosed decisions against exploring all the avenues open to nuclear-weapons development—decisions which might not have been taken in the Soviet Union when Red scientists reached such points. Dr. Teller testified that in the fall of 1945, he had offered to head the Los Alamos Laboratory's theoretical division if one of two conditions were met: either that he be allowed to test "something like twelve fission weapons per year" or "we would go into a thorough investigation of the thermonuclear question."

The thermonuclear question, of course, was not pursued until 1949.

Only 3 to 6 people out of 1,000 or more at the Los Alamos Laboratory worked on the thermonuclear bomb, and then only off and on, between 1945 and 1949, Dr. Teller testified.[36]

"Popularly expressing and crudely expressing the state of affairs, in spite of my working there and in spite of some reports being issued, I can say that the work was virtually at a standstill," Dr. Teller told the Oppenheimer Board.

In the period from 1945 to 1949, Dr. Teller estimated that less than one-third of his own time had been spent on thermonuclear development.

The first factor, then, casting doubt on the extent of the United States lead over the Soviet Union is the acknowledged periodic delay in the American program in contrast to the assumed Soviet program for "running scared." The second factor could be a miscalculation of Soviet advancement. The United States intelligence network has put the date of the first Soviet test at August, 1949. By the end of 1949, however, the United States and the Soviet Union had exploded the same number of weapons. The two nuclear powers, then, may well have "started even" in 1949 instead of with the United States in a four-year lead.

The Soviet news agency Tass, in September, 1949, reported that the Soviet Union had had the bomb secret and atomic weapons since 1947. A Molotov statement of November 6, 1948, and a Vishinsky speech of October 1, 1948, were cited by Tass as corroborating evidence.

Soviet historians and encyclopedists are notorious for rewriting history.

They are capable of rewriting it in advance as well as after the fact. On the other hand, American intelligence is not a particularly accurate chronicler of events behind the Iron Curtain. And Soviet boasts in advance of American detection of Soviet achievements have, in both the nuclear and space fields, had an uncomfortable way of being substantiated.

It will not be claimed here that either the Soviet Union or the United States is ahead in nuclear-weapons technology. It would be fatuous to claim to know. On the other hand, one can draw on past experience. Such as:

United States intelligence has underestimated Soviet technology on many occasions in the past, in aircraft development, in tactical nuclear weapons, in rocket thrust, in rocket accuracy; Vishinsky, Molotov, Malenkov, Khrushchev have made claims about nuclear development that were first ridiculed or downgraded by the United States, later substantiated. On other occasions, good intelligence estimates have simply been ignored by the policy-makers.

Today, Soviet generals are claiming they have the most advanced nuclear weaponry in the world. Not all the claims of the Soviet generals need be believed; but there is reason for the sideline observer to entertain strong doubts about the confidence of American officials in its lead, measured in years, over the Soviet Union in nuclear-weapons technology.

One estimate, for instance, was that the United States had a three-to-four-year lead over the Soviet Union when the voluntary moratoriums began in early November, 1958.[37]

If the Soviet Union had succeeded in testing secretly during the honor-system moratorium in 1959, 1960, and 1961, the presumed American lead could have been wiped out. The Soviet test series of 1961 reportedly showed the Kremlin had forged ahead in some phases of nuclear-weapons development.

Dr. Teller had this view of the status of United States nuclear devolopment compared with the Russians in the spring of 1961:

> If you want to assume that the Russians have used the opportunity of clandestine testing, we may have in that period lost much or all of our advantage if we had it in the beginning. I think it is likely that as of 1958, we were ahead of the Russians. But I also believe that our knowledge on the point who is ahead of whom is fragmentary, and I would not be sure about that point. But about this I am sure; if the Russians have used the intervening interval for continued testing during the time that our hands were and still are tied, they could have made very great progress. In every two-year period in the past the Russians had made great progress and I don't see why in the last two-year period they would not have done likewise.

This could apply "more easily," Dr. Teller said, to small nuclear weapons "than to anything else, because explosions of small nuclear weapons can be hidden without any trouble whatsoever."

The argument that the world should quit testing nuclear weapons while the United States was ahead may well have been based on a false premise.

The Catastrophe of Secrecy

The hazards of secrecy in a democracy have seldom been better illustrated than in the nuclear-test-ban field. If the general public had known, for instance, in 1958, the hazardous basis on which American scientists went into the Conference of Experts to devise a nuclear test ban, there would have been a much healthier wariness about the outcome. But the 1958 Bethe Panel operated completely in secret.

If the true results of the Hardtack II series had not been withheld from Thanksgiving, 1958, until the summer of 1959, it would not have been so easy for the Soviet Union (and the United States) to build up a case for continuing the test talks on the hopelessly unrealistic basis devised.

If the world had known of Dr. Harold Brown's 1958 warning and Dr. Fisk's 1959 statement about the utter ineffectiveness of on-site inspection, this bogus "court of last resort" and Prime Minister Macmillan's ill-advised quota plan would never have gained the stature they did.

If all Western scientists had known that Dr. Hans Bethe had "proved" that decoupling of underground nuclear explosions was "impossible" in 1958, the Latter theory might have been produced much sooner and would have gained more of the attention it deserved.

The traditional interaction of democratic forces, fully informed, was deliberately suppressed in the nuclear-test-ban debate.

"Now, what happens when secrecy intervenes?" the Nobel Prize Winner for Physics, Dr. I. I. Rabi, inquires:

> Pathetic and profound ignorance of the facts in their proper context does not prevent the policymakers outside of government from carrying on in the field of atomic energy as if all were clear to them. They gather a rumor here, a leak there, and off they go. Ignorant or learned, they take a stand, and public opinion is formed. Our Government cannot act strongly without ample support from public opinion. For wise action, an informed public opinion is necessary. When secrecy intervenes, an informed public opinion can hardly exist. Too often we have, instead, a manipulated public opinion formed by leaks, half truths, innuendoes, and sometimes by outright distortion of the actual facts.[38]

Without the checks and balances of the open, democratic system, without the application of many brilliant minds to every fundamental problem, the quality of decision-making was inevitably diluted.

The American public never has had the benefit of a Joint Chiefs of Staff appraisal of the effect of a nuclear test ban on the nation's defense position. This is in contrast to other issues, where the Administration has either boasted of collective Joint Chiefs' support or has allowed the opinions of the individual members of the Joint Chiefs to be made known through Congress.

Thomas E. Murray, an Atomic Energy Commissioner from 1950 to 1957, was familiar during that period with the JCS position. He has said: "If the Joint Chiefs of Staff were asked—and the American people are entitled to pose this question—whether our test policy is endangering our over-all national defense position, their answer would be yes." [39]

Opinions of the Joint Chiefs were buried further underground in the Kennedy Administration than in the Eisenhower era. Their concern about the test ban, however, was undiminished, despite its suppression.

The Special Government Information Subcommittee of the House Committee Operations, headed by Congressman John E. Moss from California, stated the secrecy problem this way:

> The only real national security lies in scientific progress. Scientific progress relies heavily on a free exchange of scientific ideas. Excessive restrictions on the free exchange of ideas defeat national security. By compounding security regulations with restrictive rules, by adding "need to know" requirements to clearance procedures, the Federal Government has mired the American scientist in a swamp of secrecy.[40]

Senator Humphrey, Chairman of the Disarmament Subcommittee of the Senate Foreign Relations Committee, told the Moss Subcommittee of his problems with secrecy in 1959:

> It is not my intention to suggest that the specific cases I cite be investigated further. Rather, it is to show that information is withheld for reasons that cannot be justified in the name of national security and to stress the need for vigilance on this matter by all congressional committees.
>
> Over the past year the Subcommittee on Disarmament held a number of hearings, many of them in executive session. In all cases the executive session was held because the witness requested it. Usually, after such a session the transcript of the hearing was submitted to the Executive agency or agencies involved for review. The Executive agency then marked those parts of the testimony that, in its opinion, should remain classified. In order to determine whether this classification was justified, the Committee and its staff reviewed carefully the testimony after it was returned by the Executive officials. When the reason for the classification was not self-evident, the Executive officials were questioned about it. Frequently a reason other than security was given for restricting the information. When these erroneous reasons were pointed out, the executive officials often lifted the classification label. . . .
>
> The cases which follow illustrate the various points I wish to bring out.

1. The Central Intelligence Agency, in reviewing testimony given by a noted scientist, had classified a passage of the testimony. When questioned as to why, the CIA official indicated he did not agree with the conclusion of the scientist and incorrect information should not be given out. When challenged further on the point, the CIA representative agreed to let the scientist's conclusions stand. [This referred to testimony of Dr. Hans Bethe on page 1539 of the Hearings of the Subcommittee on Disarmament, Control and Reduction of Armaments. Dr. Bethe was discussing the number of earthquakes occurring each year in the U.S.S.R. and China at given yields.]

2. The Atomic Energy Commission at first classified portions of testimony given by one of its chiefs of division that there was no evidence that the Soviet Union was developing, testing, or producing so-called clean nuclear weapons; that is, weapons with reduced radioactive fallout. The commission was asked whether it was not in the interest of the United States to have this information brought out. The Commission reviewed the matter and decided that the information was of interest and agreed to leave in that portion of the testimony. [This referred to testimony by Brigadier General Alfred D. Starbird, page 1394 of the Disarmament Subcommittee Hearings, Control and Reduction of Armaments, Part 16.] . . .

3. The Department of the Army and the Department of Defense classified testimony relating to the results of Operation Sagebrush, simulated war maneuvers of the Armed Forces using tactical nuclear weapons. The Army refused to remove this classification even after it was pointed out that at the time of the maneuvers in October, 1955, a reporter wrote extensive stories about them and that these news accounts could only have been written as a result of considerable background briefings on the part of the military officers. Part of the reason why the Army wished to continue to classify the information, according to one officer, was that the results indicated the Army didn't know quite what it was doing in the maneuvers. Even if this were true, said the officer, the information should not be released. [This refers to testimony of General Maxwell D. Taylor before the Disarmament Subcommittee, "Disarmament in Foreign Policy," Part I, p. 140.]

4. The Department of the Army requested the elimination from the record to be published several portions of testimony submitted by Army Chief of Staff General Maxwell Taylor. When challenged on the classification, over 90 per cent of what had been taken out was restored. Among the passages finally declassified were those containing general discussions of new nuclear-weapons development and the tactical uses of these weapons. They also put back statements the General had made on the necessity of improving our nonatomic- or conventional-weapons capabilities if a nuclear-weapons test ban should go into effect, general information on the fabrication of nuclear weapons, expressions of opinion regarding the reliability of agreements with the U.S.S.R., views on the psychological impact of the nuclear-test suspension on people around the world, and the effects of nuclear fallout. [Ibid, pages 116–19, 133, and 136.]

5. The government continues to classify significant information dealing

with seismology, the study of earthquakes and movements in the interior of the earth. This includes testimony given before the Disarmament Subcommittee and documents submitted to the Subcommittee by Executive agencies. The Subcommittee has never received a satisfactory explanation as to why such studies should be kept secret. [This referred to the Berkner Panel report, which was eventually published. The Humphrey point, however, is still valid: It should have been released much earlier.]

Senator Humphrey ended his statement with the comment that "in most cases overclassification of information is not a deliberate effort to deceive the people or to protect the government from criticism. Generally, I think it is due to a habit of being overcautious, in other words, to follow the rule to classify when in doubt."

Dr. Edward Teller, in an article in *The New Leader* in 1960, stated his opposition to secrecy in these terms:

We have sought our safety in secrecy which is officially designated "security." What is the present value of this security? It has failed to prevent our worst enemies from acquiring every one of our major technical secrets. It has not delayed any country with fissionable materials from detonating an atomic bomb. To restrict the full functioning of the democratic process in order to buy this kind of "security" seems to indicate a diminished interest in democracy itself.

There is a further and deeper aspect to this question. Public interest in our secrets is not great. The average citizen is willing to leave the question of dangerous weapons to the specialist who is "cleared." Many citizens seem averse to giving thought to the distasteful problem of these weapons.

They would rather abolish the weapons themselves than learn about them. They do not even stop to inquire carefully how the question of secrets and weapons affect their fully justified and paramount desire for peace.

In another article, Dr. Teller discussed the costs of nuclear secrecy:

We have paid dearly. . . . We have erected artificial barriers between other free nations and ourselves. In an age which requires common action to build a lawful world-community, we have accepted the divisive power of secrecy.

Even our discussions with our closest allies have found secrecy standing in the way.

The French were forced to make an independent effort in order to explode an atomic bomb. Would it not have been wiser to employ the great talents of French scientists in a common undertaking, aimed at increasing Western security?

How can we expect that NATO shall develop the best plan for defense when the instruments of defense are not fully known to all participants? In order to be prepared, one has to foresee possible future weapon developments. This cannot be done as long as we keep our secrets.

Our own technical efforts are hampered by secrecy. If secrecy were abolished, the ideas of the whole scientific community would become available for our defense.

Today defense is discussed behind closed doors by highly able but limited groups of experts. Fast technical progress demands the widest participation.

All these arguments are important but in my opinion the greatest damage has been done in a different way.

We live in a democracy. Our collective actions are determined by the will of the people. This will cannot be reasonably guided in an atmosphere of secrecy.

I have given arguments to show that our people are misled when they believe that nuclear tests can be controlled. They would not have been misled if all the facts had been available to them all the time. The very aura of secrecy, which surrounds all matters nuclear, has prevented open discussion and has given rise to an emotional approach and to our present predicament.

Our society needs freedom of information if it is to function properly.

Details of military operation can and should be kept secret. We must not broadcast the positions of our nuclear submarines. But there are extremely strong arguments for complete freedom of technical information.

I do not propose that all our secrets should be declassified promptly but I do propose that in the next two or three years our secrecy policy should be carefully re-examined. I hope that such a re-examination will lead to an orderly liquidation of all technical secrets.

This we owe to our hopes for disarmament. We owe it to the unity of the Western world and we owe it to the unhampered exercise of the sovereign rights of our people.

Parade of Inconsistencies

In the course of the development of argumentation on the nuclear test-ban there sprang up a crop of tangled inconsistencies that defied efforts to disentangle. The inconsistencies were by no means monopolized by any one faction or nation or bloc.

1. The whole world has agreed on the urgent need for a damping of the arms race, but has spent more than four years trying to obtain an agreement that would not significantly reduce arms tensions—nuclear-warhead production would not be stopped, nuclear stockpiles would not be reduced, and no arms reductions would be made as a result of a test ban.

2. Many have argued that the United States is ahead of the Soviet Union in nuclear weapons and therefore should strive for an agreement to stop all tests while enjoying an advantage. But these same people used to argue that the Soviet Union is eager to stop testing. How the Soviet Union could voluntarily—and eagerly—accept a permanent disadvantage in the arms race has never been explained satisfactorily.

3. The Soviet Union has persistently demanded that the nuclear powers make a simple declaration renouncing all use of nuclear weapons. She is ostensibly willing to trust two potential enemies in such a declaration, but singularly unwilling to trust a single neutral administrator of the test-ban inspection system.

4. The Soviet Union has frequently claimed that limited nuclear war would be impossible—but has developed a formidable spectrum of small nuclear warheads for battlefield, or limited-war, use.

5. After denouncing Adlai Stevenson in 1956 for proposing a partial test ban, President Eisenhower in 1958 proclaimed a unilateral test ban on all nuclear-weapons tests, large and small.

6. After insisting for years that the cardinal principle of American disarmament policy was to provide for effective inspection accompanying any disarmament move, President Eisenhower subscribed to a unilateral moratorium on testing without any inspection at all, not even ineffective inspection. Later he agreed to an uninspected moratorium on small nuclear tests below the threshold represented by a seismic magnitude of 4.75.

7. Two American Presidents hesitated to resume nuclear tests, supposedly because of the politically unfavorable impression it would leave abroad. Yet both of them permitted their representatives at Geneva to threaten that a violation of the treaty would be followed by swift resumption of testing by the West. If world opinion would disapprove testing before a violation why would it not disapprove after a violation, especially if it were sufficiently ambiguous to provoke an international debate over whether a violation had actually occurred?

8. The same people who claim that the Russians are not really interested in tactical nuclear weapons also claim that the United States should press for a test ban so the Russians could not catch up with the United States—in tactical nuclear-weapons development.

9. Advocates of a test ban have often alleged that one of the principal by-products of success in the treaty negotiations would be to increase United States intelligence on the Soviet Union. But whenever the effectiveness of the proposed inspection system is questioned, the answer invariably comes back that traditional intelligence channels can be relied upon to do a better job than any international inspectorate that could be set up under the test-ban control system. Either the intelligence net presently operating in the Soviet Union is adequate or it is inadequate, but it cannot be both.

10. The United States, while professing as one of its main objectives in the nuclear test-ban negotiations the halting of a spread in nuclear-weapons knowledge to other nations, has itself been spreading nuclear-weapons information and parts to eight of its NATO allies: Canada, France, Greece, the Federal Republic of Germany, Italy, Netherlands, Turkey, and Britain.

11. Test-ban advocates said Russia could not afford to cheat, because she would be grievously embarrassed if she were caught. But the Communists dared to cheat on the Korean and Indochinese armistice agreements and seemed to bear up extremely well, if they suffered any embarrassment at all. The Russians later forced abandonment of the whole premise when they resumed testing in September, 1961, boasted of it, and tried to intimidate the world.

12. Many Administration officials helping to make disarmament policy have *assumed* that the Soviet Union has not been testing secretly since November, 1958. These same people have argued, however, that a costly twenty-station network inside the Soviet Union and a group of inspection teams conducting twenty on-site investigations a year would be necessary to detect underground tests of 20 kilotons or above. If it were safe to assume for nearly three years that the Soviet Union was not testing, it is difficult to see why an elaborate inspection system was thought necessary.

13. One of the favorite arguments offered on behalf of a test ban has been that there was nothing of further significance to be learned about nuclear weapons. But if nuclear-weapons development had already reached the point of diminishing returns, it would seem to be a waste of time to erect into a central feature of our disarmament policy a test-ban that would be meaningless when achieved.

14. Some people used to argue that a nuclear test ban really would not prevent the United States from getting a weapon to knock out enemy launching bases: To compensate for clumsy warheads all that had to be done was to improve the guidance of the missile-delivery systems, which would not be controlled. If the test ban would not prevent weapons development, where does its value lay? On the other hand, if the aim was genuine disarmament why was not the United States pressing as hard for control of missile development as for control of warhead development?

15. Advocates of the test ban usually were the same people who emphasized the need to guard against surprise attack and the dangers of accidental war. Yet they were willing to see a test ban take full effect before nuclear-weapons systems had been fully proof-tested. The area of proof-testing nuclear weapons was one of the most important in the prevention of accidental war. Reliability depended on frequent tests of the stockpile.

16. Dr. Edward Teller and all the advocates of resumed testing frequently volunteered their willingness to renounce tests in the atmosphere on the grounds these could be policed. But their own calculations had shown that even atmospheric testing could not be policed. Even if the Geneva control net were in operation, shots of several kilotons could pass without notice in the South Pacific; in the Pacific area near the

equator; or in thunderstorms, especially over water, so that the debris would be instantly washed out of the atmosphere and quickly dispersed.

17. All factions in the Administration accepted the possibility of decoupling up to a theoretical factor of 300, but they negotiated as if no decoupling possibility existed. When the threshold was set at magnitude 4.75, it was almost invariably defined as the equivalent of a nineteen- or twenty-kiloton explosion. Rarely if ever was it spelled out clearly that the threshold, translated accurately, was twenty kilotons Nevada-tuff coupled or six to sixty megatons decoupled. Getting a full decoupling factor of 300 to 3,000 for a 6- to 60-megaton shot admittedly might be impractical because of the size of the hole required. But decoupling factors of less than 300 were deemed quite feasible. Furthermore, the so-called twenty-kiloton threshold applied only in Nevada tuff. Actually the 4.75 threshold was later discovered to permit tests of 70 to 150 kilotons, fully coupled, in dry alluvium.

18. Practically every scientist with any experience in this field knows that nuclear technology is in its infancy. They know, too, that no one nation has a monopoly on advancement in the field, and that treaties cannot enforce thought control or keep scientists from thinking. Nevertheless, many scientists advising the government on disarmament policies have purveyed the notion that, for the sake of obtaining a treaty, it is safe for the United States to try to deprive itself indefinitely of the opportunity for making further progress in nuclear technology—in the scientific knowledge of seismic and outer-space phenomena, in the peaceful applications of nuclear explosions, and in offensive- and defensive-weapons developments of substantial significance.

Lessons

There are some lessons to be drawn from the history of the nuclear test-ban issue. One of the first is that it is extremely dangerous to put off a showdown with "world opinion" over issues vital to the national security. The United States got involved in a nuclear test-ban negotiation more because it "wanted to be nice" to the rest of the world than because it believed its own security interests would be served. It may or may not have been true that wiping out the danger of nuclear war would have been in the national interest, if it were even possible. But it was clearly perceived in the days before 1958 that a nuclear test ban alone could not possibly accomplish this. Later, the United States stumbled rather than walked into the test-ban ambush, humoring the worriers of the world, who depended on the United States for protection, rather than leading them. Humoring the fainthearted, when confronted with a ruthless adversary like Soviet communism, has proved to be a dangerous game.

If one measures it in terms of risking lives, bodily injury, or damage to future generations, the cost of humoring the fainthearted could well be thousands or millions of lives. The test ban could not outlaw nuclear war. It merely assures a dirty nuclear war if one were fought—and an untold higher cost in human misery from radioactive fallout.

Another lesson is that science and technology are advancing at such a swift rate that the old methods of negotiating treaties are hopelessly inadequate for achieving disarmament agreements. Science no longer stands still in any field. Changes are constant, unpredictable, and at paces that vary from the swift to the quantum jump. Whatever system of arms control we contrive, it must be able to survive scientific change. Inspection and control systems cannot be rigid; they must be extremely flexible to take account of this incessant scientific progress.

Scientific progress frequently left the diplomats discussing difficulties that had disappeared or become irrelevant. One can imagine the problems that would confront the control system once a test ban were in effect. Procedures would have to be revamped every few months, new platoons of inspectors with new fields of competence would have to be injected into the system periodically. In former times diplomacy had an answer: Generalize the agreement. But in the explosive age in which we live, generalizations are tantamount to complete ineffectiveness. On the other hand, detailed agreements are outdated before they can be printed.

Diplomatic "lead time" in achieving agreement, once the technological basis has been laid, extends into years, even decades. Meanwhile the technological basis changes.

The problem is to find some system to take into account the rapid pace of scientific progress. What the system should be, few pretend to know, and those who do pretend probably do not.

The quest for the test ban has shown, also, that singling out specific weapons systems for control is not feasible. The test ban, of course, could not properly be said to control even one full weapons system; instead, it would have merely slowed down development of the warheads for several systems. The delivery component, the airplane or rocket, was still being developed at top speed. And warhead production, on previously-engineered designs, was proceeding unchecked. One extremely dangerous "delivery system," hand carrying by secret agents, was not even a matter for discussion or concern.

But suppose, optimistically, that ten years of negotiations could bring the entire nuclear-rocket weapons system, whether land-based or sea-based, under effective control. That would still leave the whole spectrum of chemical- and biological-weapons systems untouched. These are not widely discussed. But both the Soviet Union and the United States have acknowledged they are prepared for this kind of warfare. During the

Korean War the Communist bloc launched a gigantic propaganda campaign accusing the United States of using "germ warfare," in what the West regarded apprehensively as the familiar Red technique of the thief crying "thief!"

There are at least as many if not more technical problems involved in chemical and biological warfare as in the nuclear field. But suppose the past experience enabled the negotiators to cut the "lead time" for an effective ban on chemical and biological warfare to five years. In the next fifteen years who is to say how many new weapons systems will have sprung up. This approach to the problem appears to be a losing game.

Wars and conflicts short of war are waged over a broad, complex spectrum. In recent years, the spectrum has been widened even more by the Communists. Meaningful disarmament, then, cannot be approached on so selective a basis.

Unfortunately, weapons systems are proliferating so fast—ask the budget-makers—that achieving a balance or a safe "mix" in a progressively disarming world has become nearly impossible.

To summarize, the piecemeal approach to disarmament is ineffective; the broad-spectrum approach is physically impossible. Disarmament by conventional means has proved to be what it has been before, a mirage.

Unless, that is, there would be some way to assure all the world, through complete openness, that no power was seeking military advantage or planning attack.

Another lesson of the test-ban exercise: Beware of the wishful thinkers. Deep fears always give rise to wishful thinking. Deep fears of nuclear weapons gave rise to wishful thinking that a nuclear test-ban could somehow send the threat of nuclear war away. The wishful thinkers overpowered the realists.

Soviet psychology took skillful advantage of the wishful thinkers.

We wished so hard for a test ban that we based our control system on hopelessly inadequate science. When it was shown to be hopelessly inadequate, in the spring of 1958, we simply closed our eyes to the facts and went along with the hopes. When the Hardtack II series showed us again that the science was inadequate, we put away a few hopes but still thought, wishfully, that a partial test ban could be salvaged. All the while, we were wishfully closing our eyes to the inadequacies of on-site inspection, the hopelessness of fixing responsibilities for nuclear tests, even if they were discovered and identified. The public wanted to believe that nuclear war could be avoided by a test ban and was willing to follow anyone who told them it was possible. It was a failure of leadership that the American people were never asked to face up to the hard realities.

Putting the lesson another way: Beware the enemy who tells you things you want to hear. A corollary is better known: Don't underestimate the potential of Soviet propaganda that seems obviously transparent to the sophisticated. It can still dupe the unsophisticated and may force the world to act irrationally.

The success of the Soviet campaign to stygmatize nuclear weapons, to inhibit the Western ability to use nuclear weapons and to slow nuclear-weapons development shows that the West cannot afford to sit back and rely on the "common sense" of the world. It is a necessity for the West to educate on a saturation basis, if the Soviet Union misleads on a saturation basis.

For instance, we could do worse than start now to point out, on a saturation basis, that the Soviet Union itself now relies on the stygmatized nuclear weapons; that failure of the United States to use nuclear weapons first might expose the free nations of Eurasia to superior Soviet conventional attack.

Here are other lessons to be learned:

1. Inspection programs would better be thought out in advance, in great detail—and tested—by the United States itself, to protect all its major national interests, before negotiations can be undertaken with the Soviet Union. The false first step at the 1958 Conference of Experts proved this.

2. Clean national strategy lines must be laid down before one can undertake serious disarmament negotiations. Part of the vaccillation in the American position on the test ban was due to lack of resolution on a grand national strategy.

3. Building national strength while negotiating disarmament is basically contradictory. Therefore, there will be frequent contradictory moments when those portions of the national effort to make America strong contradict, or at least oppose, efforts to halt the arms race. Until disarmament is more than a propaganda mirage, the arms race *always* rates priority.

4. Dependence of political negotiators on expert military and scientific advice has been made very clear. The need for developing a new kind of diplomat with broad military and scientific background is indisputable. The aim would not be to take military and scientific advisers out of the picture but to help the diplomat understand the advice—and heed it rather than ignore it.

5. Procrastination in taking hard decisions is self-defeating. The American negotiating position has suffered a damaging blow in the protracted Geneva negotiations on a nuclear test ban. It will be hard in the future for the Soviet Union to forget that it was able to draw the United States into a three-year moratorium, against its better judgment, merely by holding out the bait of a nonexistent first step toward disarmament. The United States went into the negotiations with two resolves: first, to insist on inspection of any disarmament; second, to test the sincerity of

the Soviet Union. Neither of the American resolves were maintained. The United States accepted an inspection system that was really a bad joke and kept its seat in the negotiations many months after it was clear the Soviet Union was not sincere. The dead end was clearly visible, certainly at the end of the Technical Working Group II conference in December, 1959, if it had not been clear earlier.

Perhaps it salves the conscience to think that the United States held off nuclear tests for thirty-four months, hoping against hope that the Soviet Union might be persuaded to accept a test ban. But, from the Kremlin, these years since 1958 must have looked like a triumph for the men who had succeeded in putting the American testing program into a strait jacket. It is all the more tragic to know that the American policymakers should have been fully forewarned. More importantly, Dr. Harold Brown, who subsequently became the Director of Research at the Defense Department, had warned that the test ban was really a will-o'-the-wisp.

History may yet look back on the nuclear-test-ban idea as one of the grand delusions of the twentieth century, grander by far, for instance, than the Soviet ruse that it was building a big fleet of long-range bombers, or that the Russians had invented everything important since the wheel.

It should be taken as a sobering warning that the Soviet Union was able, by a clever combination of propaganda manipulation and diabolical statesmanship to have tied up the United States testing program with so shabbily camouflaged a technique.

If the Americans let it happen again, either in the test field or general disarmament or some other area, we will have no one to blame but ourselves if Communism becomes the wave of the future.

Appendix I

REPORT OF THE CONFERENCE OF EXPERTS TO STUDY THE
METHODS OF DETECTING VIOLATIONS OF A POSSIBLE
AGREEMENT ON THE SUSPENSION OF NUCLEAR TESTS
AUGUST 21, 1958

Contents

I. INTRODUCTION

A. In accordance with an agreement reached as a result of an exchange of letters between the Chairman of the Council of Ministers of the Union of Soviet Socialist Republics, N. S. Khrushchev, and the President of the United States of America, Dwight D. Eisenhower, regarding the calling of a conference of experts to study the possibility of detecting violations of a possible agreement on the suspension of nuclear tests, there began on 1 July 1958, in Geneva, in the Palais des Nations, a conference of, on the one hand, experts from Western countries and, on the other hand, delegations of experts of the Union of Soviet Socialist Republics, the Polish People's Republic, the Czechoslovak Republic and the People's Republic of Romania.

B. The Secretary-General of the United Nations was represented at the Conference by his Personal Representative, Mr. T. G. Narayanan. Conference facilities and Secretariat services were provided by the United Nations. The Experts express their appreciation for the good offices of the Secretary-General and his Personal Representative, and for the services of the Secretariat staff attached to the Conference.

C. The agenda for the Conference, adopted on 4 July, included the following main questions:

1. Exchange of opinions on the problem of the various methods for detecting atomic explosions and on other general problems of the Conference deliberations.

2. Determination of a list of basic methods of systematic observations for phenomena indicative of an explosion.

3. A system for controlling the observance of an agreement on the cessation of nuclear tests.

4. Drawing up a report of experts to the governments of those countries repre-

sented at the Conference, with conclusions and suggestions regarding a system for controlling the observance of an agreement on the cessation of nuclear tests.

D. The Conference held thirty official sessions and completed its work on 21 August 1958. By prior agreement the Conference held its sessions in private.

E. The Conference of Experts considered the phenomena accompanying nuclear explosions set off under various conditions.

F. Some of these phenomena, namely the acoustic waves occurring when there are explosions in air and in water, the seismic oscillations that occur when there are explosions on the ground, under the ground, and underwater, the radio pulses that are produced when there are explosions in the atmosphere, and the optical and gamma radiation when propagated over long distances, serve to indicate explosions and to estimate their time and place.

G. When nuclear explosions occur in the atmosphere the radioactive debris which is formed mixes in the atmosphere, and is dispersed over great distances. If a nuclear explosion is set off in the ocean or in the earth's crust, the radioactive debris will remain concentrated close to the site of the explosion for a considerable time.

H. The sensitivity of modern physical, chemical, and geophysical methods of measurement makes it possible to detect nuclear explosions by the indications described above at considerable distances, as hereafter described. Thus it is known that explosions of high yield which are set off on the surface of the earth and in the lower part of the atmosphere can be detected without difficulty at points of the globe which are very remote from the site of the explosion. On the other hand, explosions which are of low yield (a few kilotons) can be detected with good reliability, given the present state of observational techniques, only if there is a specially set up control system such as that suggested in Section IV of this report.

I. A basic difficulty in detecting and identifying small explosions arises because many natural phenomena (earthquakes, thunderstorms, and others) give signals which are similar to those produced by explosions, or which by their presence hinder the detection of the signals sought.

J. The discrimination of the signals of natural events from signals of explosions is aided by a careful analysis of the recorded data, taking into account readings obtained at several points. Those remaining unidentified events which could be suspected as being nuclear explosions might be resolved by inspection of the site.

K. The Conference of Experts has considered the methods of detecting nuclear explosions by the acoustic, hydroacoustic, and seismic oscillations which they produce in the air, water, or in the earth's crust, and, also the detection of explosions by the electromagnetic oscillations which are propagated from them, and by the radioactive debris that the explosions cause.

L. The Conference has examined the effectiveness and limitations of each of these methods for the detection of nuclear explosions and it has agreed that the combined use of the various methods considerably facilitates the detection and identification of nuclear explosions.

M. After examining the separate methods, the Conference examined the question of the technical equipment of the control system necessary to detect and identify nuclear explosions, and, after that, it passed to the question of the control system as a whole.

N. As a result of the examination of these questions the Conference reached the conclusion that it is technically feasible to set up, with the capabilities and limitations indicated in Section IV of this report, a workable and effective control system for the detection of violations of an agreement on the world-wide cessation of nuclear-weapons tests.

O. In the present report information is given about the various methods of detection and identification of nuclear explosions, about the technical equipment of a control system and about a control system as a whole. Copies of the individual documents containing the conclusions adopted by the Conference on each of the questions mentioned are attached to the present report. Verbatim records and working documents in the working languages of the Conference will follow as soon as they are available for attachment to the report.

II. Basic Methods for Detection and Identification of Nuclear Explosions

A. Conclusions as to the Applicability of the Method of Recording Acoustic Waves for the Detection of Nuclear Explosions

The Conference of Experts examined the process of propagation of the acoustic waves caused by nuclear explosions and the methods of recording these waves with the aim of determining the possibility of using them for detecting nuclear explosions.

1. When there are explosions in air, a strong air acoustic wave is formed which propagates over large distances. An indication of the amplitude of the air pressure wave is given by a formula which is approximately valid for a homogeneous atmosphere and according to which this amplitude is proportional to the cube root of the yield and inversely proportional to the distance. However, the amplitude of this acoustic wave is strongly dependent upon meteorological conditions and cannot be predicted accurately by a simple formula of such a kind. The observed amplitude in certain cases can be five times larger or smaller than that predicted by a formulation which includes only the energy release and the distance to detecting station.

2. Existing apparatus of special design can detect the air wave from a one-kiloton explosion in the air above local background noise at relatively large distances.

The detection capability of a single station is strongly dependent upon the orientation of the propagation path to the station with respect to the upper winds. When the upper winds are mainly in one direction, a one-kiloton explosion can be detected with a high degree of confidence downwind at a distance of 2,000 to 3,000 kilometers and upwind at a distance of 500 kilometers. When the upper winds are erratic and the average wind is small, such as frequently happens in the spring and fall, detection of a one-kiloton explosion can be accomplished with a similar degree of confidence to a distance of approximately 1,300 kilometers independently of the direction. On the basis of the records from three stations, the location of the explosion can be determined with an accuracy of better than 100 kilometers.

3. The acoustic apparatus at control posts at the above distances from an explosion can detect explosions which occur between the surface and a height of 30 kilometers. A reasonable extrapolation of existing experience indicates that for explosions taking place up to an altitude of about 50 kilometers there should not be a great change in the detectability of the acoustic wave. Whether a substantial acoustic wave will be generated at higher altitudes is not well known from direct experiment or from any theoretical considerations so far discussed. Deep underground and underwater explosions do not produce air waves sufficiently intense for detection purposes.

An underwater explosion in the oceans generates very strong underwater sound waves (hydroacoustic), which even in the case of small explosions can be detected at distances of about 10,000 kilometers.

4. Acoustic waves which resemble in certain cases the acoustic signals of nuclear explosions may be produced by natural events (primarily meteoric, volcanic, or submarine disturbances). In such cases the identification of the event as natural or as a nuclear explosion must be based on a comparison of acoustic data with those obtained by aid of other methods.

5. It is noted that methods of recording of pressure waves may be further improved to increase the precision and the sensitivity, and to eliminate background noise and spurious signals.

B. Conclusions as to the Applicability of the Method of Using Radioactive Debris for Detecting and Subsequently Identifying Nuclear Explosions.

The Conference of Experts has studied the process of the dissemination of radioactive debris resulting from a nuclear explosion and has considered the collection of samples of radioactive debris and its analysis as one of the methods for detecting and subsequently identifying nuclear explosions.

1. When an explosion occurs a considerable quantity of radioactive debris is produced. If the explosion is based on a fission reaction then this quantity amounts to 3×10^8 curies per one kiloton TNT-equivalent of the energy of the explosion as of one hour after the reaction. Thermonuclear reactions will lead to the formation of carbon-14, tritium, and other radioactive substances which result from neutron irradiation and which, in principle, can also be used to detect an explosion.

2. When nuclear explosions occur between the earth's surface and a height of approximately ten kilometers the radioactive debris is thrown into the atmosphere where it is carried by winds to great distances. The concentration of this radioactive debris is greatly influenced by the vertical and horizontal distribution of the wind in the troposphere and in the lower layers of the stratosphere. The concentration is also decreased as a consequence of washing out by rain and gravitational deposition.

3. The distribution by height of the radioactive debris carried in the atmosphere will depend in the first place on the energy of the explosion, on the conditions in which the explosion took place (i.e., on the earth, under the earth, or in the air) and on the meteorological conditions at the moment of explosion. In the case of low-energy explosions in the air up to a height of approximately ten kilometers the radioactive debris will initially concentrate in a small volume below the tropopause. This debris will gradually get disseminated both horizontally and vertically in the troposphere and in the course of a period of from one to thirty days (depending on the turbulence of the atmosphere, the wind structure, and the dimensions of the particles which carry the radioactive substances) it can be detected close to the earth's surface, as also at various heights up to the tropopause.

4. The spreading of the cloud in the atmosphere is determined by many meteorological processes. As a result of the action of these processes the cloud is bound to reach a stage when it is mixed in a vertical direction and spread in a horizontal direction in such a way as to afford the most convenient conditions for taking samples.

Calculations and experimental data give ground for considering that this stage will be reached in the period between the fifth and twentieth day of the existence of the cloud. Before that period the cloud may be too small, both in its horizontal and its vertical extent. After thirty days have expired a considerable part of the radioactive debris will decay and a sample will constitute a lesser proportion of the natural or other background, thereby making more difficult the detection and identification of an explosion.

5. Existing radiochemical techniques make it possible to detect and identify fresh decay products in a sample of radioactive debris containing about 10^8 fissions. The time of origin of this fresh debris can be determined within 5 to 10 per cent of its age if the sample contains about 10^{10} fissions and is not contaminated to any considerable extent by old fission products.

6. The taking of samples on the surface of the earth by a network of control posts makes it possible to carry out continual monitoring of the contamination of the air at many separate points by means of air filtration and also by collecting radioactive fallout and fallout in rain. If control posts are disposed at distances of the order of 2,000 to 3,000 kilometers then an explosion with an energy of one kiloton set off in the troposphere (0–10 kilometers above the surface of the earth) will be detected with a high degree of reliability in the period of five to twenty days although the place of explosion will be determined with some error. Calculation shows that with favorable meteorological conditions an explosion of even lesser energy can be detected in this way.

In the course of the period of time of from two to five days after an explosion of energy equivalent to one kiloton the collection of a sample of radioactive debris from the explosion which is suitable for analysis can be effected in the air by an aircraft if the area of the supposed location of the cloud is known approximately. The taking of such a sample will make it possible to establish approximately the point of the explosion by means of using meteorological data for back-tracking the trajectory of movement of the cloud.

7. Underground or underwater explosions set off at shallow depths and accompanied

by the throwing up of earth or water can also be identified by the method of collecting radioactive samples although with lesser reliability than for explosions of the same energy in the troposphere.

8. The Conference of Experts considers that systematic measurements of radioactive substances in the air and also the collection of radioactive aerosols deposited on the ground and measurements of the radioactivity of precipitation can be successfully used for the detection of nuclear explosions and also, in many cases, for assessing certain parameters relating to them even in the absence of other indications.

The utilization for a regular control service, as a method for detecting nuclear explosions, of the taking of samples of the air by aircraft over oceans can be used for detecting nuclear explosions. For this purpose use should be made of existing aircraft flights over the oceans which are carried out by various countries for the purposes of meteorological observations.

9. The Conference of Experts considers that the method of taking samples of radioactive debris can also be used successfully for subsequent investigation of the fact of a nuclear explosion in those cases when there are appropriate indications from other methods.

For this purpose, it is possible to use the detection of radioactive debris remaining at the point of the supposed explosion (on the earth's surface, under the earth, in the water) and also the determination of the presence of a radioactive cloud in the period between two and five days after a supposed explosion in the atmosphere in the area where the cloud is calculated to be by the time of investigation.

In such a case, search for the radioactive cloud can be made on an aircraft having equipment for the taking of a sample of radioactive debris. To this end use should be made chiefly of the aircraft flights over the oceans made for the purposes of meteorological observations.

10. In some cases use can be made of aircraft flights over the territories of the U.S.A., the U.S.S.R., the U.K., and other countries to collect air samples for the purpose of checking on data obtained by other methods of detection of nuclear explosions.

The Experts consider that to accomplish this task it would be quite sufficient to make use of the aircraft of the country being overflown and that in such cases it is sufficient that flights for the purpose specified should be made along routes laid down in advance. Representatives of the U.S.S.R., the U.S.A., the U.K., or other States participating in the operation of the control system may be on board these aircraft in the capacity of observers.

11. The Experts note that in the course of time the sensitivity and efficiency of the method of collecting radioactive debris will increase, as a consequence of the atmosphere becoming cleared of the radioactive products it contains, and also as a result of the perfection of the techniques for collecting and analyzing samples.

C. Conclusions as to the Applicability of the Method of Recording Seismic Waves for the Detection of Nuclear Explosions.

The Conference has considered the processes of propagation of seismic waves generated by nuclear explosions and the methods for recording these waves for the purpose of determining the possibility of using them for the detection of underground and underwater nuclear explosions.

1. When nuclear explosions occur under the ground or under the water, longitudinal, transverse, and surface waves are formed and get propagated to great distances. The first longitudinal wave is the most important, both for detecting an explosion and for determining the place of the explosion, and also for distinguishing an earthquake from explosions. Transverse and surface waves also help to define the nature of a seismic perturbation.

2. Longitudinal seismic waves caused by underground nuclear explosions set off under conditions analogous to those in which the Rainier* shot occurred can be de-

---

* The underground nuclear explosion "Rainier" with an energy of 1.7 kilotons (Nevada) was set off in unfavorable conditions for transferring energy to the ground. However, even worse conditions of coupling are possible.

tected and the direction of first motion of the longitudinal wave can be determined at a distance of approximately 1,000 kilometers, and also at distances of approximately 2,000–3,500 kilometers at sites which are considerably more quiet than the average for: (*a*) explosions of the order of one kiloton recorded during periods of favorable noise conditions; (*b*) explosions of the order of five kilotons recorded during periods of unfavorable noise conditions.

It must be noted that all seismic stations situated at thousands of kilometers from one another cannot have an identically high or identically low level of background at one and the same time.

3. Conditions for detection and identification of underwater explosions set off in shallow water but at a sufficient depth, are considerably more favorable than conditions for detecting underground explosions.

4. Control posts carrying out seismic observations should be put at sites with a minimal level of microseismic background, such as are possible in internal continental regions. Such stations, when provided with arrays of seismographs, can ensure the obtaining of the data indicated above. However, at stations which are in unfavorable regions such as coastal and island regions the noise level will be higher than at quiet stations inside continents. In these cases for detection and determination of the sign of first motion the energy of the explosion must increase in the ratio of the power of 3/2 with respect to the increase of background level. This is in part compensated by the fact that quiet stations inside continents will register more powerful explosions at distances of from 2,000 to 3,500 kilometers. Bursts with an energy of five kilotons and more will be detected by quiet stations placed at the distances named.

5. The majority of earthquakes can be distinguished from explosions with a high degree of reliability if the direction of first motion of the longitudinal wave is clearly registered at five or more seismic stations on various bearings from the epicenter. Thus, not less than 90 per cent of all earthquakes taking place in continents can be identified. The remaining 10 per cent or less of cases will require the analysis of additional seismograms where this is possible; and for this purpose use must also be made of the data of the existing network of seismic stations. If required, these supplementary stations should be further equipped with improved apparatus. In relatively aseismic areas it is sufficient merely to define the position of the epicenter. In this connexion cases of detection of seismic events will be regarded as suspicious and will require further investigation with the help of other methods. For those cases which remain unidentified inspection of the region will be necessary.

In regions where the regular disposition of seismic stations in quiet conditions is not possible, the percentage of correct identification of earthquakes will be less.

With modern methods and making use of the data of several surrounding seismic stations the area within which an epicenter is localized can be assessed as approximately 100–200 square kilometers.

6. It is noted that the range and accuracy of recording and identifying underground nuclear explosions can be improved in the future by means of perfecting the methods of recording seismic waves, both by way of perfecting apparatus and also by way of perfecting the methods for differentiating an earthquake from explosions.

D. CONCLUSIONS ON THE APPLICABILITY OF THE METHOD OF RECORDING OF RADIO SIGNALS FOR THE DETECTION OF NUCLEAR EXPLOSIONS.

The Conference of Experts considered the generation and propagation of radio pulses originating from a nuclear explosion and the methods of recording these signals in order to determine the possibility of using them for the detection of nuclear explosions.

1. In the case of a nuclear explosion in the atmosphere, there arises a powerful electromagnetic radiation (radio signal), caused by the gamma radiation accompanying the explosion. In the case of underground, underwater, or specially shielded explosions radio emissions are not expected which can be recorded at great distances by modern techniques.

When the explosion is carried out on or above the surface of the earth (water) and without specially constructed layers to absorb gamma rays, the energy and spectral distribution of the radio signal are such that its essential components are propagated over the whole terrestrial globe. The strength of the radio signal depends upon certain features of the construction of the bomb and on the altitude of the explosion. An explosion of one-kiloton yield can be detected by means of radio signals at distances exceeding 6,000 kilometers assuming that in the neighborhood of the receiving station there is no high noise level from local thunderstorms or other sources.

By radio direction finding methods, it is possible to determine the azimuth of the signal source with an accuracy of about 2°, i.e., about 30 kilometers at a distance of 1,000 kilometers. The time of production of the signal may be established with an accuracy of several milliseconds. The attainment of such accuracy depends on the choice of sufficiently flat location and on the absence of electrical interference at the receiving site.

2. Lightning flashes emit radio signals in the same frequency range and act as interference for the method of detection of a nuclear explosion by means of its radio signal.

Close to the source of radiation, the forms of radio signals from lightning and from nuclear explosions examined to date are quite different. However, at distances exceeding 1,000 kilometers, due to the distortion of the form of radio signals in the wave guide formed by the earth and the ionosphere, the form of radio signals from some individual lightning flashes is similar to the signal from nuclear explosions. The number of signals from lightning flashes recorded by apparatus without using special techniques of signal selection depends on the sensitivity of the apparatus and on the locality, and can amount to from ten to several hundred signals per second. Existing techniques can be applied to exclude automatically the preponderant majority of signals from lightning. The distinction of the remaining signals due to atmospherics from those due to nuclear explosions requires the application of special methods of discrimination, including criteria on form of signal, spectral distribution and distance to source of radiation.

In the present state of the technique of the discrimination of signals in some individual cases the record of a signal cannot be identified either as coming from a nuclear explosion or from lightning.

3. The Conference of Experts recommends that further research should be carried out in order to understand more fully the physical properties of atmospherics involved in differentiating signals from nuclear explosions and atmospherics, by means of the development of the theory of this problem, the collection and systematization of data about atmospherics and the development of suitable automatic instruments. The Conference considers that there are good prospects for improvement of procedures of signal discrimination.

4. Theoretical considerations suggest that recording of radio signals can be used to detect nuclear explosions occurring at altitudes up to the order of 1,000 kilometers.

E. CONCLUSIONS ON THE METHODS OF DETECTION OF NUCLEAR EXPLOSIONS CARRIED OUT AT HIGH ALTITUDE (MORE THAN 30 TO 50 KILOMETERS) ABOVE THE EARTH

The Conference of Experts has given theoretical consideration to the gamma radiation and neutrons resulting from a nuclear explosion and the conditions of recording them from earth satellites; and to optical phenomena and ionization of the air in the upper layers of the atmosphere in the case of a high altitude explosion (altitudes above 30–50 kilometers) and has arrived at the following conclusions:

1. A kiloton nuclear explosion produces at its source delayed gamma-rays from fission products, and prompt gamma-rays and neutrons. The number of prompt gamma-rays and neutrons depends upon the construction of the device and upon the materials surrounding it. The delayed gamma-rays are insignificantly affected by these factors. At a distance of 10^4 kilometers *in vacuo*, typical quantities of radiation from a one-kiloton fission explosion are:

a. Delayed gamma-rays: 10^4 quanta/cm^2 during the first second;

b. Prompt gamma-rays:* 10^2 quanta/cm^2 distributed over a time of about 10^{-7} second;

c. Neutrons: 10^4 neutrons/cm^2 distributed over a time of a few seconds.

The cosmic background at the height at which earth satellites orbit is under study at the present time, attention being paid to the quantity, nature, and energy of the particles; however, on the basis of preliminary data, it can be considered that the detection of an explosion from an earth satellite is possible, by means of registering the gamma-rays accompanying the nuclear reaction, neglecting shielding, and also by means of registering the gamma-rays of the fission products and the neutrons. If both prompt gamma-rays and neutrons are registered, it is possible to get some idea of the distance to the explosion. The use of gamma-rays from a nuclear explosion will make it possible to detect the explosion in cosmic space at a distance of the order of hundreds of thousands of kilometers from the earth. Estimate of the maximum distance for the detection requires data concerning the magnitude of the cosmic radiation at the orbit of the earth satellite. If there is an explosion at a height of 30–50 kilometers and above, and if the height at which the earth satellite orbits is some thousands of kilometers, one can neglect the absorption of gamma quanta in the upper layers of the atmosphere. The Conference of Experts considers that it is possible to use for the detection of nuclear explosions at high altitudes the registration of gamma radiation and neutrons with properly instrumented earth satellites.

2. In the case of an explosion at a great height light will be emitted at the point of the explosion and there will be luminescence in the upper layers of the atmosphere under the action of X rays and fast atoms from the materials in the device. Light phenomena may be detectable from the surface of the earth in clear weather at night with the help of simple apparatus; in daytime with the help of more sensitive apparatus. In cloudy weather the detection of optical phenomena from stations on the earth's surface would probably be extremely difficult.

The radiation from a nuclear explosion creates in the upper layers of the atmosphere a region of increased ionization which is detectable by the absorption of cosmic radio signals or by anomalies in the propagation of radio waves.

Our knowledge of the absorption of cosmic noise by ionospheric phenomena is not sufficient to determine the number of natural events similar to those resulting from a nuclear explosion.

The Conference of Experts considers that it is possible to use the recording of ionospheric phenomena, using appropriate radio techniques, and of optical phenomena for the detection of nuclear explosions at high altitudes.

3. The Conference of Experts has not considered the problem of the detection of nuclear explosions which might be conducted in cosmic space at distances of millions of kilometers from the earth.

F. The Conference has recommended the inclusion of the first four of these methods in the number of basic methods for detecting nuclear explosions by means of a network of control posts, and considers it possible to use several methods for detection of nuclear explosions at high altitudes as stated in II-E-1 and II-E-2.

III. Conclusions on the Question of the Technical Equipment of the Control System for the Detection and Identification of Nuclear Explosions

The Conference of Experts has considered the questions related to the technical equipment of a control net intended to detect and identify nuclear explosions, and has come to the following conclusions:

1. The posts of the control net situated in continents should regularly be equipped

---

* Special shielding of the exploding device can considerably reduce the gamma radiation accompanying the reaction, but cannot reduce the radiation from fission products. However, such shielding involves increasing by several times the weight of the whole device.

with apparatus for the detection of explosions by the acoustic and seismic methods and also by the methods of recording radio signals and of collecting radio signals and of collecting radioactive debris.

2. Certain posts situated on islands or near the shores of oceans should be equipped, in addition to the methods just mentioned, with apparatus for hydroacoustic detection of explosions.

3. Posts located on ships stationed or drifting within specified ocean areas should be equipped with apparatus for the detection of explosions by the method of collecting radioactive debris and by the hydroacoustic method. The method of recording radio signals and the acoustic method might also be used on ships if suitable equipment is developed, but the effectiveness of these two methods, particularly the acoustic one, will be considerably less than on land.

4. The apparatus installed at posts of the control network must be uniform and must satisfy the following basic technical requirements:

A. SEISMIC APPARATUS

The seismic apparatus of the control post should include:

(1) Approximately ten short-period vertical seismographs dispersed over a distance of 1.5–3 kilometers and connected to the recording system by lines of cable. The seismographs should have a maximum magnification of the order of 10^6 at a frequency of one c.p.s. and a receiving band adequate to reproduce the characteristic form of the seismic signal;

(2) Two horizontal seismographs with the parameters indicated in point (1);

(3) One three-component installation of long-period seismographs having a broad receiving band and a constant magnification of the order of 10^3 to 2×10^3 in the period range 1–10 seconds;

(4) One three-component installation of seismographs with a narrow receiving band and magnification of the order of 3×10^4 when $T = 2$–2.5 seconds;

(5) At certain posts one three-component installation of long-period seismographs with magnification of the order of 10^4 to 2×10^4 at periods of $T = 25$ seconds;

(6) Auxiliary equipment necessary in order to get precise records of the seismic signal; recording devices, chronometers, power supply units and apparatus for receiving automatic radio-signals giving correct time.

The seismic apparatus should be installed in places with a minimal level of microseismic background, away from industrial areas, and on outcrops of bedrock (where possible). The seismographs should be installed in suitable vaults.

The area required for installing the seismic apparatus should be about 3×3 kilometers.

B. ACOUSTIC APPARATUS

(1) The infra-acoustic equipment for a control post should include not less than three sets of microbarographic units each of which should have: a system for averaging out turbulent noise, a pressure sensing unit, a transmission line, and appropriate electronic amplifiers and automatic writing instruments;

(2) The sensitivity of the microbarographic stations must ensure recording of acoustic signals in the period range 0.5–40 seconds, with an amplitude of 0.1 dynes/cm²;

(3) The pressure sensing units of the microbarographs should be dispersed at about ten kilometers from one another in order to determine the direction of arrival of the acoustic signal and the speed of propagation of the signal;

(4) The hydroacoustic apparatus for a post, which is recommended for use only in oceanic zones, should include several hydrophones placed in the main submarine sound channel.

The hydrophones should be connected with the recording station on the coast by cables. Recordings of the hydroacoustic signal should be made in several frequency subranges, covering a general frequency range of from one cycle per second to several thousand cycles per second.

The infra-acoustic equipment operates best in areas of low surface winds and flat terrain covered with trees or shrubs.

C. Apparatus for Recording a Radio Signal

The apparatus for recording a radio signal should consist of:

(1) A loop-shaped radio direction finder or a radio direction finder with vertical antennas dispersed 4–5 kilometers from one another, with a frequency range of 10–15 kilocycles per second which will detect signals as low as 2 millivolts per meter;

(2) A device for recording the form of the signal, the device to provide recording of the form of the radio pulse in a frequency range 500 c.p.s. to 200 kilocycles per second when the intensity of the field is 10 millivolts per meter and more;

(3) An automatic selecting device based on separating out the characteristic electromagnetic signals accompanying nuclear explosions by their form, by their spectral density, and by their amplitude, and a device for analyzing the signal spectrum that provides display of the spectral density of the signal in the frequency range 6–100 kilocycles per second. Although existing techniques exclude the preponderant majority of signals from lightning, further advantage will be taken of information from the acoustic, seismic, or other basic methods of detection to aid in further discrimination between signals from nuclear explosions and from lightning flashes;

(4) The requisite measuring and auxiliary apparatus and also power supply units and means for obtaining correct radio time signals.

The site on which the antennas and the electromagnetic recording apparatus are disposed should be on flat or rolling terrain with about 300 meters clear space around the antennas, and distant from sources of electrical interferences, power lines, and communications lines.

D. Apparatus for Collecting and Analyzing Radioactive Debris

The apparatus for collecting and analyzing radioactive debris should include:

(1) A large filtering installation with a through-put capacity of 2×10^4 cubic meters of air over 10–24 hours, and which is used on a 24-hour basis;

(2) Equipment for collecting radioactive depositions—a surface with about 100 square meters area should be used. During dry weather, the surface can be washed down to collect dry fallout;

(3) A laboratory for simple radiochemical analysis.

Apparatus should be located in open areas, preferably on high ground, with high precipitation frequency. Apparatus should not be located in cut-off valleys or near regions with high natural background.

E. Apparatus Installed on Aircraft for Collecting Radioactive Debris and Detection of a Radioactive Cloud

(1) A filtering installation for aircraft should provide for the collection of the maximum quantity of the products of radioactive decay, the rate of filtering being about 3,500 cubic meters an hour.

(2) The aircraft utilized for the collection of radioactive debris should have equipment for the comparatively fast determination of the presence of fresh radioactive debris.

(3) A small radiochemical laboratory will be located at each base for routine aircraft-sampling flights.

Aircraft flights over ocean areas should be laid out as nearly as possible in approximately a north-south direction, and located near the sides of the major continents, as well as in the center of oceans remote from continents.

5. All the apparatus of the control posts should be designed for reliable continuous operation.

6. Improved apparatus and techniques should be actively developed and expeditiously incorporated into the control system for the purpose of continuously improving the effectiveness for the detection and identification of nuclear explosions.

IV. Conclusions on a Control System for Detecting Violations
of a Possible Agreement on the Suspension of Nuclear Tests

The Conference of Experts, having considered a control system for detecting violations of a possible agreement on the suspension of nuclear tests, has come to the conclusion that the methods for detecting nuclear explosions available at the present time, viz., the method of collecting samples of radioactive debris, the methods of recording seismic, acoustic, and hydroacoustic waves, and the radio-signal method, along with the use of on-site inspection of unidentified events which could be suspected of being nuclear explosions, make it possible to detect and identify nuclear explosions, including low yield explosions (one to five kilotons). The Conference has therefore come to the conclusion that it is technically feasible to establish, with the capabilities and limitations indicated below, a workable and effective control system to detect violations of an agreement on the world-wide suspension of nuclear-weapons tests.

The Conference of Experts has come to the following conclusions regarding such a system:

1. The control system should be under the direction of an international control organ which would ensure the coordination of the activities of the control system in such a way that the system would satisfy the following technical requirements and perform the functions involved:

a. The development, testing, and acceptance of the measuring apparatus and of the equipment, and stating the criteria for the siting of the control posts;

b. Carrying out at the control posts and on aircraft, mentioned in item 3 and 5 of the present Conclusions, of continuous and effective observations for the phenomena which make it possible to detect nuclear explosions by the use of the methods recommended by the Conference;

c. Reliable communication, with the aid of existing channels where they are suitable for this purpose, between the international control organ on the one hand and, on the other hand, the control posts and the bases from which the regular aircraft flights are carried out; communications and transportation should ensure the speedy transmission of the results of observations, of data (including samples), of reports, and of necessary supplies;

d. Means of transport of personnel of the control posts in accordance with their duties and, so far as necessary, for the staff of the international control organ;

e. Timely analysis and processing of the data from the observations of the control posts with the aim of speedily identifying events which could be suspected of being nuclear explosions, and in order to be able to report thereon in such manner as is considered by governments to be appropriate;

f. Timely inspection of unidentified events which could be suspected of being nuclear explosions, in accordance with item 6 of the present Conclusions;

g. Staffing of the control system (the network of control posts on land, on ships, and on aircraft, and also the staff of the international control organ) with qualified personnel having appropriate fields of specialization;

h. Providing assistance in putting into effect a scientific research program, with the aim of raising the scientific standard of the system.

2. A network of control posts is characterized by three main parameters: (*a*) the minimum yield adopted for the nuclear explosion or the natural events giving equivalent signals; (*b*) the number of control posts; (*c*) the probability of correct identification of natural events, particularly earthquakes.

The dependence between these parameters is such that with an increase in the yield of the explosion or the number of control posts the probability of detection and identification increases, and the number of unidentified events suspected of being a nuclear explosion decreases. On the other hand, for the identification of the increased number of unidentified events resulting from a smaller number of control posts it would be necessary to increase the number of on-site inspections or to make greater use of information coming from sources not subordinate to the international control organ or, if necessary, both.

The Conference considers that the problem of detecting and identifying underground explosions is one of the most difficult, and that, to a large extent, it determines the characteristics of the network of control posts.

3. The network of control posts would include from 160 to 170 land-based control posts (equipped in accordance with Section III of this report) and about 10 ships. Of these 160–170 control posts, about 100–110 would be situated in continents, 20 on large oceanic islands, and 40 on small oceanic islands; however, the exact number of control posts within the limits indicated above, can be determined only in the process of actually disposing them around the globe, taking into account the presence of noise at the sites at which they are located, and other circumstances.

The spacing between the control posts in continental aseismic areas would be about 1,700 kilometers, and in seismic areas about 1,000 kilometers. The spacing between the control posts in ocean areas would vary between 2,000 and more than 3,500 kilometers; the spacing between island control posts in seismic areas would be about 1,000 kilometers. This would lead to the following approximate distribution of control posts over the globe (with a network including 110 continental posts): North America, 24; Europe, 6; Asia, 37; Australia, 7; South America, 16; Africa, 16; Antarctica, 4; together with 60 control posts on islands and about 10 ships.

4. The tasks of the personnel of the control posts would include the ensuring of the normal functioning of apparatus, the preliminary processing of data received, and the forwarding of these data to the international control organ and to the government of the country on whose territory the control post is located in such a manner as may be considered appropriate by governments.

In order to carry out the tasks required one might need for each control post about thirty persons with various qualifications and fields of specialization, and also some persons for the auxiliary servicing staff.

5. In addition to the basic network described, air sampling would be accomplished by aircraft carrying out regular flights along north-south routes over the oceans along the peripheries of the Atlantic and Pacific Oceans, and also over areas of the oceans which are remote from surface control posts.

When it is necessary to investigate whether a radioactive cloud is present, in the case of detection of an unidentified event which could be suspected of being a nuclear explosion, special aircraft flights would be organized in order to collect samples of radioactive debris in accordance with Section II-B-10.

6. When the control posts detect an event which cannot be identified by the international control organ and which could be suspected of being a nuclear explosion, the international control organ can send an inspection group to the site of this event in order to determine whether a nuclear explosion had taken place or not. The group would be provided with equipment and apparatus appropriate to its task in each case. The inspection group would forward a report on the investigation it had carried out to the international control organ, and to the government of the country on the territory of which the investigation was made in such a manner as may be considered appropriate by governments.

7. The network of control posts disposed as described, together with the use of aircraft as described, would have the following effectiveness, subject to the qualifications discussed in items 8 and 9:

a. Good probability of detecting and identifying nuclear explosions of yields down to about 1 kiloton, taking place on the surface of the earth and up to 10 kilometer altitude, and good probability of detecting, but not always of identifying, explosions taking place at altitudes from 10 to 50 kilometers. In these cases the independent methods enumerated in Sections II-A, II-B, and II-D would be used.

b. Good probability of detecting nuclear explosions of one-kiloton yield set off deep in the open ocean. In this case, use would be made of the independent hydroacoustic and seismic methods described in Sections II-A and II-C.

The identification of underwater explosions can, in comparatively rare cases, be made more difficult by natural events which give similar hydroacoustic and seismic signals.

c. Good probability of recording seismic signals from deep underground nuclear explosions in continents equivalent to one kiloton and above. In this case use would be made of the seismic method described in Section II-C.

The problem of identifying deep underground explosions is considered in item 8.

8. Along with the observation of signals of possible underground explosions the control posts would record at the same time a considerable number of similar signals from natural earthquakes. Although, with the present state of knowledge and techniques, the network of control posts would be unable to distinguish the signals from underground explosions from those of some earthquakes, it could identify as being of natural origin about 90 per cent of the continental earthquakes, whose signals are equivalent to five kilotons, and a small percentage of continental earthquakes equivalent to one kiloton.*

It has been estimated on the basis of existing data that the number of earthquakes which would be undistinguishable on the basis of their seismic signals from deep underground nuclear explosions of about five-kiloton yield could be in continental areas from 20 to 100 a year. Those unidentified events which could be suspected of being nuclear explosions would be inspected as described in item 6.

The capability of the control system to identify underground nuclear explosions of one- to five-kiloton yield depends on:

a. The small fraction of earthquakes that can be identified on the basis of data obtained from the control posts alone;

b. The fraction of earthquakes that can be identified with the aid of supplementary data obtained from existing seismic stations; and

c. The fraction of events still left unidentified which could be suspected of being nuclear explosions and for which the international control organ carries out inspection in accordance with item 6.

Although the control system would have great difficulty in obtaining positive identification of a carefully concealed deep underground nuclear explosion, there would always be a possibility of detection of such a violation by inspection.

The on-site inspection carried out by the international control organ in accordance with item 6 would be able to identify with good probability underwater nuclear explosions with a yield of one kiloton and above.

9. The Conference notes that in certain special cases the capability of detecting nuclear explosions would be reduced; for instance, when explosions are set off in those areas of the ocean where the number of control posts is small and the meteorological conditions are unfavorable; in the case of shallow underground explosions; when explosions are set off on islands in seismic regions; and in some other cases when the explosion is carefully concealed. In some cases it would be impossible to determine exactly the area in which a nuclear explosion that had been detected took place.

However, the Conference considers that, whatever the precautionary measures adopted by a violator, he could not be guaranteed against exposure, particularly if account is taken of the carrying out of inspection at the site of the suspected explosion.

10. The system described does not include specific means to detect and identify nuclear explosions at high altitudes (above 30–50 kilometers). The Conference has formulated its findings on the methods of detecting nuclear explosions set off at altitudes greater than 30–50 kilometers and has characterized these methods in Section II-E.

11. The Conference of Experts recommends the control system described above for consideration by governments.

---

* The Conference notes that in order to increase the percentage of earthquakes of less than 5 kiloton yield which could be identified, it would be appropriate to supplement the data from the control posts by trustworthy data from the best existing seismic stations. The results of the observations of these seismic stations should, for this purpose, be made available to the international control organ, and the equipment of the seismic stations suitable for this purpose could be improved by using the best modern apparatus.

The following experts participated as delegates at the Conference:

Western Experts
Dr. James B. Fisk
Dr. Robert F. Bacher
Sir John Cockcroft
Dr. Ernest O. Lawrence
Sir William Penny
Prof. Yves André Rocard
Dr. O. M. Solandt

Delegations of:
Union of Soviet Socialist Republics
E. K. Fedorov
N. N. Semenov
I. E. Tamm
M. A. Sadovski
O. I. Leipunski
I. P. Pasechnik
K. E. Gubkin
S. K. Tsarapkin

Polish People's Republic
M. Miesowicz
L. Jurkiewicz
M. Blusztajn

Czechoslovak Republic
Č. Simáně
F. Běhounek
A. Zátopek
Z. Trhlik

People's Republic of Romania
H. Hulubei

Appendix II

CONFERENCE ON THE DISCONTINUANCE OF
NUCLEAR WEAPON TESTS

Draft Treaty on the Discontinuance of
Nuclear Weapon Tests

The United States and United Kingdom Delegations to the Conference on the
Discontinuance of Nuclear Weapon Tests introduced in the Conference on April 18,
1961, the full text of a Treaty for the Discontinuance of Nuclear Weapon Tests consisting of twenty-four Articles and three Annexes, a number of which have already
been adopted by the Conference. Both the United States and United Kingdom Delegations declared their readiness immediately to sign a treaty along the lines of the draft
submitted.

The Treaty completely prohibits weapon-test explosions in the atmosphere, in outer-
space, underwater, and—except for explosions producing smaller seismic signals—underground. Tests producing such explosions would be temporarily prohibited through a
moratorium voluntarily undertaken by each nuclear power, while an effort was made
through a seismic research program to improve methods of monitoring them with a
view to lowering the Treaty threshold.

A world-wide control-post net of 180 stations is to be set up, under the Treaty,
within six years; in the same period, earth- and solar-satellite systems are to be launched
to detect outer-space explosions.

Unidentified seismic events are to be inspected by teams of specialists. Control operations are undertaken by an international staff so constituted as to avoid self-inspection.

Nuclear explosions for research and other peaceful purposes are permitted under
strict safeguards.

Thus, for the first time since it began, the Conference has before it a complete treaty
with provisions for adequate controls, on the basis of which the nuclear test-ban negotiations can be brought to a successful conclusion.

[Asterisks denote articles agreed upon by the three negotiating powers.]

Preamble*

The Parties to this Treaty

Pursuing the aim of reducing international competition in armaments and in the
development of new weapons of war;

Endeavoring to take a practical step towards the achievement of the objectives of the
United Nations in the field of disarmament, including the eventual elimination and
prohibition of nuclear weapons under effective international control and the use of
atomic energy for peaceful purposes only;

Desirous of bringing about the permanent discontinuance of nuclear-weapon-test
explosions;

Recognizing that the establishment and continuous operation of effective international control is essential to the achievement of this objective;

Hoping that all other countries will also join in undertaking not to carry out nuclear-
weapon tests and to ensure the satisfactory operation of that control throughout the
world;

Confident that a discontinuance of such tests under effective control will make possible progress toward agreement on measures of disarmament

Have agreed as follows:

Article 1. Obligations to Discontinue

1. Each of the Parties to this Treaty undertakes, subject to the provisions of this
Treaty and its Annexes: (a) to prohibit and prevent the carrying out of nuclear-weapon-

test explosions at any place under its jurisdiction or control and; (*b*) to refrain from causing, encouraging, or in any way participating in, the carrying out of nuclear-weapon-test explosions anywhere.

2. The obligations under paragraph 1 of this Article shall apply to all nuclear-weapon-test explosions except those underground explosions which are recorded as seismic events of less than magnitude 4.75.

ARTICLE 2.* ESTABLISHMENT OF CONTROL ORGANIZATION

1. For the purpose of assuring that the obligations assumed in this Treaty are carried out by the Parties, there is hereby established a Control Organization, hereinafter referred to as "the Organization," upon the terms and conditions set forth in this Treaty and the Annexes thereto.

2. Each of the Parties agrees to cooperate promptly and fully with the Organization established under paragraph 1 of this Article and to assist the Organization in the discharge of its responsibilities pursuant to the provisions of this Treaty and the provisions of any agreements which the Parties shall have concluded with the Organization.

ARTICLE 3. ELEMENTS OF CONTROL ORGANIZATION

1. The Organization established under Article 2 of this Treaty shall consist of: a Control Commission, hereinafter referred to as "the Commission"; a Detection and Identification System, hereinafter referred to as "the System"; a Chief Executive Officer, hereinafter referred to as "the Administrator"; and a Conference of Parties to the Treaty, hereinafter referred to as "the Conference."

2. The Headquarters of the Organization shall be located at Vienna.

ARTICLE 4. COMPOSITION OF CONTROL COMMISSION[1]

[1] The above revised text is submitted in the context of the statements made by the United States and United Kingdom Representatives at the 274th, 286th, and 289th meetings, to the effect that the United States and United Kingdom Governments are prepared to accept the above text provided expressly, and not otherwise, that agreement is reached by his Conference upon a control system which is reliable, rapid, and effective—such as is set forth in other Articles and Annexes of the present draft-treaty proposal—and provided that agreement is reached upon all other Treaty Articles and Annexes.

1. The Commission shall consist of the following Parties:

a. The Union of Soviet Socialist Republics, the United Kingdom of Great Britain and Northern Ireland, and the United States of America, as original Parties to this Treaty; and

b. Eight other Parties to the Treaty elected by the Conference as follows: Three Parties associated with the U.S.S.R.; two Parties associated with either the United Kingdom or the United States; three Parties not associated with any of the original Parties.

2. The Parties referred to in paragraph 1-B of this Article shall be elected and shall serve for a period of two years; they shall be eligible for re-election.

3. The Parties elected to the first-elected Commission shall serve from the time of their election until the end of the third regular session of the Conference. The Parties elected at the third regular session of the Conference, and those elected biennially thereafter, shall serve from the end of the Conference at which they were elected until the end of the Conference which elects their successors.

4. Each member of the Commission shall have one representative.

ARTICLE 5. PARTIES OR OTHER COUNTRIES ASSOCIATED WITH THE ORIGINAL PARTIES

The determination whether a Party or other country is at any time to be regarded for the purposes of this Treaty as associated with any of the original Parties shall be made by the Preparatory Commission or by the Commission. However, in any case in which advice is jointly tendered by the three original Parties, the determination shall be made in accordance with that advice.

Article 6. Functions of the Control Commission

1. The Commission shall establish procedures and standards for the installation and operation of all elements of the System, and shall maintain supervision over the System to ensure its timely installation and effective operation in accordance with the terms of this Treaty and its Annexes. The Commission shall determine, after consultation with the Parties concerned, the extent to which existing launching, tracking, and data receiving and transmission facilities should be used in the installation and operation of the satellite systems.

2. *a.* The Commission shall appoint the Administrator; this appointment shall require the concurring votes of the original Parties.

b. (*i*) Subject to the approval of the Commission in each case, the Administrator shall appoint five Deputy Administrators, including one first Deputy Administrator who shall act in place of the Administrator in case of absence or vacancy.

(*ii*) Approval by the Commission of the appointment of the First Deputy Administrator shall require the concurring votes of the original Parties.

(*iii*) Appointment by the Administrator of two Deputy Administrators shall be made upon the recommendation, or with the approval of the Government of the U.S.S.R.; appointment of the two other Deputy Administrators shall be made upon the recommendation, or with the approval, of the Governments of the United Kingdom and the United States.

c. The term of office of the Administrator shall be a period of three years. The initial term of office of the First Deputy Administrator shall be a period of two years; subsequently, the term of office of the First Deputy Administrator shall be a period of three years. The term of office of the other Deputy Administrators shall be a period of three years.

d. The Administrator and the Deputy Administrators shall be eligible for reappointment. An Administrator or Deputy Administrator appointed to fill a vacancy which has occurred before the expiration of the term provided for by this Article shall hold office only for the remainder of his predecessor's term but shall be eligible for reappointment.

3. The Commission shall establish procedures for disseminating to all Parties and interested scientific organizations data produced by the System.

4. The Commission shall submit to the Conference an annual report and such special reports as the Commission deems necessary on the operation of the System and on the activities of the Commission and the Administrator in carrying on their respective responsibilities. The Commission shall also prepare for the Conference such reports as the Organization may make to the United Nations.

5. Except for the location of the Headquarters of the Organization, the Commission shall decide upon the location of components of the System. Such decisions shall be taken in agreement with the Party exercising jurisdiction or control over the territory on which the component is to be located. If any location recommended by the Commission should be unacceptable to the Party concerned, the Party shall provide, without undue delay, an alternative location which in the judgment of the Commission meets the requirements of the System, in accordance with the provisions of this Treaty and its Annexes.

6. The Commission shall lay down permanent flight routes, for use by special aircraft sampling missions, over the territory under the jurisdiction or control of each Party. Such flight routes shall be laid down in agreement with the Party concerned and in accordance with the standards set forth in Article 7 of Annex I. If a permanent flight route which the Commission desires to lay down should be unacceptable to the Party concerned, the Party shall provide, without undue delay, an alternative route which in the judgment of the Commission meets the requirements of the System.

7. The Commission may conclude agreements with any State or authority to aid in carrying out of the provisions of this Treaty and its Annexes.

8. The Commission shall ensure that the most effective and up-to-date equipment and techniques are incorporated in the System and, to this end, shall ensure that an adequate research and development program is carried out.

9. The Commission shall establish procedures for the implementation of Article 13 on detonations for peaceful purposes.

10. In addition to the functions referred to in the preceding paragraphs of this Article, the Commission shall perform such other functions as are provided for in this Treaty and its Annexes.

Article 7. Procedures of the Control Commission

1. The Commission shall be so organized as to be able to function continuously.

2. The Commission shall meet at such times as it may determine, or within twenty-four hours at the request of any member. All members shall be notified in advance of meetings of the Commission. The meetings shall take place at the Headquarters of the Organization unless otherwise determined by the Commission.

3. The Commission shall adopt its own rules of procedure including the method of selecting its chairman.

4. Any Party to the Treaty which does not have a representative on the Commission may participate, without vote, in the discussion of any question brought before the Commission whenever the latter considers that the interests of that Party are specially affected.

5. Except as otherwise expressly provided in this Treaty, decisions of the Commission shall be made by a simple majority of the members present and voting. Each member of the Commission shall have one vote.

Article 8.* The Conference

1. The Conference consisting of representatives of Parties to this Treaty shall meet in regular annual session and in such special sessions as shall be convened by the Administrator at the request of the Commission or of a majority of Parties to the Treaty. The sessions shall take place at the Headquarters of the Organization unless otherwise determined by the Conference.

2. At such sessions, each Party to the Treaty shall be represented by not more than three delegates who may be accompanied by alternates and advisers. The cost of attendance of any delegation shall be borne by the State concerned.

3. The Conference shall elect a President and such other officers as may be required at the beginning of each session. They shall hold office for the duration of the session. The Conference, subject to the provisions of this Treaty, shall adopt its own rules of procedure. Each Party to the Treaty shall have one vote. Decisions on budgetary matters shall be made pursuant to Article 15 and decisions on amendments pursuant to Article 23. Decision on other questions, including the determination of additional questions or categories of questions to be decided by a two-thirds majority, shall be made by a simple majority of the Parties to the Treaty present and voting.

4. The Conference may discuss any questions or any matters within the scope of this Treaty or relating to the powers and functions of any organs provided for in this Treaty and may make recommendations to the Parties or to the Commission or to both on any such questions or matters.

5. The Conference shall:

a. elect States to serve on the Commission in accordance with Article 4;

b. consider the annual and any special report of the Commission;

c. approve the budget recommended by the Commission in accordance with paragraph 1 of Article 15;

d. approve reports to be submitted to the United Nations as required by any relationship agreement between the Organization and the United Nations or return them to the Commission with the recommendations of the Conference;

e. approve any agreement or agreements between the Organization and the United Nations or other organizations as provided in Article 17, or return such agreement with its recommendations to the Commission for resubmission to the Conference;

f. approve amendments to this Treaty in accordance with Article 23.

6. The Conference shall have the authority:

a. to take decisions on any matter specifically referred to the Conference for this purpose by the Commission;

b. to propose matters for consideration by the Commission and request from the Commission reports on any matter relating to the functions of the Commission.

ARTICLE 9. ADMINISTRATOR AND INTERNATIONAL STAFF

1. The Administrator shall be the chief executive officer of the System and the head of the staff of the Organization. He shall be responsible to the Commission and, under its supervision, shall carry out its policy directives. He shall have executive responsibility for the installation and operation of the System under procedures and standards established by the Commission. He shall provide to the Commission such advice, reports and assistance as the Commission may request.

2. The Administrator and the staff shall not seek or receive instructions concerning the performance of their duties for any authority external to the Organization. They shall refrain from any action which might reflect on their status as international officials and employees responsible only to the Organization. Each Party undertakes to respect the international character of the responsibilities of the Administrator and staff and not to seek to influence them in the discharge of their duties.

3. Except as otherwise provided in this Treaty, the Administrator shall appoint, organize, and direct the staff of the Organization in accordance with the following provisions:

a. The staff shall include such qualified scientific, technical, and other personnel as may be required to carry out the functions of the Organization with the highest standards of efficiency, technical competence, and integrity.

b. The staffing of individual components of the System shall be designed so as to ensure maximum operating efficiency.

c. In keeping with the foregoing stipulations, the staff of the Organization shall be recruited on as wide a geographical basis as possible from personnel recommended by, or acceptable to, the governments of the countries of which they are nationals and acceptable to the Administrator, subject to the following provisions:

(*i*) The permanent administrative, scientific, and technical staff of the Headquarters of the Organization shall, as a whole and at all levels, be composed in equal proportions of nationals of the U.S.S.R., nationals of the United Kingdom or the United States, and nationals of other countries. In cases where deputies, other than the Deputy Administrators, to senior officials of the Organization Headquarters are appointed, a national of the U.S.S.R. shall have a deputy who is a national of the United Kingdom or of the United States, and a national of the United Kingdom or the United States shall have a deputy who is a national of the U.S.S.R.

(*ii*) In land control posts situated on territory under the jurisdiction or control of any of the original Parties, the scientific and technical staff of each post shall be composed in equal proportions of nationals of the U.S.S.R., nationals of the United Kingdom or the United States, and nationals of other countries. In the appointment of nationals of other countries, preference shall be given, subject to other provisions of subparagraph (*c*) of this Article, to nationals of countries exercising jurisdiction or control over territory upon which control posts are to be established.

(*iii*) In land control posts situated on territory under the jurisdiction or control of Parties other than the original Parties, no more than one-third of the scientific and technical staff of each post shall be composed of nationals of the country exercising jurisdiction or control over the territory on which the control post is situated.

(*iv*) The supporting and auxiliary staffs of each land control post shall, wherever possible, be composed of nationals of the country exercising jurisdiction or control over the territory on which the control post is located.

(*v*) The scientific and technical staffs of control posts on ships or in areas not under the jurisdiction or control of sovereign states and the members of the staff of the Organization selected by the Administrator for the purposes of paragraph 3 of Article 11 of Annex I shall be composed in equal proportions of nationals of the U.S.S.R., nationals of the United Kingdom or the United States, and nationals of other countries.

(*vi*) The chief or acting chief of each control post shall be a national of a country other than that exercising jurisdiction or control over a territory on which the control post is situated. If the country exercising jurisdiction or control over such territory is associated with an original Party, the chief or acting chief of the control post shall be a national of other than such original Party or a country associated with it.

(*vii*) The chief or acting chief of each control post situated on territory under the jurisdiction or control of the United States or the United Kingdom shall be a national of the U.S.S.R., the chief or acting chief of each control post situated on territory under the jurisdiction or control of the U.S.S.R. shall be a national of the United States or the United Kingdom.

(*viii*) The scientific and technical staffs of on-site inspection groups shall be composed of technically qualified personnel who are not nationals of the country exercising jurisdiction or control over the territory in which the event under investigation may have occurred. The Party exercising jurisdiction or control over such territory may designate one or more observers to accompany the inspection group.

(*ix*) The scientific and technical staff of any on-site inspection group despatched to conduct an inspection on territory under the jurisdiction or control of the U.S.S.R. shall be composed of nationals of the United States or the United Kingdom; the scientific and technical staff of any on-site inspection group despatched to conduct an inspection on territory under the jurisdiction or control of the United States or the United Kingdom shall be composed of nationals of the U.S.S.R.

(*x*) The U.S.S.R. or the United Kingdom and the United States may authorize the Administrator to depart from the requirements of subparagraphs (*i*) through (*ix*) above, insofar as they concern the appointment of their respective nationals to scientific and technical staff positions, either in favor of the nationals of another Party or other Parties or without restriction. In each case, the original Party or Parties concerned shall furnish the Administrator in writing with the authorization, including the period of its duration. Notwithstanding the authorization made under this paragraph, the nationals so appointed shall be considered, for the purposes of subparagraphs (*i*), (*ii*), and (*v*) to be nationals of the original Party authorizing the departure.

(*xi*) In making appointments under subparagraphs (*i*), (*ii*), (*iii*), and (*v*), the Administrator shall ensure that the administrative, scientific and technical staff of the Headquarters of the Organization, and the scientific and technical staff of each control post, shall be so composed that the total number of nationals of the U.S.S.R. and of countries associated with it shall be equal to the total number of nationals of the United States and the United Kingdom and of countries associated with either of them.

(*xii*) Any adjustment to the proportions in subparagraphs (*i*), (*ii*), and (*v*) above, which may be unavoidable for practical reasons, shall be kept to the minimum, and a compensating adjustment shall, whenever possible, be made elsewhere in the System.

d. Regulations governing the appointment, remuneration, and dismissal of staff shall be approved by the Commission.

4. The Administrator shall prepare for the Commission the budget estimates of the Organization.

5. The Administrator shall develop and arrange for the execution of a program of research and development for the continuing improvement of the equipment and techniques used in all components of the System, and shall from time to time make recommendations to the Commission regarding improvements to be incorporated in the System. The program may, with the approval of the Commission, include detonations performed to test the effectiveness of the System. Any nuclear detonations for this purpose shall be conducted under the procedures set forth in Article 13.

6. The Administrator shall prepare recommendations for approval by the Commission regarding:

(*a*) specific sites for all components of the System; (*b*) specific flight patterns for routine air sampling flights; (*c*) the number and base location of inspection groups; (*d*) the equipping of all components of the System and the standards and specifications which equipment to be used therein must meet.

7. a. When special aircraft sampling missions are undertaken, the Administrator shall appoint two qualified members of the Organization staff to accompany each

aircraft as technical operators. The technical operators shall, in accordance with the provisions of Article 7 of Annex I, verify the execution of the agreed flight plan; operate the sampling equipment; direct sampling operation; make appropriate arrangements for the safe delivery to the Organization of the samples collected; and report on the mission to the Administrator.

b. (*i*) The technical operators shall not be nationals of (*a*) any Party exercising jurisdiction or control over territory in which the event under investigation may have occurred, or of (*b*) any original Party which may be associated with the Party in paragraph 7*b* (*i*) (*a*) of this Article, or of (*c*) any Party which may be associated with any original Party to which paragraphs 7*b* (*i*) (*a*) or 7*b* (*i*) (*b*) of this Article may refer; nor, subject to the provisions of subparagraph *b* (*ii*), shall they be nationals of any Party exercising jurisdiction or control over territory in the air space over which samples may be taken.

(*ii*) On flights investigating events which may have occurred in territory under the jurisdiction or control of the U.S.S.R., the technical operators shall be nationals of the United Kingdom or the United States. On flights investigating events which may have occurred in territory under the jurisdiction or control of the United Kingdom or the United States, the technical operators shall be nationals of the U.S.S.R.

c. Any Party exercising jurisdiction or control over territory in which the event under investigation may have occurred or in the air space over which samples are to be taken may designate an observer to accompany the technical operators on the flight.

8. The Administrator shall determine when special aircraft sampling missions are required in accordance with the terms of Article 7 of Annex I and shall have authority to order the despatch of such missions. For missions whose purpose is the collection of samples over the territory of a Party or Parties, the Administrator shall select routes from among the permanent flight routes laid down by the Commission in accordance with paragraph 6 of Article 6; before despatch of the mission, the Administrator shall notify all Parties over whose territories it will fly and shall inform them of the routes selected.

9. The Administrator shall forward to the Commission within twenty-four hours after receipt all reports submitted to him by inspection teams and special aircraft missions, together with any relevant data and analyses.

10. The Administrator shall encourage and facilitate the participation by personnel of components of the System in programs of basic scientific research, to the extent that such participation would not interfere with their primary duties.

11. In addition to the functions referred to in the preceding paragraphs of this Article, the Administrator shall perform such other functions as are provided for in this Treaty and its Annexes.

ARTICLE 10. ON-SITE INSPECTION OF SEISMIC EVENTS

1. *a.* The Administrator shall certify immediately by public notice at the Headquarters of the Organization whenever he determines that an event eligible for on-site inspection in accordance with the provisions of Article 8 of Annex I has occurred. This certification shall include a specification of the time of origin and location of the seismic event, the area eligible for inspection (hereinafter referred to as the "certified area"), and the data and analysis upon which the determination of eligibility was made. The Administrator shall make every effort to make this certification within seventy-two hours after the occurrence of the event.

b. Whenever the Administrator is informed through the Organization that a seismic event of seismic magnitude of 4.75 or above which is located by the System has occurred, and if the event is not immediately rendered ineligible for on-site inspection in accordance with the provisions of Article 8 of Annex I, he shall immediately make public at the Headquarters of the Organization all data relating to such a seismic event which could be of assistance (*i*) to any Party exercising its right to request an on-site inspection under paragraphs 2 and 3 of this Article, or (*ii*) to the Commission in its decision whether to issue a directive under paragraph 4 of this Article.

The Administrator shall make every effort to make this data public within seventy-two hours after the occurrence of all events referred to in this subparagraph, except for those events which have subsequently been found ineligible for on-site inspection in accordance with subparagraphs 3c and 3d of Article 8 of Annex I.

2. *a.* If any portion of the certified area lies in territory under the jurisdiction or control of any of the original Parties, the Administrator shall immediately despatch an inspection group to carry out an on-site inspection of such portion of the certified area in accordance with Annex I, provided that:

(*i*) The U.S.S.R. requests the inspection of such portion of the certified area which lies in territory under the jurisdiction or control of the United Kingdom or the United States, and the current annual number of inspections for the Party liable to inspection is not exhausted, or

(*ii*) The United Kingdom or the United States requests the inspection of such portion of the certified area which lies in territory under the jurisdiction or control of the U.S.S.R. and the current annual number of inspections for the U.S.S.R. is not exhausted, and

(*iii*) The request for inspection is made to the Administrator not later than fifteen days after the Administrator has made public all data relating to the seismic event in question, as specified in paragraph 1b of this Article.

b. An original Party requesting an on-site inspection pursuant to this paragraph shall simultaneously inform the other original Parties.

3. *a.* If any portion of a certified area lies in territory under the jurisdiction or control of a Party other than an original Party, any Party may, not later than fifteen days after the Administrator has made public at the Headquarters of the Organization all data relating to the seismic event in question as specified in paragraph 1b of this Article, request the Commission to direct an on-site inspection of such portion of the certified area.

b. The Commission shall consider and decide upon any such request within forty-eight hours after its receipt. If a certified area lies in territory under the jurisdiction or control of more than one Party, other than an original Party, the Commission shall make a separate decision as to the inspection of that portion of the certified area on the territory of each Party concerned. If the current annual number of inspections of the Party liable to inspection is not exhausted, and if the Commission decides that the request to direct an on-site inspection should be complied with, the Commission shall direct the Administrator to carry out an on-site inspection of the certified area lying in that Party's territory in accordance with Annex I.

c. If any portion of a certified area lies in territory under the jurisdiction or control of a Party represented on the Commission, that Party shall not participate in the decision as to the inspection of such portion of the certified area.

d. If any portion of a certified area lies in territory under the jurisdiction or control of a Party associated with an original Party, that original Party and Parties associated with it which are represented on the Commission shall not participate in the decision as to the inspection of such portion of the certified area.

4. *a.* If any portion of a certified area lies in an area not under the jurisdiction or control of any sovereign state, the Administrator shall decide whether to undertake an on-site inspection. The Administrator shall notify the Commission of his decision whether to undertake an on-site inspection and shall make every effort to do so within seventy-two hours after the occurrence of the event. After the Administrator notifies the Commission that he has decided to undertake an on-site inspection, he shall proceed to have the inspection carried out unless he is otherwise directed by the Commission within forty-eight hours of such notification.

b. The Commission may direct the Administrator to inspect a certified area not under the jurisdiction or control of any sovereign state, if the Administrator has not already proceeded to do so, not later than fifteen days after the Administrator has made public at the Headquarters of the Organization all data relating to the seismic event in question as specified in paragraph 1b of this Article.

c. All on-site inspections under this paragraph shall be carried out in accordance with Annex I.

5. The number of on-site inspections which may be carried out in territory under the jurisdiction or control of each of the original Parties, pursuant to paragraph 2 of this Article, shall be twenty inspections in each annual period.

6. *a.* The number of on-site inspections which may be carried out in each annual period in territory under the jurisdiction or control of a Party other than an original Party, pursuant to paragraph 3 of this Article, shall be, with respect to each such Party, two, or such higher number as the Commission may, after consultation with the Party, determine by a two-thirds majority of those present and voting.

b. Pending the determination of a Party's number by the Commission, the provisional number for that Party shall be one inspection in each annual period for each 500,000 square kilometers or remaining fraction thereof of territory under its jurisdiction or control, except that for each Party the provisional number shall be at least two inspections in each annual period. Inspections carried out under a Party's provisional number shall be deducted from the number subsequently determined for that Party for the annual period in which such inspections were initiated. In the case of acceding Parties, the Preparatory Commission shall, after consultation with such Parties, promptly recommend, for subsequent approval by the enlarged Preparatory Commission an appropriate number of inspections to be carried out in each annual period within territory under the jurisdiction or control of such Parties.

7. The number of on-site inspections for each Party shall be reviewed by the Commission within three years after this Treaty enters into force and annually thereafter. In light of each such review, which shall take full account of practical experience in the operation of the System and of measures taken to maintain or improve its effectiveness, the Commission may fix revised numbers, provided that no number (A) shall be less than two, (B) nor less than 20 per cent of the average annual number of events of seismic magnitude 4.75 or above which are located by the System in accordance with paragraph 2 of Article 8 of Annex I, provided that when criteria for the identification of seismic events eligible for on-site inspection are agreed, no less than 30 per cent of the events remaining unidentified after the application of such criteria, occurring in territory under the jurisdiction or control of the Party to which the number relates. Such average annual number shall be based on data from control posts and research programs undertaken by the Commission in accordance with the provisions of Article 6 for a period prescribed by the Commission.

8. The liability of a Party to on-site inspections pursuant to paragraph 2 or 3 of this Article shall commence from the date on which the Treaty enters into force for that Party. The annual period in which the number of on-site inspections for each Party may be carried out shall commence on the date of entry into force of the Treaty and thereafter on the anniversary of that date in each succeeding year. In the case of a Party which deposits its instrument of ratification or acceptance after the date of entry into force of the Treaty, the number of on-site inspections which may be carried out in territory under its jurisdiction or control in the period remaining before the next anniversary of the date of entry into force of the Treaty shall bear the same proportion to its number determined in accordance with paragraph 6 of this Article, as that period bears to one year, but shall not be less than two. If the number of on-site inspections calculated in accordance with the preceding sentence includes a fraction, that fraction shall, if it is smaller than one-half, be disregarded, or, if it is one-half or greater, be regarded as equivalent to one.

9. Notwithstanding any other provision of this Article, the Commission may direct the Administrator to carry out on-site inspection in territory under the jurisdiction or control of any Party either at the request of such Party or pursuant to an agreement made by such Party prior to or subsequent to signature of the Treaty. Inspections carried out under this paragraph shall not be deducted from a Party's number. Inspections carried out pursuant to paragraphs 2 and 3 of this Article shall take priority over inspections carried out under this paragraph.

10. The Administrator shall make available to all Parties to the Treaty within twenty-four hours after receipt all reports submitted to him by on-site inspection groups, together with any relevant data and analyses.

Article 11.* Installation and Operation of the System in Parties' Territories

Each of the original Parties and all other Parties to this Treaty agree to accept on territory under their jurisdiction or control components of the System which is established on the basis of the "Report of the Conference of Experts to Study the Methods of Detecting Violations of a Possible Agreement on the Suspension of Nuclear Tests" of August 20, 1958, the "Report of the Technical Working Group on the Detection and Identification of High-Altitude Nuclear Explosions" of July 15, 1959, and the "Conclusion of Technical Working Group II Regarding Possible Improvements of Techniques and Instrumentation" of December 18, 1959, and shall be installed and shall operate in accordance with the provisions of this Treaty and its Annexes.

Article 12.* Undertakings Concerning Cooperation with the System

1. Each of the Parties undertakes to assure that adequate and expeditious transportation is available from the point of entry, or within its territory, to the site of any element of the System or any area where an on-site inspection is to be conducted.

2. Each of the Parties undertakes to enter into appropriate arrangements with the Commission for the utilization of existing meteorological and commercial aircraft flights over ocean areas for routine air-sampling purposes.

3. Each of the Parties undertakes to enter into appropriate arrangements with the Commission to have aircraft immediately available for special flights, carried out pursuant to the provisions of Article 9 and Article 7 of Annex I, over territory under its jurisdiction or control or to permit such special flights by aircraft forming part of the System.

4. Each of the Parties undertakes to enter into appropriate arrangements with the Commission for the utilization of existing weather or geophysical exploration vessels for use as components of the System.

5. Each of the Parties undertakes to give inspection groups, despatched pursuant to the provisions of Article 10, immediate and undisputed access to the area in which an on-site inspection is to be conducted, to refrain from interference with any operation of an inspection group and to give such groups the assistance they may require in the performance of their mission.

6. Each of the Parties undertakes to enter into appropriate arrangements with the Commission: for the design, construction, and provision of necessary satellite vehicles; for the provision and use of launching sites and launching vehicles; for the establishment and operation of stations to track satellites and to receive and analyze data from such satellites; and for the establishment and carrying out of a research program to measure background levels in space and to develop the necessary equipment and techniques to put effective space monitoring control systems into operation.

Article 13. Detonations for Peaceful Purposes

1. Each of the Parties to this Treaty undertakes to detonate, or assist others in the detonation of, nuclear devices for peaceful purposes only in accordance with the provisions of this Article. The detonations carried out pursuant to the provisions of this Article shall not be regarded as a violation of Article 1.

2. A Party intending to carry out or assist in such a detonation shall provide the Commission, at least four months in advance of the proposed detonation date, with a plan containing the following information: (a) the date, site and purpose of the proposed detonation; (b) the procedure it will follow to comply with paragraph 4 of this Article; (c) the expected yield of the device; (d) the measures to be taken to ensure that there will be no substantial fallout outside the immediate vicinity; and (e) the measurements to be taken and any experimentation to be conducted therewith.

3. Within two months after the receipt of the plan, the Commission shall authorize the Party to proceed with, or assist in, the proposed detonation, unless the Commission shall find that such detonation would not be carried out in accordance with paragraph 4 of this Article. If, as a result of observations at the proposed site, the Commission determines that there is a lack of compliance with paragraph 4, it shall immediately

so notify the Party planning to conduct or assist in the detonation. The Party shall thereupon refrain from carrying out or assisting in the detonation until notified by the Commission that it has determined that the detonation will be carried out in accordance with paragraph 4.

4. Each of the original Parties shall be given an adequate opportunity at a designated inspection site to inspect externally and internally any nuclear device to be detonated pursuant to this Article and to examine detailed drawings of the device, provided that such detailed drawings may not be reproduced or taken away from the inspection site. The device to be detonated shall, after inspection and reassembly, be under the continual surveillance of members of the Organization staff until detonation.

5. Members of the Organization staff shall, in addition to maintaining surveillance of the device to be detonated, observe all preparation for, and the actual firing of, the device and shall at all times have unrestricted access to the vicinity of the detonation to ensure that the device employed is the one provided in accordance with paragraph 4 of this Article.

6. Representatives of the original Parties shall be given adequate opportunity to accompany and to participate with members of the Organization staff in the exercise of their functions under paragraphs 4 and 5 of this Article.

7. The Commission may, with the concurring votes of the original Parties, provide for any other system of safeguards to ensure that nuclear detonations for peaceful purposes are carried out in accordance with the objectives of this Treaty.

ARTICLE 14.* PERIODIC REVIEW OF THE SYSTEM

1. Three years after the coming into force of this Treaty, the Commission shall review the System established under this Treaty in order to:

   a. evaluate its effectiveness for verifying compliance with the obligations set forth in Articles 1 and 13 of this Treaty;

   b. determine in the light of experience and scientific progress whether any specific improvements should be made or new elements added to the System;

   c. consider such measures to improve or maintain the effectiveness of the System as may be proposed by any Party to the Treaty in the light of experience in the operation of the Treaty.

2. The System may be reviewed by the Commission annually thereafter for the same purpose upon request of the Conference or any of the original Parties.

ARTICLE 15. FINANCE

1. Annual budget estimates for the expenses of the Organization shall be submitted to the Commission by the Administrator. After receipt of these estimates, the Commission shall submit a proposed budget to the Conference. The Conference may approve the budget as submitted or return it to the Commission with recommendations. If the budget is returned, the Commission shall then submit a further budget to the Conference for its approval.

2. The expenses of the Organization shall be borne by the Parties in accordance with a scale fixed by the Conference on the basis of recommendations submitted by the Commission as part of each annual budget. The annual contributions of the U.S.S.R. and the United States shall be equal.

3. Any party desiring to pay its assessments, in whole or in part, by supplying materials, services, equipment, or facilities shall make its offer in writing to the Commission. Within ninety days after receipt of the offer, the Commission shall determine whether to accept the offer, in whole or in part, and shall notify the Party of its decision. The Commission shall not accept such an offer unless the materials, services, equipment, or facilities offered by the Party meet the standards prescribed by the Commission and are readily usable.

4. Subject to the rules and limitations approved by the Conference, the Commission shall have the authority to exercise borrowing powers on behalf of the Organization without, however, imposing on the Parties to this Treaty any individual liability in respect of a loan or loans entered into pursuant to this authority.

5. Decisions of the Commission and of the Conference on all financial questions

shall be made by a majority of those present and voting. However, decisions by the Commission on the scale of contributions to be recommended and on the total amount of each annual budget shall require the concurring votes of the original Parties.

ARTICLE 16. PRIVILEGES AND IMMUNITIES

The privileges and immunities which the Organization, its staff, and the representatives of Parties shall be granted by the Parties, and the legal capacity which the Organization shall enjoy in the territory of each of the Parties, shall be as set forth in Annex II of this Treaty.

ARTICLE 17.* RELATIONSHIPS WITH OTHER INTERNATIONAL ORGANIZATIONS

1. The Commission, with the approval of the Conference, is authorized to enter into an agreement or agreements establishing an appropriate relationship between the Organization and the United Nations.

2. The Commission, with the approval of the Conference, shall arrange for the Organization to be brought into an appropriate relationship with any international organization which may in the future be established among any of the Parties to this Treaty to supervise disarmament and arms-control measures.

ARTICLE 18.* ANNEXES

The Annexes to this Treaty form an integral part of this Treaty.

ARTICLE 19. PARTIES TO THE TREATY

1. The essential Parties to this Treaty shall be:

a. the Union of Soviet Socialist Republics, the United Kingdom of Great Britain and Northern Ireland, and the United States of America, referred to herein as the "original Parties";

b. any other State whose adherence is decided by the Commission to be necessary for the achievement of the fundamental Treaty purpose of securing an effectively controlled permanent discontinuance of nuclear-weapon-test explosions on a world-wide basis or to permit the installation of elements of control as required by the provisions of Annex I. If any State which is proposed to be the subject of a decision in accordance with the preceding sentence is associated with an original Party for the purposes of this Treaty, that original Party and any State associated with it for the purposes of this Treaty shall abstain from voting in the decision.

2. The signature and ratification or the acceptance of this Treaty by all the States designated in paragraph 1*a* and any State whose adherence is decided to be necessary in accordance with paragraph 1*b* shall be required for the fulfillment of the provisions of this Article.

3. Any other State desiring to adhere, whose adherence the Preparatory Commission or the Commission decides would contribute to the achievement of the purposes of this Treaty, may become a Party.

ARTICLE 20.* SIGNATURE, RATIFICATION, ACCEPTANCE AND ENTRY INTO FORCE

1. This Treaty shall be open for signature by the states referred to in paragraph 1*a* of Article 19. The signatory states shall become Parties to this Treaty by deposit of instruments of ratification.

2. Instruments of ratification and instruments of acceptance by states adhering pursuant to paragraphs 1*b* and 3 of Article 19 shall be deposited with the Government of _____ hereby designated as Depositary Government.

3. Ratification or acceptance of this Treaty shall be effected by states in accordance with their respective constitutional processes.

4. This Treaty, apart from Annex III, shall enter into force when all the original Parties have deposited instruments of ratification thereof.

5. The Depositary Government shall promptly inform all signatory states of the date of deposit of each instrument of ratification and of each instrument of acceptance and the date of entry into force of this Treaty. The Depositary Government shall promptly inform all Parties of the dates on which states become Parties to this Treaty.

6. Annex III of this Treaty shall come into force on the day after this Treaty shall have been signed by the original Parties.

ARTICLE 21.* REGISTRATION

1. This Treaty shall be registered by the Depositary Government pursuant to Article 102 of the Charter of the United Nations.

2. Agreements between the Organization and any Party to this Treaty or any other State or public international organization shall be submitted for registration by the Commission with the United Nations.

ARTICLE 22.* DURATION

This Treaty shall remain in force indefinitely subject to the inherent right of a Party to withdraw and be relieved of obligations hereunder if the provisions of the Treaty and its Annexes, including those providing for the timely installation and effective operation of the control system, are not being fulfilled and observed.

ARTICLE 23.* AMENDMENTS

Amendments to this Treaty and its Annexes shall enter into force for all Parties to the Treaty when they have been adopted by a vote of two-thirds of the members of the Conference and ratified in accordance with their respective constitutional processes by two-thirds of the Parties to this Treaty, including all the original Parties.

ARTICLE 24.* AUTHENTIC TEXTS

This Treaty, of which the English and Russian texts are equally authentic, shall be deposited in the archives of the Depositary Government. Duly certified copies of this Treaty shall be transmitted by the Depositary Government to the Governments of the other signatory States and to the Governments of States which become Parties to this Treaty pursuant to paragraphs 1b and 3 of Article 19.

IN WITNESS WHEREOF the undersigned, duly authorized, have signed this Treaty.

DONE at _____, this ____ day of ____, one thousand nine hundred and sixty-one.

ANNEX I

DETECTION AND IDENTIFICATION SYSTEM

PART I. DESCRIPTION
ARTICLE 1.

The System established in this Treaty shall include the features set forth herein which are derived from the "Report of the Conference of Experts to Study the Methods of Detecting Violations of a Possible Agreement on the Suspension of Nuclear Tests" of August 20, 1958, the "Report of the Technical Working Group on the Detection and Identification of High Altitude Nuclear Explosions" of July 15, 1959, and the "Conclusion of Technical Working Group II Regarding Possible Improvements of Techniques and Instrumentation" of December 18, 1959.

ARTICLE 2.

1. The System shall, when completely established and unless otherwise decided in accordance with the provisions of this Treaty, consist of the following components: A Headquarters, regional offices, land control posts and ship-based control posts, systems of satellites, radiochemistry laboratories, air- and water-sampling facilities, on-site inspection facilities, and communications facilities. Upon recommendation of the Administrator, the Commission may decide, with the affirmative votes of the original Parties, to add components as may be appropriate for detecting and identifying nuclear explosions.

2. The general characteristics of the System shall be as follows:

a. The land control posts shall be uniformly equipped with apparatus for the collection of radioactive debris and for the recording of acoustic waves, seismic waves, electromagnetic signals, fluorescence of the upper atmosphere, visible light, and cosmic noise absorption.

b. A number of control posts situated on islands or near the shore lines of oceans shall be equipped, in addition to the methods mentioned in paragraph *2a* of this Article, with apparatus for the recording of hydroacoustic waves. Certain control posts in areas not covered by existing weather stations (e.g., Southern Hemisphere) shall include meteorological equipment and personnel necessary to obtain data on air-mass movements in order to predict the course of any air mass suspected to contain debris from nuclear explosions.

c. Control posts located on ships, which shall be stationed within specified ocean areas, shall be uniformly equipped with apparatus for the collection of radioactive debris and for the recording of hydroacoustic waves, fluorescence of the upper atmosphere, and visible light. The methods of recording electromagnetic signals and cosmic noise absorption may also be used on ships at the discretion of the Administrator.

d. Aircraft and vessels for air- and water-sampling operations shall be suitably equipped with apparatus for the collection of radioactive debris from the air and from the water.

e. On-site inspection groups shall be appropriately manned and equipped to carry out on-site inspections to determine the nature of unidentified events which could be suspected of being nuclear explosions.

f. Satellites in terrestrial and solar orbits shall be suitably equipped with apparatus for recording delayed and prompt gamma-rays, X rays, neutrons, and electrons trapped in the earth's magnetic field.

g. Suitably located ground stations shall be equipped to launch, track, and to transmit to and receive data from satellites.

Part II. Components

Article 3. Headquarters

1. *The Headquarters of the System* shall include directorates for Administration, for Supply, for Technical Operations, and for Field Operations. Technical Operations shall be comprised of a Research and Development Center and a Data Analysis Center which shall include a Central Radiochemical Laboratory. Field Operations shall be comprised of a Central Inspection Office, a Communications Center and an Operations Center which shall include a Weather Center. Administration shall include offices for Finance and Personnel; and Supply shall include offices for System Construction and for Supply and Maintenance.

2. *The Research and Development Center* shall have the necessary professional staff and facilities to conduct, either directly or by contract, research and development programs for developing and improving equipment and techniques for detection and identification of nuclear explosions.

3. *The Data Analysis Center* shall have the necessary professional staff and facilities for evaluating all data received from components of the System. All data from the components of the System shall be reported directly to the Data Analysis Center, whose functions shall include:

a. To analyze all data received from all components of the System.

b. To determine and report strictly on the basis of this analysis the time and place of occurrence and the magnitude or equivalent yield of: (*i*) an event for which the data is sufficient to establish its nature as a nuclear explosion; (*ii*) an event which is identifiable on the basis of the data as a natural geophysical disturbance; (*iii*) an event which is not identifiable on the basis of the data as natural and which therefore could be suspected of being a nuclear explosion.

c. To examine continuously the work of the components of the System to ensure the maintenance of a high degree of technical proficiency.

4. *The Central Radiochemical Laboratory* shall have the necessary professional staff and facilities to perform radiochemical and physical analyses of samples received from control posts, ships, aerial-sampling centers, or other components of the System. The Central Radiochemical Laboratory shall analyze the samples for fission products and

other nuclides to confirm the origin of the debris as being from a nuclear detonation as opposed to some other type of nuclear reaction. In addition, the Central Radiochemical Laboratory shall review for accuracy the findings of these components of the System concerning the characteristics and age of any nuclear debris involved. The Central Radiochemical Laboratory shall also be responsible for developing test procedures for use at field laboratories as required to ensure uniformity in analysis and measurement techniques throughout the System.

5. *The Central Inspection Office* shall have the necessary professional staff and facilities to direct on-site inspection of events which cannot be identified as natural events and which could be suspected of being nuclear explosions. The Central Inspection Office shall organize and maintain inspection groups on an alert basis and shall be responsible, when so directed, for the dispatch of these groups to areas designated for inspection as soon as possible following notification by the Administrator. For these purposes the Central Inspection Office shall be responsible for:

a. Rapid development of a plan for movement of the inspection group to the area of the event in consultation with the Party or Parties exercising jurisdiction or control over territory in which the inspection is to take place;

b. Rapid movement of inspection personnel and equipment to the area;

c. Direction of the inspection groups and for the conduct of the inspection in the suspect area, including provisions for additional staff, equipment and supplies deemed necessary by the inspection group.

6. *The Communications Center* shall have the necessary professional staff and facilities to ensure rapid and reliable communications with control posts, ships, aerial-sampling centers, regional offices, and satellite-tracking stations. "Rapid and reliable communications" is defined as such a communications network as will ensure an exchange of accurate and complete messages with any of the components of the System within eight hours.

7. *The Operations Center* shall have the necessary professional staff and facilities to control all field operations, excluding on-site inspection. The Operations Center shall control the launching and positioning of satellites, as well as the movement of aircraft, vessels, equipment, and personnel which are deployed for the purpose of conducting air- and water-sampling operations. It shall maintain complete and current information on the operational status of each component of the System, including aerial-sampling flights over the oceans and over territories under the jurisdiction or control of Parties to this Treaty. The Operations Center will ensure that steps are taken to maintain all components of the System at all times in a high state of operational readiness to perform their assigned functions.

8. *The Weather Center* shall have the necessary professional staff and facilities to prepare forecasts of air-mass trajectories from any point at which a nuclear explosion is suspected to have occurred for use in vectoring aerial-sampling flights to intercept these air masses. The Weather Center shall be provided by wire or radio with weather data from existing national weather networks under the control of the Parties. Appropriate arrangements shall be made for other national or international networks to supply weather data to the Weather Center by wire or radio. In addition, the Weather Center shall be provided with weather data from special weather detachments established in accordance with paragraph 2*b* of Article 2 of this Annex.

Article 4. Regional Offices

1. Regional Offices shall be established as the Commission determines to be necessary for the effective administration and operation of the System.

2. Each Regional Office shall perform the following functions:

a. Provide logistic support to and administrative supervision over components of the System operating in its region;

b. Provide necessary support and administrative assistance to inspection groups operating in its region;

c. Maintain liaison with national and local authorities in its region in connection with its performance of the above functions and in particular to ensure the expeditious transportation and local support of inspection groups.

ARTICLE 5. LAND CONTROL POSTS

1. The network of control posts shall, when completely established include at least 170 land control posts. Unless otherwise determined under paragraph 2 below, the spacing between control posts shall be about 1,700 kilometers in continental aseismic areas, about 1,000 kilometers in continental seismic areas, and between 1,000 and about 3,500 kilometers in ocean areas.

2. The number of control posts to be installed in the U.S.S.R., United Kingdom, and United States shall be as specified in Article 17 of this Annex. Except for the number of control posts to be installed in the U.S.S.R., United Kingdom, and United States, the Commission shall determine, on the basis of the foregoing standards of spacing, the number of control posts to be installed in other territories under the jurisdiction or control of the original Parties and all territories under the jurisdiction or control of Parties other than the original Parties to the Treaty. With the approval of the Commission and of the Party concerned, the control posts may be arranged in an alternative distribution within territory under the jurisdiction or control of a Party if, in the view of the Commission, such a redistribution will result in an improvement in the capabilities of the System.

3. Specific sites for control posts shall be selected in a manner to give the maximum over-all capability to the System. The siting of individual control posts shall be determined primarily on the basis of the seismic requirement. However, in the event that two or more suitable seismic sites are found in the desired areas, a final selection of the location of the control posts shall be made with due consideration of siting-requirements of the other methods of detection set forth in Article 2 of this Annex. In the event that no control-post location fulfilling seismic requirements is found that permits satisfactory operation of other detection equipment as set forth in this Annex, the Administrator may direct the installation of such equipment at a more favorable location. In the event that after a control post is established, the background seismic noise increases above acceptable limits due to human or other activity, the Administrator, after consultation with the Party, may direct that the control post may be moved to another location.

4. All land control posts shall maintain continuous operation of apparatus for the collection of radioactive debris and for the recording of fluorescence of the upper atmosphere, visible light, cosmic noise absorption, acoustic waves, seismic waves, and electromagnetic signals. Control posts situated on islands or near the shorelines of oceans shall, in addition, maintain continuous operation of apparatus for the recording of hydroacoustic waves. In addition, equipment may be operated at certain land control posts to track and to transmit to and receive data from satellites.

ARTICLE 6. SHIP-BASED CONTROL POSTS

1. The network of control posts shall, when completely established, include a system of ship-based control posts, which shall be employed in ocean areas which do not contain suitable islands. There shall be a sufficient number of ships to maintain a capability for continuous operation of four stations each in the North Pacific and South Pacific Oceans and one station each in the North Atlantic and Indian Oceans.

2. Ship-based control posts shall maintain continuous operation of apparatus for the collection of radioactive debris and for the recording of hydroacoustic waves, fluorescence of the upper atmosphere, and visible light. Equipment for recording electromagnetic signals and cosmic noise absorption may also be used on ships at the discretion of the Administrator.

ARTICLE 7. AIR AND WATER SAMPLING OPERATIONS

1. Daily, routine air-sampling flights shall be conducted at several different altitudes over ocean areas in approximately a north-south direction near the sides of continents, as well as in the center of remote ocean areas such as the Central Pacific, the Indian Ocean west of Australia, and the North Atlantic Ocean, for the purpose of detecting nuclear explosions by the method of collecting radioactive debris.

2. Special aircraft-sampling flights shall be conducted to search for a possible radio-active cloud for the purpose of collecting samples of radioactive debris within two to five days after the date of origin of the debris. Special sampling flights shall be initiated whenever fresh radioactive debris has been detected by a routine air-sampling flight or by a control post or when acoustic signals recorded at control posts establish the time and position of a possible explosion in the atmosphere. In each instance, the flight routes of the aircraft shall be selected on the basis of meteorological trajectory forecasts from the location of the suspected event, and the aircraft shall search at several different altitudes.

3. Special aircraft flights undertaken over territory under the jurisdiction or control of Parties shall be conducted, on instruction of the Administrator in accordance with Article 9 of the Treaty, over permanent flight routes as set out by the Commission in accordance with Article 6 of the Treaty. Such permanent flight routes shall be laid down in advance in such number and geographical location that, according to meteorological data, interception of any cloud containing radioactive debris will be assured within two to five days of the suspected event. Sampling aircraft to be used over territory under the jurisdiction or control of Parties shall be located in or near permanent flight routes and shall be maintained in a high state of operational readiness to conduct the sampling flights directed by the Administrator.

4. Special aircraft flights over ocean areas shall be conducted from aircraft-sampling centers distributed uniformly throughout the Northern and Southern Hemispheres. When the area to be covered by such flights is remote from any one of the centers, operations will be staged out of the nearest airfield, and necessary supplies which cannot be procured locally will be airlifted from the nearest center.

5. Water-sampling operations, by ships and/or aircraft, shall be conducted for the purpose of collecting samples of water suspected of containing radioactive debris whenever hydroacoustic signals recorded at control posts establish the time and position of a possible underwater explosion. Suitably equipped aircraft and/or vessels shall be deployed in such a manner that water-sampling operations can be conducted at the site of the event within four days after such operations are directed by the Administrator.

6. *a.* Radiochemical laboratories shall be located at each of the aerial sampling centers established in accordance with paragraph 4 above. Laboratories at aerial sampling centers shall be equipped to carry out all the necessary radiochemical analytical techniques required to determine the presence of fresh debris and to ascertain the date of origin of the debris with a precision consistent with the most modern radiochemical dating techniques. This shall be done by using as many dating techniques as sample-size and age of the debris permit.

b. Upon termination of a sampling flight, samples shall be assayed by suitable instruments, for example gamma spectrometers. Samples shall be divided in equal parts. One part shall be sent to the nearest radiochemical laboratory, and the other part shall be sent to the Central Radiochemical Laboratory for further analysis with an indication as to which are suspected of containing fresh fission products.

c. Water samples shall be assayed by suitable instruments as soon as practicable following sample collection, and those samples suspected of containing fresh fission products shall be divided in equal parts. One part shall be sent to the nearest radiochemical laboratory and the other to the Central Radiochemical Laboratory for analysis.

Article 8. Criteria for On-Site Inspection of Seismic Events

1. A seismic event which is located by the criteria in paragraph 2 of this Article and which is determined to be of seismic magnitude 4.75 or greater shall be eligible for on-site inspection unless rendered ineligible for inspection by the fulfillment of any of the criteria in paragraph 3 of this Article.

2. A seismic event shall be considered to be located when seismic signals, whose frequencies, amplitudes, durations, and velocities are consistent with those of the waves from earthquakes or explosions, are recorded at a sufficient number of control posts to

establish the approximate time and position of the event. This requires at least four clearly measurably arrival times of identifiable phases which are mutually consistent to within plus or minus three seconds. These four consistent arrival times must include P-wave arrival times at three different control posts.

3. A located seismic event shall be ineligible for inspection if, and only if, it fulfills one or more of the following criteria:

a. Its depth of focus is established as below sixty kilometers.

b. Its epicentral location is established to be in the deep open ocean, and the event is unaccompanied by a hydroacoustic signal consistent with the seismic epicenter and origin time.

c. It is established to be a foreshock of a seismic event of at least magnitude 6 which has been clearly identified as an earthquake by the criteria in subparagraphs (*a*) and (*b*) above. For this purpose a "foreshock" is defined as one of a sequence of earthquakes which occurs less than forty-eight hours before the main shock and which has an epicenter within ten kilometers of the epicenter of the main shock.

d. it is established to be an aftershock of a seismic event of at least magnitude 6 which has been clearly identified as an earthquake by the criteria in subparagraphs (*a*) and (*b*) above. For this purpose, an "aftershock" is defined as one of a sequence of earthquakes which occurs less than one week after the main shock and which has an epicenter within ten kilometers of the epicenter of the main shock.

4. In cases where adequately precise regional travel-time curves are available, and where consistent arrival times are available from control posts surrounding the epicenter, that is, from control posts at least one of which lies in every possible 90-degree sector around the epicenter, the area eligible for inspection will be 200 square kilometers. In cases where adequately precise regional travel time curves are not available, or where data from control posts lying in every possible 90-degree sector around the epicenter are not available, an area of 500 square kilometers shall be eligible for inspection. The area eligible for inspection shall be chosen so as to have the highest likelihood of containing the epicenter.

5. The basic data for all criteria shall be obtained from control posts.

6. Within three years after the entry into force of this Treaty and annually thereafter, the Commission shall review the provisions of this Article. Notwithstanding the provisions of Article 23, the Commission may at any time, with the concurring votes of the original Parties, amend the provisions of this Article. Such amendments shall be binding on all Parties to this Treaty.

ARTICLE 9. A SEISMIC EVENT EQUAL TO OR GREATER THAN MAGNITUDE 4.75

1. "A seismic event equal to or greater than magnitude 4.75" is a seismic event whose apparent magnitude M as measured by the formula M equals Q plus log (A/GT) is equal to or greater than 4.75 at one-half or more of the control posts which measure the quantity "A" and which are located at distances greater than 16 degrees and less than 90 degrees from the epicenter. The symbols in the formula M equals Q plus log (A/GT) are defined as follows:

a. "A" is one-half of the maximum peak positive-to-negative amplitude (displacement), expressed in microns in the record of the first five cycles of the P waves made by a short-period vertical-component seismograph with characteristics which will permit operation of single seismometers at quiet stations with magnification greater than ten to the sixth power at the frequency of peak response. "A" is measured if it exceeds three times the arithmetical mean of the ten greatest peak amplitudes of the noise oscillations recorded during the preceding two minutes. Noises, the periods of which differ from the signal period by not more than one and one-half times, are counted. The noise amplitude and period are determined by the same procedure as for the signal.

b. "T" is the time, measured in seconds, between the first of the peaks used in determining "A" and the next following peak of the same sign.

c. "G" is the steady state magnification of the seismograph at period T.

d. "Q" is given as a function of distance in the following table:

Distance	Q	Distance	Q	Distance	Q
16 Degrees	5.9	41 Degrees	6.5	66 Degrees	7.0
17	5.9	42	6.5	67	7.0
18	5.9	43	6.5	68	7.0
19	6.0	44	6.5	69	7.0
20	6.0	45	6.7	70	6.9
21	6.1	46	6.8	71	6.9
22	6.2	47	6.9	72	6.9
23	6.3	48	6.9	73	6.9
24	6.3	49	6.8	74	6.8
25	6.5	50	6.7	75	6.8
26	6.4	51	6.7	76	6.9
27	6.5	52	6.7	77	6.9
28	6.6	53	6.7	78	6.9
29	6.6	54	6.8	79	6.8
30	6.6	55	6.8	80	6.7
31	6.7	56	6.8	81	6.8
32	6.7	57	6.8	82	6.9
33	6.7	58	6.8	83	7.0
34	6.7	59	6.8	84	7.0
35	6.7	60	6.8	85	7.0
36	6.6	61	6.9	86	6.9
37	6.5	62	7.0	87	7.0
38	6.5	63	6.9	88	7.1
39	6.4	64	7.0	89	7.0
40	6.4	65	7.0	90	7.0

ARTICLE 10. INSPECTION GROUPS

1. Inspection groups shall be established and maintained to conduct on-site inspections as directed by the Administrator. They shall be based at a number of locations sufficient to insure prompt arrival and logistical support at the site of any unidentified continental or maritime event. Inspection groups shall be responsible for the collection and preliminary evaluation of evidence concerning the nature of the event in question. They shall remain in the inspection area until recalled by the Administrator.

2. Each inspection group shall be staffed with scientific, technical, and other personnel qualified to perform the duties required in the conduct of an on-site inspection.

3. Each inspection group shall, when dispatched, conduct any inspection directed by the Administrator in a prompt and efficient manner and shall be authorized to:

a. Establish a local base of operations.

b. Establish and maintain communications with its permanent base, the Central Inspection Office, and, as required, other components of the System.

c. Consult with local officials and individuals.

d. Conduct low-altitude aerial inspection of the area eligible for inspection, utilizing such techniques as may be necessary for this purpose, including, but not limited to, photographic, electromagnetic, magnetic, infrared, and radioactivity surveys.

e. Conduct surface and subsurface inspection in the area eligible for inspection for all evidence which may in any way relate to the nature of the event, utilizing such techniques as may be necessary for this purpose, including, but not limited to, drilling for radioactive samples for scientific analysis.

f. Utilize such other means of investigation on site as would be likely to produce relevant data.

4. Each inspection group shall submit to the Administrator periodic progress reports during the course of any inspection and a final report upon the conclusion of the inspection operation. Copies of these reports shall be sent to the Party or Parties exer-

cising jurisdiction or control over the territory in which the inspection is being or has been carried out.

5. Each inspection group shall have available for its use the technical apparatus and facilities necessary for the performance of a prompt and efficient inspection operation. Such apparatus and facilities shall include, but shall not be limited to, the following:

a. Portable seismographs for recording aftershocks, geophysical equipment for seismic profiling, detection equipment for locating metallic articles, radiation detectors, equipment for collecting radioactive samples on the surface, drilling equipment for obtaining underground radioactive samples, portable laboratory equipment for field radiochemical analysis, and photographic equipment.

b. Appropriate surface and air transport for rapid movement to an inspection area along routes prescribed by the host country, and for the operation and logistics of the inspection group.

c. Appropriate aircraft for the conduct of low-altitude aerial reconnaissance of the inspection area for evidence of the nature of the event in question.

d. Appropriate vessels for the conduct of inspection of maritime events.

e. Technically suitable and reliable communications equipment to establish and maintain contact with its permanent base of operations, the Central Inspection Office, and, as required, other System components.

ARTICLE 11. HIGH ALTITUDE SYSTEMS

1. The high-altitude systems, which are based upon the recommendations contained in the "Report of the Technical Working Group on the Detection and Identification of High Altitude Nuclear Explosions," of July 15, 1959, are established for the purpose of providing, when in effective operation, a level of capability not less than that estimated by the Technical Working Group in sections A and B of their Report. The techniques and instrumentation for the detection and identification of nuclear explosions at high altitudes shall comprise apparatus installed at control posts and ground stations as specified in Articles 2, 5, and 6 of this Annex, together with satellite systems.

Satellite systems shall be so positioned in orbits as to provide maximum capability for detecting nuclear explosions as follows:

a. One or more satellites (trapped-electron satellites) placed in an appropriate terrestrial elliptical orbit and suitably instrumented with counters for recording electrons trapped in the earth's magnetic field. A satellite shall be replaced when it can no longer record or transmit the required data to ground stations.

b. At least six satellites (far-earth satellites) placed in terrestrial orbits at altitudes of more than 30,000 kilometers so as to be continuously outside the earth's trapped-radiation belts. Three of the satellites shall be nearly equally spaced in the same orbital plane, and three satellites shall be similarly placed in a second orbital plane positioned at approximately right angles to the first. Each satellite shall be suitably equipped with instruments for recording prompt and delayed gamma-rays, X rays, and neutrons. A satellite shall be replaced when it can no longer record and transmit to ground stations the required data from any three of the four methods of detection as set forth in this subparagraph. In addition, satellites shall be replaced when the System (*i*) no longer provides complete surveillance of the earth, or (*ii*) no longer provides surveillance in all directions in space lying outside the orbits of the System's component satellites by means of the X-ray detection method from at least three satellites.

c. At least four satellites (solar satellites) placed in appropriate solar orbits and suitably equipped with instruments, including those for recording X rays. A satellite shall be replaced when it can no longer record and transmit to ground stations the required data on X-ray signals.

2. Each satellite requiring replacement shall be replaced as rapidly as possible.

3. Each satellite shall carry apparatus for verifying the performance of its equipment. Each satellite shall be inspected immediately prior to launching to ensure its instruments meet the detection requirements and that the satellite includes nothing which might interfere with the performance of its equipment. After inspection, the launching of each satellite shall be observed. This inspection and the subsequent ob-

servation of the launching of the satellite shall be performed by members of the staff of the Organization selected by the Administrator in accordance with the principles set forth in subparagraph 3*c* (*v*) of Article 9.

Part III. Data Reporting and Evaluation

Article 12.

1. All components of the System shall immediately examine all records obtained. When data which meet criteria established by the Headquarters of the System are observed, they shall be reported by wire or radio to the Data Analysis Center. All components of the System shall provide additional data to the Center upon its request. In addition, all original data and records obtained by all components of the System shall be forwarded expeditiously to the Headquarters of the System. Reliable electronic transmission of data and frequent collection of records and materials by aircraft shall be incorporated in the reporting system.

2. The equipment at control posts, ships, satellite-tracking, and data transmitting and receiving stations, and air- and water-sampling centers shall be examined periodically by technical personnel from the Headquarters of the System for the purpose of ensuring the validity of the data transmitted from these components to Headquarters.

Part IV. Support Facilities

Article 13. Communications

The System shall have rapid and reliable communications between its components and Headquarters and shall have the right to install, maintain, and operate communications facilities, including radio networks, using existing channels when they are suitable for this purpose. The network must be capable of ensuring an exchange of accurate and complete messages between the Headquarters and any component of the System within eight hours. Provisions shall be made for the receipt of standard time signals by all components of the System which record geophysical data. Provisions shall also be made for transmission to the System Headquarters of all weather data required by the Weather Center as set forth in paragraph 8 of Article 3 of this Annex.

Article 14. Supplies and Services

1. The System Headquarters shall manage resources of the System for supplies and services by such means as: establishing procurement, construction, and transportation criteria; publishing instructions for operation and maintenance of equipment; receiving and processing supply and maintenance reports from the elements of the System, and establishing specification and performance standards for equipment.

2. The System Headquarters shall ensure that technical equipment meets required performance standards before authorizing acceptance of the equipment for use in the System.

3. Maximum use shall be made of sources of supply of nontechnical equipment indigenous to the area where facilities of the System are located. Support equipment and supplies shall be locally procured where possible by the Regional Offices or control posts.

Article 15. System Phasing

The controls provided for in this Treaty shall be progressively extended, and the components of the System installed in three phases, in order to achieve and ensure world-wide compliance with the obligations of this Treaty. The subphases of Phase I shall begin within three months after the Treaty enters into force. Subphase I-A shall be completed within two years after the Treaty enters into force. Subphase I-B shall be completed within four years after the Treaty enters into force. Phase II shall begin within one year after the Treaty enters into force, and shall be completed within five years after the Treaty enters into force. Phase III shall begin within two years after the Treaty enters into force and shall be completed within six years after the Treaty enters into force. Each control post and each other facility shall be put into operation, in whole or in part, as it is installed, and the System shall be fully operational within six years after the Treaty enters into force. The Commission may, however, decide, with the affirmative votes of the original Parties, to postpone, add to, or refrain from establishing any part of Phase I, II, and III.

ARTICLE 16. PHASING OF HEADQUARTERS

The Headquarters of the System shall be established at the beginning of Phase I and shall be expanded through Phase I and subsequent phases as required to provide effective administration and operation of the System.

ARTICLE 17. CONTROL POST PHASING

Land control posts and control posts on ships shall be established as follows:

	Phase			
	I-A	I-B	II	III
U.S.S.R.	9	9	–	–
U.S.	6	4	–	–
U.K.	1	–	–	–
Oceanic Islands	20	–	16	24
Ships	10	–	–	–
Australia	–	–	4	3
Asia (non-U.S.S.R.)	–	–	21	–
Europe (non-U.S.S.R.)	–	–	3	–
North America and Greenland	–	–	14	–
Africa	–	–	7	9
South America	–	–	6	10
Antarctica	–	–	–	4
	46	13	71	50

ARTICLE 18. AIRCRAFT-SAMPLING PHASING

Aircraft-sampling facilities shall be established and made fully operational within two years after the Treaty enters into force.

ARTICLE 19. SATELLITE-SYSTEMS PHASING

Subject to the provisions of Article 11 of this Annex, satellite systems shall be installed as follows:

	Phase			
	I-A	I-B	II	III
Trapped-electron satellites	1	–	–	–
Far-earth satellites	–	6	–	–
Solar satellites	–	–	–	4
	1	6	–	4

ARTICLE 20. INSPECTION GROUP PHASING

Inspection groups shall be established from the beginning of Phase I. A sufficient number of groups shall be maintained to carry out inspections at any time in the numbers which, in accordance with the terms of this Treaty and its Annexes, may currently be required.

ARTICLE 21. COMMUNICATIONS PHASING

A survey of communications requirements shall be performed at the beginning of each phase. Elements of the communications system shall be timed to be operational so as to ensure rapid and reliable communications for each control post or other component of the System as soon as such post or other component becomes operational.

ANNEX II

PRIVILEGES AND IMMUNITIES

ARTICLE 1. DEFINITIONS

In this Annex:

1. The expression "representatives of Parties to this Treaty" includes representatives on or to any organ of the Organization established under the provisions of this Treaty, including the Conference, together with the members of their official staffs.

2. The expression "representatives of Parties to this Treaty on the Control Commission" includes all members of the official staffs of such representatives except those whose duties are clerical. For the purpose of this Annex such clerical personnel shall be deemed to come within the class of persons referred to in subparagraph (1) of this Article.

3. The expression "members of the Organization staff" includes the Administrator and all the employees of the Organization.

4. The term "expert" shall mean an individual performing a mission on behalf of the Organization either at the headquarters of the Organization or in the territory of a Party to this Treaty.

5. The term "host government" shall mean the government of the country in which the Headquarters of the Organization is located.

ARTICLE 2. JURIDICAL PERSONALITY

1. The Organization shall possess juridical personality. It shall have the capacity (*a*) to contract, (*b*) to acquire and dispose of property, (*c*) to institute and defend legal proceedings.

2. The Organization may provide for suitable identification of ships and aircraft employed on the official service of the Organization.

ARTICLE 3. PROPERTY, FUNDS AND ASSETS

1. The Organization, its property and assets, wherever located and by whomsoever held, shall enjoy immunity from every form of legal process except in so far as in any particular case the Commission, on behalf of the Organization, has expressly waived this immunity, but such express waiver of immunity shall not extend to any measure of execution or detention of property.

2. The premises of the Organization shall be inviolable. The property and assets of the Organization, wherever located and by whomsoever held, shall be immune from search, requisition, confiscation, expropriation, and any other form of interference, whether by executive, administrative, judicial, or legislative action.

3. The archives of the Organization and all documents belonging to it or held by it or by its staff or experts on its behalf shall be inviolable wherever located.

4. The Organization, without being restricted by financial controls, regulations, or moratoria of any kind, may, subject to the obligation to give effect as far as is practicable to representations made to it by any Party, exercise the following rights:

a. To hold currency of any kind and operate accounts in any currency;

b. To transfer its funds freely from, to, or within any country Party to this Treaty and convert any currency held by it into any other currency.

5. The Organization, its assets, income, and other property shall be:

a. Exempt from all direct taxes except those taxes which are in reality a charge for specific services;

b. Exempt from all customs duties, prohibitions, and restrictions on imports and exports in respect of articles imported or exported by the Organization for its official use; articles imported under such exemption shall not be disposed of, by sale or by gift, in the country into which they are imported except under conditions approved by the Government of that country;

c. Exempt from all customs duties, prohibitions, and restrictions on imports and exports in respect of its publications.

6. The Organization shall be exempt from taxes imposed directly on its expenditure

transactions but not exempt from those taxes which are in reality a charge for specific services.

ARTICLE 4. COMMUNICATIONS

1. Each Party shall take appropriate steps necessary to ensure that its domestic and international telecommunication services accord to telecommunications of the Organization treatment at least equal to government telecommunications with respect to priority of transmission, and accord these telecommunications higher priority, i.e., special priority as accorded to the United Nations Organization in emergencies, when requested, and that rates charged shall be no higher than minimum government rates. Postal communications shall be handled in the most expeditious manner possible.

2. No censorship shall be applied to the official correspondence and other official communications of the Organization.

3. The Organization shall have the right to use codes known to all Parties and to despatch and receive by courier or in sealed bags only official correspondence, other official communications, and objects intended for official use. Such couriers and sealed bags shall have the same immunities and privileges as diplomatic couriers and bags.

4. Nothing in paragraphs 2 and 3 of this Article shall be construed to preclude the adoption of appropriate security precautions to be determined by agreement between a Party and the Organization.

ARTICLE 5. REPRESENTATIVES OF PARTIES TO THIS TREATY

1. Representatives of Parties to this Treaty on the Control Commission shall enjoy, in the territory of the host government, the same privileges and immunities as the host government accords diplomatic envoys accredited to it.

2. Representatives of Parties to this Treaty on the Control Commission shall enjoy, while present in the territory of another Party in the discharge of Commission duties, the same privileges and immunities as the Party accords diplomatic envoys accredited to it.

3. Representatives of Parties to this Treaty shall enjoy, while present in the territory of the host government and while in the territory of another Party in the discharge of their official duties and during their journey to and from the place of meeting, the following privileges and immunities:

a. Immunity from arrest, detention, or any legal process with respect to words spoken or written and acts done by them in their official capacity;

b. Inviolability for all their official papers and documents;

c. The right to use codes, couriers, and sealed bags in communicating with their Governments, their staffs, and with the Organization;

d. The same exemption in respect of themselves and their spouses from immigration restrictions, aliens' registration, and national service obligations as is accorded to comparable categories of the staffs of diplomatic missions;

e. The same facilities with respect to currency or exchange restrictions as are accorded to comparable categories of the staffs of diplomatic missions;

f. The same immunities and facilities with respect to their personal baggage as are accorded to comparable categories of the staffs of diplomatic missions;

g. The right to import free of duty their furniture and effects at the time of first arrival to take up their posts in the territory of a Party and, on the termination of their functions there, to re-export such furniture and effects free of duty; furniture and effects so imported shall not be disposed of, by sale or by gift, in such territory except under conditions approved by the Government thereof.

4. A representative to whom this Article applies shall, during any period when he is present in the territory of another Party for the discharge of his duties, be exempt from taxation on his official salary and emoluments, and where the legal incidence of any other form of taxation depends upon residence, any such period shall, for the purposes of determining his liability to taxation, be treated as not being a period of residence in that territory.

5. The Administrator shall communicate to the Parties concerned the names of the

representatives and members of their official staffs to whom paragraph 2 of this Article applies and the probable duration of their stay in the territories of such other Parties.

6. The privileges and immunities accorded under paragraphs 1, 2, and 3 are not for the personal benefit of the individuals themselves, but in order to safeguard the independent exercise of their functions in connection with the Organization. Consequently, a Party not only has the right, but is under a duty to waive the immunity of its representatives and their staffs in any case where, in its opinion, the immunity would impede the course of justice and can be waived without prejudice to the purposes for which the immunity is accorded.

7. The provisions of paragraphs 1 to 5 above shall not require any Party to grant any of the privileges or immunities referred to therein to any person who is its national or any person who is its representative or is a member of the staff of such representative.

ARTICLE 6. ORGANIZATIONAL STAFF AND EXPERTS

1. The Administrator and the deputies of the Administrator shall be accorded the privileges and immunities normally accorded to diplomatic envoys.

2. All other members of the Organization staff shall be accorded the following privileges and immunities:

a. Immunity from arrest or detention whenever assigned to a control post, an inspection group, or a routine or special flight; and at all times immunity from arrest, detention, or any legal process with respect to words spoken or written and acts done by them in the performance of their official functions;

b. The same facilities with respect to currency or exchange restrictions as are accorded to comparable categories of the staffs of diplomatic missions;

c. The same immunities and facilities with respect to their personal baggage as are accorded to comparable categories of the staffs of diplomatic missions;

d. The same exemption from immigration restrictions, aliens' registration and national service obligations for themselves, their spouses, and members of their immediate families residing with them and dependent on them as is accorded to comparable categories of the staffs of diplomatic missions;

e. The same repatriation facilities in time of international crisis for themselves, their spouses, and members of their immediate families residing with them and dependent on them, as are accorded to comparable categories of the staffs of diplomatic missions;

f. The right to import free of duty their furniture and effects at the time of first arrival to take up their posts in the territory of a Party and, on the termination of their functions there, to re-export such furniture and effects free of duty; furniture and effects so imported shall not be disposed of, by sale or by gift, in such territory except under conditions approved by the Government thereof.

3. Every expert performing a mission for the Organization either at the headquarters of the Organization or in the territory of a Party shall be accorded the following privileges and immunities:

a. Immunity from arrest or detention;

b. Immunity from legal process in respect to words spoken or written and acts done by him in the performance of his official functions;

c. The same exemption from immigration restrictions, aliens' registration, and national service obligations as is accorded to comparable categories of the staffs of diplomatic missions;

d. Immunities and privileges specified in items (*b*) and (*c*) of paragraph 2 of this Article.

4. Every member of the Organization staff and every expert shall be exempt from taxation on the salaries and emoluments paid to him by the Organization.

5. The Administrator shall keep the Parties currently informed as to each individual to whom any of the foregoing paragraphs of this Article is applicable. A Party shall always be entitled to notification of the name and responsibility of any such individual before his arrival for official duties in the territory of that Party, so that it may have an opportunity to comment to the Administrator upon the proposed assignment of such expert or member of the Organization staff.

6. Privileges and immunities are granted to members of the Organization staff and

to experts in the interests of the Organization and not for the personal benefit of the individuals themselves. The Administrator shall have the right and the duty to waive the immunity of any such individual in any case where the immunity would impede the course of justice and can be waived without prejudice to the interests of the Organization. In the case of the Administrator, his immunity may be waived by the Commission provided the Commission finds the immunity would impede the course of justice and can be waived without prejudice to the interests of the Organization.

7. The provisions of paragraphs 1 to 4 inclusive above shall not require any Party to grant any of the privileges or immunities referred to therein to any person who is its national, except:

a. Immunity from arrest, detention, or any legal process with respect to words spoken or written and acts done by him in the performance of his official functions for the Organization;

b. Facilities with respect to currency or exchange restrictions so far as necessary for the effective exercise of his functions.

ARTICLE 7. ABUSES OF PRIVILEGES

1. The Organization shall at all times cooperate with the appropriate authorities of Parties to facilitate the proper administration of justice, secure the observance of police regulations, and prevent the occurrence of an abuse of the privileges and immunities set out in this Annex.

2. If any Party considers that there has been an abuse of the privilege of residence in its territory or of any other privilege or immunity granted by this Annex, the following procedure shall be adopted:

a. In the case of an abuse by the Administrator, consultations shall be held between the Party and the Commission to determine the action to be taken.

b. In the case of an abuse by any individual referred to in paragraphs (*a*) or (*b*) of Article 1, the Party which considers that there has been an abuse may, after consultation with the Party whose representative is concerned and in accordance with the diplomatic procedure applicable to diplomatic envoys accredited to the former Party, require the representative to leave its territory.

c. In the case of an abuse by an individual referred to in paragraphs 2 and 3 of Article 6, the Party which considers that there has been an abuse may, after consultation with the Administrator and, in the event of disagreement, with the Commission, require the Administrator to arrange for an immediate replacement.

ARTICLE 8. LAISSEZ-PASSER

1. Members of the staff of the Organization and experts on missions on behalf of the Organization shall be entitled to use a special *laissez-passer* procedure modeled on the United Nations *laissez-passer* procedure, to be evolved by the Administrator pursuant to regulations approved by the Commission.

2. Parties shall recognize and accept the Organization *laissez-passer* issued to members of the staff of the Organization and to experts on missions on behalf of the Organization as valid travel documents.

3. Members of the staff of the Organization and experts traveling on the Organization *laissez-passer* on the business of the Organization, shall be granted the same facilities for travel as are accorded to comparable categories of the staffs of diplomatic missions.

ARTICLE 9. INTERPRETATION AND SUPPLEMENTARY AGREEMENTS

1. The provisions of this Annex shall be interpreted in the light of the functions with which the Organization is entrusted by this Treaty and its Annexes.

2. The provisions of this Annex shall in no way limit or prejudice the privileges and immunities which have been, or may hereafter be, accorded to the Organization by a State by reason of the location, in the territory of that State, of the headquarters or other components and agencies of the Organization. The Organization may conclude with any Party or Parties agreements supplementing the provisions of this Annex, so far as that Party or those Parties are concerned.

ANNEX III*

The Preparatory Commission

1. A Preparatory Commission, consisting of one representative from each of the original Parties to this Treaty, shall come into existence on the day after this Treaty shall have been signed by all the original Parties. The Preparatory Commission shall remain in existence until the Control Commission has been elected in accordance with Article 4 of this Treaty.

2. Except as provided in Section 5 of this Annex, the Preparatory Commission shall take decisions by agreement among the three original Parties, adopt its own rules of procedure, meet as often as necessary and determine its own place of meeting. It shall appoint an executive secretary and such staff as shall be necessary, who shall exercise such powers and perform such duties as the Preparatory Commission may determine.

3. The expenses of the Preparatory Commission may be met by a loan provided by the United Nations or by advances from governments. The repayment of loans shall be included as an item in the budget for the Control Organization's first financial period. The Preparatory Commission shall make the necessary arrangements with the appropriate authorities of the United Nations for repayment of the loan. Advances from governments may be set off against assessments of the governments concerned levied in accordance with the provisions of Article 15.

4. Pending deposit of instruments of ratification of the Treaty by all the original Parties, the Preparatory Commission shall:

a. Conduct preliminary technical studies and consultations with regard to the location, installation, and equipping of control posts and other components of the Control Organization, including:

(*i*) geological and topographic map studies of the geographical areas of the world where control posts are to be located;

(*ii*) consultations with technical representatives of the original Parties for the purpose of adopting standard construction designs for control posts and regional offices and of choosing types of equipment for each of the methods of detection;

(*iii*) studies of the surveys which will be required for selecting sites for control posts and other components;

(*iv*) studies of communication requirements;

(*v*) consultations with the original Parties for equipping and utilizing their aircraft for routine flights and vessels to be stationed in accordance with the Treaty and its Annexes;

(*vi*) studies of requirements for standard time transmission and reception to ensure accurate relative time at all control posts and other components of the Control Organization.

b. Draw up detailed requirements and regulations for the staffing of the Organization and invite applications for posts to be filled during the initial operations of the Organization;

c. Draw up requirements and invite applications for the post of Administrator;

d. Recommend the site in Vienna of the permanent Headquarters of the Organization; draw up recommendations for the provisions of a Headquarters agreement defining the status of the Organization and its rights and relationship with the host country;

e. Draw up detailed plans for the day-to-day technical and administrative operations of the Organization;

f. Draw up for submission to the Conference the budget for the Organization's first financial period and a recommended scale of assessment;

g. In conjunction with the United Nations, initiate the preparation of a draft agreement which would be in accordance with Article 17 of this Treaty;

h. Make arrangements for the convening of the first Conference, to be held not later than six months from the date instruments of ratification have been deposited by all the original Parties.

5. *a.* On the day after deposit of instruments of ratification of the Treaty by all the original Parties, or as soon thereafter as possible, the Preparatory Commission shall be

enlarged, to consist of one representative from each of the original Parties to this Treaty and one representative from eight other states, chosen by agreement between the three original Parties from among those states which at that time have deposited instruments of ratification of the Treaty.

b. The Preparatory Commission thus enlarged shall exercise the powers conferred upon the Control Commission by the Treaty, in accordance with the procedures therein specified for the Control Commission. After the Preparatory Commission has been enlarged and pending the appointment of the Administrator, the executive secretary of the Preparatory Commission shall exercise the powers conferred upon the Administrator by the Treaty.

c. Pending the enlargement of the Preparatory Commission pursuant to paragraph (*a*) of this Section, the Preparatory Commission shall continue to exercise only those functions listed in Section 4 of this Annex.

Notes

PART I: FALLOUT—FACTS AND MYTHS

CHAPTER 1: *Biological Effects of Radiation*

1. W. F. Libby, Paper for the Swiss Academy of Medical Sciences, March 27, 1958.
2. Received in "one shot" over a short period of time, usually measured in hours or a few days.
3. Federal Radiation Council, "Background Material for the Development of Radiation Protection Standards," May 13, 1960, pp. 5–6.
4. *Ibid*, p. 7.
5. *Ibid*.
6. 1957 Joint Atomic Energy Committee Hearings, p. 1058 ff.
7. FRC, *op. cit.*, p. 10, para. 2.35.
8. Dr. Austin M. Brues of the Argonne National Laboratory recited this scientific parable at the 1957 JAEC Hearings: "The late Dr. Egon Lorenz . . . carried out the lowest level experiment in chronic irradiation that has been done, giving mice a little over 0.1 roentgen daily throughout their life. He found, and thus confirmed an earlier experiment, that the irradiated mice developed more leukemias than those that were not irradiated but their average life span was almost 10 per cent longer. What a mouse would do in this case if he had a free choice I am not sure."
9. "Proponents on both sides of the argument are agreed that it would take millions and more likely billions of mice to settle the point directly," Austin Brues, Argonne National Laboratory, 1959 JAEC Hearings, p. 1380. "This is because of the very small proportions of population that would be involved at fallout levels even under the most extreme guesses that have been made."
10. Dr. Lloyd W. Law, National Cancer Institute, USPHS, 1959 JAEC Hearings, p. 1420.
11. FRC, *op. cit.*, p. 11, para. 2.40.
12. Charles Dunham, 1959 JAEC Hearings, p. 12.
13. *Ibid*.
14. Douglas Grahn, Geneticist, Division of Biology and Medicine, AEC, "Radiation-induced Life Shortening and Associated Effects," 1959 JAEC Hearings, p. 8, ff.
15. FRC, *op. cit.*, p. 17.
16. Brues, 1960 JAEC Handbook on "Radiation Protection Criteria and Standards," pp. 409–10. "We may quite properly ask ourselves whether radiation is something so radically different in its action from other noxious agents that we must use different criteria in evaluating it. Quite frankly we don't know, and the chief reason why we don't know is our lack of the same detailed information about other hazards—chemical and dietary hazards in particular—which we have about radiation."
17. Brues, Argonne National Laboratory, Lemont, Illinois, 1959 JAEC Hearings, p. 1399.
18. "I once made a calculation by exactly the same means as are used in the calculations of the maximum permissible concentration [of radiation], comparing lung cancer with radium cancer and derived a Maximum Permissible Concentration—occupational criteria—of 2.4 cigarettes a day. An off-site MPC would be one every four days. The only assumption made here was that cigarettes are the causative agent."—Brues, 1957 JAEC Hearings, p. 933.
19. Dr. Hardin Jones, University of California Radiation Laboratory, as quoted in Teller and Latter, *Our Nuclear Future*, Criterion, 1958, p. 124.
20. *Ibid*.

21. Brues, Argonne National Laboratory, *Critique of the Linear Theory of Carcinogenesis*, Science, 421650-59 Vol. II, 30. Also 1959 JAEC Hearings, p. 1392.

22. Brues, 1959 JAEC Hearings.

23. Assuming there is no test-ban.

PART II: TEST-BAN MOVEMENTS AND NEGOTIATIONS

CHAPTER 2: *The Background*

1. Dr. Vannevar Bush, Oppenheimer Hearings, April 23, 1954, p. 562.

2. Bush, *ibid.*, pp. 564–65. Dr. Bush based this on the assumption, now outmoded, that cities and "soft" military bases would be the principal targets in a nuclear war.

3. Rabi, *ibid.*, p. 455.

4. Truman, *Memoirs*, Vol. II.

5. Congressional Record, Senate, 83rd Cong., First sess., Joint Resolution No. 89, June 15, 1953, p. 6292.

6. Kosta Telegadas, U.S. Weather Bureau, "Announced Nuclear Detonations," November, 1959.

7. Atomic Energy Commission, "The Effects of High-Yield Nuclear Explosions," February, 1955, p. 13.

8. AEC, "Some Effects of Ionizing Radiation on Human Beings," July, 1956, p. 6.

9. Across West Executive Avenue, in the White House compound, to the old, ornate State-Navy Building, renamed the Executive Offices Building. Mr. Eisenhower held his press conferences in the old Indian Treaty Room on the fourth floor.

10. Brookhaven National Laboratory, "Medical Survey of Marshallese Two Years After Exposure to Fallout Radiation," March, 1956.

11. *Ibid.*

12. Lapp, "Civil Defense Faces New Peril," *Bulletin of Atomic Scientists*.

13. Executive Branch Memorandum, October 24, 1956.

CHAPTER 3: *1955*

1. *Disarmament, The Intensified Effort, 1955–1958*, Dept. of State, October, 1960.

2. *Ibid.*, p. 9.

3. Soviet Proposal introduced in the Disarmament Subcommittee: Reduction of Armaments, the Prohibition of Atomic Weapons, and the Elimination of the Threat of a New War, May 10, 1955, United Nations doc. DC/SC1/26/Rev.2, May 10, 1955 (also doc. DC/71, annex 15) in Disarmament Commission "Official Records: Supplement for April to December, 1955, pp. 17–25.

4. Address by Soviet Premier Bulganin at the Warsaw Conference of the Eastern European States, May 11, 1955, as quoted in Tass Text in Dept. of State files. *Documents on Disarmament, 1945–1959*, Volume I, pp. 469–70.

5. *Disarmament, the Intensified Effort, 1955–1958*, Dept. of State, October 1960, p. 10.

6. *Ibid.*, p. 11.

7. *Ibid.*

8. *Ibid.*, p. 12.

9. *Ibid.*, p. 13.

10. Executive Memorandum, October 24, 1956, para. 43.

11. *The Geneva Conference of Heads of Government, July 18–23, 1955*, Dept. of State Publication 6046, 1955, pp. 55–56.

12. The Atomic Energy Commission complicated its own problems when it used its influence to keep Dr. H. J. Muller, the geneticist, away from the Geneva Atoms for Peace Conference, later tried to smooth the affair over by having the paper he was to present included in the record. Early in October, AEC Chairman Strauss apologized

for the "snafu." Dr. Muller had been critical of the AEC and this incident served to confirm suspicions that the AEC had something to hide.

13. Moscow Radio Broadcast, August 12, 1955.

14. Macmillan Statement, Geneva Foreign Ministers Meeting, November 10, 1955. MFM/DOC/50, Nov. 11, 1955, *The Geneva Meeting of Foreign Ministers, October 27–November 16, 1955*, Dept. of State, pp. 195–199.

CHAPTER 4: 1956

1. Secretary Dulles, Dept. of State press release, No. 15, January 11, 1956.

2. *Disarmament, the Intensified Effort*, Dept. of State Publication 7070, October, 1960 (Revised), pp. 23–24.

3. U.N. doc. DC/SC.1/42, April 3, 1956.

4. U.N. doc. DC/84, May 23, 1956.

5. Thomas E. Murray, Statement before Subcommittee on Disarmament of the Committee on Foreign Relations, April 12, 1956. This is an interesting disclosure, coming as it did five years before the Soviet Union's 100-megaton-bomb boasts.

6. Humphrey Subcommittee Hearings, April 12, 1958, Part 17, pp. 1468–69.

7. *New York Times*, October 22, 1956.

8. *New York Times*, October 25, 1956.

9. U.N. doc. DC/87 July 3, 1956.

10. U.N. doc. DC/88, July 3, 1956.

11. U.N. doc. DC/92, July 10, 1956.

12. U.N. doc. DC/98, July 31, 1956.

13. Dept. of State Historical Office *Chronology of the Development of United States Disarmament Policy, 1953–1960*, February 1960, p. 8.

14. *Disarmament, the Intensified Effort*, p. 27.

15. U.N. doc. DC/97, July 16, 1956.

16. Atomic Energy Commission release, September 21, 1956.

17. *New York Herald Tribune*, October 12, 1956, p. 11.

18. *Op. cit.*

19. Secretary of State Dulles told the Senate Disarmament Subcommittee (1956 Hearings, part 2, page 54) on February 29, 1956, he did not think it would be possible to achieve an inspection system 100 per cent mechanically complete but if risks could be reduced to small enough proportions, these risks might be balanced against the serious risk of continuing the arms race. British Marshal of the Royal Air Force Sir John Slessor had written in "Air Power," Vol. 3, No. 1 (October, 1955), p. 5, that: "A system of control and inspection to be absolutely 100 per cent cast-iron-proof against bad faith would mean that the agents of the international control organ would have to be free to go literally anywhere they chose." He expressed doubt whether British, Americans or Russians would soon accept this.

20. No 20-megaton American explosion has been made a matter of public record.

21. Again he was assuming all H-bombs were large.

22. A careful word, easily confused with "immeasurable," but meaning simply that no one could measure what damage would be caused.

23. Some American officials speculated that the Soviet Union had been trying to draw a sharper Eisenhower reaction in the hope this might help Mr. Stevenson at the polls on November 6. Returning this note, or other drastic response, might have played into Mr. Bulganin's hands as well as Mr. Stevenson's, some thought.

24. Associated Press, October 14, 1957. This was at least partly correct; Mr. Stevenson did not have it straight that H-bombs could be large or small.

CHAPTER 5: 1957

1. Lodge Statement to General Assembly First Committee, *Dept. of State Bull.*, Feb. 11, 1957, pp. 225–28.

2. *Dept. of State Bull.*, Feb. 11, 1957, pp. 228–29. Statement at 824th meeting of the First Committee of the General Assembly.

3. Eleventh General Assembly Resolution 1011.

4. *Disarmament, the Intensified Effort, 1955–1958*, Dept. of State Pub. 7070, October, 1960, p. 31.

5. *Dept. of State Bull.*, June 3, 1957, pp. 902–3.

6. *Dept. of State Bull.*, April 8, 1957, p. 562.

7. U.N. doc. DC/SC.1/PV.89, Mar. 20, 1957, pp. 2–14.

8. Gallup Poll, reported in the Congressional Record, Senate, 85th Cong., First sess., June 17, 1957, p. 9318.

9. *Disarmament, the Intensified Effort*, p. 35.

10. U.N. doc. DC/SC.1/PV.88, March 19, 1957, p. 17.

11. U.N. doc. DC/SC.1/PV.93, March 27, 1957.

12. U.N. doc. DC/SC.1/PV.95, pp. 15–20.

13. *Op. cit.*

14. *Dept. of State Bull*, June 3, 1957, pp. 901–2.

15. *Disarmament, the Intensified Effort*.

16. U.N. doc. DC/SC.1/PV. 117, May 27, 1957, p. 3.

17. *Disarmament, the Intensified Effort*, p. 41.

18. *Ibid.*, pp. 41–42.

19. U.N. doc. DC/SC.1/60, July 29, 1957.

20. U.N. doc. DC/SC.1/PV. 123, June 20, 1957, p. 2.

21. U.N. doc. DC/SC.1/PV. 124, June 25, 1957, pp. 2–5.

22. *Disarmament, the Intensified Effort*, p. 42.

23. U.N. doc. DC/SC.1/PV. 128, July 2, 1957, p. 35.

24. U.N. doc. DC/SC.1/PV.129, July 3, 1957, p. 2.

25. U.N. doc. DC/SC.1/PV. 138, July 19, 1957, pp. 2–15.

26. *Dept. of State Bull.*, August 12, 1957, pp. 267–72.

27. U.N. doc. DC/SC.1/62/Rev.1, August 2, 1957.

28. U.N. doc. DC/SC.1/PV.149, pp. 20–25.

29. U.N. doc. DC/SC.1/65/Rev. 1, August 27, 1957, Annex 4.

30. *Disarmament, the Intensified Effort*, p. 50.

31. White House Statement by the President, August 28, 1957.

32. *Disarmament, the Intensified Effort*, p. 48.

33. U.N. doc. DC/SC.1/66, August 29, 1957.

34. *New York Times*, March 19, 1957, p. 11.

35. *New York Times*, September 20, 1957, p. 5.

36. Cf. Lodge, list of concessions in speech before U.N. General Assembly Political Committee, US/UN press release 2763, October 10, 1957.

37. Press Conference, September 10, 1957.

38. Lodge Statement to the First Committee of the General Assembly, US/UN Press Release 2763, October 10, 1957.

39. David Griggs and Edward Teller, "Deep Underground Test Shots," UCRL–4659, February 21, 1956.

40. Libby, Statement before Senate Disarmament Subcommittee, March 6, 1958.

41. "Phenomenology of Contained Nuclear Explosions," University of California Radiation Laboratory 5124, Rev. I.

42. *Ibid.*

43. *Ibid.*

44. Seismographs are uniformly calibrated so that the peaks and valleys recorded from earth movements on the seismograph's chart can be measured and judged to give a relative reading of the intensity of the earth movement.

45. Libby, *op. cit.*

46. Senate Disarmament Subcommittee Hearings, January 28, 1959.

47. Gerald W. Johnson, Gene T. Pelsor, Roger G. Preston and Charles E. Violet, "The Underground Nuclear Detonation of September 19, 1957, Rainier, Operation Plumbbob," February 4, 1958.

48. Roger E. Batzel, "Radioactivity Associated with Underground Nuclear Explosions," UCRL 5623, June 23, 1959, p. 9.

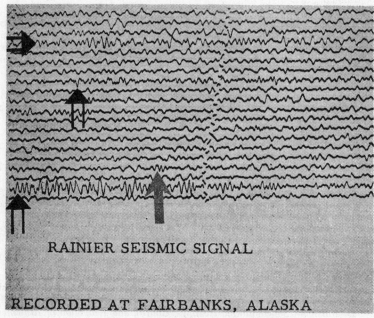

RAINIER SEISMIC SIGNAL

RECORDED AT FAIRBANKS, ALASKA

FIGURE 3: Seismic Detection of Rainier

CHAPTER 6: 1958

1. Disarmament Subcommittee Hearings, *Control and Reduction of Armaments*, Part 14, February 28, 1958, p. 1337, ff.
2. Associated Press, February 28, 1958.
3. This letter has never been made public.
4. State Dept. Press Release No. 158, March 31, 1958.
5. The Soviet Union resumed testing on September 30, 1958.
6. Disarmament Subcommittee Hearings, Part 16, March 12 and 25, 1958.
7. Indicates classified comments were removed.
8. A proposed nuclear weapon with little blast and heat effect, but with high output of neutrons which can kill humans without destroying structures.
9. Disarmament Subcommittee Hearings, *Control and Reduction of Armaments*, Part 16, 1425.
10. *Ibid.*, p. 1438.
11. *Ibid.*, p. 1449.
12. Richter or Gutenberg-Richter scale, to be discussed at greater length later in this section.
13. This was 10 times the estimate of Dr. Orear, but an underestimate as was later discovered.
14. Senator Symington recalled that "in England in 1941 just north of Birmingham, they had the Bolton-Paul plant, and they were terrified that the Germans were going to destroy it. So they built a phony plant about five miles off and they carefully left a bucket on the roof or something in order that it could be seen by a good camera. That plant was destroyed five times by the Germans. The plant that they really did camou-

flage was never touched. That is the type and character of thing you are going to get into if you are going to really want to cheat." Disarmament Subcommittee Hearings, *Control and Reduction of Armaments*, Part 17, April 17, 1958, p. 1540.

15. *Ibid.*, p. 1542.

16. *Ibid.*, p. 1544.

17. The Neutral Nations Supervisory Commission in Korea, composed of Switzerland, Sweden, Poland, and Czechoslovakia, was frustrated by the two Communist members from conducting effective inspections in North Korea. As a result, there were great build-ups of military equipment in North Korea in violation of the 1953 armistice agreement.

18. An assumption whose foundations were questioned by some.

19. Don Tocher, Seismologist, University of California, letter of April 17, 1958 to Senator Humphrey, reported in Disarmament Subcommittee Hearings, *Control and Reduction of Armaments*, Staff Study No. 10, June 23, 1958, pp. 583–84.

20. *Ibid.*, p. 504.

21. Letter by Dr. Carl F. Romney to Senator Humphrey. May 16, 1958.

22. Letter by Mr. Gutenberg to Senate Disarmament Subcommittee, April 23, 1958, Subcommittee Staff Study No. 10, June 23, 1958, p. 532 and letter by Dr. Richter to the Subcommittee, p. 575.

23. Richter letter of April 18, 1958, to Senator Humphrey, *op. cit.*, pp. 576–77. It should be noted that despite Dr. Richter's misgivings his magnitude scale became deeply involved in the nuclear-test issue. President Eisenhower later proposed, and the Soviet Union accepted, a "threshold" of 4.75 above which no nuclear tests were to be allowed.

24. Haskell, letter of June 2, 1958, to Senator Hubert Humphrey, Disarmament Subcommittee Staff Study No. 10, p. 534 ff.

25. Poulter letter to Senator Humphrey, April 15, 1958, *ibid.*, p. 569.

26. Dr. B. F. Howell, Jr., Head, Department of Geophysics and Geochemistry, Pennsylvania State University, April 17 letter to Senator Humphrey, *ibid.*, p. 543 ff.

27. Disarmament Subcommittee Hearings, *Control and Reduction of Armaments*, Part 17, April 17, p. 1529.

28. *Ibid.*, p. 1584.

29. Press release by Senator Humphrey, March 31, 1958.

30. Statement by Senator Humphrey on Senate Floor, April 3, 1958.

31. Eisenhower letter to Khrushchev, April 8, 1958, *Dept. of State Bull.*, April 28, 1958, pp. 679–80.

32. *Ibid.*

33. Ambassador Lodge, as the Republican Vice Presidential nominee, boasted frequently that the United States had never lost a vote in the United Nations.

34. In 1961, the General Assembly did.

35. Events bore him out, eventually, but not before the Russians got an uninspected test-suspension of 34 months.

36. Soviet Memorandum, May 5, 1958, *Dept. of State Bull.*, July 7, 1958, pp. 17-22. This memo also returned to an earlier Soviet position that tests should be banned "forever," not suspended for a definite period of time. This position was again reversed during the treaty negotiations.

37. Khrushchev letter to President Eisenhower May 9, 1958, *Dept. of State Bull.*, June 9, 1958, pp. 940–42.

38. U.N. doc. DC/SC.1/PV. 94, pp. 13–14.

39. Eisenhower letter to Khrushchev, May 24, 1958, *Dept. of State Bull.*, June 9, 1958, p. 939.

40. Dept. of State Press Release 319, June 10, 1958.

41. *Ibid.*

42. Aide-Memoire from the Soviet Foreign Ministry to the American Embassy, June 25, 1958, as reported in *Documents on Disarmament, 1945–1949*, Vol. II, Dept. of State.

43. Speech at Soviet-Czechoslovak meeting. Moscow Radio broadcast, July 12, 1958.

44. Conference of Experts, EXP/NUC/PV.3, July 4, 1958, pp. 27–30.
45. Conf. of Experts, PV.4, July 5, p. 5.
46. *Ibid.*, pp. 62–65.
47. Conf. of Experts, PV.7, July 9, pp. 62–70.
48. *Ibid.*, pp. 71–75.
49. Conference of Experts Report, EXP/NUC/28, August 20, 1958, Part II, paragraph 4.
50. Conference of Experts, EXP/NUC/PV.7, July 9, 1958, pp. 82–95.
51. *Ibid.*, In answer to a question from Dr. Fedorov, Sir William said 1010 fissions are produced by an explosion with the power of 10^{-13} kilotons, or one ten-billionth of a ton in equivalent TNT power.
52. Doyle Northrup, Experts, PV.8, pp. 87–88.
53. Experts, PV.14, July 17, pp. 53–55.
54. Experts, PV.16, July 21, p. 26.
55. *Ibid.*, p. 17.
56. Experts, PV.11, July 14, pp. 6–7.
57. Experts, PV.2, July 2, pp. 4–6.
58. Experts, PV.11, p. 41.
59. *Ibid.*, pp. 77-78.
60. Experts, PV.12, July 15, p. 92.
61. Experts, PV.13, July 16, p. 36.
62. Experts, PV.14, July 17, p. 101.
63. A blind spot at intermediate range in which seismic signals cannot be detected.
64. Experts, PV.14, July 17, pp. 107–110.
65. Experts, PV.15, July 18, p. 11.
66. If a nuclear test-ban treaty were to be agreed upon and signed by Italy, that country thus would become a candidate for many on-site inspections. Earthquakes there would appear naturally as explosions.
67. While no conclusion was written into the report, American scientists said it had been "generally agreed in the discussions" that two negative first motions, that is seismic signals of rarefactions, would be sufficient to identify an underground disturbance as an earthquake—and thus remove the requirement for on-site inspection. Dr. Hans Bethe, Senate Disarmament Subcommittee Hearings, *Disarmament in Foreign Policy*, Part I, February 2, 1959, p. 174.
68. As we have seen, 95 per cent of all underground disturbances could be correctly identified simply by calling all of them earthquakes. Tests could hardly amount to 5 per cent, even if many nations were active.
69. U.S. Bureau of the Census, 1960.
70. Dr. Romney, Senate Disarmament Subcommittee Hearings, *Disarmament in Foreign Policy*, January 28, 1959, Part I, p. 22.
71. Dr. Fisk and Dr. Romney, *op. cit.*, p. 13.
72. Conference of Experts, EXP/NUC/PV.19, July 24, p. 17.
73. Dr. Latter, Experts, PV.16, July 21, pp. 38–40.
74. Experts, PV.20, July 25, p. 7.
75. Experts, PV.17, July 22, pp. 67–70.
76. Experts, PV.21, July 28, p. 78.
77. Experts, PV.22, July 30, Annex 3.
78. Experts, PV.25, August 1, p. 21.
79. *Ibid.*
80. *Ibid.*, p. 22.
81. This could be an interesting principle to hark back to in case a control system is set up and it is proved inadequate.
82. Doyle Northrup gave the conference this definition of aseismic areas: "Someone in our delegation has defined as an aseismic area one where there is no seismograph. We feel that when this network is in being many of the areas that may now be considered aseismic will reveal activity of the order of magnitude of three to four earthquakes."
83. Experts, PV.22, July 30, p. 26.

84. The Soviet Union later agreed that the inspection system could be administered by a neutral, but returned in 1961 to the parity principle.

85. Experts, PV.22, July 30, p. 31.

86. *Ibid.*, p. 36.

87. *Ibid.*, pp. 47–50.

88. *Ibid.*

89. Experts, PV.23, July 31, p. 31.

90. After Dr. Brown's presentation, the Soviet Academician Sadovski told a wry joke about Dr. Brown's "optimism." According to an anecdote current in Russia, he said, "When an optimist is asked how he evaluates an existing situation, he says that it is very bad but no doubt will become even worse; whereas a pessimist, when asked the same question, says that the situation is so terrible that it could not get any worse. I think Dr. Brown's optimism is precisely of the kind to which I have just referred."

91. Experts, PV.23, July 31, p. 3.

92. *Ibid.*, p. 41.

93. *Ibid.*, p. 56.

94. *Ibid.*, pp. 62–65.

95. *Ibid.* See question by Dr. Carl Romney, pp. 72–76.

96. Dr. Fedorov, Experts, PV.25, August 4, p. 31.

97. Experts, PV.23, July 31, pp. 78–80. Whether the additional 50 were connected with their remote test-detection system was an intriguing question the conference did not pursue.

98. Experts, PV.25, August 4, p. 61.

99. Experts, PV.26, August 5, p. 31.

100. *Ibid.*, pp. 32–35.

101. *Ibid.*, pp. 42–45.

102. Participants in the conference had forgotten these remarks by Dr. Semenov when the author inquired about this point. They said they had no recollection that the Soviet Union was ready at any point to settle for a 300-station network.

103. Doyle Northrup, Experts, PV.26, August 5, p. 46.

104. Experts, PV.27, pp. 27–30.

105. Annex 3, Conference of Experts Report, EXP/NUC/19, August 20, 1958, Rev. 2, August 19, 1958.

106. Conference of Experts, EXP/NUC/PV.7, July 9, 1958.

107. Experts, PV.16, July 21, p. 61 ff.

108. Dr. Fisk reported at a later conference that geophones had not been helpful in locating the Rainier shot.

109. Experts, PV.16, July 21, pp. 87–90.

110. *Ibid.*, pp. 103–5.

111. This assumes that the hole would be bored only about 2,000 feet; there is no assurance that a violator would make things that easy. He might go twice that depth or farther. Who could be sure?

112. Brown, Experts, PV.21, July 28, p. 49.

113. *Ibid.*, p. 51.

114. *Ibid.*, pp. 37–41.

115. Sir William Penney, Experts, PV.26, August 5, p. 51.

116. Experts, PV.21, July 28, p. 61.

117. Experts, PV.8, p. 71.

118. Dr. Harold Brown, 1960 Joint Committee Hearings, "Technical Aspects of Detection and Inspection Controls of a Nuclear Weapon Test Ban," April 19, 1960, p. 7.

119. The reference to youth was a crack at the tender age of Dr. Harold Brown and Dr. Richard Latter, then in their early thirties.

120. Experts, PV.21, July 28, pp. 72–76. This conflicted with Dr. Fedorov's great emphasis on traces of human activity.

121. *Ibid.*, p. 77.

122. Experts, PV.24, August 1, pp. 18–20.

123. Experts, PV.23, July 31, p. 87.

CHAPTER 7: *Optimism Unbounded*

1. Ambassador Lodge, Senate Disarmament Subcommittee Hearings, *Disarmament in Foreign Policy*, Part II, pp. 316–17. February 5, 1959.
2. U.N. doc. A/3896/Rev. 1, October 6, 1958.
3. *Dept. of State Bull.*, September 8, 1958, p. 378.
4. Note from the Soviet Foreign Ministry to the American Embassy, August 30, 1958, U.N. doc. A/3904, September 9, 1958.
5. These extravagant exaggerations were allowed to stand unchallenged publicly.
6. Note from the American Embassy to the Soviet Foreign Ministry, September 10, 1958, *Dept. of State Bull.*, September 29, 1958, p. 503.

CHAPTER 8: *Hardtack II*

1. Gerald W. Johnson and Charles E. Violet, *Phenomenology of Contained Nuclear Explosions*, UCRL-5124, Rev. 1. (December, 1958), p. 24.
2. For further information see *The Neptune Event, A Nuclear Explosive Cratering Experiment*, by A. Vay Shelton, Milo D. Nordyke, and Robert H. Goeckermann, UCRL-5766, April 19, 1960.
3. *Op. cit.*, p. 19.
4. Berkner Panel Report, 1960 Joint Atomic Energy Committee Hearings, p. 699.
5. UCRL-5124, p. 24.
6. Johnson and Violet, *op. cit.*
7. *Radioactivity Associated with Underground Nuclear Explosions*, by Roger E. Batzel, UCRL-5623 (June 23, 1959), p. 9.
8. *Ibid.*, p. 10.
9. Mr. Eisenhower resisted whatever impulses he may have had to follow the military administrative technique of replacing erring subordinates. Dr. Bethe, chairman of the panel which had produced the optimistic 1958 report (against the advice of many other scientists) was retained. So was Dr. Killian. Both continued to give their advice on other aspects of the test problem.
10. White House Press Release, January 5, 1959.
11. Those favoring a test ban later objected, however, that this sentence made no mention of new uses discovered for shadow-zone signals.
12. *Disarmament and Foreign Policy*, Senate Disarmament Subcommittee Hearings, January 28, 30, and February 2, 1959, p. 17.
13. *Ibid.*
14. *Ibid.*, p. 19.
15. When the Bethe Panel was preparing for the Conference of Experts.
16. An example of the difficulties "scientific" compromise brings. The Senator apparently did not know that the estimate of 100, advanced by the Americans, was based on science, meager as it was, while the figure of 20 was produced by the Russians out of thin air. The 20 was finally accepted for inclusion in the experts report without mention of American reservations as to its validity.
17. *Disarmament and Foreign Policy*, p. 30.
18. The Senator may have been thinking of an area 5 or 10 miles on a side, varying from 25 to 100 square miles. These areas conform more closely to accepted claims of accuracy for seismology.
19. *Disarmament and Foreign Policy*, p. 166.
20. Earlier witnesses had estimated the signal at 33 per cent of previous calculation. Measurements in this area are never precise but Dr. Bethe was, characteristically, on the optimistic side.
21. Testimony was given in executive session and this indicates portions were omitted here for security reasons.
22. Report of the Conference of Experts, EXP/NUC/28, August 20, 1958, Part III, E (6). "Improved apparatus and techniques should be actively developed and expeditiously incorporated into the control system for the purpose of continuously

improving the effectiveness for the detection and identification of nuclear weapons."

23. Dr. Romney indicated a year later that the project had run into difficulties. It was difficult to anchor the seismograph in the mud encountered at those depths, and equipment corrosion was another problem.

24. Others were not as optimistic about making the unmanned stations tamper-proof.

CHAPTER 9: *The Big Hole*

1. Conference of Experts, EXP/NUC/PV.14, July 17, pp. 82–85.

2. His brother, Dr. Richard Latter, had participated in the Geneva Conference of 1958.

3. Rand Corporation, Press release, December 22, 1959.

4. Some of his testimony was censored, but not at points which would logically have led to the subject of decoupling.

5. *Op. cit.*, p. 166.

6. For the Panel's detailed technical report on requirements for the research program see *The Need for Fundamental Research in Seismology*, by the Panel on Seismic Improvement, March 31, 1959, a State Department document. A summary of the findings of the Panel is contained in Dept. of State Press Release, June 12, 1951.

7. Dr. Carl Romney, *The Need for Fundamental Research in Seismology*, Panel of Seismic Improvement, Appendix 18, p. 7.

8. Rand Corporation Report, R-348. The four authors indicated their work had been undertaken with the encouragement of Dr. Edward Teller, Director of the Lawrence Radiation Laboratory at Livermore. They said they were "grateful to him for important technical advice." Professor D. T. Griggs, of the University of California at Los Angeles, who had collaborated with Dr. Teller in exploring the possibilities of underground nuclear testing, was also mentioned for his "valuable criticism" in development of the theory.

9. Dept. of State Press Release, Summary Report of the Panel of Seismic Improvement, June 12, 1959, p. 4.

CHAPTER 10: *Treaty Conference*

1. *Geneva Conference on the Discontinuance of Nuclear Weapon Tests*, Dept. of State Publication 7000, General Foreign Policy Series 157, released October 1960, p. 8.

2. Dept. of State Press Release 615, August 26, 1959.

3. *Documents on Disarmament, 1945–1959*, Dept. of State Publication 7008, Vol. II, p. 1441.

4. News Conference statement by Secretary of State Dulles, October 28, *Dept. of State Bull.*, November 17, 1958, p. 768.

5. General Assembly Resolution 1252 of the 13th General Assembly, November 4, 1958, Part A, 1,2.

6. Tass statement, November 14, 1958, U.N. doc. A/4015, December 1, 1958.

7. William J. Gehron, Public Affairs Officer, Office of the Special Assistant to the Secretary for Disarmament and Atomic Energy, Dept. of State Publication 7090, released October, 1960, p. 2.

8. Senator Gore, Senate Disarmament Subcommittee hearings, *Technical Problems and the Geneva Test Ban Negotiations*, February 4, 1960, p. 21.

9. *Ibid.*

10. Geneva Conference Document GEN/DNT/PV.37, pp. 3–10.

11. Dept. of State Publication 7090, *op. cit.*, p. 3.

12. Soviet Government statement, Conference Document GEN/DNT/26, January 26, 1959.

13. *Dept. of State Bull.*, February 9, 1959, pp. 188–89.

14. Hearings of the Senate Subcommittee on Disarmament, Part I, January 28–February 2, 1959, pp. 33–51.

15. *Ibid.*, p. 181.

16. *Ibid.*, pp. 33–51.

17. *Ibid.*

18. Concluding speech, 21st Congress of the Communist Party of the Soviet Union, February 5, 1959; Moscow Radio Broadcast, February 5, 1959.

19. Press release quoting remarks of Senator Hubert H. Humphrey on the Senate Floor, May 7, 1959.

20. Eisenhower April 13 letter, *Dept. of State Bull.*, May 18, 1959, pp. 704–5.

21. This in effect put Mr. Macmillan in the position of suggesting two plans at the same time, one calling for a comprehensive ban including a quota of on-site inspections to police underground explosions, the other a first-phase approach which would obviate the need for on-site inspections altogether.

22. *Dept. of State Bull.*, May 18, 1959, p. 705.

23. *Documents on Disarmament, 1948–1959*, Dept. of State Publication 7008, Vol. II, p. 1399.

24. *Ibid.*, pp. 1400–1401; Lloyd's statement to House of Commons, April 27, 1959.

25. *Dept. of State Bull.*, June 8, 1959, pp. 825–26.

26. *Ibid.*, pp. 826–27.

27. The testing power could rig two satellites on one booster, perhaps like the Breb, the small radiation satellite which was fired as a "piggyback" rider from Transit IIa, a navigational test satellite, on June 22, 1960.—*Information Please Almanac*, 1961, p. 62.

28. Summary analysis of 1960 JAEC Hearings, May 1960, p. 55.

29. Dr. Wolfgang H. Panofsky, High Energy Physics Laboratory, Stanford University, testimony before the 1960 Joint Congressional Atomic Energy Committee Hearings, *Technical Aspects of Detection and Inspection Controls of the Nuclear Weapons Test Ban*, April 19, p. 36.

30. Joint Press Release, No. B-94, June 15, 1959.

31. "Because of the fact that there are regions in space which a violator can use, where there is a definite lack of methods, and particularly because of the fact that the methods which are available have in many cases a background and false signal rate which cannot be fully evaluated at this time, we believe that a multiplicity of methods is extremely desirable. We are not anywhere as near to certainty of coverage by multiplicity as we are in the case of ground stations."—Dr. Wolfgang Panofsky, GEN/DNT/HAT/PV.17, p. 41–45.

32. Dr. Fedorov, GEN/DNT/HAT/PV.20, p. 13.

33. Gehron, *op. cit.*

34. Dr. Panofsky, U.S. Chairman, Technical Working Group I, June 27, 1959, GEN/DNT/HAT/PV.6, p. 16.

35. *Ibid.*, pp. 16–17.

36. Panofsky, *ibid.*, pp. 33–35.

37. GEN/DNT/HAT/PV.17, July 8, 1959, p. 56.

38. GEN/DNT/HAT/PV.18, p. 17; GEN/DNT/HAT/PV.17, pp. 52–55.

39. None of these radiations were detectable from the earth because the atmosphere kept them from penetrating.

40. Panofsky, GEN/DNT/HAT/PV.7, p. 31.

41. Dr. Hulme, Chairman of the United Kingdom delegation, *op. cit.*, p. 46.

42. Panofsky, *op. cit.*, pp. 47–50.

43. Panofsky, *ibid.*, p. 51.

44. Panofsky, *ibid.*, p. 52.

45. Panofsky, *ibid.*, p. 53.

46. Life of the satellite system was estimated to be one to two years.—TWG II, GEN/DNT/HAT/PV.14, July 7, p. 72.

47. Panofsky, *op. cit.*, pp. 56-57.

48. Panofsky, *ibid.*, p. 101.

49. Hulme, *ibid.*, p. 41.

50. Verbatim record of the Technical Working Group on the Detection and Identification of High-Altitude Nuclear Explosions, GEN/DNT/HAT/PV.3, pp. 61–62.

51. *Ibid.*, p. 62.

52. Joint Committee's Summary Analysis of Hearings, April 19–22, 1960, p. 61.

53. *Op. cit.*

54. Panofsky, 1960 Joint Atomic Energy Committee Hearings, April 19, p. 51.

55. Panofsky, TWG I, PV.6, pp. 31–32.

56. Dr. Panofsky, in the 1960 Joint Atomic Energy Committee hearings, told Representative Holifield that he would "certainly not" consider one X-ray signal from one satellite as a reliable determination that a violation had occurred. "If it was seen by several satellites I think it would be considered to be such."—*Hearings on Technical Aspects of Detection and Inspection Controls of a Nuclear Test Ban*, April 19, p. 53.

57. GEN/DNT/HAT/PV.15, p. 57.

58. How this figure was arrived at is not clear. The Geneva Conference of Experts had estimated there would be 20 to 100 unidentified events per year above five kilotons. Taking the median, that would be 60 inspections per year above five kilotons, since all of these would be investigated. This would leave 25 inspections below the five-kiloton threshold, reflecting an estimate of only 125 earthquakes below five kilotons that would need investigation. Actually seismologists estimated that there would be thousands below the five-kiloton threshold.

59. *Documents on Disarmament, 1945–1959*, Vol. II, p. 1441. This pledge also was booby-trapped. The promise was not to resume tests *in the Soviet Union* unless the Western powers resumed.

60. General Assembly Resolution 1402 (XLV) November 21, 1959, UN doc. A/Res.1402 (XIV) November 25, 1959, UN doc. A/Res. 1379 (XIV) November 23, 1959.

61. This "commitment" Senator Humphrey was to honor a year later by suggesting that the United States could not continue a test-ban beyond June, 1961.

62. The 25 to 50 inspections apparently referred to those inside the Soviet Union. It was a figure that stood a better chance than 366 inspections to get Soviet acceptance, but how much better was impossible to tell. Moscow was still offering only "a few."

63. Senator John F. Kennedy, *The Strategy of Peace*, Harper, 1960.

Chapter 11: *Technical Working Group II*

1. M. A. Sadovski, Technical Working Group II, PV.1, pp. 18–20.

2. *Ibid.*, p. 66.

3. *Ibid.*, p. 68.

4. Technical Working Group II, PV.2, p. 76.

5. TWG II, PV.3, p. 16.

6. *Ibid.*, pp. 23–25.

7. *Ibid.*, Add. 1.

8. TWG II, PV.10, p. 6 ff.

9. Senate Disarmament Subcommittee Hearings, *Technical Problems and the Geneva Test Ban Negotiations*, February 4, 1960, p. 38.

10. TWG II, PV.4, pp. 20–40.

11. *Ibid.*

12. TWG II, PV.5, p. 41.

13. TWG II, PV.6, p. 6.

14. *Ibid.*

15. *Ibid.*, p. 56.

16. TWG II, PV.7, p. 46.

17. TWG II, PV.12, pp. 33–35.

18. TWG II, PV.7, p. 57 ff.

19. *Ibid.*, pp. 107–10.

20. TWG II, PV.10, pp. 63–65.

21. *Ibid.*, p. 66 ff.

22. *Ibid.*, p. 86.

23. *Ibid.*, p. 96.

24. *Ibid.*, p. 101. As already noted, an erroneous claim.

25. TWG II, PV.11, p. 6.

26. *Ibid.*, p. 16 ff.
27. *Ibid.*, pp. 27–30 ff.
28. *Ibid.*, p. 37.
29. TWG II, PV.16, pp. 15–16.
30. This was later to be confirmed by American experiments.
31. TWG II, PV.16, p. 31.
32. TWG II, PV.8, p. 76 ff.
33. TWG II, PV.9. The Bethe arithmetic was not correct, incidentally. The number of drillings would have been 100,000 instead of 500,000.
34. *Ibid.*, p. 17.
35. TWG II, PV.11, pp. 57–60.
36. TWG II, PV.8, p. 87 ff.
37. TWG II, PV.12, p. 56.
38. *Ibid.*, p. 56 ff.
39. TWG II, PV.13, pp. 43–45.
40. TWG II, PV.14, p. 21.
41. TWG II, PV.15, p. 81.
42. TWG II, PV.17, pp. 92–95.
43. *Ibid.*, pp. 97–100.
44. *Ibid.*, pp. 46, 67–70.
45. TWG II, PV.20, p. 31 ff.
46. TWG II, PV 21, pp. 76–80.
47. TWG II letter to Chairman of the Conference on the Discontinuance of Nuclear Weapons Tests, Annex 2, p. 6, December 18, 1959.
48. Letter by American delegation at Technical Working Group II to Chairman of the Conference on the Discontinuance of Nuclear Weapons Tests, Annex 4, p. 4, December 18, 1959.
49. GEN/DNT/TWG II, PV.9/Annex 3, p. 5.
50. It still had not as this manuscript went to press.
51. Dr. James Brown Fisk, testimony before Senate Disarmament Subcommittee, *Technical Problems on the Geneva Test Ban Negotiations*, February 5, 1960, p. 7.
52. *Op. cit.*, p. 35.
53. Presidential Press Conference, February 11, 1960. Mr. Eisenhower's sensitivity to the distinction between laboratory testing and weapons testing was being expressed here for the second time, and indicated an Administration awareness of the difficulty and importance of defining nuclear tests.
54. Sir Michael Wright remarked later in the same meeting at which the American proposal was made: "We have had the advantage—I think I might say that all of us have had the advantage—of some advance notice of the United States proposals."—Verbatim record of the 170th Plenary meeting of the Conference of the Discontinuance of Nuclear Weapons Tests, February 11, reproduced p. 547, 1960 Joint Atomic Energy Commission Hearings, Part II.
55. *Washington Evening Star*, February 11, 1960, p. A-5.
56. *Op. cit.*, p. 553–54.
57. *Ibid.*, p. 563.
58. Ambassador Tsarapkin, *op. cit.*, p. 572.
59. *Op. cit.*, p. 580.
60. *Op. cit.*, p. 585.
61. As quoted by Ambassador Wadsworth at the Geneva negotiations, March 21.
62. Speaking of the 250-mile spacing, Dr. Edward Teller told the Joint Atomic Energy Committee hearings later that he believed such a system would require several inspections *per day* in order to convert it into a reasonably reliable one.—1960 JAEC Hearings, Part I, p. 196.
63. Letter by Dr. Herbert Jehle, Professor of Physics, George Washington University, to Ambassador James J. Wadsworth, March 10, 1960, as quoted in 1960 JAEC Hearings, Part I, p. 415.
64. Tass, March 23, 1960.
65. White House Press Release from Camp David, by James C. Hagerty, Press

Secretary to the President, and Leslie Glass, Minister of Information, the British Embassy, March 29, 1960.

PART III: The 1960 Joint Committee Hearings

Chapter 12: *Probability Almost Zero*

1. 1960 JAEC Hearings, Part I, p. 208.
2. Later calculations raised the decoupling factor to 350.
3. Later refinements set the factor at 150.
4. L. P. Meade, 1960 JAEC Hearings, p. 146.
5. Mr. Meade's reference was from a 1939 article in the *Bulletin of the American Association of Petroleum Geologists*.
6. Mr. Meade's explanation (page 154, 1960 Joint Atomic Energy Committee Hearings) followed inquiries about a March, 1960, issue of *Nuclear Information*, a publication of the Greater St. Louis Citizen's Committee for Nuclear Information, a long-time foe of nuclear testing. An article by Dr. John Ong, Assistant Professor of Mechanical Engineering of Washington University, St. Louis, had estimated it would take three years and four months and cost $50 million to build an 800-foot diameter hole in salt. The project would produce insuperable problems of concealment, he said. Dr. Ong estimated there were only a dozen salt domes in the United States suitable for the operation. Mr. Meade commented that the Ong method "looks to me like . . . it is the hard way to do it . . . it would seem to me that he is not at all familiar with the solution mining practice in common use in the chemical industries."
7. Summary analysis of 1960 JAEC Hearings, *Technical Aspects of Detection and Inspection Controls of a Nuclear Weapons Test Ban*, May, 1960, pp. 27–29.
8. Using the alternative formulas for setting the annual number of on-site inspections, however, one now obtained different results. If one asked for 20 per cent of the total (123) one would seek 25 on-site inspections per year. If the quota were figured on the basis of 30 per cent of the unidentified events, the result would be 21 on-site inspections.

Chapter 13: *The Network*

1. 1960 JAEC Hearings, April 21, p. 320.
2. System of radar stations built inside the Arctic circle in Canada.
3. "On the basis of our study we recommend that the number be cut down to something like 31 instead of 100 because of practical difficulties of finding 100 satisfactory locations within an area of a two-mile circle," Dr. Peterson said. 1960 JAEC Hearings, p. 325.
4. Summary analysis of 1960 JAEC Hearings, *Technical Aspects of Detection and Inspection Controls of a Nuclear Weapons Test Ban*, May, 1960, p. 12.
5. 1960 JAEC Hearings, Part I, p. 332.
6. Summary analysis, 1960 JAEC Hearings, p. 9.
7. This was an optimistic assumption in view of the experience at the United Nations, where the United States was one of the few countries that met its obligations. The Soviet Union was not anxious for the inspection system to succeed in the Soviet Union. In the Congo situation, Moscow refused to pay any of the United Nations expenses.
8. Summary analysis, 1960 JAEC Hearings, May, 1960, p. 45.
9. *Ibid.*, p. 44.
10. *Ibid.*
11. Dr. Richard Latter, 1960 JAEC Hearings, pp. 93–94.
12. Hearings and Summary analysis, 1960 JAEC Hearings, May, 1960, Footnote 3, p. 9.
13. *Ibid.*, p. 9.
14. *Ibid.*

15. 1960 JAEC Hearings, pp. 175–76.
16. Dr. Bethe later sent a letter to the JAEC suggesting that, because of the large territory within the Soviet Union that is aseismic he would estimate that a spacing of 400 kilometers, rather than 200, "would suffice," so that "if this number is accepted for the aseismic regions, the total number of unmanned stations in the U.S.S.R. may be reduced to about 200."—1960 JAEC Hearings supplementary remarks by H. A. Bethe, p. 183.
17. 1960 JAEC Hearings, p. 177.
18. *Ibid.*, p. 167.

CHAPTER 14: *Judgment Withheld*

1. Summary analysis, 1960 JAEC Hearings, May, 1960, p. 67.

PART IV: THE KENNEDY YEARS

CHAPTER 15: *One More Try Fails . . .*

1. Geneva Conference on the Discontinuance of Nuclear Weapons Tests, PV.293, p. 3.
2. *Ibid.*, p. 10.
3. Press release by Congressman Chet Holifield, June 14, 1961.
4. Moscow speech by Premier Khrushchev, English translation by Tass, June 21, 1961.
5. Geneva Conference on the Discontinuance of Nuclear Weapons Tests, United States Disarmament Administration, Dept. of State Publication 7258, October, 1961, p. 179 ff.
6. Premier Khrushchev staged a too-sly stunt on February 2, 1962 to prove American test-detection apparatus was better than Washington was willing to admit. He ordered a "secret" underground shot—the only one generally known to have been exploded beneath the surface of the earth by the Soviet Union. The United States promptly announced detection of the explosion and Mr. Khrushchev claimed proof the United States had sensitive enough equipment to catch all sneak nuclear shots. But the explosion had been in the range of 40 to 60 kilotons—well above the threshold about which the United States worries. It had been in an area where few earthquakes are known to have been recorded, so the suspicion of a nuclear shot was already well supported. More important, the test was made in an area previously identified as a nuclear test site.
7. Ambassador Arthur H. Dean, "U.S. Outlines New Position on Test Ban Treaty," statement at 69th Plenary Session of the Conference of the 18-Nation Committee on Disarmament at Geneva, Switzerland, August 14, 1962. (France did not participate in the conference so it was also referred to as a 17-nation meeting.)
8. *Ibid.*
9. *Ibid.*
10. *Ibid.*

CHAPTER 16: *But the Quest Goes On*

1. Khrushchev letter to President Kennedy, December 19, 1962. He was again trying to introduce a principle that the distrustful West could not accept, that underground nuclear tests could not be conducted in cities, or other populated areas.
2. President Kennedy's letter to Chairman Khrushchev, December 28, 1962.
3. Chairman Khrushchev's letter to President Kennedy, January 7, 1963.
4. Dr. Edward Teller, Paper for the Republican Conference Committee on Nuclear Testing, February 1, 1963.
5. Letter by Mr. Fisher to Washington *Post*, March 4, 1963.
6. Dr. Ruina, JAEC Hearings, March 5, 1963.
7. Theodore A. George, ARPA, JAEC Hearings, March 7, 1963.
8. As quoted by Representative Hosmer, JAEC Hearings, March 5–8, 1963.

PART V: An Appraisal

1. There exists the possibility that the United States has developed and stockpiled among its military capabilities agents of chemical and biological warfare, with appropriate delivery systems, to counter Soviet thrusts in other ways than by using nuclear weapons. If United States military security is that good this book, most of the debate on the nuclear test ban, and most of the negotiations, as well as most of the effort in the great Pentagon building on the southern banks of the Potomac, become mere hot air. It is of course extremely doubtful that an open society could pull off such a sweeping diversionary maneuver as this implies. But there is no one in high government office who gives any hint in his day-to-day contacts of this outside chance. The possibility of a major scientific breakthrough going unknown through the development, production, and stockpiling stages is much more real on the Soviet side than the American.

2. The Bay of Pigs adventure came as close as the United States has come recently to violating our tradition.

3. *New York Times*, July 31, 1952, p. 6.

4. *Handbook on Radiation Protection Criteria and Standards*, Joint Atomic Energy Committee, pp. 1619–20.

5. Walter Robertson, Assistant Secretary of State for Far East Affairs, before Senate Disarmament Subcommittee Hearings, *Disarmament in Foreign Policy*, Part II, February 23, 1959, p. 380.

6. *Ibid.*

7. *Ibid.*, p. 382.

8. Fred Charles Ikle, *Foreign Affairs*, April, 1961, p. 211.

9. Ikle, *ibid.*, p. 212.

10. Churchill, *While England Slept*, Putnam, 1938, p. 333.

11. G. I. Pokrovskiy, *Gornyi Zhurnal* (*Mining Journal*), Vol. I, No. 5 (1956), pp. 29–32.

12. Senate Disarmament Subcommittee Hearings, *Disarmament in Foreign Policy*, January 28, 1958, Part I, p. 11.

13. Reuters, November 28, 1960.

14. President Nasser had reported the establishment of an Atomic Energy Commission and plans for building a power reactor and a nuclear physics laboratory in 1957. *New York Times*, July 23, 1957, p. 9.

15. Stassen, Disarmament Subcommittee Negotiations of 1957, U.N., DC/PV.134, p. 19.

16. U.N. Doc. A/C.1/PV.1054, pp. 7–22.

17. *New York Times*, September 26, 1957, p. 7.

18. New China News Agency, Peking, May 11, 1960.

19. "In the private conversations that preceded the formal sessions [at the First Pugwash meeting in July 1957] one of the American participants tried to convince me that if America and Russia would formally agree to stop the testing of bombs, it would be possible to prevent additional nations from acquiring the bomb. One of our Russian colleagues, who listened to this argument, was just as skeptical about its validity as I was."—Szilard, *Bulletin of Atomic Scientists*, March 1960, p. 82.

20. "One may well ask, for instance: What is the point of going to all this trouble and expense to track down earth tremors which have their focus on Russian territory when Russia could evade the agreement, if she desired to do so, by conducting her bomb tests on Chinese territory? Of course, China could adhere to the agreement if she wanted to, but why should she do so when the agreement would preclude her from developing bombs of her own and when she was not a party to the negotiations?" —Szilard, *Bulletin of Atomic Scientists*, March 1960, p. 84.

21. Peiping New China News Agency broadcast in English to Asia and Europe, September 12, 1962, of signed article published by People's Daily the same day.

22. *New York Times*, February 17, 1961.

23. *Ibid.*

24. National Planning Association, Pamphlet No. 108, "The Nth Country Problem and Arms Control," by W. Davidon, M. Kalkstein, and C. Hohenemser.

25. *Ibid.*, pp. 27–28.

26. How accurate the three scientists' cost estimates were was open to question, however. The French government announced that its plans for developing into a nuclear power involved expenditures of about $1.2 billion over a four-year period from 1961 to 1964. France had spent some money on the project in earlier years.

27. From "1970 Without Arms Control; Implications of Modern Weapons Technology," by NPA Special Project Committee on Security through Arms Control. Washington, 1958, pp. 39–42.

28. Professor Otto Hahn of Germany, winner of the Nobel Prize for the discovery of fission of the uranium atom, says: "If the smaller countries and the underdeveloped countries receive atomic reactors, they will also be able to make atomic bombs. A reactor that produces electricity also makes plutonium, the stuff of atomic bombs."

29. *Bulletin of Atomic Scientists*, December, 1960, p. 392.

30. Truman, *Memoirs*, Vol. II, p. 298.

31. *Ibid.*

32. Members of the Committee at that time were J. Robert Oppenheimer, James B. Conant, Lee A. DuBridge, Enrico Fermi, and I. I. Rabi.

33. Truman, *Memoirs*, Vol. II, p. 302.

34. Dr. Ralph Lapp, *Atoms and People*, Harper, 1956, p. 99.

35. Dr. Teller, Oppenheimer Hearings, p. 721.

36. *Ibid.*, p. 713.

37. Senate speech by Senator Thomas J. Dodd, of Connecticut, Congressional Record, May 12, 1960.

38. Dr. I. I. Rabi, *Atlantic Monthly*, August, 1960, p. 41.

39. Murray, "Nuclear Testing and the American Security," *Orbis*, Vol. IV, No. 4.

40. Moss Subcommittee Report, "Scientific Information and the National Defense," House Report 1619, April 22, 1958.

Index